Cultural Anthropology
UNDERSTANDING OURSELVES & OTHERS

FOURTH EDITION

FOR: Leonard Crapo

Ardys Crapo

David

Shannon

Rhondda

Torrie

Andrew

Cultural Anthropology

UNDERSTANDING

OURSELVES &

OTHERS

FOURTH EDITION

RICHLEY H. CRAPO

UTAH STATE UNIVERSITY

Brown & Benchmark
PUBLISHERS

Madison, WI   Dubuque   Guilford, CT   Chicago   Toronto   London
Mexico City   Caracas   Buenos Aires   Madrid   Bogotá   Sydney

Book Team

Acquisitions Editor *Tom Romaniak*
Managing Editor *John S. L. Holland*
Production Manager *Brenda S. Filley*
Managing Art Editor *Pamela Carley*
Photo Researcher *Wendy Connal*
Developmental Editor *M. Marcuss Oslander*
Designer *Victoria Barth and Charles Vitelli*
Typesetting Supervisor *Libra Ann Cusack*
Typesetter *Juliana Arbo*
Proofreader *Diane Barker*
Graphics *Shawn Callahan, Lara M. Johnson, Laura Levine*
Permissions Coordinator *Janice M. Ward*
Marketing Manager *Pam Cooper*

PUBLISHERS

Executive Vice President and General Manager *Bob McLaughlin*
Vice President of Production and Business Development *Vickie Putman*
Director of Marketing *John Finn*

A Times Mirror Company

The credit section for this book begins on page 446
and is considered an extension of the copyright page.

Cover *© 1995 Lindsey Hebberd, Woodfin Camp & Assoc.*
Cover design *Victoria Barth*
Research by *Pamela Carley*

Library of Congress Catalog Card Number: 95-83212

ISBN 1-56134-447-8

Printed in the United States of America
by Times Mirror Higher Education Group, Inc.
2460 Kerper Boulevard, Dubuque, IA 52001

10 9 8 7 6 5 4 3 2 1

PREFACE

Anthropology, like its study, humankind, is a tremendously diverse subject that provides a richness of information and an excitement in learning for students. The challenge is to present to students a coherent and meaningful introduction. While no text is likely to fulfill the hopes and needs of all instructors, I believe *Cultural Anthropology: Understanding Ourselves and Others,* Fourth Edition, will provide the basic insights into the field that a thoughtful student ought to have as part of a contemporary liberal education. These include not only facts and theories but, most importantly, the anthropological attitude of a commitment to understanding and appreciating cultural diversity. Less than this will not prepare students for life in a culturally diverse and increasingly interdependent world.

Content and Organization

In *Cultural Anthropology: Understanding Ourselves and Others,* Fourth Edition, I have made numerous changes to the text to accommodate the needs of the majority of instructors and to keep the text accessible to students and current in a rapidly changing world.
- The major revisions include the following:
- The sequence of chapters has been substantially reordered to provide a more logical organization.
- The chapter on American culture in previous editions has been integrated throughout the text, so students can appreciate their own culture as part of the world's cultural diversity.
- A new Student Study Guide has been incorporated into the text. It contains the chapter outline, chapter objectives, a series of questions with space available for students to write their answers, and a matching test based primarily on the glossed terms in the text.
- New material has been added on careers in anthropology to provide students with a practical view of the field.
- Many ethnographical examples have been updated to provide the current status of societies in a world that is rapidly changing.
- New ethnographical examples have been included that illustrate how various cultures adapt to the modern world or how they strive to maintain their own identity.
- Timely information on the relationships between race, cultural ability, intelligence, and I.Q. has been added.
- The discussion of language has been expanded to consider language and nationalism, bilingual education, language extinction, and recent attempts to characterize language macrofamilies.
- The religion chapter has been expanded to include material on religious change, syncretism, and evidence of religion from the archaeological record.
- The illustrations have been carefully revised so that the historical record of many cultures remains, but photographs of cultures adapting to a technological modern world provide students with a balanced approach to the field of anthropology and the diversity of cultures.

Part I, The Science of Culture

The book begins with a succinct discussion of the often confusing subject of anthropology itself: the breadth of its content, its holistic perspective, its history and contemporary forms, its methods, and its ethics. This chapter has been carefully reorganized so that historical concepts are discussed early in the chapter. The section on humanistic and scientific approaches to explaining culture have been moved here from Chapter 2 to provide a more coherent definition of anthropology. Chapter 2 introduces the concept of culture, including discussions of both ideology and technology, as well as issues of cultural diversity and how different cultures respond to and influence each other. Chapter 3 outlines the concept of social organization and discusses the relationships between biology and social statuses, race as a social status, and racism as an element of social organization. The complex issue of racially defined social roles is discussed, and students begin to realize how intelligence and intelligence testing must be understood within a cultural context. Chapter 4 examines the way in which changes in social status are organized by each society into a distinctive life cycle. Finally, chapter 5 takes a detailed look at gender statuses and gender roles in social life and in the relationships between gender and social institutions such as economics, politics, and religion.

Part II, Adaptation, Cultural Change and Cultural Diversity

Building on the basic concepts of culture and social organization, the next two chapters focus on aspects of human survival, adaptation to the physical and social environments, and the infrastructural components of human social life. Chapter 6 discusses the physical environments in which societies are found, the concept of adaptation, and how human societies organize their subsistence customs in various environments. Chapter 7 presents the general principles of cultural change, discusses the demise of the world's technologically simple societies, and analyzes the plight of the peasant cultures of the developing world and of the contemporary world's indigenous and refugee peoples.

Part III, Social Institutions

The next four chapters examine the institutions of economics, marriage and the family, kinship and descent, and politics. Chapter 8 defines the universal characteristics of economic systems and emphasizes the roles of culture, symbols, and values in the economic customs of the world's societies. Chapter 9 discusses the varieties of marriage that have been recognized in human societies and surveys some of the customs and family forms that arise from these marriages. Chapter 10 discusses the human concept of descent and how it has developed into various kinship systems. Chapter 11 considers how humans solve the practical problems of social life, utilizing the various mechanisms that form the political system of each society, and outlines the basic types of political systems that have existed in the world's societies.

Part IV, Ideology and Symbolism

The final section of the text moves to the superstructure of culture, the realm of symbolism, communication, religion, the role of culture in human personality, and aesthetics. Chapter 12 begins with a consideration of the human capacity for endowing things with meaning and then examines the unique role of language as a system of meaningful symbols with which humans communicate and create their cultural order. Chapter 13 takes an in-depth look at religion, an abstract and creatively varied use of the human ability to symbolize. This chapter not only demonstrates the varieties of human religious ideology, but also points out the role religious thought plays in social organization. Chapter 14 discusses the role of culture in shaping personality, creating altered states of consciousness, and defining culture-specific psychological disorders. Chapter 15 examines the nature of expressive culture such as play, recreation, and art with consideration given both to the universal human capacity for aesthetic experience and to the cultural variables in aesthetic evaluations.

Learning Aids

A variety of learning aids has been systematically incorporated into the text. A list of chapter objectives informs students of the skills they will acquire from their study of each chapter. This is followed by an outline to aid students in recognizing the main concepts that are covered in the chapter and in understanding how they will be organized. To facilitate students' learning of the basic concepts of each chapter, all *terms* are defined in context and *boldfaced* for easy recognition. A formal definition of each term is also provided on the page where it occurs. These technical terms are also defined in an alphabetized *glossary* at the end of the book. Since learning the subject matter of a new field also involves acquiring a new vocabulary, students should be encouraged to use these glossaries as a valuable learning review. By testing their knowledge of the meaning of each term, they can readily determine which parts of each chapter need further study in preparation for tests. Each chapter ends with a summary to help students review the basic concepts that have been introduced. Each chapter also contains an annotated list of readings to guide students in further readings concerning individual topics that have been covered.

Major concepts are often illustrated by *extended narrative examples*. These provide concrete, down-to-earth examples of the material under discussion. For instance, chapter 1 introduces students to Ruth Benedict's *Patterns of*

Culture in a discussion of cultural differences in the expression of feelings, and several extended narratives about the Kwakiutl, Zuñi, and Dobuans in chapter 2 are used to illustrate these concepts and at the same time update the current lifestyles of these groups. Through the use of narrative examples drawn from the ethnographic record, students can gain a greater respect for cultural diversity as well as an insight into the underlying unity of humanity within that diversity. In so doing, they will also learn that we can better understand ourselves through an understanding of others. These narrative examples are clearly marked in the table of contents and are identified within the text by a boxed structure.

Unfamiliar cultures to which students are introduced in the extended narratives are located geographically on maps in the narrative. All references cited within the body of the text have been compiled into a single bibliography placed immediately before the index.

Ancillaries

This edition of *Cultural Anthropology: Understanding Ourselves & Others* is accompanied by an instructor's resource guide, *Teaching and Testing with Cultural Anthropology: Understanding Ourselves & Others,* Fourth Edition, prepared by myself and Lisa Clyde Nielsen. Each chapter of the instructor's resource guide contains a chapter outline, chapter objectives, glossary, chapter overview, a lecture outline, discussion questions, a set of activities for in-class use or as outside assignments, and an annotated list of suggested readings and films.

As with previous editions, questions have been prepared to provide a comprehensive test bank. This edition contains an average of 100 items per chapter or 1500 items in all. In addition to multiple-choice, true/false, and essay questions, it also includes short-answer questions. The entire test bank is available on MicroTest III, a computerized test generator.

Acknowledgments

I deeply appreciate the insightful suggestions made by the reviewers of all four editions. The publisher and I wish to thank them for their constructive criticism and expert advice.

Arthur L. Alt, College of Great Falls

Elvio Angeloni, Pasadena City College
Jeffery A. Behm, University of Wisconsin
Anne Belisari, Wright State University
Jim Bell, Linn-Benton Community College
Purnima M. Bhatt, Hood College
Anne Briton, University of Miami
William B. Brunton, North Dakota State University
James Conrad, Essex Community College
Matthew Cooper, McMaster University
John Cottier, Auburn University
Douglas Dalton, Longwood College
Mary S. de Grys, Winthrop College
James Eder, Arizona State University
Jack David Eller, University of Colorado-Denver; Teikyo Loretta Height University
Mark S. Fleisher, Washington State University
Bonita Freeman-Witthoft, West Chester University
Robert R. Gradie, University of Connecticut
Daniel A. Grossman, Cuyahoga Community College
Robert C. Harman, California State University, Long Beach
Mary T. Healey, SUNY Brockport
Vernon Jantzi, Eastern Mennonite College
Donna Jones, Drury College
Ruth M. Krulfeld, George Washington University
Diane Lichtenstein, Baldwin-Wallace College
Christine Loveland, Shippensburg University
Mary McCutcheon, George Mason University
Toby Morantz, McGill University
Reka Ferencz Mosteller, SUNY Albany
Marjorie Tallant Nam, Tallahassee Community College
Donald K. Pollack, SUNY Buffalo
Ted Presley, Abilene Christian University
Harald E. L. Prins, Kansas State University
Robert A. Randall, University of Houston
John Rushford, College of Charleston
Eugene E. Ruyle, California State University, Long Beach
Daniel Schwartz, Pima Community College
James M. Sebring, University of New Mexico
Wesley Shumar, Shippensburg University
Jay Sokolovsky, University of Maryland, Baltimore
Dorice M. Tentchoff, Oregon State University
Alaka Wali, University of Maryland
James M. Tim Wallace, North Carolina State University

Linda M. Whiteford, University of South
    Florida
Guy H. Wolf II, Towson State University
Newell Wright, Valdosta State College

Special thanks are also due to M. Marcuss Oslander who skillfully edited this and the two previous editions and whose insightful suggestions have greatly contributed to the maturation of this text, to Pamela Carley and Wendy Connal for finding the right pictures, and to Bill Ferneau for bringing the publisher and me together. I wish also to thank my wife Sharon for her patient support of my writing efforts and for her useful criticisms of the manuscript as it has evolved.

Richley H. Crapo

CONTENTS IN BRIEF

PART ONE
THE SCIENCE OF CULTURE

PART TWO
ADAPTATION, CULTURAL CHANGE, AND CULTURAL DIVERSITY

PART THREE
SOCIAL INSTITUTIONS

PART FOUR
IDEOLOGY AND SYMBOLISM

TABLE OF CONTENTS

This map shows the approximate location of the cultures introduced in this book. You will find page references to these cultures in the index.

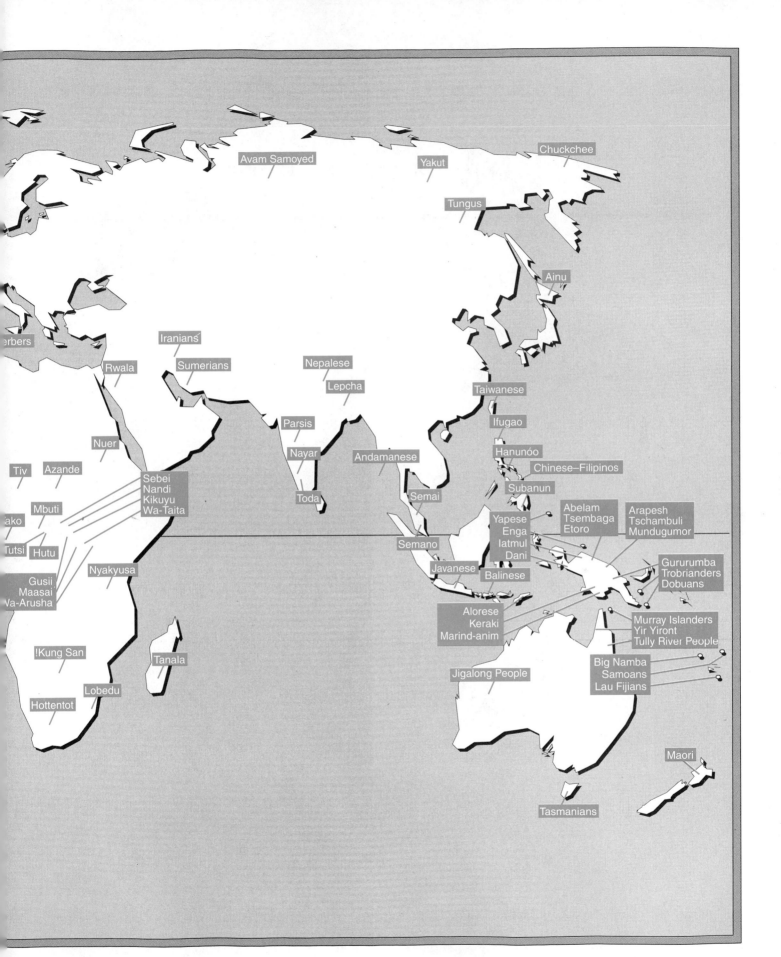

PART ONE

The Science of Culture

CHAPTER ONE
ANTHROPOLOGY: A DEFINITION

Fieldwork and participant observation are unique methods of studying cultures employed by anthropologists. As with any discipline, the field of anthropology has evolved. The prescientific view saw all non-Western cultures as degenerated forms of an earlier divine creation. This gave way to cultural evolutionism, empiricism, and eventually to the current period of specialization in which many subfields of anthropology exist, studying many different aspects of both ancient and modern societies.

CHAPTER TWO
CULTURE

The tendency of humans to share their ideas and emotions about their own natures and to develop survival strategies that they pass on to future generations as customs is the basis of culture. Various subsistence technologies derive from a society's pattern of culture and its adjustment to the environment in which it survives. Cultural relativism is the method of trying to understand another culture within its own context.

CHAPTER THREE
SOCIAL ORGANIZATION, BIOLOGY, AND CULTURE

Our status in each group with which we are affiliated is ranked by the power and prestige others expect us to have. Sometimes our statuses are achieved by effort, sometimes they are assigned to us based partly on our culture's ideas about biology. Each status requires us to know and play a variety of roles that, as they change, are often celebrated by rituals.

CHAPTER FOUR
THE LIFE CYCLE

Each culture identifies rites of passage in its own unique way. Most cultures acknowledge pregnancy, childbirth, marriage, parenthood, and death as stages in the cycle of life that determine one's status in society as well as one's relationship to others.

CHAPTER FIVE
GENDER AND CULTURE

The roles that males and females play in society are based not only on a society's perception of sex and gender, but also on its socialization values. Feminist anthropologists have studied the relationship among social power, honor, and gender, and have concluded that status is generally a measure of economic power and varies from culture to culture.

Anthropology is a discipline through which we seek to understand human nature and the broad implications of social interaction. It is at once personal yet scientific. Anthropologists study societies at first hand with a humanistic interest in their cultures and customs, but use a scientific approach to gather information that they hope will ultimately lead to a greater appreciation and acceptance of the diversity in human societies. Chapter 1 defines anthropology by detailing the historical methods that have been used and describes current ideologies. Chapter 2 defines in a multidimensional way the basic concept of culture as an institutionalized system of ideas, emotions, and survival strategies passed on from one generation to another. Chapter 3 outlines the concept of social organization and discusses the relationship between biology and culture. Chapter 4 examines the way in which changes in social status are organized by each society into a distinctive life cycle. Chapter 5 looks at gender roles in society and their relationship to social institutions such as economics, politics, and religion.

CHAPTER ONE

Anthropology: A Definition

Chapter Objectives

After reading this chapter, you should be able to:

Define anthropology as a discipline.

Describe the diversity and interrelatedness of anthropological topics.

Outline the history of anthropology.

Discuss the methods of anthropological research.

Enumerate the subdivisions of anthropology.

Analyze fieldwork in the context of the subdivisions of anthropology.

Discuss the benefits and limitations of participant observation.

Explain the basic ethics of anthropological research.

Identify the uses of cross-cultural comparison.

Explain the difference between emic and etic interpretations of culture.

Explain the difference between humanistic and scientific approaches to culture.

Characterize the individual approaches to explaining culture.

THE BREADTH OF ANTHROPOLOGY
The Holistic Perspective
Breadth in Time and Space

HISTORY OF ANTHROPOLOGY
The Prescientific Period
The Evolutionary Period
The Empiricist Period
The Functionalist Period
The Period of Specialization

METHODS OF ANTHROPOLOGICAL RESEARCH
Fieldwork
Participant Observation
Cross-Cultural Comparison

KINDS OF ANTHROPOLOGY
Academic Anthropology
Applied and Practicing Anthropology

ANTHROPOLOGICAL APPROACHES TO EXPLAINING CULTURE
Anthropology as Humanistic Interpretation
Anthropology as Scientific Explanation

◀ ***Figure 1.1*** *Anthropology Anthropology is the holistic study of diverse human societies both of the past and the present. While many cultures no longer exist as separate entities in the world, each is unique in its history and traditions.*

Many of the sciences and the humanities study humankind, but anthropology is a special way of understanding our species. In a sense, it incorporates all other ways of studying human societies. This chapter explains what anthropology is, how it gathers information about human behavior, how it tries to keep its work on an ethical basis with respect for all its subjects, how different anthropologists analyze culture, and how anthropology has evolved as a discipline.

Pothunters. Fossils. Computers in the jungle. Notetakers on garbage dumps. *Ny tykka-nu. Nyet.* Analysis. Statistics. Songs. Anthropologists seek to gather information about many different ways of life, using whatever resources are available to them at any given time.

THE BREADTH OF ANTHROPOLOGY

Anthropology is enlightening and exciting because of the breadth of its approaches to understanding the human condition. Classified by subject matter, it is one of the humanities, so anthropologists share some of the interests of philosophers, literary and art critics, translators, and historians. Classified by aspiration, anthropology is a science and shares a great deal with sociology, psychology, political science, economics, linguistics, geography, paleontology, and biology. As cultural anthropologist Eric Wolf (1964) noted over 30 years ago, anthropology uniquely bridges the gulf between the sciences and the humanities. This distinctive breadth of subject matter remains a hallmark of anthropology today.

The history of anthropology has been characterized by a dynamic tension between the two poles of science and humanism. There is a fascinating paradox about the attempt to create a science of the human condition. To understand the essence of human reality is, on the one hand, to become immersed in a network of subjective meanings, and on the other hand, to attempt to analyze a human way of life with some degree of objective accuracy. The lines between objectivity and subjectivity blur in a strange way. To analyze a society or its customs with the impersonal charts and tables of a detached observer is one way to try to avoid bias, yet it misses the essential meanings that every way of life has for its people.

How anthropologists have balanced the competing humanistic and scientific thrusts of their discipline is the essence of the history of anthropology. It has its roots among the social philosophers of the eighteenth-century Enlightenment, who perceived cultural differences to be the result of conscious human choices rather than as the end product of natural social processes. Then Victorian scholars of the nineteenth century guided anthropology into a passion for objective positivist science, but followed a model of cultural evolution that seems to us today to have been strongly motivated by a desire to portray European civilization as the inevitable goal of natural evolutionary processes. Then, in an effort to purge itself of such naive biases, it developed a passion for fieldwork and for fact collecting that gave birth both to a literary portrayal of non-Western cultures as exotic *others* and to a simultaneous call for a nonjudgmental cultural relativism. Today, anthropologists have returned to both the model of the natural sciences and to an application of the critical tools of literature and art to the study of human meanings. The former searches for causal relationships between environmental and cultural variables such as natural resources, technology, economics, and human population. The latter, an approach more like translating or novel writing, stresses the problems of how the anthropologist, as an outsider, comes to grips with the ideological and symbolic codes that make each culture meaningfully distinct.

Today, then, anthropology is an exciting mix of diverse approaches. *Cultural ecologists* explore the adaptation of cultures to different habitats. Practioners of *feminist anthropology* survey the influence of gender on social power, among other things. *Postmodernists* reinvigorate our awareness of the interpersonal processes by which anthropological insights are honed. The breadth of subject matter brings together specialists from many fields both in science and the humanities. Consider this diversity: in the past decade, the major anthropological journals have included articles on the origin and global spread of AIDS, the roles of gender in prehistoric societies, the rights of indigenous peoples throughout the world, agricultural and economic development in Third World countries, the rise and political influence of Islamic fundamentalism, and the origins and diversity of languages. Anthropology unites these and other diverse topics into a single field by taking as its goal the most complete understanding of the human condition possible. The goal of this book is to introduce you to the unity that defines the current field of cultural anthropology.

The Holistic Perspective

Anthropology is broader in its scope than other fields in which human beings are the topic of study. Its purpose is to paint a **holistic** picture of the human condition, that is, one that shows how different aspects of being human relate to and influence one another. For instance, an anthropologist who is especially interested in human economic life is likely to study how the economic customs of a society, a group of people who have a common identity, influence and are influenced by that society's physical environment, political system, religious customs, family patterns, or even its artistic endeavors. An anthropologist who is concerned with human biology might attempt to demonstrate that various frequencies of fractured vertebrae may result from different hunting practices. An anthropologist studying the language of a Native American society may attempt to determine the location of its ancestral homeland by comparing its words for plants and animals with those of other related languages and by considering the geographical distributions of those specific plants and animals for which the related languages share words.

Breadth in Time and Space

In addition to being more holistic than other fields, anthropology tends to be broad in scope because anthropologists develop their ideas about what is typical of human beings by comparing a wide range of different human groups before drawing their conclusions. For instance, most of the ideas set forth in a contemporary textbook on abnormal psychology are based on research that has been carried out in Europe or North America in societies whose people differ relatively little in upbringing and life experiences. By contrast, a typical anthropological textbook describing the character of mental illness will include comparisons among peoples as diverse as Ituri Forest pygmies, Canadian Inuit, traditional Chinese villagers, and Swedish city dwellers. Anthropologists want their ideas about human nature to be based on as wide a spectrum of human ways of life as possible. For this reason, anthropologists study people in all parts of the world in both simple and complex societies. Their perspective is based on **cross-cultural research**—research that draws data from many diverse ways of life rather than just one.

Anthropologists try to uncover as much as possible about societies of the distant past as well as about life in contemporary societies. The artifacts and fossil remains of ancient peoples are studied for clues to how people lived in the past in the hope that the knowledge gained will help us understand how we became what we are today.

HISTORY OF ANTHROPOLOGY

Although anthropology is a relatively young discipline, it has its roots in earlier attempts to learn about unfamiliar cultures. Even after anthropology became systematized as a study, it evolved through many forms.

The Prescientific Period

Anthropology owes its birth to the European expansionism of the fifteenth and sixteenth centuries. Exploration and colonization brought Europeans into contact with many diverse ways of life. Government officials who wished to exert political control over native peoples, and missionaries who desired to convert them to Christianity, were active in recording and studying the languages of native peoples.

---

holistic emphasizing the full range of relations among parts of a system and the ways the operation of those parts helps to perpetuate the whole system

cross-cultural research research that bases its conclusions on data drawn from many diverse ways of life rather than just one

FIGURE 1.2

EDWARD BURNETT TYLOR

Tylor postulated, in the nineteenth century, that culture evolved uniformly and progressively, thus making possible the idea of progress for all societies.

The Evolutionary Period

In the eighteenth cèntury, Enlightenment philosophers began to consider the establishment of a science of human society. The discipline of anthropology grew out of their speculative thought about the rules that govern all human life, the evolution of cultures, and the diversity of human ways of life.

Out of the contrast Europeans saw between their own industrialized, urban societies and smaller-scale foraging, gardening, and nonindustrialized agricultural societies grew the idea that cultures had evolved from simple beginnings to more complex civilizations. This concept of **cultural evolutionism** became the dominant view among Enlightenment scholars.

In 1735 Carolus Linnaeus had published the *Systema Naturae*, which classified plants and animals into a hierarchical system based on their degree of similarity to one another. Although Linnaeus's purpose had been simply to demonstrate the divine order of God's creation, his systematic categorization of humans and other living things suggested that living forms had achieved their current differences through evolution. The discovery of fossils of extinct animals also contributed to this idea. Toward the end of the eighteenth century, scholars began to consider the idea that biological species might also be evolving.

In 1859 Charles Darwin published *On the Origin of Species,* in which he set forth the first successful theory of the mechanisms by which evolutionary change occurs. About the same time, the discovery of the first known fossil remains of ancient humans added dramatic support to the applicability of Darwin's ideas to the human species.

In the nineteenth century, archaeology was also providing support for the idea that ways of life evolved. Excavation of the remains of prehistoric human groups showed that earlier human societies used simpler tools and lived in smaller, less sedentary communities than later human societies. In 1871 Sir Edward Burnett Tylor published *Primitive Culture,* in which he developed a theory of the evolution of religion and discussed the concept of **survivals**, remnants of earlier social customs and ideas that could be used as evidence for reconstructing the evolutionary past of societies. In 1877 a contemporary of Tylor, Lewis Henry Morgan, published another strong argument for the evolution of culture, *Ancient Society,* a book that has remained influential to this day. In 1883 Tylor became the first anthropologist to hold a position at a university and gain respect as a professional scientist, and anthropology as a professional field of study was born.

The Empiricist Period

American anthropology developed its own distinctive flavor at the beginning of the twentieth century under the leadership of Franz Boas. Originally trained in physics, Boas brought to the field of anthropology a scientific emphasis

---

cultural evolutionism the nineteenth-century emphasis on analyzing cultures in terms of their development through a series of stages from savagery to civilization

Systema Naturae the book in which Carolus Linnaeus classified plants and animals into a hierarchical system based on their degree of similarity to one another

survivals remnants of earlier social customs and ideas that can be used to reconstruct the evolutionary past of societies

FIGURE 1.3

on **empiricism.** He taught his students that the careful collection of accurate information about other ways of life was as important as the building of theory. He also vigorously condemned armchair theorizing—the building of grandiose theories based on speculation rather than on research. Boas was an empiricist who viewed science as a discipline dedicated to the recording of fact. During his career, Boas published over 700 articles dealing with topics as diverse as changes in the bodily form of descendants of American immigrants, Native American mythology, geography, and the relationships between language and thought. Boas stressed the importance of fieldwork by anthropologists. Since his day it has become the rule for students to spend a period of time studying a way of life by participating in and observing it firsthand.

It was Boas and his students who established anthropology as a field of study in major universities throughout the United States. Boas set the tone of the distinctive form that American anthropology cultivated for half a century. Beyond stressing the importance of fieldwork data collection, Boas and his students strongly rejected the idea that cultures were determined by race or that races differed from one another in their ability to learn any way of life. Similarly, Boas avoided comparing cultures in ways that carried any implication of ranking them. Instead, he stressed the importance of **cultural relativism**, the idea that it is invalid to try to evaluate other cultures in terms of Western standards, and that each way of life is best understood by its own standards of meaning and value. This idea remains a fundamental concept in anthropology to this day.

During the first half of the twentieth century, dominated by Boas, anthropologists commonly adopted the concept of **diffusion**—the spread of customs, artifacts, and ideas from one society to another—to organize their ideas about how ways of life influence each other. In the United States, the concept of diffusion led to the idea of **culture areas**, relatively small geographical regions in which different societies had come to share many similar traits through diffusion. A culture area can be exemplified by the Plains region of the United States. The Plains were occupied by dozens of different tribes whose people spoke many different languages. Yet these diverse societies had come to share many customs, dress, worldview, and values through diffusion.

FRANZ BOAS

The firsthand observation of other cultures and careful collection of data about them was Franz Boas's greatest contribution to modern anthropology.

During the first half of the twentieth century **diffusionism**, the approach to cultures

---

empiricism the viewpoint that conclusions should be based on careful observation and description, rather than on abstract theorizing

cultural relativism principle that cultural traits are best understood in the context of the cultural system of which they are a part; the attempt to avoid the narrow bias of judging a custom or entire culture on the basis of one's own cultural values; the view that meanings of behaviors are best understood when interpreted in terms of the culture of the actors

diffusion the passage of such cultural traits as customs, artifacts, and ideas from one society to another

culture areas geographical areas in which different societies share a complex of cultural traits due to similar adaptations to their environmental zone and to the effects of diffusion of cultural traits through those societies

diffusionism the early-twentieth-century approach to analyzing cultures that emphasized the historical reconstruction of the influences of one culture on another, in contrast to the more general evolutionary perspective of earlier anthropologists

RUTH BENEDICT

Benedict was instrumental in establishing the importance of studying each culture as a unique entity with its own distinctive pattern of values and customs.

that took the study of the diffusion of cultural traits as its major interest, was the dominant view in America. During this period European anthropologists were also abandoning their interest in cultural evolution and turning to their own brand of diffusionism as a means for reconstructing social history. European diffusionists felt that earlier anthropologists had placed too much emphasis on the independent invention of social traits and underrated the role of the diffusion of ideas. They traced the spread of social traits and ideas around the entire world from a small number of centers in which they believed those traits had been originally invented. Although the early diffusionist theory that all cultures derived from a small number of great cultural centers in the world has been abandoned as an oversimpliciation, the idea of diffusion itself—the borrowing of cultural traits from society to society—is still accepted as a valid concept.

The Functionalist Period

In England the diffusionist viewpoint took on its most simplistic form. The British diffusion-

ists contended that all important inventions had occurred but once, in ancient Egypt, and spread from there to other parts of the world. By the 1930s this view of human history had been replaced by an approach known as **functionalism**. Functionalists were not concerned as much with history or the origins of customs as they were with the mechanics of a society, the way in which it functioned. In their view, a society was able to continue to exist because its customs were adaptive and made it possible for people to cope with their environment and with one another. Therefore, a society's customs can be analyzed by their **functions**, their contribution to maintaining the unity and survival of the society. The main proponents of this view were Bronislaw Malinowski and Alfred Reginald Radcliffe-Brown. Both Malinowski and Radcliffe-Brown stressed the importance of fieldwork and rejected evolutionism and diffusionism. Malinowski emphasized that societies survive by making it possible for their members to meet seven biological and psychological needs: nutrition, reproduction, bodily comforts, safety, relaxation, movement, and growth. He analyzed the functions of a society's customs by how they helped the individual to meet these needs. Radcliffe-Brown, however, was concerned with the functional mechanisms that operate within society to maintain an orderly social life among its members.

The early members of the functionalist school of thought were criticized by later anthropologists for having too often assumed that every custom must have some *positive* social or cultural function, a bias that led them to ignore the possibility that there could be *dysfunctional* customs. The early functionalists tended to ignore the fact that some customs, while beneficial to some, might prove harmful to other members of the society. For instance, in addressing the issue of cultural change in Africa, Malinowski (1945) never questioned the idea that the Europeans who had invaded and con-

---

functionalism the approach to analyzing cultures by examining the mechanics of society while it is in equilibrium, as opposed to the more historical emphasis of diffusionism or the developmental emphasis of evolutionism

function the contribution that any one cultural trait makes to perpetuating the unity, equilibrium, and adaptation of a way of life within its environment

quered various African lands had a right to rule. His analysis of the colonization of Africa simply argued that "what are being given to the Africans are new conditions of existence, better adapted to their needs but always in harmony with European requirements" (p. 160), a viewpoint that certainly would have been disputed by the subordinated African populations.

The early functionalists also have been criticized for having ignored the fact that there are forms of change that can lead to equilibrium and stability. This blind spot often expressed itself as an uncritical acceptance of the status quo, a bias also exemplified by Malinowski's willingness to emphasize the benefits that Africans supposedly obtained by living under British colonial domination.

Although earlier uses of functionalism have been widely criticized, the idea that customs have an effect on other parts of a culture and its society is taken for granted today by all anthropologists. Analyzing the functions of customs is probably the most common single technique used in anthropological discussions of human life, regardless of the specific school of thought.

While functionalism was on the rise in England, one branch of American anthropology was becoming more interested in the role of psychology in ways of life. Many of the anthropologists of this tradition were students of Boas who were influenced by his interest in human psychology and worldview. The best known of these anthropologists were Ruth Benedict and Margaret Mead. In 1934, Benedict published *Patterns of Culture*, which is still among the most widely read of American anthropological works. In this book, she argued—as did the functionalists—that ways of life are integrated wholes. Unlike the functionalists, however, she found this integration in the unity of a people's mentality and values. Mead stressed the importance of childrearing practices on personality development. During the 1930s, students of **culture and personality**, or psychological anthropology, as this new subfield of anthropology came to be known, were greatly influenced by Freudian views of developmental psychology. Following World War II, their influence declined. The early practitioners of culture and personality studies have been faulted for their tendency to overgeneralize about cultural patterns, based on impressionistic stereotypes that largely ignored many variations in the behaviors of the peoples they studied.

FIGURE 1.5

MARGARET MEAD

Mead is best known for her study of culture and personality. The book Coming of Age in Samoa *is her influential study of adolescent development and behavior.*

The Period of Specialization

Since World War II, two major trends have characterized cultural anthropology. The first has been a gradual shift in ethnographic studies from fieldwork in relatively isolated non-Western, kinship-based societies toward fieldwork in Third World communities that are rural subdivisions of current nation-states. This has been a natural result of the extinction of the previously isolated groups or their gradual absorption into the politics and economics of the larger countries that have asserted increasing control over them. The second trend has been the rise of a growing number of specializations within anthropology. The two major earlier interests—the symbolic aspects of culture and the material and social conditions to which human life must adjust—have continued to be the major divisions within cultural anthropology, but many specialized subfields have developed within both of these approaches to culture.

Changes within the major professional organization for anthropologists in the United

---

culture and personality the anthropological field that studies how psychological traits and personality characteristics are influenced by culture

States illustrate the flourishing of specialized approaches and interests within the field. The major U.S. professional organization for anthropologists is the **American Anthropological Association**. Its membership, which consists of individuals from all four of the primary subfields of anthropology, has grown so much that a single, general organization is no longer adequate to meet the professional needs of its members, whose areas of specialized interest have become quite diverse. To accommodate these needs in a way that still fosters the historic goal of maintaining a holistic and integrated perspective for the field as a whole, the association was reorganized in 1984 so that it is now composed of over a dozen smaller subunits that help anthropologists coordinate their research and share their findings. Most of these affiliated societies publish their own journals, and their members meet together in smaller groups during the annual convention of the parent association. One example is the Society for Psychological Anthropology, whose members have tried to overcome the weaknesses of earlier culture and personality studies by emphasizing the use of statistical comparisons of data from many different societies. The Society for Feminist Anthropology has been formed by those who are interested in gender issues. Cultural anthropologists who are interested in cross-cultural comparative research belong to the American Ethnological Society. Anthropologists who have extended the viewpoint of their discipline to include the study of contemporary North American, Latin American, European, East Asian, and African cultures along with the non-Western cultures that were the historic focus of the field find a home in the Society for Cultural Anthropology. The Society for Humanistic Anthropology houses members who advocate the use of the same techniques that are used for analyzing written literature and folklore. They interpret other aspects of culture as a system of meaningful symbols. Anthropologists who have extended the work of ethnography to include modern film and videotaping technologies as means for recording ways of life work together within the Society for Visual Anthropology. The National Association for Practicing Anthropologists has been formed to bring together applied anthropologists who use their skills in solving cultural problems and who are often employed today in settings such as industry, private consulting firms, and government.

Despite its increasing diversity, anthropology still manages to maintain an overall identity as a unified field through the activities of the parent association. For instance, the major journal of the profession, the *American Anthropologist,* regularly publishes articles, book reviews, and correspondence of general professional interest by members of all of its affiliated organizations. The American Anthropological Association also organizes the yearly meetings that bring together members of all of its more specialized affiliates and publishes a monthly newsletter that includes listings of employment opportunities for anthropologists and information about current trends in the profession.

METHODS OF ANTHROPOLOGICAL RESEARCH

As a science, anthropology has its own distinctive research methods. These involve fieldwork and the comparative method. In cultural anthropology, these take the form of participant observation and cross-cultural comparison.

Fieldwork

The essential method of anthropological research that is shared by anthropologists regardless of their specialization is **fieldwork**—study carried out in the field for firsthand observation. Biological anthropologists may spend time in search of fossil remains of human ancestors or observing primates like chimpanzees or baboons in the wild to learn about the behavior of species closely related to our own. Archaeologists spend time in the field examining and excavating sites once occupied by human beings or even cataloging trash in a city garbage dump. Anthropological linguists work with native speakers of diverse languages to gather data firsthand about these languages and how they are used in real-life situations.

American Anthropological Association major professional organization for anthropologists in the United States

fieldwork the basic tool of anthropological research in which information is gathered from the context in which it naturally occurs

Ethnographers spend prolonged periods of time living in isolated non-Western societies, in developing countries, or in a variety of settings such as rural villages, religious communes, prisons, central city slums, or even middle-class communities in Western societies to gather data about the life and customs of those they observe.

Direct observation in natural settings is the common factor in data collection by all kinds of anthropologists. This feature contrasts with the work of other social and behavioral scientists, who have traditionally collected their data in laboratory settings, in structured interviews, or indirectly with printed questionnaires. Consider, for example, the differences in approach of a psychological anthropologist and a psychologist or sociologist interested in human aggression. A psychologist might advertise for volunteer subjects and then have these volunteers administer what they are told are electric shocks to confederates of the researcher, ostensibly to study the effects of punishment on learning but actually to study human willingness to act aggressively when told to by authority figures. Or volunteers who were exposed to a staged argument on their way to the laboratory might be compared with those volunteers who were not. Despite the insights thus gained, there are significant limitations on the usefulness of such studies. Subjects are limited to people who volunteer to come to the laboratory to participate in the research. Whether people who volunteer for such activities are typical members of society is always questionable. Furthermore, it is not always clear what a subject's willingness to follow the directions of a psychologist in a laboratory setting reveals about the same person's likelihood of participating in a riot during a blackout, getting into a bar fight, volunteering for military service during a national crisis, or committing homicide.

An anthropologist interested in human aggression would carry out research in the social environments in which violence occurs. The research would be carried out over a period of months, while the anthropologist lived among the people being studied, interacting with them in their normal, day-to-day settings, and recording examples of real aggression as it occurred. Based on repeated observations over long periods of time, the ethnographer might then suggest some general conclusions about the situations or patterns of interaction that are most likely to trigger aggressive behavior in the particular society being studied.

Participant Observation

Most ethnographic research is also carried out using what is called **participant observation**. The anthropologist lives with the subjects in the field for a long enough period to earn the trust that people require to behave in the ways they usually do when strangers, tourists, or "outsiders" are not present. Ideally, the ethnographer becomes skilled enough at following local customs to be accepted as a functioning member of the group, while maintaining sufficient objectivity about the way of life to be able to describe and analyze it fairly and impartially. In practice, complete acceptance as a member of the community being studied is rare.

Anthropologists expect to learn the native language of the people they study, since it is a kind of record and model of its speakers' understanding of themselves and their environment. It also facilitates the direct questioning of a people about their customs and the meanings of those customs. Along with simple observation, direct questioning is an important part of participant observation. Anthropologists carry out their questioning in ways that are systematic enough to uncover implicit but not normally discussed aspects of ways of life that might otherwise remain unknown. Systematic questioning requires asking the same questions of many different informants. This is done partly to verify the accuracy of what the researcher is told—after all, anthropologists are outsiders, and they may be considered fair game to informants who may resent their presence or simply enjoy the humor of deceiving them. Asking the same questions of many informants also ensures that the information obtained is typical of the ideas expressed in the community at large.

Participant observation has limitations as well as strengths. One problem is that the time and energy it requires make it impossible for anthropologists to sample more than a fraction of the many lifestyles that exist at any time, and each anthropologist is only able to spend time in a limited number of communities within any one society. Choices such as which society to study, which communities within

---

participant observation the technique of cultural anthropology in which the researcher spends a prolonged period participating with and observing subjects in their natural setting, as opposed to studying them in a laboratory setting

that society, and which members of the community to spend time with are influenced by many factors that cannot be called objectively scientific. For instance, financial limitations may determine the choice of where to do the research; national politics in the society may influence which communities are visited; and the chance meeting of a community member who belongs to a particular political, religious, or economic faction may determine who will shun or be willing to work with the anthropologist.

Another problem in the fieldwork approach is the fact that the anthropologist's very presence can alter in important ways a way of life she or he is studying. For instance, Jean Briggs (1986) noted that "the hosts must also rearrange their lives, at some cost to themselves, to include the anthropologist and to solve the problems created by the latter's presence. The disruption may be more or less severe, depending on the nature of the role that the anthropologist adopts (or is assigned) in the society" (p. 20).

Gender and Fieldwork. In the past, most anthropologists were men. Since 1984, new doctoral degrees in anthropology have been earned by an equal number of women and men ("Survey of Anthropology Ph.D.'s," 1991, p. 12). This shift toward gender balance has greatly improved ethnographic data, since the gender of fieldworkers influences the information to which they have access. For instance, lives of women may be inaccessible to a male anthropologist, and the gossip in male-only settings may be unavailable to a female anthropologist.

Because both male and female anthropologists frequently assume the gender roles of the people in the society they study, the kind of topics they choose (or are constrained) to investigate is limited, as is the kind of data that they collect. For instance, Ann Fischer's (1986) first field project was the study of Trukese mothers. Since she was pregnant at the time, the Trukese spontaneously offered her many of their views on the physiological experience of pregnancy, greatly facilitating her research. She also found that she and her husband were given rather different kinds of information. She reported that "if our field notes are compared, my husband's record the more formal aspects of culture in exactitude, while mine tend to be a running account of what was happening in the village or in the homes in which I observed.

This difference held in most of the cultures in which we did fieldwork together, although in New England I was in a better position to obtain formal interviews than was my husband. . . . Our access to data was different in every culture we studied" (p. 282). Since the lives, customs, and opinions of men and women differ in important ways in every culture, male and female anthropologists gain different insights in the field.

Ethics in Anthropological Research. Since the subjects of anthropological research are human beings, there are important ethical considerations in doing fieldwork. It is generally agreed that the first loyalties of an anthropological fieldworker must lie with the people being studied. Our work must be carried out and reported in ways that cannot be used to harm the peoples whose lives we are investigating. When an anthropologist lives for extended periods of time with a people to thoroughly absorb the details of their lives and customs, it is almost inevitable that the researcher will become privy to information that might be harmful to the welfare and dignity of the host people were it to become public knowledge. Such knowledge is expected to be held in confidence, and anthropological research is reported only in ways that ensure the anonymity of individual informants and the welfare of the communities studied.

Because anthropological research carried out among living peoples is a matter of skilled observation and inquiry, anthropologists generally have no qualms about informing their subjects about the purposes of their research. There are, of course, situations in which the gathering of specific information about people's behavior would be made more difficult by an explicit admission of what the anthropologist is seeking, either because the informants' knowledge would make them self-conscious—thereby causing them to alter their normal behavior—or because informants may sometimes say what they think the investigator would like to hear. For instance, it would probably be self-defeating to announce one's intention to count how often people violate their own rules of public etiquette, since this would warn them to be on their best behavior whenever they see you coming! Thus, anthropologists may be open about their general topic of interest without compromising their ability to observe the specific behaviors that are relevant to learning

(Continued on p. 15)

THE FIELDWORK EXPERIENCE: A CASE STUDY

After 3 years of graduate training, I prepared for my first experience in anthropological fieldwork, the study of the Shoshone language and its probability of becoming extinct. I remember one piece of advice my mentor gave me as we drove for the first time to the reservation which he had selected for my work: Don't ask directly about how many people or families lived on the reservation because such questions would raise the suspicion that I was really gathering information for the government for some nefarious purpose. I followed this advice even though it slowed considerably my building of a clear picture of the makeup of the reservation.

At first it seemed that I could not have been more fortunate in a fieldwork location. The Tribal Council had graciously offered me a rent-free ranch house that seemed luxurious. It was supplied with propane lighting, a stove, running cold water, and a propane refrigerator. It was furnished with a couch, desk, and bed. Most important of all, it actually had an indoor toilet!

My first crisis was the discovery that although the house had a mechanically perfect toilet, it was unusable. It seems a child had flushed a rubber ball down the drain. Ordinarily this might have been fixed, but the drainpipe narrowed, somewhere in the front yard, to a size smaller than the ball. Thus, my prized possession was as unfunctional as a fur-lined teacup.

The biggest initial adjustment to life in the field was loneliness. Residents of the reservation had their own work to do and lives to live. Most people were cattle ranchers, and their work kept them busy. They did not just drop everything because a young anthropologist had arrived. At first, I was at a loss to know how to go about meeting people. Residences were dispersed over the reservation. There were no stores to form a place of congregation. However, there was a third-class post office, where mail arrived and departed only weekly, a small two-room frame structure where I figured people would drop by occasionally. The reservation had no telephones, there was no television reception in the valley, and only a few houses had self-generated electricity to power even a radio, so I assumed that the mail would be an important source of information about the outside world. I stopped by the post office the next time I found it open. Mail was brought out to the reservation once a week by an automobile referred to as "the stage." People did come by to mail a letter or pick up their own deliveries, but few ever stayed long enough for me to get to know them. The one exception, of course, was the postmaster, Billy Mike, who became my first acquaintance. He expressed friendly interest in why I had come to the reservation, and spent many hours helping me learn the Shoshone dialect that was spoken locally. Eventually he introduced me to other, older members of the community.

My main task was to develop an accurate description of the roles of Shoshone and English on the reservation. I wanted to discover the rules that governed which language was likely to be spoken by which persons under various circumstances. Thus, I was interested in whether speakers' choice of language in a given conversation could be predicted by combinations of such things as the age or sex of each speaker, the topic being discussed, or the specific vocabulary items that were necessary for that topic. In essence, I was trying to characterize the degree to which English was displacing Shoshone as the language of choice in conversations as well as the ways in which the displacement was happening.

The single most difficult barrier that I was forced to grapple with was my own lack of fluency in the Shoshone language. I had been fortunate in having been able to study the language for 2 years before starting my fieldwork, but what I had learned was only "book Shoshone," and once I was on my own on the reservation it quickly became clear to me that I lacked the conversational abilities that would be needed to follow the important but subtle nuances of day-to-day speech among native Shoshone speakers. Shoshone is a fascinating language whose verbs are particularly problematic for a native English speaker who is accustomed to the need for remembering only a few variations on the past, present, and future tenses. Shoshone, by contrast, has some sixteen basic tenses that differ not only according to *when* in time the process is placed but also in the style or quality of the action. For instance, there are two simple past tenses that differ only in whether the activity was completed gradually or suddenly. Thus, the English sentence, "She died," requires in Shoshone a choice of tense that would depend on whether the cause of death was a lingering illness or a broken neck. A third past tense in Shoshone is used for activities that were completed only in a location different from where the speaker currently is. It is true, of course, that these distinctions can be made by adding the right words and phrases to the basic English sentence, but unfortunately for the native English speaker, these differences in meaning are grammatically obligatory in Shoshone and— even worse—they are accomplished with suffixes that are appended to the basic verb. Consider the three Shoshone sentences, *Ne tekka-nu* ("I ate [a leisurely meal]"), *Ne tekka-hkwa* ("I ate [quickly]"), and *Ne tekka-hkooni* ("I ate [while I was over there]"). Present tenses are equally elaborate. There is one suffix for an activity that has just recently begun, another for a process that has been going on for a specific period of time, and a third for one that is happening now but has no definite time of onset. For some time, I despaired of being able to follow the sense of even the simplest conversations. I had discovered that distinctions that a student could readily notice in a neatly typed text did not linger nearly long enough in the air when spoken. For a long time, I contented myself with collecting single words, preferably nouns.

Still, some facts about language use became apparent quite soon after my arrival. For instance, although almost everyone on the reservation whom I met spoke both Shoshone and English, there was tremendous variation in proficiency in both languages from one speaker to another. This was especially noticeable when persons of different age were compared. The oldest resident was a woman who was said to have reached her hundredth birthday and who claimed to speak no English at all. Others who ranged in age from about 60 to 80 were fluent Shoshone speakers who typically spoke English as well but with a clear Shoshone accent and an occasional difficulty with English vocabulary. Middle-aged speakers usually had nearly equal proficiency in both languages, while many of those under 40 appeared to be more at home with English than Shoshone.

Even before I could follow what was being said, I noticed that conversations in Shoshone were interspersed with English loan words regardless of the age of the speakers. When the topic dealt with technological issues, such as the repair of a water pump, English words such as *pliers, hammer,* or *wire* were common. Many words for recently adopted foods such as coffee, grapes, and oranges were also borrowed from English. Shoshone has no native obscenities, so when the Shoshone adopted the use of obscenities along with many other aspects of U.S. culture, English words and phrases were simply borrowed and used within Shoshone sentences. Here the pattern was noticeably age-related.

Situations and topics controlled language choice as well. Several families on the reservation were members of the Mormon religion, which is a major Christian denomination throughout many of the Great Basin states. Each week a non-Indian representative of this church came to the reservation to hold worship services. In this setting, the English language predominated even in conversations before and after the meeting among Shoshones who attended.

During my work with the Indians, I would typically tape-record the examples of speech that I intended to analyze later. Simultaneously, I made handwritten notes in an abbreviated style about what was happening. They contained comments on such things as the context of conversations, persons involved, and the topics being discussed as well as any spontaneous insights into linguistic or cultural aspects of the conversations that I felt might help my later analysis. At other times, for instance when I was systematically eliciting ways of saying various things, these notes became careful transcriptions of the complete responses. Each evening at home, I would type my notes to produce a separate, neater collection of field notes.

The story lines of the material I had recorded raised cultural as well as linguistic questions that also had to be answered. Why, for instance, was the weasel the animal of choice for preparing both gambling and love magic? Or when the "medicines" prepared for these purposes were "spoken to," did it imply a hearing spirit within the supernatural materials or was the speaking merely a way of manipulating the materials by invoking inanimate and unthinking supernatural forces? I made notes on such questions so that I could follow up on them.

As my work progressed, I began recording conversations and folktales that were part of the oral tradition. At the same time, I was able to cross-check the accuracy of what I had learned. Such practice enabled me eventually to follow the sense of conversations that occurred spontaneously in my presence. So I began to examine the interplay of Shoshone and English in the natural speech that was happening around me. I started recording not just when and where one of the languages seemed to be preferred over the other and how the words of one language were adopted into the other, but also how speakers might switch from one language to another as topics of their discussion changed. At the same time, as I developed an increasing facility with the native language, I started to learn things about reservation life that had not been clear through English alone. For instance, I began to learn that adults, who previously had been careful to avoid suggesting that they accepted the traditional Shoshone religious beliefs, openly discussed such matters as native curing ceremonies and native mythology when speaking Shoshone in my presence. I began to learn something of the contemporary Shoshone ideology, a worldview that incorporates both traditional Shoshone ideas and those of the U.S. mainstream.

The reservation on which I lived was one of the few places throughout the Great Basin homeland of the Shoshone that was fortunate enough to have a practicing Indian doctor, a religious curer called a *pohakante*. Willie Blackeye was highly respected and held traditional curing ceremonies about once a month for patients who came to him from throughout Nevada. He claimed that he did not speak English, but I am still not sure whether this was so or if his fostering of this belief was a means of maintaining a certain distance from what those on the reservation called "Anglo culture." But whether it was intended or not, the contrast between the predominant use of English in the setting of Mormon worship services and the dominant role of Shoshone in Willie Blackeye's curing ceremonies clearly marked the contrast between traditional and nontraditional aspects of Shoshone religious ideology. Thus, as the Indians shared with me the traditional religious lore of Coyote and the other supernatural animals that populate Shoshone mythology, words borrowed from English occurred only rarely. Stories about more recent history contained many examples of borrowed words. Finally, English was most common in gossip and tales of recent events.

My exploration of language choice among contemporary Shoshone exemplifies the holistic and integrative nature of cultural anthropology. Although the central concern of my research was a linguistic topic, I was not primarily interested in the Shoshone language as a closed system. Instead I sought to uncover the cultural rules that governed when and where one language would more likely be used than another. This forced me to examine how the Shoshone discussed their environment, their artifacts, and their economic activities. I also had to examine the social facts of Shoshone life, since their patterns of language use differed so dramatically by age. Ideology also could not be ignored, because English had not been uniformly adopted for communicating about all the various aspects of Shoshone symbolic life.

Although my personal goal was an academic one—completing the requirements for a degree in anthropology—participant observation research is not a process of detached data gathering and analysis. I could only obtain information about the use of language in real life by living with my subjects and interacting with them in their own settings. As a matter of fact, many of the important insights into the dynamics of a society come as a result of the interplay between the fieldworker and the native participants as the researcher struggles to understand the culture. It is the give-and-take of participant research that is particularly central to the anthropologist's ability to translate another culture into the idiom and metaphor of his or her own way of life. I too found that I was drawn into the life of the reservation in ways that fulfilled my own goals and, at the same time, served the values of the people I had come to study. In fact, I am fortunate to be able to still maintain some contact with those people who touched my life in meaningful ways and broadened my understanding of both the range of diversity within the human condition and the underlying similarities that make us all one human family.

about that topic. The real issue here is that anthropologists endeavor not to deceive their subjects or carry out research that serves interests that differ from the community's own. Clandestine or secret research is frowned on by most anthropologists. One way of avoiding conflicts of interest over allegiance to the people studied and to others with differing political aims is to avoid accepting research assignments that the funding agency requires be carried out in secrecy.

The anthropologist's second allegiance is to the expansion of a scientifically respectable body of knowledge about the human condition. Thus, anthropologists seek to do everything in their power to collect accurate information and to make it openly available to others in a form that does not violate their informants' rights or compromise their dignity. It is common practice for anthropologists to provide copies of their research reports and publications to the communities they are studying. This ensures integrity in the research process and loyalty to the values of the subjects, and it also makes it possible for the fruits of anthropological research to be used by the subjects for their own benefit.

Cross-Cultural Comparison

The third component of anthropological research is **cross-cultural comparison**—examination of the varied ways a certain aspect of

---

cross-cultural comparison basing general conclusions about the nature of culture and its influence on society on the comparison of a diverse sample of cultures from many parts of the world, so that those conclusions will be generally valid for the human condition as a whole

TABLE 1.1   **CORRELATIONS BETWEEN SEXUAL RESTRICTIVENESS AND MARRIAGE CELEBRATIONS**

		Sexual Restrictiveness		
		Low	Medium or High	Total
Marriage Celebration	Small	11	7	18
	Moderate or Elaborate	4	28	32
	Total	15	35	

In a sample of 50 societies from the Human Relations Area Files (HRAF), researchers have verified a relationship between few premarital sexual restrictions on women and simple weddings, and extensive premarital sexual restrictions on women and elaborate weddings.

Source: Adapted from *Varieties of Sexual Experience: An Anthropological Perspective on Human Sexuality* by S. G. Frayzer, 1985, New Haven, CT: Human Relations Area Files, p. 328.

human life is treated in many different cultures. For instance, an ethnologist who is interested in examining the general rules that relate to aggression in any society might compare the ethnographic data from a broad range of human societies to determine what social factors are consistent predictors of specific forms of aggression.

Anthropological fieldworkers are especially skilled at providing insights into the relationship of a custom to its broader social context. Their in-depth exposure to a particular way of life allows them to notice in detail how one part of a culture influences another. Yet, to develop truly useful generalizations about the ways in which culture functions, it is necessary to demonstrate that relationships that appear to be valid in one culture will hold true for others under like circumstances. Cross-cultural research is the typical strategy that anthropologists use for this purpose. By comparing a sufficient number of historically unrelated cultures from different parts of the world, it is possible to determine, for instance, whether warfare is more likely in societies in which there are large differences in wealth between families than in societies in which all families have about the same level of wealth. Anthropologists can also determine whether sexual inequality is more likely in societies where warfare occurs between neighboring peoples who belong to the same culture than in societies where warfare occurs between members of very different cultures.

Currently, the most sophisticated collection of data on many different societies is one which was begun in 1937 by George Peter Murdock and several colleagues (1981). This collection of cross-cultural data is known today as the **Human Relations Area Files (HRAF)**. This nonprofit organization in New Haven, Connecticut, now maintains over three-quarters of a million pages of information on 335 major societal groups, each of which has been coded for the presence or absence of characteristics on a standard list of over 700 cultural and environmental traits. Use of data from the HRAF has made it possible for researchers to determine what cultural traits or environmental factors are the best predictors of the presence or absence of various customs, thereby testing their ideas about the effects of one part of a cultural system on another.

Here is a brief example of how the HRAF might be used. Suppose an anthropologist suspected that in societies where it is important for a man to be identified as the father of his wife's children, there would be both elaborate marriage rituals (to publicly proclaim the relationship between the husband and wife) and

Human Relations Area Files (HRAF) a research data pool containing information on over 335 major societal groups, each coded for the presence or absence of about 700 cultural and environmental traits

strong rules to limit a woman's sexual behavior outside marriage. Simple weddings with few sexual restrictions on the woman might likely be found in other societies where males and females are considered equals. There should, however, be few societies in which one is prominent and the other absent. If we examined a sample of societies from the HRAF files to check how likely it is that these two traits occur together, we would find that, although there are exceptions, elaborate weddings and restrictions on women's sexual behavior do tend to go together, as do simple weddings and few sexual restrictions (see Table 1.1).

KINDS OF ANTHROPOLOGY

Anthropologists work in two main settings. About 80 percent are employed in academic settings where their research and teaching emphasize the exploration of knowledge about the human condition. In recent times, however, an increasing number of anthropologists find employment in settings that permit them to apply their knowledge and research skills to the practical problems of human society.

Academic Anthropology

There are four main types of academic anthropologists: cultural anthropologists, archaeologists, anthropological linguists, and physical anthropologists. Generally speaking, **cultural anthropologists** are interested in understanding the rules that govern ways of life, or **cultures**. They study the customs of human societies to discover what leads to their similarities and differences. As a part of their training, cultural anthropologists are usually expected to spend a prolonged period of time—often a year or more—living in a society that practices customs usually very different from those of their own, participating in that way of life, and recording the customs of that society as accurately as possible.

Cultural anthropologists who specialize in recording the customs of human societies are called **ethnographers**. Their descriptions of human ways of life are called **ethnographies**. Other cultural anthropologists known as **ethnologists** attempt to unravel the general laws

that guide the development of human ways of life. They have their own specialties, such as people's economic life, political systems, marriages, family and childrearing practices, art, religious practices and beliefs, or psychological traits. The specializations within this branch of anthropology tend to overlap with the interests of professionals in the other behavioral and social sciences within a university. Yet, cultural anthropology has a distinctive contribution to make: to show how each part of human life, be it language, politics, economics, family life or religion, fits into a way of life as a whole. In a sense, other social and behavioral scientists study the various parts in isolation from one another, while the cultural anthropologist is interested in how these relate to the broader context of human life.

Archaeologists, like cultural anthropologists, are interested in understanding ways of life but specialize in cultures that have ceased to exist. Archaeologists reconstruct the history and the culture of a society from the objects or artifacts its people left behind. The fieldwork of the archaeologist involves the careful, painstaking excavation of places where people have lived. The skills required for the work of excavating a site include surveying, map making, photography, and others necessary for the preservation of information about each object unearthed, including exactly where it was located compared to every other object discovered.

Unfortunately, preserving a site is difficult for many reasons. Natural phenomena such as floods, ice, lightning-induced fires, and wind

---

cultural anthropologists anthropologists who specialize in the study of specific cultures or of culture in general

culture a learned system of beliefs, feelings, and rules for living around which a group of people organize their lives; a way of life of a particular society

ethnographers cultural anthropologists who spend prolonged periods living with and describing the cultures of specific peoples

ethnographies descriptions of customs, beliefs, and values of individual societies

ethnologists cultural anthropologists who formulate general laws of culture based on the study of the ethnographies of many diverse societies

archaeologists cultural anthropologists who study the material remains of earlier societies in order to reconstruct their cultures

RECREATING STONE TOOLS TO LEARN THE ANCIENT MAKERS' WAYS

Last summer Kathy Schick and Nicholas Toth drove out to Oregon, bought 2,000 pounds of obsidian, quartizite and basalt from three quarries, hauled it back to their home here in a rental truck and dumped it in their backyard. For Dr. Toth and Dr. Schick, a husband-and-wife team of archeologists at Indiana University, the load of rocks is a vehicle in interpreting human evolution.

Over the next few years they, their students, volunteers and a pygmy chimpanzee named Kanzi, well known in the anthropology community for his participation in language experiments, will flake the stones into tools, just as humans' hominid ancestors did beginning 2.5 million years ago. The lithic experiments are part of their project to investigate human origins and evolution through technology.

"If anything defines the human condition, it's tools and technology," said Dr. Toth, who, with Dr. Schick, founded the university's Center for Research into the Anthropological Foundations of Technology in 1986, when they were junior members of the anthropology faculty. As hominids started using tools and becoming carnivores, they began to "produce simulated biological organs—slashing, crushing organs," Dr. Toth said.

"You see a reduction in the size of the teeth and jaws because we're replacing biology through technology," he continued. . . .

Next year, working with a radioneurologist, they plan to make tools out of stone themselves while their brains are being imaged by positron emission tomography. The experiment may show whether there is a correlation between tool making and other cognitive skills, such as language. . . .

Building on the work of a few other lithic toolmakers, he began flaking stones and testing out the products. Dr. Schick soon joined in these efforts, which included butchering various animals, including a few elephants. (All had died of natural causes.)

From the experiments Dr. Toth developed an important hypothesis about Oldowan tools, the simple flaked stone implements that first appeared 2.5 million years ago and were named by Dr. Mary Leakey and Dr. Louis Leakey, the archeologists.

"The easy but now erroneous inference was that because of their different shapes, the cores were the tools," Dr. Schick said of these implements.

But in their experimental butcheries, Dr. Toth and Dr. Schick found that the small flakes struck from a core were much more effective in cutting than the core itself. With an obsidian flake they could slice through the one-inch-thick hide of an elephant. When the blade dulled, after about five minutes of work, they simply hammered on the core with a large stone to get another flake.

"When people think of stone they think 'primitive, not functional,' but you can't get anything sharper than a flake," Dr. Toth said.

Far from being waste products, known as débitage, the flakes were at least as useful to early hominids as the chunky cores, they concluded.

Their experiments also shed light on the brains of the early hominids—probably Homo habilis—who used these tools. Dr. Toth noticed that flakes struck side by side from a core exhibited different features depending on whether the toolmaker held the stone hammer in his left or right hand. Analyzing the flakes he had produced, Dr. Toth, who is right-handed, found that of those that showed such differences, 56 percent of them had right-handed features and 44 percent of them left-handed features. He established this ratio as being consistent with the pattern produced by a right-handed person. An analysis of flakes found at Koobi Fora showed a ratio of 57 to 43. From this Dr. Toth inferred that the hominids who made the tools had been preferentially right-handed. Modern-day humans are 90 percent right-handed and are the only known creatures to show such a pronounced preference for one hand. Dr. Toth's work suggests that for whatever reason, the brains of these tool-makers were already profoundly lateralized.

From: "Recreating Stone Tools to Learn the Ancient Makers' Ways," by B. Fowler, December 20, 1994, *New York Times*, pp. C1, C12.

can cause a site to be damaged irreparably. Human interference with the landscape can also take its toll:

Archaeological sites may be bulldozed into nonexistence during the construction of a road or building. They may be covered by the lake created by a new dam. The Olmec site of La Venta in western Tabasco, Mexico, one of the oldest centers of civilization in the Western Hemisphere, is now an oil refinery.

More dramatic is the impact of deliberate

vandalism. Archaeological sites of tremendous public interest have been destroyed with increasing frequency in the United States in recent years. For instance, one of the most impressive prehistoric Native American rock art murals in the United States, a mural created at least 600 years ago in Butler Wash, Utah, has been severely damaged on two occasions by vandals using spray paint to cover the original paintings. In the United States, such vandalism and *pothunting* by collectors has doubled during the last decade, and as many as 90 percent of surveyed archaeological sites have been damaged, spurred by a now illegal multimillion-dollar artifact industry. (Cowley, 1989)

To analyze the materials obtained in an excavation, the archaeologist may use skills similar to those of botanists, zoologists, geologists, physicists, and other laboratory scientists, since the original environment of the site must be reconstructed. The archaeologist at this stage may seek to answer such questions as what plants and animals were being eaten and whether these foods were domestic or wild, what the native plants and animals suggest about the climate of the site, or how the materials left behind may provide clues about the age of the site. After such questions have been answered, the work of the archaeologist becomes much like that of the historian and the cultural anthropologist. The goal at this point becomes the description of a way of life and its history.

Anthropological linguists are interested in the role of language in human life. They may be concerned with the origins of language, the biological characteristics of human beings that make it possible for them to use language, the ways in which languages change, or how language is used in daily life. Unlike linguists in other fields, anthropological linguists are chiefly concerned not with language for its own sake, but with the relationships between language and the human condition. Like cultural anthropologists or archaeologists, anthropological linguists may devote their efforts to fieldwork. In the field, the anthropological linguist may record the little-known languages of the world, the oral traditions, the music, the poetry, the styles of speaking, or the social and geographical dialects that are characteristic of a people. Other anthropological linguists with more theoretical interests may study the data

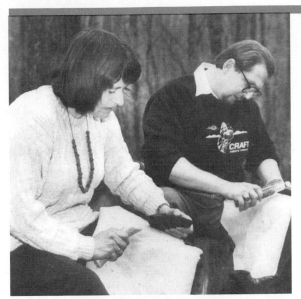

FIGURE 1.6

DR. KATHY SCHICK AND DR. NICHOLAS TOTH

Husband and wife archaeologists Kathy Schick and Nicholas Toth use antlers to shape obsidian tools just as our hominid ancestors did 2.5 million years ago. Schick and Toth plan to have their brains imaged by positron emission tomography while they are making tools out of stone, which may show whether there is a correlation between toolmaking and cognitive skills such as language.

from many related languages, much as the ethnologist compares the customs of different societies.

Physical anthropologists are also sometimes called **biological anthropologists**. The purpose of their research is to answer a variety of questions concerning the origins of the human species, its evolutionary history, and the current biological variation among the peoples of the world. Some physical anthropologists study the fossilized skeletal remains of our

---

anthropological linguists cultural anthropologists who specialize in the study of communication, human languages, and their role in human social life

physical (biological) anthropologists anthropologists who specialize in the study of the evolutionary origins of the human species, the relationships between the human species and other living primates, the physical variations within the human species today, and the relationships between human biology and our species' cultural capacities

biological anthropologists physical anthropologists

FIGURE 1.7

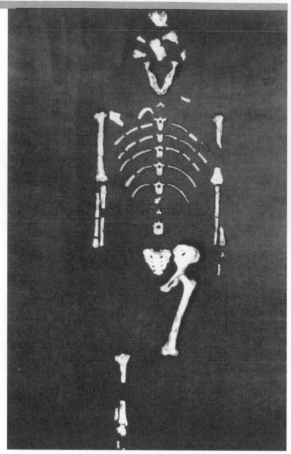

"LUCY"

Some physical anthropologists study the fossilized skeletal remains of early hominids, or human ancestors. Lucy, an Australophithecus afarensis *skeleton found in Ethiopia in 1974, is one of the oldest skeletons found, being roughly 3.5 million years old; paleontologists recently found bones and teeth of a 4-million-year-old erect-walking hominid in Kenya and remains of a 4.4-million-year-old hominid in Ethiopia.*

early human ancestors and their close relatives, with the goal of developing an accurate picture of the evolution of our species. Others have a more specialized interest, like learning about the diseases from which ancient peoples suffered. Some physical anthropologists specialize in studying how the biological characteristics of contemporary peoples differ from one another and how these differences may have come about. There are even physical anthropologists who devote themselves to the study of the biology and behavior of our close nonhuman relatives, like the chimpanzees, gorillas, and monkeys, to learn more about the similarities and differences between us.

As diverse as the specialized interests of different anthropologists may be, what unifies them is their common desire to better understand the nature of humans and to relate their research to the broader picture of the human condition. It is this integrating tendency that is characteristic of the anthropological enterprise and differentiates it from other disciplines that study humans.

Applied and Practicing Anthropology

Randolph Fillmore (1989) of the American Anthropological Association's Information Services reported that "nonacademic employment is expanding as anthropology Ph.D.'s fill career niches once exclusively filled by sociologists, economists, and other social scientists. These latter jobs consist of managing research programs in private firms, government agencies, and nonprofit associations, societies and institutes" (p. 32). Applied anthropologists who use their skills to solve a variety of practical human problems now do consulting for the World Bank and work for companies that do independent consulting in Third World development projects. They work as business consultants for GM, Xerox, Nissan, and other corporations. In the United States, they are employed by the Centers for Disease Control and Prevention, state health departments, the Bureau of Land Management, the Bureau of Indian Affairs, and the U.S. Park Service. They also find employment in private companies that do cultural and human resource management studies throughout the United States.

As anthropologists have studied the problems of nonindustrial populations and of the urban and rural poor in industrialized societies, many have felt a growing obligation to apply their insights to achieve constructive change in areas such as overcoming the cycle of poverty in peasant societies. Because of these and other social concerns, the subfield of anthropology called **applied anthropology** was created. John van Willigen (1986) suggests that the work of applied anthropology falls mainly into three

(Continued on p. 22)

applied anthropology use of anthropological skills and insights to aid in the process of cultural development in nonindustrialized parts of the world or to aid in private and public policy making

STEVEN SIMMS, ARCHAEOLOGIST

I am an archaeologist specializing in prehistoric foragers and farmers of the western United States and in the reconstruction of the ecosystems in which they lived. This also makes me a cultural anthropologist. The idea that these are inseparable is central to describing how I perceive our discipline, what we should be doing, and what our contribution to knowledge is. It was also central in establishing my professional path beginning in my undergraduate days at the University of Utah when I shifted among biology, cultural anthropology, sociology, and archaeology.

Archaeology can be exotic. Experiences abound, whether it be the excitement of excavating a centuries-old campsite in Nevada where the log huts people lived in still stand, or the awe of excavating dozens of human burials exposed by flooding at the edges of the Great Salt Lake in Utah. Sometimes the most exciting experiences come from the challenge of organizing field projects involving dozens of people in often remote locations. Nevertheless, archaeology is primarily a scholarly discipline, anchored in library research. Without the broader context provided by those who have preceded us, comparative knowledge from other places, and a body of theory to help define issues, archaeology would be simply another collector's hobby. Thus for me, archaeology is a perfect way to blend an appreciation for the intellectual life with a love of natural history.

This does not mean one has to know everything about everything. Rather, one needs to develop a system of knowledge that can organize and comprehend the "forest" as more than the mere sum of the trees within it. Anthropology attempts this in several ways. One way that reflects my interest in ecology (the science of relationships) is by recognizing that all human evolution and behavior is always a product of both culture and nature. These facets of human behavior cannot be understood as percentages of influence, by saying, for instance, such and such a behavior is 10 percent genetic and 90 percent cultural. All behaviors, whether it be the execution of language, the characteristics of diet, the shape of intelligence, the patterns of sharing and theft, or the patterns of homosexuality, have both biological and cultural components. Furthermore, it is pointless to quibble about which is more important because they are inextricably linked. Anthropology is the only field that comprehends behavior this way.

The thing archaeologists struggle with most is understanding the past from the fragmentary and indirect material remains left behind, whether these remains be a faint fire hearth, debris from making tools, the outline of a house, the empty shell of a storage pit, exotic objects imported from other places, or the regional patterns these things form and how they change through time.

The concern with knowing about this huge past led me back into cultural anthropology during the past decade, when I participated in fieldwork in the "ethnoarchaeology" of a living group of Bedouin pastoralists in Jordan. This tribe of Bedouin were, until recently, engaged in many traditional practices. In short, we watched people who camped as a way of life change their environment as they went about their lives. In effect, we watched them create archaeological sites by observing the way behavior shaped the material record of the sites they occupied and worked at. Studies like this are improving the ability of archaeologists to "decode" a very tricky past. There is more, however. We found that by linking an archaeological study of the Bedouin group with a study of their ethnohistory using travelers' accounts and government records, along with an ethnographic study including the recording of oral history, food sharing and storage, and genealogy, that we could develop a much more comprehensive picture of a living group. Recently, the study was taken one step further when we became advocates for this Bedouin group who are encountering rapid modernization and face the challenge of preserving their cultural identity and self-direction in the face of colossal outside influences in a rapidly changing Near Eastern country. By all measures, I guess this is applied cultural anthropology.

Thus the power of anthropology is in the appreciation for the subtleties of culture, and historical nuance, but without ever losing sight of the fact that the forest itself—culture, nature, and the sweep of time is greater than the sum of its parts and constitutes a subject of study as a whole. For any educated person in the modern world, knowledge of how things fit together and how there is unity in what has come to be called the "multicultural" is useful knowledge. It is also empowering knowledge in a world that often seems a fragmented tangle of loose ends, ethnic division, religious squabbles, and competing and often ad hoc ideologies. Anthropology certainly does not offer an ideology, but it offers a lens to disentangle these concerns.

domains: information, policy, and action. The domain of information includes gathering and analyzing information that is relevant to the change process. The anthropologist's work in policy creation is typically a matter of providing policymakers with useful information or of analyzing research data. The domain of action includes the things actually done by anthropologists and intervention strategies that they bring to bear in change efforts.

Others who are also interested in applying anthropological approaches to analyzing and solving real-world problems prefer the term **practicing anthropologist**. This is particularly true of those who find full-time employment in private corporations or government agencies, working in an extremely wide range of settings such as agriculture, alcohol and drug use, disaster research, geriatric services, industry and business, military, policy making, social impact assessment, urban development, or wildlife management.

ANTHROPOLOGICAL APPROACHES TO EXPLAINING CULTURE

Anthropology has characteristics of both the humanities and the sciences. The humanistic aspect of anthropology stems from our desire to know and understand other cultures. Anthropologists with a humanistic orientation approach the study of cultures as translators who try to make the symbols of one culture understandable in terms of those of another. They attempt to portray and interpret the customs, values, worldview, or art of one culture so that they can be appreciated by readers accustomed to a different language and way of viewing life. The scientific approach searches for more mechanistic, cause-and-effect explanations of how particular cultures have developed their distinctive characteristics, and for causes of **cultural universals**. The focus is on the role culture plays in human adaptation to the environment and survival.

This dual quality of anthropology, the humanistic desire to understand and appreciate other cultures as systems of meanings and the scientific attempt to explain cultures as mechanistic systems, manifests itself in various ways. For instance, ethnographers distinguish be-

tween emic and etic descriptions of cultures, a distinction first made by Kenneth Pike (1967, p. 8). An **emic analysis** of a culture, though written for outsiders, is one that portrays a culture and its meaningfulness as the insider understands it. As Charles Frake (1964) has pointed out, such a model may incorrectly predict the actual behavior of the people whose culture it describes, and still be valid—so long as the native member of that culture is equally surprised by the error (p. 112). Ward Goodenough (1956) has suggested that the adequacy of an emic model of culture can be tested in two ways: it must not do violence to the native's own feel for the structure of what is described, and it must provide an outsider with whatever knowledge is necessary to talk about the culture or behave in the same way as a native (p. 261).

An **etic analysis** creates a model of a culture by using cross-culturally valid categories, that is, categories that anthropologists have found to be generally useful for describing all cultures. Such models invariably describe each culture in ways that seem alien to its own participants, but that facilitate comparisons between cultures and the discovery of universal principles in the structure and functioning of cultures. According to Marvin Harris (1968), "Etic statements are verified when independent observers using similar operations agree that a given event has occurred," and etic models are valid insofar as they accurately predict the behavior of the native participants of a culture (p. 575).

Anthropology as Humanistic Interpretation

Anthropology is a humanistic discipline in its goal of broadening our understanding of culture as a meaningful system. As Clifford Geertz (1973) put it, "The aim of anthropology is the enlargement of the universe of human dis-

---

practicing anthropologist anthropologist who applies anthropological approaches to analyzing and solving real-world problems

cultural universals those characteristics of human life that can be found in all human ways of life

emic analysis description of a culture as it would have meaning for an insider

etic analysis description of a culture in categories based on universal principles

TRISH CLAY, PRACTICING ANTHROPOLOGIST

I am a practicing anthropologist working for the National Marine Fisheries Service (NMFS), a government agency that oversees regulation of fishing in federal waters off the U.S. coast. I began this job in 1992 upon finishing my Ph.D. dissertation. Prior to that I taught anthropology at Indiana University–Purdue University at Indianapolis, while finishing my degree. I had done applied work between undergraduate and graduate school, with a regional development corporation of the Venezuelan government. This is not the anthropology I originally expected to do, but it is an anthropology I love.

In high school I thought I wanted to be a chemical engineer. In college, I took an introductory anthropology course and immediately changed my major. I think, though, that several experiences with living abroad as a child had primed me for anthropology. My father, a mathematician, had taught in Ghana for a year on a Fulbright Lectureship. Later, when I was 17, he took a position with a university in Venezuela, where he remained for 7 years. That was the beginning of my Venezuelan connection.

As an undergrad, I had a strong interest in language and ended up with a double major in anthropology and modern languages. I had learned Spanish in Venezuela and had studied French since the fifth grade. I took a couple of courses in German, and spent my sophomore year in France under an exchange program. Within anthropology, I took many linguistics and symbolic anthropology courses, and thought I would end up as an anthropological linguist.

I came across an opening at the regional development corporation in Venezuela. I worked there for 18 months, doing small ethnographic studies. While there, I became interested in the government's programs for fishermen. When I re-turned to graduate school, that became the basis for my dissertation.

My dissertation fieldwork looked at government-sponsored marketing cooperatives and analyzed their organization in relation to traditional marketing systems. My current job involves a very different fishery from the one in Venezuela—in terms of the level of technology, the types of species, and the levels of stock abundance, but also revolves around government programs and fishermen. About half of my work is fieldwork, time spent on the docks, on vessels, or in fishermen's homes, where I solicited information on preferred fishing grounds and fishing strategies, gathered demographic information such as age and ethnic affiliation of harvesters, and determined the level of involvement of other family members and relatives. This work is used by fishery managers in formulating and evaluating fishery management plans. I am also expected to publish these results in peer-reviewed journals. The other half of my job is policy analysis and review of such areas as social impact assessments, fishery management plans, and environmental impact statements.

The specialty area of fisheries anthropology is relatively new, only really developing in the 1960s though there had been famous early studies of fishing people such as those by Malinowski. The hiring of fisheries anthropologists by government is even less developed. While the first fisheries anthropologist position was created by NMFS in the early 1970s, mine, in 1992, was the second. Social and economic impacts of fisheries policy are gaining public attention, however, so interest in the field is growing in government circles. Funding, however, has so far lagged behind the expressions of relevance. Nonetheless, this is an exciting field and one that may expand over the next decade.

course" (p. 14). In seeking to understand what other ways of life mean to those who live them, anthropologists have much in common with translators of foreign languages. The Talmudic scholar Jacob Neusner (1979) described the anthropologist's role as that of a translator who makes the insider's point of view meaningful to the outsider: "Anthropologists study the character of humanity in all its richness and diversity. What impresses me in their work is their ability to undertake the work of interpretation of what is thrice alien—strange people, speaking a strange language, about things we-

know-not-what—and to translate into knowledge accessible to us the character and the conscience of an alien world-view" (p. 17). The humanistic problem of how to understand other cultures has also been likened to translation by Jean-Paul Dumont (1978): "Interpretation . . . can refer to three rather different matters: an oral recitation, a reasonable explanation, and a translation from another language. . . . In all three cases, something foreign, strange, separated in time, space or experience is made familiar, present, comprehensible: something requiring representation, explanation or trans-

FIGURE 1.8

CLAUDE LÉVI-STRAUSS

The founder of structuralism, Lévi-Strauss proposes that the human mind perceives and classifies the world around it in a dualistic fashion. In books such as The Savage Mind, *he suggests that this cognitive process is a universal phenomenon that manifests itself in humans in every society in the world.*

lation is somehow 'brought to understanding'—is interpreted" (p. 14).

The skill at interpreting cultures and explaining the significance of seemingly strange customs is probably the central feature of anthropology in the public mind—a skill analogous to that of a translator. On a deeper level, the interpretation of cultures can include the study of patterns within the symbolism, language, and ideology of a culture using analytical styles analogous to those of literary interpretation or art criticism. Anthropologists who specialize in the study of religion, art, folklore, and the influence of culture on human personality are often drawn toward the humanistic or interpretive end of the anthropological spectrum. The major traditions within cultural anthropology that stress the interpretation of culture include structuralism, interpretive anthropology, hermeneutic anthropology, and ethnoscience.

Structuralism.   One of the best-known interpretive approaches is structuralism, a branch of anthropological analysis founded by the

French anthropologist Claude Lévi-Strauss (1958/1967). The viewpoint of **structuralism** is that beneath all of the superficial diversity of cultures is an underlying unity that reflects the tendency of the human mind first to think in terms of contrasts and opposites such as black versus white, good versus bad, or female versus male and, second, to resolve the dilemmas that some opposing ideas create. According to Lévi-Strauss, it is the nature of the human mind to construct these logical contrasting categories because of the inherent dual structure of the human mind. Lévi-Strauss (1969, 1970) finds evidence of symbolic dualities in all aspects of human culture, from mythology to kinship systems. For instance, he has asserted the existence of a regularity of kinship relationships wherein two of the kinship pairs uncle/nephew, brother/sister, father/son, and husband/wife will always be emotionally positive, while the other two will be emotionally negative. The combinations vary from society to society, but the duality of two positive and two negative relations among these four kinship pairs is always maintained. In other words, if the father/son relationship is warm and close, then the husband/wife relationship in the same society will be typically cold and distant.

For a common example of how opposites permeate human thought, consider the duality inherent in the symbols and themes of the Cinderella story. A poor young girl works in the house of a rich old woman. The girl is beautiful but unkempt; her stepsisters are ugly but well cared for. Her stepmother is mean and evil; her fairy godmother is the epitome of goodness. In the story, symbols of nature are transformed into symbols of culture. Several tiny mice become the large and beautiful domestic horses that pull the coach, which is a transformed pumpkin. Two rats are transformed into elegantly dressed coachmen. Cinderella herself is transformed into a princess on the night of the ball, temporarily surpassing the superior status of her stepsisters. Her temporary triumph is made permanent after the original midnight time limit through the intervention of a paradoxical object, a slipper made of fragile glass—the only magical item that is strong enough to

---

structuralism Lévi-Strauss's concept of the underlying unity of all cultures, represented in the tendency to think in dualities

transcend time and survive past the midnight barrier. Another duality brings the story to a close when the slipper fits only the tiny foot of Cinderella, not the huge feet of her stepsisters.

Like Lévi-Strauss, Mary Douglas has tried to clarify the order that underlies human cultural symbolism. She argues that concepts of something unclean—either hygienically or spiritually—are intimately related to a culture's concepts of orderliness. When people categorize the world of their experience, they impose a symbolic order on it. No system of human thought perfectly mirrors the complex world in which people find themselves, so there are always things that do not seem to fit a particular classification system. Because they do not fit the normal system, they are thought of as opposite or as abnormal, disgusting, unclean, or spiritually polluting. Such things are often tabooed, or forbidden, and the very act of avoiding them helps perpetuate people's sense that the world around them is as orderly as their symbolic system for classifying it.

Douglas (1966) has illustrated her approach to symbolism by examining the food taboos of Leviticus. The ancient Hebrews classified the world of living creatures into the three basic types that corresponded to the three realms described in Genesis, the heavens, the earth, and the waters. Birds flew in the heavens and had feathers. Animals had feet and walked, hopped, or jumped. Fish swam in the waters and had scales and fins. Living things that did not fit properly into any of the categories that were believed to have been pronounced good by God in the Genesis story were spiritually unclean. Thus, locusts that flew instead of hopping or sea animals such as the octopus or shellfish that had no scales or fins were "abominations." By mixing the characteristics thought to be appropriate to each category, these creatures seemed to cross the boundaries of creation and to oppose the order that Hebrew culture attributed to God's act of creating things in their proper forms. Therefore, they were classified as taboo foods.

Interpretive Anthropology. The anthropological approach that most parallels that of translation is known as **interpretive anthropology**, which attempts to explain how each element of a culture relates meaningfully to its original context. Interpretive anthropologists do not search for general principles that govern human cultures. Instead, they view each cul-

ture as a distinct configuration of meanings that must be understood on its own terms. An important proponent of this approach is Geertz (1973), who has characterized the approach of interpretive anthropology as an attempt to understand "the native's point of view . . . to figure out what the devil they think they are up to" (p. 58). His analysis of the cockfight as a cultural obsession in Bali is an example of interpretive anthropology at its best. Cockfights are an important occasion for gambling by the owners of the cocks, their relatives, and other spectators. The matches become statements about the honor, dignity, prestige, and respect of the owners themselves because of the high stakes in the wagers between the owners of the cocks (1972).

Geertz shows how, in its imagery, the fighting cock is both a powerful symbol of Balinese concepts of masculinity and, simultaneously, of animals, the antithesis of all that is human. Metaphors about cocks abound in Balinese discourse about men, and the word for cock, *sabung*, is used with meanings such as "hero," "warrior," "man of parts," "lady-killer," or "tough guy." The owner of each cock identifies with his animal and the masculinity it represents, but this identification also implies that there is a darker, nonhuman side to men's nature—a fact that is also evident in the ritual symbolism of the cockfight. A match between two cocks, each armed with razor-sharp steel spurs, is "a wing-beating, head-thrusting, leg-kicking explosion of animal fury" (p. 8) that may last as long as 5 minutes and ends with the death of one animal. Each fight is prefaced with rituals and chants, because the deaths that end each fight are regarded as sacrifices to demons that control the natural evils of Balinese life such as illness, crop failure, or volcanic eruptions. Thus, cockfights bring their participants into the realm of "the powers of darkness" with which humans must contend for success in life.

Hermeneutic Anthropology. During the past several decades, some anthropologists have attempted to make more explicit the process by which the anthropologist comes to understand an alien culture. This approach, called

---

interpretive anthropology approach that attempts to explain how each element of a culture relates meaningfully to its original context

hermeneutic anthropology (from the Greek word for "interpretation"), examines the interaction of the fieldworker and the native informant, the interplay between observer and the observed. Achieving insight into how members of another culture think and feel about what the fieldworker does and says modifies the anthropologist's own understanding of the culture.

Hermeneutic anthropology is an outgrowth of the ideas of the French philosopher Paul Ricoeur, who emphasized the role of understanding others as a means for self-understanding. Ricoeur's ideas have been incorporated into the anthropological process by Paul Rabinow (1977), who has referred to the mutual attempts of the fieldworker and informant to understand one another as "the dialectic of fieldwork" (p. 39). The anthropologist is very much in the forefront of the narrative, never an "objective" analyst behind the scenes. The biases of the fieldworker are themselves usually brought to light as he or she grapples with the experience in the attempt to make sense of it. Readers are similarly exposed to the emotional and intellectual dilemmas experienced by the native informants as they too are sometimes forced to come to grips with new ways of perceiving themselves and their own culture because of their work with anthropologists.

Postmodernist Anthropology.   As the cultures of the world have come to influence each other and have become more alike, anthropologists have redirected their fields of study from the isolated "exotic" cultures of traditional anthropology, which hardly exist anymore, to *contemporary* non-Western Third World traditions. Anthropologists have begun to borrow many of the tools and much of the jargon developed by other disciplines such as philosophy, gender and minority studies, and literature to communicate about cultural diversity from an increasingly international perspective.

This not yet unified but increasingly popular approach to ethnographic writing has come to be most widely known as **postmodernist anthropology**. It emphasizes that each culture must be portrayed as "an open-ended, creative dialogue of subcultures, of insiders and outsiders, of diverse factions" (Clifford, 1983, p. 137). By rejecting the notion that culture is a homogeneous system, postmodernism also denies the authority of any one mode of anthropological interpretation. Instead, postmodernists explore the diversity of meanings in human life and emphasize the exploration of cultural meanings as a cooperative quest. The anthropologist and native members of a society participate in a dialogue that evokes a variety of meanings and viewpoints and that recognizes that "there are always alternative interpretations" (Marcus, 1986, p. 191).

A number of European philosophers and intellectuals such as Jacques Lacan (1967), Michel Foucault (1977), Jacques Derrida (1976), and Pierre Bourdieu (1977) have had a major influence on postmodernist anthropology. They have expanded the anthropological concept of cultural relativism into a logical attack on the privileged status of Western scientific thought. This redefinition of Western science as merely one ideology among a multitude of equally valid Western and non-Western ways of conceiving of the human condition implies that anthropology itself has no claim on any superior validity as a purely "objective" commentary on other societies.

The most influential postmodernist anthropologists today are James Clifford, George Marcus, and Michael Fischer. These and other postmodernists have reinvigorated ethnographic writing. They have criticized traditional ethnographies that claimed to achieve true scientific objectivity. Postmodernist ethnographies portray a culture "as open-ended, ambiguous, and in flux" (Marcus & Cushman, 1982, p. 45).

Postmodernists also emphasize the participant half of participant-observation. Their work is characterized by the portrayal of the dialectic interplay of anthropologists and the people with whom they participate. For instance, the word "I" is much more common in postmodernist ethnographies than it ever was before. In part, this stems from the fact that postmodernist ethnographers are now living

---

hermeneutic anthropology approach that examines the interaction between fieldworker and native informant

postmodernist anthropology a humanistic approach to anthropology that rejects the notion of ethnography as a detached, scientifically objective process and proposes the view that culture is composed of a constantly changing, open-ended, and ambiguous system of meanings that are negotiated and renegotiated by members of society as they interact

among literate peoples, who not only have developed their own traditions, but who also can communicate about them fairly easily. Postmodernist ethnographers, therefore, collaborate with the people they live with rather than simply "describe" them.

The typical postmodernist ethnography is based on a **dialogic model**, a form of writing that, like a dialogue, brings the interaction of the anthropologist and the native members of a society into the forefront of the document. Postmodernists also emphasize the importance of diversity within, as well as among, cultures. For instance, Clifford (1983) uses the concept of **polyphony** to describe the diversity of voices and viewpoints within every human group that embodies the dynamic nature of every culture.

Ethnoscience. An approach to cultural interpretation in which a systematic description of a culture as it is perceived by its own people and developed by studying the linguistic categories that informants use to discuss their culture is called **ethnoscience**, or sometimes **cognitive anthropology**. This is accomplished by skillfully formulating and asking appropriate questions that encourage informants to define the boundaries of each concept and its relationship to other concepts. In so doing, the ethnoscientist makes explicit the hierarchy of categories into which a society subdivides the world of its experience. In effect, ethnoscientists construct a dictionary of the native language and culture.

The systematic approach of ethnoscience results in extremely detailed and accurate descriptions of how people classify those things they talk about. One result of the rigor of this approach is that it tends to focus on rather specific and limited parts of an entire culture. Although, in theory, it might be possible to eventually outline the knowledge of an entire culture by such methods, ethnoscientists have been unable to describe more than a fraction of any single culture. For instance, Goodenough (1956) has suggested methods for systematically describing the kinship system of a society. Conklin (1956) has examined the color categories of the Hanunóo of the Philippines. Frake (1961) has outlined how the Subanun of Mindanao diagnose the various types of diseases recognized in their culture, and (1964) has described the native categories of Subanun "religious behavior."

Anthropology as Scientific Explanation

While much of culture exists in the symbolic realm of ideas—the beliefs and feelings of an ideology—there is also a practical aspect of culture that makes it possible for a people to survive physically. Each culture, as a system of common understandings, serves as a form of social bonding and also as the action plan by which a human society interacts with its natural environment to fulfill its survival needs. Anthropologists whose interests lean toward the scientific goal of explaining and predicting human behavior emphasize the practical influences of social life, human biological and psychological needs, technology, and the environment in their descriptions of how the symbolic or ideological elements of culture arise. Their concern is for isolating the factors that give rise to the diverse cultures of the world and for developing models that show how these factors determine the form that a culture develops. The major traditions among these anthropologists include British structural-functionalism, American functionalism, Marxist anthropology, neofunctionalism, cultural ecology, sociobiology, and cultural materialism.

British Structural-Functionalism. British anthropologists have long emphasized the importance of **social structure**, the network of social relations among members of a society, in creating the basic customs of each culture. Their approach, called **social anthropology**, was founded by Radcliffe-Brown (1949). In the small-scale societies that were most often stud-

---

dialogic model an approach to ethnographic narrative that engages the anthropologist and natives of a culture in a give-and-take exploration of cultural meanings

polyphony diversity of viewpoints within a single culture

ethnoscience (cognitive anthropology) approach that aims to systematically describe a culture by analyzing the linguistic categories used by informants to discuss their society

cognitive anthropology ethnoscience

social structure the part of social organization made up of groups and their relationships with each other

social anthropology Radcliffe-Brown's approach emphasizing the importance of social interactions in determining the customs of a culture

ied by anthropologists, kinship ties were determinants of how people were expected to treat one another. Because of the concern of Radcliffe-Brown and his colleagues for how a society's customs functioned to maintain its social structure, the analytical method of social anthropology has been given the name **structural-functionalism**.

American Functionalism.

American anthropology was more influenced by the views of Malinowski (1935), who asserted that cultural customs function primarily to support seven basic human **biological and psychological needs** that must be dealt with by every society: nutrition, reproduction, bodily comforts, safety, relaxation, movement, and growth. Malinowski's list is probably an incomplete summary of human survival needs, but it can be used to illustrate that cultural variation is constrained by the practical necessities of human survival. A culture can only survive if it responds effectively to its members' survival needs.

As cultural creatures, we human beings do not meet our biological and psychological needs directly. Instead, we fulfill our needs as the culture of our social group prescribes. In no society do people eat every edible plant or animal available to them. People eat only those things their culture defines as "foods," and they exclude from their diets other items of equal nutritional value. For instance, in parts of East Asia dog meat is considered a delicacy, while the Western custom of eating cheese and yogurt is considered disgusting.

Similarly, in no society is the need for reproduction fulfilled by allowing all people to mate indiscriminately. In every society, sexual acts are controlled by cultural rules, such as those determining appropriate partners, when and where sexual acts may occur, and how those acts should actually be performed. For instance, among the Navajo of the southwestern United States, sexual intercourse is forbidden between any persons of known familial relationship, no matter how distant. The pre-Conquest Quechua Indians of the Andes, on the other hand, expected their emperor, the Inca, to mate with his full sister.

The need for bodily comforts is dealt with in each society by prescribing certain forms of housing and clothing as acceptable. These cultural patterns also provide each individual in the society with a plan for making minor improvements in his or her immediate environment.

Each culture also includes plans of action for ensuring safety in dangerous situations. These include guidelines for conduct when walking down a dark street alone, when lost, or when attacked by an animal or by a human enemy. Human skills in coping with danger vary from culture to culture.

The needs for relaxation, movement, and growth are met in culturally patterned rhythms of work and sleep, exercise and rest, recreation and practical activities. Each society trains its young in the way of life of its people and teaches its members the skills they must acquire at each stage of their lives.

Neoevolutionism.

Interest in the evolution of cultures was reintroduced by Leslie White (1943), who suggested that cultural evolution could be measured by the per capita energy that a technology allows people to draw from their environment (pp. 168–169). White's approach to cultural evolution has been called **neoevolutionism**. His view describes culture as "a mechanism for harnessing energy and of putting it to work" (p. 390). The technological system determines the way in which a society must be organized, even those parts of culture that are not directly related to survival. Thus, White's view of cultural evolution incorporates the concept of culture into a system in which technology, the human relationships that make up a society, and nontechnological beliefs and feelings each influence one another, but in which technology is the guiding force of cultural change.

In White's concept of neoevolutionism, **technology** is described as the tools and tech-

---

structural-functionalism approach based on the analytical method of social anthropology that focuses on ways in which societies' customs function to maintain their social structure

biological and psychological needs the needs for nutrition, reproduction, bodily comforts, safety, relaxation, movement, and growth

neoevolutionism a view of cultural evolution that describes culture as "a mechanism for harnessing energy and of putting it to work" and that measures cultural evolution by the amount of energy that a society's technology harnesses per capita per year

technology tools and techniques through which human beings harness the energy available in their environment

niques used to extract resources from the environment and the knowledge and skills for making and using them. Every culture must include valid ways of coping with the natural environment, the source of energies and raw materials used to fulfill group and individual needs. In every society, objects are manufactured and used in undertakings ranging from recreation and worship to basic survival. Technology provides ways in which the forces of nature, whether physical or biological, are captured, transformed, and utilized to preserve human life and provide comfort. In fact, a human society might well be described as the organized patterns of human interaction through which the energies of nature are channeled from person to person.

According to White (1971), those activities that are most related to survival—the provision of food, shelter, and defense—have the biggest influence on how the rest of a cultural system is organized. Regardless of how simple or how complex a society is, its tool kit and technological know-how include the means for solving these problems and most directly influence the nature of a culture.

Multilinear Evolutionism. Julian Steward (1955), another twentieth-century cultural evolutionist, placed greater emphasis than did White on tracing the courses of evolutionary change followed by individual cultures, an approach he referred to as **multilinear evolution**. Like White, he emphasized the ways in which people adapted to their environments as determining the characteristics of the rest of their culture. Unlike White, he had little interest in broad generalizations about cultural evolution. Instead, he advocated a more empirical approach to tracing the specific course of evolution followed by each culture, an approach that he believed would discover both differences and "limited parallels of form, function, and sequence" among them (p. 19).

Marxist Anthropology. Karl Marx and Friedrich Engels were the first students of history to attempt to develop a deterministic theory of social change. Their viewpoint was that all history was the outcome of the conflicting economic interests of the various social classes. **Marxist anthropology** espouses this theme and focuses on the role of social conflict, especially economic and political conflict, in determining the conditions under which people live. For in-

stance, a Marxist anthropologist, in explaining the slow pace of economic change in a nonindustrialized nation, would suggest that one important factor is that the lands worked by many rural farmers are owned by nonresident members of the upper class. In such a situation, social policies that might benefit the landless food producers would conflict with the economic interests of the landowners, who are likely to have greater influence over governmental policy decisions than are the farm workers. Thus, the Marxist anthropologist would point to the conflicting interests of the producers and owners as a barrier to economic development.

Neofunctionalism. An application of Marx's emphasis on the existence of conflict in social life and its relationship to stability in cultural systems is the hallmark of **neofunctionalism**. The neofunctionalist might point to the conflicting party ideologies in U.S. politics as a part of the system by which stability is maintained in the United States. In a two-party political system, each party strives to obtain the votes of more than half of the electorate in order to have its candidate elected. The conflict between the two parties and the positions of any two competing candidates are expressed in language that portrays them as being at opposite ends of the political spectrum, yet both parties must actually be somewhere near the center of the political spectrum represented by U.S. voters. Thus, a campaign process that emphasizes conflicting values and political commitments is the means by which the central majority of voters are wooed by politicians who, once elected, are likely to be neither extremely liberal nor extremely conservative in practice.

---

multilinear evolution an approach to cultural evolution that emphasizes the divergent paths that each culture follows as it adapts to its local environment

Marxist anthropology the study of the effects of class conflict on social and cultural change

neofunctionalism contemporary approach to studying functional processes of cultural systems, with emphasis on the ways in which conflict may be one of the mechanisms by which cultural stability is maintained

FIGURE 1.9

ANNETTE WEINER

Dr. Weiner has conducted considerable research in the Trobriand Islands, Papua New Guinea, and some in Western Samoa. She is particularly interested in the study of gender, sexuality, and the part that women play in societies around the world.

Feminist Anthropology. The specialization known as **feminist anthropology** is a recent model in anthropology that shares Marxist anthropology and neofunctionalism's common concern for how conflict and inequities of power can play themselves out in human life. The defining characteristic of feminist anthropology is its specific interest in how gender-related differences influence social life. Although gender is always a central variable in feminist analysis of social life, these theorists also appreciate the ways in which access to social power is unequally distributed based on a variety of other social categories such as class, ethnic, and racial distinctions. Therefore, feminist anthropologists are among those, such as the symbolic and postmodernist anthropologists, who are most likely to stress the importance of diversity and dialogue and meaning in any culture. They are unique in their ability to bridge the gulf between humanist and scientist that more clearly separates practitioners of the other approaches to anthropology.

Cultural Ecology. In the approach known as **cultural ecology**, the study of the adjustment of ways of life to different habitats, it is as-

sumed that culture is an adaptive mechanism, and that those customs that improve a society's ability to adapt to its environment are the ones that are most likely to survive. This viewpoint is similar to that which biologists apply to evolution, so it is not surprising that cultural ecologists such as Andrew Vayda and Roy Rappaport (1968) have included the interaction of both culture and biology in their description of single adaptive systems. Thus, cultural ecologists view culture as part of a larger system that includes the natural environment and its interaction with human and animal populations and human customs.

Rappaport's (1967, 1968) analysis of the Tsembaga Maring people of New Guinea has become a classic illustration of the cultural ecological approach. The Tsembaga were tropical forest horticulturalists who grew taro, yams, sweet potatoes, and manioc, and raised pigs. The root crops were a daily staple for the Tsembaga diet, but pigs were eaten only in ceremonial events that formed part of a longer cycle of warfare and peace between neighboring villages. When the size of the herds was small, pigs were easy to care for. They foraged for themselves during the day, and their rooting in the gardens actually aided in the cultivation of the soil.

As the herds grew, however, increasing proportions of garden crops were expended on feeding pigs. Finally, after a period of about 11 years, the costs of maintaining the herds became so great that the adult pigs began to be slaughtered in ceremonies that marked the beginning of a period of warfare between neighboring villages. The fighting continued for a period of weeks until one of the villages was routed. Its survivors abandoned their homes and sought refuge with their kin in other villages. Meanwhile, the victors slaughtered the loser's herds and destroyed their gardens and houses.

At the end of each war, the major ceremonial slaughter of pigs occurred, as the winners gave thanks to their ancestors for their victory and rewarded with gifts of meat the allies who had helped. The size of the herds returned to manageable numbers, and a truce remained in effect between the victors and the vanquished

---

feminist anthropology the study of the ways in which social power interacts with gender

cultural ecology the study of the ways in which cultures adapt to their specific habitats

FIGURE 1.10

TSEMBAGA MARING PIG CEREMONY

The Tsembaga Maring pig ceremony illustrates the concept of culture as part of ecological approach. When the herd of pigs becomes too large to manage, *the Tsembaga engage in a ritual slaughter intended to reduce the herds and stabilize the ecological balance among pigs, humans, and their environment.*

until the herds had once again grown large enough that they had to be culled.

Rappaport believed that the Tsembaga pig ceremonies supported the long-term balance between the human population and the food supply. Alliances were more easily formed by villages that could demonstrate their ability to support herds large enough to attract supporters, who then would be rewarded during the pig slaughter ceremonies. So, the Tsembaga were motivated not to cull their herds as a source of protein throughout the year. Since the ceremonial slaughter was an integral part of the warfare process, conflicts between villages happened only periodically in a cycle that prevented human population growth from overtaxing the available land resources and geographically redistributed those who survived, while their garden plots returned to nature and regenerated themselves.

Sociobiology.   Like cultural ecologists, sociobiologists assume that adaptive behavior is more likely to survive than nonadaptive behavior, but unlike cultural ecologists, the concept of culture is given a less central role in the interpretation of the adaptive process. The emphasis in **sociobiology** is on the evolution of

human genetic predispositions for adaptive ways of behaving that will maximize the reproductive success of human groups. In sociobiological thinking, culture is basically a system of reproductive strategies and cultural traits that are common in our species because they have been favored by biological evolution.

As one example, sociobiologists such as Pierre Van den Berghe and David Barash (1977) note that many cultures permit or even encourage men to have more than one wife, while very few societies encourage the opposite practice of a woman having several husbands. This, they argue, is because the reproductive success of men and women is normally enhanced by the former marriage pattern. For males, reproductive success is improved by having many mates. But for females, each pregnancy represents a great expenditure of energy, so their reproductive success is enhanced by a lasting union with a single male whose characteristics will improve her children's chances of surviving. Thus, the common custom of plural mar-

(Continued on p. 33)

_____

sociobiology approach that emphasizes the role of natural selection on genetic predispositions for specific behaviors

PRACTICAL REASONS FOR DOBUAN PARANOIA

According to Reo Fortune (1932), the Dobuans had a fierce mistrust of one another, a mistrust that bordered on paranoia. Their life was filled with sorcery. Food never grew without magic and neighbors engaged in magical theft of one another's crops; the winds did not blow except by magic; sex occurred only when one was bewitched; and all death was believed to have been caused by sorcery, with the surviving spouse the probable sorcerer. It would have been a mistake, though, to interpret Dobuan ideology as rampant mental illness. When the Dobuan outlook on life, nature, and their fellow Dobuans was seen as a cultural adaptation to their unhappy circumstances, it made a great deal of sense.

The Dobuans lived on rocky, volcanic islands that had only sparse pockets of soil that were much less productive than those of their Melanesian neighbors. Their extremely small villages never numbered more than about 25 people and they made their living from gardens they cut from the jungle. Their staple food was the yam, but the meagerness of their environment made hunger a constant threat, even though they lived in small and scattered groups. There was never enough food and everyone went hungry for several months before each planting time to make sure there would be enough seed yams. Eating one's seed yams was the ultimate mistake, for not even a person's own family would provide new ones to someone who had proven to be such a failure. Dobuan economic life was characterized by fierce and secretive competitiveness, even within families. Husbands and wives maintained separate gardens and, although they worked together and pooled their food, they did not share seed yams.

The death of a Dobuan created severe economic obligations for the in-laws. During the period of mourning, a surviving husband had to work the gardens of his deceased wife, her parents, and her brothers and sisters, while his own brothers and sisters had the added work of caring for his. After the burial, the kin of the survivor had to make a large payment of food and yams to the relatives of the deceased. At the death of a man, his wife's children were required to cook a mash of bananas and taro, a starchy root plant, and deliver it to the relatives of their father. After the mourning period was over, the children were never again permitted to enter the village of their father or to eat food from his garden.

Is it any wonder that with conditions of economic hardship such as these, the Dobuans were not a trusting people? They lived in a world of limited resources, and their concept that one could prosper only at the expense of another was not unrealistic. This unhappy outlook on life was exaggerated when they tried to gain a symbolic modicum of security in an insecure life. Like peoples the world around, the Dobuans sought security in religion. To the Dobuans, nature was not the kind provider; it was magic alone that assured the growth of crops. Yams, the Dobuans believed, would only grow with the aid of incantations inherited from one's mother's family. When hunger still occurred each year, the Dobuans salvaged the emotional security that religion brings at an awful cost—by attributing their poor harvest to the sorcery of their neighbors. They thus affirmed that their magic did work, and in fact was so powerful that it could be used to steal the yams of others. In simplest terms, the Dobuans traded the fear of possible starvation for a mistrust of their fellow humans.

DOBUANS

The Dobuans lived on the rocky volcanic islands of Melanesia. They made their living from gardens they cut from the jungle, but their harsh environment made hunger a constant threat. Their numbers began to decline as early as 1884 when many were taken into slavery. Currently, about 900 Dobuans work as professionals or in government service.

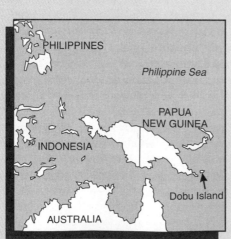

PHILIPPINES

Philippine Sea

PAPUA NEW GUINEA

INDONESIA

Dobu Island

AUSTRALIA

riage for men is based on the biologically evolved behavioral tendencies of both men and women. The sociobiological emphasis has not always been accepted by the traditional cultural anthropologists whose interests have centered on culture, but some aspects of sociobiology have been integrated into the approaches of some biological anthropologists and cultural anthropologists who are interested in human adaptations to their environments and in relationships between biology and the cultural capacities of the human species.

Cultural Materialism.   The approach known as **cultural materialism** also shares cultural ecology's interest in the human relationship with the environment, but adds a hierarchy of technological and social variables to explain the ideology of a particular culture. Harris (1979), the anthropologist who gave cultural materialism its impetus, has summarized the major behavioral categories within which culture is manifest. He also proposed that all are ultimately linked to practical responses to the world. The first of these behavioral categories is the **mode of production**, the technology and practices by which people expand or limit their basic subsistence production in their specific habitat. A culture's mode of production includes its subsistence technology, technological relationships to ecosystems, and work patterns. The second category is the **mode of reproduction**, the technology and practices by which a people expand, limit, and maintain their population. Discussions of mode of reproduction would touch on matters of demography; mating patterns; fertility, natality, and mortality; nurturance of infants; medical control of demographic patterns; and contraception, abortion, and infanticide.

Domestic economy—the organization of reproduction and basic production, exchange, and consumption within the family or household—comes next in Harris's model. This is the realm of family structure, domestic division of labor, domestic socialization, age and sex roles within the family, and domestic discipline. Next comes the category of **political economy**—the organization of reproduction, production, exchange, and consumption outside the domestic setting. Here one finds the political organization of society, its factions, clubs, associations, and corporations. Here also is nondomestic division of labor, taxation, and tribute, as well as public education, class, caste, urban and rural organization, and the mechanisms of social control and warfare. The final category, according to Harris, is the **behavioral superstructure**, the realm of art, music, dance, literature, advertising, rituals, sports, games, hobbies, and science.

Each of these behavioral categories has a corresponding component within the system of culture. The last, the behavioral superstructure, is most intimately centered within ideology, the symbolic core of culture, and the furthest removed from the mundane influences of practical living. A link exists, nonetheless. Harris contends that the modes of production and reproduction have a major influence on the characteristics of the domestic and political economy, which in turn influence the behavioral superstructure of a culture. In brief, the means by which a people survive and maintain their population within an environment influence their social customs and even the more purely symbolic parts of human life.

---

cultural materialism approach that analyzes technological and social variables in explaining ideological facts of culture

mode of production the work practices by which people apply their subsistence technology within a particular environment

mode of reproduction the technology and practices operating within a particular social environment that influence the size of the society's population

domestic economy the reproductive, economic, and social behaviors that characterize life within the family or household

political economy the reproductive, economic, and social behaviors that are typical of life outside the family or household

behavioral superstructure those behaviors most closely linked to a culture's ideology, including art, ritual, recreation, philosophy, and science

CHAPTER SUMMARY

1. Anthropology is the broadest of the disciplines studying the human condition, for it draws on fields as diverse as philosophy, art, economics, linguistics, and biology for its conclusions.

2. Anthropology grew out of eighteenth-century European Enlightenment attempts to explain the diversity of cultures that had been encountered during the prior centuries of world exploration and colonial expansion.

3. Anthropological history has emphasized various models for analyzing cultural differences. Its early period was dominated by an evolutionary perspective. Early evolutionist models gave way to a greater interest in a more particularistic focus complemented by a heavy emphasis on fieldwork as a means of data collection. Starting in the 1930s, most anthropology was dominated by functionalist analysis; more recently there has been a proliferation of many different schools of thought.

4. Even when working for governmental or commercial employers, anthropologists try to maintain an ethical approach that safeguards the interests of the people they are hired to study.

5. In cultural anthropology, these take the form of participant observation and cross-cultural comparison.

6. While most anthropologists continue their work through universities, applied and practicing anthropologists are bringing their skills to nonacademic settings.

7. The major fields of anthropology itself are cultural anthropology, archaeology, anthropological linguistics, and physical anthropology. They all utilize the same basic anthropological methods of fieldwork and comparative studies.

8. The two main models—culture as a symbolic system and culture as an adaptation to the environment—are represented by a number of new specialized subfields in anthropology, including feminist anthropology, psychological anthropology, visual anthropology, humanistic anthropology, and applied anthropology.

ANNOTATED READINGS

Angeloni, E. (Ed.). (1995). *Annual editions: Anthropology 95/96* (18th ed.). Guilford, CT: Dushkin Publishing Group/Brown & Benchmark Publishers. An annually revised collection of significant articles on contemporary issues in cultural anthropology.

Borofsyky, R. (Ed.). (1994). *Assessing cultural anthropology*. New York: McGraw-Hill. A collection of essays that express the diversity of viewpoints in contemporary anthropological thought.

Chambers, E. (1985). *Applied anthropology: A practical guide*. Englewood Cliffs, NJ: Prentice Hall. An overview of applied anthropology with an emphasis on its relation to policy and its application in both Western and non-Western settings.

Clifford, J., & Marcus, G. (Eds.). (1986). *Writing culture: The process and politics of ethnography*. Berkeley, CA: University of California Press. A collection of explorative writings by postmodernist anthropologists.

DeVita, P. R. (Ed.). (1990). *The humbled anthropologist: Tales from the Pacific*. Belmont, CA: Wadsworth. Accounts by 20 anthropologists of errors that they made and misunderstandings that they had during their fieldwork.

Harris, M. (1968). *The rise of anthropological theory: A history of theories of culture*. New York: Thomas Y. Crowell. An authoritative and comprehensive history of cultural anthropology by a leading figure in contemporary anthropology. Must reading for students who have decided to major in anthropology.

Lévi-Strauss, C. (1967). *Structural anthropology* (C. Jacobsen & B. G. Schoepf, Trans.). New York: Basic Books. (Original work published 1958). Seventeen articles by the founder of structural anthropology, including the application of linguistic techniques to the study of culture.

Lowie, R. H. (1937). *The history of ethnological theory.* New York: Holt, Rinehart & Winston. The traditional view of the history of cultural anthropology in a readable style.

Moore, H. (1988). *Feminism and anthropology.* Minneapolis, MN: University of Minnesota Press. Provides a good general overview of feminist perspectives in anthropology.

Morgan, S. (Ed.). (1989). *Gender and anthropology: Critical reviews for reseach and teaching.* Washington, DC: American Anthropological Association. A review of gender studies that covers both gender roles in the major world regions and a variety of general issues pertaining to gender.

Rappaport, R. A. (1968). *Pigs for the ancestors: Ritual in the ecology of a New Guinea people.* New Haven, CT: Yale University Press. An excellent illustration of the approach of cultural ecology applied to the analysis of warfare among the Tsembaga Maring of New Guinea.

Ruby J. (Ed.). (1982). *A crack in the mirror: Reflexive perspectives in anthropology.* Philadelphia: University of Pennsylvania Press. A collection of studies by ethnographers who forthrightly discuss the anthropologist's role in reflexive anthropological research.

Spradley, J. F. (1980). *Participant observation.* New York: Holt, Rinehart, & Winston. A step-by-step overview of how ethnographic research is conducted.

Strathern, A. (1993). *Landmarks: Reflections on anthropology.* Kent, OH: Kent State University Press. Essays and lectures on fieldwork and theory in cultural anthropology that also provide interesting insights into the perspectives of a number of historically important anthropologists.

van Willigen, J. (1986). *Applied anthropology: An introduction.* New York: Bergin & Garvey. A basic introduction to the field of applied anthropology.

CHAPTER TWO

Culture

CHAPTER OBJECTIVES

After reading this chapter, you should be able to:

Explain the nature of culture.

Define ideology.

Discuss ideological communication.

Explain the relationship between beliefs and feelings.

Enumerate the differences between real and ideal culture.

Discuss the ways cultures may influence each other.

Outline the various emotional reactions people have to other societies and cultures.

Analyze the values of cultural relativism.

Explain the causes of culture shock.

Recognize how scientific and humanistic approaches to culture influence the ways culture is conceptualized.

◀ ***Figure* 2.1** Intercultural Influences *Despite the now quite common influence of one culture upon another around the world, most social groups still make an effort to retain some of their traditions. These American Indians watch some traditional dances of the Mohawk, Hopi, Apache, and 22 other tribes at the Thunderbird American Midsummer Powwow at the Queens County Farm Museum in Floral Park, New York.*

CULTURE

IDEOLOGY

Ideological Communication
Beliefs
Feelings
Cultural Change

CULTURAL DIFFERENCES

Intercultural Influences
Ethnocentrism
Cultural Relativism

VIEWPOINTS ABOUT CULTURE

Diversity in Conceptualizing Culture
The Unity and Diversity of Cultures
Culture Shock

Unlike other animals, we humans have a persistent tendency to try to make sense of our existence and to share those understandings with others of our group. We also feel a necessity to alter the environment so that we can survive more comfortably and predictably. These ideas and survival strategies are institutionalized and perpetuated as culture, the subject of this chapter. After analyzing the systematic patterning of beliefs, feelings, and ways of surviving, we must note that these patterns differ from one society to the next, commonly resulting in misunderstandings and mistrust between human groups.

Cockfights. Dogfights. Boxing matches. Blanket giveaways. Pig slaughters. Sacred cows. Basket moon. Harvest moon. Man in the moon. Grass skirts. Banana leaf skirts. Silk skirts. One man's diamond is another man's coal. Humans identify their world and their place in it according to what they learn from their environment, their ancestors, their families, and their schools. And despite the explosion of communications technology, one woman's diamond is still, for the most part, another woman's coal.

CULTURE

Human beings are social animals. We live in communities that may be parts of larger social groups called societies. A **society** is a group of people who conceive of themselves as distinct from other groups. All human groups develop complex systems of ideas, feelings, and survival strategies and pass them from one generation to the next. Anthropologists call the system of ideas, feelings, and survival strategies of a particular human group the **culture** of that group. Great diversity exists among anthropologists' definitions of culture. Alfred Kroeber and Clyde Kluckhohn (1952) surveyed 158 definitions of culture by other social and behavioral scientists. They found that the concept of culture always centered on the idea that there is a system to the beliefs and feelings that unify a human group and give it an identity as a society. Those who share this way of life may be aware of some parts of the system, whereas

their awareness of other parts of the system may be implicit in their customary behavior without their being conscious of it.

Behaviors that are guided by culture are learned, rather than acquired through biological inheritance. Thus, instincts, innate reflexes, and other biologically predetermined responses are not a part of culture. Some parts of a culture are taught explicitly; others are learned by direct and indirect observation of the behaviors of others.

In learning the customs of their culture, people are taught that they share some "common understandings" with one another and that others expect them to follow those customs. Our North American culture gives particular meanings to behaviors such as shaking hands and applauding a performance. Our common understanding about the use of these behaviors lets us know when we should perform them. A definite awkwardness or embarrassment is felt by everyone involved if someone does either behavior at the wrong time or place. In this sense, much of a way of life is like a set of rules about how one ought to live. These parts of culture, like the rules of a game, give structure and continuity to the social life of each human group. The predictability that culture lends to a people's behavior gives them security since it allows them to anticipate the behavior of others, including those they are meeting for the first time. Therefore, the parts of culture that are explicitly taught are often thought of as the *proper* ways of behaving.

Participating in a shared and traditional system of customs also gives life a sense of meaningfulness. Thus, attending the World Series, the Super Bowl, prom night, rock concerts, and sunbathing on a crowded beach are activities that help the people of the United States conceive of themselves as a society with its own distinctive culture. Customs, objects, and events acquire meanings for the participants

---

society a group of human beings who conceive of themselves as distinct from other such groups

culture a learned system of beliefs, feelings, and rules for living around which a group of people organize their lives; a way of life of a particular society

WHERE SUBURBAN TRIBES GATHER
FOR SAND AND SURF

This excerpt (in a somewhat tongue-in-cheek way) illustrates the power of customs in identifying groups and how the culture defines rules and develops values for different subcultures within the larger one.

Like a Bedouin to his tribesmen, Richard Dupras called to the families gathered round him on the burning midday sands: "How many people did we have at dinner the other night?"

"Thirty-five," the satisfying answer came.

This is the annual gathering of the suburban tribes on the sands of the Jersey Shore, where time seems to pass at a biblical pace, the years counted according to the generations of new in-laws and babies sharing the beach, chairs, umbrellas, cottage. Throw a handful of sand on the beach here and in neighboring resorts like Lavallette and it is hard not to hit a three-generation encampment.

"We first came here 30 years ago, after our first six children," said Mr. Dupras of Somerville. "John, how long have you come here?" he asked a son-in-law, John Hughes, still dripping from a swim.

"Since I was a baby, in Manasquan," Mr. Hughes replied. "These are my roots." He stopped and smiled. "I used to swim in the water until, when I closed my eyes at night, all I saw were waves coming at me."

Time can seem to be suspended in the filmy sunlight that hangs over these beaches because so little has changed in all the decades since northern New Jersey's suburbs created summer outposts on this strip of oceanfront along Barnegat Bay.

Ocean Beach, the Levittown of shore resorts, has 3,000 modest cottages crammed from bay to dunes along two dozen lanes named for fish and fowl (as in Tuna Way). In the last 10 years, it has survived winter storms, recession, pollution and, a sign of how out of whack that decade was, 1980's real-estate speculators.

Now Tuna and the other ways look like they always have, a treeless camp of squat cottages next to a wide beach and the Atlantic. The beach is as wide as ever, despite the storms, and as full of children, and the water looks its cleanest in years. For beach people, who do not spend their days inside, the essentials are here for as little as $500 or $600 a week. Rentals are strong, sales are up. . . .

In many ways the developers of this long strip of sand re-created the suburbs from which their buyers came, complete with their preoccupation with status. To elegant Bay Head and nouveau Mantoloking, the motels and boardwalk of Seaside Heights seem honky-tonk and the tiny lots of Ocean Beach are rinky-dink. . . .

Pat Grappone of Rutherford, who bought a cottage three years ago, 20 years after her first vacation here, said, "The only thing that's different is that these cottages are $90,000 now. But if anything, it seems better now. Maybe because we own.

"You know what's nice here?" she said. "Around 6 o'clock, all the men down at the water fishing."

From: "Where Suburban Tribes Gather for Sand and Surf," by George Judson, July 15, 1993, *New York Times,* pp. B1, B8.

and may be thought of as **symbols** of the culture. Clothing, for example, is chosen not only to protect our bodies from the elements—but also to convey symbolic messages that may be interpreted by others according to the shared meanings of our culture.

Earlier anthropologists tended to use the concept of culture as if there were no diversity within the "common understandings" of a people. This was an easy oversimplification in an era in which most fieldwork was done in small-scale societies of 50 to 300, where it is easier to stress the commonalities of thought and values that are expressed. But anthropologists who did their research in societies with larger populations could hardly ignore the fact that their descriptions of a society's culture had to take into account the fact that a culture is not fixed and changeless with a universally accepted pattern of customs, ideas, and feelings even within the same society. Awareness of this diversity within a culture led to the concept of **subcultures**, variations within a culture that are shared by different groups within a society.

symbol an object or event that represents another object or event only because of the agreement among people that it will

subcultures the geographical or social variations that occur within the cultures of societies with large populations

FIGURE 2.2

SUBURBAN CLAN

Pat and Jack Grappone and Cosmo and Addi Pavone are members of a suburban tribe that gather for sand and surf. They are responding to one of the imperatives of culture: participation in a shared and traditional system of customs. Attending the World Series, the Super Bowl, prom night, and rock concerts, and sunbathing on a crowded beach are activities that help the people of the United States conceive of themselves as a society with its own distinctive culture.

The recognition that each culture may be made up of subcultures, much as languages may have various dialects, emphasizes the fact that cultures are not static. Some recent anthropologists, especially feminist anthropologists, postmodernist anthropologists, and others, have emphasized the processes by which diverse viewpoints, values, and ways of behaving are negotiated by members of a society. In these approaches, the concept of culture is viewed as consisting of a polyphony of voices rather than as a solo melody.

Many anthropologists in the first half of this century emphasized the integrated quality of the values and beliefs that were characteristic of each culture, and described each as a self-consistent system of meanings. Today, we are more likely to acknowledge that even when there are important regularities within the symbolic patterns that make up a culture, those patterns are neither rigidly present nor necessarily consistently adhered to in the behavior of people. Thus, despite some degree of internal consistency, any culture may include contradictory beliefs and competing values.

but people are not conscious of all of them. They may never explicitly state an underlying rule to which they seem to be conforming, yet the regularity in their behavior may be obvious to an outsider. Suppose we observed that members of a certain society always took care to lock the doors and windows of their homes and automobiles when leaving them, that they never left their bicycles unlocked when they entered a store, and that they never left valuable items unattended or in open view even at home. We might conclude that these people believe that some of their members are likely to steal, even if they never say so directly. If we were further reporting on our observations, we would include in our description of their culture the implicit rule of maintaining the security of one's own possessions, even if these people did not explicitly refer to such a rule when speaking among themselves.

A culture, then, includes all the rules and regulations that govern a way of life, both conscious, formally stated beliefs and feelings—called an **ideology**—and unconscious, informal, or implicit beliefs and feelings.

IDEOLOGY

Within any culture, there are regularities in how people act, think, feel, and communicate,

ideology the consciously shared beliefs and feelings that members of a society consider characteristic of themselves

FIGURE 2.3

CULTURAL DIVERSITY

Feminist and postmodernist anthropologists have emphasized the diversity that exists within a culture and the interactional influences that researchers and the people that they're studying can have on one another.

Ideological Communication

As people communicate about themselves and their environment, they build a consensus about the nature of humankind and the universe in which it exists. Much communication among members of the same society is done to reinforce this consensus. Such **ideological communication** is an important way in which people identify themselves as members of a group, declare their allegiance to it, and define their rules for behaving in the group. It frequently takes the form of highly ritualized acts, such as a pledge of allegiance to a flag or some other symbol of the group, recitation of articles of faith, or singing of hymns that glorify the doctrines of the group. Ritual affirmations of one's social solidarity with others may, of course, be less formally structured, as in so-called "small talk," the content of which is nonetheless highly predictable. For instance, North Americans recognize that the greeting "How are you?" is not a request for information but simply the opening gambit of a ritual communication of friendship and willingness to interact. The more or less predictable response—"I'm fine, thank you"—is not a measure of one's actual state of health, but an affirmation of the same willingness to interact and a declaration that one shares the same cultural code of symbolic behavior. Such ritual reaffirmations of mutuality may be interspersed throughout an entire conversation in stereotyped communications, as in a discussion of the weather. Although ideological communication conveys little information, it reinforces the existing conventions about reality and our place in it. So it is through the efforts we devote to ideological communication that we construct and reconstruct the meaningfulness of the world. As Clifford Geertz (1973), an anthropologist who stresses the need to understand the symbols around which people organize their lives, poetically described it, we humans are "suspended in webs of significance" (p. 5) that we ourselves spin.

_____

ideological communication communication that reaffirms people's allegiance to their groups and creates a sense of community by asserting its ideology

Beliefs

An ideology has two main interacting components: a subsystem of beliefs and a subsystem of feelings. **Beliefs** are the means by which people make sense of their experiences; they are the ideas that they hold to be true, factual, or real. By contrast, **feelings** are a people's inner reactions, emotions, or desires concerning experiences. Although beliefs are judgments about facts, they are not always the result of rational analysis of experience. Thus, emotions, attitudes, and values—aspects of the feeling system—may ultimately determine what people believe. Within limits set by the necessities of survival, persons may choose to believe what is pleasing to believe, what they want to believe, and what they think they ought to believe. Once people are convinced of the truth of a new set of beliefs, then, they may change some of their previous feelings to make it easier to maintain those new beliefs.

Conformity to a Belief System.   People in each society have their own distinctive patterns of thought about the nature of reality. These beliefs reflect what those who share a culture regard as true: "God exists"; "The sky is blue"; "Geese fly south for the winter"; "Spilling salt causes bad luck."

The knowledge of a society is taught to its children either implicitly or explicitly, as *the proper way* of understanding the world. Thus, as children, we learn that the other members of our society share a system of thought and a pattern of thinking about the nature of the world. For example, North Americans grow up under a formal educational system in which mechanical models sometimes are used to demonstrate the plausibility of the idea that the moon is a sphere, the apparent shape of which depends on the relative positions of the sun, the moon, and the earth. By contrast, the Shoshone Indians of the western U.S. Great Basin area traditionally explained the phases of the moon by describing it as shaped like a bowl or basket rather than a sphere. The phase of the moon was thought to be simply a matter of which side of the moon was facing the observer: a crescent moon was a side view, and a full moon was the outside convex bottom.

We obtain full acceptance as members of our group by conforming to the ways in which others think. Cultural ideas are imposed on us through rewards for conformity and punish-

ments for deviance. Individuals who violate their culture's rules for proper thinking are likely to experience punishment ranging from a mild reproof or laughter to severe sanctions such as banishment, imprisonment, or death. In the contemporary United States, normal people do not "hear voices." Those who do may find themselves placed in mental hospitals "for their own good" or "for the safety of others." In other times and places, those who heard voices have been honored as spiritual teachers. North American school children are rewarded for believing that the moon is a sphere and punished for believing otherwise. During my fieldwork on an isolated Shoshone reservation in the late 1960s, I discovered that my attempt to describe the moon as a sphere evoked either argument or skeptical looks, and my desire for acceptance soon silenced my expression of deviant views.

Widespread acceptance of a system of beliefs gives people a sense of identity as a group. A people's knowledge that they share a set of beliefs gives them a feeling of security and a sense of belonging. When people become conscious of their shared beliefs, especially if they assign a name to their system of beliefs, this part of their ideology may begin to function as an active, driving force in their lives. Such conscious systems are particularly common in complex societies. They are most dramatically illustrated by the named religions and political factions that can command the loyalties of great masses of people.

Types of Belief Systems.   Every society tends to develop two different kinds of belief systems: scientific and nonscientific. The former occurs because a certain degree of practical insight into the nature of the world and its workings is necessary for any society to survive. Beliefs about such matters as how to obtain food and shelter or how to set broken bones must be based on pragmatic rather than emotional judgments if they are to be useful. The beliefs that arise from the search for practical solutions to mundane problems of living

---

beliefs ideas people hold about what is factual or real

feelings subjective reactions to experiences as pleasant or unpleasant, good or bad. Feelings include emotions, attitudes, values, and drives

may be referred to as the **scientific beliefs** of a society.

The second basic type of belief found in every culture grows out of a people's feelings about their existence. These **nonscientific beliefs** are often formally organized within the framework of religious and artistic philosophies that portray the universe and express (sometimes in the guise of descriptions of reality) deeply valued feelings about the world in which people find themselves. Strong emotional commitments may also exist in politics or recreation. These, too, are often guided by beliefs that express the members' deeply held feelings.

Feelings

Feelings and beliefs tend to strengthen each other. Our feelings may be the motivation for believing things for which no objective support exists. Beliefs may, in turn, validate our feelings. When we believe that our feelings are the same ones that other people experience in the same situations, we are more confident that they are valid. Recognizing that our feelings are shared by others also supports our sense of belonging to a definable group.

Four major kinds of feelings find their idealized expression within an ideology: emotions, attitudes, values, and drives.

Emotions. An **emotion** is a reaction to experience as pleasant or unpleasant, to varying degrees. As we mature, we learn to distinguish many subtle variations on the two basic emotional themes of pleasantness and unpleasantness, such as delight, elation, affection, love, mirth, happiness, surprise, or exultation, and contempt, anger, distress, terror, or grief. Which emotions we learn to experience in various circumstances depends on the culture in which we are raised.

Each society trains its members to associate certain emotions with certain situations and to experience each emotion at differing intensities in different settings. For instance, J. Briggs (1970) found the expression of anger to be almost totally taboo among one Inuit group, and Levy (1973) found almost no expression of anger among the Tahitians he studied, while very elaborate customs for the display of anger exist among the New Guinea Kaluli (Schieffelin, 1983) and the Yąnomamö of Brazil and Venezuela (Chagnon, 1983). Marston Bates (1967), a zoologist, illustrated how some foods, which are con-

FIGURE 2.4

CULTURAL INFLUENCES ON FOOD
The physiological reaction to food choice is based on an emotional experience learned as a part of one's culture. Thus, it is culture that determines that cow meat is acceptable food in the United States, that dog meat is acceptable food in parts of East Asia, and that the grubs pictured here are acceptable food in Australia.

sidered delicacies to people in some cultures, can be disgusting to people of other cultures:

Even though repugnance to a particular food has a cultural rather than a physiological basis, the aversion can still cause a strong physiological reaction. The big lizards called iguanas are a highly prized food item in almost all parts of tropical America where they are found; the meat has a delicate, chicken-like flavor. But for some reason lizards are not eaten in Europe or the United States, perhaps because we do not have any suitable species: our lizards are for the most part too small to be of much use as food. But whatever the reason,

scientific beliefs beliefs that are based on the desire to solve the practical day-to-day problems of living
nonscientific beliefs beliefs that grow out of people's feelings
emotion a pleasant or unpleasant subjective reaction to an experience, characterized by varying degrees of muscle tension and changes in respiration and heart rate

we clearly regard lizards as unsuitable for eating. We once served iguana at a dinner party in South America. The subject had been thoroughly discussed, and we thought everyone understood what he was eating. Certainly all the guests ate with gusto. But as the conversation continued during the meal, a French lady who was present suddenly realized that the iguana she had been eating *était un lézard* and became violently nauseated, although a few minutes before she had considered the meat delicious.

I remember once, in the llanos of Colombia, sharing a dish of toasted ants at a remote farmhouse. This was my first voluntary experience with ants—I have eaten lots of them involuntarily, raw, when they just taste sour—and I found the toasted ants have a pleasant, nutty flavor. My host and I fell into conversation about the general question of what people eat or do not eat and I remarked that in my country people ate the legs of frogs. The very thought of this filled my ant-eating friends with horror; it was as though I had mentioned some repulsive sex habit. (pp. 21–22)

Cultures also differ in how strongly or mildly feelings should be expressed and in which emotional experiences are most commonly emphasized. According to the French anthropologist Claude Lévi-Strauss (1950), "The thresholds of excitement, the limits of resistance are different in each culture. The 'impossible' effort, the 'unbearable' pain, the 'unbounded' pleasure are less individual functions than criteria sanctioned by collective approval, and disapproval" (p. xii). Cultural differences in emotional intensity were illustrated by Ruth Benedict, author of one of the most widely read anthropological books ever printed, *Patterns of Culture* (1934). For instance, she cited the late nineteenth-century Kwakiutl culture of Vancouver Island as one in which the expression of strong emotion—especially feelings of extreme self-worth bordering on megalomania—was encouraged. She described their religious ceremonies in the following words:

In their religious ceremonies the final thing they strove for was ecstasy. The chief dancer, at least at the high point of his performance, should lose normal control of himself and be rapt into another state of existence. He should froth at the mouth, tremble violently and ab-

normally, do deeds which would be terrible in a normal state. Some dancers were tethered by four ropes held by attendants, so that they might not do irreparable damage in their frenzy. (pp. 175–176)

Benedict contrasted the Kwakiutl with the Zuñi of the early 1900s. The Zuñi, who lived in the southwestern part of the United States, had a culture that encouraged moderation in the expression of all feelings. Zuñi rituals were monotonous in contrast with those of the Kwakiutl. They consisted of long, memorized recitations that had to be performed with word-perfect precision. The Zuñi had no individualized prayers; personal prayers were also memorized and recited word for word. As an illustration of how Zuñi culture required moderation in emotion, Benedict cited the case of a woman whose husband had been involved in a long extramarital affair. She and her family ignored the situation, but after she was exhorted by a white trader to take some action, the wife did so by not washing her husband's clothes. In her words, "Then he knew that I knew that everybody knew, and he stopped going with the girl" (p. 108). No argument, no yelling and crying. Just a mild indication that her wifely status was in question. For a Zuñi husband, this message was strong enough.

For the Dobuans, a people of Melanesia whose culture was studied in the early 1900s by Reo Fortune (1932), the dominant feelings were animosity and a mistrust that bordered on paranoia. These feelings permeated their customs. For instance, even husband and wife would not share food for fear that they might poison each other. All deaths were regarded as murders. In deaths that other people might ascribe to natural causes, black magic was the assumed weapon, with the surviving spouse the most likely suspect as the murderer. Dobuans assumed that their spouses were unfaithful whenever the opportunity existed, so they bribed their children to spy on each other. Benedict (1934) described Dobuan paranoia:

The formula that corresponds to our thank-you upon receiving a gift is, "If you now poison me, how should I repay you?" (p. 166)

Similar contrasts in the degree to which emotions are encouraged or inhibited have been reported by other anthropologists. For instance, Byron Good, Mary-Jo Good, and Robert

THE KWAKIUTL, ZUÑI, AND DOBUANS TODAY

In 1996, the Kwakiutl work at commercial fishing, in logging, in a variety of service industries, and as employees of government. The original Kwakiutl population count is not known, but it was heavily reduced by disease before 1835, when it had dropped to 8,575. After continued declines that reduced the Kwakiutl to fewer than 1,000 people in 1929, the population has risen to about 4,000, a figure that is still significantly below its original levels.

The famous Kwakiutl potlatches (discussed on p. 52), with their lavish, competitive giveaways, were outlawed by the Canadian government in the 1920s. Arrests and confiscation of ceremonial paraphernalia led to an end to Kwakiutl ceremonial life until its revival in recent times. These efforts by both the Canadian government and church leaders to undermine traditional Kwakiutl culture and economic life played an important role in incorporating the Kwakiutl, who had survived the earlier, socially disruptive population declines, into Canadian society. The acculturation of the Kwakiutl included the replacement of their traditional religious beliefs with those of Christianity under the influence of strong missionary efforts. Today, most Kwakiutl are Anglican Christians. Some belong to evangelical Protestant churches. Nevertheless, original Kwakiutl religious symbolism survives among contemporary Kwakiutl artists whose artwork is sold in many stores on Vancouver Island and elsewhere.

Today, the Zuñi, who actually call themselves the Ashiwi, live on the Zuñi Reservation in west-central New Mexico. They number over 8,000 people, many of whom occupy a pueblo, or village, that they call Itiwana, "the Middle Place." The pueblo, also called Zuñi, has lost most of its traditional outward form. It now has paved streets, sidewalks, and streetlights. Other Zuñi live outside the pueblo on various parts of the 655-square-mile reservation, which was established in 1877 and represents only about 3 percent of the land the Zuñi originally considered their territory. An unknown number live outside the reservation.

The Zuñi's traditional horticultural economy of maize, beans, squash, and other crops was supplemented by various European domesticates introduced by the Spanish, who also introduced the Zuñi to cattle and sheep. Since their introduction, these animals have become an important source of income to the Zuñi. Many households supplement their incomes through the production of jewelry and other home crafts that are sold both on and off the reservation. Employment off the reservation has also attracted many of the Zuñi to neighboring cities.

Zuñi women continue to have high status in their society, but Americanization has shifted Zuñi inheritance patterns, which once followed maternal lines, to the common U.S. pattern of inheritance through either male or female lines. Homes and farmlands are now owned privately rather than by clans. However, the maternal clans continue to exist and play prominent roles, for instance in ceremonial activities.

Since 1970, the Zuñi have been governed by an elected tribal council, headed by a governor and advised by an Indian agent appointed by the U.S. secretary of the interior. Traditional Zuñi religious life is still very much alive, and its religious leaders, who were the traditional heads of the Zuñi theocratic government, still have great influence in the politics of the reservation. Zuñi Catholics, though a minority, make up another important political faction within the pueblo.

Dobu Island currently has a population of about 900 inhabitants, far fewer than the estimated 2,000 Dobuans of 1891. Their population decline began as early as 1884, when "blackbirders" or slavers took a number of Dobuans into slavery and killed others. By the early 1890s, copra (coconut meat) traders had entered Dobu along with Christian missionaries, and European diseases had begun to kill many of the Dobuans.

Now, Dobuans are all followers of Christianity, although traditional practices of magic, witchcraft, and sorcery have not been lost. Dobuans still speak of yams as persons, who will leave their owners' gardens if they are not treated with the proper magical rituals and respect. They work as clerks, medical doctors, lawyers, and Christian ministers, run their own businesses, and are employed by the local Dobuan government or by the provincial government of Papua-New Guinea as public servants. Several Dobuans have run for national parliament.

(see *reference maps,* pp. 32, 49, 52)

Moradi (1985) have described the various ways in which profound sadness and sorrow are expected to be expressed in Iranian culture, where such feelings have deep personal and religious value. They report, for instance: "Pious Shi'ite Moslems gather weekly to hear the cruel martyrdom of Hossein, the grandson of the Prophet, commemorated in poetry and preaching and to respond with open weeping. Their secular literature is filled with melancholy and despair. Tragedy, injustice, and martyrdom are central to Iranian political philosophy and historical experience." In Iranian culture sadness is equated with personal depth and thoughtfulness, while boisterous talking and joking is considered unmannerly. Likewise, Gananeth Obeyesekere (1985) expressed surprise when what to him was quite an ordinary Buddhist Sri Lankan expression of hopelessness, suffering, and sorrow was perceived by a psychologist in the United States as evidence of clinical depression. Similarly, the Yąnomamö culture described by Napoleon Chagnon (1977) fosters strong emotional involvement between individuals, and anthropologist Clifford Geertz (1973) described Javanese culture as encouraging individuals to maintain psychological states of "smoothness" and calm.

Attitudes. Our **attitudes** are statements of our preferences, our likes and dislikes that are more generalized than our specific emotional reactions to situations. Attitudes need not correspond to the pleasantness or unpleasantness of the emotions associated with an activity. Skydiving, for instance, may create conflicting emotions: fear and exhilaration. A general attitude toward high adventure—liking or disliking it—determines which way the scales will tip. Probably in every society individuals are taught to dislike or feel neutral about some situations that may lead to pleasant emotions and to like other situations in which they experience unpleasant emotions. Athletes may learn to crave the exercise that their goals demand, even though they dread the pain that attends each workout; soldiers may be taught to seek the very situations of battle that arouse their deepest fears; and people who have broken the habit of smoking or drinking can be among the most outspoken opponents of tobacco or alcohol.

Values. The third part of the feeling subsystem of an ideology is **values**: feelings about what should or should not be considered good and bad. Values play a role in so many parts of life, that it is useful to distinguish between various kinds of values. **Morality** consists of those values that demand respect for the rights of other humans. It includes, for instance, rules

against theft as well as positive obligations toward others, such as fulfilling promises and nurturing one's dependent children. Those values that govern manners and define what is considered courteous or civil ways of communicating with others are called **etiquette**. Such values do not function, like moral values, to prevent victimization of others or to meet the needs of those for whose welfare we are responsible. Rather, they create a comfortable social distance between individuals that make moral conflicts less likely. For instance, in English the word "please" has the effect of making it clear that a request is not to be taken as a demand. **Piety** is composed of distinctly religious values that define our purely spiritual obligations, including right and wrong conduct that affect our relationship with the supernatural. Jewish dietary laws, Mormon rules against drinking alcohol or coffee, and the Blue Laws outlawing liquor sales on Sundays fall into this category. **Aesthetics**, or rules that govern feelings about beauty and ugliness, also control our judgments about whether things are compatible with one another. Most Americans, for instance, would regard Greek columns as an inappropriate feature on a ranch-style house.

The values of different cultures can be amazingly diverse, to the extent that what is held to be supremely desirable by the members of one society may be despised by another. That which one people holds dear as a religious or moral obligation of the most sacred kind may be viewed as sacrilegious or immoral by another. When the Samoans were first met by Europeans, women did not cover their breasts in public. Indeed, to do so would have been considered highly improper and immodest by the traditional Samoans. In contemporary

---

attitude a subjective reaction to an experience expressed in positive or negative terms

values feelings about what should be considered good, bad, moral, or immoral; the ideals that people long for but do not necessarily pursue

morality values concerning proper and improper ways of treating other human beings

etiquette values that govern manners and define what is considered courteous or civil ways of communicating with others

piety values concerning the treatment of nature and the supernatural

aesthetics values concerning beauty and the compatibility of things

FIGURE 2.5

COMPETITION

Competitiveness is a major drive in the American psyche, manifesting itself in economic situations, social situations, and in sports. Even children learn to keep score in games, and pick those for their teams who will help them win.

Europe, an opposing set of evaluations prevails concerning public exposure of the breast; yet, the European woman is quite unconcerned about exposing the back of her neck in public, an act that would have resulted in strong disapproval in traditional Chinese society.

When they were first described by anthropologists, the Toda of India had no word for adultery in their language. They considered it highly immoral for a man to begrudge another man his wife's sexual favors. On the other hand, they had strong rules against being seen eating in public. Among the Dobuan islanders in the first part of the twentieth century, being happy was not a valued emotional state. In contrast, the Founding Fathers of the U.S. government declared the pursuit of happiness to be one of the fundamental values of society. In the United States today, competitiveness seems fundamental to much of day-to-day life, while the early nineteenth-century Hopi of the southwestern United States carefully taught their children that it was wrong to shame others by outdoing them in competitive situations. The child who finished a race first was expected to take care not to do so the next time around.

Drives. Jules Henry (1963) suggested a distinction between what he calls drives and values. **Drives** are motives that people actually pursue, sometimes at great cost, rather than those to which they merely give lip service. Since it is in pursuit of their culture's drives that people invest their time and energy, drives represent the things that people value most strongly in the practical sense. They also are the source of stresses in life. What Henry calls *values* represent ideals that people long for but do not necessarily pursue. They are often opposites of drives, since they might give release from the stresses created by the pursuit of drives. Henry describes the roles of drives and values:

> Drives are what urge us blindly into getting bigger, into going further into outer space and into destructive competition; values are the sentiments that work in the opposite direction. Drives belong to the occupational world; values to the world of family and friendly intimacy. Drives animate the hurly-burly of business, the armed forces and all those parts of our culture where getting ahead, rising in social scale, outstripping others, and merely

drives the ideals that people actively pursue, sometimes at great cost, rather than those to which they merely give lip service

surviving in the struggle are the absorbing functions of life. When values appear in these areas, they act largely as brakes, on drivenness. (p. 14)

In the United States, status climbing and upward social mobility are drives derived from competitive circumstances. The extreme emphasis on competition as a social good even carries over into the realm of relaxation and recreation. Even though people assert the idealized value that "it's not who wins the game, but how you play the game" that counts, this statement is probably best understood as a wistful but unrealistic protestation against the practicalities of a way of life in which "nice guys finish last." Those who follow the mainstream U.S. culture continue to teach their children to keep score when playing games, a practice that the traditional Zuñi of the American Southwest would have eschewed as abhorrent.

Material acquisitiveness also must be seen as a manifestation of competitiveness. In a society in which, by Old World standards, the majority has never suffered from a lack of physical security or even luxury, materialism is best understood as a manifestation of the competitive desire to "keep up with the Joneses," that is, as evidence of one's competitive success. Social movement often is accompanied by physical mobility—the expansiveness of U.S. society and the "don't fence me in" restlessness.

The idealized values that counter the implicit conflict and potential hostility in competition include relaxed interpersonal relations, friendliness, frankness, love, kindness, decency, openness, and good sportsmanship. Charity and generosity also are valued as contrasts to the drive to make a profit. Simplicity, idealization of the idyllic pastoral life, and the myth of the noble savage are values that counterbalance the drives of material acquisitiveness.

Cultural Change

The various terms and categories used to define culture may give the false impression that a culture can be completely and accurately described by a simple listing of its characteristics as if they were homogeneous, fixed, and unchanging. Unfortunately, it is just not that simple. For culture is a dynamic system, and every culture is in a constant state of flux. Indeed, although we may speak glibly about a consensus or about "typical" beliefs or feelings, such descriptions are as inaccurate a portrayal of a culture as a snapshot is of a waterfall or a whirlwind. In the real world of human life, individuals differ from one another in many ways. So it is more accurate to think of culture as a system of symbols, customs, ideas, and feelings that is constantly being negotiated and redefined by members of a society as they interact and communicate with one another. It is also this dynamism that allows—indeed, impels—each culture to change with the passing of time.

As useful as a description of a culture may be, no culture is, or ever was, set in stone. At best, any description of a culture merely evokes images of a way of life as it was perceived by the one who has described it at some point in time. Even that image will have lost some of its dynamism, some of its variety, in the telling. Just as an automobile repair manual fails to capture the dynamism of an idling engine, a description of a way of life may suggest homogeneity and stasis where diversity and change really exist.

Ideal vs. Real Culture.   It is important to note that culture is a system of *ideals* for behavior, but that people do not always follow the guidelines of their culture. Sometimes, for example, individuals violate cultural ideals about proper communication behavior, as North Americans do when they behave rudely to show their anger. Sometimes people violate their culture's ideals for personal gain at the expense of others, but most of the time their failure to conform to cultural ideals is not consciously intended. For instance, very few U.S. drivers make technically legal stops at stop signs, but most do not think of themselves as breaking the law as they make their near-stops and proceed.

In studying culture, one must recognize that there is a difference between what is called **ideal culture** and **real culture**. The former refers to the ways in which people describe their

---

ideal culture the ways people perceive their own customs and behaviors, often more a reflection of their feelings and ideals about what they should be than an accurate assessment of what they are

real culture culture portrayed in terms of the actually observable behaviors of a people

way of life; the latter to how they actually behave. People's behavior can sometimes be quite different from a description of their ideal culture. This can be a matter of individual nonconformity to cultural rules or in some cases nearly everyone may customarily do things differently from what one might expect from listening to what they say about their customs.

This difference between real and ideal culture can be dramatic even in the case of formal rules that people are supposed to obey. The next time you are at a busy street corner governed by a four-way stop, spend a few minutes keeping track of how few drivers actually make full and legal stops.

IDEAL AND REAL CULTURE AMONG THE TRADITIONAL ZUÑI

Descriptions of the ideals embodied in a culture's rules for living are not always the same as descriptions of the people's actual behavior. Ruth Benedict's portrayal of the Zuñi of the U.S. Southwest, and presumably their portrayal of themselves to her, was one of a culture in which emotional excess and individualism were held to a minimum. The Zuñi avoided selecting as leaders people that they believed sought the office. They carefully taught their children to avoid competition and conflict. Their ritual life idealized emotional restraint. Benedict (1934) claimed of the Zuñi that "Drunkenness is repulsive to them" (p. 82), that violence was so rare that only a single case of homicide could be remembered in village history, and that "Suicide is too violent an act, even in its most casual forms, for most Pueblos to contemplate. They have no idea what it could be" (p. 117).

These cultural ideals, however, do not give an accurate picture of the realities of Zuñi life. Varieties of behavior occurred among the Zuñi as they occur in all other societies. According to Ruth Bunzel (1952), the Zuñi were often split into factions that disagreed about whether anthropologists should be accepted in the village. There was rivalry along religious lines as well. Li An-Che (1937) claimed that "A strife of immense magnitude took place between the Catholic and Protestant elements" (p. 69). Zuñi initiation of children into adult life, like initiations at other pueblos, involved severe whippings (Roth, 1963). Village ceremonies were often marred by drunkenness (Barnouw, 1963). Violence was not nonexistent in Zuñi life, and although their culture might foster a reticence to discuss it, even suicides did occur (Hoebel, 1949).

Culture provides guidelines that mold people's behavior, but there are conditions under which deviance from the guidelines may be more common than conformity to them. One of these conditions is the effect of contact with other societies and their customs. Was Zuñi life more emotionally

constrained before its political and economic subordination within the U.S. nation-state? This may well have been the case, since contact with more powerful societies can be especially disruptive to the internal harmony of a way of life. Certainly the alcoholism must be understood, at least in part, as a result of disruptive outside influence on Zuñi life. Probably we will never know how much pre-contact Zuñi behavior deviated from Benedict's portrayal, but we should remember that ideal culture and behavior are never identical.

ZUÑI

The Zuñi occupy a small territory in the U.S. Southwest. They describe their ideal culture as one that encourages cooperation, friendliness, and peacefulness. In reality, however, their culture has been influenced by the alcohol and violence that surrounds them.

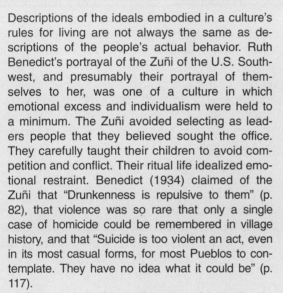

Cultural Differences

Cultures differ greatly in their ideologies and practical responses to their varying environments. When very different peoples come in contact with each other, usually the one with less political and economic power is changed by the other. Even when both maintain their integrity, members of differing groups may find it difficult to understand and appreciate each other's ways. In this section, we will look at intercultural influences, intercultural prejudices, ethnocentrism (the attitude that one's own culture is the only proper way of life), and cultural relativism (understanding and appreciating other cultures in their own terms).

Intercultural Influences

Contact between two cultures can bring tremendous change to both societies, or especially to one of them when they differ greatly in economic and political power. Sometimes the extinction of native populations is carried out by systematic acts of war, and sometimes it is a less extreme process of assimilation. Nevertheless, the transition from the original way of life to a socially dependent status is never without turmoil. Cultural subordination of one way of life by another, even when it occurs peaceably, can be a shattering experience.

Time and time again, anthropologists have described the tragic effects on the world's agricultural peoples of contact with the industrialized nations of the world. Diseases introduced from the more densely populated societies sometimes decimate the local population. The awareness that other peoples are more powerful and have more luxuries than they do is a blow to the cultural pride that unifies a society. Often, contact with another society is followed by a rise in the rate of internal conflict, alcoholism, and suicide. For the Kwakiutl, contact with Europeans may have led to exaggerated— and destructive—attempts to display wealth and power.

Ethnocentrism

When people learn about groups whose ideologies and adaptive strategies differ from their own, they may have little understanding or appreciation of those differences. People grow up under the nurturance of their group, identify themselves as members of the group, and learn to fulfill their needs by living according to its culture. Often, the training of children in the ways of the group is communicated expressly by contrasting them with the supposed behaviors of outsiders: "Other parents may let their children come to the table like that, but in our family we wash our hands before eating!" Such expressions teach children the patterns of behavior expected of group members, but they also communicate a disapproval of outsiders.

In complex societies with large populations, people may learn to express prejudices about the superiority of their own groups over other competing ones *within* the society. The expression of these prejudices may vary from the good-natured jibes of members of one political party toward those in the "loyal opposition" or the friendly but serious theological disagreements between neighbors of different religious persuasions to the very confrontational hostilities exchanged between political demonstrators, such as the exchanges that sometimes occur in the United States over issues like gun control or abortion.

In all societies it is common for people to feel prejudices against groups whose cultures differ from their own. This attitude that the culture of one's own society is the naturally superior one, the standard by which all other cultures should be judged, and that cultures different from one's own are inferior, is such a common way of reacting to others' customs that it is given a special name by anthropologists: **ethnocentrism**, centered in one's *ethnos*, the Greek word for a people or a nation, is found in every culture. People allow their judgments about human nature and about the relative merits of different ways of life to be guided by ideas and values that are centered narrowly on the way of life of their own society.

Ethnocentrism serves a society by creating greater feelings of group unity. Individuals affirm their loyalty to the ideals of their society when they communicate with one another about the superiority of their way of life over other cultures. This enhances their sense of

---

ethnocentrism the attitude that one's own culture is the only good one and that the more other cultures differ from one's own, the more inferior they are

identity. A shared sense of group superiority—especially during its overt communication between group members—can help them overlook internal differences and prevent conflicts that could otherwise decrease the ability of the group to undertake effectively coordinated action.

For most of human history, societies have been smaller than the nations of today, and most people have interacted only with members of their own society. Under such circumstances, the role of ethnocentrism in helping a society to survive by motivating its members to support one another in their common goals has probably outweighed its negative aspects. However, ethnocentrism definitely has a darker side. It is a direct barrier to understanding among peoples of diverse customs and values. It enhances enmity between societies and can be a motivation for conflict among peoples whose lives are guided by different cultures.

Ethnocentrism stands in fundamental conflict with the goals of anthropology: the recognition of the common humanity of all human beings and the understanding of the causes of cultural differences. To many students, much of the appeal of the field of anthropology has been its intriguing discussions of the unending variety of customs grown out of what, from the viewpoint of the uninitiated, may seem like strange and exotic, unexpected, and even startlingly different values. A people's values generally make perfectly good sense when seen and explained in the context of their cultural system as a whole.

Cultural Relativism

The alternative to ethnocentrism is **cultural relativism**, the idea that the significance of an act is best understood by the standards of the actor's own cultural milieu. Relativism is not an idea unique to anthropology. In every culture, people interpret the meaning of a thing depending on the context in which it occurs. For instance, we might react very differently to seeing someone lying in a gutter in an inner city ghetto versus finding someone lying face down in an office in the financial district of the same city. In the first situation we might assume, perhaps mistakenly, that the person was simply drunk, while in the second setting the possibility of a heart attack would probably come to mind more quickly. The symbolic basis of all cultural systems invariably leads to variations in the meanings of things from situation to situ-

FIGURE 2.6

POTLATCH
The Kwakiutl of the Pacific Northwest coast of North America stage periodic potlatches as a means of enhancing the status of the host chief. The more he gives away, the greater his status. Performing the hamat'sa dance, shown at this W. T. Cranmer potlatch in Alert Bay, British Columbia, in 1983, is an inherited right of the dancer and is considered one of the most important events at a potlatch.

ation. People who share the same culture learn to take the context of one another's acts into account when they are trying to communicate. Of course, intergroup prejudices sometimes interfere with people's efforts to understand one another, even within the same culture.

Anthropologists have come to value cultural relativism as a first step toward understanding other cultures. A relativistic view of other cultures holds all ways of life to be equally valid sources of information about human nature. Relativism, as a research tool, reminds us that even customs that seem inhu-

(Continued on p. 53)

cultural relativism the principle that cultural traits are best understood in the context of the cultural system of which they are a part; the attempt to avoid the narrow bias of judging the value of a custom or entire culture on the basis of the values of one's own culture; the view that meanings of behaviors are best understood when interpreted in terms of the culture of the actors

THE KWAKIUTL POTLATCH: A REACTION TO EUROPEAN CONTACT?

The Kwakiutl, the indigenous population of Vancouver Island and the British Columbia coast, were described by Franz Boas (Codere, 1967), who visited them first in 1886, and by Ruth Benedict, one of Boas's students. When Boas observed them, the Kwakiutl, who now call themselves Kwakwaka̱'wakw, were a people whose culture encouraged emotional extremes, channeled into fierce competition for status between individuals and groups. According to Benedict (1934), "The object of all Kwakiutl enterprises was to show oneself superior to one's rivals. This will to superiority they exhibited in the most uninhibited fashion. It found expression in uncensored self-glorification and ridicule of all comers" (p. 190).

The expansiveness in the Kwakiutl personality was seen at the great giveaway *potlatches*, ceremonial feasts at which gifts were lavishly given to guests as part of a public announcement of an important event in the life of the host, such as his claim to having achieved a higher social status. The most dramatic of the potlatches were those at which the Kwakiutl sought to shame their rivals with demonstrations of the unmatchable superiority of their wealth by lavishly giving away food, blankets, and other valuable property. To show the host's disdain for surplus wealth, gallons of fish oil were poured by "slaves" through the smoke-holes of their longhouses onto the fires to make them blaze higher. Blankets were ripped to shreds, and holes were chopped in the bottoms of boats. Sometimes entire villages were burned by a chief and the slaves put to death in the extremes of conspicuous consumption. At potlatch feasts, a chief's retainers sang hymns of praise such as the following one reported by Benedict:

I am the great chief who makes people ashamed.
I am the great chief who makes people ashamed.
Our chief brings shame to the faces.
Our chief brings jealousy to the faces.
Our chief makes people cover their faces by
*   what he is continually doing in this world,*
Giving again and again oil feasts to all the tribes.
(p. 190)

What are we to make of such extremes? To Benedict, the Kwakiutl behavior simply illustrated the diversity of culture, but later anthropologists placed this behavior in better perspective. The Kwakiutl described by Boas and Benedict had long been in contact with the Europeans. Intensive trade for almost 40 years before Boas's first visit had greatly affected their culture, and many of the extremes he observed were exaggerations of their earlier customs—exaggerations that arose as attempts to adjust to the effects of European contact. Helen Codere (1950) points to the core of the problem: smallpox and other diseases introduced by contact with Europeans decimated the Kwakiutl population, which had fallen to less than a tenth of its original size by the time Boas first met them. Marvin Harris (1974) believes that this population shrinkage and the loss of many working-age people to employment away from the Kwakiutl villages greatly intensified the competition for labor; at the same time, European wages brought unexpected wealth into the Kwakiutl economy, which was also being flooded with blankets and other trade goods in return for native furs. The native practice, common in many small-scale societies, of holding communal feasts at which food is redistributed by the chiefs to the poor, was modified into celebrations of material wealth by which the chiefs tried unsuccessfully to attract people back to the villages.

KWAKIUTL

Indigenous to Vancouver Island and the coast of British Columbia, the Kwakiutl have been acculturated both by Canadian customs and by Christianity. Their original religious symbolism, however, survives among Kwakiutl artists.

mane or irrational according to our own values must be described and analyzed as objectively as possible if we wish to develop scientifically valid understandings of human behavior. Relativism reminds us that all cultures have customs that seem bizarre or repugnant to outsiders. For instance, both electroconvulsive treatment for depression and the use of machines for measuring heartbeat, blood pressure, and respiration to determine whether a person is lying might well seem inhumane or irrational to people whose cultures do not include these practices.

Cultural relativism grew out of a recognition that cultures can be quite diverse in the meanings they assign to the same behaviors and in the values they embody. However, cultural relativism is *not* the same as ethical or moral relativism, the idea that since there are no absolute or universal standards that are shared by all cultures for deciding what is right or wrong then all values can be rejected as arbitrary and any custom is as acceptable as any other. Cultural relativism is not the claim that "anything goes" and does not imply that we must abandon our own values or accept customs that are personally repugnant to us. Rather, it is a methodological tool for *understanding* other cultures and their customs, including customs that we might not like. We need not, for instance, come to value infanticide in order to understand the roles it may play in peoples' lives in a society where it is customary. What cultural relativism requires of us is simply that we do not confuse our own feelings about such a custom with understanding it. To do the latter, we must investigate the meanings the custom has for those who practice it and the functions it may fulfill in their society.

As a result of working among peoples with ways of life very different from their own, anthropological fieldworkers commonly find that the preconceived notions they bring with them do not help them understand what is going on in the culture they are studying. Cut off from their own people and their accustomed way of life, it is they who must learn to understand the meanings of the symbols of the people they are living with, rather than the other way around. The anthropological imperative is "Respect or fail!" Learning to understand the language and the customs as they are understood by the insiders of the group is often a clear and basic necessity for survival in a foreign culture. It can also be prerequisite to the work of gath-

FIGURE 2.7

CULTURAL RELATIVISM

A culture's symbolic systems of communication, customs, and habits are unique and can best be understood by others in relationship to the situation in which they occur. People from other cultures visiting the United States would probably find it difficult to understand the significance of masked figures going from door to door late in October with a request for treats. Only when they viewed it as a cultural custom of celebrating All Hallow's Eve would they be able to place it in the proper perspective.

ering accurate information about a culture or of developing insights about how it might have come to be the way it is and why it functions the way it does. The necessity of interpreting the meaning or value of an act within the culture in which it is found, that is, from a cultural relativistic viewpoint, has been long recognized within anthropology as a fundamental first step in learning to understand a culture as a coherent system of meaningful symbols.

Elizabeth Hahn (1990) illustrates the difficulties that ethnocentrism can impose on puzzling out the meanings of cultural behavior. Her fieldwork took her to the island of Tongatapu in Tonga. After a frustrating period of isolation in which she was unable to establish a relationship with anyone, Hahn decided to visit a government official:

He greeted me in standard office dress—a white long-sleeved shirt and necktie, a dark brown *tupenu* (a Tongan skirt), and a *ta'ovala* (a Tongan mat) secured around his waist by a braided cord of coconut fiber. The walls of his office were lined from floor to ceiling with papers, and reports of the Central Planning Department. I wondered how to make my vague and observation-oriented project seem like something worthwhile. Here were Tongans themselves engaged in the process of writing about and planning change in their culture and I, a foreigner, was going to have something interesting to say about their social processes, someone who half the time couldn't seem to find her way around the tiny capital of Nuku'alofa? But he was very cordial and soon put me at ease. He seemed to be willing to talk to me for longer than the polite five-minute chat. Here at last was someone to whom I could explain what I was trying to accomplish in Tonga. Indeed, he listened and he asked thoughtful questions. I fought the urge to lean over and hug him. I was having my first "anthropological" discussion—one professional to another. And then it happened—in the middle of one of my explanations, he started raising and wiggling his eyebrows at me. I was taken completely off guard and stammered to a stop. He stopped. No sooner had I resumed talking than he started giving me the eye again. We started and stopped several times. I began to get very angry. There he was, looking so innocent with a quizzical expression on his face, as if *I* were the one doing something odd. How dare he come on to me? How dare he feign interest in my project just so he could flirt with me? I decided to ignore him, but I also made a mental check of other people in the building who might be within earshot of the open office door. I did not want to be alone with him. He acted as if everything was just fine and made no reference to his pass at me. Both of us ignored the glitch even though we undoubtedly thought the other was a bit strange. As our conversation ended, I thanked him for his time, shook his hand, and departed with my head spinning. (p. 73)

End of incident? No. Some time later, while Hahn was talking to a Tongan woman, the woman began to wiggle her eyebrows in the same way, and Hahn began to reinterpret the possible meanings of the gesture:

Was she making a joke or some sort of non-verbal comment? Was she teasing me? Her laughing eyes seemed to draw me in. Had a joke been made that I was too naive to catch? I acted as though I understood, smiled, and after a few minutes, in mindless imitation, I moved my eyebrows up and down as smoothly as possible. It worked well and we had this very lively and civil conversation. I wondered how she could keep it up for so long—it felt sort of like wiggling your ears. Back in my room, I repeated the gesture in the mirror—yep, that's it all right. I felt silly. I felt like an impostor, I was certainly becoming entangled but I had no idea what I was doing. But it was also exhilarating—like flying blindly through the clouds and emerging unscathed. (p. 74)

As she interacted with other people, Hahn eventually decided the gesture did not seem to fit her idea that it might express a joke that she had missed and eventually came to realize that it was "a simple, elegant expression of affirmation—a gesture that draws the participants to each other's eyes, giving an intensity and intimacy to a friendly exchange," a conclusion that she later confirmed by a direct inquiry to a friend (p. 74).

It is not always an easy task to describe customs in terms that people who follow a different way of life can comprehend. This is especially true when we try to explain things that we ourselves have always taken for granted. Our experiences are so common in our own culture that we rarely need to talk about them or explain them—even to ourselves. This can pose problems when people of quite different cultural backgrounds attempt to communicate. Barre Toelken (1979) described an experience during his fieldwork among the Navajo that illustrates such a difficulty:

I had lived with the Navajo family of old Little Wagon for several months before he politely asked me early one morning what kind of noise I was making on my wrist every day. I tried to explain to him that my watch was a means of measuring time, but of course since the Navajos have no word for time as we know it, and because I was still learning the Navajo language, I had no way to explain it to him. My first impulse was to believe that I could simply describe what time was like and why it was important to know it and where I was in relationship to it, but I was brought up abruptly by my realizing that nothing I could say to the old man made any sense to him at all. I pointed out to him how the hands went around a dial that was marked off in equal sections. I then told him that by watching where the hands were I could determine what kinds of things I should be doing. "Like what?" he asked in Navajo. "Well, eating. It tells me when to eat." "Don't your people eat when they are hungry? We eat when we are hungry if there is food." "Well, yes, we eat when we are hungry; that is, no, we eat three times a day, and we are not supposed to eat between times." "Why not?" "Well, it's not healthy." "Why is that?" And so on. I tried another tack. I said that this machine told me when I needed to do those things that were necessary in order to make my living (there is no Navajo word for *work* that sets it apart from other useful and normal things a person might do). The old man asked, "Aren't those things that you do anyway? What is it that this tells you to do that you wouldn't do anyway?" "Well, it tells me when to go out and look for rocks [there was no Navajo word for uranium at the time], and then my company will know how much to pay me." "Do you mean if you lost that machine, you would stop looking for rocks?" "Well, no, I guess I wouldn't." Finally, in exasperation, I said that the watch actually was my reference point to some larger ongoing process outdoors, and this seemed to satisfy the old man. But later, when we were outside that afternoon, he stopped me and held me by the elbow and asked, "Where is it? That which is happening out here?" Beginning to be even more frustrated, I said, "Well, the sun comes up and goes down, doesn't it?" "Yes," he agreed expectantly. "Well, I guess I can't explain it to you. It's nothing, after all. It's all inside the watch. All it does is just go around and make noise." "I thought so," he said." (pp. 277–278)

VIEWPOINTS ABOUT CULTURE

Throughout the history of anthropology, culture has been variously conceptualized and defined by each school of thought within the field. Anthropology has always played a role in bridging the gap that has traditionally separated the sciences and the humanities. Thus, the diversity of viewpoints ranges from the scientific to the humanistic.

Diversity in Conceptualizing Culture

The competing ways in which different anthropologists have portrayed culture reflect the relative influence of physical science and humanities models for understanding the human condition. These two competing strains in anthropological history can be exemplified by the contrasting views of two students of Franz Boas in the early part of this century. In 1915 Alfred Kroeber declared that culture, "though carried by men and existing through them, is an entity in itself, and of another order from life" (p. 285). What he meant was that although culture is a human phenomenon, it cannot be understood by studying human biology or psychology. Instead, culture is a "superorganic" phenomenon (Kroeber, 1917) that must be studied as a phenomenon in its own right to identify the lawful characteristics that govern cultural processes.

Kroeber's ideas differed markedly from those of his teacher, Boas, and most of Boas's students, who paid much more attention to the role of human individuals in the history of each culture they studied. The most vigorous attack on Kroeber's concept of culture as a superorganic phenomenon was carried out by another of Boas's students, Edward Sapir (1934). Sapir, who was particularly interested in the human use of language, argued that the superorganic view of culture was an unjustified reification, since "the true locus of culture is in the interactions of specific individuals and, on the subjective side, in the world of meanings which each of these individuals may unconsciously abstract for himself from his participation in these interactions" (p. 236). To Sapir (1934), Kroeber's concept of culture was too concrete and fixed, since it portrayed culture as "a neatly packaged up assemblage of forms of behavior handed over piecemeal, but without serious breakage, to the passively inquiring child" (p. 414). Sapir conceived of the transfer of culture as a process in which each child interpreted, evaluated, and modified every cultural pattern during the process of socialization.

These two approaches to the concept of culture have competed with one another throughout the history of anthropology. Those who follow some variant of Kroeber's definition share a scientific interest in the discovery of the laws that govern cultural processes and emphasize the customs and institutions such as politics and economics by which society adapts to its natural environment. Those whose vision of culture comes closer to Sapir's humanistic focus emphasize the role of human discourse and narratives in defining the meaning of social life and nature.

Whether culture is best understood as a distinctively human adaptive mechanism that can be studied without reference to the individual members of society or as a system of ideas and feelings that are given form through the dialogues that individuals create and use as they negotiate their way through daily life may never be fully resolved. In one form or another, however, culture can be seen as the unifying concept of the field of anthropology.

The Unity and Diversity of Cultures

Throughout its history, anthropology has embodied an interest in both the diversity and unity of cultures throughout the world. Approaches that emphasize the diversity of cultures have tended to focus on the unique customs, beliefs, and values that give each culture its distinctive identity. Such approaches were particularly common in the earlier days of anthropological research, when fieldwork often took anthropologists far from home to small and relatively isolated societies. When carried to an extreme, the emphasis on the diversity of human ways of life has often focused on non-Western cultures that might seem exotic. But an underlying goal of the anthropological descriptions of other cultures has always been to make other cultures understandable. This search for unity within diversity has been carried out by humanistically oriented anthropologists who demonstrate how each part of a way of life fits coherently into a broader system of meanings of each culture. They find parallels between otherwise alien customs and analogous elements of the daily life that one knows and understands.

Culture Shock

Anthropologists who engage in fieldwork in a culture that differs from the one in which they grew up often experience a period of disorientation or even depression known as **culture shock** before they become acclimatized to their new environment. Even tourists who travel for only a short time outside their own nations may experience culture shock, and unless they are prepared for its impact, they may simply transform their own distress into a motive for prejudice against their host society.

Today, the world is much more homogeneous and interdependent than it was in the early days of anthropological fieldwork. It has been largely taken over by states and governments that assert their sovereignty over all peoples within their boundaries. Thus, there are fewer truly simple, isolated societies like those that anthropologists once preferred to study. Nearly all of these independent, small-scale societies are now extinct or have changed tremendously to cope with the influences of the industrializing world around them.

Missionaries and traders have brought about many of these changes even in relatively remote areas. The search for new sources of income and for resources valued by the industries of the cities have brought many kinds of immigrants into the frontier territories that were once occupied by societies that had no direct experience with external governments.

Most ethnographic fieldwork, therefore, is carried out today among the rural and urban descendents of peoples like the Dobuans studied by Reo Fortune, the Zuñi of Ruth Benedict's time, or the Kwakiutl described by Franz Boas. Culture shock is still an experience that ethnographers must cope with, but in some ways it has become a more subtle phenomenon. The economic and political interconnectedness of most of the world's people has made us all more alike in many superficial ways. The Yąnomamö wear t-shirts and running shorts. The Navajo wear jeans and drive automobiles. Zuñi pottery and jewelry can be found in department stores. In many cases, the peoples whose lives and customs ethnographers study today speak the national language of the countries in which they live. It has become easy for anthropologists to approach their fieldwork with naïveté, expecting fewer differences and misunderstandings than they actually discover because superficial similarities can mask important deeper cultural differences that may not have been lost.

(Continued on p. 58)

culture shock the loneliness and depression that are often experienced when one is in a foreign cultural setting

DOING FIELDWORK AMONG THE YĄNOMAMÖ

Napoleon Chagnon (1983), an anthropologist who conducted his research among the Yąnomamö Indians of Venezuela, has described his initial reaction to that people when he first met them in 1966. The Yąnomamö were an extremely fierce and warlike people who valued and cultivated extremes of aggressive behavior unequaled in many parts of the world. Their use of hallucinogenic drugs in their religious rituals added to their distinctive cultural configuration. Although it is certainly not typical of an anthropologist's first day in the field, Chagnon's uncommonly frank revelation of his feelings on first exposure to a non-Western culture gives some sense of the psychological effects of radical changes in one's symbolic environment and the ease with which ethnocentric prejudices might arise and preclude even the first steps towards the objective study of other ways of life.

We arrived at the village, Bisaasi-teri, about 2:00 p.m. and docked the boat along the muddy bank at the terminus of the path used by the Indians to fetch their drinking water. It was hot and muggy, and my clothing was soaked with perspiration. It clung uncomfortably to my body, as it did thereafter for the remainder of the work. The small, biting gnats were out in astronomical numbers, for it was the beginning of the dry season. My face and hands were swollen from the venom of their numerous stings. In just a few moments I was to meet my first Yąnomamö, my first primitive man. What would it be like? . . .

My heart began to pound as we approached the village and heard the buzz of activity within the circular compound. Mr. Barker commented that he was anxious to see if any changes had taken place while he was away and wondered how many of them had died during his absence. I felt into my back pocket to make sure that my notebook was still there and felt personally more secure when I touched it. Otherwise, I would not have known what to do with my hands.

The entrance to the village was covered over with brush and dry palm leaves. We pushed them aside to expose the low opening to the village. The excitement of meeting my first Indians was almost unbearable as I duck-waddled through the low passage into the village clearing.

I looked up and gasped when I saw a dozen burly, naked, filthy, hideous men staring at us down the shafts of their drawn arrows! Immense wads of green tobacco were stuck between their lower teeth and lips making them look even more hideous, and strands of dark-green slime dripped or hung from their noses. We arrived at the village while the men were blowing a hallucinogenic drug up their noses. One of the side effects of the drug is a runny nose. The mucus is always saturated with the green powder and the Indians usually let it run freely from their nostrils. My next discovery was that there were a dozen or so vicious, underfed dogs snapping at my legs, circling me as if I were going to be their next meal. I just stood there holding my notebook, helpless and pathetic. Then the stench of the decaying vegetation and filth struck me and I almost got sick. I was horrified. What sort of a welcome was this for the person who came here to live with you and learn your way of life, to become friends with you? They put their weapons down when they recognized Barker and returned to their chanting, keeping a nervous eye on the village entrances.

We had arrived just after a serious fight. Seven women had been abducted the day before by a neighboring group, and the local men and their guests had just that morning recovered five of them in a brutal club fight that nearly ended in a shooting war. The abductors, angry because they lost five of the seven captives, vowed to raid the Bisaasi-teri. When we arrived and entered the village unexpectedly, the Indians feared that we were the raiders. On several occasions during the next two hours the men in the village jumped to their feet, armed themselves, and waited nervously for the noise outside the village to be identified. My enthusiasm for collecting ethnographic curiosities diminished in proportion to the number of times such an alarm was raised. In fact, I was relieved when Mr. Barker suggested that we sleep across the river for the evening. It would be safer over there.

As we walked down the path to the boat, I pondered the wisdom of having decided to spend a year and a half with this tribe before I had even seen what they were like. I am not ashamed to admit, either, that had there been a diplomatic way out, I would have ended my fieldwork then and there. I did not look forward to the next day when I would be left alone with the Indians; I did not speak a word of their language, and they are decidedly different from what I had imagined them to be. The whole situation was depressing, and I wondered why I ever decided to switch from civil engineering to anthropology in the first place.

I had not eaten all day, I was soaking wet from perspiration, the gnats were biting me, and I was covered with red pigment, the result of a dozen or so complete examinations I had been given by as many burly Indians. These examinations capped an otherwise grim day. The Indians would blow their noses into their hands, flick as much of the mucus off that would separate in a snap of the wrist, wipe the residue into their hair, and then carefully examine my face, arms, legs, hair, and the contents of my pockets. I asked Mr. Barker how to say "Your hands are dirty"; my comments were met by the Indians in the following way: They would "clean" their hands by spitting a quantity of slimy tobacco juice into them, rub them together, and then proceed with the examination.

YĄNOMAMÖ

Xingu National Park is an area that borders Venezuela and Brazil, where the Yąanomamö and several other tribes hope to preserve a way of life that won't be affected by pollution caused by miners, disease caused by intruders, and cultural assimilation.

Mr. Barker and I crossed the river and slung our hammocks. When he pulled his hammock out of a rubber bag, a heavy, disagreeable odor of mildewed cotton came with it. "Even the missionaries are filthy," I thought to myself. Within two weeks, everything I owned smelled the same way, and I lived with that odor for the remainder of the fieldwork. My own habits of personal cleanliness reached such levels that I didn't even mind being examined by the Indians, as I was not much cleaner than they were after I had adjusted to the circumstances. (pp. 9–12)

Today, the Yąanomamö no longer live the kind of life Napoleon Chagnon witnessed. Miners, loggers, and many others have encroached on their land, destroying the forest and spreading disease (see Chapter 7, p. 173).

CHAPTER SUMMARY

1. Culture consists of the learned ideas and survival strategies that unify members of a particular human group. Group members are conscious that some of their beliefs and feelings are shaped by the ideology of their culture.

2. Facing different environments with differing ideas about how one should live, cultures have evolved along different lines. Variations are often so extreme that people from different cultures have a hard time understanding each other's ways.

3. Cultural relativism, in which we try to make sense of the values and behaviors of other cultures within their own contexts, has long been used by anthropologists to encourage better understanding among all peoples.

4. Fieldwork can be a psychologically difficult experience, since the meanings and values of the fieldworker's own culture may not be useful guides for understanding or responding acceptably to the customs the fieldworker is trying to comprehend. The sense of isolation and feelings of depres-

sion that can result from being immersed in another culture are referred to as culture shock.

5. The two ways in which anthropologists study culture focus on it either as a su-perorganic phenomena with regularities that can be scientifically understood, or as a system of meanings that are embodied in the dialogues that occur among the individual members of each society.

ANNOTATED READINGS

Benedict, R. (1934). *Patterns of culture.* Boston: Houghton Mifflin. A classic description of three cultures with very different value systems.

Fernea, E. W. (1989). *Guests of the sheik: An ethnography of an Iraqi village.* New York: Doubleday. An engrossing account of women's life in the 1960s in the rural village of El Nahra in southern Iraq.

Fox, R. G. (Ed.). (1991). *Recapturing anthropology: Working in the present.* Santa Fe, NM: School of American Research Press. A collection of viewpoints on the production of anthropological descriptions of life in contemporary societies.

Geertz, C. (Ed.). (1971). *Myth, symbol, and culture.* New York: W. W. Norton. An important collection of essays on culture as a symbolic system.

Harris, M. (1974). *Cows, pigs, wars and witches: The riddles of culture.* New York: Random House. An exciting popular illustration of the cultural materialist approach to explaining human customs.

Hsu, F. L. K. (1983). *Rugged individualism reconsidered: Essays in psychological anthropology.* Knoxville, TN: University of Tennessee Press. Comparisons of traditional Chinese and U.S. cultures by an anthropologist who was born in China.

Rabinow, P. (1977). *Reflections on fieldwork in Morocco.* Berkeley, CA: University of California Press. A description of how an anthropologist's encounters with Moroccans shaped his understanding of Moroccan culture.

Steedly, M. M. (1993). *Hanging without a rope: Narrative experience in colonial and postcolonial Karland.* Princeton, NJ: Princeton University Press. An ethnography of the lives and history of the Karo of North Sumatra, Indonesia, as depicted through their stories and memories.

Tedlock, B. (1992). *The beautiful and the dangerous: Encounter with the Zuñi Indians.* New York: Viking. A wonderfully readable description of life and fieldwork in the contemporary town of Zuñi, New Mexico.

CHAPTER THREE

Social Organization, Biology, and Culture

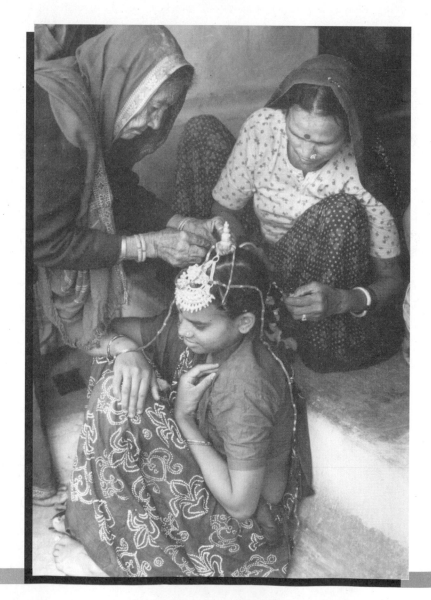

Chapter Objectives

After reading this chapter, you should be able to:

Define the concept of social organization and its parts.

Discuss the relationships between status, roles, and division of labor.

Explain the relationship of rank to power and prestige.

Compare and contrast the concepts of class and caste.

Discuss the nature and functions of master statuses.

Explain the nature of minorities.

Explain the relationships between biology and statuses.

Discuss the scientific fallacies of racism.

Analyze the social functions of racism.

◀ ***Figure 3.1*** *Status All relationships a person may have with others are called statuses and exist in pairs. These women in India illustrate complementary statuses in that the three different generations are expected to behave in ways that reflect their hierarchical statuses as grandmothers, mothers, and daughters.*

Organizational Patterns

Groups
Statuses and Roles
Division of Labor
Rank
Contextual Cues
Master Statuses

Biological Traits and Social Statuses

Biology and Socially Learned Roles
Race, Cultural Ability, and Intelligence

Nowhere are all people treated equally. In every society, people are organized into groups and levels of honor and social power. Categorizing people on the basis of distinctions such as the kind of work they do or their relationships to each other has the benefit of making social life efficient, orderly, and predictable. But some ways of categorizing people lead to inequalities that are unrelated to people's innate abilities. Such discriminations are made on the basis of historically derived, and therefore culturally diverse, ideas about categories such as race and sex. After examining patterns of social organization and the ways in which biological characteristics are sometimes the basis for assigning different statuses, we consider racism and its functions in society and its lack of scientific validity.

Tinker. Tailor. Soldier. Sailor. Rich man. Poor man. Beggar man. Thief. Imagine yourself digging through old greasy tinfoil and moldy orange peels for your daily dinner. Or imagine yourself in a London Fog trenchcoat on a foggy London morning cautiously peering around a corner to catch a glimpse of the spy carrying an alligator briefcase. Imagine yourself growing up Black in the hills of South Africa or White in the Australian outback. Wherever you find yourself in society, your identity is determined both by biology and by culture.

ORGANIZATIONAL PATTERNS

Throughout human history, cultural continuity has been maintained by symbolic communication among members of a particular society. The pattern of that communication is determined by how society is organized. The **social organization** of a society consists of (1) the various groups that form the society; (2) the statuses that individuals may hold; (3) the division of labor, or the way in which the tasks of society are distributed among individuals and groups; and (4) the rank accorded to each group and status.

Groups

Every human society is a **group**, whose members perceive their common identity because of the culture that binds them together. All human societies that have been studied subdivide into smaller groups that coalesce from time to time for specialized activities. Such groups have geographical boundaries, specifiable members, a common activity engaged in by members, and a division of labor. Basketball fans scattered across the country are not a group, for example, but spectators at a specific game are. When a group is formally organized, it may have an explicitly formulated ideology and a goal-oriented "game plan" or set of procedures for carrying out the activity that brings its members together.

The members of social groups generally identify themselves symbolically with a name or some other emblem of their group identity. Commonly, the identifying emblem indicates the activity that draws the members together or represents some other important aspect of the group's characteristics. Thus, the group identity of the United States of America is symbolized by a flag that portrays the political unity of that society's 50 states by a group of 50 stars. The Great Seal of the United States of America contains the image of an eagle clutching an olive branch and arrows, symbols of peace and war, which suggest that the major purpose of the nation as a political entity is to maintain internal order and to defend the group. A smaller, more face-to-face group, such as a basketball team, may identify itself as a unified body by naming itself and by symbolizing its athletic purpose with some symbol of its prowess, such as a charging bull or a buzzing hornet.

There will also be structured relationships between groups in every society. Interactions by groups are culturally patterned and may involve hierarchical ranking, with each group having different degrees of honor and social power. Group relationships are sometimes

---

social organization the relationships between the groups, statuses, and division of labor that structure the interaction of people within society

group two or more individuals engaged in a common activity

called the **social structure** of a society, to distinguish this aspect of social organization from other aspects such as individual statuses and roles (Service, 1962).

Statuses and Roles

Besides groups, each pattern of social organization also includes several kinds of relationships. All relationships that a person may have with others are called **statuses** and exist in pairs, such as doctor and patient, husband and wife, parent and child, or friend and friend. The **status pairs** of a society are of two types: those in which the holders of the statuses are expected to behave in different but mutually compatible ways, and those in which the holders of the statuses are expected to behave in a similar way toward one another.

Status pairs in which both parties are expected to behave in different but compatible ways are called **complementary statuses**. The status of doctor, for example, requires the existence of the complementary status of patient, that of parent implies that of offspring, and without the status of student there could be no teacher. In each of these cases, the holder of one status of the pair is expected to behave differently from the holder of the second status, and one of the statuses may have access to a greater amount of honor, social power, and/or wealth. Thus, parents have the power to train and control their children rather than the other way around, and it is the teacher who tests and assigns grades to the student.

Statuses such as friend, neighbor, enemy, colleague, or ally, on the other hand, imply the existence of two or more holders of the same status who are expected to act toward one another in similar ways. Statuses paired in this way are called **symmetrical statuses**. One cannot be an enemy unless there is someone who will respond in kind as an enemy, too (Watzlawick, Beavin, & Jackson, 1967).

In every society, each person may be involved in many different kinds of relationships and therefore have many different statuses. The same person may be a wife, a mother, a student, an employee, a friend, and a political activist. Some statuses that we have no choice about are known as **ascribed statuses**. These often include characteristics such as gender, family membership, or, in some societies, racial identity. Other statuses must be acquired during our lifetimes and may change as our posi-

tion in life changes. These statuses, such as team captain, college student, or club member, are known as **achieved statuses**.

The ways in which the holder of a status is expected to behave are called the **roles** of that status. Every status has several different roles, each of which is considered appropriate for certain times and places. For instance, in a classroom students take notes, ask and respond to questions, and occasionally take tests. At home they are expected to read and study assignments and compose term papers. Their written assignments may require that they be able to carry out library research or demonstrate other skills at information gathering. People in these situations behave in the role of student. When these same people go to a party on Saturday night, however, they assume a role other than student and behave differently.

By conforming their behavior to the role expectations of others, holders of a particular status symbolically communicate that they wish to be responded to in a manner appropriate to that specific status rather than to some other status that they might also hold. The team captain is expected to direct action on the field; off the field, the same person may be expected to listen to and respect the opinion of another

---

social structure the part of social organization made up of groups and their relationships with each other

status a culturally defined relationship that one individual may have with one or more other individuals; the position within a group that each member holds

status pair the statuses that two people acquire when they interact, and that together form a relationship

complementary statuses a pair of statuses, each of which has roles that are different from but compatible with the roles of the other

symmetrical statuses a pair of statuses, each of which has the same roles to play with respect to the other

ascribed statuses social positions that one is assumed to occupy by virtue of the group into which one happens to be born—for instance, one's sex or race

achieved statuses social positions that one acquires by demonstrating the necessary role-playing abilities

role the skills, abilities, and ways of acting toward others that belong to each status of a society

with whom he or she shares the status of friend. The various status pairs of a society form a pattern of predictable expectations that guide their interactions and simplify social relationships. When team members accept another's status as team captain, they know that during a game their appropriate relationship to the leader is that of followers. Without such role agreements, ball games—and social life— would be somewhat chaotic.

Division of Labor

The day-to-day work that must be done in any society is allocated to people through their statuses. This makes it possible for the members of society to be organized efficiently into a clear-cut, well-known, and effective **division of labor** by which all the tasks of life are accomplished.

Even in those human social systems where few specialists exist, there is some division of labor. In foraging societies, for example, age and gender are the primary bases for assigning the work of life. Even though tasks may overlap and distinctions may not be strictly enforced, males and females in all societies are generally expected to specialize in somewhat different economic activities, as are the members of different age groups. Typically, in the foraging societies men are assigned the status of hunters, while women specialize as gatherers of wild plants. Children may provide some help around the campsite, fetching water or gathering branches for the fire. Older members of the group may be relied on for their experience in interpersonal and intergroup relations to mediate disputes, negotiate with strangers, or arrange marriages. In societies in which people grow their own food, other forms of specialization develop, and the division of labor may become much more intricate. For instance, individuals or entire villages may specialize in the growing of a particular crop or the manufacture of woven goods or pottery. These are traded to other people or villages in return for their specialties. In industrialized societies, there are so many specialized occupations that a monetary system is needed to organize the exchange of labor.

Rank

Some kinds of work are valued more highly than others. **Rank** is a measure of the relative importance accorded to groups and statuses and the work that they do. Holders of highly ranked statuses and members of highly ranked groups generally have more ready access to whatever is valued in their culture than do other members of their society.

Power and Honor.   Rank has more than one component. According to Kemper (1978), the two characteristics of a status that determine its social rank are the amount of social power and honor[1] associated with it. Power and honor are measures of one's ability to influence others successfully. **Power** is the ability to exercise coercion in obtaining what is sought and to punish the failure of others to comply. **Honor** is the esteem that some statuses confer on those who hold them. The respect that comes to persons such as Supreme Court justices, ministers, or movie stars whose statuses are honored makes it easier for them to accomplish goals and influence others without coercion.

Groups, too, may be ranked in the degree of power and honor that they command. For instance, secret societies and vigilante groups are often characterized by high access to power, but their level of honor may be judged low by others. Service associations such as the Kiwanis Club or a charity fund-raising group may have little power to coerce others to contribute to their cause, but they may be highly enough respected to receive voluntary contributions.

Like groups, individual statuses may be ranked. In the United States, the occupational statuses of doctor and senator are prestigious and are each given more social power and a greater income than the lower-ranked occupations of sales clerk, mail carrier, and carpenter.

---

1. Kemper (1978) defines status as esteem based on a "relationship in which there is *voluntary compliance* [italics in original] with the wishes, desires, wants and needs of the other" (p. 378). This is the meaning of "honor" as defined in this text.

---

division of labor the rules that govern how the day-to-day work of life is divided among the holders of various statuses

rank the relative importance of a status or group as measured by the amount of power and/or honor to which it is entitled

power the ability to exercise coercion in a group in obtaining what is sought

honor the esteem some statuses confer on those who hold them

Societies differ in which statuses are most highly ranked. For instance, in industrialized nations where many of the important relationships in life are based on jobs, occupational status is a major determinant of the rank most people hold. In these societies, the loss of income that comes with retirement is often accompanied by a loss of rank. In societies where kinship relationships determine the most important roles, it is common for rank to increase with age and experience.

Class. Ranking of diverse statuses is more common in those societies that have large populations and many differentiated, highly specialized statuses or jobs. These societies are organized into a hierarchical structure that sometimes is subdivided formally into ranked classes. A **class** is a broad stratum that cuts across society and is made up of unrelated families that have more or less equal access to income and prestige. Sometimes class membership is determined by birth, and the statuses that individuals may hold during their lifetimes are limited to those of the class into which they are born. In such a case, when people are not permitted to move from one formally demarcated class to another by acquiring a new status, the classes are called **castes**.

Contextual Cues

No matter how simple or complex a society, each of its members will hold more than one status. People learn to play each of their numerous roles as they are directed by culturally defined **contextual cues**, which might be the location in which they find themselves, the date and time of day, or the statuses of other persons who are present. Thus, in the United States and Canada, holders of the status of student who find themselves in the context of a classroom during a scheduled class meeting time are expected to play one of their student roles that is appropriate to that set of cues. In another setting, students may relate to a teacher in another student-appropriate role, but one that is more appropriate to the nonclassroom setting. When the teacher leaves, the students' behavior may shift radically as they play the roles of entirely different statuses.

Sometimes conflicting contextual cues occur in the same situation, calling for different roles at the same time. In such circumstances, depending on how different those roles are

FIGURE 3.2

CASTE

The caste system in India is a complex social and religious system of ordering the members of its society. The highest rank is the Brahmin caste and the lowest, the Sudra. Beneath these are the Untouchables, not considered a part of the caste system. These untouchables perform menial tasks such as bricklaying.

from one another, the individual may experience an extreme degree of psychological disorientation and confusion technically called **role conflict**. For instance, the first time a newly married couple is visited by their parents in the couple's home, a degree of awkwardness may arise when the young couple attempt to play

(Continued on p. 67)

class a broad, ranked stratum within society made up of unrelated families that have more-or-less equal power and prestige

caste a social class determined by birth, so that an individual cannot legitimately change class membership by acquiring a new status

contextual cues culturally defined indicators such as setting, date, time of day, or the statuses of other persons present that determine which roles are appropriate and which are inappropriate to play

role conflict emotional discomfort and confusion experienced in situations in which conflicting contextual cues indicate that an individual should play the roles of more than one of his or her statuses

CASTE IN INDIA

Caste in India has been described by many anthropologists, as in classic studies by Beals (1974, 1980), Dumont (1970), Kolanda (1978), and Mandelbaum (1972). The system of organizing people socially by grouping them into castes is an ancient practice that is couched in religious concepts and differs somewhat in various parts of India. In simplified terms, there are four major kinds of castes. The first of these, the **Brahmin**, is ranked highest in ritual purity and closeness to God. Members of this caste are priests in theory, although in fact most practice other occupations. Socially, members of the Brahmin caste are accorded greater honor than are those of the lower castes even though they have less power and wealth than many members of other castes. The **Kshatriya**—warrior-rulers, nobles, and landowners—are next in honor. They are thought to be less ritually pure than the Brahmins and are subject to fewer dietary and ritual restrictions than the priestly class. Next come the **Vaisya**, the commoners, and, finally, the **Sudra**, who are the farm artisans, servants, farmers, and laborers. Below all these are the people of no caste, the so-called **Untouchables** who perform the polluted tasks of life such as removing dead cattle from the village, tanning hides, working leather, and removing human waste.

Although Indian society accords greater honor to the higher castes, it does not link freedom with this honor. Members of the higher castes are hedged about by various restrictions, most notably dietary restrictions. The Brahmins and Vaisya are expected to be strict vegetarians, although the Kshatriya may eat goat, considered a relatively clean animal, and may drink liquor. The Sudra may eat chicken (a less pure animal) as well as goat, and the Untouchables may eat any meat, including beef and pork. In varying degrees the members of higher castes also are expected to avoid physical contact with the members of lower castes.

Within each caste there are many occupational subcastes or **jatis** that are also ranked by ritual purity. Members of each jati have rights over and responsibilities to the members of other jatis. For instance, potters of the artisan class are expected to make pottery for the farmers, while the farmer is expected to present the potter with a traditional portion of his harvest. The relationships between the jatis are most noticeable when a ritual is performed. For instance, Brahmins must officiate using bowls made by the Potter jati and wearing clothes provided by the Weaver jati and washed by the Washer jati. Such rituals portray the interdependence of the various jatis and reassert the rights of each to belong to the community, since all public rituals require the cooperation of all jatis. In everyday economic life, few people in modern India actually make their living on the basis of their jati occupation. Many people may provide services for a fee or follow an occupation different from their traditional jati occupation, since most jatis have more members than are necessary for performing the service. Thus, jati occupations represent more a system of ritual than of real economic ranking.

Caste is an important social reality in contemporary India (Gargan, 1992), but with the passage of time, the traditional reciprocal economic roles of jati occupations are being undermined as imported products enter the local economies of rural India. Increasingly Indians are replacing their reliance on the services performed by members of other jatis with the use of these new imports. For instance, the use of imported dishware can reduce the need for potters, buying razor blades can take the place of visiting barbers, and gasoline-driven equipment can replace work previously done by agricultural laborers.

Hostilities sometimes arise within the system because the different castes are each accorded different amounts of honor, power, and wealth. The Hindu religious ideology helps to minimize these conflicts by asserting that individuals who conform well to the rules that govern their position in life will be rewarded by future rebirth into a higher caste. By accepting the caste system and following its rules, one may eventually attain a sufficient spiritual development to avoid being reborn into the world and its misery. Those who rebel against the rules of caste will be reborn at a lower position, thereby prolonging the cycles of reincarnation and human suffering.

Brahmin the highest-ranked Hindu caste, members of which are theoretically priests

Kshatriya the second most important of the Hindu castes, members of which were the traditional warrior-rulers, nobles, and landowners

Vaisya the third-ranked Hindu caste, comprised of commoners

Sudra the lowest of the Hindu castes, made up of farm artisans, servants, farmers, and laborers

Untouchables the lowest-status members of Hindu society who belong to none of the traditional castes and who ritually perform the polluted tasks of life

jati an occupational subcaste in Hindu society

FIGURE 3.3

MASTER STATUS

Master status is a position in society a person holds of either high or low rank that cannot be ignored.

Here men in traditional dress greet Pope John Paul II in Port Moresby, the capital of Papua New Guinea.

the role of heads of household in the presence of their parents, who have previously had a monopoly over that superior status.

When people have several statuses that are significantly different in rank, they will tend to adopt the highest status that is appropriate to the situation. The greater the importance that ranking has in a society, the more its members will attempt, wherever possible, to avoid appearing in roles of subordinate statuses. The exception to this rule is that a person who has attained a highly ranked status, such as a senator or a Nobel Prize winner, may play the role of a much lower status as a way of showing respect for his or her subordinates. U.S. presidents have been photographed in their shirt sleeves on tractors and in Native American headdresses to "humanize" themselves in the public eye.

Master Statuses

The usual pattern in which the setting determines which roles a person may play is altered when he or she holds a master status. A **master status** is one that is so strongly imbued with importance in the minds of people that it cannot be ignored. For instance, if the chief justice of the United States or a well-known actor were to appear in a college classroom on parents' visiting day, this visitor probably would not be treated as just another parent in the audience. More likely, instead of the situation's defining the status of the visitor, the situation itself would be redefined to fit the visitor's master status. Unlike an ordinary parent, such a visitor would likely be introduced to the class, and the regular lecture might even be preempted by remarks from the guest.

Master statuses may have low rank as well as high. Having a low-ranked master status can overshadow the other statuses a person may hold, even those usually held in high esteem by others. For instance, an alcoholic physician may find it difficult to acquire patients or to

master status a social status that is so important that it cannot be ignored

AN AMERICAN MASTER STATUS

In the United States and Canada, people with same-sex sexual orientation have had minority status since they have been identified as a social group. There has been some movement toward acceptance of gay men and lesbians since the Gay Liberation Movement of the late 1960s. However, homophobia, fear of and hostility toward these people, is still a common phenomenon: people with a same-sex orientation are barred from serving openly in the military; the Boy Scouts of America has denied membership to gay boys and has excluded gay men as scoutmasters; gay men and lesbians lack the legal and economic benefits of marriage, such as inheritance rights and insurance benefits that are available to heterosexuals; in 1986, the U.S. Supreme Court ruled that laws forbidding sexual intimacy between same-sex partners are constitutional. In these and in other ways, lesbians and gay men are singled out by public institutions for discrimination.

Homophobia is most likely to occur where the gender roles of men and women are particularly distinct and the roles of women are ranked below those of men. Thus, homophobia and female subordination are related phenomena. George Weinberg (1982/1985), the American psychoanalyst who coined the term *homophobia,* found that the most homophobic individuals were those who associated men's roles with the exercise of power and dominance and women's roles with passivity. Such individuals perceive people of same-gender orientation as having abandoned the traditional roles of men or women.

In the view of Adrienne Rich (1980), the subordination of women in a patriarchal society is perpetuated by the assumption that heterosexuality is the normal human state. This assumption, which she calls heterosexism, maintains male dominance by denying the validity of female viewpoints. Charlotte Bunch (1975) has argued that the oppression of gay males and lesbians and of women in general are linked phenomena, since patriachal institutions control women through heterosexist definitions that assume "that every woman either is or wants to be bonded to a man both economically and emotionally" (p. 180). Heterosexism operates in all institutions, not just in the narrow arena of sex.

Dennis Werner (1979) found that homophobia was one aspect of a broader opposition to any form of nonprocreative sex. He tested the hypothesis that attitudes toward same-sex orientation and behavior are negative where population growth is desired and permissive where population pressures are severe. He compared a sample of **pronatalist societies**, whose customs favor reproduction by forbidding practices such as abortion or infanticide that can limit population growth, with a sample of **antinatalist societies** that permit such practices. In 75 percent of the pronatalist societies, homosexuality was ridiculed, forbidden, or punished, but in 60 percent of antinatalist societies, it was permitted among at least some members of society. Thus, homophobia and the minority status of lesbians and gay males can be understood as byproducts of cultural values that encourage heterosexual marriage and procreation.

---

obtain referrals from other doctors. Having a low-ranked master status at one time in one's life can bar one from attaining more respected statuses later.

Master statuses of low social rank are sometimes given the special designation of **minorities**. Minorities in North America include many groups defined by similar characteristics such as ethnic background, religion, race, and gender. **Ethnic group** identity is based on shared customs, such as those of immigrants from various European countries, especially of southern and eastern Europe. Religious minorities, such as Muslims, Buddhists, Rastafari, Amish, Hutterites, and Mormons, also exemplify groups that have not received total acceptance as members of the U.S. or Canadian mainstream.

The definition of minorities is not necessarily a matter of numbers. In the United States, for instance, females make up slightly more than 50 percent of the population, and Blacks constitute large numerical majorities in many cities and counties. Yet birth into either of these

---

pronatalist societies societies whose customs favor reproduction and forbid abortion and infanticide

antinatalist societies societies whose customs favor low birth rates and thus permit abortion and infanticide

minorities those with a low-ranked master status, commonly but incorrectly called "minority groups"

ethnic group a group whose identity is based on shared customs, especially of immigrants

FIGURE 3.4

FEMALE ROLES

The expectation that females will follow traditional roles has changed in recent years. The fact that females have succeeded in such traditionally male roles as politician, physician, or soldier is evidence that gender roles are learned, not biologically inherited. Above, Hillary Rodham Clinton joins Prime Minister Benazir Bhutto of Pakistan at a luncheon for prominent women in Islamabad.

statuses may impede acquisition and successful use of highly ranked social statuses. Thus, U.S. women currently hold less than 15 percent of elective offices in a society in which they comprise over half of the total population, and adult Black males in the United States suffer from an unemployment rate that is twice that of the adult male workforce as a whole.

BIOLOGICAL TRAITS AND SOCIAL STATUSES

In every human society, some of the statuses that people hold are based on observed biological characteristics such as sex, degree of biological maturation, physiological handicap, or skin color. But as we shall see, how biological traits are understood depends greatly on cultural interpretations that can be highly arbitrary.

Biology and Socially Learned Roles

From birth individual children may differ from one another in behavioral capacities or generalized tendencies, such as activity level, aggressiveness, or responsiveness to stimuli. Such differences are innate and may result from biologically inherited hormonal and neurological factors. Social roles, on the other hand, are not inherited biologically, but rather, as cultural phenomena, are learned. Our inborn predispositions may influence the style with which we play a role, but they do not determine the content of our roles.

Although biology alone does not control the content of social roles, beliefs about biology may. People who share some biological characteristic may be socialized into playing roles that their culture claims are a natural result of those biological traits. The result is a self-fulfilling prophecy in which playing the learned role seems to prove the culture's association of the behaviors with biology. For instance, an active female child may be subject to intensive social training that leads her to conform to a more passive and nonaggressive role because her society considers these traits attributes of the female status. Similarly, Scott (1969) has described an interesting process by which those with poor vision may acquire the status of blind persons. Having been labeled blind by legal criteria, such persons may begin to interact with various care-giving agencies. In the process of providing their services, these agencies may unwittingly encourage their poorly sighted clients to learn to perceive themselves as helpless. Learning to play the blind role inhibits the use of whatever vision the clients actually possess.

When statuses are assigned to people because of biological characteristics, the roles that they are expected to play are commonly thought of as a natural and inherent result of those biological conditions. In societies where men hold powerful statuses, the culture is apt to contain beliefs that men are somehow naturally more dominant than women. Where one racial group dominates another in the same society, the members who hold the more highly ranked statuses will generally be described as inherent leaders, while those of the subordinate race will be commonly portrayed as naturally lazy, less intelligent, and in need of guidance.

Belief in Distinct Races.   The ideologies of many societies include the idea that the human species contains distinct biological subdivisions called **races**. Although some scientists who are interested in the biological diversity within our species also use the concept of race, their studies actually reveal something quite different: *Homo sapiens* is a species in which great diversity exists in every local group and in which the frequencies of traits vary gradually from region to region. In fact, ideas of racial purity are no more than myths. Neighboring human groups are constantly exchanging genes through intermating, and no human groups are really isolated from their neighbors, even when rigid taboos exist. It has been estimated by sociologist Robert Stuckert (1966) that approximately 23 percent of persons classified as White in the United States in 1960 had at least one ancestor of African origin. Truly separate races in the sense of really distinct and biologically pure strains have never developed in the human species. Because of the flow of genetic material from group to group, the peoples who originally occupied different regions of the earth—such as Sub-Saharan Africa, Europe, East Asia, Australia, and the Americas—differ from one another in only 0.1 percent of their genetically inherited traits. Thus, the so-called "races" referred to by popular culture are not nearly so different from each other as people imagine.

Throughout most of history, people interacted only with close neighbors who differed very little from them biologically. Even if their cultures differed radically, an individual's status was likely to be framed as a nonbiological concept such as *foreigner* or *stranger*. Those who held such statuses might be treated ethnocentrically as social inferiors and would be expected to play inferior roles. But it was not until the peoples of distant parts of the world began to interact that the idea of race became a common way of identifying social contrasts between them.

The belief that humankind is divided into several major races began during the age of European colonial expansion. Travel to far-flung parts of the world brought people together from places where the most frequently observable biological traits such as skin color or hair texture differed enough to be readily noted by the travelers. These contrasts were the basis for creating racial statuses when the political need arose. Colonial expansion was undertaken to obtain economic and political benefits for the homeland. Expecting members of the colonized societies to play different roles from the colonizers supported this goal. The racial ideology helped to maintain the distinction between "us" and "them."

The criteria by which "races" are defined vary from culture to culture. Usually, they are easily observable traits such as skin color, the shape of facial features, hair color and texture, or body stature. Less observable traits such as blood type would not allow quick and easy decisions about what social roles should be played between people. In North America, skin color and hair texture are the determinants of the "race" to which one will be thought to belong. In Bolivia, on the other hand, nonbiological attributes such as clothing and dialect or accent may greatly influence other people's beliefs about one's "race."

Racial Prejudice and Discrimination.
Since racial classifications are social conventions, they differ from culture to culture. The defined racial categories may include as few as two socially relevant categories or a multitude of them. Despite the arbitrariness of racial classifications, they may seem quite real to those who have been socialized into using them. The power of social beliefs in racial differences can

---

races distinct biological subdivisions of a species

be so great that people may be dealt with on the basis of the qualities that are culturally attributed to their race rather than the qualities they actually demonstrate as individuals. Stereotypes about differences between racial groups make it possible to assign somewhat different social roles to members of the different racial groups. Wherever people are classified by race, it is common for members of different racial groups to play somewhat different social roles.

Especially when the roles that are commonly available to members of different racial groups involve a consistent ranking of one racial group over others, the differences in roles may be perpetuated by racial prejudices. **Racial prejudice** is an attitude made up of feelings of dislike and contempt for people who are thought of as belonging to a racial group different from one's own. It may be learned from and supported by the ideology of a culture, and manifest itself in institutions such as laws, public policy, and corporate practices. But prejudice is an antipathy that is felt by individuals. Racial prejudice is translated into behavior when it causes us to treat members of other racial groups differently than we would treat members of our own. Such behavior is called **racial discrimination**. While it may be the way an individual manifests his or her racial prejudice, it can also be behavior that is required by institutions such as a company policy of not hiring members of minority races, a law forbidding marriage between members of different races, or a social custom of joking about minority races. This kind of institutionally based discrimination is one of the components of **racism**, culturally mandated, institutionally supported discrimination against members of minority races.

Racism is normally supported by **racist beliefs**, which involve the mistake of thinking that expected social roles are actually inborn racial characteristics. Believing that socially imposed racial differences are innate legitimizes the subordination of one racial group to another. Though inaccurate and demeaning, racist beliefs have evolved because they serve a variety of societal needs such as supporting the political and economic goals of the dominant segments of society.

Economic and Political Roots of Racism. That such social applications of racism have consistently represented nonscientific and arbitrary judgments that serve the changing, often ethnocentric values of society is evidenced by three scientifically untenable characteristics of these racist standards. First, standards of racial classification have been highly arbitrary in biological terms, since they are socially directed to supporting the supposed "purity" of the dominant group. For instance, in the United States, anyone who admits having even one Black ancestor is commonly classified by others and treated socially as a Black—regardless of physical appearance. It would be just as logical to classify someone who has a small amount of "White blood" as a White. But the function of racial classification in the United States has been to deny equal access to economic and political power to those of other than northern European ancestry.

The second major evidence that racism, far from being scientific, grows out of the predominant social values of the day is that racist ideas about the behavioral tendencies of the "races" change with the shifting winds of public and political sentiment. Thus, in the United States of 1935, the Japanese "race" was commonly viewed as progressive, intelligent, and industrious. Only 7 years later, in 1942, the Japanese were widely viewed as an inherently cunning and treacherous "race." After 1950, as political allies of the United States, they once again came to be viewed as hardworking and progressive! Similarly, when there was a labor shortage in California during the construction of the transcontinental railway line, the Chinese who provided cheap labor were described as a frugal, sober, law-abiding "race." Then, when competition for jobs became severe and it became economically desirable to exclude further immigration of Chinese laborers, the

---

racial prejudice an attitude made up of feelings of dislike and contempt for people who are thought of as belonging to a racial group different from one's own

racial discrimination treating people differently based on their membership in different racial groups

racism culturally mandated, institutionally-supported discrimination against members of minority races that is based on and supported by cultural beliefs about innate differences between the races

racist beliefs beliefs that mistakenly attribute the causes of role differences to inborn racial predispositions rather than to social learning

AT THE RACIAL DIVIDING LINE

Greg Williams was riding a Greyhound bus headed for Muncie, Ind., when his life changed forever. The 10-year-old boy had grown up in Virginia, attending whites-only schools and swimming in whites-only pools. But on that bus ride in 1954, with his father and his brother, Greg learned the truth.

For years, his father had been "passing" as white. But in Muncie, he and all of his relatives were considered black.

"Life is going to be different from now on," Greg remembers his light-skinned father telling him and his brother that day. The boys' mother had left them, and they were headed to Indiana with their father to start over. "In Virginia you were white boys," said his father. "In Indiana you're going to be colored."

Gregory H. Williams is now 51 years old and dean of the Ohio State University College of Law. His book about his life as a boy caught between two worlds has just been published. *Life on the Color Line: The True Story of a White Boy Who Discovered He Was Black* (Dutton) tells how people treated a black boy with white skin and straight hair.

Mr. Williams's father was born to a black woman. She became pregnant in a relationship with a white man for whom she worked as a maid.

During his teen-age years in Muncie's housing projects, black boys who didn't know of Greg Williams's heritage taunted him with cries of "white motha _____." And white strangers shot him looks of shock and anger when they saw him dating black girls.

"The story is more than Greg Williams," the law dean said in an interview. "I was trying to write a story of a boy who was trying to cope with a world in which everyone wanted to make life as hard as possible because he did not fit in a category."

Across the country at the State University of New York at Buffalo, another law professor has just completed a book about not fitting in. Her story is not as dramatic as Mr. Williams's. Judy Scales-Trent grew up in a middle-class family with a strong black history. But her great-grandfather was white and she has very light skin. Her book, *Notes of a White Black Woman* (Penn State Press), describes her bitterness at life on the racial dividing line. . . .

"I wrote to make sense of my life," she says in the book's introduction. Her experience brings the meaning of race into question, she says. "Because I am a black American who is often mistaken for white, my very existence demonstrates that there is slippage between the seemingly discrete categories 'black' and 'white.' "

In an interview, Ms. Scales-Trent said American society believes that maintaining black and white as distinct racial groups serves a purpose. "I think race is created in this country to separate black and white," she says. "I think of them as terms of war."

Both Mr. Williams and Ms. Scales-Trent are considered black when their universities take account of the race of their employees. But they are also part of a growing number of mixed-race people who are waging a war of their own against

---

Chinese "race" suddenly became described as dirty, unassimilable, and even dangerous.

A third evidence that the racist approach is the handmaiden of economic and social segregation values rather than scientific values is the double standard commonly used by racists when evaluating different social groups. For instance, when two groups of White children differ in IQ scores, the explanation of the difference is commonly sought in factors such as the quality of their schooling, their social environments, or the socioeconomic positions of their parents. But when minorities and Whites differ from one another in precisely the same way, it is apt to be labeled as a "racial difference."

The racist approach has consistently failed to have any scientific validity. On the contrary, it supports social prejudices by claiming that socially created group differences are biologically determined and therefore unchangeable. Such an argument provides a political rationale for people to oppose attempts to change the current limitations in access to social prestige and political and economic power on the basis of race. For that reason, the racist argument has persisted for several centuries, even though it has never proven itself to be of any scientific value in explaining human social difference.

Slavery and Racist Beliefs.   Racism is essentially a modern phenomenon. The modern racist way of reacting to "outsiders" by claiming that they are biologically inferior, unable to learn the "superior" customs of the rac-

America's concept of race. Many people of mixed racial background are writing about their lives.

Both Ms. Scales-Trent and Mr. Williams say that despite their mixed backgrounds, America did not allow them to claim both white and black heritage. They were defined as black.

In the United States, anyone who has any black ancestors is considered black, according to F. James Davis, who recently retired from teaching sociology at Illinois State University. Mr. Davis's 1991 book, *Who Is Black? One Nation's Definition* (Penn State Press), says America defines people with black ancestors as black, even if they also have white ancestors.

Ms. Scales-Trent's book begins with entries from a diary she started in the late 1970's when she was in her 30's. She describes how white people who did not realize she is black used racial slurs in front of her. She tells of the guilt she has felt at not looking black enough. She wonders: Has she avoided discrimination—been able to rent an apartment and catch a cab—because she looks white? . . .

For his part, Mr. Williams watched the reconstruction of his racial identity happen almost overnight. It showed him that race was as much about economics and privilege as about color.

One day he was white, living in a comfortable home in a whites-only neighborhood of Virginia. But after James A. Williams's once-profitable tavern near a military base went out of business at the end of the Korean War, he felt forced to move with his sons to Indiana to find work. There, Greg Williams became black. His father could find only low-paying jobs—partly because he drank and partly because of his color—and the family lived in the toolshed his Grandma Sallie called home.

In a chapter of his book called "Learning How to Be Niggers," Mr. Williams writes about his early years in Muncie. He barely got enough to eat each day and bought his clothes at rummage sales. . . .

Life became easier for Mr. Williams when he enrolled as a freshman at Ball State University. His teachers did not discriminate against him because of his financial situation or his background. "I was able to run into a lot of teachers who were interested in my intellectual ability rather than immobilized by my heritage," he says.

Mr. Williams's book ends with his years at Ball State, but his achievements didn't stop there. He went on to earn a law degree and a Ph.D. in political science from George Washington University.

Mr. Williams has spent his career in academe, first at George Washington, then at the University of Iowa, and now at Ohio State.

In each job, says Mr. Williams, he has made a commitment to helping minority students. . . .

"I am grateful to have been able to view the world from a place few men or women have stood," he writes at the book's end. "I realize now that I am bound to live out my life in the middle of our society and hope that I can be a bridge between the races, shouldering the heavy burden that almost destroyed my youth."

From "At the Racial Dividing Line," by Robin Wilson, January 27, 1995, *Chronicle of Higher Education*, pp. A17, A20.

---

ist's own group, came into existence as a way of protecting the eighteenth- and nineteenth-century institution of slavery when voices began to speak out against it. Defenders of slavery even claimed the institution was divinely willed. For example, in 1772 the Reverend Thomas Thompson published a work entitled *The Trade in Negro Slaves on the African Coast in Accordance with Humane Principles, and with the Laws of Revealed Religion*, and in 1852 the Reverend Josiah Priest published *A Bible Defense of Slavery*.

When use of Africans as slaves began in the United States, there was little need to justify it with racist arguments. Ethnocentric values sufficed as rationales for the institution of slavery. Slave owners could claim that their slaves were better off with them than as free persons in their own allegedly inferior cultures. It was supposed that they had been given the chance to learn a superior way of life, higher moral values, the true religion, and a more enlightened way of thinking, in addition to enjoying a higher standard of living, better medical knowledge, and a longer life expectancy than if they had been permitted to remain in their former state. It could also be contended by the ethnocentrist that one could not simply discharge a slave after a few years of service because releasing a slave to his or her own devices in a complex society would be "inhumane." According to this argument, the complexity of the "superior way of life" would be more than a person taken into slavery as an

FIGURE 3.5

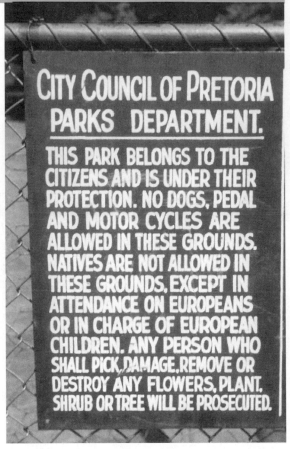

APARTHEID

In South Africa legal barriers prevented a non-White majority from achieving social equality with the dominant White minority until the system of legal inequality was dismantled between 1989 and 1994.

new way of life adequately to participate on an equal footing in a "civilized" society.

With this change from a simple ethnocentric argument to a concept of an inherent incapacity of some non-White "races," the old claim of inferiority took on an even stronger aura of inevitability. Although the old institution of slavery no longer may be used as the vehicle for the domination of one group by another, the concept of differences in the capacities of different "races" lives on as a rationale for the dominance of one culture over another or of one segment of a society over its other members.

Rationalizing Social Inequality. Looking at human differences in a racist way holds that the traits that lie within a person are responsible for his or her behavior. Such inner traits include willpower, determination, ego, inborn potentials, intellectual capacities, and the like. This tradition has made it difficult to convince many people of the value in viewing behavior as being affected by cultural factors that are outside the person. Racist thinking served as a way of rationalizing the inequalities from which the dominant members of society were benefiting. Unequal treatment of social minorities could be perceived as the result rather than the cause of the differences between the various segments of the society. Because it is an effective way of supporting the status quo, the racist approach to explaining human behavior became a common way of reacting to human behavior differences and remains unquestioned by large segments of society today, 2 centuries after it originated.

The pseudoscientific language of the racist lent an aura of propriety to the inequities that existed within society. Early European biological scientists and other scholars were given to expressing the ethnocentrism of the day in a veiled form of racist description when they examined the human species. Carolus Linnaeus's eighteenth-century classification of the animal world (1735/1956) (see chapter 1) was so carefully done that it remains the basic system used even today by biologists. Yet, his description of the human species is an excellent example of how an otherwise careful and methodical analysis can become biased by ethnocentric prejudices. In Linnaeus's classification the "European race" was described not only in such biological terms as "white, ruddy-complexioned, muscular, blue- eyed, and yellow-haired," but also in behavioral terms such as

adult could learn to cope with. Thus, it was the slaveholders' burden to take care of these "innocents" the rest of their lives. And, of course, it was only fair—so the argument ran—for them to work for their "benefactors" in return for these acts of "kindness."

Such ethnocentric rationales are not so useful when applied to the second generation of slaves. If a slave's children are exposed from infancy on to the way of life of the slave owner, they cannot be described as any less aware of how to live "properly" than any other member of the society unless one adds a new rationale to the old ethnocentric one. To continue to rationalize slavery into the second and third generations, the slave-owning group had to develop the view that the group they held in bondage was somewhat inferior in that its members were genetically unable to learn the

"governed by rites" (i.e., by customs), the "Asiatic race" as "governed by opinion," and the "African race" as "governed by whim." Thus, Linnaeus's classification of the human species is not simply biological, but racist as well.

Pseudoscientific racist characterizations have continued to be found in publications of otherwise well-educated Western writers since Linnaeus. The clothing of public prejudices in the pseudoscientific language of racism has lent the weight of scientific prestige to biases that have supported discriminatory hiring policies and social segregation by race. Such beliefs seem to be revived generation after generation despite the best efforts of the scientific community to educate the public about their groundlessness. The racist ideas in favor early in the twentieth century lost much of their appeal in the United States during World War II, when the nation was mobilized in opposition to the expansionism of Germany under the blatantly racist ideology of the Nazi government. Yet just a quarter of a century later, after the birth of the Civil Rights movement, which increased the involvement and influence of Black voters in U.S. politics, pseudoscientific racism was revived. During an inflationary period, when it was easy for many working-class U.S. Whites to perceive the political and economic gains of Blacks as displacing White workers, Arthur Jensen (1969), a prominent U.S. educational psychologist, presented a controversial argument that biological inheritance is more important than environmental experience as a determinant of human behavior. Jensen contended that human intelligence has a substantial genetic component and that race governs intellectual capacities as well as other biologically inherited traits. He concluded that the expense of government efforts to provide remedial education for disadvantaged racial minorities was unjustified.

Anthropologists and other social and behavioral scientists responded by pointing out the racist implications and the scientific fallacy in Jensen's biological interpretation of the educational and IQ test performance differences between Blacks and Whites. Although the scholarly community refused to endorse the racism behind such views, the same ideas have been reawakened again in 1994 during another period of widespread political dissatisfaction with government programs aimed at raising the economic status of minority citizens. The most widely publicized effort to assert a connection between race and intelligence has been the work of psychologist Richard J. Herrnstein and political scientist Charles Murray. Like Jensen before them, they too reveal a political agenda behind their claims about race and intelligence because their ideas oppose current government antipoverty programs. They argue that contemporary political theory is guided by "the assumption that egalitarianism is the proper ideal, however difficult to achieve in practice" (Herrnstein & Murray, 1994, p. 527) and that this ideal "underestimates the importance of the differences that separate human beings.... The systems of government that are necessary to carry out the egalitarian agenda ignore the forces . . . which lead inherently and inevitably to tyranny" (p. 532).

Thus, the concept that supposed racial differences may influence people's ability to live successfully in a society is not simply an idea of historical interest. On the contrary, it is still espoused strongly by influential people and continues to support the inequalities of opportunity that have long been linked to the minority statuses that some members of society are assigned at birth.

Legalized Racial Distinctions. Often the racism of the politically dominant segment of a society receives official sanction through legislation. Since the politically dominant segment of the United States has generally been composed of Whites, laws about supposed racial differences have often been prejudiced by ethnocentrism that was flattering to Whites. The "White way of life"—that is, northern-European-based, industrialized, capitalistic culture—was assumed to be the superior way of living and therefore the most deserving of protection by law. Since the ability to participate in a way of life was thought to be "in our blood," it followed that the most effective way of preserving the "White civilization" would be to maintain as much separation of the races as possible. Thus, at one time over three-quarters of the states in the United States had laws prohibiting interracial marriages. That is, those of non-White racial statuses were forbidden to marry Whites, although marriages between members of non-White races were not consistently forbidden. Nineteen states still had such laws in 1968 when they were struck down by the U.S. Supreme Court as unconstitutional.

A recent example of a society built on the principle of racial segregation was South Africa, in which legal barriers prevented a non-

White majority from achieving social equality with the dominant White minority until the system of legal inequality was dismantled between 1989 and 1994. South African law recognized the existence of four "races": Whites, Africans, Coloureds, and Asians. Whites were those of European ancestry, mostly descendants of Dutch Boers and English settlers. Africans were native African Blacks. Asians were people of Indian descent whose ancestors came to South Africa in the nineteenth century. Coloureds were peoples of mixed descent. The rigid separation of the "races" was maintained by laws forbidding interracial marriages, the legal requirement of segregated residence, separate systems of education, and unequal voting rights. Africans made up over 71 percent of the population but lacked voting rights that would give them a corresponding influence over the government. The government defined Africans as citizens of various "homelands," reserves that had been set aside for their occupation. South African cities, on the other hand, were set apart by law for White residents only. Non-White laborers who worked in the cities resided in townships located outside the cities. Although Whites represented only 16 percent of the population, they received by far the greatest social benefits. For instance, while the African unemployment rate would be as high as 30 percent, White unemployment was below 10 percent. This was partly because the White-dominated government was the single largest employer of Whites; 40 percent worked for the bureaucracy. Thus, through control of the government, South African Whites maintained a system of political and economic privilege based on race. The first all-race election was finally held in 1994, when Nelson Mandela was elected president.

Germany under Nazi rule is another example of the extremes to which a racist ideology can lead. After first enacting a series of discriminatory laws and creating ethnic ghettos much like those later seen in South Africa, Hitler's regime systematically exterminated about 6 million Jews and millions of other people of southern and eastern European ancestry in the name of purifying the Aryan "race."

Economic and Health Costs of Racism.
Different ways of treating socially designated races are not without their cost. Consider this example based on information from the *Statistical Abstract of the United States* (U.S. Bureau of the Census, 1994): by 1995, the White life expectancy was expected to reach 76.8 years, 4.4 years more than that of African Americans. The difference can be attributed to a higher infant mortality rate among African Americans, inadequate access to medical treatment and hospital facilities, and the debilitating effects of segregation, lower-class jobs, and high unemployment rates. Thus, currently, in every generation of 76.8 years, 4.4 years of life are denied to 33 million African Americans, an equivalent of 145.2 million years of human life wasted needlessly.

It is in effects such as the lowered life expectancies and living standards among those who hold minority racial statuses that racism makes itself felt in its most harmful way. To those who feel its effects, even more abhorrent than ethnocentrism or racial prejudice is the fact that these attitudes may become the basis of social policies, supported by the weight of law or custom, which then perpetuate arbitrary and harmful inequalities between peoples.

Race, Cultural Ability, and Intelligence

Discriminatory treatment of socially defined "racial" groups is generally rationalized by the idea that different races are biologically endowed with different abilities. Yet there is no scientific evidence that any racial group is superior or inferior to any other in its innate cultural abilities. Neither is there any evidence of racial differences in individuals' abilities to learn and adequately participate in any cultural system when they are given an equal opportunity to learn the necessary skills.

Anthropological researchers who have studied human lifeways around the world have reported again and again that biological differences seem to be no barrier to sharing a way of life. They report that common ways of living, customs, and values are sometimes spread over several regions occupied by peoples of different biological backgrounds. How people go about their lives is determined by their experiences in life and their opportunities to implement what they learn through that experience. A child of British parentage whisked away at birth and raised by adoptive Asian foster parents will learn and value the customs of his or her Asian peers and speak an Asiatic language with the same accent as his or her Asian playmates. Nothing in the biological makeup of such a child would impel him or her to value the British political system or to speak with a British accent.

Yet the argument continues to arise that some races are inherently less capable of full participation in a particular society. In the United States, the form of logical thought that is measured by intelligence tests is a highly valued social skill, and much has been made of the fact that some so-called "races" seem to score higher on these tests than others. When **IQ (intelligence quotient)** scores are grouped by race, there is a difference of approximately 15 points between the average of Blacks and Whites on most of the tests of intellectual skills commonly used in the United States. In this section, we will look closely at nonbiological factors that may influence these test scores, including differences in education, language, socioeconomic background, motivation, and cultural biases in the tests themselves.

The Instability of Test Scores. Contrary to popular belief, an individual's IQ score is far from a stable measure of an unchanging trait. Changes in such things as the quality of schools can influence performance on IQ tests. Evidence for this began to accumulate during World War I, when the U.S. Army carried out a massive intelligence testing program of personnel from many civilian backgrounds and it was found that Blacks in some northern states scored higher on IQ tests than did Whites in some southern states. Several studies have demonstrated that environmental factors are able to affect IQ scores by much more than 15 points in individual cases. In one study of 12-year-old Black New York City schoolchildren, most of whom had come from southern states, it was found that those who had lived in the city for more than 7 years scored 20 points higher on IQ tests than those who had lived there for 2 years or less (Downs & Bleibtreu, 1972). It has also been demonstrated that our IQ continues to rise while we attend school and begins to decline again when we leave the academic setting. The school environment keeps students actively engaged in the use of precisely those skills that are called on when they take an intelligence test. A group's average IQ score is therefore influenced by the quality and length of its education.

The fallacy that IQ test scores reflect an inborn level of mental ability is best illustrated by the rapid changes that have occurred in average IQ test scores throughout the world in the past half century. James R. Flynn (1987) examined IQ test results from 14 nations over periods of time and found a consistant pattern of massive changes in the average scores. For instance, in the Netherlands between 1952 and 1982, the average IQ score for 18-year-old males increased by 21 points. This change was so dramatic that by 1982, 1 in 4 (25.25 percent) Dutch 18-year-olds had IQs of 130 or higher, compared with 2.27 percent in 1952! Between 1951 and 1975, the average Japanese IQ score of children ages 6 through 15 changed from 100 to 120. For all 20 nations combined, the rate of increase averaged 0.588 IQ points per year on those tests that psychologists often describe as the most "culture free." Flynn concluded that such major changes from one generation to the next could not be explained if IQ tests truly measure intelligence that is defined as a biologically inherited ability.

Language Effects on IQ Scores. Dialect or language differences may be another important variable affecting the average intelligence test scores of different groups. Even when tests are not specifically about one's knowledge of spelling and grammar, taking intelligence tests requires the use of language skills simply to read any written instructions or understand the test questions. It is only to be expected that immigrants whose native languages differ from the one in which the tests are written would perform poorly on such tests, regardless of race.

Chandler and Platkos (1969) clearly demonstrated the language bias in intelligence testing in one California school district by reevaluating the intelligence test scores of its Spanish-speaking children with a Spanish-language intelligence test. Most of the children who had previously been classified as "educable mentally retarded" on the basis of the earlier English-language tests achieved a normal score, and some of them achieved above-average scores. In the United States, the centuries of social segregation of Blacks from Whites has led to the development of a distinctive Black English venacular (see chapter 12, p. 312) that differs greatly from the Standard American English that is rewarded with high grades in schools and invariably used in tests of intelli-

---

IQ (intelligence quotient) a standardized score on an intelligence test

THE ELLIS ISLAND PROJECT: A STUDY IN THE MISUSE OF INTELLIGENCE TESTS

In 1913, Henry H. Goddard (1913, 1917) a psychologist who believed that "social diseases" such as immorality, criminality, and insanity were biologically inherited, carried out a research project for the U.S. Public Health Service on Ellis Island (Chase, 1977). After testing the ability of European immigrants who were entering the United States through Ellis Island, he reported that there was an especially high incidence of "feeble mindedness" among southern and eastern European immigrants. For instance, he contended that 87 percent of the Russian immigrants, 83 percent of the Jews, 80 percent of the Hungarians, and 79 percent of the Italians were feebleminded! Since it was believed that these immigrants' inability to score well on these tests would be inherited by their descendants, admitting them to the United States was considered potentially dangerous. As a result, in following years there was a great increase in the deportation of immigrants who scored poorly on intelligence tests.

Incredible as it may seem today, these judgments—and the policy decisions that were affected by them—were made on the basis of English-language tests, administered orally through an interpreter. Goddard purposely had his assistants test people who appeared to them to be "feeble minded." The immigrants who were so tested were not even a random sample of all immigrants but were selected from those who arrived by third-class passage, most of whom had little or no formal education. The effects of such testing methods are aptly portrayed in the words of Stephen Jay Gould (1981):

> Consider a group of frightened men and women who speak no English and who have just endured an oceanic voyage in steerage. Most are poor and have never gone to school; many have never held a pencil or pen in their hand. They march off the boat; one of Goddard's intuitive women takes them aside shortly thereafter, sits them down, hands them a pencil, and asks them to reproduce on paper a figure shown to them a moment ago, but now withdrawn from their sight. Could their failure be a result of testing conditions, of weakness, fear, or confusion, rather than of innate stupidity? Goddard did not think so. Incredibly he attributed the low scores of these immigrants to a biological deficit in their intellectual capacities rather than to problems in the testing procedures.

gence. Since the Standard American English has much more in common with the dialects spoken by most Whites than it does with the Black English vernacular, there is a strong linguistic bias against Black students built into intelligence tests used today.

Social Background and IQ Scores.   Those who hold different racial statuses in the United States historically have had unequal opportunities to achieve highly valued social positions and high-income occupations. As a result, the races are socially and economically stratified in the United States. According to the U.S. Bureau of the Census, Whites possess a disproportionate share of the higher socioeconomic statuses and non-Whites are disproportionately relegated to low socioeconomic positions. Since intelligence tests are generally designed by well-educated, well-paid professionals, such as psychologists who have doctoral degrees from universities, those who do best on such tests are generally those who have the most in common with the authors of the tests. Thus, social groups who have been strongly segregated and otherwise denied participation in the mainstream of U.S. culture tend to receive lower scores on such tests.

If socioeconomic class differences are held constant when evaluating IQ scores—that is, if persons of similar social, educational, and economic backgrounds are compared—all socially designated races generally achieve equivalent IQ scores. For instance, Zena Blau (1981) carried out a study of 579 Black and White mothers and their fifth- and sixth-grade children in Chicago area communities. When she compared Black children with White children of similar social and economic rank, the difference in the average scores of the two groups was reduced by 40 percent. Religious background also influences the intellectual development of a child. For instance, Hofstadter (1963) has discussed the anti-intellectualism of the evangelical fundamentalist churches—their opposition to science, modern secular education, and the secularization of life that has resulted from industrialization and urbanization. Since a fundamentalist religious background is much more common among Blacks than among Whites in the United States, this influence on Black-White IQ differences is an important one. In Blau's sample (1981), for instance, two-thirds of the Black students had a fundamentalist religious background. When she compared Black and White students of similar socioeconomic and religious backgrounds, the difference between the average IQ scores of the two groups dropped to only four points. Among high-socioeconomic-status Protestants and nondenominational and nonreligious children, there were no IQ score differences between Black and White children.

Cultural Bias in IQ Tests.   IQ tests themselves are not flawless. For most of their history, intelligence tests have been popularly perceived as scientific measures of an individual's innate intellectual potential. Yet, from the beginning, they have contained questions that assumed a knowledge of societal experiences, practices, values, and ways of thinking that were characteristic of the higher socioeconomic classes. For instance, an intelligence test once used to measure the mental abilities of grammar school children included the question: "Pick the word that doesn't belong: (a) cello, (b) harp, (c) drum, (d) violin, (e) guitar." Some 85 percent of the high socioeconomic class children recognized that "drum," the only non-stringed instrument, was the item that "did not belong." However, 45 percent of the low socioeconomic class children, who were less likely to have ever seen a cello or a harp, failed to answer this question in the way the testers perceived as correct. The test authors had failed to recognize this potential class bias in the question.

Similarly, during the economic depression of the 1930s elementary school children of poor families in the United States were said to be less intelligent than children of families with higher incomes when in response to an intelligence test question "The color of milk is: (a) white, (b) black, (c) red, (d) blue," they selected the answer "blue." According to the psychologists who prepared the test, that was an incorrect response. Yet these children were simply describing reality as they had experienced it: from economic necessity, poor families during

the Depression were apt to be consumers of skim milk that does, in fact, have a slightly bluish cast. In the dialect of the day, skim milk was called "blue John." Thus their answer was not incorrect in their own experience. A few years ago, a colleague working in the African state of Malawi found the following item on a test that was being used to assess the intelligence of Malawi students: "If ten crows are sitting on a fence and you shoot one, how many will be left?" The response "nine," based on the arithmetic operation of subtracting one from ten, was scored as the correct response and was considered evidence of a student's intellectual skill. It was finally noticed, however, that many of the children who were tested failed to answer this seemingly simple arithmetic problem correctly and that they tended to respond with the same "incorrect" response of "zero." The reason for their "error" was their rural background. It gave them a more realistic appraisal of the behavior of birds—which fly away when shot at—than was held by the author of the test, who had selected the answer on the basis of a purely academic frame of reference. One could not ask for a better example of the effects of different life experiences on the ways of interpreting a test question.

Intelligence Labeling as Self-Fulfilling Prophecy.   Scores achieved on tests of intellectual skills are often used as criteria for making judgments concerning schoolchildren that may influence their future academic careers. They may, for instance, lead to assigning students either to accelerated classes or those for "slow learners." Once assigned, the original categorization of students as "superior" or "slow" may continue through the years. Later teachers may be influenced in their own expectations about students on the basis of the original labeling.

Rist (1970) described a 3-year observational study of a class of ghetto children that illustrated how the school system may unwittingly reinforce the class differences among their families. The kindergarten teacher of these children made judgments about their intellectual skills and assigned them to different groups within the class. This categorization was reflected in the seating arrangement of the students. Those placed at the first table were those whom she described as "fast learners," while those at the last two tables "had no idea of what was going on in the classroom." Rist contends that the criterion for assigning the children to these groups was actually the degree to which the children conformed to several middle-class U.S. characteristics. That is, the real differences between the children consisted of such things as the degree to which they used Standard American English, their neatness and cleanliness, and whether their parents were educated, employed, and living together.

Rist further noted that this initial placement of the students—based on the kindergarten teacher's impressions during the first 8 days of class—persisted into later grades. The students' achievement was influenced by the way the teachers acted toward them, which in turn corresponded to the expectations for their behavior that were implicit in the original classifications. The initial perception of each succeeding teacher was influenced by preconceptions based on knowledge of how the students were categorized and how they performed in the previous grade. This example illustrates the possibility that socially biased judgments about supposed differences of innate ability may be a cause of later differences in the performance of students, differences that are used to justify the "accuracy" and even propriety of the original practice of classifying the students.

It is not difficult to imagine how labels such as "slow learner" or "superior student" may hinder or aid their bearers through the rest of their school careers. Students who are labeled "above average" are apt to receive endless encouragements to "live up to their potential" and enroll in intellectually valued subjects that lead to a college career and highly valued occupations. Students labeled "below average," on the other hand, are more likely to be encouraged to enroll in subjects that are less intellectually stimulating; when they fall behind in their work, they are less likely to be pushed because it is believed they will grow "frustrated" if more is demanded of them than they are capable of doing. These students are likely to end their scholastic careers earlier and with less training. Thus, intelligence tests on which labeling and expectations are based may serve as vehicles for inhibiting social and economic mobility.

The Impossibility of Culture-Free Testing. Recently, psychologists and educators have attempted to salvage the use of intelligence tests by redesigning them to minimize their most obvious cultural biases. They have hoped to thereby create so-called **"culture-free" intelligence tests**. However, even if the specific items in a test do reflect knowledge available to one segment of society, their life experiences may lead to differences in the ways they respond to the tasks. Cultural learning affects the way we perform any task. If one style of response is regarded as more appropriate than others, even a "culture-free" test will result in higher scores for members of the society who respond in that style, just as older so-called "intelligence" tests have always done. It is impossible to create a measure of pure, environmentally uninfluenced, biological intelligence, since all human beings are raised in a social environment that will influence their behavior as inevitably as their genetically inherited biological qualities will. Culture, in other words, is not just in the tests; it is in the test-takers as well.

What happens if we remove the influences of U.S. culture on the performance of Black and White children? Klaus Eyferth (1959) carried out an interesting study of children born in Germany after World War II to German mothers and fathers from the occupation troops. Since the children were reared in Germany, the differences between Black and White U.S. subcultures were not present. When Eyferth compared the IQ scores of biracial children whose fathers were Black with those whose fathers were White, he found that the two groups were virtually identical in their IQ test performance. This study strongly indicates that U.S. Black-White IQ differences are not racial in origin, but are the results of being reared in different U.S. subcultures.

"culture-free" intelligence tests tests that are not biased in favor of the values and life experiences (the "culture") of any one segment of a society

CHAPTER SUMMARY

1. None of us operates totally independently as isolated, self-sufficient individuals. Each of us lives within a society, and all societies organize their members into groups of various sorts and divide labor among their members.

2. Our social life is also characterized by relationships with many people, each of which involves a status.

3. Each status carries various role expectations defined by our society.

4. Statuses are ranked in power and honor by our society, with some—master statuses—considered so significant that their high or low rank outweighs that of all other statuses. Low-ranked master statuses are the defining feature of minority groups.

5. Statuses are sometimes assigned on the basis of observable biological facts, such as age, sex, and skin color.

6. Racism confuses the social roles played by minority groups with biology as a cause of behavior.

7. Racist thinking prevents minority group members from having equal access to economic and political power.

8. The role expectations that accompany minority group status have little or no relationship to our innate characteristics; they are cultural phenomena, socially learned and enforced.

9. Intelligence test scores are influenced by culture.

ANNOTATED READINGS

Dahlberg, F. (Ed.). (1981). *Woman the gatherer*. New Haven, CT: Yale University Press. Six articles on women's roles from cross-cultural and evolutionary perspectives.

Dalby, L. (1985). *Geisha*. New York: Vintage Books. A beautifully written and copiously illustrated description of geisha life.

Friedl, E. (1975). *Women and men*. New York: Holt, Rinehart & Winston. A brief but information-packed overview of gender roles and their relationships to variations in culture. Must reading for the anthropology major.

Gould, S. J. (1981). *The mismeasure of man*. New York: W. W. Norton. A study of the history of intelligence testing that concludes that the idea of racial differences in intelligence was invalid.

Martin, M. K., & Voorhies, B. (1975). *Female of the species*. New York: Columbia University Press.

An examination of the status of women in societies of varying social complexity.

Moore, H. (1988). *Feminism and anthropology*. Ithaca, NY: Cornell University Press. A good general overview of feminist perspectives on gender.

Moran, M. (1990). *Civilized women: Gender and prestige in southeastern Liberia*. Ithaca, NY: Cornell University Press. A recent ethnography on the cultural construction of gender in West Africa.

Rosaldo, M. Z., & Lamphere, L. (Eds.). (1974). *Woman, culture, and society*. Stanford, CA: Stanford University Press. Discussions by female anthropologists of their observations of the status of women in a variety of societies.

Shipman, P. (1994). *The evolution of racism: Human differences and the use and abuse of science*. New York: Simon & Schuster. Examines the ways scientific research about race has been used and misused.

CHAPTER FOUR

The Life Cycle

Analyze the social and psychological functions of rites of passage.

Describe the more common customs in the world concerning pregnancy and childbirth.

Explain the three forms of learning that play a role in socialization.

Describe the more common customs in the world concerning sexuality and puberty.

Describe the more common customs in the world concerning marriage and divorce.

Describe the more common customs in the world concerning old age and death.

◀ *Figure 4.1* *Ritual* *This Shinnecock man and Black-foot woman, who are pictured at the annual Father Sky Native American Festival in Inwood Park, New York City, are wearing traditional Native American regalia. Native American powwows sometimes involve potlatches that mark an individual's coming of age.*

THE LIFE CYCLE
Rites of Passage
Pregnancy, Childbirth, and Naming
Enculturation, Childhood, and
    Adolescence
Courtship and Marriage
Parenthood
Divorce
Old Age
Death

Many of the social statuses that we acquire follow one another in a definite sequence from birth to death, known as the life cycle, and are commonly recognized in cultures throughout the world. It is particularly common to publicly celebrate status changes: to proclaim the addition of a new member of the human community shortly after birth, to announce the passage from childhood to adulthood around the time of puberty, to move from an unmarried to married status, and to adjust to the loss of a member of the community at death.

Neonate. Infant. Rug rat. Toddler. Child. Youngster. Adolescent. Young adult. Employee. Husband. Wife. Parent. Retiree. Wherever you find yourself in society, your identity goes through culturally defined status changes throughout your life. Their predictability can facilitate your movement through various positions within your community's social organization and can foster psychological security when your life undergoes major changes.

THE LIFE CYCLE

Arnold Van Gennep (1908/1960) has pointed out that as we move from one status to another within the **life cycle**, the life events and status changes that are typically experienced by individuals are commonly proclaimed to other members of society by formal rituals known as life crisis rites or rites of passage.

Rites of Passage

Ceremonies such as christenings, puberty rituals, marriages, and funerals, which we hold whenever a member of society undergoes an important change in status within the life cycle of the group, are considered **rites of passage**. They symbolically dramatize how important status changes are in the eyes of society and help to maintain stability and order while society adjusts to culturally significant changes in people's lives. The acquisition of a new status calls for the successful adoption of a new set of roles by the person who is moving into the new phase of life. The formal dramatization of these changes in a ritual of status change may

be psychologically beneficial to those who are beginning roles that they have not practiced before, and to other members of society who must also adopt new ways of relating to them. Four public symbolic rituals are commonly celebrated throughout the world: naming ceremonies, which confer human status on the new member of society and proclaim the parenthood of its caretakers; puberty celebrations, which confer adult status; marriages, which legitimize new sexual, economic, and childrearing obligations; and funerals, which proclaim the loss of human status by the deceased and restructure the ongoing social order.

Pregnancy, Childbirth, and Naming

The first life-cycle change is associated with birth. Yet even before that obviously major event, our parents are experiencing the status changes of pregnancy. The biological facts of conception, pregnancy, and the birth process are interpreted differently among various cultures. After birth, each society also has its specific ways of raising us.

Pregnancy. People in most societies believe that pregnancy is a result of sexual intercourse, but conception itself is explained in a variety of ways. Often the child is thought of as developing from semen, menstrual blood, or both. In many societies, both the mother and the father are believed to contribute during intercourse to the conception and sometimes to the growth of the child. Sometimes, however, the role of one parent is more important in explaining the origin of the child. For instance, in ancient Greece, the father was thought to plant the child in the mother as one might plant a seed in the field. The mother merely carried the father's child as it grew. Such a metaphor was not uncommon in horticultural societies in which men were dominant. In other societies, where men and women had equal status, the symbols of procreation might emphasize the role of both father and mother in conception. In a few cases, women were thought to become pregnant without the aid of a husband.

---

life cycle the status changes from birth to death that are typical of a particular society

rite of passage (life crisis rite) a ritual that formalizes a major change in social status

On the surface, some societies appear to be unaware of the link between intercourse and conception. Walter E. Roth claimed that the indigenous people of the Tully River of North Queensland, Australia, were ignorant of the role of sex in pregnancy:

> A woman begets children because (a) she has been sitting over the fire on which she has roasted a particular species of black bream, which must have been given to her by the prospective father, (b) she has purposely gone a-hunting and caught a certain kind of bullfrog, (c) some men may have told her to be in an interesting condition, or (d) she may dream of having the child put inside her. (quoted in Leach, 1969, p. 87)

On the other hand, Tully River people were aware that copulation causes pregnancy in animals. It is unlikely, therefore, that they were unaware that sex caused pregnancy in humans in a purely physiological sense. However, in any culture, people's ideas about humans are never straightforward descriptions of observed fact, uninfluenced by their values. Their denial of the role of sex in human pregnancy was not simple ignorance; it was a symbolic affirmation of their ideologically important values. According to Leach (1969), the pregnancy beliefs of the people of Tully River are ways of affirming that "the relationship between the woman's child and the clansmen of the woman's husband stems from public recognition of the bonds of marriage, rather than from the facts of cohabitation" (p. 87). The people of Tully River believe that pregnancy is "caused" by a woman's catching the right kind of bullfrog in the same sense that Christians believe that a wife's fertility is "caused" by the rice thrown at her at the end of her wedding ceremony.

Pregnancy Rituals.   Pregnancy is a time of potential anxiety, since it is fraught with possible negative outcomes such as miscarriage, physical defects in the baby, or death in childbirth for either the infant or the mother. Such anxieties cause people to turn to symbolic **pregnancy rituals** to protect the child and pregnant woman and to aid in a successful birth. These rituals are frequently expected to apply to the husband as well as the pregnant woman. They generally take the form of taboos against doing things that have some similarity to the feared outcomes. For instance, the Great Basin

FIGURE 4.2

RITES OF PASSAGE

Rites of passage symbolically dramatize significant changes in people's lives. They not only help the person adjust to his or her new role, but also help other members of the family or of society understand new ways of relating to the person. In Roman Catholic countries such as Mexico, an important ritual in a person's spiritual growth is the taking of the sacrament of Holy Communion. These girls prepare for the ritual with candles, prayer books, and rosary beads.

Shoshone forbid a pregnant woman or her husband to eat either the mud hen, which they call the "fool's hen," or the trout, which flops about when one catches it, since the former might result in the child's being stupid and the latter in its becoming entangled in the umbilical cord during labor.

Among the Aztecs of Mexico, pregnant women were forbidden to look at an eclipse of the sun, which they called *Tonaltiu qualo*, meaning "The sun is being eaten," since to see this phenomenon might result in a lip defect, such

---

pregnancy rituals religious rules such as taboos designed to protect the unborn child and the mother during pregnancy and childbirth or admonitions to engage in acts believed to be a positive influence on the developing child

CONCEPTION WITHOUT SEX IN THE TROBRIAND ISLANDERS' IDEOLOGY

Very few societies view conception as being caused spiritually rather than sexually. Most notable, though, for such beliefs are the native peoples of Australia and the native inhabitants of the Trobriand Islands. Bronislaw Malinowski (1929), who contributed to the development of anthropological research and analytic methods, lived for years among the Trobriand Islanders during World War I. He reported their beliefs about conception in a book ethnocentrically entitled *The Sexual Life of Savages*, from which the following account is derived.

The Trobrianders' ideas about conception are related to their beliefs in reincarnation. The Trobrianders believe that after death the spirit *(baloma)* of a person goes to Tuma, the Island of the Dead, where it enjoys a happier life than that of mortals. Periodically it rejuvenates itself until it decides to return to the world of mortals. Then it transforms itself into a small spirit-infant. The spirit-infant is brought to a human mother-to-be by an older controlling spirit, who usually appears to the woman in a dream to inform her that she is about to become pregnant. This controlling spirit is most often either a maternal relative of the woman or her father.

After revealing its intentions, the controlling spirit lays the child in the woman's head, causing blood from her body to rush there before descending to the womb with the spirit-child. Although intercourse may open the way for the child, it is not thought to cause conception. Actual entry of the child into the mother's womb is ap-

parently thought to be by way of the vagina, since the Trobrianders insist that a virgin is unable to conceive because of her "tightness." After conception the woman's menstrual flow is said to cease because the mother's blood nourishes the body of the infant and helps to build it.

According to Malinowski, the combination of mystical and physiological features of these pregnancy beliefs provided a complete theory of how human life originates. In addition, Malinowski noted that Trobriand social, economic, and political life was carried out within a matrilineal society in which the members of social groups shared maternal ancestors. Thus, in day-to-day social life maternity was a much more influential fact than paternity. Malinowski concluded that the Trobriand ideology of reproduction "also gives a good theoretical foundation for matriliny; for the whole process of introducing new life into a community lies between the spirit world and the female organism. There is no room for any sort of physical paternity" (p. 179).

Malinowski contrasted the Trobrianders' mother-oriented system of thought with the more male-oriented ideology of the missionaries who sought to convert them to a Christian belief system:

We must realize that in the cardinal dogma of God the Father and God the Son, the sacrifice of the only Son and the filial love of man to his Maker would completely misfire in a matrilineal society, where the relation between a father and son is decreed by tribal laws to be that of two strangers, where all personal unity

as harelip, in the unborn child. As a prophylactic against the effects of accidentally seeing an eclipse, the Aztec mother-to-be might wear an obsidian blade over her breast to protect the child.

On the other hand, some pregnancy rules require behaviors that are similar to the characteristics of a good birth. The Shoshone father was encouraged to hunt the otter, since this animal is known for its enjoyment of sliding down slippery riverbanks, much as the child was hoped to pass easily through the birth canal. Like many other cultures, U.S. culture includes several traditional pregnancy taboos and admonitions. One of these is the idea of **marking**. According to this belief, children may be influenced by things that are done by or that hap-

pen to their mothers during pregnancy. For instance, birthmarks might be attributed to the mother's having eaten too many strawberries, raspberries, or other red foods. The most common expression of the concept of marking in the United States today is in admonitions to do things believed to influence the child in positive ways. For instance, a pregnant woman may hear that by spending time listening to classical music, reading good literature, and immersing herself in art she may predispose her child to similar pursuits. The concept of the

---

marking the idea that the behaviors of a woman during pregnancy may influence the physical or psychological characteristics of the unborn child

between them is denied, and where all family obligations are associated with mother-line. We cannot, then, wonder that paternity must be among the principal truths to be inculcated by proselytizing Christians. Otherwise the dogma of the Trinity would have to be translated into matrilineal terms, and we should have to speak of a God-kadala *(mother's brother), a* God-sister's-son, *and a divine* baloma *spirit. But apart from any doctrinal difficulty, the missionaries are earnestly engaged in propagating sexual morality as we conceive it, in which endeavor the idea of the sexual act as having serious consequences to family life is indispensable.* (pp. 186–187)

The Trobrianders vehemently opposed the idea of physiological paternity, a belief that is well-suited to a society with a strong patriarchal ideology but not to their own. They characterized the missionaries' belief that sex is the cause of conception as an absurdity and the missionaries, therefore, as liars. For example, Malinowski quotes one of his informants as saying, "Not at all, the missionaries are mistaken, unmarried girls continually have intercourse, in fact they overflow with seminal fluid, and yet have no children" (p. 188). By native logic, if sex were the cause of pregnancy, the unmarried girls would become pregnant more often than older married women, since they engage in sexual intercourse much more often. Yet it is the older married women who have the most children. Another informant argued, "Copulation alone cannot produce a child. Night after night, for years, girls copulate. No child

comes" (p. 189), contending thereby that the empirical evidence did not support the view of a relationship between sex and pregnancy. Malinowski also tells us that, "one of my informants told me that after over a year's absence he returned to find a newly born child at home. He volunteered this statement as an illustration and final proof of the truth that sexual intercourse had nothing to do with conception. And it must be remembered that no native would ever discuss any subject in which the slightest suspicion of his wife's fidelity would be involved" (p. 193).

According to Annette Weiner (1988), the contemporary Trobrianders, who no longer disagree with Western ideas about procreation, continue to use the concept of "virgin birth" as a way of avoiding public shame over infidelity. Weiner, relying on myths and old people's beliefs, argues that the Trobriand ideas about spirits causing pregnancy may have served this purpose even in Malinowski's day. She believes that the implicit understanding that both sexes are part of the process of reproduction existed in ideas that, although spirits cause the pregnancy, sexual intercourse is necessary for the development of the fetus *after* conception: "A man develops and maintains the growth of the fetus through repeated sexual intercourse with his wife" (p. 123).

The Trobriand Islanders' denial that sex causes conception symbolically supported their emphasis on inheritance of both property and familial authority through the mother's line. The concept of a paternal role in the creation of a child would challenge the kinship system around which their political and economic life was built.

marking of an unborn child by its mother parallels the idea that, after birth, mothers have the principal psychological influence on the development of the child and therefore usually receive greater credit or blame for what the child becomes than other individuals.

Abortion. Abortion has been practiced throughout history and in most societies that have been studied by anthropologists. For instance, George Devereux (1967) examined a sample of 350 nonindustrialized societies and reported that intentionally induced abortions were "an absolutely universal phenomenon" (p. 98). More recently, abortion has been studied by anthropologist Suzanne Frayser (1985). Using a sample of 47 societies for which data

on attitudes about abortion was available, she found that most societies publicly disapprove of abortion primarily because they are most commonly performed when the circumstances of pregnancy are socially unacceptable, for instance, when the pregnant woman is unmarried.

Devereux (1955) examined the methods of abortion in 400 societies that lacked modern medical techniques. He listed 16 techniques that women commonly use to terminate their pregnancies. They include doing strenuous activity, squeezing or jolting the belly, inserting foreign objects or noxious fluids into the uterus, or taking drugs to harm the fetus or cause it to be expelled. These traditional techniques are generally ineffective and are as likely to harm or kill the woman as the fetus.

In contrast, medical techniques developed in this century and now available in most parts of the world are, when carried out during the first trimester, safer than pregnancy itself.

About 1.6 million legal abortions occur in the United States each year. Between 90.5 and 93 percent of these are performed during the first 12 weeks of pregnancy. A total of 99.2 percent are performed before 20 weeks, and only about 100 in the whole country (less than 0.01 percent) are performed after 24 weeks. It is estimated that about 46 percent of U.S. women will have an abortion at some time in their lives. Although the frequency of abortions has not increased significantly since *Roe v. Wade* and is no greater than it was in the 1860s, abortion has become a major political issue in the United States (Doerr & Prescott, 1990, p. xv).

Two sociologists, Steven Nock and Paul Kingston (1990), argue that U.S. abortion politics is really a conflict about women's roles. They assert that antiabortion activists "believe men and women to be intrinsically different in their social roles. Women, such individuals believe, are destined to be mothers first and foremost. Because motherhood is women's natural role, anything that makes it less central or less important makes women less important" (p. 209). In their view, "The abortion debate pits traditional women and men against nontraditional men and women. In a very real sense, the argument is over how we view women: Are they equal to men?" (p. 210).

The view that abortion politics is motivated by gender-related values is supported by the research of James Prescott (1990), a cross-cultural psychologist. He compared the voting records of legislators in Canada and the United States and found that those with antiabortion records were more likely than those with a prochoice voting record to support capital punishment, the Vietnam War, and military aid to the Nicaraguan Contras. They were also more likely to oppose handgun controls, the use of medical heroin for dying patients, and to support the illegality of fornication and adultery and the punishment of prostitution. He concluded that opposition to abortion is related to male dominance, opposition to equality for women, and moral fundamentalism.

Prescott found a similar pattern of social values concerning abortion and gender roles in a cross-cultural survey. He compared cultures that denied a woman the right to abortion with those that permitted abortions and found that antiabortion cultures were also most likely to have practiced slavery, the torture, killing, and mutilation of prisoners of war, the exploitation of women and children, the punishment and/or rejection of premarital and extramarital sex, and the definition of family membership in terms of fatherhood alone (p. 109). In other words, nonindustrialized abortion-intolerant societies have tended to be warlike ones in which the patriarchal domination of women and other minorities was the basis of social life.

It has also been suggested that cultural values concerning abortion are related to the perceived need for population growth. When it is not considered important, women have great latitude in aborting a pregnancy; when it is considered important to increase family size, women often face strict rules against abortion. For instance, Stephen Mosher (1983) has documented the strong governmental role in limiting family size in the People's Republic of China that has led in some instances to coercive pressure on women who have previously had children to undergo abortions, sometimes as late as in the seventh month of pregnancy. In other countries in which the government has supported a population growth policy, women's access to contraceptive information and abortion has been denied by governmental action. Romania under Nicolae Ceauşescu—who was overthrown in December of 1989—is a prime illustration of such a country. Karen Breslau (1990), a *Newsweek* correspondent in Bucharest, reported that in 1966, Ceauşescu declared, "The fetus is the property of the entire society" and "Anyone who avoids having children is a deserter who abandons the laws of national continuity" (p. 35). Under his prochildbirth policy, Romania's birthrate nearly doubled. The law forbade sexuality education and abortion. Women were required to be given pregnancy tests every three months. Pregnant women who miscarried were called in for questioning on suspicion of having had an illegal abortion, and those who did not have children were charged a "celibacy tax" that could be as much as 10 percent of their monthly salaries.

Birth.   In most societies, when the woman enters labor she is attended by one or more women who have already experienced childbirth themselves and who help her through the process. Most commonly, birth occurs with the woman assuming a kneeling or squatting position, a posture that facilitates the birth process more than the reclining position traditionally used in many Western hospitals. These upright birthing positions have a beneficial effect on the angle of the birth canal and take advantage of gravity in aiding the passage of the infant.

It is only in recent years that Western medicine has begun to abandon its customary treatment of women in labor as if they were ill patients undergoing a surgical procedure. With pressure from women's groups, the role of the woman in her labor has been redefined as an active partner with others involved in the birthing process, and changes have begun to be made in the woman's posture during childbirth that facilitate her role and not simply that of the medical personnel.

For most Americans and Canadians the preferred place for the delivery still is a hospital in the presence of the physician and one or more nurses. North Americans generally regard it as desirable for a woman to seek the services of a physician starting about two months into her pregnancy. This doctor will evaluate the health of the woman, check the progress of the pregnancy, and deliver the baby if it is carried to term. However, this ideal is not always possible for those with low incomes, due to the high costs of medical treatment and hospital care.

There is an increasing return to the less expensive system of delivery at home with the aid of a nurse-midwife who, at the same time, offers more personalized care than does the hospital system. Many hospitals, in turn, are beginning to shift from the use of specialized labor and delivery rooms to the use of birthing rooms, which can save as much as half the hospital costs for a normal delivery.

Couvade. A few societies, most commonly gardening societies that occupy tropical forest environments, have a custom known as the **couvade**, in which the husband acts as if he is going through labor while his wife is giving birth to their child. This ritual is often performed with the intent of providing religious protection for the newborn child by misdirecting any potentially harmful supernatural powers away from the actual birth that is in process elsewhere.

Why would such a practice be more likely in tropical forests? The groundwork for answering this question was laid by John Whiting (1964), who showed that in environments with protein scarcity—many tropical forest crops do

FIGURE 4.3

BIRTH

The most common method of giving birth in non-Western societies is for the woman to assume a squatting position. This !Kung San woman is preparing to give birth, with an older woman in attendance who will assist her.

not have all the amino acids necessary for protein building—children tend to be nursed for long periods. This protects the child from suffering from protein deficiency in its early developmental period. Prolonged nursing is facilitated by rules against the nursing mother's having sex for several years after the birth of a child, since another pregnancy would require weaning the first child. The sex taboo, however, does not prevent the husband from having other wives and continuing his sex life during this period in their households. One result of this arrangement is that a male child spends his early years with no male role model in residence in his mother's household.

If male solidarity is extremely important—for instance, where warfare is common—male puberty rites, where the boy proves his manhood by enduring pain, may be one way of helping him finally break his sexual identifica-

(Continued on p. 91)

_____

couvade a custom in which the husband acts as if he gives birth to his child

NISA'S FIRST LABOR

Marjorie Shostak (1983) has written a fascinating biography of a !Kung San woman, Nisa. The !Kung are the northern linguistic subdivision of the San people, all of whom were foragers in traditional times. The San as a whole occupied lands in Botswana, Namibia, Angola, and South Africa. The !Kung San live mostly in Botswana and Namibia. Nisa's home was in northwest Botswana. !Kung San women faced childbirth without medical facilities or the help of traditional midwives, although they were often helped to give birth by their own or their husband's female relatives. About one woman died for every 500 births, and infant and child death was common. Nisa's account of her first birth is dramatic:

> I lay there and felt the pains as they came, over and over again. Then I felt something wet, the beginning of the childbirth. I thought, "Eh hey, maybe it is the child." I got up, took a blanket and covered Tashay with it; he was still sleeping. Then I took another blanket and my smaller duiker skin covering and I left. Was I not the only one? The only other woman was Tashay's grandmother, and she was asleep in her hut. So, just as I was, I left.

> I walked a short distance from the village and sat down beside a tree. I sat there and waited; she wasn't ready to be born. I lay down, but she still didn't come out. I sat up again. I leaned against the tree and began to feel the labor. The pains came over and over, again and again. It felt as though the baby was trying to jump right out! Then the pains stopped. I said, "Why doesn't it hurry up and come out? Why doesn't it come out so I can rest? What does it want inside me that it just stays in there? Won't God help me to have it come out quickly?"

> As I said that, the baby started to be born. I thought, "I won't cry out. I'll just sit here. Look, it's already being born and I'll be fine." But it really hurt! I cried out, but only to myself. I thought, "Oh, I almost cried out in my in-laws' village." Then I thought, "Has my child already been born?" Because I wasn't really sure; I thought I might only have been sick. That's why I hadn't told anyone when I left the village.

> After she was born, I sat there; I didn't know what to do. I had no sense. She lay there moving her arms about, trying to suck on her fingers. She started to cry. I just sat there, looking at her. I thought, "Is this my child? Who gave birth to this child?" Then I thought, "A big thing like that? How could it possibly have come out from my genitals?" I sat there and looked at her, looked and looked and looked.

> The cold started to grab me. I covered her with my duiker skin that had been covering my stomach and pulled the larger kaross over myself. Soon, the afterbirth came down and I buried it. I started to shiver. I just sat there, trembling with the cold. I still hadn't tied the umbilical cord. I looked at her and thought, "She's no longer crying. I'll leave her here and go to the village to bring back some coals for a fire." (pp. 193–194)

Today, 62,000 San people live in the Kalahari desert of Botswana, Namibia, and Angola. None survive in South Africa. Between 2,000 and 5,000 of the San continue to forage, but their food resources are becoming scarcer as agriculture and cattle ranching expands in the areas that surround them. Most of the San have been forced to adopt work as day laborers on neighboring ranches and farms or have migrated to nearby towns in search of work. Their unemployment rate in the towns is high and the San standard of living is probably lower than it was traditionally. Modern medical facilities at the time of childbirth are as inaccessible today as they were when Nisa gave birth to her first child.

!KUNG SAN

The !Kung (pronounced with a click of the tongue first) are a division of the San people. Today they live in the Kalahari desert of Botswana, Namibia, and Angola, but since their food resources are becoming scarce, they have been forced to work on neighboring farms rather than forage. Medical facilities are as inaccessible today as they were when Nisa gave birth.

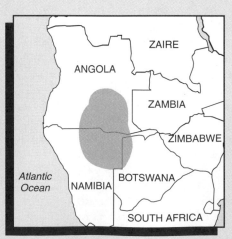

ROMAN CATHOLIC BAPTISM

The rite of baptism is normally practiced shortly after the birth of a child as the first religious rite of passage for Roman Catholics. As is common throughout the world for rites of passage for infants, the baptismal rite includes naming the child and introducing it to others present as a new member of the community.

The rite of baptism ideally takes place on Sunday in the presence of other church members, relatives, and friends. It begins with the godfather and godmother presenting the child for baptism. The priest meets them at the door of the church. The priest asks them "What name do you give your child?" to which they respond with the name of the child. Then, using the name to identify the child, the priest asks the godparents what they are requesting in behalf of the child, to which they respond, "Baptism." Thereupon the priest charges the godparents with their responsibility for the spiritual training of the child. After they agree to accept this duty, the priest welcomes them in behalf of the church and traces the sign of the cross on the forehead of the child.

The welcoming of the child to the church is followed by scriptural readings regarding the rite of baptism and a short sermon on the significance of baptism. This may be followed by a brief period while all present are invited to pray silently. The congregation is then led in a vocal prayer regarding the death and resurrection of Jesus, who is asked to receive the child into the church and to grant that the godparents will be examples of faith to the child. The priest then prays for God to free the child from sin and to send the Holy Spirit to the child, after which the child is anointed with consecrated oil.

After being anointed, the child is taken to the baptismal font, where the priest reads a blessing reminding all those present that water is a rich symbol of the grace of God and of religious cleansing. The priest baptizes the child by immersing it in the water or by pouring water on it three times while saying, "I baptize you in the name of the Father, and of the Son, and of the Holy Spirit."

Following the baptism, the congregation sings a short hymn, the child is anointed again, and clothed with a white garment provided by the family. The priest lights a candle, a symbol of the light of Christ, and reminds the godparents of their duty to help the child walk in the light and to keep the flame of faith alive in the child's heart.

---

tion with his mother and prove clearly that he has entered the masculine domain. Munroe, Munroe, and Whiting (1973) have argued that the couvade is a possible alternative to male puberty rites. Because the psychological identification with the female role is never fully lost, the couvade occurs as a symbolic acting out of the female role at the time of childbirth. Be this as it may, the link between the couvade and protein-deficient environments is clear. For instance, the couvade is not found in certain tropical forests such as those of Southeast Asia where pigs and chickens have been domesticated or where vegetable foods are grown that provide all the amino acids necessary for protein synthesis by the human body.

Although many do not find Munroe, Munroe, and Whiting's rather Freudian interpretation of the significance of the couvade completely satisfactory, the custom does make sense in a rather pragmatic way: since the father will be absent from the home in which his child will be raised, the couvade publicly affirms his paternity.

Naming. The next important symbolic act in the life of a newborn baby is its **naming ceremony**. In this ritual the baby is officially received into the community of human beings and symbolically given human status by acquiring a human name. In the birth or naming ritual, the infant is commonly brought into contact with those aspects of life that are of central concern to the members of the society into which it is being received. Thus, among the Samoans of Polynesia and the Yahgan of southernmost Argentina (Cooper, 1946; Murdock, 1934; Service, 1978), both of whom relied heavily on sea products as their main source of food, the newborn child was bathed in the sea shortly after birth. The Mbuti Pygmy of the Ituri Forest of Africa (Gibbs, 1965) grow no food but obtain all their basic needs from the uncultivated resources of the forest; they therefore speak of the forest as their parent and their

---

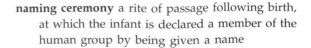

naming ceremony a rite of passage following birth, at which the infant is declared a member of the human group by being given a name

provider. They initiate their children into the human group in a ritual in which vines from the forest are tied around the children's ankles, wrists, and waists, thereby bringing them into contact with their future livelihood.

In the United States parents begin selecting a name for the child months before the birth. Most families have no formal customary rules for selecting the name, such as a requirement to name the child after a particular relative, but many choose to do so. Since the selection of the name is largely an aesthetic issue, the popularity of different names rises and falls over the generations much as do fashions in dress. Names are officially given without ceremony immediately after birth when the attending physician fills out a birth certificate to be filed in the county records. A religious naming ceremony may be conducted for the child a few weeks later.

Enculturation, Childhood, and Adolescence

From birth through adolescence, we humans are raised in some kind of family setting according to the dictates of our culture. Our upbringing usually includes some restrictions on free expression of our sexuality, including taboos against intercourse with certain family members. In many societies, our attainment of sexual maturity is marked by special puberty rites honoring our passage into adulthood.

Enculturation Process.   The process by which children learn the culture that guides the life of members of their society is known as **enculturation** or **socialization**. Even before they begin to communicate in the language of their society, those around them have begun to mold their behavior so that it will conform to the rules for living that make up their culture.

In the United States people socialize their children differently depending on the sex of the child. Symbolically, the color pink is associated with girls and blue with boys as appropriate for clothing and decorations of the baby's crib. It has been noted that mothers speak more to girl babies than to boys, and fathers tend to play in a rougher, more jostling fashion with their male children. Before six months of age, male babies are touched more frequently by their mothers than are girls, but after six months of age the opposite is true. Boys are given less emotional support throughout the

rest of their lives and learn rapidly that "big boys don't cry." Instead of emotional support from others, they are encouraged to obtain pleasure from success in competition and in demonstrating skill and physical coordination. Girls are encouraged to take care in making themselves pretty, and their clothing is often designed more for eye appeal than for practicality in play. By and large, differences in the socialization of children reflect a stereotype of gender differences that views males as strong, active, unemotional, logical, dominant, independent, aggressive, and competitive and females as weak, passive, emotional, intuitive, supportive, dependent, sociable, status-conscious, shy, patient, and vain. In the past 20 years, stereotypes such as these have changed tremendously among university students and other young people but less so for U.S. society at large.

Anthropologists have long asserted that enculturation occurs partly by imitation and partly by direct teaching through language. In imitative learning, which Edward Hall (1959) calls **informal learning**, learners are on their own to simply observe how others do something and then to keep trying it themselves until they "get the hang of it." Much of what we have learned informally is done automatically, without awareness or concentration and with little or no feeling. Learning informally how to behave in a situation results in a lot of variation in the personal styles of each individual and a generally greater tolerance for such differences. The range of permitted variation in customs that are learned by this trial-and-error method also makes it easier for such customs to gradually change by adapting older ways of doing things to new situations. The range of individual differences within informally learned customs makes the boundaries between successful conformity and rule breaking somewhat fuzzy and the rules that govern proper behavior in informally learned areas of life may literally "go without saying." Nevertheless, there are limits on how differently an individual may perform informally learned customs and still be accepted. Since the rules are not spelled out

---

enculturation (socialization) the process by which children learn the customs, beliefs, and values of their culture

socialization enculturation

informal learning learning by imitation

and members of the group have not been taught how to talk about those rules or their violation, awareness that informally learned rules are being broken takes the form of rapidly mounting anxiety in all present until someone acts to deal with the rule violation. According to Hall, in Japan tension over the breaking of informal rules is expressed by giggling and laughter, while in the United States the nervous anxiety may take the form of anger or withdrawal.

Learning that occurs when language is used to admonish us for violating a custom is called **formal learning**. The teacher expresses disapproval of our behavior and suggests an alternative way as the proper, moral, or good way to act. We are conscious of the rules we are following if we learned them formally, since talking about them was part of the learning. Formal ways of doing things are endowed with deep feelings by the participants, and their violation leads to tremendous insecurity in those who rely on them to order and structure their lives. For this same reason, formally learned customs are slow to change.

It is also possible to teach a custom by talking about it, but without expressing disappointment or disapproval of the learner's rule-breaking behavior. Instead, the new way of acting is explained by giving the logical reason that lies behind it. This form of learning has been called **technical learning** by Hall. People are most highly conscious of technically learned behaviors, since they are generally given explanations for their implementation. Technical learning is especially important in settings in which practical skills are taught, for instance when parents explain to children the most effective way to do something like tie shoelaces or use a new tool. Little emotion is associated with material learned in this way, because the emphasis is on efficiency or effectiveness rather than propriety. Technically learned customs may be replaced readily by new technical ways of dealing with the same situation.

Childhood and Adolescent Sexual Socialization. Before we are able to play the role of adults with complete success, we must acquire knowledge of the sexual customs of our society. Most societies deal with this necessity in a fairly matter-of-fact way. According to Clellan Ford and Frank Beach (1951), 34 percent of the 95 societies whose sexual customs they surveyed had little or no restriction on sexual experimentation in childhood. Examples of peoples whose attitudes toward childhood sexuality were **permissive** are the Lepcha, an agricultural society in the Himalayas, and the Trobrianders, who live on one of the Melanesian islands. According to Ford and Beach, the Lepcha believed that sexual activity is necessary in order for girls to grow up. Therefore, most girls were regularly engaging in full sexual intercourse by the age of 11 or 12. Among the Trobrianders, boys of 10 to 12 years of age and girls of 6 to 8 years are given explicit sexual training by older companions.

Fifty-one percent of the societies Ford and Beach studied were **semirestrictive**: young people were expected to follow certain rules of etiquette in their exploration of their sexuality, although no severe punishments were imposed for violations. Only 15 percent of these societies were truly **restrictive** of childhood sexuality, and such patterns were most common where male solidarity was economically or politically important and where class distinctions or differences in wealth were important matters. This is certainly understandable, since adults in such societies are likely to have a greater vested interest in the future marriage plans of their children. The more carefully the sexuality of unmarried persons is controlled, the greater are their parents' options in selecting marriage partners for their children.

In the United States, adolescents explore their identities as social beings during the teenage period as they practice the skills necessary to achieve an independent adult status. Acceptance by their peers becomes extremely important, and adolescents begin to create a sense of independent functioning by adopting new val-

---

formal learning learning that proceeds by admonition and correction of the learner's errors, with emotional emphasis on the importance of behaving acceptably

technical learning learning that occurs when the logical rationales for specific ways of doing things—rather than emotional pressure to behave in that way—are given to the learner

permissive societies those that are tolerant of childhood sexual experimentation

semirestrictive societies those that accept childhood sexual experimentation so long as those involved follow established rules of etiquette and discretion

restrictive societies societies that do not accept childhood sexual experimentation

ues that are in harmony with their peer group and with the social milieu outside their family. In this period of dating, adolescents begin to learn the skills of courtship and lay the foundations for their adult sexual identities. Although ideals historically have required that both sex and pregnancy be delayed until after the marriage ceremony, this is no longer the case in practice. According to the Alan Guttmacher Institute (1994), among young people in the United States who turned 18 between 1986 through 1988, 56 percent of the women and 73 percent of the men had experienced sexual intercourse by this age (p. 20). In 1991 there were 1,150,000 reported pregnancies among adolescent women aged 19 and under. About half of these pregnancies were ended through abortion, and 368,500 (31 percent) culminated in births out of wedlock (Alan Guttmacher Institute, 1994; *U.S. Bureau of the Census,* 1994).

Puberty Rituals.   Near the time individuals reach biological maturity, it is common for a **puberty ritual** or **adulthood ritual** to be held. This ritual signals the transition from childhood to adulthood and impresses on both the child and his or her community that the old roles of childhood are to be set aside and that she or he should be treated as an adult.

In the dominant North American culture, some of the traditional rites of passage are relatively weak or sometimes lacking. For instance, few people in the United States experience any form of true puberty ritual as they near adulthood. Instead we have several less significant transitions, each of which confers some of the rights of adulthood: obtaining a driver's license during the teenage years, graduating from high school, gaining the right to vote at the age of 18, and becoming old enough to drink alcoholic beverages legally at the age of 21. This lack of a clear puberty ritual often creates confusion about the roles we are expected to play and leaves individuals to wrestle alone with what in the U.S. culture is commonly called an "identity crisis." The existence of this expression in everyday language is evidence of how extensive role confusion is in this society. It suggests the benefits that rites of passage may provide to a society's members by helping them maintain a greater sense of self-confidence as they undergo the normal changes experienced by members of their group.

Not all societies practice puberty rituals, but they are relatively common. In Yehudi Co-hen's (1964) examination of 65 societies, 46 had puberty rituals, while 19 did not. He divided these societies into two groups: those with nuclear families only (minimal families that consist only of parents and their children) and those with complex family organizations such as lineages and clans in which many related individuals participate in family affairs (see chapter 10). He found that in societies based on the nuclear family, where children would be trained from an early age to be socially independent, the probability of puberty rituals was smaller than in those societies with more complex families, where children were trained to play an interdependent, cooperative role with many other family members.

Social circumstances that foster interdependent role playing can lock people into their current roles and make change difficult without the aid of a mechanism for transformation from one status to another. The puberty ceremony symbolically redefines the child as an adult in a dramatic, public fashion that is difficult for those involved to ignore. The ritual proclaims the changes in rights and responsibilities that everyone in the group must recognize.

Puberty Rites for Males.   For boys, puberty rituals seem to be most dramatic when the transition from boyhood to manhood is potentially difficult. Under such circumstances, male puberty rituals are often severe and painful ordeals, involving ceremonies such as **circumcision** (the surgical removal of the foreskin), **scarification** of the body (decorating the body with a pattern made of scars), tattooing, and the filing or knocking out of front teeth as indicators of adult status.

Whiting, Kluckhohn, and Anthony (1958) found that circumcision of males as a part of initiation rituals is especially associated with three social customs: a taboo on sex between husband and wife for a year or more after the

---

puberty ritual a rite of passage that formalizes the change from the status of child to the status of adult

adulthood ritual puberty ritual

circumcision the surgical removal of the foreskin from the penis

scarification decorating the body by cutting designs in it and treating them with ashes or other material to ensure that they will produce raised scars

FIGURE 4.4

PUBERTY RITE FOR FEMALES

This 12-year-old girl from the Kuria tribe has just been circumcised without anesthesia. She carries an umbrella and shilling notes hang from her headdress. The people of her village, dressed in tree branches, clap and sing to her. Female genital mutilation, a painful and sometimes dangerous practice traditionally thought to guard virginity and discourage sexual intercourse, remains common in more than 20 African countries in spite of the opposition of many women and some heads of state.

birth of a child, the sharing of sleeping quarters by mother and child with the father's quarters elsewhere, and the establishment of residence by a married couple near the husband's relatives. The first two of these customs make it more difficult for a male child to identify with the male role, since the most available adult role model is the mother. The third, residence of couples near the husband's relatives, is common where male solidarity is important among adults. The conflict between the need to identify with the male group as an adult and the relatively weak childhood tie between father and son makes the transition from childhood to adulthood a stressful one. Hence the dramatic ritualizing of the status change through which a boy proves to the adult male community that he is capable of adopting the adult male role.

Puberty Rites for Females.   J. Brown (1963) found that about half of a sample of 60 societies practiced puberty rituals for girls. These rituals are more likely to occur in societies where the residences of newly married couples are estab-

lished near the wife's relatives than in societies where daughters leave home when they marry. The puberty ritual emphasizes the young woman's new role. The more important a woman's labor is to the family food supply, the more likely it is that female puberty rituals will be practiced. As with male initiation rituals, painful ceremonies are most likely in societies where the transition from childhood to adult roles is most difficult. For girls, this occurs in those societies where mothers and daughters share sleeping quarters while the father sleeps elsewhere.

In many societies where male dominance over women is an important fact of life, the genitals of female children are mutilated, a practice called **female circumcision**. Hosken (1980) describes the most common forms, their effects, and the cultural settings in which they occur.

---

female circumcision mutilation of female genitals, including infibulation and excision, a symbol of male dominance in some societies

FRANCE FIGHTS FEMALE GENITAL MUTILATION BY AFRICAN IMMIGRANTS

As she rose in a Paris courtroom, a small figure in a black lawyer's robe, Linda Weil-Curiel talked so softly that the judge and the jury had to lean forward to hear her argument.

"This is butchery invented to control women," Miss Weil-Curiel told the court. She was speaking as a member of the prosecution team in the trial of a woman accused of allowing the genital mutilation of her daughter, a tradition widely practiced in parts of Africa for centuries.

Since African immigrants brought the custom to France more than a decade ago and their babies began to arrive at local hospitals bleeding, infected, sometimes dead as a result of surgery at home, Miss Weil-Curiel has become the country's leading crusader against the practice.

Her actions have already led to 15 trials involving more than 30 families, making France the first nation to bring criminal charges against those who perform this female mutilation. . . .

The prosecutions have also become part of the larger debate over how a society should deal with immigrants' customs which it finds unacceptable. Britain, Sweden, and Switzerland in recent years have passed laws against female genital mutilation, but they have not prosecuted it. Last month, a bill banning the practice in the United States was introduced in Congress.

In the dock on a recent day was Bintou Fofana Diarra, an immigrant from Mali. She was accused of complicity in mutilating her three-month-old baby, an act that landed the little girl in a Paris hospital for three weeks and nearly caused her death. A distraught Mrs. Diarra testified that she did it for the good of the child, "to make her like the other girls so that she could find a husband."

The operation, she conceded, was done secretly in her home. But she said it is normal in Mali. According to United Nations reports, sexual mutilation affects millions of mostly Muslim women in more than 25 countries, across the central belt of Africa as well as in Yemen, Oman, Malaysia and Indonesia. The mutilation involves cutting off all or part of a young girl's clitoris and labia, and in some cases stitching her vagina closed until marriage. . . .

Miss Weil-Curiel said that during trials here, ethnologists and physicians often come down on different sides of the issue. During Mrs. Diarra's trial, a French ethnologist argued that Africans should not be punished because they act under social pressure.

He said that people cite different reasons for the centuries-old practice, such as the erroneous belief that the Koran commands it, that it is more hygienic, that it keeps a girl chaste, that without the ritual she cannot get a husband and therefore the family cannot get a dowry. One father recently told a Paris court that he had his infant cut "so that later she will behave herself."

Doctors who have treated mutilated women told the court that these women often cannot achieve orgasm and often develop hard scars, cysts, swellings or infections. Dr. Marie-Hélène Franjou, director of a Government maternity clinic at Yvelines, near Paris, said the procedure often causes lifelong problems, including complications in childbirth. . . .

In her office, Miss Weil-Curiel, who is 50, says that change has been slow since the first mutilation trial in 1983. She says she has pinned her hopes on the small but growing movement of African women, founded in Senegal in 1984, who are fighting the practice at home. But in France and in Europe, she said, not enough is done because the problem deals with women's sexuality and embarrasses people.

"If immigrants cut off a girl's ear in the name of tradition, there would be an outcry," she said. "But here the sex of a future woman is cut off and people are willing to defend it or turn away." It is up to women, she said, "to force this onto government agendas."

From "French Prosecutor Fighting Girl-Mutilation by Migrants" by Marlise Simons, November 23, 1993, *New York Times*, p. A13.

Infibulation—an operation performed mostly in childhood by which the sides of the vulva are closed over the vagina—is particularly common where the virginity of wives is important. Following infibulation, sexual intercourse is not possible until the barrier created by the operation is cut, usually by the husband. Deinfibulation is extremely painful. It can result in severe bleeding and can lead to tetanus and other infections that can damage the fallopian tubes and cause sterility. Deaths from medical complications are not uncommon.

---

infibulation surgical closing of the female vulva over the vagina

COURTSHIP IN SAMOA

In traditional Samoa before contact with Europeans, children were unshielded from the facts of sex, birth, and death. Growing up sharing a house with no walls with 50 or 60 relatives, they did not develop the kind of shame that is connected with sex in societies where privacy is more common. Chastity in daughters was a mark of prestige for families, but, as in all societies, sexual experimentation occurred discreetly. Mead (1928) believed that both men and women were equally free to choose their partners, and her informants claimed that the European concepts of fidelity and jealousy were unheard of.

Etiquette required that a rendezvous be arranged through a go-between, called a *soa*. An unmarried woman might invite a suitor to spend the night with her in her family's home if she did not wish to meet him elsewhere. In such a case, the young man would enter the house after dark when other family members were already asleep and leave before they awoke.

This form of courtship gave rise to a custom known as **sleep crawling**, in which an unpopular youth or jilted lover might sneak into the house of a young woman without invitation, in the hope that she might be expecting another lover and allow him to stay once she had discovered the deception. Freeman (1983) regards this as a form of rape and believes that a great deal of competition occurred among young men in this practice, due to the great emphasis that Samoan families placed on competition for status and on the chastity of their daughters as a symbol of their family honor. If the woman was not favorably disposed to the sleep crawler, she had the option of rousing her household to chase, ridicule, and beat the intruder for adopting such tactics. If he were publicly identified, a sleep crawler was disgraced and would not be entertained or considered for marriage by other women.

Informal clandestine love affairs in Samoa would eventually lead to the development of more or less permanent primary sexual liaisons between couples that were, in effect, a form of trial marriage. If the couple desired to formalize their relationship by marriage, a courtship process was required in which a go-between would accompany the lover to the woman's family and plead his case for him. After repeated visits, the actual proposal of marriage would be made by the go-between. If the marriage was acceptable to the family, a ceremony would be arranged in which elaborate gift giving took place between the two families.

SAMOANS

On the island of Samoa in the South Pacific, courtship was generally discreet and sexual liaisons occurred under cover of darkness. Sleep crawling was a focus of courtship in which a young man would hope to gain favor with a woman by sneaking into her room at night uninvited and so impressing her that he would be invited to stay.

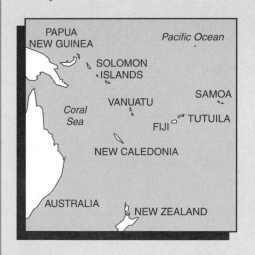

Excision—removal of the pleasure-sensitive clitoris—is performed to reduce a woman's sexual sensations and, thereby, her interest in sex. This is thought to increase her fidelity in marriage, especially in societies where polygyny (where men are permitted to have more than one wife) is practiced, and legitimate opportunities for heterosexual intercourse are less common for wives than for husbands. Excision is sometimes thought to increase female fertility, so it is also practiced to ensure that a woman will have many children.

---

excision surgical removal of all or part of the female clitoris

sleep crawling a Samoan sexual practice in which an uninvited youth would enter a young woman's house after dark with the intent of seduction

FIGURE 4.5

MARRIAGE RITUAL

The marriage ritual differs greatly from culture to culture, and weddings in the United States frequently combine elements from different traditions. In this Hindu ceremony in the United States, the bridegroom wears a combination of formal Western and Indian clothing, while the rituals follow Hindu traditions. Here, the bride and bridegroom, along with the priest and family members, grasp a symbolic vessel, a lota, *traditionally thought to ensure an auspicious beginning for the marriage.*

Female genital mutilation is most common today in the most populous areas of East, Central, and West Africa, in some Middle Eastern countries, including Egypt and the southern Arabian Peninsula, and in some parts of Indonesia and Malaysia. Excision is practiced by Christian Copts in Egypt, as well as by Egyptian Moslems and by non-Moslem groups in the 26 African countries where it has been documented. Furthermore, although infibulation was not a traditional Western practice, excision was practiced by European and American surgeons into the twentieth century as a supposed cure for masturbation and nymphomania, a negative label for sexual desire in females (Barker-Banfield, 1983).

Although the practice of female circumcision is still common, it has started to encounter opposition in recent years by a growing number of African and European women who have become concerned especially about the medical dangers it can pose. Efforts by women acting through the United Nations have led a few heads of state to take a position against female circumcision. For instance, Thomas Sankara of Burkina Faso spoke out against female circumcision before he was deposed in 1991. Presidents Abdou Diouf of Senegal and Daniel arap Moi of Kenya have also publicly opposed the practice. Yet, female circumcision continues to have widespread support, not only because of the weight of tradition but also because, for many, the practice became a form of resistance to colonial interference earlier in this century.

Courtship and Marriage

Following the puberty or adulthood ritual, the next common rite of passage is marriage. Cultures handle courtship and mate selection in many different ways. In many societies, marital partners are selected by parents. In others, especially those in which children will establish their own households that are economically independent of their parents, courtship and choice of spouse is a responsibility of the young adults themselves.

Nonmarital Sex.   Following puberty, the majority of societies are quite tolerant of sexual experimentation before marriage. Frayser (1985) found that 64 percent of her cross-cultural sample of 61 societies had little or no restriction on premarital sexual relations. According to Ford and Beach (1952), the least permissive societies are, as might be expected, those in which wealth and class differences cause parents to have the greatest interest in controlling the marital choices of their children, and societies in which the economic and political position of families is based on male solidarity.

Marriage Ritual.   Once an agreement for marriage partners has been achieved between the families, the actual ritual of marriage may occur. Marriage rituals vary tremendously from society to society. They may involve elaborate symbolism and drama or they may be as simple as a public announcement by a couple that they consider themselves married. Where formal rituals of marriage are customary, the symbolism often emphasizes the union being created between the two families. It may also portray the relations, especially those of a stressful nature, that are expected to exist between the couple and their respective in-laws. For instance, among the Aztecs of Mexico the bride was carried, like a burden, on the back of the old woman who had acted as her matchmaker to the place of the marriage. After lectures by the elders of both families about their new responsibilities as married persons, the capes of the couple were tied together into a knot by which they were joined in marriage.

G. W. Stow (1905) described a South African !Kung San marriage ritual, which is no longer practiced, in which the bride was captured by the bridegroom and his family or friends from her defending relatives. During the wedding feast the groom was expected to seize hold of the bride. Then the two families began to fight while the bride's family focused their attention on beating the groom with their digging sticks. The groom had to succeed in holding onto his bride during this beating for the marriage ritual to be complete. Had he failed, he would have lost his bride.

In Western societies the notion that the government had authority to regulate marriages did not exist before the Middle Ages. Instead, as has been common in many non-Western societies throughout the world, marriages were created by the negotiation of a contract between the couple or between their respective families. No religious or governmental ceremonies were required since their creation was simply a matter of family law. Between the eighth century and the year 1000 the ceremonies that created marriages continued to be organized by families or individuals, but sometimes members of some of the more important, upper-class members of society were honored with a ritual blessing of the unions in church ceremonies that generally preceded the actual wedding ceremony that was still performed according to the secular customs of family law. Gradually, nonfamily authorities became more involved in the regulation of marriages. Landowners, for instance, began to require the peasants who worked their land to obtain their permission to marry and establish new households, since marriages among the peasants could involve the movement of workers from the properties of one landowner to those of another. Governments

FIGURE 4.6

ORTHODOX JEWISH WEDDING IN THE UNITED STATES

At an Orthodox Jewish wedding, the bride dances in a circle with other women and girls to mark the joy of the occasion, while the bridegroom dances in a separate circle with male guests. While romantic love is the dominant ideal within the U.S. courtship and marriage system, many Orthodox communities retain a formalized process of introduction for unmarried young people within the community who are prospective marital partners.

encouraged the local religious leaders to take responsibility for keeping records of marriages and religious marriage rituals became more common. In western European countries, it was not until the year 1215 that religious wedding ceremonies began to be required by church authorities for a marriage to be legitimate. The governmental regulation of marriage through the requirement that couples apply to the state for a license to marry did not become a part of the Western concept of legitimate marriage until the middle of the sixteenth century. As the state began to assert its authority to determine the legitimacy of marriage, the earlier secular form of marriage through family contracts was replaced by marriage by a governmental official as an alternative to a religious marriage ceremony, which governments also recognized as valid under secular law.

Marriage in the United States. Couples in the United States are marrying later today than they were a generation ago. The median age of males marrying for the first time is nearly 26 years, and for females it is slightly over 23 years. The ideal of romantic love as a basis for marriage is perhaps nowhere else in

FIGURE 4.7

PARENTHOOD

Becoming a parent involves a culturally defined status change that entails new obligations. In China, where most women work outside the home, fathers may share in child care responsibilities.

the world so strongly supported as it is in the United States.

Why is romantic love such an important ideal in the U.S. courtship and marriage system? One factor, certainly, is the economic unimportance of the nuclear family as a unit of production in the country. As industrialization undermined the economic role of the extended family, the marital choices of children grew increasingly independent of parental authority. As parental decision making in the choice of mates declined, emotional attraction grew increasingly central to the process of mate selection. Another factor in the maintenance of the ideal of romantic love appears to be the dependent economic status of women. The romantic ideal stresses the role of women as objects of love, valued for their emotional, aesthetic, nurturing, and moral contributions to society rather than for their economic productivity and practical contributions outside the domestic sphere. This romanticizing of women as economically dependent love objects con-

trasts with actual current marriage practices in which over half of married women are employed outside the home.

Just how does mate selection actually proceed? Several researchers suggest a model that involves a sequence of stages. First, proximity is an important factor. People are most likely to get together with those whom they are likely to encounter. Thus, in spite of their mobility, most people in the United States actually marry a partner who lives within a few miles of them. Ineichen (1979) found that almost 65 percent of a sample of 232 married couples lived in the same city before they married, most of them coming from the same area or adjacent areas of the city.

Initial attraction is likely to be based on superficial, easily observable characteristics such as physical attractiveness, dress, and evidence of social power and prestige. After meeting one another, couples' compatibility of values and attitudes is especially important. Agreement on religious, sexual, familial, and political values is a good predictor of the development of a stable relationship (Kerkhoff & Davis, 1962). Burgess and Wallin (1953) found that engaged couples were remarkably similar in their physical attractiveness, physical health, mental health, social popularity, race, religion, parents' educational levels, parents' incomes, and the quality of their parents' marriages. Thus, similarity seems to be an important element in the attraction that leads to relationships.

Parenthood

With marriage may come children, turning the social unit into a family. The relationship between spouses generally changes at the birth of the first child. It creates new obligations for the husband and wife and new demands on their time and energy. Their domestic roles must be adjusted to accommodate their new status as parents. No longer will they have as much exclusive time for each other.

In societies in which the family organization is important economically and politically, entry into parenthood may be formally indicated by a change in the parents' names. Using this custom, called **teknonymy**, a parent might be called Father of Lynn or Mother of Kay.

---

teknonymy the custom of referring to a person as the parent of his or her child rather than by birth name

Teknonymy is most often practiced by men in societies in which the couple takes up residence with or near the wife's family. Women may practice it as well, but in fewer societies. In either case, it reflects an elevation in the social rank of the individual, since because of the birth of the child he or she is no longer considered an outsider to the family with which the couple resides. The name change calls attention to the greater bond that now exists between the new parent and the in-laws.

Divorce

Not all marriages last until the death of a spouse. In the United States, for instance, between 30 percent and 40 percent of marriages are likely to end in divorce. Around the world, there are societies with higher and lower rates of divorce. Reasons for divorce vary, but impotence, infertility, infidelity, laziness, and simple incompatibility are common justifications. In three-quarters of the nonindustrialized societies that have been studied by anthropologists, women and men have been more or less equal in their right to divorce (Murdock, 1957).

Cross-cultural variations in divorce rates make it possible to discover some of the factors that make divorce less likely. The payment of a marriage gift to the bride's family gives her family a vested interest in the stability of the marriage, since the groom's family is likely to demand return of the payment if the marriage is dissolved. The dowry, a transfer of wealth in the opposite direction, has a similar effect of stabilizing marriage ties. When the couple lives in an extended family, relatives are also likely to have a stabilizing effect on their marriage. Matrilocality, discussed in chapter 9, "Marriage and the Family," also is associated with a low divorce rate. Perhaps this is because the control over property that this form of residence gives to women is associated with greater-than-usual social power and honor for women and little familial authority for the husband, who resides with his in-laws. Under these conditions, the frequency of abusive behavior by the husband is also likely to be relatively low.

Old Age

Many of us want to grow older, but we do not want to grow old. The negative feelings we have about aging are partly related to the loss of health and strength that accompany the bio-logical process. Socially, aging may also bring a loss of our accustomed rank. What are the factors that contribute to the loss of social power and honor that old age brings in societies such as our own? Cross-cultural research sheds some light on this question.

When postmarital residence rules require a couple to live near one spouse's parents, it is easier for the parents to continue their roles as family heads into their old age. In societies in which the family is a cooperating economic or political group, an older person's status as family head can be a major determinant of his or her rank in life. According to a study of nonindustrialized societies by Lee and Kezis (1979), nuclear families lack a structure in which parents can maintain their role of family heads into old age. Older people are more likely to have high-ranked statuses in societies in which they live with related married couples and in societies in which descent is traced through only one of the parents (patrilineal or matrilineal societies) rather than through both. However, if an extended family is too large to be easily led by a single family head or couple, decisions may actually be made by smaller groups within the extended family. When the political power or wealth of a family is not consistently related to a particular lineage, parents' rank is not so likely to rise with age as in a system in which it is.

In all societies, the elderly are accorded more respect if they are economically productive. Thus, in industrialized societies where rank is associated closely with wealth and income, the social rank of the elderly tends to decline markedly at retirement.

Death

Simple and obvious criteria such as the absence of breathing, heartbeat, or reaction to pain have been used in societies throughout the world to determine when **biological death** has occurred. With the development of a technology to measure brain functioning directly, in the United States and other industrialized societies, more emphasis seems to be directed toward defining death as the cessation of activity in the cerebral cortex of the brain, the center of intellectual and

---

biological death measured by cessation of such organic functions as breathing, heartbeat, reaction to pain, or brain functioning

FIGURE 4.8

DEATH

A major change in a family or society is the death of one of its members. Many societies have elaborate rituals to help the spirit of the deceased in its journey in the afterlife as well as to help those left behind to adjust to the loss. At this Chinese wake service in the United States, friends and relatives mourn a woman who was killed during a robbery.

conscious processes. However, these criteria may not always agree with one another. For instance, the cerebral cortex may no longer be active while the heart and lungs continue to operate, or a person may be comatose and unresponsive to pain, yet later report having been fully aware of the surroundings. Life-support systems used to maintain the vital functions of comatose patients whose heart and lungs have stopped functioning further complicate the process of determining biological death.

Psychological death refers to the process by which people prepare themselves subjectively for their impending biological death. Elisabeth Kübler-Ross (1969), who studied dying patients' responses to their circumstances in U.S. hospitals, identified five coping patterns that patients exhibit as distinct stages in the process of coming to terms with their impending deaths. Others (Corr, 1993) have since suggested that these reactions do not necessarily

occur in any specific sequence and that some individuals may not experience all five. The first reaction described by Kübler-Ross is *denial*. Patients refuse to accept the correctness of the diagnosis, insisting that some error has been made or that their records have been confused with those of someone else. Their basic attitude might be summed up as, "There must be some mistake; this cannot be happening to me!" The second response of patients to learning that they are dying is *anger*, which is characterized by rage, envy, and resentment. In this reaction, the dominant question is, "Why me, why not someone else?" The anger may be directed at anyone at hand—other patients, doctors, nurses, even family members who come to visit and comfort the person. The third reaction is

psychological death the process by which one subjectively prepares for impending biological death

THE MAPUCHE DEATH AND BURIAL RITUAL

According to Louis Faron (1961, 1968), the Mapuche, a native people of southern Chile, believed that death is caused by spiritual powers. The forces of evil known as *wekufe* were usually brought into play by a sorcerer-witch called *akalku*. When a person died, the corpse became dangerous to those who had to deal with it. One or two members of the household washed the corpse, clothed it in its finest garments, and laid it out for display on an altar in the house. After four days, the body was transferred to a canoe-shaped coffin that had been carved from a split tree trunk.

The relatives, especially the women of the family, mourned and lamented the loss, tore their garments, and promised revenge for the death, which they believed to have been caused by sorcery. Then came the wake or "Black Gathering." First, the house was purified of evil spirits to prevent them from capturing the soul of the deceased. This was done by horsemen who surrounded the house and shouted at the evil spirits who invariably came in search of the souls of the dead. A four-day-and-night vigil by the relatives followed. This was important, since how the deceased spent eternity—either among the ancestors or in the underworld of witches—depended not on how he or she had lived but on how the mourners conducted themselves during the death ritual. It was their behavior that prevented the witches from stealing parts of the corpse for use in creating a new evil spirit.

After the four days of vigil, the corpse was taken to a bier in a field. There the deceased was praised in several speeches. The coffin was then painted black and decorated with cinnamon, apple, and the shrub maqui. A large wooden cross, a symbol borrowed from Catholicism, was placed at the head of the coffin, which faced toward the east.

The guests, who might number over 1,000, then assembled in the mourning houses and were fed a ceremonial meal provided by the family of the deceased. The men were greeted by the host and the female guests by a female relative of the deceased, in separate groups. Although many feared to do so, it was customary for the guests to look on the face of the corpse. Small gifts, belongings, and a packet of food were dropped into the coffin to accompany the deceased on the journey to the afterworld of the ancestors.

Only the closest relatives finally accompanied the coffin to the graveyard. As they returned from the cemetery, ashes were scattered along the way to prevent the spirit from returning to bother the living.

MAPUCHE

The Mapuche, people native to southern Chile, followed several rituals upon the death of a loved one. They focused on evil spirits as the cause of death. The behavior of the relatives during the "Black Gathering," or wake, was believed to influence how the deceased spent eternity.

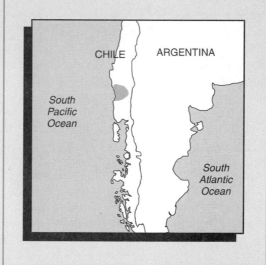

---

one of *bargaining* for more time. In this coping strategy, patients seek a slight extension of their deadline—to allow doing something "for one last time" or some similar request, in return for which they vow to live a better life. *Depression* is the fourth response, in which the dying person mourns because of the approaching loss of people and things that have been meaningful in his or her life. Finally, some patients respond with acceptance, a kind of quiet expectation. Acceptance is not a state of happiness but one

social death the point at which people respond to a person with the behaviors appropriate to one who is biologically dead

of rest in which there are almost no strong feelings and the patient's interests narrow as he or she gradually withdraws from everyday life in preparation for what is about to happen. This may be a time of great distress for the patient's family, since they may feel rejected by his or her withdrawal and lack of interest in their visits.

Socially, death brings about the final change of status in the human life cycle—the change from a human status to a nonhuman one. **Social death** is the point at which other people begin to relate to a dying person with behaviors and actions that are appropriate toward someone already dead. Like psychological death, social death may occur before biological death. W. H. Rivers (1926) reported that among the Melanesians, the word *mate*, which means "dead person," was applied not only to the biologically dead but also to individuals who were gravely ill, close to death, and to the very old who were likely to die soon. The Melanesians, of course, distinguished between biological *mate* and social *mate*. The purpose of referring to those who were close to death as *mate* was that they were treated socially as if they were dead. Such persons might be buried alive so that they could proceed to a more pleasant afterlife rather than linger among the living under the unpleasant circumstances of extreme age or terminal illness. Among the Inuit of the Arctic, the survival of hunting families would be endangered if they slowed their wanderings through arctic wastes in search of food to allow the aged or infirm to keep up. Eventually, at the urging of the afflicted party, the Inuit might hold a funeral ceremony and say goodbye to the one who had

to be left behind to die so that others might live.

Since all societies must restructure their social relations so that the work of the world may be continued after the death of a member, social death is found in each society. The most dramatic aspect of this social custom is manifest in **funeral rituals**. Funeral rituals provide a mechanism for dealing with and disposing of the body of the deceased and, at the same time, provide a setting in which the survivors can be encouraged to adjust themselves to the person's now permanent absence. As a part of this second role of funeral rituals, issues of inheritance of property rights and of passing on the statuses of the deceased to new persons are dealt with in many societies during or immediately following the funeral.

Death in the United States has been largely removed from the familial context by other social institutions that have taken over the management of the dying and the dead. Hospitals and nursing homes care for the terminally ill and insulate the surviving family members from much of the dying process. People are likely to die in either a hospital or a nursing home, often in isolation from their family members. Traditionally, doctors and nurses have tended to avoid telling terminal patients that they were dying. A specialized funeral industry exists to take care of the practical necessities preparatory to burial, and to usher the survivors through the funeral and mourning process.

---

funeral ritual a rite of passage that formalizes the removal of an individual from the status of living member of the social group

---

CHAPTER SUMMARY

1. We change in many ways through life, but some of our changes are not unique to us. Rather, they are signs that we are passing through predictable stages in the life cycle.

2. The major stages discussed here are birth, socialization during childhood, marriage, family formation, old age, and death.

3. Societies shape these changes in culture-specific ways, with only a few universals or near-universals such as the incest taboo.

4. Life-cycle changes may be marked by customs such as pregnancy taboos, *couvade*, naming ceremonies, puberty rituals, marriage negotiations, marriage rituals, establishment of residence, divorce, and funeral

rites, each of which has specific cultural meanings and purposes.

5. In the United States, birth is being treated more personally than in the past, but socialization of children sometimes perpetuates outdated stereotypes.

6. U.S. adolescents turn to their peer groups for socialization and sex, with a high rate of teenage pregnancies. Marriages are occurring later and breaking up sooner.

7. In the United States, illness is treated according to a medical model, with the elderly placed in institutions to die.

ANNOTATED READINGS

Ginsberg, F. (1989). *Contested lives: The abortion debate in an American community.* Berkeley, CA: University of California Press. An ethnographic study of the grassroots abortion politics in a U.S. community.

Kenyatta, J. (1962). *Facing Mount Kenya: The tribal life of the Gikuyu.* New York: Random House. An excellent description of Kikuyu life by a Kikuyu anthropologist who went on to become prime minister and president of Kenya. Especially good chapters on life-cycle rituals.

Moffatt, M. (1989). *Coming of age in New Jersey: College and American culture.* New Brunswick, NJ: Rutgers University Press. An anthropological study of the sexual and academic adventures of adolescents at a major U.S. university in the 1980s.

Shostak, M. (1983). *Nisa: The story of a !Kung woman.* New York: Random House. A fascinating account of the life history of a woman in a foraging society.

Simmons, L. W. (Ed.). (1942). *Sun Chief: The autobiography of a Hopi Indian.* New Haven, CT: Yale University Press. An autobiographical account of the life of a Hopi chief, Don Talayesva.

Van Gennep, A. (1960 [1908]). *The rites of passage* (S. T. Kimball, trans.). Chicago: University of Chicago Press. The classic discussion of the major changes in status that are celebrated in ritual.

CHAPTER FIVE

Gender and Culture

Chapter Objectives

After reading this chapter, you should be able to:

Distinguish between sex and gender.

List some of the common sexual differences in humans.

Discuss cultural differences that have existed in gender roles.

Recognize the effects of gender stereotypes on the roles we learn to play.

Explain the concept of third and fourth genders.

Outline the common patterns of division of labor by gender.

Explain the influences of kinship, economics, religion, and warfare on the relative power and honor accorded the different genders.

Discuss the various aspects of women's rights as human rights.

Discuss the relationships between religion and gender differences.

SEX AND GENDER
Sexual Differences
Gender

DIVERSITY IN MALE AND FEMALE ROLES
Socialization of Gender Differences
Common Patterns in Division of Labor
Gender Roles and Subsistence

THIRD AND FOURTH GENDERS
The Berdache
The Hijra
The Transvestite

GENDER, POWER, AND HONOR
Gender Stratification
Gender in Patrilineal Societies
Male Dominance
Gender in Matrilineal Societies
Matrifocality
The Causes of Gender Inequality

GENDER AND RELIGION
Gender Symbolism
Gender in the Religious Institution

WOMEN'S RIGHTS AS HUMAN RIGHTS
Economic Exploitation
Equality in Family Law
Reproductive Rights
Violence
Political Rights

◀ ***Figure* 5.1** *Undermining Gender Stereotypes* *Gender stereotypes, preconceived ideas about the distinction between appropriate "male" behaviors and roles and appropriate "female" ones, have been challenged by women who have entered political life. Aung San Suu Kyi has been the leader of democratic opposition to the military government in the southeast Asian state of Myanmar (formerly Burma), where politics have historically been dominated by men. After she was put under house arrest by the government in 1989, her party won nationwide elections in 1990, but the results were nullified by the government. She was awarded the Nobel Peace Prize in 1991 but remained under confinement until the summer of 1995.*

In all societies, ideas about differences between men and women influence the ways in which social roles are assigned. Not all cultures limit gender roles to two categories. In some, the genders of men and women are complemented by an alternative third or even a fourth gender category. A society assigns its genders different degrees of social power and honor. When there are significant differences, the men's roles are typically accorded greater rank. Such differences are influenced by kinship systems, the nature of warfare, and the economic aspects of each society. Religion typically provides support for gender role differences, and the gender characteristics of society are typically incorporated into mythology and other religious symbols. The privileged status of men's social roles found in many societies has often caused women's rights to be neglected.

Man, woman, macho, lady, hunk, broad. We have many different words that have both political and personal significance for the countless ways humans behave in male or female roles. They reveal much about our culture and our attitudes about our social roles. In this chapter, we will explore the ways in which culture molds our beliefs and feelings about sex and gender.

SEX AND GENDER

The word "sex" is often used as a synonym for "gender" by the public, but anthropologists give different meanings to each word. The term **sex** refers to biological distinctions such as the chromosomal, hormonal, or physical differences between males and females. **Gender** defines the social statuses and roles that people are socialized into based on cultural concepts about the sexes. In this chapter we will look at some of the complexities of both sex and gender.

Sexual Differences

Humans are biological creatures as well as cultural beings. Females and males differ biologically in various ways. Genetically, women have two X chromosomes, and men have an X and a Y. Since only males carry the Y chromosome, the sex of a child is determined by whether it received an X or a Y chromosome from its father.

Males and females differ in both their primary sexual characteristics, such as genitals and reproductive organs, and the secondary sexual characteristics that develop during puberty, such as breasts in females and low-pitched voices and a broad distribution of body hair in males. Physiologically, males in the human species are slightly larger than females on average, a characteristic known as **sexual dimorphism**. The sexes also generally differ in how strength is manifested. Males typically are able to exert higher levels of energy for short periods, while females tend to have greater endurance and are generally hardier. This distinction can be noticed at all stages of development. For instance, a higher percentage of spontaneous abortions tend to be males, and females seem to have a naturally higher life expectancy, although this is counteracted in many societies by lifestyles that increase women's mortality rates.

Some studies also point to basic psychological differences between the sexes. Beatrice Whiting and John Whiting (1975) carried out an in-depth study of children in six different societies, where they found a number of psychological characteristics that crosscut cultural boundaries. For instance, boys and girls both showed dependence, but expressed it in different ways: girls tended to seek help and contact, while boys sought attention and approval. They found no differences between boys and girls in seeking and offering friendship to others, and they found that girls behaved as actively as boys. Some differences in the behavior of boys and girls in the six societies, however, were discovered. Boys played more aggressively and in larger groups than girls did, and older boys were more likely to respond to aggression with aggression. Thus, there appear to be some general psychological characteristics that distinguish the sexes even in childhood.

---

sex biological distinctions such as the chromosomal, hormonal, or physical differences between males and females

gender social statuses assigned on the basis of cultural concepts about the sexes

sexual dimorphism marked differentiation in size and form of the sexes

Gender

Gender is a social identity that consists of the roles a person is expected to play because of his or her sex. Whereas we are born with sexual characteristics, our gender is something we must learn. All cultures recognize the existence of at least two genders: females are normally socialized into the roles that lead them into a social identity as women, while males learn men's roles.

Gender Stereotypes. It is not surprising that the average differences between males and females figure into **gender stereotypes**, preconceived ideas about how women and men differ in their personality traits, behavioral skills, and predispositions. However, it is a mistake to believe that biology is the *cause* of gender differences. In the first place, biological differences are average distinctions between males and females as groups, but there is a range of individual differences within both sexes, and they overlap more than they differ in most characteristics. Thus, some males may have greater endurance than most females, and some females may be able to exert more strength than most males. If biology *caused* gender differences, then they too would be merely statistical averages between what males and females did socially. But gender differences do not simply arise out of our predispositions to play various roles. Rather, gender stereotypes are *guidelines* that tell us how we are expected to act. It is our culture's gender stereotypes, not biology, that most directly channel us into our different gender roles. Sometimes gender stereotypes become so important that people refuse to acknowledge that individuals of one sex are capable of playing roles usually expected of members of the other sex. Rigid enforcement of gender stereotypes that prevents individuals from playing roles that are not those of their own sex is called **sexism**.

DIVERSITY IN MALE AND FEMALE ROLES

Since gender is culturally defined, there are significant differences from culture to culture in the specific roles of men and women. What is thought of as masculine or feminine behavior in one culture may not be thought of in the same way in another culture. Such differences are influenced by many factors such as environmental resources, economics, kinship, politics, and religion. In this section we will explore diversity within gender.

Socialization of Gender Differences

Anthropologists have noted that in every society there are socialization practices that result in differences from the typically expected North American patterns of male and female personalities.

The well-known anthropologist Margaret Mead did fieldwork (1950) among three New Guinea societies in which the ideologies about sex roles were quite different. Her descriptions of the Arapesh, Mundugumor, and Tschambuli make it clear that how people think about being masculine or feminine is highly variable and determined by culture rather than by any absolute dictates of biology. Although there were gender role differences among the Arapesh, no basic temperamental differences were thought to exist between males and females. Neither men nor women were believed to be driven by spontaneous sexuality, and violence, although tolerated, was not linked with either sex. Men were expected to be gentle, unacquisitive, and cooperative. Women were taught to accept anything out of the ordinary without curiosity. From childhood, they had been actively discouraged from asking questions about anything unusual and from engaging in speculative thought, a pastime that was encouraged in boys.

The people of a not-too-distant tribe, the Mundugumor, were quite different in their attitudes about the sexes. The Mundugumor were headhunters and cannibals, and the life of a male was characterized by fighting and the competitive acquisition of women through warfare. They assumed that there was a natural hostility between members of the same sex. As a result, inheritance of most property crossed sex boundaries with each generation from father to daughter and from mother to son. Compatibly with their way of life, both males and

gender stereotypes preconceived ideas about what behaviors and roles are considered "masculine" or "feminine"

sexism the belief that differences in the sex roles of males and females are biologically determined

MALE AND FEMALE ROLES IN IRAN

For an in-depth example of socially patterned status differences between males and females, we can look at Iranian men and women. According to Behnam (1985), the traditional Muslim family traced its ancestry through the father, tended toward marriage between cousins, favored polygyny, and was male dominated. The Iranian family was an autonomous economic unit in production as well as consumption. This lent it great cohesiveness, and the decision making for the domestic group lay in the hands of the male hierarchy within the family. According to Nassehi-Behnam (1985), the economic role of the family made marriage an important union between two family lines, so marital choices were a matter of great importance, with preparations sometimes beginning at birth.

In wealthy Iranian families, the symbolic distinction between the private intimacy of the household and the profane external world of strangers was portrayed by dividing the house into two areas, the private (*andaruni*) interior of the home, the area of the wife, and the public (*biruni*) area of the man, the threshold between the home and the outside world. Although the men of the family could enter the private areas of the home, the women were excluded from the public areas.

The responsibility of the woman for domestic work was emphasized by the Islamic religious traditions. The exemplary models of the division of labor within a marriage were Ali, the brother of Muhammad, and Ali's wife, Fatimah. In Islamic *hadith* or sacred tradition, Fatimah took responsibility for the domestic affairs, such as grinding the flour, baking the bread, and sweeping the house, while Ali took responsibility for all work outside the door of the house, such as bringing the firewood and obtaining food for the family. In the words of Allah as recorded in the *Qur'an* (4:34), "Men are the protectors and maintainers of women because God has given the one more [strength] than the other, because they support them from their means." Men, in other words, are thought to excel women in natural strength, so it is their responsibility to support their wives. Since a son will bear the economic responsibility of supporting a wife, a daughter need not inherit as much as a son. The *Qur'an* (4:11) specifies that "God [thus] directs you as regards your children's [inheritance]: to the male, a portion equal to that of two females."

Industrialization has created many strains on the traditional Iranian family structure. Urbanization has drawn many people away from rural areas. Housing problems in the cities make it difficult for extended families to maintain a common residence, further fragmenting the earlier family hierarchies. Industrialization also created increasing opportunities for women to be employed,

FIGURE 5.2

IRANIAN DRESS CODE

Roles for men and women in Iran follow a long tradition of Muslim heritage, but industrialization and revolution have combined to cause some changes. Women's work is still legally restricted, but the dress code now allows women to wear colorful garments and to show some of their hair beneath their scarves. These shoppers in Teheran illustrate the traditional hair covering (on the right) and the modern.

females were raised to have violent social personalities and to place no value on sensuality. For instance, breast-feeding of infants was done in a utilitarian way, with no hint of pleasure; nursing was carried out only to give food and never for comfort from fright or pain.

Finally, the Tschambuli, a third nearby group, did distinguish personality differences between men and women, although these expectations differed radically from role expectations of men and women in North America. The Tschambuli preferred marriages in which a man had many wives. Ancestry was traced through the men of the family. Men owned the houses and the land and officially "owned" their wives. But in practice, women held the main power in society. It was they who made most of the economic decisions, and they took the initiative in social life. For instance, Tschambuli women were socialized to be sexually aggressive, while the men, who were shy in

making divorce easier, since employment permits women to support themselves following divorce. Thus, the divorce rate is three times as high in urban areas as in rural areas (Nassehi-Behnam, 1985).

The Islamic revolution of 1979 brought attempts to reestablish the old male/female distinctions, with an increased application of Islamic religious principles in family law and values and the repeal of the Family Protection Laws passed in 1972, which had granted women the right to divorce, the right to an education and to work without their husbands' consent, and the right to custody of the children as well as restrictions on polygyny. The new government made the wearing of the veil by women in public mandatory, women's employment was restricted, and coeducational schooling was terminated as being contrary to Islam.

The efforts of the postrevolutionary government to root out all evidence of Western influence from Iranian life were particularly strong during the 1980s. The Islamic dress code became an important symbol of political loyalty. According to Katayon Ghazi, women who failed to wear the long veil, or chador, and to cover all parts of their bodies except their faces and hands "were harassed and arrested by the revolutionary Komiteh, the Islamic national morality authority, in its crackdown on what were termed obscene trends." Vio-

lations of the dress code resulted in imprisonment, flogging, or a heavy fine. For instance, displaying rouge and mascara in public was punishable by 70 lashes. Ghazi reports that Abolhassan Bani-Sadr, the first president after the revolution, asserted "that women must cover every strand of hair because 'research proved female hair had a kind of radiance' that might be tempting to men" (Ghazi, 1991, p. A4).

By 1991, civil and revolutionary forces had become integrated. The Komiteh merged with the local police forces. This stabilization of the government has reduced some of the zeal with which public morality had been enforced previously. Women's work is still legally restricted, and their testimony remains invalid in court. Women still lack the right to divorce or to leave the country without their husbands' permission. But enforcement of the dress code has been relaxed. Now, according to Ghazi, "most of the violators rounded up on Mohseni Square and herded into buses face far lighter penalties," such as detainment at the Center for Combating Sins for a maximum of 24 hours or even immediate release upon signing a commitment to observe the law (p. A4). Under these relaxed standards, some women have begun to wear more colorful garments and let perhaps an inch of hair show from beneath their scarves.

adolescence, were not. Mead (1950) summarized her findings:

> Here, admittedly looking for light on the subject of sex differences, I found three tribes all conveniently within a hundred mile area. In one, both men and women act as we [North Americans] expect women to act—in a mild parental responsive way; in the second, both act as we expect men to act—in a fierce initiating fashion; and in the third, the men act according to our stereotype for women—are catty, wear curls and go shopping, while the women are energetic, managerial, unadorned partners. (p. vi)

These extremely contrasting examples demonstrate that the personalities of men and women in any one society are not unambiguous manifestations of inherent characteristics that are fixed by nature. Rather, they are mani-

festations of each society's culturally patterned role expectations.

Common Patterns in Division of Labor

In spite of differences in how gender roles may be structured, there is a pattern to differences in roles that are commonly assigned to women and men. A cross-cultural study by Murdock and Provost (1973) revealed that throughout the world, males are almost always responsible for hunting large land and sea animals and game birds and for trapping smaller animals. They are usually expected to fish, to herd large animals, collect wild honey, and to clear the land and prepare it for planting. Women are usually involved in gathering wild plant foods. Other food production activities, such as collecting shellfish, caring for small animals, milking animals, and planting, tending, and harvesting crops, are not consistently assigned to either men or women. As a matter of fact, such tasks are often roles of either gender. Men usually butcher animals, while women most often cook, prepare vegetable foods, drinks, and dairy products, launder, carry water, and collect fuel. Preserving meat or fish for future use may be done by either men or women or by both.

The common division of labor that Murdock reported for food getting and preparation most often associates men with work that requires strength or rapid bursts of energy and women with work in which lower levels of strength are required for longer periods. This pattern seems to apply to other areas of work as well. For instance, men typically do woodworking, including felling trees, preparing wood, and building boats. They also are almost always the ones who mine and quarry stone, smelt ores, and work with bone, horn, and shell. Men usually build houses and make nets and ropes. On the other hand, spinning yarn is almost always done by women. Either or both genders prepare skins and make leather products, baskets, mats, clothing, or pottery. Whyte (1978a) has added to Murdock's list by noting that it is almost always men who are involved in warfare and who hold most positions of political leadership. Weisner and Gallimore (1977) have noted that child care is usually carried out by women.

According to J. K. Brown (1970), two other biological factors besides strength and metabolism also have an influence on gender roles: pregnancy and lactation. Since women of childbearing age in most parts of the world spend about half of their time either pregnant or nursing children, it is easy to see why women's roles usually include most of the child care responsibilities as well as other duties that can be carried out while pregnant or tending children. By contrast, men's roles include many activities that take them away from home for long periods, or activities that, although done near the home, must be done without the interruption that child care would involve. In addition, many male activities would be dangerous to children.

The common gender differences in tasks that seem unrelated to either strength or child care may simply be secondary effects of tasks that can be explained in these ways. For instance, men's involvement in making musical instruments is probably influenced by their other work with wood, just as their work at making nets and ropes may arise from the common use of these tools in activities such as fishing, trapping, and smelting. Although men's prominence in warfare may be related to their typically greater size and proportion of muscle to body weight, it is also true that many of men's roles, such as hunting and fishing, take them away from home to locations where strangers are more likely to be encountered. The weapons of war are also typically the same kinds of tools that men are accustomed to using in activities such as hunting. In small-scale societies, the association of men with warfare most certainly increases their likelihood of entering positions of political leadership where decisions are made about matters such as relations with neighboring groups of potential enemies.

Gender Roles and Subsistence

Women in the United States now represent about 46 percent of the paid labor force, and the typical family has two incomes. Nevertheless, women's income has not achieved equality with that of men, and married women's incomes average only about a quarter that of their husbands. This inequality helps to perpetuate women's greater involvement in contemporary U.S. domestic roles. Even when husbands and wives are employed for the same number of hours a week, U.S. women continue to bear the primary responsibility for shopping for groceries and clothing, cooking, doing the family laundry, and caring for the children.

A look at the broad range of human cultures shows clearly that the U.S. division of labor in which men have greater control over family income and women have more responsibilities at home is far from inevitable. Rather, the relative contribution of men and women to subsistence varies considerably, depending on how food is obtained. For instance, women in some foraging societies contribute as much as 80 percent of the calories their families eat (Service, 1962; Lee & DeVore, 1968b; Tanaka, 1977). However, on average women's subsistence production in *all* foraging societies represents about 28 percent of the family's food. Women's subsistence contribution tends to be larger than that in societies that practice horticulture or agriculture without irrigation. Peggy Sanday (1973) has reported that women produce from about 33 percent to about 45 percent of the subsistence in such societies (see Figure 5.3). However, more complex forms of food production technology, such as irrigation-based agriculture, are associated with heavy labor.

FIGURE 5.3

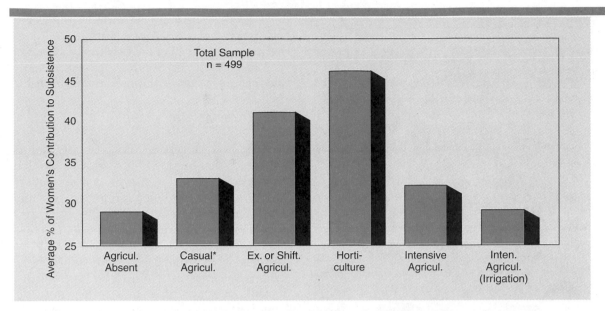

RELATIONSHIP BETWEEN TYPE AND INTENSITY OF AGRICULTURE AND AVERAGE PERCENTAGE OF WOMEN'S CONTRIBUTION TO SUBSISTENCE

*Less than 5% of total sample.

Source: From Peggy R. Sanday, "Toward a Theory of the Status of Women," *American Anthropologist, 75* (1973), p. 1691. Reproduced by permission of the American Anthropological Association.

The subsistence contribution of women is low in societies that practice intensive agriculture and is as low as that of foraging women where irrigation is part of the agricultural work. Although industrialized technology reduces the amount of physical labor women must perform well below the levels that are common in agrarian societies, the process of becoming industrialized involves increased poverty and deprivation among women in the lower social classes and rural women.

THIRD AND FOURTH GENDERS

Although all cultures have at least two genders, there are some in which third or fourth genders exist. These typically involve a change of the usual association of men's roles with the male sex and of women's roles with females. Three examples of third and fourth genders are the berdache, the hijra, and the transvestite.

The Berdache

A number of indigenous North American societies had a social status that has come to be known as the **berdache**, a female or male who had adopted a sex role that mixed the gender characteristics of both sexes. The berdache was particularly common among men of Plains Indians tribes where warfare was an almost sacred preoccupation and where the male role placed strong emphasis on demonstrations of pride, bravery, and daring. So the presence of the berdache has long been thought of as a cultural alternative for men who lacked the skill or interest in the aggressive pursuits of the traditional male role (Hoebel, 1949, p. 459). Such a man might instead opt for the life of a berdache by adopting the dress, work, and mannerisms of a woman.

The berdaches held a sacred status in many Native American societies. Often they played important ceremonial roles, and in some cases all shamans were required to be berdaches. A female who became a berdache actually moved up the status hierarchy and might achieve wealth and social prominence by doing so, since the change allowed her to participate in what were considered the more advantageous male pursuits such as trade. A berdache "man"

---

berdache a social status in which males and females adopt the role of the other sex; considered a third gender in some societies

FIGURE 5.4

BERDACHE

The last of the Crow male berdaches, Finds-Them-and-Kills-Them, illustrates the cross-dressing characteristic of this gender role. Males who assumed some of the work, dress, and behavior of a woman were accepted into their community because the berdache was a legitimate way to express a personality that was not compatible with the traditional Plains Indian man's role.

might marry and even rear children by having another man impregnate his wife, or a berdache "woman" might hire another woman as a surrogate mother.

The Hijra

Serena Nanda (1985, 1990) has described the *hijra*, a socially recognized third gender in India. The hijra, most of whom live in cities in north India, are regarded as neither male nor female, but their roles include elements of both. Like the berdaches of the North American Indians, the hijra gender also includes religious roles. As devotees of the Mother Goddess Baluchara Mata, the hijra are expected to undergo a surgical removal of their external genitalia and to live an asexual life. Their sexual abstinence is believed to be a source of sacredness that allows the hijra to give blessings of fertility, prosperity, and health or to cause infertility through their curses. The hijra perform as musicians and dancers at christenings and at weddings. In these roles, the hijra are spiritually identified with the Hindu god Shiva, who also plays the roles of singer, dancer, eunuch, and transvestite.

The Transvestite

Third and fourth gender roles generally include the expectation of cross-dressing or mixed-gender dressing, behavior known as **transvestism**. The transvestite fulfilled a common expectation of the berdache gender role of the indigenous people of North America and the behavior continues today in contemporary India. In societies in which third or fourth genders are accepted, it serves as a noticeable symbol of a person's special status. In societies in which only two genders are recognized, transvestism tends to be stigmatized and serves a somewhat different function. In these societies, people participate in cross-dressing for brief periods, in rituals, for recreation, or as a form of psychological release from gender-related role stresses. For instance, Richard Doctor (1988), who surveyed research on transvestism, found that in the United States and Europe, transvestism is most often engaged in by heterosexual males in covert settings.

GENDER, POWER, AND HONOR

The approach that analyzes culture and society by examining the relationships among social power, social honor, and gender is called **feminist anthropology**. Studies by feminist anthropologists have revealed some important new insights into the causes of inequality between women and men.

Sanday (1974) has suggested four measures of the social power of women's rank: (1) female control of material things such as land, produce, and crafts outside the domestic unit; (2) demand for women's produce outside the fam-

---

transvestism cross-dressing or mixed-gender dressing, a common part of the berdache gender role and of the Western transvestite status

feminist anthropology the anthropological approach that studies the relationships among social power, social honor, and gender

ily unit locally or in external markets; (3) women's right to participate in the political process in a way that influences policy affecting those outside their domestic unit; and (4) the presence of female solidarity groups that protect women's political or economic interests. She found that women's rank, evaluated by these measures, varied considerably from society to society, and that when women's economic contribution to subsistence was very high or very low compared to men's, women's power tended to be low. It was in the middle range, where men and women cooperated in subsistence production and contributed more or less equally to the economy, that women's social power was greatest. This suggests that economic dependency functions to perpetuate low levels of power for women, but that when women become the major economic mainstay of families, men tend to find other spheres for exerting their social power.

Gender Stratification

The differences in social power and honor that may exist between men and women are termed **gender stratification**. When there is no significant gender stratification, men and women are more or less equal in the deference and respect they receive and in their abilities to influence political decision making. This can be the case even when women do not normally hold political offices. Where gender stratification is significant, however, women's social power or honor, or both, are low.

In extreme cases of female subordination, women, stigmatized as inferior and spiritually dangerous to men, are in danger of rape, physical and psychological abuse, and murder. Such behaviors that inflict harm on females may even become accepted as valid customs under various circumstances. Carole Sheffield (1987) has called customs that employ violence against females and help maintain male control and domination of females through intimidation **sexual terrorism**.

Rape as Social Control. In some societies, rape or the threat of rape has been used as a mechanism for controlling women's behavior. For instance, Thomas Gregor (1982) described the Mehinaku of central Brazil, who segregated men and women and had a very strict division of labor by gender. The men's house was a sacred place and a social club from

which women were excluded. When women violated rules that forbade them from observing the sacred things of men, the Mehinaku used gang rape as punishment.

Among the Cheyenne Indians of the North American Plains, a wife who committed adultery could be punished by gang rape at the husband's request. He would invite the 30 to 40 unmarried men who were members of his military association but not members of his wife's clan to rape her. If she survived the ordeal, she still was stigmatized for the rest of her life.

Chinese Footbinding. Chinese footbinding is a form of physical abuse that became accepted as a custom. Until the 1920s many Chinese families bound the feet of their young daughters very tightly to keep them small into adulthood, a trait that was regarded as beautiful. According to Howard Levy (1966), the custom began within the upper class and demonstrated that a man should support a wife who could not walk well enough to work. Small feet became symbols of aristocracy and beauty, so the practice spread into the middle and even working classes. Normal feet, like those of farm women who had to work, were ridiculed as ugly. The process of binding involved extreme pain and led to permanent deformation of the woman's feet. The custom of footbinding was particularly difficult for poorer women whose feet had been bound but who had to walk in spite of the pain because they had to work. In the late 1920s the Chinese government exerted tremendous pressure against its people to end the custom.

Physical Abuse. The physical abuse of women is a major worldwide problem. For instance, Lori Heise (1989a) notes that "in Bangkok, Thailand, a reported 50 percent of married women are beaten regularly by their husbands. In the barrios of Quito, Ecuador, 80 percent of women are said to have been physically abused. And in Nicaragua, 44 percent of men admit to beating their wives or girlfriends. Equally shocking statistics can be found in the industrial world" (p. B1). According to physi-

---

gender stratification systematic differences in power and honor between men and women

sexual terrorism customs that employ violence against females in order to maintain male domination

cian Teri Randall (1990), in the United States abuse by a partner or spouse is the single most common cause of injury to women and visits by women to emergency rooms in hospitals. Injuries from abuse by husband or lover are more common than injuries from automobile accidents, muggings, and rapes combined. The annual cost of family violence in the United States includes $44 million direct costs, 175,000 days missed from paid work, 21,000 hospitalizations, 99,800 days of hospitalization, 28,700 emergency room visits, and 39,900 doctor visits. In a study by Jean Abbott, Robin Johnson, Jane Koziol-McLain, and Steven Lowenstein (1995) in Denver, Colorado, 54.2 percent of women reported having experienced domestic violence during their lifetimes, and 11.7 percent of these patients were seeking medical attention for domestic violence-related problems. The researchers also found that 12 percent of the women had been battered in the past 30 days. This was consistent with the results of a survey by physicians B. Elliot and M. Johnson (1995) of an outpatient clinic in a midwestern U.S. city with a population of 85,000, in which 12 percent of women reported currently being involved in a battering relationship.

Suttee. Another example of sexual terrorism was the custom of the suttee that was practiced in nineteenth-century India. A Hindu widow was expected to demonstrate her fidelity and love for her deceased husband by joining him on his funeral pyre. In traditional Hindu communities, the woman's status was defined so intensely in terms of her relationship with a husband that a widow was not permitted to remarry. A widow's sexual behavior would have dishonored her family. Her devotion to her husband, whom she should have loved and honored as a god, was expected to be so great that she would not have wished to survive without him. Mary Daly (1978) reports that since widows had no acceptable means of surviving, those who did not follow the custom of the suttee were sometimes forced into the fire by their relatives.

Purdah. Family honor is extremely important in many Islamic countries, and often deeply depends on the sexual purity of the female members of the family. That purity is ensured by the practice of purdah, or seclusion, in which women remain isolated from public view. Common features of purdah are the re-

striction of women to the inner parts of the home when guests are present and the rule of women's being veiled when outside the home. Violations of the rules of purdah are severely punished in some countries that follow the custom. Gideon M. Kressel (1981) analyzed societies where the murder of a sister or daughter is practiced to restore family honor when she has been publicly accused of consorting with a male. The act need not have included sexual intercourse. For instance, Kressel cites the example of a 13-year-old who was drowned after she had been berated by her brother when he caught her holding hands with a boy. The attacker is usually a brother, but is also frequently the father. The victim is most often in her teens, but may be a married woman. The homicide generally occurs after a public attack on the family's honor that the family is unable to address by other means, such as arranging a marriage between the couple. An arranged union may be problematic, however. If the boy is of a lower-ranked lineage, the marriage may not be acceptable to the girl's father, since it would lower the esteem of his lineage. Kressel believes that such homicides allow patrilineal kin groups to demonstrate their loyalty to the values of the society in which they are competing for social standing. They enhance the family's prestige and demonstrate the religious commitment of the attacker to societal values.

Gender in Patrilineal Societies

Patrilineal societies, especially those that also practice patrilocal residence, (see chapter 9, p. 238) provide a strong structural basis for the subordination of women. Patrilineality defines children by their relationship to their father and his relatives, thereby reinforcing the symbolism of male authority within families. It also can be the basis for uniting brothers in fraternal groups whose solidarity in work and warfare can perpetuate male economic dominance and aggressive roles that carry over into the domestic setting. Patrilocal residence further reinforces male dominance, since it separates married women from their birth families and brings them under the authority of their husbands' relatives. Female subordination in patrilineal, patrilocal societies is not inevitable, however. The structural disadvantages of these societies can be counterbalanced by other economic and political forces, a fact that will be discussed in the section of this chapter on matrifocality.

(Continued on p. 118)

WOMEN AND THE LAW IN THE VICTORIAN UNITED STATES

In some cases, the dominant role of men in the political institutions of society can be quite strongly entrenched and supported by ideas about the incompatability of political roles and women's nature. In such cases, the denial of women's access to full participation in society's formal political life can even be rationalized as a means of "protecting" women. The following excerpts from a decision by the Wisconsin Supreme Court in 1875 illustrate this "protective" rhetoric very well. In this decision Justice Edward G. Ryan denied Lavinia Goodell, one of the few women lawyers in the United States at that time, the right to argue one of her cases before that court:

In the Matter of the Motion to Admit Miss Lavinia Goodell to the Bar of This Court . . .

This is the first application for admission of a female to the bar of this court. And it is just matter for congratulation that it is made in favor of a lady whose character raises no personal objection, something perhaps not always to be looked for in women who forsake the ways of their sex for the ways of ours. . . .

So we find no statutory authority for the admission of females to the bar of any court of this state. And, with all the respect and sympathy for this lady which all men owe to all good women, we cannot regret that we do not. We cannot but think the common law wise in excluding women from the profession of the law. The profession enters largely into the well being of society; and, to be honorably filled and safely to society, exacts the devotion of life. The law of nature destines and qualifies the female sex for the bearing and nurture of the children of our race and for the custody of the homes of the world and their maintenance in love and honor. And all life-long callings of women, inconsistent with these radical and sacred duties of their sex, as is the profession of the law, are departures from the order of nature; and when voluntary, treason against it.

The cruel chances of life sometimes baffle both sexes, and may leave women free from the peculiar duties of their sex. These may need employment, and should be welcome to any not derogatory to their sex and its proprieties, or inconsistent with the good order of society. But it is public policy to provide for the sex, not for its superfluous members; and not to tempt women from the proper duties of their sex by opening to them duties peculiar to ours.

There are many employments in life not unfit for female character. The profession of the law is surely not one of these.

The peculiar qualities of womanhood, its gentle graces, its quick sensibility, its tender susceptibility, its purity, its delicacy, its emotional impulses, its subordination of hard reason to sympathetic feeling, are surely not qualifications for forensic strife. Nature has tempered woman as little for the juridical conflicts of the court room, as for the physical conflicts of the battle-field. Womanhood is moulded for gentler and better things. And it is not the saints of the world who chiefly give employment to our profession. It has essentially and habitually to do with all that is selfish and malicious, knavish and criminal, course and brutal, repulsive and obscene, in human life.

It would be revolting to all female sense of the innocence and sanctity of their sex, shocking to man's reverence for womanhood and faith in woman, on which hinge all the better affections and humanities of life, that woman should be permitted to mix professionally in all the nastiness of the world which finds its way into courts of justice; all the unclean issues, all the collateral questions of sodomy, incest, rape, seduction, fornication, adultery, pregnancy, bastardy, legitimacy, prostitution, lascivious cohabitation, abortion, infanticide, obscene publications, libel and slander of sex, impotence, divorce: all the nameless catalogue of indecencies, *la chronique scandaleuse* [the scandalous chronicle] of all the vices and all the infirmities of all society, with which the profession has to deal, and which go towards filling judicial reports which must be read for accurate knowledge of the law. This is bad enough for men.

We hold in too high reverence the sex without which, as is truly and beautifully written, *le commencement de la vie est sans secours, le milieu sans plaisir, et le fin sans consolation* [the beginning of life is without assistance, the middle is without pleasure, and the end without consolation], voluntarily to commit it to such studies and such occupations. *Non tali auxilio nec defensoribus istis* [Not with such help or with those defenders], should judicial contests be upheld. Reverence for all womanhood would suffer in the public spectacle of woman so instructed and so engaged. . . .

By the Court.—The motion is denied.
(39 Wis. 232 [1875])

Sexual Equality in Vanatinai Society

Anthropologists have long been attracted to South Pacific islands for more than the warm breezes and sparkling lagoons. They go to such places seeking in the simpler societies the rudiments of human community, sometimes glimpsing a rough-hewn harmony beyond the experience of more complex societies.

So it was for Dr. Maria Lepowsky, who in 1978 became the first and only anthropologist to live with the people of Sudest Island—or to use the local name, Vanatinai, meaning motherland. This is a sparsely populated island in the Louisiade Archipelago of Papua New Guinea, which extends southeast of New Guinea and separates the Solomon and the Coral seas. The people there are an anthropologist's dream because they have had only minimal contact with Western colonialism and missionaries.

The longer Dr. Lepowsky observed the people, sharing their daily lives for two years and learning their rituals and ideologies, the more she realized that life on Vanatinai was different from other societies in one fundamental respect. Men and women were living and working as virtual equals. This was, she concluded, a striking example of what anthropologists call a gender-egalitarian culture, and perhaps the first one to be studied in detail by any anthropologist.

"It is not a place where men and women live in perfect harmony and where the privileges and burdens of both sexes are exactly equal," Dr. Lepowsky said, "but it comes close."

Close enough, she said, to challenge the position of some theorists in anthropology that male dominance is universal or somehow inherent in human cultures and that only its forms and intensity vary. The new findings suggest instead that the island's culture could serve as a model of what a sex-egalitarian society would be like and a countermodel to relations between the sexes and ideologies in nearly all other cultures. . . .

Dr. Lepowsky acknowledged that the island's small population of 2,300 and remoteness favored the development and preservation of such a society. On Vanatinai, everyone participates in community decisions, meeting face to face, instead of delegating power to a few leaders, who might tend to be men. Vanatinai has no chief.

Another factor, she said, is that the culture is matrilineal, with kinship traced through the mother's clan and women inheriting and owning land and other property. Other matrilineal societies do not approach equality of the sexes. But on Vanatinai, the central position of women in island life is said to be taubwaragha, which means both "ancient" and "the way of the ancestors."

Dr. Lepowsky found evidence of the equality on every hand. Unlike other Pacific cultures, Vanatinai has no special men's meeting houses or male cult activities. The language is gender-neutral, with no pronouns like he or she. Boys as well as girls care for younger siblings, and men are expected to share in child care as fathers. In many other New Guinea societies, which consider women inferior to men, menstruation is thought of as a form of pollution and menstruating women must go into seclusion, but not on Vanatinai. Women there also have as much sexual freedom as men.

Young people on the island are considered to be adults once they have entered into a stable marriage. They frequently marry several times before they settle into a lasting relationship. The new husband is expected to spend several months to a year in "bride service," living with and working for the wife's parents and presumably earning their approval. Later on, the couple normally alternates living with the wife's kin and the husband's.

Although their god of creation is a male named Rodyo, the mythology includes powerful female spirits and the theme of the "wise woman." Both

Male Dominance

A fundamental concept for understanding male dominance is the idea of **patriarchy**, a form of society in which access to social power and prestige is unequally distributed by gender to men. The culture and customs of a patriarchal society assume that male privilege is normal, and both men and women in such societies may resist challenges to patriarchal institutions. The structure of a patriarchy can make it extremely difficult for members to perceive or acknowledge that some of their customs function in ways that victimize women. As a matter of fact, most of us live in societies in which the privileges of power and prestige are unequally divided in a variety of ways besides gender: race, ethnic origins, religion, and various other social statuses. Gender is but one of the many ways in which inequality can be manifested.

---

patriarchy a form of society in which access to social power and prestige is available primarily to men

men and women have access to supernatural power through communication with ancestors and other spirits. Women as well as men can possess special knowledge of magical spells and ritual techniques, sources of power in the community. Either a man or woman can preside over the crucial public ritual at the time of planting yams, one of the island's main crops. . . .

[W]omen on Vanatinai have equal access to the culture's most significant form of authority and influence. Through hard work, ritual generosity and acquisition of supernatural knowledge, anyone may achieve the gender-blind title of gia, or giver. It is a version of the "big man" on other islands, who gains prestige by accumulating goods and then giving them away at ritual feasts.

On Vanatinai, Dr. Lepowsky reported, women figure prominently in the acquisition of ceremonial valuables like shell necklaces and greenstone ax blades. They may lead their own expeditions to other islands to trade for these goods. It is a "dramatic indicator of the sexually egalitarian nature of the culture," she said.

In some ways, though, it is not perfectly egalitarian. Dr. Lepowsky observed that younger women were likely to spend more time caring for children and gardening and less on building reputations as a giver.

"The average woman spends more of her time sweeping up the pig excrement that dots the hamlet," she wrote. "The average man spends more time hunting wild boar in the rain forest with his spear. His hunting is more highly valued and accorded more prestige by both sexes than her daily maintenance of hamlet cleanliness and household order."

Nonetheless, Dr. Lepowsky concluded, "the example of Vanatinai shows that the subjugation of women by men is not a human universal, and it is not inevitable."

VANATINAI SOCIETY

The people of Sudest Island, or Vanatinai have developed a nearly perfect gender-egalitarian culture. The women have as much authority and influence as the men; anyone may achieve the gender-blind title of gia, or giver. Women have as much sexual freedom as do men, and may lead their own expeditions to other islands to trade for ceremonial goods. Their society challenges the concept that male dominance is universal and inevitable.

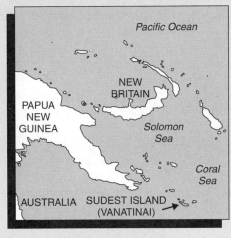
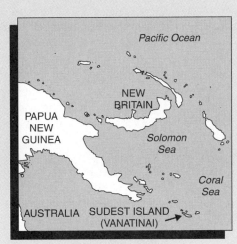
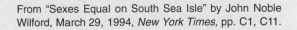

From "Sexes Equal on South Sea Isle" by John Noble Wilford, March 29, 1994, *New York Times*, pp. C1, C11.

Gender in Matrilineal Societies

Whyte (1978b) examined a cross-cultural sample and found that there was a tendency for women's status to be higher where descent groups were matrilineal and marital residence was matrilocal. In these societies, women often owned property, including houses and food-producing land, held economic responsibilities such as setting prices and marketing produce, and wielded substantial influence in the day-to-day running of community affairs.

Matrifocality

Nancy Tanner (1974) discussed the concept of **matrifocality**, a form of social system in which high female status is maintained by the absence of men and female control of food production. Matrifocality is common in matrilineal socie-

---

matrifocality a form of society in which high social status is assumed by females primarily because they control food production and because the male is absent much of the time

FIGURE 5.5

MATRILINEAL SOCIETIES

Women often own property, hold economic responsibilities, and market produce, thus gaining high status in matrilineal societies. These Minangkabau women of Malaysia own their ancestral rice fields and thus wield considerable power in their society.

ties, but may also occur in patrilineal societies. For instance, the Ibo of eastern Nigeria is a patrilineal society that follows a patrilocal residence rule at marriage. Ibo men enter polygynous marriages, but since they are involved in long-distance trading that keeps them away much of the time, each wife has her own house and garden and controls the products of her own labor. Marketing of surplus produce occurs locally, where the prices are set by a women's organization. The independence that this matrifocal lifestyle promotes functions to keep women's status high even in this patrilineal, patrilocal society.

Matriarchies.   The idea of *matriarchies*, societies in which men are dominated politically and economically by women, is a common mythological theme in many male-dominated societies. Peggy Sanday (1981) found that such myths are particularly common in societies where men are the nominal authority figures in families but where women actually have a great deal of autonomy. In these societies, myths of an earlier matriarchy may be indicative of a degree of male anxiety about his authority. It was even suggested by some anthropologists in the last century that there may have been an early period in the evolution of cultures in which matriarchy was the normal social order. However, anthropological fieldwork has never discovered an existing matriar-

chal society, and the idea that such societies may have existed in the past is rejected by almost all anthropologists today (Bamberger, 1974).

The Causes of Gender Inequality

Various causes have been suggested for gender inequality. Prominent among these have been men's role in warfare and the economic division of labor by gender.

Warfare.   Marvin Harris (1974) points out that the dominance of males in nonindustrialized societies is likely when the male role in warfare is compatible with their day-to-day domination of local community life. Thus, in societies in which warfare is waged primarily between neighboring communities, the type of conflict called internal warfare in chapter 11, the aggressive role of males as warriors is carried over into their daily social roles as leaders of their local communities and families. In such societies, women are expected to play subordinated roles and are often treated as objects of barter between warriors. Divale and Harris (1976) have noted that internal warfare correlates with an unbalanced sex ratio in which there are fewer women than men, which results from the high value placed on sons in these warlike societies and is partly brought about by the practice of female infanticide. Because the sex ratio imbalance then makes it difficult for young men to find wives, a man's desire to prove his valor in battle and thus obtain a wife can be a powerful psychological motive for participation in warfare.

The role of warfare in the subordination of women does not hold in external warfare when it (or economic activities such as long-distance trade) removes men from their local communities for prolonged periods. The day-to-day economic and political life of local communities is then in the hands of women, and inheritance is typically handed down from mother to child. In such societies, women often have high rank, and men's aggressive warrior roles convey no special privileges on the men when they return home, since property is owned and inherited by women.

Economics.   Lisette Josephides (1985) contends that male access to strategic resources is a primary factor in male dominance over women. Friedl (1975) has argued that the cru-

NONTRADITIONAL FEMALE ROLES

Women who move into nontraditional roles may invite social antagonism in some cultures. In South Asia, however, women have been elected leaders of a number of countries; Benazir Bhutto has twice been chosen prime minister of Pakistan. Here she reviews a female unit of the army.

cial issue in the control of economic goods is whether men have exclusive rights to decide how these goods will be used and distributed outside the domestic setting. For instance, the distribution of meat by hunters in foraging bands, the distribution of economic goods by bigmen in horticultural tribes, or the predominance of men in managerial positions that control other employees' salaries can be a source of male dominance when women do not also participate in these roles. In societies where men monopolize these activities, women's contribution to family income might equal or excel that of men, but they are still likely to experience subordination. In effect, male control over the extradomestic use of goods, including resources produced by women, becomes a means for "buying" higher status. Heidi Hartmann (1976) argues that the indirect and impersonal mechanisms of control that emerged with capitalism perpetuated male control over women by enforcing lower wages for women by job segregation, thereby creating pressure for women to marry. This not only advantages men both economically and domestically, but also creates a vicious cycle of subordination for women.

Sanday (1973) has suggested that men's absence from the local community for long-distance trade or for working in distant towns may give women greater local control over important economic resources, but she also has pointed out (1974) that women's economic productivity is not necessarily reflected in greater social respect. For instance, according to Siegfried Frederick Nadel (1952), among the Nupe of Nigeria, women's economic position is generally much better than their husbands', but Nupe men fear and resent women openly.

The importance of women's control over valued economic resources is illustrated in many western African societies such as the Ibo, where women's roles included the sale of produce in markets controlled by women. In these societies, women had very high social standing. Similarly, among the Plains Indians of the United States, male and female economic roles were very different. Men hunted the bison, an extremely important resource that provided not only food, but also hides, sinew, and bones used to make many tools. However, in spite of men's very aggressive roles when it came to intertribal warfare or the policing of village life,

Plains women had very high status that derived, at least in part, from growing the plant foods that were the staples of the Plains diet. The beans and corn that they grew met people's nutritional needs for protein even when men brought in no meat from the hunt. Thus, Plains women owned and controlled a critical resource that freed them from economic dependence on men. These examples contrast with the lot of many New Guinea highlands women whose work in the family gardens and in managing the care of the family pig herds was the basic source of food and wealth. Although they produced these goods, the property and produce were considered to be owned by their husbands, so women lacked control over the fruits of their own labor and had rather low social standing.

Mary Nelson (1989) suggests that social change in the roles of women can be a source of antagonism towards them by men. For instance, the Inquisition occurred in Europe during a time when women were entering new forms of employment. Hundreds of thousands of women, particularly those who were not following their traditional gender roles, were accused of witchcraft and put to death—a practice that came to an end soon after men as well as women became potential targets of witchcraft accusations.

In the contemporary secular cultures of the West, many women who move from earlier traditional gender roles to those less traditional are commonly victims of social antagonism. For instance, in the United States, employed women have been accused of causing a supposed decline in family values and an increase in social problems among children. Even psychiatric labeling sometimes has been used to legitimize the victimization of women. In the last century, women who did not conform to mainstream values about gender roles sometimes found themselves defined as mentally ill. More recently, several new gender-related diagnostic categories have been suggested by U.S. mental health practitioners, including one, Self-Defeating Personality Disorder, that portrays battered women as provokers of their own abuse, and another, Paraphilic Coercive Disorder, that potentially could be used by a man as a legal defense against rape. These controversial categories stimulated much debate, and neither achieved the status of official diagnostic categories in the 1994 revision of the American Psychiatric Association's diagnostic manual.

GENDER AND RELIGION

The institution of religion is a powerful force in molding people's attitudes and values. The ideology of religion includes, among other things, creation mythologies using gender symbolism and religious rules that tend to verify men's and women's roles in society. The gendered division of labor within the social structure of religious groups also tends to reflect gender stratification within their societies and is often interpreted as evidence for supernatural support for similar gender stratification in society at large. Thus, religion is often a prominent factor in maintaining gender stratification.

Gender Symbolism

Numerous studies have documented the ways in which a culture's symbolism expresses the social roles of men and women (see Ortner, 1974, and Strathern, 1980). Sanday (1981) has shown that gender differences often manifest themselves in the descriptions of the world. For instance, in societies in which women are markedly subordinate to men, untamed nature is often regarded as symbolically female in contrast with the "masculine" realm of culture. Patriarchal societies also typically emphasize masculine deities in their mythologies, while egalitarian societies often utilize feminine symbolism. For instance, in egalitarian Iroquois society, the supreme creator was a female deity, the Ancient Bodied One, and it was her daughter who gave birth to humans. On the other hand, the Mosaic deity, Yahweh, was a war god who led the Hebrews in their conquest of Canaan and the building of a kingdom.

Where men's and women's roles are equal in everyday life, female deities are prominent in creation stories, and female symbolism predominates: birth, creativity, and progress usually originate from *within* something such as water or earth. Female creators work alone or in conjunction with male deities, and bring forth humans from the earth, mold them from clay, transform them from plants or animals, or carve them from wood. The symbolism of female deities is illustrated by the creation story of the Yuchi Indians of North Carolina, reported by Speck (1909): Humans originated from the union of the earth with a drop of menstrual blood that had fallen from the Sun, a female deity (pp. 205–207).

In contrast, where women's roles are markedly subordinate to those of men, the religious symbolism of creation typically emphasizes male gods who come down from the sky, and themes of warfare, aggression, and sexuality. In these societies, humans are usually created out of the god's body, by acts of sexual intercourse or through self-fertilization by the god. In male-dominant societies, things that are identified with women may be regarded as supernaturally dangerous, especially to men. For instance, according to M. Meggitt (1964), men of the Enga of the western New Guinea highlands obtained their wives from competing neighbors and said, "We marry the people we fight" (p. 218). Enga men believed that women's menstrual blood was a dangerous substance that could destroy men's ability to achieve wealth, pigs, or success in war.

Male-dominant societies also often use cultural symbolism that characterizes females as the originators of various forms of evil, such as sin, illness, and death. For instance, in the Judeo-Christian story of the origin of human beings, it is Eve who succumbs to the temptation of the serpent and commits the first sin, the cause of death and the curse of pain in childbirth. In Greek mythology, illness, greed, and death were released into the world through Pandora's impulsiveness and uncontrolled curiosity.

Gender in the Religious Institution

Where gender equality is present, women's roles are likely to include those of religious practitioners. For instance, among many of the egalitarian Indians of northern California, shamans were always women. Gender stratification, on the other hand, is often associated with practices such as segregating male and female worshippers, excluding women from religious roles, or restricting them to shamanistic rituals that are subordinate to the ecclesiastical rituals of male priests. Thus, the exclusive ceremonial men's houses of South America and the New Guinea highlands, and comparable ceremonial groups among aboriginal Australians, had political, economic, and religious functions that fostered male dominance. Women were typically forbidden to participate in or even observe the religious rituals practiced by men in these settings. In other male-dominant socie-

FIGURE 5.7

MEN'S HOUSE

In many societies, males attempt to retain sole knowledge of myths of human origin and the nature of the supernatural. They exclude women and children from their initiation rites and their separate residences. This is the interior of a men's house in New Guinea.

ties, women maintained a separate religious system. For instance, in many Middle Eastern countries where men may hold a number of different positions as ritual practitioners within Islam, the dominant ecclesiastical religion, women may participate in a variety of "women's cults" in which female shamans enter trances and become possessed by spirits to serve as mediums, diviners, and curers for their clients. Similarly, according to I. M. Lewis (1971), Korean shamanism, a religious form that contrasts with the ecclesiastical role of male priests, is primarily a women's activity, providing them with a psychological outlet for the stresses of their subordinated roles in Korean secular life. According to E. Bourguignon and L. Greenberg (1973), in these male-dominant settings, spirit possession symbolism figures prominently in women's religious ritualism.

SEX-BASED PERSECUTION AS A BASIS FOR ASYLUM IN THE UNITED STATES

Thanks to the efforts of feminist lawyers from the Women Refugees Project at Harvard Law School and individuals from 35 other groups, the United States became the second country in the world [in addition to Canada] to offer political asylum to women persecuted because of their gender. The new guidelines, announced by the Immigration and Naturalization Service (INS) on May 26, formally recognize rape, domestic abuse, genital mutilation, slavery, forced marriage, and other forms of violence against women as potential grounds for protection. Women are eligible for asylum as long as they can prove that their personal political beliefs made them a specific target of state persecution.

In the past, sexual violence has been viewed by the INS and immigration courts largely as a private act, even when committed by soldiers or government officials. Rape, for example, was often seen as a street crime rather than as a form of torture or punishment.

But partly because of the mass rape of women in Bosnia and increased awareness of such issues as domestic violence, the INS acknowledged that there are distinct forms of persecution suffered only by women. . . .

Along with these new guidelines, two other recent developments constitute a new way of applying existing political asylum laws to women. The Inter-American Commission for Human Rights of the Organization of the American States issued a report saying that rape was used as a form of political torture to Haiti. And the Board of Immigration Appeal established as a precedent the asylum of a Haitian woman who was raped in retaliation for her support for President Jean-Bertrand Aristide.

From "Women Refugees Offered Asylum for Gender Violence" by Linda Wong, July 1995, *Sojourner, 20* (11), p. 20.

WOMEN'S RIGHTS AS HUMAN RIGHTS

A number of countries that have signed international human rights documents that include guarantees of equal treatment of women regularly cite religious values concerning the "sanctity of the family" as grounds for not enforcing these clauses. For instance, Rebecca Cook (1990) reports that Bangladesh, Egypt, Iraq, Libya, and Tunisia have accepted the UN's 1979 Convention on the Elimination of All Forms of Discrimination against Women, but reserve the right not to follow its obligations when they conflict with Islamic law. Malawi, too, excepts obligations wherever they conflict with its customary law. Iraq, South Korea, and Turkey have maintained the right not to grant women the same rights as men to acquire, change, or retain their nationality. And in Cyprus, Egypt, Iraq, Jamaica, South Korea, Thailand, and Tunisia, where children are deemed to have the nationality of their father, the convention is not accepted. Leslie Calman (1987) has argued that since "women generally have had little influence over political definitions of 'public' moral-

ity, the primacy of this value over that of individual rights is detrimental to women" (p. 1).

One major effect of the inequality of women in patriarchal societies is the cultural tendency to equate "human" more readily with men than with women. This is more than a simple matter of semantics. It has tremendous practical significance that adversely impacts women. One effect of this distinction is that the international political concern for "human rights" often focuses on those rights that are of greatest concern to men. For instance, Calman has discussed the fact that political rights violations against women have frequently been treated as a *woman's* issue rather than as a *human* rights issue. M. Mejer (1985), has given an exemplary account of this contrast, documenting the difficulties of women in obtaining refugee status when they have fled violent and coercive situations. When political issues that concern the violation of women's rights are discussed, they are often treated as a different and less important category.

Margaret Schuler (1986) has summarized some of the major categories of human rights violations that frequently affect women in particular: (1) economic exploitation, including the failure of governments to provide minimum

ANNOUNCEMENT OF PEACE PRIZE

OSLO, Oct. 16 (AP)—Following is the Norwegian Nobel Committee's announcement today that the 1992 Peace Prize had been awarded to Rigoberta Menchú of Guatemala:

The Norwegian Nobel Committee has decided to award the Nobel Peace Prize for 1992 to Rigoberta Menchú from Guatemala, in recognition of her work for social justice and ethno-cultural reconciliation based on respect for the rights of indigenous peoples.

Like many other countries in South and Central America, Guatemala has experienced great tension between the descendants of European immigrants and the native Indian population. In the 1970's and 1980's, that tension came to a head in the large-scale repression of Indian peoples. Menchú has come to play an increasingly prominent part as an advocate of native rights.

Rigoberta Menchú grew up in poverty, in a family that has undergone the most brutal suppression and persecution. In her social and political work, she has always borne in mind that the long-term objective of the struggle is peace.

Today, Rigoberta Menchú stands out as a vivid symbol of peace and reconciliation across ethnic, cultural and social dividing lines, in her own country, on the American continent and in the world.

From *New York Times*, Oct. 17, 1992, p. 1.

QUICHÉ INDIAN

Rigoberta Menchú, a Quiché Indian from Guatemala in Central America, won the Nobel Peace Prize in 1992. She has worked to prevent violence against indigenous people in her native Guatemala and for peace around the world.

---

wage laws for occupations filled primarily by women, and the lack of day-care rights; (2) lack of equal treatment of women by family law (such as the failure of governments to grant women the right to obtain a divorce and the imposition of greater punishments for crimes such as adultery, and the lack of inheritance rights); (3) denial of reproductive rights (including the right to contraceptive information, access to safe contraceptive technologies, the right to obtain medically safe abortions, and the right to bear children); and (4) violence and exploitation (including domestic violence, rape, sexual harassment, and coerced prostitution). Calman adds that women's human rights should also be understood to include political rights (such as the right to vote and to hold public office) and the right to an education.

Economic Exploitation

However poverty is measured, women comprise a major and growing proportion of the

FIGURE 5.8

RIGOBERTA MENCHÚ

Human rights violations around the world have a cultural tendency to be considered more relevant to males than to females. Rigoberta Menchú, a Quiché Indian from Guatemala, has fought to restore rights not only to her own people, but to all people throughout the Americas. She was awarded the Nobel Peace Prize in 1992.

WHAT'S IN A NAME?

In the United States it has been a tradition until recently for a woman to adopt her husband's surname when she marries. The custom is still so common that the government routinely cooperates in name changes with a minimum of formality. It is a rather easy matter for a woman to obtain a new driver's license with a new surname by merely showing a marriage certificate. In Utah, however, two women recently discovered that it is not as easy for that change to be reversed following a divorce.

In 1988 Wendy Jean Alldridge Jorgenson attempted to have her driver's license reissued under her birth name, Alldridge. She presented the motor vehicles department with her divorce decree and her birth certificate. Although the state still had a record of the earlier license under her birth name, she was informed that the department's unwritten policy was to make such a change only if a woman obtained a judicial order to that effect. Ms. Alldridge challenged the legality of the policy in court. In October 1989 U.S. District Judge J. Thomas Greene ruled against her. He informed Ms. Alldridge that she had two alternatives. The first was to have her divorce decree amended to include the name change, which would require her to seek her ex-husband's permission. Otherwise, it would be necessary for her to go through the costly process of requesting a

legal name change in court. Ms. Alldridge tried to have the judge's decision overturned, but the 10th U.S. Circuit Court of Appeals upheld the lower court's decision in April 1991.

Utah is not unique in the United States in assuming that a woman's identity and her name depend on her relationship to a man. In 1990, Lucille Anne Riccitelli of Providence, Rhode Island, decided to resume her birth name to honor her father after he died without any sons. She was successful in having the name on her driver's license and Social Security card changed, but when she tried to change her name on a joint bank account that she and her mother had at Fleet National Bank, they insisted on a court document to validate the name change. Probate Judge Anthony B. Sciarretta told Ms. Riccitelli that she would have to get her husband's permission before he would grant her request for the name change. Although Ms. Riccitelli's husband, Edward Martin, supported his wife's wish to use her father's surname, she and her husband agreed that requiring his consent was inappropriate, since the requirement treated Ms. Riccitelli as if she were a minor without independent legal rights. Nevertheless, Judge Sciarretta denied her petition because she refused to obtain her husband's permission.

---

world's poor today. This trend is known as the **feminization of poverty**. Poverty is especially a problem of older women and younger women with children. Worldwide, a third of all households are headed by women. Since women receive less income than men in all countries, and since they are so much more likely than men to have to bear the expense of childrearing alone when a family is headed by one parent, it is not surprising that women are generally poorer than men.

In the United States, the trend toward the poor being primarily women and children began after World War II. According to information from the U.S. Census Bureau, as of 1990 about two-thirds of all people living in poverty in the United States were female. The problem of poverty in single-parent families is particularly acute, since child-care responsibilities often mean choosing between day-care expenses that make employment unprofitable or accepting low-paid, part-time work that is more

compatible with less expensive ways of organizing child care, such as pooling work and babysitting with friends or relatives. For many women neither of these options proves successful, and the circumstances of single-parent life force them into dependence on the welfare system. Currently, about half of women in poverty are more or less permanently reliant on public welfare or on the support of friends or relatives.

Equality in Family Law

The family is considered a separate entity in legal matters. For instance, the enforcement of laws pertaining to families is under the authority of kinship groups in chiefdoms. In societies with state governments that monopolize the

---

feminization of poverty a growing trend in which women comprise a large proportion of the world's poor

right to use force, the law often treats the family as a special institution. Laws that do not support the traditional customs of family life may exempt the family from the usual rules of law. Even when family life is not exempted from the principles of law that might impinge on it, enforcement of those laws may not be rigorous. Thus, the legal rights of men and women may differ significantly in matters that members of society perceive as related to the family.

The insularity of the family makes it an institution in which gender inequality can lead to abuses that are not publicly addressed. Thus, in many societies a husband can avoid the charge of murder by asserting that the killing was done in defense of "family honor." For instance, until 1989 Brazilian courts accepted the defense of family honor in cases where it judged that the killing was in response to a wife's adultery.

The right to choose one's own spouse and the right to divorce are not equally available to men and women in many societies. For instance, Gail Cairns (1984) reports that in nine Latin American countries, the grounds for divorce are not the same for men and women. In five countries adultery by a husband is grounds for divorce only if it involves a public scandal, while adultery by a wife is sufficient grounds for a husband to be granted a divorce. In El Salvador, a woman is not permitted to remarry for 300 days after the final divorce decree. In Israel a husband's consent is generally required for a Jewish divorce, and in Middle Eastern countries that follow Islamic law, a similar rule applies unless an exemption is granted by a cleric.

Reproductive Rights

The right to control one's own reproductive life is limited in various ways in most of the countries of the world today. For instance, Mosher (1983) has documented the strong governmental role in limiting family size in the People's Republic of China. Under a legal policy that limits each family to having only one child, women who become pregnant a second time have been put under strong pressure to terminate their pregnancies. In some instances women have been coerced into undergoing unwanted abortions as late as in the seventh month of pregnancy. Diana Russell and Nicole Van de Ven (1976) reported that during the 1960s, Puerto Rico's government policy of con-

FIGURE 5.9

LIMITS ON REPRODUCTIVE RIGHTS
China's one-child-per-family policy has involved both rewards for couples that have only one child and measures such as forced abortions for women who conceive a second time. This couple is pictured with their daughter in Hohhot, Inner Mongolia; because of the policy there have been reports of female infanticide by couples who want a boy instead of a girl.

trolling population growth had resulted in 35 percent of women of childbearing age being sterilized, in most cases without the use of the sterilization consent form required by law. Research indicated that 19.5 percent of these women reported health complications, and 10 percent reported that their relationships suffered as a result of their sterilization.

While some countries have imposed limitations on women's reproductive rights, others, by government action, have limited or denied women's access to contraceptive information and abortion. As described in Chapter 4, p. 88, the extremes that such a policy took in Romania under the regime of Nicolae Ceaușescu, where government was concerned for the nation's low birth rate, practically mandated pregnancy. Romanian law forbade sexuality education, contraception, and abortion. Women who failed to conceive were fined a "celibacy tax" of up to 10 percent of their salaries, and pregnant women who miscarried were suspected of having had an abortion and were summoned for questioning. These policies ended in December 1989 when Ceauşescu was overthrown. Although the Romanian policies represent an extreme, government efforts to increase population are still pursued in many countries through policies that restrict or deny women family planning services.

Violence

While physical abuse by partners is the most common form of violence against women worldwide, there are many other sources of physical harm that commonly impact women more than men. For example, Mitra Das (1989) has documented the rise in frequency of dowry-related wife burnings in parts of India. These developed because of the economic changes that resulted from industrialization, which has particularly affected lower-caste families, for whom large dowries have become increasingly important. Decades ago, dowries in India were gifts that a woman received from her parents when she married. Now, the dowry gifts are paid to her in-laws, who many times perceive them to be inadequate, instead of to the bride. Dowry deaths, often caused by setting fire to a kerosene-doused woman, were described as "kitchen accidents." Such a death allowed the family to acquire another dowry when the husband remarried. The problem has become so common that the Ahmedabad Women's Action Group has estimated that as many as 1,000 women may have been burned alive in Gujarat, India, in 1987.

Political Rights

In many countries today, women are denied political rights in a variety of ways. For instance, in Kuwait and Bhutan, men, but not women, have the right to vote. In other cases, human rights violations occur against both men and women, but the violations of women's rights are systematically different from the political abuses that are experienced by men. For instance, both women and men are involved in cases of arrest and detention without trial in a variety of countries and may experience torture as political prisoners. However, politically motivated violence against women frequently involves rape as an aspect of political torture, as witnessed most recently in Haiti and Bosnia-Herzegovina (Adams, 1989; Ashworth, 1986; Anonymous, 1987, Anonymous 1989; Heise, 1989b; Tambiah, 1986). Sexual slavery is another human rights violation that particularly affects women. Women in various parts of the world are held forcibly in slavery today, but because this practice is associated with forced prostitution, it has not been addressed as a "human rights" issue in such institutions as the United Nations. Member nations are not required to submit statistics on the practice. Women forced into prostitution under such conditions have not been recognized as deserving of refugee status and receive no special protections, but have, in some countries, been arrested and imprisoned even though their participation in prostitution had been involuntary.

CHAPTER SUMMARY

1. Gender is a social and cultural identity that consists of the roles a person is expected to play because of his or her sex.

2. There is great cross-cultural variety in how the genders are perceived.

3. Some societies have more than two gender categories.

4. In many societies, men's gender roles have greater privilege with respect to power and honor.

5. The presence or absence of male dominance is influenced by a society's kinship system, the nature of its warfare, and its economic customs.

6. Religion provides supernatural support for society's gender-role traditions and portrays gender differences in the symbolism of its creation stories.

7. Women's human rights have often been ignored in areas such as economics, family law, reproductive rights, protection from violence, and political rights.

ANNOTATED READINGS

Blackwood, E. (Ed.). (1986). *The many faces of homosexuality: Anthropological approaches to homosexual behavior.* New York: Harrington Park Press. A collection of important anthropological articles that examine homosexual roles in a variety of cultural and theoretical contexts.

di Leonardo, M. (Ed.). (1991). *Gender at the crossroads of knowledge: Feminist anthropology in a postmodern era.* Berkeley, CA: University of California Press. A collection of specialized essays on feminist anthropological studies of gender and society.

Ginsburg, F., & Tsing, A. (Eds.). (1990). *Uncertain terms: Negotiating gender in U.S. culture.* Boston: Beacon Press. A collection of essays on gender in the United States.

Moore, H. (1988). *Feminism and anthropology.* Minneapolis, MN: University of Minnesota Press. Provides a good general overview of feminist perspectives in anthropology.

Morgan, S. (Ed.). (1989). *Gender and anthropology: Critical reviews for research and teaching.* Washington, DC: American Anthropological Association. A review of gender studies that covers both gender roles in the major world regions and a variety of general issues pertaining to gender.

Nanda, S. (1990). *Neither man nor woman: The Hijras of India.* Belmont, CA: Wadsworth Publishing Company. An excellent account of a third gender in India.

Roscoe, W. (1991). *The Zuñi man-woman.* Albuquerque, NM: University of New Mexico Press. The life history of We'wha, the most well known Zuñi berdache.

Sanday, P. R. (1981). *Female power and male dominance: On the origins of sexual inequality.* New York: Cambridge University Press. A cross-cultural examination of sex role inequality and the ways in which sex role differences are symbolized.

Sanday, P. R., & Gallagher, R. (Eds.). (1990). *Beyond the second sex: New directions in the anthropology of gender.* Philadelphia: University of Pennsylvania Press. A collection of challenging essays that incorporates new approaches to analzying gender and culture, including insights into the diversity of ways that culture and gender can be perceived.

PART TWO

Adaptation, Cultural Change, and Cultural Diversity

CHAPTER SIX
ENVIRONMENT, ADAPTATION, AND SUBSISTENCE

Humans have learned to live in such diverse environments as icy polar lands and rainy tropical forests. Foraging and food domestication are the two ways societies acquire food, a basic survival need for any society. Each has its implications for how people organize the rest of their lives. Industrialization of agriculture is a modern adaptation of the food-gathering process that has had a profound effect on the cultural and social developments of the societies that use it.

CHAPTER SEVEN
CULTURAL EVOLUTION AND THE CONTEMPORARY WORLD

The dynamics of change are predicated on the readiness of a culture to accept and adapt to it. Innovations and change may take the form of invention, discovery, borrowing, or diffusion. As specific adjustments to the natural environment or as responses to neighboring societies and their cultures, cultural change has dramatically altered life in many nations. Simple nonstate societies are few in number today due to the rapid expansion of state societies into their territories. Although industrialization has brought great power to some nations, the majority of the world's peoples still live as peasant food-producers in politically and economically subordinated segments of nation-states.

We humans must learn to adapt first to our physical environment and then to the cultural environment we have constructed if we are to survive as individuals and as societies. Chapter 6 illustrates the diversity of physical environments around the world and the subsistence technologies that have been developed to aid in adaptation. Human cultural systems are dynamic. The pace of change is rapidly accelerating today as societies communicate more easily with one another and learn to adapt more readily to a complex, technological way of life. Chapter 7 details this process of cultural evolution, focusing on the interrelationships among technology, social organization, and ideology and illustrates how this process affects contemporary world societies.

CHAPTER SIX

Environment, Adaptation, and Subsistence

After reading this chapter, you should be able to:

Discuss the relationship between cultural areas and natural environments.

Characterize the world's major natural environments.

Explain the concept of carrying capacity.

Discuss the concept of adaptation in the context of biology and culture.

Define subsistence adaptation.

Discuss foraging as a subsistence adaptation.

Explain optimal foraging theory.

Discuss the major theories of the origin of food production.

Describe the kinds of food production.

Relate the different kinds of food production to the natural environments in which they are usually found.

◀ **Figure 6.1** *Adaptation* *The definition of adaptation includes changes in the organism in response to the environment, and changes in the environment caused by the organism. This family lives in the Atlas Mountain region of Morocco. Their clothing and tent structure protects them from driving winds and searing heat.*

Human societies occupy territories, and their customs must enable them to cope with their environments if they are to survive. In this chapter we will examine the different kinds of environments that are found around the world, and discuss the ways in which societies have adjusted to different conditions by using the resources that their environments make available.

Oats, peas, beans, and barley grow. And potatoes. And tomatoes. Except in times of drought, or too much rain, or Japanese beetles. How long could you survive if you had to grow all your vegetables in your backyard and hunt for your meat in your neighborhood? Would your problems differ if you lived in Alaska or Arizona? Consider the source of your lunch or dinner if you had no supermarket or McDonald's to supply it. Imagine your life without hamburgers and french fries. Imagine eating mostly rice every day. Or sushi. Or snake meat. You would probably love it. Humans have learned to adapt to many diverse types of foods.

ENVIRONMENTAL DIVERSITY

Human beings are unusual among the many species of animals in having successfully occupied so many different environments. Approximately 5 billion human beings are found in habitats as diverse as arctic regions, deserts, and tropical rain forests. Throughout the world, people have managed to survive challenging physical circumstances, and they have learned to exploit an amazing variety of food resources. To understand the success of the human animal in adapting to a complex natural world, it helps to be aware of the different specific environments in which people are found today.

Cultural and Natural Areas

Alfred Kroeber (1939), a U.S. anthropologist, noted that the culture areas of native North Americans tended to have boundaries that corresponded with important differences in their natural environments. The correspondence be-

tween cultural and natural areas can be understood in several ways. For instance, the diffusion of cultural traits from one society to another is influenced by the environment and by natural boundaries that inhibit communication, trade, and other forms of interaction between peoples. This is not simply because such boundaries are necessarily physical barriers that are difficult to cross—although they sometimes can be—but more importantly because all aspects of a culture are in varying degrees adaptive responses to the environments in which they are found. This is particularly true of culturally governed customs that pertain to obtaining food, to shelter, and to defense technologies. Societies occupying the same or similar natural environments may readily borrow cultural traditions from one another that are relevant to successful adaptation. On the other hand, such adaptive cultural traits are less likely to be of interest to neighboring peoples who occupy different habitats.

Natural Environments

Preston James (1959) has classified the world into eight major types of natural environments that are characterized by important differences in climate, vegetation, and animal life. These differences are based, in part, on latitude and proximity to oceans and mountain ranges, each of which plays a role in determining both the resources that are available and the kinds of problems that people encounter in feeding themselves.

Mixed Forests.   In temperate climates there are **mixed forests**, such as those of eastern North America, that are made up of conifers and broadleaf trees. They are often accompanied by rolling plains and open areas in which the fertile soil provides an ideal situation for contemporary agricultural societies. So even though they represent only 7 percent of the earth's land surface, they are occupied today by about 43 percent of the human population. Prior to the development of iron tools, when it was more difficult to cut down the trees, these lands may not have held such a large proportion of the human species.

---

mixed forests regions of conifers and broadleaf trees in temperate climates

Scrub Forests. Regions between coasts and mountains that have mild, wet winters and hot, dry summers are **scrub forests** that attract a disproportionate share of human population. These areas, such as much of coastal California, represent only 1 percent of the land, but are home to 5 percent of the earth's human occupants.

Tropical Forests. Regions such as the Amazon Basin of Brazil that have warm climates and abundant rainfall, plant, and animal life are **tropical forests**. Although they cover only 10 percent of the earth's surface, 28 percent of the human species live in tropical forests.

Since heavy rainfall leaches away important soil nutrients and since tropical forest soils are typically high in acidity, they are not particularly productive as agricultural lands. Gardening techniques that rely on periodic changes in garden sites are common. Domesticated pigs have been used as food by some societies that occupy tropical forests, most particularly in southeast Asia and the Melanesian, Micronesian, and Polynesian islands of the Pacific.

Mountain Lands. Highly complex landforms of **mountain lands** such as the Rocky Mountains or Appalachians of North America include a variety of environments, often within short distances of one another. The major environmental differences relate to (1) climate differences that are influenced by elevation and (2) local differences in rainfall and sunlight within a mountain area. For instance, slopes on the eastern sides of mountains near oceans receive greater rainfall than do the western sides, and northern and southern slopes typically receive different amounts of sunlight. These differences result in numerous different plant and animal communities that occupy specific environments within the entire mountain region. Mountain lands seem to have provided few resources to peoples who lacked domesticated foods, except at elevations below 6,000 feet above sea level, but have proven most useful to pastoralists and agricultural peoples; they represent 12 percent of the globe's land area and are occupied by 7 percent of the world's people.

Grasslands. Twenty-six percent of the earth's surface is covered by **grasslands**, a greater area than any other type of environment. Yet only 10 percent of the human species inhabit grassland areas. There are three basic types of grasslands that differ in climate and in the predominant type of grass: steppes, prairies, and savannas. **Steppes**, such as the vast treeless stretches of southeastern Europe and Asia, have dry climates and extreme temperature changes during the year. Their grasses are short, hardy varieties that can tolerate their dry environment. **Prairies**, such as the North American Great Plains, have wetter climates and, consequently, support taller varieties of grass. **Savannas**, similar to some treeless plains of Florida, are found in tropical areas and are characterized by tall grasses and drought-resistant undergrowth.

Grasslands can be exploited usefully by hunters because of the large game animals, especially foraging herd animals, that occupy them. Pastoralists find them productive, since they are equally good environments for domesticated grazing animals such as cattle and sheep. Gardening in these environments is difficult without a plow or machine technology, since the grass-dominated soils are difficult to prepare for planting.

Arid Lands. The low annual rainfall in desert **arid lands**, such as parts of the southwestern United States and Great Basin, results in much of the land being sparsely covered by various plants such as grasses and low-growing desert shrubs that are capable of surviving on limited amounts of water. Isolated fertile pockets with year-round water may occur within arid lands, the only spots in which rainfall gardening is possible. Plant cultivation

---

scrub forests regions between coasts and mountains with mild, wet winters and hot, dry summers

tropical forests regions with warm climates and abundant rainfall, plants, and animal life

mountain lands a variety of highland environments, often within short distances of one another

grasslands areas that cover 26 percent of the earth's surface, with grasses of different types

steppes areas that cover stretches of southeastern Europe and Asia, with a short, hardy variety of grass

prairies areas with tall varieties of grass that tolerate wetter climates

savannas tropical areas of tall grasses and drought-resistant undergrowth

arid lands areas of low annual rainfall and sparse cover with low-growing desert shrubs

FIGURE 6.2

CARRYING CAPACITY

If a population cannot stabilize itself quickly enough at the carrying capacity of its environment, it may experience widespread famine. Some families simply leave an area that has limited resources, such as this one leaving the drought-stricken area of the Karal region in Chad.

outside these areas requires irrigation, and pastoralism is possible but not as productive as it is in grasslands. So arid lands have typically supported dispersed bands of foragers, whose collecting of wild plants and hunting of animals permits them to live in very small nomadic groups that exploit large territories. Thus, deserts compose 18 percent of the world's land mass but only 6 percent of its people. Yet they are still not the most sparsely settled of the earth's environments.

Boreal Forests. Boreas, the Greek god of the north wind, gives his name to heavily wooded regions, mostly dominated by coniferous trees, the **boreal forests**. Because the climatic conditions are colder and less favorable for plant domestication than are those of other forested regions, the boreal forests such as the logging and mining areas of northern Ontario have attracted few human inhabitants. They represent 10 percent of the land surface of the world, but only 1 percent of the human species occupies these forests.

Polar Lands. Regions of cold climates near the north and south poles, **polar lands** are made up of **ice zones** of permanent snow and ice; **tun-**dras, level or undulating treeless plains in the arctic and subarctic regions of North America, Asia, and Scandinavia; and **taigas**, swampy, coniferous forests of the northern lands south of the tundras. These are the least densely occupied environments of the world, representing 16 percent of its land area, but containing less than 1 percent of the people of the earth. The weather of the polar lands may be continually below freezing, and even those areas farthest from the poles have short growing seasons and, therefore, few plants. As a result, polar lands do not easily support any of the basic subsistence technologies. Until recently, they have been successfully occupied only by foraging peoples who have emphasized the hunting of both land and sea mammals and fishing.

---

boreal forests heavily wooded regions dominated by coniferous trees

polar lands regions of cold climates near North and South poles

ice zones regions of permanent snow and ice

tundras level or undulating treeless plains in the arctic and subarctic regions of North America, Asia, and Scandinavia

taigas swampy coniferous forests of the northern lands south of the tundras

Carrying Capacity

The different natural environments of the world are not equally accessible to living creatures, including human beings. One measure of the ability of species to survive on the resources available to them in a particular environment is the **carrying capacity**, that is, the upper limit on population determined by the characteristics of that environment. Population can be limited by such things as the food resources naturally available in an environment, the potential fertility of the soil for food production, climate, and the available water resources. The most crucial factor in determining the upper limit to which population can grow is the vital resource that is least available, since a population cannot be sustained at a level that makes its needs for any single resource greater than is consistently available, no matter how abundant the other resources may be.

Generally speaking, populations tend to stabilize at levels somewhat below the theoretical carrying capacity of their environments. The reason for this is that as populations grow toward the limit set by the available resources, competition between individuals for the resources will increase, so the effort and costs that must be expended to sustain each member of a population grow as well. The increased costs can offset the growth, making it increasingly difficult for the population as a whole to meet its needs. If this happens, the rate of population growth tends to stabilize gradually somewhere below the level that could be sustained in theory. This common pattern of regulating growth does have exceptions. When the growth rate is rapid enough, for instance, it's possible for a population to exceed the carrying capacity of its environment and thus experience general decimation due to starvation.

BIOLOGICAL AND CULTURAL ADAPTATION

The adjustment of an organism to a particular environment, **adaptation** is a two-way process, since it involves both changes in the organism in response to the demands of the environment and changes in the environment brought about by the organism. Adaptations in the organism can include biological and cultural changes that both facilitate and improve its adjustment to a particular environment.

Biological evolution is one of the means by which living species, including human beings, are able to adjust to an environment. Over a period of time, natural conditions select, or determine, which biological traits are most likely to be weeded out of a species and which are likely to remain. This process was called **natural selection** by Charles Darwin (1859/1965), who first systematically described parallels between the natural adaptation of a species and the "artificial" adaptation of breeding stock produced over many generations.

Biological anthropologists would be quick to cite examples of ways in which human beings have adapted to different environments around the world. For instance, the human trunk, head, arms, and legs tend to be longer and thinner in hot dry environments, while rounder and more compact body parts are associated with cold environments. The former traits create greater surface areas from which excess heat can be radiated efficiently from the body through evaporation of sweat. In cold environments where heat loss can endanger life, such traits would be less adaptive than the more compact shapes that make heat retention easier. Adaptive benefits have been suggested for other human differences, such as variations in average lung capacities at different elevations and skin color at different latitudes. For instance, the darkest skin tones consistently occur within about 15 degrees north or south of the equator in all parts of the world. Lighter skin shades are found as one moves further north or south. Natural selection seems to have adjusted skin tone to variations in the amount of sunlight that reach the surface of the earth. The interaction of sunlight with the skin produces vitamin D, which is found naturally in very few foods. The right amount of this vitamin is important to the human body, since both too much and too little can be fatal. Pigmentation filters out sunlight that passes through the

carrying capacity a particular environment's ability to support a species on the available resources

adaptation adjustment of an organism to a particular environment

natural selection the process whereby those members of a species that are better adapted to their environment contribute more offspring to succeeding generations than do other members

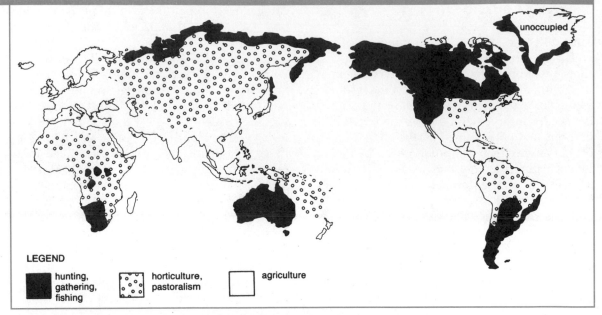

SUBSISTENCE TECHNOLOGIES OF 1600 C.E.

This map shows the worldwide range of subsistence technologies in 1600 C.E.

skin, and thus the adaptation of skin color is darkest near the equator, where it prevents overproduction of vitamin D. Away from the equator, where sunlight must pass through a greater layer of the atmosphere before it reaches the human skin, progressively lighter skin tones aid in the absorption of sunlight and thus avoid the problem of too little vitamin D production.

More interesting to cultural anthropologists are the ways in which human beings are able to adjust to their diverse environments by changing their habits, customs, and cultures. Culturally governed changes in behavior make it possible for humans to adjust successfully to new environments quite quickly. Biological evolution is a much slower process. For instance, fashioning animal skins and furs into warm clothing, using dog-sledge transportation, and constructing igloos from the icy environment probably do more to explain the ability of Inuit peoples to survive so successfully in the arctic north than does Inuit body stature.

SUBSISTENCE ADAPTATIONS AND THE ENVIRONMENT

The study of **subsistence** is the study of how people obtain the necessities of life, particularly

food, from their environment. It is in the study of food getting that we see most clearly how the forces of nature set limits and provide possibilities for human social and cultural life and how human **subsistence technologies**, the tools and techniques for obtaining food, help people adapt to their environments around the world.

Foraging

The oldest, simplest, and least specialized of human subsistence technologies is **foraging**, a food-collecting system based on fishing, hunting wild animals, and gathering wild plant foods. Foraging lifestyles predate the evolution of completely modern forms of *Homo sapiens*, who were present in Africa and the Near East at least 50,000 years ago and in western Europe by 40,000 years ago. It is clear that although survival by foraging is all but extinct today, it has a longer history as a basis for human survival than any other means of subsistence. Foraging was the only way in which people obtained food until about 10,000 years ago,

---

subsistence how people obtain the necessities of life, particularly food, from the environment

subsistence technology the tools and techniques by which people obtain food

foraging a subsistence technology based on gathering wild plant foods, hunting, and fishing

when the first experimentation with plant and animal domestication began in the Near East.

The principal subsistence tools in those few remaining cultures that still live by foraging are digging sticks, clubs, spears, bows and arrows, fishing devices, traps, fire, and containers for storing, cooling, and transporting food. Tools are general purpose and few in number, since they must be made on the spot when needed or transported as the people move from place to place in the quest for food. According to Alan Lomax and Conrad Arensberg (1977), who surveyed the subsistence systems of 1,308 societies, "The emphasis is on hand skills rather than tools" (p. 668). Since individual skill is critical to success in the quest for food, foragers generally socialize their children to be independent and assertive and to rely on their own initiative rather than to be compliant to the demands of others.

Since hunting and gathering technologies rely on naturally occurring wild foods, foragers are unable to live year round in groups as large as those supported by food domestication. Therefore, social mechanisms more complex than the family are not necessary for organizing the political and economic lives of foragers. They lack governments and warfare and tend to be highly mobile, especially when hunting provides a major portion of their food supply.

Considering the small size of their social groups, it is hardly surprising that foragers generally have been less politically powerful than food domesticators, and when in competition with them, foragers have usually been at a disadvantage. As a result, they continued to exist until recently primarily in those areas of the earth of marginal interest to the plant and animal domesticators: the arctic wastes, the tundras, deserts, and tropical environments.

Today, there are few peoples left who rely primarily or entirely on foraging. Some of the Inuit of the Canadian arctic have returned to a tradition of self-sufficient hunting after a period of acculturation. Despite the European intrusion, many of the !Kung San people of the southwestern African desert maintained a foraging lifestyle until the 1970s outside South Africa, where they are no longer found. But especially since the mid-1970s, the San have undergone severe acculturation as governmental policies have aided the expansion of cattle herding into their traditional lands. Most San have been forced to find new ways to survive, such as working as herders for neighboring cat-

FIGURE 6.4

FORAGING

Hunter-gatherers, or foragers, rely on the fish, game, or plants readily available in their environment for food. The oldest form of subsistence, foraging is being replaced in many areas of the world by some form of agriculture more suited to feeding large numbers of people. This Kalahari San is digging for bulbs after the rainy season.

tle owners. There are about 62,000 San in the desert of Botswana, Namibia, and Angola. Of these, only between 2,000 and 5,000 might still be called foragers. About 4,000 aboriginal Australians have managed to maintain a semi-nomadic foraging way of life within nationally established reserves. Some tropical forest foragers, such as the Agta of northeastern Luzon, can still be found in the Philippines. Several tropical forest peoples of South America, such as the Ach of eastern Paraguay, still forage periodically despite efforts of the government to introduce them to agriculture. The Mbuti and other Pygmies of Africa's Ituri forest are among the most numerous foragers today, numbering about 40,000 persons. Their ability to retreat into the forest has kept their traditional lifestyle

PYGMY NET AND ARCHERY HUNTING IN THE ITURI FOREST

The Ituri Forest Pygmy of Zaire are a foraging people with an emphasis on hunting. Their adaptation to a tropical forest environment, described by Colin Turnbull (1961), illustrates the interplay of technology and environment by which a society adjusts to its surroundings while meeting its subsistence needs. The Pygmies are divided into two major groups that differ in their primary food-getting technology and that have resulting differences in their social organization. One part of the Pygmy population, the Efe, emphasizes archery; the other, called Mbuti, are net hunters.

For about 10 months of each year, the net hunters live deeper in the forest than do the archers, in communities of up to 30 families. Their hunt, as Turnbull describes it, is a communal affair:

> The net-hunting technique calls for each family to set up its net and fasten it to the net on each side (every elementary family owns one net, up to three hundred feet in length). As the men and youths are silently forming this semicircle, the women and girls form an opposite one, and at a given signal from the men, close in, beating the undergrowth with branches and making a distinctive whooping cry.
>
> Any animal falling into the nets is immediately killed with a spear, and the owner of the net into which it fell will give it to his wife to put in her basket. If the animal is too large for this, it is cut up and divided on the spot; otherwise the division takes place back in camp. The ultimate sharing follows no clear-cut kinship lines, though the owner of the net and the owner of the spear that killed the animal have first priority. Momentary individual needs seem to be given much more consideration, and portions will be given to those who were un-

able to come on the hunt or whose nets trapped no game. (pp. 296–297)

The remaining two months of the year are a time of plenty in the forest. Game is so abundant during this period, called the honey season, that smaller groups of related families can readily provide for their own needs without participating in communal hunts. During this period, the community tends to break up into smaller groups that go their own way until food becomes scarce enough to warrant cooperating in larger groups again.

The Pygmies who are bow-and-arrow hunters follow the opposite yearly cycle of dispersal and congregation. They occupy lands near the edges of the forest that are less productive than the interior areas, partly because these areas have been changed by the presence of commercial plantations, mining activities, tourism, missions, and roads. Through most of the year the archer Pygmies wander in groups of three or four brothers and their families. Hunting is done only by men, who climb trees near game trails and wait for the opportunity to shoot animals that pass by or are flushed by the hunters' dogs. The food is carried back to the camp, where it is divided. Women in these groups do not participate in the hunt, but collect vegetable foods near the camp and take care of domestic chores. The archery hunters also supplement their food gathering by engaging in trade with nearby farming villagers outside the forest, a resource that is less used by the net hunters.

Once a year, during the honey season, game becomes abundant enough even in the territories of the archers to make communal hunts more

viable, but it, too, is threatened as logging makes inroads into their territory.

Band Cultures.   Foraging forms the subsistence base of a societal type known as the **band** (see chapter 11). Bands are typically small groups based on kinship, with labor divided only by age and sex, sharing of resources, temporary leadership roles, material possessions limited by nomadism, and ideals reflecting these features. Wild foods are a sparse resource for people with no other means of survival. The poor environments occupied by foragers in re-

cent times are unable to support more than about one person per five square miles, and in some places as few as one person per 500 square miles.

Nomadism and Material Culture.   Without a domestication technology, people must follow

---

band a seminomadic, kinship-based society with no full-time government, economically based on a foraging subsistence technology

productive than archery. During this short season, the bow-and-arrow hunters coalesce into a larger community that cooperates in a hunt very like that of the net hunters, although no actual nets are used. According to Turnbull, the communal hunt of the honey season

> not only reaffirms the unity of the archery band as a whole, it also provides an opportunity for discussion of matters of general interest, such as betrothals, or the election of a new headman. . . . It is a time for general socializing, for song and dance (much of which is of ritual significance), and ultimately for the realignment of the smaller sections whose composition is never the same year after year. Petty hostilities and jealousies are removed during this festive season, which lasts about two months; old friendships are renewed and new friendships formed. (p. 301)

The contrasting yearly cycles of the two groups of Pygmies are an interesting illustration of how environmental differences can influence the customs of a culture. Although historical documentation does not recount the actual development of these two patterns of Pygmy life, it is conceivable that they arose in response to a decline in game in the forest fringes due to road building and other exploitation of forest resources by the non-Pygmy newcomers.

Today, the Ituri Forest Pygmies remain one of the largest foraging populations in the world, since the forest provides some isolation from encroaching food domesticators. The Mbuti number about 40,000, who live in bands of between 10 and 70 people. Deforestation has reduced the food resources of the Mbuti, and many have taken up agriculture or accepted

FOREST PYGMY

The Pygmy in Zaire, in Central Africa, remain one of the largest foraging populations in the world. They are divided into two types of foragers: the Efe emphasize archery and the Mbuti, net hunting. But because deforestation has greatly reduced their food resources, some Pygmies have turned to agriculture or employment on nearby farms and plantations to sustain themselves.

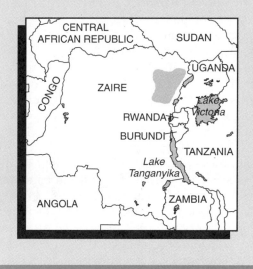

employment on neighboring Bantu farms and coffee plantations.

their food supply. This seminomadic pattern has an influence on the nature of a band society's material technology. Band-level peoples cannot afford to have as many different kinds of specialized tools as are commonly found among more sedentary peoples. Each tool must be able to serve many different functions and be easily carried to a new hunting ground. For instance, the Australian boomerang served not only as a throwing weapon used in the hunt but also as a flat working surface when making other tools, a digging tool, a club, a scraping tool, and a percussion musical instrument.

Group Structure. According to Julian Steward (1955) and Elman R. Service (1962), the hunting and gathering technology places certain functional demands on the social organization of the band-level culture. Permanent social groups cannot be very large. The local group that works and lives together averages about 50 people in contemporary band societies and rarely exceeds 100 people. The local groups of band cultures may have been somewhat larger in earlier times, when bands occupied areas with more abundant resources than are now found in the marginal areas to which they have been restricted by the expansion of more powerful societies. Nevertheless, wild food resources cannot maintain large local groups except in very lush environments, since the larger the group is, the farther individuals must travel from their base of operations in their quest for food.

As a general rule, in the small, local groups of band cultures, most individuals will be related, either by descent, which is commonly traced through both men and women, or by marriage. This community is the basic institution in a band society for organizing the education of children, social etiquette, and economic, political, military, and judicial practices.

Division of Labor.

The only specialization of labor in a band culture is that based on differences of gender and age. In a band society supported by the sparse resources of wild foods, the most economical division of subsistence labor usually assigns the work of hunting to the men, while the gathering of wild plants near the camp is done by the women and older children. This specialization of labor is an adaptation to pregnancy in the female and the need for prolonged nursing of infants. Although these two biological facts might hinder her as a hunter, the woman still can be an important provider of plant foods gathered locally during periods of pregnancy and lactation. Elman R. Service (1962), R. B. Lee and Ivan DeVore (1968a), and J. Tanaka (1977) have estimated that women sometimes provide as much as 80 percent of the calories in the diets of people who survive by hunting and gathering. However, in circumstances where a rigid differentiation is not important for the survival of the group, men, women, and children may play overlapping roles. In hunting and gathering societies in areas with plentiful wild foods, men may often gather wild plants as well as hunt; and men, women, and children may frequently work together in cooperative hunting activities.

The relative emphasis that each foraging group places on plant gathering, hunting, and fishing depends on the nature of each local environment. These differences influence the gender relationships within foraging societies. Ernestine Friedl (1975) has suggested that the division of labor by gender in foraging societies takes one of four major forms, depending on the subsistence adaptation of the foraging groups to their specific environments: individual foraging, communal foraging, plant-focused foraging, and animal-focused foraging.

Individual Foraging.

Subsistence based on individual foraging is common in environments in which meat is a relatively unimportant resource. In **individual foraging**, both men and women are expected to gather their own plant foods, but men provide primarily for themselves while women forage for themselves and their children. Only a small amount of time is devoted to hunting in this subsistence pattern. Men and women are typically equal in social power and prestige in these foraging societies.

Communal Foraging.

In environments where the major meat resource is fish or small game, and plant foods are most easily collected by cooperative labor, **communal foraging** is common. Hunting is usually accomplished by driving animals toward nets where they are killed by the men of the group. In communal foraging, the game is normally divided at the site among all the families who participated, so no particular prestige is gained by men from their role in hunting. The joint participation of women and men in the subsistence activities of communal foraging societies usually results in a relative equality between them.

Plant-Focused Foraging.

Societies in environments where plant resources can readily supply the majority of the food from areas nearby engage primarily in **plant-focused foraging**. These groups that emphasize plant collecting are usually the least rigid about separating the roles of men and women. While men are occupied with hunting larger animals that may have to be pursued for long distances over a period of days, women gather plant foods near the camp, an activity that typically provides between 60 and 70 percent of the group's food. Nevertheless, men's social prestige and power are often high when compared with women's, because whenever they bring more meat to camp than their own families can use, they share the surplus with the hunters of other

---

individual foraging men and women each gather their own plant foods, with women providing for the children

communal foraging cooperative food gathering where fish and small game are meat resources and plants are easily collected

plant-focused foraging gathering of plant resources that are readily available, allowing hunting expeditions far from campsite

families and are given high status by their neighbors as a result. In contrast, the plant foods that women provide to their own families are the basic staple of life. They are readily available to all, so there is no need for women to share the fruits of their labor outside their own families. Thus, women lack access to a means for raising their status in the way men do. Parallels in North America that illustrate how income produced for consumption within the family does not translate as readily into social power or prestige outside the domestic setting are kitchen gardens and food canning. While these may be sources of personal pride or even respect among a small circle of neighbors, they do not have the same impact on a woman's wider public influence as a high salary, part of which may be spent on such things as hosting parties for colleagues. In this unbalanced system, when men share food with nonrelatives, their status rises in a way that emphasizes the dependence of women on men for the important resource that men provide.

Animal-Focused Foraging.   Environments that offer little in the way of plant foods may be occupied by foragers when fish and animal life are abundant enough. In **animal-focused foraging,** fish and large game hunted by men are the basic food. In this subsistence system, women do not contribute directly to the food supply, but bear domestic responsibilities, including the processing of the meat and skins brought in by the men. Often in those societies, men make the tools that women use. Especially where the meat resources are large game animals, the pursuit of which can encourage high levels of competitiveness and aggression in hunters, the economic dependence of women on men can result in low social status for women.

Optimal Foraging Theory

Nowhere do people use every possible available resource in their environment. Insects, for instance, are a source of protein that is ignored by a great many cultures. Dogs and cats are quite common in North American and European societies, but are culturally defined as pets rather than as foods. Some species of dogs were raised for their food value by the Aztecs, and both dogs and cats are marketed in various parts of the Orient where milk products traditionally have not been favored as foods. This

FIGURE 6.5

INUIT SEAL HUNT
After a period of acculturation, some of the Inuit, or Eskimos, of the Canadian arctic have returned to self-sufficient hunting and fishing. This hunter uses modern technological methods to bring home his seal from Bathurst Inlet.

selectivity in the cultural definition of potential food resources exists even in societies that rely on the simplest of food-getting technologies that permit only foraging for wild foods.

Optimal foraging theory is a way of trying to explain why some foods are emphasized more than others, and why some are regularly ignored by collectors of wild foods. Basically, optimal foraging theory asserts that the likelihood of foragers using a potential food resource is directly proportional to the calories it offers as food per unit of effort required to obtain and prepare it for eating. The greater the caloric cost of obtaining and preparing a given

---

animal-focused foraging fish and animal life provide basic food supply where plants are scarce
optimal foraging theory principle that foragers use food resources in direct proportion to the caloric effort required to obtain them

food, the less likely it will be sought. When all potential foods in a given environment are ranked from the one with the highest rate of return on effort expended to the one with the least payoff, it will be found that those foods at the top of the list will be the ones that are most commonly used in the diet. Items lower on the list will be less and less often used. When the full dietary requirements of a foraging group are considered, there is some point on the entire list below which it is unlikely that potential foods will ever be sought except under unusual circumstances.

Optimal foraging theory is useful for answering a number of questions about food-collecting activities. For instance, it would be ethnocentric to suggest that insects are not used as foods by most societies because insects are unaesthetic as foods. The idea that their nutritional value is lower than that of other animals is simply incorrect. However, the tendency of many societies to ignore the nutritional value of many insects that exist in their environment does make sense on the purely practical level suggested by optimal foraging theory: The high amount of effort that an individual would usually have to expend to gather enough of them to prepare a meal simply makes most insects too costly to be worth the effort in most environments most of the time. Of course there are exceptions. The aboriginal Shoshone of the Great Basin desert of the United States were regularly plagued by infestations of grasshoppers in sufficient numbers so that it was quite cost effective to simply dig a trench, cover its bottom with hot coals, and then just wait until it filled itself with roasted grasshoppers. In such a situation, the usual predictions of optimal foraging theory would not be violated if grasshoppers became a temporary important addition to the normal yearly diet, as they did regularly for the Shoshone.

Of course, a plant or animal may be collected for reasons other than its value as food. The tribes of the North American Great Plains hunted the bison as an important food resource, but they also used its hide for leather, its tendons for making bows, and its horns and bones for making various tools. Similarly, an animal or plant low on the list as a food resource might be sought and eaten anyway when its other uses added to its food value make the effort worthwhile. However, the basic principle of optimal foraging theory is not really violated by such considerations. The return

on invested effort is still the best predictor of a resource's being utilized, whether the return is calculated in terms of food calories or in terms of any other units of value that contribute to the survival of a social group.

Food Production

Although the shift to food domestication had been viewed by the early cultural evolutionists as progress, current anthropological thinking holds that foraging has its advantages, too. Judging from the few groups that still practice hunting and gathering, ways of life based on foraging are usually quite satisfactory in their ability to meet the needs of people. Population density is generally low, and the communities of cooperating individuals are never very large. Under these circumstances, it is simple for the local group to move quickly from place to place. As a result, food shortages are rare among hunters and gatherers. In addition, nomadic or seminomadic hunters and gatherers, unlike sedentary peoples, do not live amidst their own refuse. This factor, plus the low population densities that are characteristic of foragers, means that the epidemics that often plague peoples who live under crowded conditions are also rare. Furthermore, Marvin Harris (1977) has pointed out that foragers have a much shorter workweek than do food domesticators. For instance, the southern African !Kung foragers need to work only about three hours a day to obtain a nutritious diet, even though their desert environment is not nearly so lush as most of the areas occupied by hunting and gathering peoples before the rise of farming.

Rise of the Contemporary World System. Today, the subsistence systems of the world's various nations are no longer independent entities determined solely by the economic needs of local peoples who interact with their natural environments. Rather, the subsistence activities of each nation are widely interconnected in a multinational web of economic exchange that forms a world economy. The core of this world economy is formed by the world's developed industrial nations, especially western Europe and the United States, whose industries extract tremendous wealth in the form of natural resources from the nations of the less developed countries of the world. This interdependence between the underdeveloped and developed

OPTIMAL FORAGING, AMERICAN SUBSISTENCE, AND CULTURE

The return on invested effort influences food choices in North America, just as it has in other societies. As in foraging situations, how we manage our resources depends on factors such as the income available for investing in food and the relative scarcity of things to eat. For the typical member of the civilian labor force who works eight hours a day, the equivalent of invested effort consists of the money available for the food budget and the time available to buy it.

Variation in food choice is influenced by family income. For instance, the home-prepared meals of higher-income families include more meats and a larger variety of vegetable-based foods, while the meals of those on tighter budgets are correspondingly higher in less expensive foods such as pastas and foods high in fats. Today much food is eaten outside the home either as recreation or as sustenance during work or school hours. Food choices made during work hours are often a catch-as-catch-can affair, influenced by what is most readily available in a limited time: Should I grab something from the vending machine in the snack room, or do I have time to slip over to McDonald's? Pizza Hut delivers, but I can't afford that at work too often, especially if I choose that for an evening meal occasionally.

Did you ever notice how your best-intended diet plans go by the wayside on nights out? Have you ever seen any low-calorie, fat-free choices at a movie theatre? Who can pass up buttered popcorn at the movies—or chocolate-covered almonds and a soda? Would baseball really be baseball without a hot dog, a hot pretzel, or an ice-cream cone? Maybe they don't fit my diet plan, but after all, there aren't a lot of choices in those settings. Should I really do without, because everything is either too fatty, too sweet, or too expensive? Not me! The choices we make from what is available are influenced by how hungry we feel and what we will get for the dollar spent.

Of course, maximizing return for cost among available options is not the only factor that influences our choices. Culture also plays a role, both among foragers and in societies with industrialized agriculture. In both cases, religious food taboos may restrict choices. The forager may ignore a totemic animal, and the American may avoid nonkosher foods, alcohol, or meat for religious reasons. American ideas about "healthy eating" have also changed our food habits in the last decade, so that steak has given way to pasta, ice cream has given way to frozen yogurt, and potato chips have given way to pretzels. Ethnic diversity in food tastes within American society has also increased the variety of foods that are now available in the same city or town. French, German, Italian, Japanese, Chinese, Thai, and Mexican restaurants may be found within a short distance of one another. In sum, food choices are influenced by a complex mix of availability, nutritional benefits, cost, and cultural factors such as status differences, ethnicity, and religion.

nations has been referred to as **neocolonialism**, because it has much in common with the economic exploitation of colonial nations by the colonial empires of the last century. Unlike traditional economic exploitation of colonial resources, however, the current system does not dominate the colonial regions as subordinate areas of a political empire. Instead, underdeveloped nations are economically so dependent on their participation in the world system that they are financially unable to extricate themselves. The specialized roles of underdeveloped countries within the world system makes it difficult for them to develop their economies, since the goals of development may be, to various degrees, incompatible with the current subsistence systems of these countries.

The global economic interdependence of today's world is not a totally one-sided system. Although the economic roles of developed nations provide their societies with the world's highest standards of living, they too are dependent upon the continued participation of undeveloped countries in the world economic system. Thus, although the economies of less developed nations may be extremely depend-

---

neocolonialism the contemporary world system of economic exploitation of underdeveloped nations by the developed centers of economic power, in which underdeveloped nations' participation is enforced by economic necessity rather than by political coercion.

ent on an inflow of loans that allows them to improve their productivity and create new possibilities for employing their growing urban populations, defaults on these loans by impoverished debtor nations would be disastrous for the industrialized countries, whose economies would be impacted if these loans were not repaid. For instance, in 1995 the United States played a major role in helping Mexico avoid defaulting on its international loans. Although this move was not politically popular within the United States, it was not simply a humanistic decision on the part of the U.S. government, since U.S. banks have been major sources of loans to Mexico. If Mexico were allowed to default on its international debts, which in 1995 had reached $150 billion, the loss to American banks would have had tremendous impact on the entire U.S. economy. Today, there are no truly self-sufficient economies, and despite the inequalities of the average per capita incomes and standards of living of participating nations, those nations are interdependent parts of the world economic system.

The Trend toward Food Domestication

Between 10,000 and 18,000 years ago, the lifestyle of the foragers of southwest Asia began to change. Along the hilly flanks of the mountains of the Near East, there was sufficient rainfall for abundant wild grains to grow without cultivation. Foragers in these zones were able to gather a variety of wild foods in different seasons and preserve them in storage pits for off-season use. Food storage made a more sedentary life possible even while exploiting wild cereal crops that were native to the area. These wild cereals could be harvested easily by lightly beating the stems so that the seeds would break loose and fall into a basket. After grinding with stone tools, the tough seeds could be prepared for eating in a variety of ways. The use of these wild grains resulted in a more sedentary life and population growth, and laid the foundation for the eventual domestication of plants and animals.

The rise of population that may have led to food domestication can be accounted for by the interplay between human fertility and **sedentarism** (a settled rather than nomadic lifestyle). Following the birth of a child, a woman will not again begin ovulation so long as less than 20 to 25 percent of her body weight con-

sists of fat (Frisch and McArthur, 1974; Frisch, 1975). This figure represents the approximate amount of calories that a fetus needs to develop to full term. That is, before a fertile woman will be able to conceive, her body must store enough calories of energy to nourish a developing fetus for a nine-month pregnancy. In active nomadic populations this threshold of body fat is more difficult to achieve than in sedentary populations, since the foragers burn more food energy themselves and their diets are likely to be lower in carbohydrates and higher in protein. Because nursing one child takes about 1,000 calories a day, it is unlikely that a woman will become pregnant as long as she is nursing if she lives in a seminomadic hunting and gathering society. Since nursing is likely to continue for the first three years of an infant's life in most societies, the level of fertility is, on the average, much lower in hunting and gathering societies than in sedentary societies using domesticated foods. The span of childbearing years is also shorter, for the onset of menstruation occurs later in hunting and gathering societies because a hunting and gathering diet is rich in protein. In demonstration of these theories, Richard B. Lee (1972) and Gina B. Kolata (1974) have reported growth in fertility and population among those !Kung hunter-gatherers who abandoned their native seminomadic way of life for a more sedentary food production economy.

Esther Boserup (1965) argued, on the other hand, that population growth may have been a cause for the food domestication. It would have created pressure for more effective control over the food supply than was possible with the simple gathering of wild plants. Robert Sussman (1972) pointed out that population growth eventually made it necessary for people to move into less productive areas around the margins of the zones where wild grains grew in natural abundance, and Lewis Binford (1968) and Kent Flannery (1969/1971) believe that it was in these marginal zones that people found it necessary to seek more direct human control over their food supply. People began to keep near to the home base a few animals such as sheep, goats, dogs, and cattle, which had previously been hunted. This practice ensured a steady supply of meat as well as other useful

---

sedentarism living in permanent or semipermanent settlements

products such as hides, milk, and milk products. By experimenting in how to plant seeds, people acquired grains as dietary supplements in areas where they had not been common previously.

The process that led to the domestication of plants and animals began as early as 13,000 years ago. It is not possible to place a precise date on its origins, since the shift to food domestication was a gradual process. There is even some debate about where the earliest center of food domestication was. Some archaeological evidence has suggested that it may have occurred in southeast Asia. Nevertheless, the process is best documented in the Near East. Because the distinction between the remains of wild and domesticated plants and animals is subtle, what are considered earlier materials simply may represent plants and animals in the process of being domesticated. It is safe to say, however, that by 9000 B.C.E. goats and sheep had been domesticated in the Near East, and barley and wheat were domesticated by 7000 B.C.E. in the same area. Cattle and pigs also were under human control by 7000 B.C.E. The domesticated grains differed from their wild relatives in that the crop domesticators favored larger seeds. As the seeds evolved to a larger size under human influence, the grain was more firmly attached to the stems and could no longer be harvested easily by shaking the stems over a basket. Thus, the domestication of grains required the simultaneous evolution of a new technology for use in the harvest, including knife blades and sickles for cutting bunches of stems. Such tool kits were in use in the ancient Near East by 7000 B.C.E.

Simple Food Domestication. The simplest form of food production is **horticulture**, a simple form of gardening that involves only the planting, weeding, harvesting, and storage of foodstuffs. There is no use of the plow, draft animals, fertilization of the soil, or crop rotation, all of which are characteristic of more complex agricultural technologies. Techniques for irrigating the gardens are simple and do not include large-scale irrigation canals that require more heavy labor to build or maintain than can be performed by close relatives. The most common hand tools used in labor-intensive horticultural tribes are the digging stick and the hoe. Most horticulturalists have some domestic animals with which they supplement their diets, but animals are never the source of the bulk of their diet.

FIGURE 6.6

HORTICULTURE

The subsistence technology of horticulture provides people with food in a simple uncomplicated way. This African woman in a village on the Ivory Coast is pounding grain into flour.

A horticultural technology provides a more reliable subsistence and produces more food per acre than does a hunting and gathering technology, so peoples with horticultural technologies live in larger communities than do foragers. Their denser populations give them correspondingly greater political power than foragers have, so horticultural societies are much more widespread. Four hundred years ago, they were found primarily in the tropical forest areas of South America, in many parts of North America, in most areas of Africa, throughout the islands of the Pacific, and in some of the Asian mainland. Nevertheless, the

---

horticulture cultivation of crops using simple hand tools such as the hoe and digging stick and without fertilization of the soil, crop rotation, and often without irrigation

THE SHUARA OF ECUADOR AND PERU

The Shuara are a horticultural people, popularly known as the Jívaro, who have been described by Michael Harner (1972). They live within the higher reaches of the Amazonian tropical forest of eastern Ecuador and Peru. Their basic subsistence food is a starchy root crop called manioc, but they also grow maize, sweet potatoes, squash, beans, peanuts, bananas, plantains, and papayas. These foods are supplemented by fish and game such as monkeys, birds, and peccaries.

Gardens are prepared near the living site by a group of men who belong to the same family. Undergrowth is cleared from a garden area, and the small trees are ringed by removing a strip of bark from the entire circumference of each one to weaken them. When the larger trees are felled, originally with stone axes and in more recent times with steel axes, they take with them the smaller weakened trees in their vicinity, since their canopies are interwoven with vines and other jungle growth. Several months later, after the brush and trees have dried, the garden area is burned. Then the gardens are planted and an elliptical, palm-thatched house is erected. The gardening itself is done by the women of the group.

Men hunt to supplement their families' diets with meat. Small game such as monkeys and birds are shot with blowgun darts that are coated with curare, a poison that suppresses the breathing reflex of the animal. Since a monkey is likely to try to pull out the dart, it is notched so that it will break off easily and leave the poisoned tip inside the animal. Within a few minutes, animals shot with the poisoned darts drop from the trees. Since the blowgun is such a silent weapon, it is often possible for a skilled hunter to pick off several monkeys from a troop before the others become alarmed. Larger game may be killed with spears, or in recent times, with shotguns or rifles. Fish are taken with traps, nets, or spears. The Jívaro (Shuara) have an unusual technique of poisoning the water and the fish in it. They build a dam to contain the fish and, using natural plants such as barbasco shrub and masu, pour the sap into the water. The poison stuns the fish so they can be speared. Little ecological damage is done by this method.

SHUARA (JÍVARO)

Living in the tropical rain forests of Ecuador and Peru, the Shuara, also known as Jívaro, subsist primarily on carbohydrate crops such as manioc, sweet potatoes, and corn. They use slash-and-burn agriculture to grow their crops and supplement their diet by hunting small game and spearing fish after they first poison them in dammed-up pools of water.

simple tools of horticulturalists give them relatively little control over the productivity of the land they cultivate, so there are natural limits on their distribution throughout the world. Horticultural communities were typically found in areas with warm or temperate climates favorable to the domestication of plants.

The simpler forms of horticulture are known as **extensive** or **shifting cultivation** because they use the same gardens for only a few years followed by letting the land remain idle for several years to renew its fertility. Since gardens must be shifted to new plots, horticultural work is extended to plots farther from home than would be required if the same plots could be reused perpetually. So tribal societies that rely on shifting cultivation are only semiseden-

---

extensive cultivation horticulture that involves the use of land for short periods followed by periods of letting the land stand idle for several years

shifting cultivation extensive cultivation

FIGURE 6.7

SLASH-AND-BURN CULTIVATION

Horticulturalists use simple tools such as hoes and digging sticks to plant their crops. In order to clear a plot of land for planting, they cut down or slash the trees and brush and then burn them. The ashes that remain act as fertilizer for the soil. This type of food production is also known as shifting cultivation, since a new plot of ground may be started every planting season.

tary, since entire communities may have to be moved to new locations occasionally to open up new gardening lands.

Depending on the characteristics of the natural environments in which it occurs, extensive cultivation may take one of two forms: slash-and-burn horticulture or dry-land gardening. **Slash-and-burn cultivation**, also known as **swidden horticulture**, is common in tropical forest environments and in savannas, where clearing the land requires heavy labor. The trees and vegetation that are cut away are left to dry and then burned before a crop can be planted. Garden plots are cultivated for several years, during which they may become less and less productive as their nutrients are depleted. Then the fields are allowed to lie fallow for a period of up to 9 or 10 years before they are cleared and worked again. Typically, gardeners who use the slash-and-burn technique have several gardens, each of which has been cultivated for a different length of time, so that each year the oldest may be abandoned to nature while an-

other, abandoned previously, is again prepared for use. Ultimately, after several cycles of use and abandonment of plots, the soil will have become so depleted that the forest does not grow back, and entirely new gardens must be prepared. Eventually, gardens may be so far from the original village that an entire settlement of several hundred people may relocate to a more convenient area.

Dry-land gardening is carried out in arid environments. The major problem in dry-land gardening is getting sufficient water to the

---

slash-and-burn cultivation a form of farming in which the land is prepared by cutting and burning the natural growth and in which several plots, in various stages of soil depletion, are worked in a cycle

swidden horticulture slash-and-burn horticulture

dry-land gardening horticulture is carried out in arid environments with the aid of simple supplemental watering techniques

FIGURE 6.8

PASTORALISM

Pastoralists focus on animal husbandry as their primary source of food. Depending on the environment, some pastoralists migrate with their herds of cattle, yaks, llamas, or camels to favorable foraging areas. Camels are found primarily in northern Africa and the Arabian peninsula. This Turkana nomad is milking a camel.

crops. Some small canals may be used to channel available water resources such as the seasonal runoff of rainwater from higher land. However, in the absence of major, reliable water sources such as rivers, large irrigation projects that require heavy cooperative labor are not a part of this system. In drier periods water may have to be hand-carried to individual plants in gardens.

In nonforested regions where cereal crops predominate, the settlements of horticulturalists may be more permanent than those of tropical forest farmers. Particularly in drier climates, horticulturalists may engage in some hand-watering of plants or limited irrigation of fields, but irrigation is not so common or complex as in agriculturally based societies.

Horticultural Tribes.   When hunting and gathering subsistence technology gave way to sedentarism and the domestication of plants and animals, a more complex societal type

arose called the **tribe**. In tribal societies population may approach 100 people per square mile. Local groups must maintain more or less permanent residence near the planted gardens from which they draw their food. These groups can grow to be quite large in comparison with the local groups of hunting and gathering peoples. According to Marshall D. Sahlins (1960), the communities of contemporary horticultural societies have up to 200 to 250 residents. While the local groups in bands may comprise anywhere from one to a dozen families that are loosely interrelated by ties of marriage, a tribal community may consist of as many as 20 residential families. Often, these families may be grouped into a number of larger kin groups that are united to one another by ties of common ancestry. These kinship groups are the basic units of tribal government.

Control over the food supply allows horticulturalists to live in larger local groups than foragers. Several hundred people may live together in villages throughout the year. Housing is more permanent and house construction more elaborate than are the temporary shelters of foragers. Village life necessitates greater accommodation to the presence of others, so childrearing necessarily emphasizes compliance and responsibility over independence and assertiveness in children. Family organization tends to be more elaborate among horticulturalists than among foragers, since a large number of family members may reside in the same location over many generations.

The authority of the family organization in the lives of its individual members is great, since the family is the basic governing institution in horticultural villages. Each family may be a politically autonomous component of the village except in matters that affect the common welfare. Such matters tend to be dealt with by a council of family leaders from the entire village, who seek to achieve a consensus on how to handle the problem. The greater numbers and more complex social organization of horticulturalists and the need for control of the land as a source of income make warfare a common element of life in horticulturally based societies.

(Continued on p. 152)

tribe a semisedentary society that is governed by kinship groups and economically based on extensive horticulture or pastoralism

THE NORTHERN TUNGUS REINDEER HERDERS OF SIBERIA

The northern Tungus, many of whom identify themselves as the Evenki, occupy much of eastern Siberia. Their environment is in the treeless tundra and forested taiga zones of the northern polar region, where plant cultivation is impractical. Their source of livelihood is reindeer herding and hunting.

The Tungus keep a domesticated variety of reindeer that they milk and use for riding and as pack animals, much as horses are used among their southern neighbors. Natural dangers such as wolves make it difficult to increase the herd, and as many as half the herd may be lost each winter. Normally, herd reindeer are only eaten at a few ceremonial events or when a weak animal is culled from the herd to prevent it from breeding; they are not a regular source of meat. The primary sources of meat in the Tungus diet are wild reindeer, deer, elk, bear, wolves, and boars that are obtained by hunting and trapping.

The Tungus must travel with their herds as they migrate between their summer and winter pasturages. The northern tundra is the preferred feeding ground during the short summer, because lichens and other foods are more plentiful than in the forest lands to the south. During the four months of summer, the herds are plagued by mosquitoes and gadflies, so the reindeer feed at night and congregate in the daytime around smoky fires built by the Tungus to repel the pests. For the rest of the year, the herds move south and pasture during the day, so that they can be protected at night from wolves.

The summer home of the Tungusic family is a birch bark lodge. In the winter, when the herds must travel constantly to forage for food beneath the snow, the home is a small skin tent occupied by a nuclear family. The husband is responsible for trapping and hunting and heavy labor around the camp, while the wife milks and cares for the herds and takes charge of the routine domestic chores. The husband's hunting and trapping activities are important, since they provide food, skins for clothing and tents, and furs that are used to trade for useful items such as rifles and metal utensils. This leaves the wife with a great deal of responsibility for the herds in the absence of her husband, including moving it to new grazing areas when this is necessary.

The northern Tungus's way of life became difficult to document during the Soviet Union's control of their territory, but it is clear that the northern Tungus's culture has changed dramatically. Frances Svenson (1980) reported that the introduction of alcohol into the society had disastrous effects, including many deaths among the Evenki. Efforts by the Soviet Union to collectivize the Siberian herds met with great resistance and led to the loss of about two-thirds of the animals. The building of early-warning radar sites, airstrips, and missile facilities in northern Siberia is believed to have resulted in the loss of lands by many of the Siberian herders, including the Tungus.

TUNGUS

A herding tribe in the territory of eastern Siberia, the Tungus depend on their reindeer and the land on which they graze to support themselves. During the Soviet Union's control of their territory, alcohol was introduced with disastrous effects on the health of the tribe, and the building of radar sites, airstrips, and missile facilities in northern Siberia has greatly reduced the amount of grazing land available to the tribe.

FIGURE 6.9

RAISED-FIELD FARMING

Clark L. Erickson, an archaeologist at the University of Pennsylvania, has been studying the remains of raised-field farming systems in Llanos de Moxos, an area east of the Andes in Bolivia, South America. In this system, rectangular plots were built up about three feet above ground level, were from 10 to 30 feet wide, and from 100 to 1,300 feet long. Canals, about 10 to 30 feet wide, were excavated to a depth of about three feet below ground level. They collected excess rain water and provided drainage for the fields.

Pastoralism.   A more specialized form of domestication technology is **pastoralism**, which focuses on animal husbandry as the major source of food. It is practiced in tribal societies found in areas unsuited to plant cultivation: the arctic, the subarctic, deserts, mountains, and grasslands. Pastoralism is thus probably of more recent origin than horticulture. Indeed, it is commonly argued that pastoralism in most parts of the world developed as farming peoples expanded into environmentally less productive zones and adjusted by relying more heavily on domestic animals as their basic source of income. Most pastoralists do supplement their diets with food grown in simple gardens, but plant growing is always subordinated to the demands of their animal husbandry. Thus pastoralism typically requires large areas of land and a somewhat migratory way of life called **transhumance**, the pastoralist practice of moving their animals between at least two different primary foraging areas at different elevations in different seasons. Pastoralism is the predominant means of subsistence in environ-

ments such as deserts, grasslands, savannas, and mountains that are unable reliably to sustain horticultural or nonindustrialized agricultural production.

There are several types of pastoralism that occupy somewhat different environments, depending on the animal that is the primary subsistence resource. Cattle herding was most common throughout sub-Saharan Africa, particularly throughout equatorial and east Africa, southern Africa, and parts of Madagascar. Cattle herding was also found in limited areas in the northern part of South America among the Goajiro, a people of mixed Native American and African origins. Many of the cattle-herding peoples combined pastoralism with some plant cultivation. Camels were the basis for pastoral-

(Continued on p. 154)

_____

pastoralism a subsistence technology based on animal husbandry

transhumance a form of pastoralism in which only a part of the group moves with the herd; some stay in villages and grow crops year round

FARMING LESSONS FROM PREHISTORY

For four or five months at a stretch, much of the vast savanna of Llanos de Moxos in northeastern Bolivia is under water. For the rest of the year, the flat landscape lies parched under the tropical sun.

An environment like that would seem to be good for little, least of all for farming. But the pre-historic peoples of the region did farm their land, on a vast scale. They were able to do so, for hundreds of years, because they came up with an ingenious response to the alternating floods and dry spells: Build the growing fields up above the water level and surround them with canals to capture the excess moisture.

Clark L. Erickson thinks those ancient farmers have something to teach their late-20th-century descendants.

Since 1990, Dr. Erickson, an archaeologist at the University of Pennsylvania, has been studying the remains of raised-field farming systems in the Llanos de Moxos that date back some 2,000 years. More than a traditional archaeological dig, however, the project he heads is also an experiment in building and farming raised fields. He and his colleagues want to learn not only how the ancient system might have worked, but also whether it might be put to use again by the peasants who now live in the region.

"I'm convinced that, technologically, this system is sound," Dr. Erickson says. "It's great. It's sustainable agriculture."

The Llanos de Moxos, which roughly coincides with the political boundaries of the Bolivian department (or state) of the Beni, lies east of the Andes in the area of South America known as Amazonia. The tropical lowlands are mostly flat savanna, or grassland, with some stands of dense forest on higher ground along the rivers. For much of the rainy season, from December through May, the savanna is covered by a thin sheet of water, although at certain times and places the ground may be several feet under.

Through the 1950's, experts believed that such an inhospitable environment could not have supported a large, culturally advanced population. In 1961, however, William M. Denevan, a geographer recently retired from the University of Wisconsin at Madison, working with an oil-company geologist, found the remains of prehistoric raised fields in the Llanos de Moxos.

"The Amazon is an area of very poor soils," he says. "Add to that the problem of flooding. To find that these areas were once cultivated was quite dramatic." . . .

The rectangular plots were built up roughly three feet above ground level, and were from 10 to 30 feet wide and from 100 to 1,300 feet long. Between the fields were canals, also 10 to 30 feet wide, that had been excavated to a depth of about three feet below ground level.

The excavated fields have provided a lot of information about phases of construction and the crops that were grown. But the ancient soil cannot tell researchers all they want to know, including such things as how productive the fields were or how much labor was required to build and maintain them—or why the system had been largely abandoned by the time the Spanish arrived in the 16th century. To try to answer some of those questions, Dr. Erickson turned to a method known as "experimental archaeology," which involves recreating things like ancient dwellings or tools as a way to determine how they might have been made and used. . . .

Data gathered by members of Dr. Erickson's project—added to information from research on raised-field sites elsewhere—reveal a good deal about why ancient farmers found the system advantageous.

Raising the fields, for example, increases the thickness of the topsoil in the area where crops are grown. The canals not only hold excess rain water, but also provide drainage for plots that would otherwise be water-logged. Muck from the bottom of the canals is rich in nutrients and can be used as a kind of "green manure" for the fields.

The proof, though, is in the plants. Among the crops Erickson has cultivated are bananas, maize, and beans, and their yields have usually exceeded those of local peasants using slash-and-burn methods. In the 1992–93 growing season, when heavy rains rotted the plants in ground-level plots, the raised fields produced the only manioc (cassava) in the area.

Dr. Erickson's scholarly work on the Bolivian raised fields also has a practical side. Unlike many other archaeologists, he is an active proponent of applying ancient knowledge to future development. In the Llanos de Moxos, he and his Bolivian colleagues are attempting to re-introduce the raised-field system as a viable means of economic support for the region's farmers. . . .

Erickson and others . . . believe that raised-field agriculture could be a key to the sustainable development of indigenous territories.

Raised fields, Erickson argues, can be built with simple tools, and do not require the large financial and technological investment that many third-world development projects call for. The initial construction of the fields is labor intensive, he adds, but subsequent maintenance is not, making the fields relatively cost-effective.

From "Farming Lessons from Prehistory" by Ellen K. Coughlin, February 17, 1995, *The Chronicle of Higher Education*, pp. A10, A15.

ism throughout northern Africa and the Arabian Peninsula. Reindeer herding was particularly important among various peoples of the far north, including the Lapps of the northern Scandinavian subarctic and various peoples in Siberia. Yak herding was limited to the high mountain regions of the Himalayan area. A similar, geographically limited form of pastoralism was found in the Andes of South America, where llama herding in combination with agricultural production was important for societies such as the Inca who dominated the area at the time of European contact. Mixed pastoralism, the predominant type throughout western Asia north of India, combined a variety of animals such as sheep, goats, horses, and cattle.

Since they occupy territory that is often marginal and unproductive, pastoralists are generally unable to produce everything they need. Therefore, they must obtain some goods from neighboring horticultural or agricultural peoples. This is often accomplished by trade, but sometimes it is more profitable to raid their more sedentary neighbors. Especially when the animals they keep, such as horses or camels, give them great mobility, these peoples can carry out their raids rapidly with little warning and leave quickly afterwards.

Since the herds of pastoralists are vulnerable to theft, pastoralists must constantly be with their herds and live in perpetual readiness for conflict. Warfare is a prominent fact of life in pastoral tribes. Thus, childrearing emphasizes obedience, deference to authority figures, and a competitive and socially dominant role for male warriors.

Intensive Cultivation.   In extensive cultivation, gardens cycle between years of cultivation and years of idleness (see p. 148). In contrast, **intensive cultivation** involves a smaller number of fields that are used year after year. Intensification has a variety of causes. Crops available in some environments may lend themselves to more intensive use of the same fields. For instance, fruit trees that bear year after year may make it possible to utilize the intensive cultivation of some gardens while fields used for other crops are still being cultivated extensively. New food-growing techniques can also bring about more intensive use of fields. For instance, food growers may intensify their cultivation techniques by the addition of more complex irrigation methods or crop rotation. The increased productivity allows com-

munities to become completely sedentary and local populations to reach larger levels characteristic of chiefdoms, societies that support full-time governmental authorities and even hierarchies of political authorities that unite many communities under the same government (see chapter 11, p. 266).

Intensive cultivation forms a continuum of increasing productivity. The most productive levels, referred to as **agriculture**, include the use of such tools and techniques as animal fertilizers, crop rotation, draft animals, and the plow. Agriculture is much more recent than horticulture, being a scant 6,000 years old, but it has proven to be a very successful form of subsistence, and agricultural societies have become the largest, most widespread, most dominant peoples in the world and occupy the most productive parts of the world's surface. An important feature of the social changes brought about by agriculture is the development of true states, societies with cities, large populations, true social classes, and full-time governments that monopolize all legal authority (see chapter 11, p. 269).

The simplest form of agriculture is **nonindustrialized (traditional) agriculture**. In this form, the major tools are hand implements such as the hoe, shovel, and animal-drawn plow. Crops are grown for local consumption, but the use of the plow, animal-derived fertilizers, and irrigation results in greater productivity than is usual in extensive cultivation, so that market crops may also be produced. Use of the plow and animal or human fertilizer to enhance the productivity of the soil makes agriculture more land intensive than labor intensive. While horticulturalists can expand their populations only by opening new land to cultivation, land-intensive agriculture can allow farmers to support population growth by increasing the output of their fields. The populations of towns occupied by agricultural peoples commonly number in the thousands or tens of

---

intensive cultivation the use of food growing techniques that permit permanent use of the same fields

agriculture the form of intensive cultivation that uses tools and techniques such as irrigation, animal traction, and fertilization of the soil

nonindustrialized (traditional) agriculture intensive cultivation using simple tools such as hoes, shovels, and animal-drawn plows

NONINDUSTRIALIZED AGRICULTURE

Agriculture makes use of more complicated technology than horticulture to produce food. The use of plows pulled by draft animals and simple organic fertilizers characterize the complexity of nonindustrialized agriculture. Tending his cornfield, Romá Neria Franco guides his mule near Tenango del Aire, Mexico.

thousands. Such large groups require a high degree of specialization and the presence of a system of government that is not based solely on the authority of the family organization. Because of the large urban populations that agriculture can support, agricultural societies frequently have class distinctions with inherited differences in political power and wealth within the local communities.

Industrialized Agriculture. The form of food production that relies most heavily on technological means for harnessing energy, such as fossil fuels and hydroelectric power rather than human or animal labor, is **industrialized agriculture**. Currently, its tool kit includes motorized equipment such as tillers, tractors, and harvesters. Chemical fertilizers are used to enhance the productivity of the soil, herbicides are used to minimize unwanted plants that compete with crops for water and soil nutrients, and pesticides play an important role in minimizing crop destruction by insects. Industrialized agriculturalists not only irrigate their fields, but also may employ various techniques for modifying the effects of adverse weather conditions—for instance, by shading crops or artificially maintaining higher temperatures around their plants during periods of cold weather.

Industrialized agricultural techniques create high yields with relatively little investment of human labor. On the other hand, these techniques are very inefficient in terms of the ratio of energy used to produce food to the number of calories yielded. By comparison, in horticulture, human labor is intense, but represents

---

traditional agriculture nonindustrialized agriculture
industrialized agriculture the use of an industrialized technology and other techniques such as chemical soil fertilization to obtain high levels of food production per acre

almost the entire investment of energy for producing food. In preindustrialized agriculture, human labor is supplemented by the work of draft animals such as oxen whose upkeep, along with the costs of manufacturing tools such as the plow, results in a much greater investment in producing each year's crop. Industrialized agriculture carries this to an extreme. In addition to human labor on the farm, it requires the work of specialists who manufacture and maintain farm equipment, petroleum products such as gasoline and oil to fuel the equipment, and chemical fertilizers, herbicides, and pesticides to increase yields. There are also costs in transporting produce to factories, in packaging the food, in delivering the packaged goods to markets, and in marketing them. Susan Brown and J. Clair Batty (1976) estimated that the energy to produce, process, package, transport, market, purchase, prepare, and eat a single can of corn that contained 269 calories of digestible food energy could easily require the expenditure of 5,384 calories of energy by the time the dishwasher finished running. Thus, industrialized agriculture is tremendously productive in that a small number of people are able to provide enough food to support a large population, but extremely inefficient in requiring much more energy to produce per calorie than do production systems that rely on human and animal labor. Industrialized agriculture also has other costs in its long-term impact on the environment. For instance, pesticides can migrate from the fields to which they are applied into the groundwater and neighboring streams, where they can adversely affect humans and other animals. Industrialized farm equipment can also cause faster loss of topsoil than preindustrialized farming.

High-yield production techniques, coupled with an industrialized system of transportation to carry the produce over great distances, have made possible the rise of farms of tremendous acreage. An industrialized agriculture nevertheless operates at great costs, when one measures the amount of energy required to produce food. But it is so productive that in the United States less than 3 percent of the population is involved in food production.

Societies whose subsistence technology is industrialized agriculture invariably support sufficiently large populations that they must be organized by full-time governments that monopolize political power. The populations commonly number in the millions or hundreds of millions. Indeed, individual cities in industrialized societies may number in the tens of millions.

CHAPTER SUMMARY

1. Natural environments place limits on the characteristics of the cultures that societies have developed in different parts of the world.

2. Each environment contains the particular resources that a society may use to meet its people's survival needs.

3. The use of some resources provides opportunities for the development of large social groups and tremendous social complexity, while the use of others may severely restrict the size and complexity of a society.

4. One traditional way of categorizing the world's natural environments divides the world into eight basic habitats: mixed forests, scrub forests, tropical forests, mountain lands, grasslands, arid lands, boreal forests, and polar lands.

5. Each of these environments has a unique set of resources that provide opportunities and set limits on cultural development.

6. In adapting to the world's various environments, human societies have developed a variety of subsistence technologies, including foraging, horticulture, pastoralism, traditional agriculture, and industrialized agriculture.

ANNOTATED READINGS

Cohen, Y. (Ed.). (1974). *Man in adaptation: The cultural present.* Chicago: Aldine. A collection of articles about the environmental adaptations of pastoral and farming societies.

Douglas, M., & Isherwood, B. (1979). *The world of goods: Toward an anthropology of consumption.* New York: W. W. Norton. Discusses economic theories of consumption and how anthropologists might study consumption.

Duke, P. G., & Wilson M. (1995). *Beyond subsistence: Plains archaeology and the postprocessual critique.* Tuscaloosa: University of Alabama Press. An examination of the North American Great Plains from an environmental archaeology perspective.

Gish, J. W. (1993). *Subsistence and environment.* Albuquerque: Office of Contract Archaeology and Maxwell Museum of Anthropology, University of New Mexico. An examination of prehistoric subsistence practices within the environments of North America, based on archaeological evidence.

Harris, M. (1986). *Good to eat.* New York: Harper & Row. A collection of essays on the reasons for cultural differences in what is eaten, by the founder of the cultural materialistic approach to studying culture.

James, P. E. (with collaboration by H. V. B. Kline, Jr.). (1959). *A geography of man.* Boston: Ginn. An influential attempt to classify the world's major primary environments.

Kroeber, A. (1939). *Cultural and natural areas of native North America.* University of California Publications in American Archaeology and Ethnology, vol. 38. The first systematic anthropological demonstration of the relationships between cultural areas and natural environments.

Lean, G., & Henrichson, D. (1994). *Atlas of the environment.* Santa Barbara, CA: ABC-CLIO. An atlas of the world's contemporary environmental characteristics.

Lustig-Arecco, V. (1975). *Technology: Strategies for survival.* New York: Holt, Rinehart & Winston. An examination of the role of technology in the adaptation of hunters, pastoralists, and farmers.

Rappaport, R. (1967). *Pigs for the ancestors: Ritual in the ecology of a Papua New Guinea people.* New Haven, CT: Yale University Press. A cultural ecological analysis of the Tsembaga Maring that emphasizes the role of pig herding as a regulatory mechanism in Tsembaga warfare.

Vayda, A. (Ed.). (1969). *Environment and cultural behavior: Ecological studies in cultural anthropology.* New York: Natural History Press. A classic collection of writings that illustrates the cultural ecological approach to understanding human customs in the social, demographic, and environmental contexts in which they are found.

Wallerstein, I. (1974). *The modern world-system.* New York: Academic Press. The pioneering statement about the origins of the world economic system.

CHAPTER SEVEN

Cultural Evolution and the Contemporary World

After reading this chapter, you should be able to:

Discuss how cultural change occurs.

Analyze the interrelationships among the three cultural subsystems: technology, social organization, and ideology.

Contrast specific and general evolution.

Explain the principles of cultural evolution.

Discuss the nature and causes of alienation.

Discuss the processes of acculturation, ethnocide, and genocide.

Analyze the process of industrialization.

Compare and contrast developed and underdeveloped societies.

Discuss feudal and colonial peasantries.

Describe contemporary peasantries.

Explain the work of applied anthropology.

Explain the role of population control in developing nations.

◀ *Figure 7.1 Culture Dynamics Cultural changes may arise within a society or may result from the influence of one society on another. As this Samburu Warrior illustrates, technology has infiltrated even the desolate regions of northern Kenya. Cellular phones and computers are bringing all the world's cultures closer together.*

Human cultural systems do not remain stable forever. In adjusting to the world around them, to the effects of population growth, and to the influence of other groups, human beings adopt new and different ways of manipulating their environment, of organizing themselves, and of thinking and communicating. Over the millennia, societies have evolved from simple hunting and gathering ways of life to extremely complex ones based upon industrialized technologies. In this chapter we will explore the process of cultural change and the forces that have influenced the rise of societies that have greater technological and social complexity. We will consider whether technological progress is synonymous with progress in the quality of life. We will also examine the diverse contemporary world, in which hunting and gathering cultures that have changed little over thousands of years coexist with rapidly modernizing industrial cultures whose trappings range from superhighways, heart transplants, and cable television to polluted air and water. Between these two extremes, the mass of humanity are peasants, living from the land by hand labor, with little income for luxury goods.

Tai chi. Cannes. PC compatible. Yeltsin. Clinton. Bosnia and Herzegovina. Are we becoming a global culture? Is there any area of the world that has not seen the golden arches? Or not felt the influence of a microchip? What has made us what we are, and how do we maintain individual and cultural autonomy in a world that is becoming culturally unified?

THE PROCESS OF CHANGE

Cultural traits are subject to many change-promoting influences, both internal and external. As one trait changes, others also shift, ultimately altering the nature of the entire cultural system.

Cultural Dynamics

No culture is completely static. Cultural changes may arise within a society, or they may result from the cultural influence of one society on another. The primary forms of change are innovation, diffusion, and acculturation.

Innovation. The development of any new characteristic within a culture that occurs as a result of discovery or invention can be called an **innovation**. **Discovery** involves noticing something that has not been noticed before, while **inventions** involve putting previous cultural elements together in some new way. Discoveries and inventions do not occur randomly, since the current cultural pattern of thinking in any society prepares people to notice or accept some new things more readily than others, and cultural values will favor some forms of change over others. If innovations depart too radically from the current way of thinking, they may not be valued or may even seem bizarre to most members of society and, thus, will not be accepted. In a culture with a high degree of role specialization, it is possible for some members of society to have experiences that are so uncommon in society at large that the insights they produce will be regarded as insignificant, foolish, or of no practical use. For instance, Gregor Mendel, a nineteenth-century Austrian monk, spent years cultivating plants, and in the process developed revolutionary new ideas about genetics that were shelved for years. It was only much later that growing interest in evolutionary theory among biologists provided a place where Mendel's discoveries proved to be very useful and enlightening to the scientific community.

Diffusion. Cultural changes that occur as a result of the influence of one society on another are referred to as **diffusion**. Anthropologists generally distinguish between two forms of diffusion: **direct borrowing** of traits and

---

innovation changes in a culture as a result of discovery or invention

discovery the development of new insights and ideas

invention the act of combining preexisting cultural traits in new ways

diffusion the passage of a cultural trait such as customs, artifacts, and ideas from one society to another

direct borrowing the adopting of a cultural trait by one society from another with relatively little change in form, as exemplified by traits acquired through trade or imitation

FIGURE 7.2

ACCULTURATION

The Ainu, an indigenous people who live on Hokkaido, Japan's northernmost island, are fighting to maintain their own autonomous culture rather than be completely assimilated by the Japanese. The battle is being led by Masanori Toyooka, on the right. He hopes to obtain four islands as a home for the Ainu from the Russians, who seized them in World War II. Fusae Doi, on the left, works with him to preserve Ainu handicrafts.

stimulus diffusion, in which the idea of the trait rather than the trait itself passes from one people to another. In both cases, the trait is likely to be modified in form, use, and meaning, to fit into the way of life of the recipient society. But the greatest changes occur in stimulus diffusion when the trait is created anew by the borrowing society to meet its own needs.

Tobacco provides an example of what changes occur in a directly borrowed trait. It was originally used in religious rituals in Native American cultures. In the process of being assimilated by other cultures, both the crop and methods of its preparation have been greatly modified (Linton, 1936). It is now used in most parts of the world as a recreational substance, rather than for religious purposes. The transmission of writing from Mesopotamia to Egypt illustrates how the form of a trait may be changed when it is borrowed through stimulus diffusion. It is believed by many that the idea of writing was borrowed by the Egyptians, but instead of using Mesopotamian written symbols, the Egyptians created entirely new pictorial forms to write their own language.

Acculturation. When two or more cultures interact intensely so that they change in the process of adjusting to each other, anthropologists term the adjustments **acculturation**. The process of cultural change may begin before members of the two societies actually meet, as technological traits from one society are traded through intermediary societies until they reach far distant groups. But acculturation occurs most dramatically when two societies are interacting directly. As each adopts the other's technological, social, and ideological traits, it becomes more like the other. When one of the societies is politically, economically, and technologically less powerful than the other, it will change the most. When this process is carried to an extreme, the subordinate culture can

stimulus diffusion the borrowing of the idea for a cultural trait by one society from another, with the implementation of that idea being more or less determined within the borrowing culture

acculturation the process in which one culture adapts to the influence of another culture by borrowing many of its traits

change so much that it is hardly distinguishable from the dominant one. As a more powerful society extends its boundaries and politically subordinates a less powerful people within its own native territory, the indigenous people generally come to have very little influence on the political decision making of the society that governs them.

The process of acculturation can take place forcibly, for instance, through military domination. It can also occur more peaceably through mechanisms such as trade. As members of the less powerful society seek to acquire useful materials from their more powerful trade partners, their own way of life changes in the process. Acculturation can eventually lead to the extinction of an entire culture even though its people survive (see also p. 170).

The general long-term effects of the interaction of societies of unequal power have been formulated by David Kaplan (1960) as the **Law of Cultural Dominance**: "That cultural system which more effectively exploits the energy resources of a given environment will tend to spread in the environment at the expense of less effective systems." Any interacting cultures have some effect on each other. But, since more traits flow from the dominant to the subordinate culture, the latter is the one more likely to be radically altered—if it survives the effects of contact with the more powerful society at all.

The Law of Cultural Dominance is not an invariable process. Cultures differ in their receptivity to acculturation on the basis of their degree of evolutionary adaptation. Some technologically simple societies have been remarkably resistant to the effects of cultural change at the hands of more powerful societies. Ruth Benedict (1934) pointed out long ago that the Pueblo Indians have had a long history of rather successful resistance to the effects of cultural traits of neighboring peoples. Nevertheless, in the general evolutionary scheme, societies with greater technological control over energy resources have fairly consistently expanded while technologically simple societies are becoming fewer each year.

Interrelationships among Technology, Social Organization, and Ideology

Change may begin within any aspect of culture, but is likely then to affect other aspects of culture as well. The major goals of culture-guided behaviors are manipulation of the external environment with a technology, social interaction within a social organization, and symbolic expression of experiences that are made meaningful by a shared ideology. These three major subsystems of culture—technology, social organization, and ideology—are related, and change within any one will affect the others (see Fig. 7.3).

Evolution through Technological Change. Some anthropologists consider technology—the means by which energy is drawn from the environment and used within a society—to be the area most likely to be the leading edge of cultural change. Leslie White (1971) formalized this idea as the **Basic Law of Cultural Evolution**: "Other factors remaining constant, culture evolves as the amount of energy harnessed per capita per year is increased, or as the efficiency of the technological means of putting the energy to work is increased" (pp. 368–369). Due to the extreme reliance of humans on tools to maintain life, changes in the tool kit of a society have profound effects on the nature of the society itself and on a people's understanding of the world.

The economy has the most immediate technological effect on the social organization, because its structure determines the division of labor in the production and distribution of subsistence goods. Population size is affected too: the more effective a subsistence technology becomes at providing energy beyond the minimum necessary for survival, the larger the population will grow. As the population expands, there will be a corresponding increase in the complexity of the social organization and other parts of the technology. With increasing numbers of statuses and specialization—and interdependence of statuses—new and more complex means of political control will develop. New specialized political statuses take over roles previously fulfilled by kinship. Societies with the most complex technologies also

---

Law of Cultural Dominance the principle that the cultural system that effectively exploits the energy resources of a given environment has the tendency to spread into that environment at the expense of less effective systems

Basic Law of Cultural Evolution the concept that increases in energy harnessed or in efficiency of its use through technological change are the primary cause of cultural evolution

FIGURE 7.3

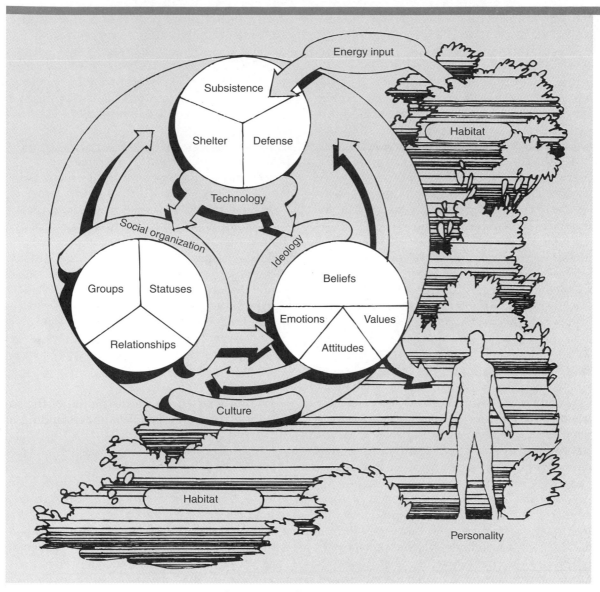

CULTURAL SUBSYSTEMS

This chart shows the relationship of the cultural subsystems of technology, social organization, and ideology. Change in any one will affect the others.

tend to be those that are most highly stratified with ranked statuses, some of which have access to great amounts of power, prestige, and control over the material wealth of the society.

Technological changes will be reflected in ideological adjustments, first as new informal patterns of ideas and feelings arise and later as the formal, conscious ideology finally accommodates to the new circumstances. The ideology may reflect technological or social innovation by actually adding new beliefs.

A classic example of the effects of technological change on social organization and ideology is the case described by Sharp (1952) of

the introduction of steel hatchets to the Yir Yiront, an Australian hunting and gathering society that had previously known only the stone axe. Among the Yir Yiront, stone axes were manufactured only by adult men and were exclusively their makers' property. They were, however, commonly used by women, by men who owned no axe of their own, and by children, all of whom had to borrow one from an adult male kinsman. The process reinforced the authority of the kinship system that structured the society, and the axes themselves served as symbols of masculinity and male dominance in the social and economic system. Enter the

European missionaries, who attempted to help the Yir Yiront "improve their conditions of life" by distributing or trading to everyone steel axes which, being technologically more efficient tools, were to help the natives "progress." What the missionaries did not understand was that this change undermined the authority of the adult males of the society and eventually had a disruptive effect on the economic system of the Yir Yiront as well, since their trade with neighboring peoples was motivated by the need to acquire stone to manufacture the axes. The festive annual gatherings at which trade previously had occurred began to lose their social importance and excitement as trading partnerships weakened. A married man might find it easier to obtain a steel axe from white men by selling his wife's services as a prostitute than by traditional means, which was hardly the sort of "progress" anticipated by the European missionaries.

Evolution through Social Change. Cultural change may begin not only within the technological subsystem but also within the social organization. As a population grows, the number of social relationships increases, and new ways of coordinating society are needed. New statuses and institutions arise in response to these pressures. In very simple societies, the family is the fundamental institution of social control. It educates the young, produces food and other economic goods, carries out judicial activities when members violate important rules, and performs other "governmental" functions. As societies increase in population and density, new institutions arise to help coordinate human interaction. One important new institution is the special-interest nonkinship association—groups such as the local militia composed of all young men of the group, the voluntary fire brigade, or the harvest cooperative group. Larger-scale societies begin to develop full-time specialists and other new statuses and groups such as full-time governmental specialists, draft laborers, religious leaders, and standing armies.

As the social organization becomes more complex, cultural changes are reflected in the society's technology and ideology. For instance, when producers begin to specialize in the manufacture of a given item, it tends to become more standardized in form. Ideologically, as governmental specialization develops, members of the society increasingly value order and stability, even at the expense of individual autonomy.

Evolution through Ideological Change. Adjustments in the cultural subsystems that are initiated in the ideological realm may be exemplified by processes such as the birth of a new religious or political philosophy. When successful, the new doctrine is proclaimed by a social body organized by the author of the new teachings. New ideologies thus give rise to new social structures, which, in turn, influence the functioning of the culture's technology.

An ideology may, on the other hand, slow the process of change. The Old Order Amish of Pennsylvania are a well-known example of a social body that for ideological reasons has remained highly resistant to the complex technological changes that have occurred among surrounding communities. The Amish have maintained a horse-and-buggy transportation system, a horse-drawn plow subsistence technology, and a home life largely unaffected by the presence of radios, televisions, and other common North American household appliances.

CULTURAL EVOLUTIONARY THEORY

The observable differences among tribes, bands, chiefdoms, and states have led a number of anthropologists to speculate about whether these levels constitute developmental stages in the advance toward civilization, the progress of societies from one stage to another, or improvements in the quality of life. In asking such questions, they have tried to formulate general laws that can be applied to the process of cultural evolution in all societies.

Specific and General Evolution

The existence of extensive parallels in the development of early civilizations suggests that the evolution of ways of life is as orderly as biological evolution. Marshall Sahlins and Elman R. Service (1960) and Service (1971) have clarified the regularity of cultural evolution by pointing out that cultures change in two fundamentally different ways: (1) through a process of **specific evolution**, or change in the

---

specific evolution change in the direction of increasing adaptive specialization

direction of increasing adaptive specialization; and (2) through a process of **general evolution**, or change in the direction of increasing complexity. In the first, a way of life becomes more adjusted to its specific environmental circumstances—in a word, more specialized. In the second, new parts of a total environment are drawn upon by the cultural system. As a culture becomes more complex, it relates to its environment in radically new ways, harnessing greater amounts of energy for new uses. Qualitative change is the hallmark of general evolution.

While biological changes cannot be passed from one species to another, the traits that arise in one culture may pass over into another. Thus, the evolutionary development of cultures must be seen in terms of the interplay of the specific and general evolutionary changes that occur within cultures and the interactions between cultures.

Stabilization vs. Evolutionary Potential

It is the interaction between cultures that makes possible an interplay between the forces of specific and general evolution. Acting alone, specific evolution leads ultimately to stability. If a culture were ever to achieve a perfect adaptation to its environment, any further change would be maladaptive. If a way of life is relatively inefficient in helping a society to deal with its environment, it is a simple matter for a people to improve their adjustment to the circumstances. However, the more efficient a way of life becomes in making use of the resources available to a people, the more expensive and difficult it becomes to implement each new increase in efficiency, so that change in the direction of greater adaptation gradually slows and a way of life becomes more stable. This fact has been referred to by Thomas Harding (1960) as the **Principle of Stabilization**. On the basis of this principle, Sahlins and Service (1960) have formulated what they call the **Law of Evolutionary Potential**, which states that a culture's capacity to move from one general evolutionary stage to another varies inversely with its degree of specific evolutionary adaptation.

If it were not for general evolution, interacting cultures would continue increasing their adaptations to their environments and to each other until a final stability would be achieved among them. But, as we have seen, under cer-

tain circumstances cultures may adapt to their environment in ways that cause a qualitative change in social complexity and power. General evolutionary change inevitably disrupts the previous balance of power between neighboring societies. As each new general evolutionary stage is achieved, societies at the new level expand at the expense of simpler, less powerful cultures. Some of these simpler societies may be absorbed. Others may be driven out of their territory or annihilated as the more complex society expands in population and acquires new territory. Still others may adopt the new technology themselves and thus enter the new level of general evolution. The latter will eventually need to improve the efficiency of their use of the technology that made the transition to the new stage possible. As this process occurs, the earlier dominant societies of this stage are likely to achieve a high degree of social stability sooner than latecomers do.

Leapfrogging

When considered in light of the Law of Evolutionary Potential, the first culture to make the transition from one general evolutionary level to the next becomes specialized in a technology, making it difficult for it to move to an even more complex stage. Instead, it is the backwater cultures, those that are less specifically adapted to their current situation, that have the greatest chance to leap ahead in power and complexity by adopting and implementing radically new technologies. This fact has been formulated into another general law of cultural evolution, called the **Law of Local Discontinuity of Progress**. This law states that successive stages of general evolutionary change are not likely to be achieved

---

general evolution change in the direction of increasing complexity

Principle of Stabilization the concept that the more efficient a culture becomes at harnessing energy for society, the more expensive and difficult it becomes to implement new means of increasing efficiency

Law of Evolutionary Potential the concept that a culture's capacity to move from one general evolutionary stage to another varies inversely with the degree of its specific evolutionary adaptation to its environment

Law of Local Discontinuity of Progress the idea that the successive stages of general evolutionary change are not likely to occur in the same locality

in the same locality. General evolutionary change tends to occur in a kind of leapfrogging way, with the dominant centers of world power shifting from one area to another over the centuries.

Service (1971) has argued that this leapfrogging process is likely to continue into the future. It is his contention that, should no unpredictable factor such as a war intervene, the most likely course of future events is one in which Western civilization will be eclipsed by some of the currently underdeveloped nations. "Those nations that are now the most advanced in the present coal and oil complex have less potential for the full and efficient use of the industry of the future than certain hitherto 'underdeveloped' regions which could build a new civilization well-adapted to such a base" (p. 42). Other anthropologists believe that the current balance of power between the more developed and less developed nations is not likely to change because it is now maintained by a web of economic interdependencies worldwide in scope.

The forces of industrialization, of course, are still spreading gradually throughout the world. In Western Europe and North America, the process was one that began with quite small-scale industries and expanded to the large and complex international industrial corporations of today over a period of centuries. The social, political, and ideological life of these regions was gradually transformed to fit the needs of the developing industrial complex. Those areas of the world that are just now beginning the process of industrialization are naturally seeking to do so quickly. In Service's words, "They will begin with the latest and most advanced of the known technologies and attempt to create the complete industrial complex at once, skipping whole epochs of our development" (pp. 44–45).

Service has suggested that, in the process of worldwide industrialization, at least some of the developing nations may surpass the status of the United States and the (former) Soviet Union as the world's dominant powers, both politically and economically. However, other factors besides a culture's ability to change readily must be considered in assessing trends in cultural development. Part of the adjustment of a culture to its specific environment is its relationship to other cultures with which it must interact. In the contemporary world, the global nature of economic forces and the political and economic influences of the world's dominant nations are major factors in how the rest of the world's cultures are changing. It is quite possible that these influences will inhibit the traditional leapfrogging pattern of cultural change.

Progress?

Does technological progress also produce progress in quality of life? The major changes that occur in societies when technologies harness more energy are increases in population, in the number of statuses and groups, and in the specialization of roles. Inherent in these changes is an increased interdependence of everyone in society. Individuals have less autonomy and less ability to fulfill their own needs and must rely upon others to perform necessary tasks for which they themselves lack the skills. In general, family continues to play a role as an economic group in consumption, but tends to lose its role as a production and distribution group. The role of kinship as an economic and political force also declines. In the realm of ideology, more and more facets of life need to be understood in mechanistic rather than spiritual terms, for the role of religion declines as a culture becomes more generally evolved. All of these trends tend to make the lives of individuals less and less secure and stable.

Alienation. The major psychological effect of individuals' decreasing autonomy and control over their own lives is referred to as **alienation**. The concept of alienation is most strongly associated with Karl Marx (1961), who argued in 1844 that alienation develops when the work of individuals ceases to satisfy human needs directly and becomes instead merely a means of satisfying those needs indirectly. In the simplest societies, individual roles are highly generalized, and each individual possesses most of the skills necessary for survival. For instance, if a woman is hungry, she takes up a basket and a digging stick (often of her own making) and goes in search of food. This direct relationship between work and personal needs leads to a sense of fulfillment in work. As societies become more complex, however, persons work not to satisfy their immediate physical needs but merely to obtain some ob-

---

alienation dissociation of workers from ownership of things they produce, accompanied by feelings of powerlessness and boredom

FIGURE 7.4

TECHNOLOGICAL PROGRESS

These Shinto priests perform an elaborate purification rite for the safety of a prototype of Japan's new FSX fighter. While new technology may boost a nation's economy, religious traditions may have to be adjusted so that their rites take account of those changes.

ject such as money that can later be used to satisfy those needs. The labor is a step removed from the purpose for which it is ultimately performed. A telephone operator may spend the day pushing buttons in service of others, an activity that has no obvious connection with obtaining food or shelter or any other personal need. He or she may receive payment for this work only once a month and is not likely to feel the same personal satisfaction in that daily work as does the hunter in manufacturing the salmon spear or rabbit snare that will be used to obtain the day's meal.

The effects of alienation are multiplied when individuals must work for others in order to survive. Under such conditions, even the direct products of a worker's labor do not belong to him or her, and this lack of control reduces the sense of satisfaction for having created some useful or aesthetic object.

High specialization of labor also leads to competition among interdependent spe-

cialists. Each attempts to obtain the most possible from his or her goods or services at the expense of others. Such competition also increases the sense of alienation from society, which is a source of human security and meaningfulness.

The first anthropologist to emphasize the concept of alienation in the study of human cultures was Edward Sapir (1924). He went so far as to suggest that cultures could be rated in terms of how "inherently harmonious, balanced, self-satisfactory" they are, a view that has received little attention from other anthropologists. Although he did not suggest that there is a direct relationship between the complexity of a society and the degree to which its culture is "a spiritual hybrid of contradictory patches, of water-tight compartments of consciousness that avoid participation in a harmonious synthesis" (p. 410), there is an obvious parallel between his views and Marx's concept of alienation.

WESTERN SHOSHONE LAND RIGHTS IN THE UNITED STATES

Denying indigenous peoples the right to control their own lives is not just a thing of the past. It continues to occur wherever indigenous peoples are found. The ongoing political contest between the Western Shoshone of the North American Great Basin region and the U.S. government is just one powerful example of how once-sovereign societies lose their autonomy to powerful nations.

In 1863 the U.S. government signed the Treaty of Ruby Valley with the Western Shoshone, who occupied a 43,000-square-mile territory that included parts of southern California, the eastern half of Nevada, and parts of Idaho. This treaty was unusual in the history of relationships between the United States and American Indian societies because it ceded no land to the United States, which was still involved in a civil war and was concerned with ensuring the continued flow of gold from California. The Shoshone did agree to end warfare against the United States and to allow the construction of roads, railways, and telegraph lines through mining settlements within their territory. Over the next 125 years, the U.S. government obtained billions of dollars worth of resources from Western Shoshone lands under this arrangement.

During the 1920s conflicts over land use increased between the Shoshone and non-Indian settlers. In 1934 the U.S. government installed a tribal council form of government among the Shoshone, a system that was fundamentally different from their traditional way of governing. In 1946 Congress created the Indian Claims Commission, which would be authorized to adjudicate Native American land claims against the United States. The legislation authorized lawyers who represented Indians in such cases to be paid 10 percent of any awards the commission made to Indians. In the same year, the Bureau of Indian Affairs persuaded one group of Shoshone, the Temoak Bank, to file a claim for compensation for the loss of Shoshone lands. The Temoak understood the purpose of this claim to be the recovery of their control over their traditional lands.

The law firm appointed by the Bureau of Indian Affairs to represent the Shoshone was the same one that had drafted the legislation creating the claims commission. Other Western Shoshone bands protested that their land had never been ceded to the United States, and that to accept compensation would amount to selling their lands. In 1951 the law firm petitioned the claims commission to recognize that its actions in behalf of the Temoak Shoshone actually represented the interests of the entire Western Shoshone people. A group of Temoak Shoshone were selected by the law firm as the "exclusive representatives" of the Western Shoshone. Those who disagreed with its plans were dismissed from the group. Despite objections by the majority of the Shoshone

THE VANISHING OF NONSTATE SOCIETIES

As the cultures of the world evolved, societies at each new general evolutionary level were technologically and socially more powerful than those of the preceding levels. Throughout the history of cultural evolution, societies with less dense populations have been displaced by those with technologies that have allowed their populations to grow increasingly powerful. Tribes have displaced bands, and chiefdoms have expanded at the expense of both band and tribal peoples. The process continues today as the state-level societies take control of territories that once belonged to nonstate peoples. As this happens, more and more of the nonstate societies of the world are becoming extinct.

Indigenous Peoples

Today, relatively few bands, tribes, and chiefdoms still exist, and the number is declining each year. The expansion of state societies into territories once occupied by nonstate societies has given rise to groups called **indigenous people**, who are the native people of an area now controlled by a state political system within which they have little or no influence. Today, about 200 million people, or less than 4 percent of the world's population, have this status. As we shall see, however, most indigenous people do not continue to live their ancestral way of life. Those who do are an even smaller minority.

---

indigenous people a group of people whose occupation of an area precedes the state political system that now controls that area, and who have little or no influence within that political system

involved, the petition was granted by the commission. The Temoak and other Shoshone soon learned that the law firm was not attempting to secure a ruling that would recognize their ownership of their traditional land; instead it was seeking a monetary award.

In 1962, the Indian Claims Commission noted that it had been "unable to discover any formal extinguishment" of Western Shoshone lands in Nevada. However, on February 11, 1966, the law firm that ostensibly represented the Shoshone's interests *against* U.S encroachment on Shoshone lands *stipulated* that the Shoshone had ceded 24 million acres of land to the United States (including 16 million acres that were occupied by no one but Shoshone Indians), and arbitrarily fixed the date of that stipulated loss as July 1, 1872, the middle day of the year, but otherwise a date of no known historical significance. The law firm requested that these lost lands be paid for and that land values in mid-1872 be used to compute the amount of the compensation. In 1972 the Indian Claims Commission concluded that the lands of the Western Shoshone had been "taken" in the nineteenth century by "gradual encroachment of whites, settlers and others."

Since the Temoak were now convinced that their lawyers were serving the interests of the U.S. government, instead of Indian interests, the Temoak fired the law firm as their agents. However, the Bureau of Indian Affairs refused to recognize the right of the Temoak to do so and continued to renew the firm's contract "in the Indians' behalf." In effect, the lawyers were now being employed by the government to act as representatives of the Indians against their clients' own wishes and to pursue a course of argument favored by the government.

The Western Shoshone hired their own lawyer and appealed the commission's ruling in the U.S. Court of Claims. The court refused to rule on the issue of who held title to the traditional Shoshone lands, but awarded the Shoshone $26,154,600 for the loss of 24 million acres, land that by 1979 values would have been worth more than $40 billion. The law firm that had been contracted by the Bureau of Indian Affairs was paid $2.5 million "for services rendered."

To pay the Shoshone for the lands they had now lost, the U.S. Department of Interior transferred $26,145,189.89 (the amount of the award less $9,410.11 as an offset against goods it claimed the government had delivered to the Shoshone in the 1870s) into a trust account held by the U.S. Treasury Department in behalf of the Shoshone. Accumulating interest since 1979, this money now amounts to 70 million dollars. The Western Shoshone have refused to accept receipt of this money since that date. Their purpose had never been to sell their territory, but to gain recognition of their ownership of it. As of June 1995, the Western Shoshone have unsuccessfully continued their efforts to reassert their sovereignty over their traditional lands.

According to Burger (1987), indigenous peoples live on all five continents. They are found in about half of the 161 member states of the United Nations. In North America there are about 2.5 million Native Americans. There are between 25 and 30 million indigenous Indian people in Central and South America and about 60,000 Sami (formerly known as Lapps) in Scandinavia. Maoris make up about 240,000 of New Zealand's population. There are about 250,000 Aboriginal Australians. Over 14 million indigenous peoples live in Africa. The remaining 136 million are found in Asia: about 6.5 million in the Philippines, 11 million in Myanmar, 500,000 in Thailand, 51 million in India, and 67 million in China.

Once, the ancestors of today's indigenous peoples occupied most of the world. Conquest and colonization changed that. Many have been dispossessed of their traditional lands and have resettled. Those whose lands were of little use to the national economies of the conquering states remain in their native territories, although even these people have typically been forced into restricted areas such as the Indian reservations of the United States. The territories of today's indigenous peoples, such as deserts, tundras, forests, mountains, and islands, can be termed **frontier areas**, lands that are unproductive for industrialized agriculture. But the insulation that frontier areas have provided for their inhabitants in the past is weakening. Their natural resources are gradually attracting more and more outsiders, both individuals and corporations, which are seeking to exploit them for the benefit of the more urbanized economies of the states that claim sovereignty over

---

frontier areas lands unproductive for industrialized agriculture that are opened to settlement by national governments that do not recognize the claims of the indigenous population

FIGURE 7.5

GENOCIDE

The systematic destruction of a people has taken place around the world. While the tragedy in Bosnia-Herzegovina is the most publicized, genocide is occurring in other places around the world as well. These are the remains of people killed in ethnic fighting between the Hutu and Tutsi tribes in Rwanda in Africa. Villagers look on as their remains are moved to the village of Gatonde for a proper reburial.

them. In many places around the world, indigenous peoples are disappearing because of these outside influences.

Extinction

Although there are still 200 million indigenous people in the world, many indigenous cultures have become extinct. There are three general ways in which indigenous cultures disappear: acculturation, ethnocide, and genocide.

Acculturation.   When two previously distinct cultures come in contact, they both change. This process, called acculturation, was discussed in detail on p. 162. We should note here, however, that while acculturation generally causes both cultures to change, it can change a culture so much that it soon loses most of its own traditional characteristics and in effect becomes extinct.

Ethnocide.   Sometimes the destruction of a traditional way of life is carried out by deliberate, systematic policies of the dominant culture. Such a process is called **ethnocide**. The effect of ethnocide is that a group is denied the right to enjoy, develop, and disseminate its own traditional culture and language. Politically dominant societies may legally require that indigenous peoples send their children to schools that train them in the dominant culture and language. In some cases these are boarding schools, where the children must live for long periods of time, far from their own families. Often the use of their native language is not only discouraged but also forbidden and punished. Removed from the normal process of socialization in their own native culture, they return home ill-equipped to carry on their parents' way of life. Missionary efforts also have contributed to the destruction of indigenous ways of life by attacking traditional religious beliefs and working for the abolition of all forms of marriage other than monogamy (Ribiero, 1971; Walker, 1972).

Genocide.   Related to ethnocide, the destruction of a culture, is the practice of **genocide**, the systematic destruction of a people. Many of the indigenous people of the world have been and are being systematically exterminated. Military campaigns against native peoples have been only one way in which the extinction of whole societies has occurred. Biological warfare also has been used. In the earlier days of U.S. history, clothing and blankets infected with smallpox and other diseases were distributed to some Native Americans, ostensibly as gifts. Colonial people also had given gifts of poisoned foods to indigenous people and had sometimes hunted them for sport (Bonwick, 1870; Calder, 1874; Horwood, 1969). In the past decade in many parts of Latin America, Indians have been killed by settlers moving onto their traditional lands. This private warfare is carried out with guns, bombs, dynamite, and even rapid-fire weapons from helicopters by private individuals, while national governments have turned a blind eye to the killing. In some cases, despite the presence of indigenous people, government agencies have declared traditional native lands to be "empty"

ethnocide the systematic destruction of a traditional way of life
genocide the systematic extermination of a people

and therefore legitimately available for settling by nonindigenous farmers, miners, and land speculators. For instance, in 1978, in the Department of Alta Verpaz, Guatemala, non-Indian landowners tried to evict Kekchi Indians from lands they had lived on for generations. When the Indians protested to the mayor in the nearby town of Panzos, 100 were killed and 300 wounded. Within four years the federal government had defined all Indians as "subversives," and a military campaign against them had begun. In 1982, government forces massacred 302 Chuj Indians in the village of Finca San Francisco in the Department of Huehuetenango. The only survivors were 20 men who were away from the village at the time. Over a six-month period, between 2,000 and 10,000 Indians were killed by government forces. As of 1992, over a million people have been displaced from their homelands by these conflicts, and about 200,000 have left the country to find refuge in other parts of Central America.

Thomas Gregor (1983) describes the impact of the immigration of nonindigenous people into one Latin American country:

> In 1500 explorer Pedro Cabral landed on the coast of Brazil and claimed its lands and native peoples for the Portuguese empire. Since that time Brazilian Indians have been killed by European diseases and bounty hunters, forced off their land by squatters and speculators, and enslaved by ranchers and mine owners. Today the Indians, numbering less than one-tenth of the precontact population, inhabit the most remote regions of the country. (p. 1)

The effects of such violence have penetrated even into indigenous groups that have had little direct contact with outsiders. Gregor focuses on the Mehinaku, a single village tribe that lives in a vast protected reservation in the Mato Grosso of Brazil. Despite their official protection and relative isolation, contact with Brazilians has been sufficient to undermine the security of their lives. Gregor quotes one Mehinaku villager as saying, "Last night my dream was very bad. I dreamed of a white man" (p. 1). According to the Mehinaku, such dreams portend illness. The symbolism is apt since, in the words of Gregor, "In the early 1960s, almost 20 percent of the tribe died in a measles epidemic, and the villagers continue to suffer from imported diseases for which they have neither natural nor acquired immunity" (p. 2).

THE EFFECTS OF INDUSTRIALIZATION

One fundamental factor sealing the doom of many nonstate societies and altering the nature of all the world's cultures has been **industrialization**. Beginning with the Industrial Revolution in Great Britain in the latter half of the eighteenth century, many cultures have joined the movement away from home production of goods to large-scale, mechanized factory production requiring great inputs of capital. This shift has brought profound alterations in all aspects of life, including changes in economic systems, growth of populations, and concentration of people around cities. Even those societies that have not industrialized are now defined and affected by their lack of industry.

Indigenous Peoples Today

In response to the influx of outside forces such as the logging and mining industries, indigenous peoples throughout the world are forming organizations to influence both national and international policies that affect their autonomy. According to Julian Burger (1987), one of the major causes of this coalescence of indigenous organizations has been the "massive explosion of demand for natural resources on the world market . . . [that] has stimulated vigorous exploration and exploitation" of the territories of indigenous peoples (p. 44). For instance, in 1974 the International Indian Treaty Council was formed in the United States to bring Native American concerns before international bodies such as the United Nations. It obtained status as a nongovernmental consultative organization at the United Nations in 1977. In 1978 Native Americans also formed the Indian Law Resource Center to support Indian legal rights in the U.S. court system and through international groups such as the UN Commission on Human Rights. Many such organizations now exist throughout most of the world. A similar international organization, the World Council of Indigenous Peoples, was organized in 1975. Its members are made up of delegates who

---

industrialization the process of change from an economy based on home production of goods to one based on large-scale, mechanized factory production

FIGURE 7.6

FOURTH WORLD CONFERENCE ON WOMEN

Women of indigenous cultures from all over the world met at The Fourth World Conference on Women in Beijing, China, in 1995, to formulate the first United Nations document spelling out the political, economic, and sexual rights of women. While *not binding, it is influential, particularly in those countries where women currently have few rights. These delegates, including Adelaide Moundele-Ngollo from the Congo, (left), visited the Great Wall during a break in the conference.*

now represent over 35 million of the world's indigenous peoples. In 1982, in response to the demands of indigenous peoples' organizations, the UN Commission on Human Rights "established an annual Working Group on Indigenous Populations to gather information about the situation of indigenous peoples world-wide and make recommendations about future international laws to protect their rights" (Burger, 1987, p. 61).

Developed and Underdeveloped Societies

Societies may be categorized in a number of ways. One simple distinction commonly is made on the basis of industrialization. **Developed countries** are the industrialized nations of the world: primarily the countries of North America and Europe, along with Japan, Taiwan, Russia, and a few others. **Underdeveloped countries** are the remaining, largely nonindustrialized societies of the world, including most of Africa, Asia, and Latin America. The distinction between developed and

underdeveloped countries is widely used, but the dichotomy is simpler than the reality it represents. The world's underdeveloped countries vary from extremely poverty-stricken societies in which hunger and starvation are daily problems to others that have incorporated a great deal of industrialized technology into their economy and will soon be viewed as developed countries. Those underdeveloped countries that are making major gains in industrialization are sometimes referred to as **developing countries** in recognition of the changes that they are undergoing.

As of mid-1995, nearly four-fifths of the human population lived in underdeveloped nations (Haub & Yanagishita, 1995). Living standards are very low in these areas, and

(Continued on p. 174)

---

developed country nation in which industrialization has become the primary basis of the economy

underdeveloped country nation with a largely nonindustrialized economy

developing country underdeveloped nation undergoing industrialization

THE YĄNOMAMÖ TODAY

Frontier lands occupied by indigenous people often attract citizens of the larger nation states, who then claim sovereignty over them. The Yąnomamö of Brazil and Venezuela have experienced a large influx of Venezuelan and Brazilian farmers, loggers, and miners who are radically changing their ancestral environments in the hopes of quick profits. Like other indigenous peoples who are not well represented in the governments that control them, the Yąnomamö and their traditional way of life have received little protection from either the Venezuelan or Brazilian governments. For instance, in 1975 about 4,500 of Brazil's 10,000 Yąnomamö Indians lived in an area of northern Amazonia that the government had ostensibly set aside as a reserve to protect them from outside incursion. But this land, now called the Yąnomamö Park, has continued to attract mining companies and illegal settlers. By June 1991, some 45,000 gold and tin miners had entered Yąnomamö lands, and opposition to the establishment of a Yąnomamö reserve was strong. For instance, in response to protests about the incursion of others into the Yąnomamö Park, the governor of Roraima, Brazil, said, "An area as rich as this, with gold, diamonds and uranium, cannot afford the luxury of preserving half a dozen Indian tribes which are holding up development" (Wright, 1982, p. 29).

The cavalier attitude of government leaders to the plight of the Yąnomamö is particularly interesting when actual government practice is contrasted with what one might expect if the legal rights of the Yąnomamö were actually enforced. For instance, Brazilian law guarantees the rights of Indian peoples to their land. The Indian Statute of December 19, 1973 gave "the Indians and native communities in the terms of the constitution, permanent possession of the land they inhabit, recognizing their right to exclusive usufruct of the natural wealth and all the utilities existing on that land" (Act No. 6001, Art. 2, Par. IX). The act also required the government to formally define the exact boundaries of the lands of each Indian group within five years. Nevertheless, by 1978, only a third of the native Indian territories had been formally defined, and the National Indian Foundation (FUNAI), the government agency charged with the protection of Indian rights, had been taking no action against the non-Indian colonizers who had entered these areas.

In addition to losing their lands to the more powerful immigrants who have laid claim to the resources they contain, the Yąnomamö have suffered tremendously from the diseases that have come with the immigrants. The Venezuelan Yąnomamö have experienced epidemics of measles and whooping cough that have killed as many as 30 percent of some communities, and they are currently threatened with extinction by diseases such as tuberculosis and malaria. In their isolated frontier setting, the Yąnomamö lack the immunity and the medical facilities to protect them from these diseases.

Efforts to acculturate the Yąnomamö have included the use of enforced recruitment of Yąnomamö children into a boarding school far from their homes. Jacques Lizot has described how Yąnomamö children were enticed away from their homes with candy, soft drinks, or invitations to ride on motor boats, and then taken to the boarding school with no explanation to their parents. There, every effort was made to eliminate all vestiges of their Yąnomamö identities: their hair was cut, their names were changed, and they were required to survive on foods to which they were unaccustomed, while the adults proceeded to "educate" them about their own inferiority and the necessity of learning a new language and new customs.

The Yąnomamö, like other indigenous peoples, have escalated their efforts to control their own destinies. One Yąnomamö leader, Davi Kopenawa Yanomami, has described the current plight of his people:

My Yąnomami people know, they see what is happening to our community, and they see what is happening to our relatives in other communities. They are terrified of the miners, of the [polluted] rivers.

The miners invaded our reserve and came to our communities feigning friendship; they lied to us, they tricked us Indians, and we were taken in. Then their numbers grew; many more arrived, and they began bringing in machinery that polluted the river. The pollution killed the fish and the shrimp, everything that lived in our rivers. (Albert, 1991, p. 52)

The outcome of the Yąnomamö efforts to obtain self-determination within a protected reserve is still in question, and their efforts to affect public opinion and national policy continue. However, they recently experienced one important breakthrough in their efforts toward their cultural survival. On November 15, 1992, then–Brazilian president Fernando Collor de Mello established the long-promised reserve for the Yąnomamö Indians. The Brazilian reserve is situated next to a similar Venezuelan Yąnomamö reserve, and the two reserves contain 68,331 square miles of land.

FIGURE 7.7

CATEMACO SHAMAN

In Catemaco, a Mexican town with a tradition of witchcraft, Jorge Jáuregui, otherwise known as the Infernal Goat, worries that the North American Free Trade Agreement of 1992 will adversely affect his ability to cure people in the traditional way with dried tree bark, dead snakes, and magic potions.

their current economies often will not support industrial development. Most underdeveloped countries suffer from severe shortages of land, capital, or labor. Land is often largely owned by a small, elite minority, with the remainder severely fragmented into plots too small to do more than meet the minimal needs of the families who farm them. The results of the absence of capital include roads that are impassable when it rains, schools that lack enough books, and per capita incomes that are extremely low. The average per capita gross national product of the underdeveloped nations is $1,030, compared with $17,270 for the developed world (Haub & Yanagishita, 1995). The population of the underdeveloped world is a more rural one than that of developed countries: while 74 percent of the people in developed societies live in urban areas, only 37 percent of the people in underdeveloped countries do so (Haub & Yanagishita, 1995). As developing countries are drawn into the worldwide network of industrialized economies, they change in a variety of ways that are discussed in the sections of this chapter that follow.

Economic Change

Industrialization has greatly influenced the economic and social life of societies in which it has occurred. Preindustrial economies are fundamentally systems of family-based production, with the food and other goods produced used primarily by the families themselves. Farming peoples who produce for their own consumption are more likely to diversify into as many as 20 to 30 different kinds of crops and animals. This diversity minimizes their risks and maximizes their autonomy. Trade exists mostly to distribute the surpluses from the family and community stock rather than to specialize in the production of food or other goods for the purpose of trade. Market-oriented farmers tend to invest in a smaller number of more specialized crops for sale, produce less for their own consumption, and rely more on their cash incomes to purchase the foods and other commodities their families need.

Changes in the economic role of domestic production also tend to impact gender relations within the family. For instance, June Nash

TABLE 7.1

WORLD'S TEN LARGEST CITIES

1950	Population (in millions)	1995	Population (in millions)	2000 (proj.)	Population (in millions)
1. New York–NE New Jersey	12.3	1. Tokyo-Yokohama	28.5	1. Tokyo-Yokohama	30.0
2. London	10.4	2. Mexico City	23.9	2. Mexico City	27.9
3. Rhine-Ruhr	6.9	3. São Paulo	21.5	3. São Paulo	25.4
4. Tokyo-Yokohama	6.7	4. Seoul	19.1	4. Seoul	22.0
5. Shanghai, Mainland	5.8	5. New York–NE New Jersey	14.6	5. Bombay	15.4
6. Paris	5.5	6. Osaka-Kobe-Kyoto	14.1	6. New York–NE New Jersey	14.6
7. Buenos Aires	5.3	7. Bombay	13.5	7. Osaka-Kobe-Kyoto	14.3
8. Chicago–NW Indiana	4.9	8. Calcutta	12.9	8. Teheran	14.3
9. Moscow	4.8	9. Rio de Janeiro	12.8	9. Rio de Janeiro	14.2
10. Calcutta	4.6	10. Buenos Aires	12.2	10. Calcutta	14.1

Sources: 1950 information from United Nations, Department of International Economic and Social Affairs, 1985. 1995 and 2000 information from the 1995 *Information Please Almanac, 1994*, Boston and New York: Houghton Mifflin, p. 130.

(1993) found that change toward market economics in one Mayan community in Mexico has had very different implications for the lives of men and women. Women continue to manufacture pottery by the traditional technique of coiling clay into pots that are finished by open firing. Thirty years ago, pots were made for local use. Now the marketing of pottery is an important source of family income that is used for the purchase of such things as trucks, cattle, and education for male children. Thus, increased integration into the industrialized market system has resulted in great costs for women, whose labor has intensified and education declined, while education and mobility have increased for men.

With industrialization comes a major increase in the number of specialized occupations. It has created a great demand for wage laborers at centralized locations who do not produce their own food, thus creating a situation where the economy is no longer a family-oriented subsistence activity but a market-oriented enterprise.

Industry also fosters the production of non-essential food crops, such as cocoa and coffee, and nonfood products, such as wool for textiles or sisal for twine and cordage manufacture. So industrialization fosters a move of a large per-centage of farmers away from staple food production. In an industrialized economy, the food-producing sector of farming becomes increasingly mechanized and competitive, so that small-scale farms become less viable.

Urbanization

Agriculture created towns and cities long before industrialization began, but industrialization greatly fostered the growth of cities. Since the large-scale manufacture of marketable goods and trade go hand in hand as industrialization proceeds, industrialized centers of manufacture tend to be located in urban centers along the routes of trade. As industry produces a growing demand for labor, workers are drawn out of rural areas into the cities to find employment, and urban areas grow in population.

In 1900 only 13.6 percent of the world's population lived in cities. By 1995 the portion of the world's population living in urban areas had risen to 43 percent (Haub & Yanagishita, 1995), and it is expected to climb to 60 percent by the year 2020. Part of the process of urbanization has been an increase in the size of cities. In 1950 there were only 2 cities with more than 10 million inhabitants: the New York–New Jersey urban complex and London. In

FIGURE 7.8

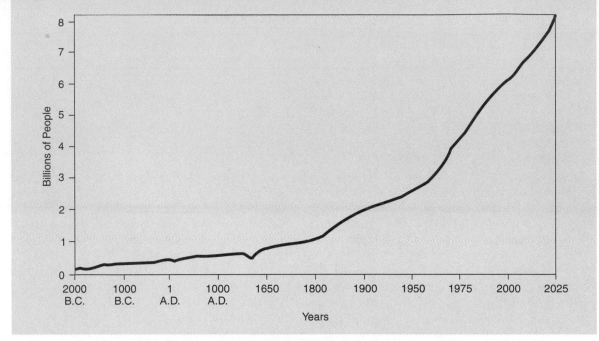

WORLD POPULATION GROWTH THROUGH HISTORY

The growth of the population of the world has historically been a long, slow process until the Industrial Revolution, which initiated a rapid growth period.

1995 there were 14 such cities, the largest of which was Tokyo-Yokohama with 30 million people (see Table 7.1 on page 175).

World Population Growth

In addition to becoming more concentrated in cities, the world's population has grown as industrialization has increased our life expectancy, described in the next section, "Industrialization and the Quality of Life." The history of human population can be described as a long period of slow growth followed by a relatively recent explosion that reached its fastest rate of expansion in 1965, when world population was increasing at about 2 percent per year. The period of slow growth ended with the development of agriculture about 10,000 years ago; the continuing rapid explosion started with the Industrial Revolution.

A third of a million years ago, in the time of *Homo erectus*, the human population of the entire world was less than 1 million people. When food domestication began, about 10,000 years ago, there were still fewer than 10 million people in the world. By the year 1 C.E. the figure was about 300 million. It reached 500 million in 1650, and the first billion was achieved about 1800. By July 1986 the figure had reached 5 bil-

lion. While the world required more than 300,000 years to reach a population of one billion, the second billion took only about 130 years, the third just 30 years, the fourth only 15 years, and the fifth a mere 11 years!

Industrialization and the Quality of Life

Industrialization does provide benefits. It makes possible a level of productivity much greater than that based on hand labor, which frees many members of society to pursue the specialized occupations that do not exist in preindustrial societies. Thus, industrialization brings to society new goods and new services, not only raising the standard of living but also extending life expectancy through better nutrition and security from famine, improved housing and sanitation, and a decline in the rate of infectious diseases and lower mortality rates in all age categories because of immunization and specialized medical care.

But industrialization also has its costs. Growth in industry is paralleled by growth in air and water pollution. As population grows, increased demand for goods can lead to the depletion of nonrenewable resources such as minerals and fossil fuels and to the overuse of potentially renewable ones. The urban growth that an expanding population fosters brings crowding and its attendant problems of unemployment, poverty, poor health and nutrition, and crime. It is ironic that industrialization can create both many new jobs and high unemployment, wealth and poverty, abundant foods and poor nutrition. Many of these problems grow out of the fact that although industrialization creates wealth, that wealth is not necessarily equitably distributed. Indeed, the process of industrialization has, without exception, been accompanied by increasing disparities in the wealth, power, and honor of the social classes that are part of all state-level societies. At times, these inequities can be the source of major social problems.

Another effect of the spread of industrialization is the increasing economic interdependence of the entire world. Over a decade ago, Eric Wolf (1982) wrote:

> On one level it has become a commonplace to say that we all inhabit "one world." There are ecological connections: New York suffers from the Hong Kong flu; the grapevines of Europe are destroyed by American plant lice. There are demographic connections: Jamaicans migrate to London; Chinese migrate to Singapore. There are economic connections: a shutdown of oil wells on the Persian Gulf halts generating plants in Ohio; a balance of payments unfavorable to the United States drains American dollars into bank accounts in Frankfurt or Yokohama; Italians produce Fiat automobiles in the Soviet Union; Japanese build a hydro-electric system in Ceylon. There are political connections: wars begun in Europe unleash reverberations around the globe; American troops intervene on the rim of Asia; Finns guard the border between Israel and Egypt. (p. 3)

The interconnectedness of the world is even greater today.

PEASANT CULTURES

Since the beginning of urbanization, the contrast between urban centers of power and wealth and less influential rural food-producing areas has been a fact of human life. As societies have grown more urbanized, the gulf between the elite decision makers and the less powerful rural subsistence workers has increased so that the majority of the human population now consists of a largely rural class of politically and economically uninfluential poor whose labors make the benefits of elite life possible. This disenfranchised class, known as **peasants**, is mostly made up of food producers whose economic life centers on using family-based labor, and who consume most of what they grow. Since peasants must produce their own food, they do not specialize in cash crops. They may produce some crops for sale, or hire out their own labor to supplement their incomes, but their cash incomes are too low to change their material condition and, consequently, their socially subordinate status. Typically, peasants use nonindustrialized, hand-labor techniques that yield only a minimal subsistence for their own families. Yet, in a seeming contradiction, they need large families to ensure that they have enough labor to produce the food they need. They are largely rural peoples, but some peasants live in urban areas where they can supplement their incomes from small-scale gardening with income from paid labor. Peasants are economically and politically dominated by a governing class of which they are not a part. They rarely control their own political destinies. Their food production is generally part of the larger society's economy, but they have little influence on its operation. In most societies, peasants do not own the land that they work.

Feudal Peasantries

In preindustrial times, peasants were part of political systems in which local aristocratic leaders, who claimed ownership of the land, granted the **feudal peasants** the privilege to use the land to grow their own food in return for rent or service. According to G. Dalton (1969), the relationship between peasant and

---

peasants people who use nonindustrialized, labor-intensive techniques for producing food and who are politically and economically subordinate to a governing class of which they are not a part and with whom they have little influence

feudal peasants food producers in preindustrialized societies who pay rent or perform service for the privilege of farming lands owned by local aristocratic officials, who, in turn, have obligations to provide police and military protection, judicial services, and care for the peasants in times of hardship

lord in feudal times involved responsibilities and obligations on the part of the landowner as well as the peasant. For instance, the feudal lord provided military and police protection for the peasants, settled disputes, and fed them in times of hardship. Peasants' lack of land ownership has probably always been a source of dissatisfaction in most feudal societies (Wolf, 1969), but the conditions of peasant life likely worsened following industrialization, when contracted wage labor replaced the earlier paternalistic feudal system, and the peasant was forced to provide for all his own needs. In the industrialized economic system, the obligations of the propertied classes end with the payment of the wage.

Colonial Peasantries

Near the end of the fifteenth century, new ship-building technologies heralded the beginning of an age of European seafaring exploration and empire building. European imperialism included the military control of much of the American continents by Spain, followed by Portuguese colonization of parts of South America. Through military force Spain extracted vast amounts of wealth from the areas it controlled by forcing the native peoples to work in mines and to produce food on Spanish estates. In North America the British and the French established colonies in which the native peoples were displaced or killed by the influx of large numbers of colonial settlers. Africa and Asia were also incorporated into the worldwide European network of trade, but European colonial settlements tended to be confined to the coastal areas of these regions, where their primary role was usually to facilitate trade. By the middle of the eighteenth century, these settlements had become centers from which European colonial administrations ruled the native populations through military force and extracted valuable economic resources from the surrounding, inland areas. The resources exported from colonies included slaves, ivory, gold, and palm oil from various areas of West Africa and cotton, spices, and tea from India and Asia. Finally, during the eighteenth century, industrialization began to transform the economies of European countries from their earlier rural, feudal focus into a factory-based system built on wage labor. With the development of industrialized food production and transportation technologies, the subordination of peasantries intensified.

Colonial peasants were forced, sometimes economically and sometimes by the pressure of military might, to move from the production of food to the production of nonfood export crops and to engage in labor for pay. As Frances Moore Lappé and Joseph Collins (1977) have said:

> Colonialism destroyed the cultural patterns of production and exchange by which traditional societies in "underdeveloped" countries previously had met the needs of the people. Many precolonial social structures, while dominated by exploitative elites, had evolved a system of mutual obligations among the classes that helped to ensure at least a minimal diet for all. A friend of mine once said: "Precolonial village existence in subsistence agriculture was a limited life indeed, but it's certainly not Calcutta." The misery of starvation in the streets of Calcutta can only be understood as the end-point of a long historical process—one that has destroyed a traditional social system. (p. 76)

The colonial subordination of peasantries can be seen as a process in which some societies have been underdeveloped to the benefit of others (Rodney, 1972). Colonial administrations encouraged the production of cash crops such as cotton, cocoa, coffee, sugar, and tobacco for export at the expense of the staple foods that had been produced previously. The exports from colonial areas consisted basically of two types of commodities: luxury goods valued by consumers in the ruling nations, and resources—including slave labor for export to other colonies in need of cheap labor and raw materials for use in factories in the colonial homelands. The export crops were selected for their high-priced value in the home market relative to their shipping costs and not for their value as foods.

The shift from self-sufficient subsistence crops to the production of cash crops did not occur voluntarily among indigenous peoples. In some cases, foreign governments or private individuals claimed ownership of native lands and forced the inhabitants to work the fields as

---

colonial peasants members of peasant societies that were politically and economically dependent on a foreign state that perpetuated its economic exploitation of the peasant area by military domination

slaves, wage laborers, or dispossessed tenant farmers. The profits remained in the hands of the foreign interests. Where physical force was not used to bring about this shift to cash crop production, taxation was another means, since the indigenous population had to begin working for a wage to pay the tax. With government and private businesses pursuing the common goal of benefiting the colonial homeland, there was no motivation to set wages high for indigenous workers. Indeed, instead of wages being freely determined by the effects of "supply and demand," the necessity of a money income meant that the lower the wages were kept, the longer the laborer had to work.

As a result of the forced change to paid labor, previously self-sufficient farmers could no longer grow enough food to meet their own needs. Ironically, even though peasant peoples throughout the world are basically farmers, the peasant societies had to become major food importers to feed themselves. This locked them firmly into economic markets that were dominated by the imperial powers that ruled the colonies. By the end of the eighteenth century, the economic dependence of the colonial countries was sufficiently developed that it was no longer necessary to enforce their participation in the network of trade. Gradually, the imperial administrations loosened their holds on the local colonial governments. During the nineteenth century, British economic power eclipsed that of the European imperial rivals, which even withdrew from many of their colonies, leaving Britain as the dominant world power.

Due to the effects of imperial colonialism, the local populations of the colonies had no way to benefit from their participation in the world market. Tremendous wealth was actually being drained from their countries in the form of taxes and the products that were exported. The wealth that flowed into the country in return for the exports enriched the foreign owners of the factories and plantations but not the wage laborers who originally owned the lands and resources. As the new elite exploited increasing amounts of land in producing exports, less and less land remained for traditional uses such as growing food crops, grazing animals, or foraging for wild foods. Thus, the same process that locked the native populations of the colonial world into the international cash economy locked them into poverty as well. When imperial colonialism ended, the former colonies that had been kept in the subordinate

role of resource exporters became today's Third World countries.

The exception to this pattern of underdevelopment in European colonies were those areas such as North America and southern Africa where colonization involved the displacement of the native population by large numbers of European immigrants. These newcomers from Europe were already economically market oriented and were able to participate in the benefits of industrialization in their new homelands. Unlike the native populations of other colonial areas, they were not forced to export their products and resources without receiving an equitable level of money and useful goods in return. Neither did their participation in external markets interfere with the development of a self-sufficient farming and ranching subsistence base.

During the period from 1870 to 1914, there was a brief resurgence of imperial colonialism as the growth of industrialization outside of Britain created new demands for resources in other parts of the world, including Germany, Italy, Russia, France, Japan, and America. This new economic competition among the European industrializing nations led to renewed attempts, by both Britain and the others, to secure colonial sources of raw materials for industry in these countries. During this period 17 percent of the world's land was brought under the domination of the competing European colonial powers. However, this brief resurgence of colonial expansionism ended in military conflict among the European nations, and by the end of World War I, old-style colonialism had come to an end. Most of the earlier colonies remained economically dependent on the homelands, however, and the flow of resources from the (now former) colonial lands to the industrialized lands has continued since then.

Contemporary Peasantries

Today, as noted on page 177, most of the people in the world can be classified as peasants, members of a social class of traditional, family-based food producers who are subordinate to an urban-based administrative class in each of their societies. The economies of these societies are, themselves, highly influenced by worldwide economic forces that are beyond their control. Because of the small volume of their specialized cash crops, the peasants lack the cash flow to pay for the equipment and services

FIGURE 7.9

SOMALI PEASANT

Warring factions in Somalia have prevented many crops from being harvested in the mid-1990s. With the fall of the dictator Mohammed Siad Barre, farmers have been assisted in planting crops again in some areas. Sharif Abdul Nur plants sorghum seeds in the town of Habarre, north of Baidoa, and hopes to purchase a herd of camels, the mainstay of Somali economy. In fleeing the war, Sharif lost his 33 camels, which were stolen by the guerrillas.

that would be necessary to industrialize their farming techniques. Nor is their economic base sufficient for state taxation to sustain the bureaucratic social benefits available in urban centers. Traditional credit and rental arrangements in peasant communities are often based on commodities rather than money, and exchange is centered on small marketplaces in which individual peasants act as "penny capitalists," selling their few surplus products or selling their labor on a piecemeal basis. Since in many peasant societies much of the most productive land is owned by a wealthy elite—who long ago converted it to the production of cash crops—peasants find it difficult to produce sufficient foods on their "postage stamp" farms to meet their own nutritional needs. Much of their cash income is devoted to the purchase of food, and typically the cash incomes that they obtain prove insufficient to meet the expenses of life in an industrializing society.

Peasant societies are not all identical. They are found in various environments and use many different types of subsistence technolo-

gies. Jon Moris (1981) has outlined nine basic types of peasants exhibiting different subsistence styles today:

1. Pastoralists and ranchers in low-density populations that are spread over large territories.
2. Tenant farmers who grow one or two market crops such as coffee or hemp on irrigated farmland.
3. Laborers who live and work on large foreign-owned farms or estates and who grow export crops such as rubber or tea.
4. Farmers who rely on natural rainfall in isolated pockets of semiarid lands and hilly areas with steep slopes that are suited only for hand-growing techniques and who market only what they don't need.
5. Peasants who live by labor-intensive farming in impoverished conditions in crowded smallholdings.
6. Landless peasant workers or dispossessed tenant farmers in government-organized settlements and frontier areas.

TABLE 7.2

PER CAPITA LEVELS OF INDUSTRIALIZATION

	1750	1800	1830	1860	1880	1900	1913
Developed Countries	8	8	11	16	24	35	55
United Kingdom	10	16	25	64	87	100	115
France	9	9	12	20	28	39	59
Germany	8	8	9	15	25	52	85
United States	4	9	14	21	38	69	126
Canada	–	5	6	7	10	24	46
Third World	7	6	6	4	3	2	1
China	8	6	6	4	3	2	2
India	7	6	6	3	2	1	2

Source: Paul Bairoch, "International Industrialization Levels from 1750 to 1980," *Journal of European Economic History, 11* (Fall 1982), p. 294.

7. Aged, sick, and uneducated peasants in impoverished rural communities who depend on remittance income from younger members of the community who work in other areas.

8. Refugees and former tenant farmers who have become landless and dispossessed.

9. Peri-urban squatters who live in densely settled, often illegal communities near urban areas and support their families by gardening "postage-stamp" farms and working in the neighboring cities.

Change in Peasant Societies. Industrialization is gradually occurring in the Third World, but not at the same rate as in developed countries. In fact, under the conditions of economic change that have been described above, it should not be surprising that the per capita level of industrialization actually declined in Third World countries while it was rising in the developed world (see Table 7.2).

The economic limitations of peasant life are not easily overcome. Economist Robert Chambers (1983) has stressed the fact that rural poverty often goes unnoticed or misunderstood by outsiders. Most peasants live in conditions that are geographically or socially too far removed from the lives of urban elite policy makers for governments to understand their real needs. Thus, government efforts to improve the conditions of peasant life are often based on faulty assessments of what needs to be done. They too often fail to appreciate the necessity of incorporating peasants' own insights about their needs into the policy and process of development.

Some observers also feel that a major obstacle to change lies in the peasants' own attitudes. According to Foster (1965), life in peasant societies often leads to a rather fatalistic, dreary outlook in which the drudgery of life is not believed to bring much reward, since the achievement of one person can only be accomplished at the expense of another. Foster has called this outlook the **image of limited good**. Because of this view of life, peasants are commonly jealous of success, and peasant life contains many social pressures not to excel over one's peers. Lewis (1966) sees this lifestyle as fostering attitudes that cause peasants and other poverty-stricken people to think only of today, to spend and consume what they have right now since saving for tomorrow seems futile. Lewis calls this approach to life the **culture of poverty**. Although this outlook certainly is not the underlying cause of the impoverished conditions of peasants in most parts of the world, it can make it difficult for peasants to take part effectively in opportunities for social change.

image of limited good a fatalistic outlook common in situations of peasant poverty, in which the drudgery of life is not believed to bring much reward, since the achievement of one person can only be accomplished at the expense of another

culture of poverty an approach to life often found in situations of poverty in which actions are directed only to satisfying the needs of the present, by spending and consuming all income, because saving for the future seems futile

Eric Wolf (1966) believes there are more substantial reasons why change is difficult in peasant circumstances. Peasants are slow to join forces to overcome exploitation, because they are individually bound into vertical political ties or "patron-client" relationships with more wealthy and powerful individuals on whose aid they depend in times of need. To work with other peasants for the common good is to sever these personally advantageous ties, so peasant communities are caught in a cycle of competition among individuals and factions.

Scott (1976) points out that the status quo does provide the peasant with a buffer from adversity. Peasant community expectations have a leveling effect that limits the poverty into which any one member of the society can sink. The maintenance of "commons"—lands available to all, for instance as pasturage—is an example of the buffers against adversity that are built into the peasant community. Commercialization, according to Scott, is actually a threat to peasant security, since it undermines the mechanisms that provide that security in impoverished circumstances.

Prices in peasant markets are quite unstable and seasonally variable, since peasants market only the surplus that their families do not need for food. They tend to rely on relatives for credit and assistance, and lack sufficient cash incomes to support markets that sell factory-produced goods. Some developmental social scientists believe this situation is self-perpetuating, because reliance on family for labor and economic support leads to large family size, and increased population growth leads to reduced savings and investment. This, in turn, necessitates greater reliance on family labor and traditional means of production.

Although there are many features of life in peasant societies that make change difficult, it would be a mistake to assume that change is impossible. Peasants have been ready to revolt against the system that maintains their landlessness and poverty when opportunities for successful uprisings have presented themselves. Many social scientists believe that peaceful improvement of peasant conditions is also possible. Popkin (1979) portrays the peasant lifestyle as a rational response to the tight constraints that limit their production and to the high degree of risk they face in making a living. He contends that when markets and opportunities exist, peasants respond by increasing output.

Refugees

Another major social problem of international scope today is the increasing number of **refugees**, displaced people—largely of peasant origin—who have been forced from their homes and means of livelihood because of the fear of political persecution. They include political activists who were dissenting participants in the conflicts from which they are now fleeing, others who are targeted because they are members of some persecuted religious, ethnic, or racial group, and individuals who simply have found themselves in the middle of fighting between two or more other conflicting groups. Refugees are the products of economic imbalances and poverty, political upheavals due to war, armed conflict, civil disorder, persecution of ethnic minorities, and governmental human rights abuses.

Today, there are over 18 million refugees worldwide, 80 percent of whom are women and their children. About a third of the world's refugees are people who have been forced to cross international borders, but nearly 40 million are so-called "internal refugees" who have been forced to migrate within their own countries. The movement of such large numbers of people either within their own countries or across national borders can have a major disruptive impact on the economies of the areas in which they settle. In the eyes of governments and local citizens, the influx of large numbers of refugees who have no source of income represents a cost rather than an asset. So, typically, refugees are not welcomed. Just as the United States devotes a great investment of federal funds to inhibit the flow of Mexican nationals who are in search of employment in the United States, so too do countries in other parts of the world provide similar barriers to both economic and political refugees in their flight from intolerable conditions. International borders are sometimes closed to them, and those who are allowed to cross may find themselves in impoverished settlement camps that have little or no access to either humanitarian aid or employment.

---

refugees displaced people who have been forced from their homes and means of livelihood because of the fear of political persecution

FIGURE 7.10

SERBIAN REFUGEES

Faced with an offensive by Bosnian government forces and Bosnian Croats, as many as 40,000 Serbian civilians were forced to evacuate the town of *Sipovo in Western Bosnia. On a road near the town of Jajce, this Serbian family rests with their belongings on a horse-drawn carriage.*

Applied Anthropology and Cultural Change

Since the time of Malinowski, who first used the term **applied anthropology**, there have been attempts to use anthropological insights and analytic skills to facilitate efforts at planned social change. This work has grown in importance as governments and other organizations, such as the World Bank, have begun to focus more energy on bringing about social and economic development and aiding the process of industrialization in the Third World. One of the important insights about planned social change of this type is that economic development is not simply a matter of importing money and technology. Of what use, for instance, is a tractor in a rural area where there are no facilities for its maintenance or repair? Development requires systematic changes in the entire social infrastructure of the countries that are undergoing the process. People must be trained in the use of new technologies and in the support industries that these technologies require. Determining how to accomplish this and other changes necessitated by new ways of producing food and other needed commodities also requires the establishment of useful mechanisms of communication between the grassroots users of the new technologies and the agencies involved in introducing them. Most of the real barriers to large-scale social change efforts are social rather than purely technological. Anthropologically trained specialists bring their knowledge of social and cultural processes to bear on dealing with such problems.

Fisher (1972) describes a number of reasons why government-sponsored development projects often fail. The list demonstrates that these failures are more typically social and ideological than technological in nature.

1. Projects intended to improve the lot of the peasant poor are often designed by persons who are unfamiliar with life in the peasant community, and these projects are imposed from the outside.

---

applied anthropology the attempt to use anthropological skills and insights to aid in the process of cultural development in nonindustrialized parts of the world or to aid in private and public policy making

CUBAN REFUGEE CAMPS AT THE U.S. NAVAL BASE AT GUANTANAMO

On August 5, 1994, following riots in Havana, President Fidel Castro of Cuba announced that he would no longer prevent Cubans from trying to leave the country by sea to seek refuge in the United States. An exodus of thousands of Cubans resulted. For the previous 28 years, Cubans had had priority for entry into the United States, but the sudden influx of Cubans suggested that this policy might now prove untenable. On August 22, U.S. policy changed; 267 refugees from Cuba arrived at the U.S. naval base at Guantanamo Bay in Cuba and were refused asylum. By midnight 2,548 refugees had been picked up in the Florida Straits by U.S. Coast Guard cutters. On the next day another 3,253 refugees were detained on their way to the United States. Many had left Cuba on dangerous, homemade rafts or boats, in the hope of reaching U.S. shores. But the rapid influx of large numbers of Haitians to Florida had already created a political climate that was not receptive to new Caribbean arrivals. Under the new U.S. policy, Cuban refugees would have to prove that they had a well-founded fear of persecution if they were returned to Cuba before they could gain asylum and move to the U.S. mainland. So the refugees were brought to the Guantanamo Naval Base, where a camp had been prepared to house them. The Guantanamo base was already the temporary home for 14,616 Haitian refugees who were being held there. Three months later, the number of Cubans at the naval base had reached 24,000, and by the end of February 1995, when U.S. relatives of the Cubans were permitted to visit them, there were 28,000 being held. Additional Cubans were being held at a camp that Panama had agreed to open for the United States in September 1994.

In the beginning the refugee camps at Guantanamo consisted of tents, cots, food, and portable toilets; conditions of the settlements in Panama were also primitive. In response, there were several cases of violent unrest among the refugees in Panama and sit-ins, hunger strikes, and a number of suicide attempts among some of the refugees at Guantanamo, especially during the summer heat. The increased pressures in handling the continued inflow of Cubans led the U.S. government to ease tensions with Cuba, agreeing on May 2 to allow the detainees to enter the United States. Under this agreement, however, all new refugees leaving Cuba would be denied asylum and returned to Cuba.

However, the impact of the new policy was not immediate. By the end of April 1995, there were still 12 settlement camps at Guantanamo, and of the 31,000 refugees who had arrived by then, only about 10,000, particularly women, children, the sick, and the elderly had been given asylum and allowed to move to the United States; $35 million had been allocated to construct better facilities. Barbed wire barriers had been replaced with chain-link fences, 75 doctors and social workers had been sent to the settlements to provide medical and psychological therapy to the refugees, and there were finally plans to build a recreation center, open a store where refugees could buy personal items, and put electric lights into the tents. The expectations were that processing the remaining 21,000 refugees might take several years.

2. The governments involved sometimes fail to commit resources that are necessary for the projects to succeed.
3. Goals and resource allocations may be changed in the middle of a project without regard to the effects on work in the community setting.
4. Often, the resources may be spread too thinly to be effective in any one area.
5. Erroneous assumptions are commonly made about the effectiveness or capabilities of the institutions involved in the project, or the human element in the real work of project implementation may not be fully taken into account.

6. The various governmental ministries involved in the work may not coordinate their efforts.
7. Finally, demand for the new product created by the peasants is often insufficient for the work to become self-sustaining, and the yield or output projections may be inconsistent with the level of management available.

Since many of these problems involve social as well as purely technological issues, anthropological skills can be particularly relevant to their solution. For instance, participant observation techniques can be very useful for clarifying the real needs of the grassroots communities and for assessing how development efforts are really impacting them. Economist Robert Chambers (1983) contends that ideas expressed as "We must educate the farmers" and "We must uplift the rural poor" must be reversed: "Outsiders have first to learn *from* farmers and *from* the rural poor" (p. 201). Only they can be a valid source of information about their real needs or the problems with which they are confronted as they implement plans for economic development in their own communities. Most anthropologists, accustomed to studying local populations at the grassroots level, would concur with Chambers's criticisms of recent work: "Staff working in rural areas distance themselves from rural people, showing their separate style and standing through clothing, shoes, vehicle, office, briefcase, documents, and manner and speech. Hierarchy, authority and superiority prevent learning 'from below'" (p. 201). His critique of traditional development efforts that are imposed from the top down point to one important role for developmental anthropologists, whose tradition of participant-observation has prepared them to facilitate the flow of needed information from the bottom up.

THE FUTURE OF THE PEASANT WORLD

Alexander Robertson (1984) points to an important fact of modern development work: "Since the Second World War almost every country in the world, from Britain and Bolivia to Finland and Fiji, has had a national development plan" (p. 7). Development today is carried out within established bureaucratic structures organized and controlled by national governments and other organizations and agencies whose scope is international. Developmental anthropologists work within these structures, not apart from them.

Despite the difficulties in planned cultural change, the life of peasant villagers, who make up the majority of the world's inhabitants, is changing due primarily to the green revolution and new techniques for contraception.

The Green Revolution

The spread of scientific farming techniques is the result of what has been called the **green revolution**, the use of modern plant breeding to produce hybrid crop varieties that are much more productive than many traditional crops. The production of high-yield, fertilizer-intensive, fast-maturing crops is spreading quickly into the world's villages, along with year-round irrigation and multiple cropping. The green revolution has been particularly successful in improving the income base of peasant farmers in parts of Asia and India. By the early 1980s the introduction of irrigation systems, modern varieties of increased-yield food plants, and fertilizer technology had begun to counteract the previous inability of peasants to produce enough food to meet the demands created by population growth. The critical problem in peasant village development is achieving peasant labor productivity sufficient to counteract the strong population pressure on limited land resources. The green revolution has been one important factor in solving this problem. The successes have been great enough that a number of underdeveloped countries are becoming increasingly competitive in the world marketplace. On the other hand, many poor peasant farmers cannot afford to adopt the costly new technologies.

Population Control in Developing Nations

A second major force that has had a tremendous impact on the lives of peasant peoples in the past half-century has been the introduction of new, affordable contraception throughout much of the Third World. Scientific contraceptive technologies have proven to be an effective way of countering the problem of population pressure. For instance, Critchfield noted in 1981 that "in places as scattered as China, India's Kerala and Karnataka states, Sri Lanka, and Java and Bali in Indonesia, annual population growth rates have plummeted from 2½–3 percent in the early sixties to 1–1½ percent now—mostly in the five years from 1975 to 1980. Elsewhere, though less spectacularly, fertility [the number of children born per woman] has been declining for the first time in the modern era" (p. 322). These trends have continued in parts of the Third World where governments have advocated the widespread use of contra-

---

green revolution use of modern plant breeding to produce high-yield, fertilizer-intensive, fast-maturing crops

HOME, HOME ON THE RANGE, IN BRAZIL'S HEARTLAND

Out here in Brazil's big sky country, where the cows outnumber people and the billboards tout weed killers, Douglas Ferrell looks through the window of his air-conditioned tractor cab and sees dollar signs stretching to the horizon.

"I buy new land every year—you can make 40 percent on your investment out here," said the 40-year-old soy and cotton farmer from Pennsylvania. Starting with a 1,200-acre farm a little over a decade ago, Mr. Ferrell has increased his holdings fivefold, bought 1,100 head of cattle and the latest in tractors and combines, and started construction on the tallest farmhouse—two stories— and the biggest grain silos ever seen in these parts.

RIO VERDE'S FARMS

As a result of increased mechanization farming has become Brazil's fastest growing economic sector since 1980. This farming boom has made Brazil one of the world's top five food exporters.

One of his Mennonite neighbors recently cautioned that Mr. Ferrell was getting a "big head." But his success is part of an agricultural boom that is thrusting Brazil into the world's top ranks of food exporters.

Often overshadowed by Brazil's coastal industries, farming has been the country's fastest-growing sector since 1980. Over the last 15 years, farm production increased by 47 percent, while industrial production increased by just 11 percent.

This farming boom has made Brazil one of the world's top five "food powers" despite the fact that since 1980, the acreage under cultivation in Brazil has remained the same, and Government subsidies have been cut in half.

The productivity increases are a result of heavy investment in mechanization, typified by the brand new tractor and combines on Mr. Ferrell's farm. . . .

Brazilian farmers are so successful that they trample national borders in search of cheap land. Today, Brazilian colonists plant and harvest one-third of the soy planted in Bolivia and Paraguay, and own 4 percent of Uruguay's land.

But the region's "Green Revolution" is most visible here in the table-flat lands of the country's midwestern savannah, or cerrado.

"In 20 years, Brazil will be exporting throughout the world food produced in the cerrado," predicted Norman Borlaug, 81, the American agricultural scientist who won the Nobel Peace Prize in 1970 for research that helped bring about Asia's "Green Revolution."

Over the last 25 years, grain production in the cerrado has quadrupled to 20 million tons. And farmers only till 15 percent of the arable land in a region with an area equal to that of Britain, France, Germany, Italy, Portugal and Spain combined.

From "Home, Home on the Range, in Brazil's Heartland" by James Brooke, April 26, 1995, *New York Times*, p. A4.

ception to keep population growth from overburdening the ability of the agricultural base to provide food. Some countries such as the People's Republic of China and Singapore have adopted even stronger measures.

More than one-fifth of the human population, over 1.2 billion people, live in the People's Republic of China, and over half of those peo-

ple are under 33 years of age. Both the absolute size of the Chinese population and the large percentage of the population represented by people of reproductive age make population control a major concern in China. A high fertility rate might well overcome China's ability to feed its population in the future, much less to achieve the status of a developed nation. For these reasons, the Chinese government has taken more extreme measures than have many developing countries, and they appear to have been quite successful at reducing the fertility rate. One means of lowering the fertility rate is to delay the average age of marriage. The current legal age for marriage in China is 20 for women and 22 for men. However, the main efforts to reduce fertility involve direct intervention in family planning. As Article 53 of the revised 1978 constitution of China states, "The state advocates and encourages birth planning." Using newspapers, radio, and television, the government actively publicizes and encourages the goal of limiting births to one child per family. Bonuses, larger pensions, free health care for the child, priority in housing, and the promise of education and employment priorities for the child are all used as inducements for voluntary commitment to having only one child. County birth planning offices supply contraceptives and subsidize local health centers for IUD insertions, sterilizations, and abortions.

Peer pressure is also used to achieve the goal of one child per family in China. At the local level, the government has organized a system of fertility committees throughout the country that meet with individuals and create social pressure for conformity to government goals in family planning. Families are encouraged to publicly commit themselves to having only one child, although in deference to the strong value that Chinese peasants still place on sons, a second child is considered acceptable if the first is a daughter. Female infanticide is practiced in some rural areas of China but is not sanctioned by the Beijing government. The weight of public opinion is brought to bear on individuals who refuse to support the national goal of reduced population growth. A liberal policy on abortion and social pressure to terminate pregnancies after the second birth have reduced China's total fertility rate to only 2.74 children per family, a rate about half of what it was in 1970 and equivalent to that of developed countries.

Singapore, where nearly 3 million people occupy a mere 240 square miles, is one of the three most densely populated countries of the world. By 1969 the government began providing free family planning services, including abortion and sterilization. Government policy was to encourage small families. Women received maternity leave only for their first two children. The medical fees for the delivery of

FIGURE 7.11

BIRTH CONTROL IN CHINA

Many families in China acquiesce to the social pressures that strongly encourage each family to have only one child. Some, however, do not. In the village of Tongmuchong, southwest of Chenzhov, live what are called the "wild people" of Hunan Province. They have heard about the one-child policy but have chosen to ignore it. And in the Pearl River Delta of Guangdong Province there is a large group who live on boats, deliberately evading population control, like this woman and her children. The government, however, is becoming coercive, and in some instances, violent, with these who oppose the policy.

babies were greater for each successive child. Income tax exemptions applied only to the first two children. Subsidized housing was denied to large families. In 1983 the government began offering a cash payment equal to the average yearly income of a family in Singapore to any woman who was sterilized after her second child. Singapore's strict policies were so successful that by 1985 fertility had dropped from its earlier rate of 4.5 to only 1.4 children per family, and efforts to slow population growth were ended. In 1995 the population growth rate remained approximately the same.

In developed countries where the costs of population growth have not been felt so strongly, it is difficult for many people to accept the degree to which the governments of China and Singapore are intervening in the reproductive lives of their citizens. These measures are more readily comprehended in light of the terrible costs that high fertility rates have had in slowing the process of economic development in much of the world. Remaining underdeveloped takes its toll, not only as an absence of the material luxuries associated with industrialization, but also as hunger and high mortality rates. Life expectancy at birth in the underdeveloped countries is now 58 years, compared with 72 years in developed nations. In light of the advantages of successful development, similar governmental measures to control fertility rates may become common in other parts of the developing world.

CHAPTER SUMMARY

1. Cultures change—often in the direction of increasing complexity—through local discoveries and inventions and borrowed innovations.

2. As changes occur in technology, social organization, or ideology, they affect the whole culture, which then adjusts.

3. The interrelated signs of increasing complexity include: harnessing of more energy per capita, increased specialization of labor, greater population density, more status ranking, decreasing emphasis on kinship, decreasing individual independence, more centralized political control, and more secular ideology.

4. The changes through which societies pass may be categorized as specific evolution (adaptation and specialization) or general evolution (qualitative change toward greater complexity).

5. Specific evolution tends to stabilize a society (the Principle of Stabilization).

6. General evolution moves a society toward increasing complexity, unless such change is inhibited by the effects of the society's previous adaptation.

7. Indigenous cultures are becoming more and more scarce, either through adaptations to the dominant cultures that surround them or through forced takeovers of their ancestral lands, ethnocide, and genocide.

8. Industrialization has brought profound economic changes, population growth, concentration of population around cities, and both positive and negative effects on the quality of life.

9. The majority of the world's people are affected by these trends but still live as peasants, practicing small-scale food production for their own needs.

10. Some anthropologists apply their knowledge of societies around the world to help solve social problems.

ANNOTATED READINGS

Bernard, H. R., & Pelto, P. J. (Eds.). (1972). *Technology and social change.* New York: Macmillan. An important collection of case studies of the effects of the introduction of Western technology on a variety of cultures.

Bodley, J. H. (1990). *Victims of progress.* Mountain View, CA: Mayfield Publishing Co. A discussion of the destructive effects of contact with industrialized societies on traditional societies.

Chambers, R. (1983). *Rural development: Putting the last first.* Essex, England: Longman Scientific & Technical. A standard text on development.

Gold, S. J. (1992). *Refugee communities: A comparative field study.* Newbury Park, CA: Sage Publications. A comparative ethnographic study of Vietnamese and Soviet Jewish refugees in the United States.

Grillo, R., & Rew, A. (Eds.). (1985). *Social anthropology and development policy.* New York: Tavistock Publications. A sourcebook for developmental anthropology that is especially popular in England.

Isbister, J. (1993). *Promises not kept: The betrayal of social change in the Third World.* West Hartford, CT: Kumarian Press. A state-of-the-art examination of world development issues from political science and social science perspectives.

Robertson, A. F. (1984). *People and the state: An anthropology of planned development.* Cambridge, England: Cambridge University Press. An important book on how national governments and international agencies frame the context in which developmental anthropologists work today.

van Willigen, J. (1991). *Anthropology in use: A source book in anthropological practice.* Boulder, CO: Westview Press. Contains descriptions of how anthropologists have helped solve practical problems in many different settings.

Wulff, R. M., & Fiske, S. J. (Eds.). (1987). *Anthropological praxis: Translating knowledge into action.* Boulder, CO: Westview Press. Twenty-five award-winning essays that describe various cases where anthropological knowledge has been put to use in social change projects.

Zolberg, A. R., Suhrke, A., & Aguayo, S. (1989). *Escape from violence: Conflict and the refugee crisis in the developing world.* New York: Oxford University Press. An attempt to analyze the major refugee movements since the 1970s.

PART THREE

Social Institutions

CHAPTER EIGHT
ECONOMICS

Commodities acquire different values in different societies. Economic systems provide rules that determine how these commodities are produced, distributed, and consumed. The concepts of use rights, ownership, and division of labor are involved in production. Distribution is accomplished by some combination of reciprocal exchange, redistribution, and various types of markets. Patterns of consumption depend, in part, on need but also on status and prestige.

CHAPTER NINE
MARRIAGE AND THE FAMILY

Marriage is a social, economic, and sexual union between two individuals and two families. The most well known forms are monogamy, polygyny, and polyandry, but other less well known forms also exist. In each culture there are rules for the choice of marriage partner, and rituals for the establishment of the union. The size of the family is related to the customs that govern where a married couple lives.

CHAPTER TEN
KINSHIP AND DESCENT

Our relationship to other members of our kindred group may be defined matrilineally, patrilineally, ambilineally, or bilaterally. Groups of relatives may be organized not just by descent rules, but by economic and social conditions as well, into lineages, clans, phratries, or moities.

CHAPTER ELEVEN
POLITICS

Political power, the means of establishing and controlling public order, is organized and channeled in different ways in bands, tribes, chiefdoms, and states and may be vested in families, communities, associations, or specialized functionaries. The type of territorial political organization is dependent on the size and complexity of the community in which it is found. Where societies come to disagree with the established authority, conflict may arise and ultimately be resolved either peacefully or violently.

Humans are not isolated creatures but social ones. It is in our nature to interact with others of our species for reasons of companionship and survival. Chapter 8 examines how the values of commodities differ from culture to culture and discusses the development of economic systems. It includes a section on the research of Annette Weiner. Chapter 9 illustrates the many forms that marriage takes in societies around the world. An intimate social relationship, it is the basis for the creation of the family, the primary group to which we belong and the basic institution of social life throughout human existence. Chapter 10 describes the systems used to identify our relationships to other members of our family. Incorporating a section on gender and politics, chapter 11 examines the use of power to maintain an ordered society and to restore order when conflicts arise or rules are broken.

CHAPTER EIGHT

Economics

After reading this chapter, you should be able to:

Explain the role of culture in the definition of commodities and economic value.

Explain the roles of use rights and the ownership of resources in the process of economic production.

Discuss the concept of division of labor.

Discuss the economic differences among the U.S. social classes.

Define the three forms of economic distribution.

Relate the forms of economic distribution to the four societal types.

Compare and contrast subsistence economies and consumer economies.

Define status income and explain its economic functions.

Discuss the four systems of economic control.

Relate the four systems of economic control to the four societal types.

Explain how population growth affects U.S. life.

◀ **Figure 8.1** *Market Exchange   Market exchange involves the buying and selling of goods. It can become an impersonal type of transaction in industrialized states where the exchange depends on supply and demand rather than on knowing the seller. These Peruvians buy and sell their goods in open air markets.*

In this chapter we will discuss how economic systems work in different societies. We will first examine how cultures define what they value as potential economic commodities. We will consider how the relative values of commodities may vary from culture to culture, how cultural values as well as survival needs may influence the level of demand that may exist for a given commodity, and how cultures differ in the motives that are defined as normal reasons for economic exchanges. Economic systems will then be examined in terms of cultural differences in the control and use of resources, the production of valued goods and services, and in the distribution and consumption of goods and services.

Yen. Pieces of eight. Bull market. Penny candy. How long do you think you or your family could survive if you had to grow all the fruit and vegetables you needed? Or how many cows do you think you could raise on a tiny balcony on a high-rise apartment on the East Side of New York City? What kind of house do you think you'd live in if you had to build your own from the resources available in your immediate area? If your neighbor had more trees than you did and you had more chickens, what system would you devise to exchange the items you both need?

DEFINITION OF ECONOMIC SYSTEMS

The system by which people obtain or produce, distribute, and consume valued material goods and services is called **economics**. An economic system includes the subsistence customs most concerned with the production of needed goods discussed in chapter 6, as well as the rules that govern what is done with those goods and how they are used. In this chapter, we will examine in more detail how people organize themselves socially to facilitate the production, exchange, and use of goods and services.

The Cultural Definition of Commodity

Cultures differ in what they define as useful or valuable, that is, as **commodities**. People work to produce food, provide themselves with shelter, and defend and reproduce themselves in all cultures. However, as was pointed out in the discussion of culture, the specific goods and services that constitute food, shelter, or means of defense differ from society to society. For instance, milk and dairy products were unacceptable foods for adults in traditional East Asian cultures, while North Americans reject the use of dog or snake meat, both of which are eaten in various parts of Asia. These differences may be accounted for in part by an extension of the principle of optimal foraging discussed in chapter 6. Essentially, this is the idea that when people work they generally try to maximize the returns that they gain from their efforts. Although few would argue with such a principle in general, it alone is not sufficient to account for the diversity of things that people endow with economic value throughout the world. An overzealous application of the principle would imply that people would rely on the minimum number of food types necessary to meet their nutritional needs. Nowhere do people do so, however, except where they are forced to by dire circumstances. We seek variety in our diets and even expend extra effort on special occasions to obtain and prepare unusual delicacies.

Cultural differences are even greater when we consider the range of variation that exists in pleasurable activities that are not mandated by survival needs. Consider, for instance, art, recreation, and religion. Although each category is a cultural universal, and even though the psychological principles that guide people's behavior in each category may also be universal, the specific behaviors and objects people find beautiful, sacred, or fun are not readily predictable.

Intangible Property. Cultural variation in the definition of commodities to be produced, ex-

(Continued on p. 196)

---

economics system by which people obtain or produce, distribute, and consume material goods and services

commodities goods, services, and intangible items that are determined to be useful or valuable in a particular culture

SEAWEED FARMING

Benson U. Dakay hefted a tangled, soggy gray-green clump and shook it slightly.

"This is what it's all about," he said. "Seaweed."

The man known in the Philippines as the Seaweed King grinned, glanced around the warehouse piled with bags of the ocean's greenery and declared: "Seaweed is growing. Seaweed is growing fast."

One of eight children who inherited a small trading business and a mosquito-repellent company from his father, who was an orphan from Fujian Province in China, the 40-year-old Mr. Dakay has built an empire on seaweed here in the southern Philippines. . . .

During the late 1960's, Mr. Dakay said he wondered about the European companies that were increasingly interested in buying seaweed harvested from the ocean, packing it up and shipping it to Europe for processing. Here in Cebu, seaweed had been part of the local diet for generations, but there seemed little use for the stuff beyond an appearance in a salad bowl.

"We were dealing with the Europeans," he said, of his father's trading company. "We were supplying the French and some to the Danish. The Danes were putting up a buying station. I started organizing farmers to gather wild seaweed. But the whole thing became depleted after five years. There wasn't any more seaweed."

About the same time, a researcher from the University of Hawaii was experimenting here with the idea of seaweed farms, examining whether seaweed could be raised like any other crop.

"The Government began providing some support for seaweed farming," said Filipina Scott, who heads the marine biology section at the University of San Carlos here. "It began very slowly, but then began to take off."

For Mr. Dakay, the success of seaweed farming marked the beginning of the real commercialization of the seaweed industry in the Philippines, the transformation from gathering natural seaweed to organized farming. "Farming was the key," he explained.

Beginning with the farmers who had earlier gathered wild seaweed, Mr. Dakay and Government fisheries and aquatic resources agents began urging farmers throughout the archipelago to create and tend sea farms of about two and a half acres each. The farms were created by stringing nylon cord from stakes and tying seaweed seedlings to the cords. By the beginning of this year, nearly 100,000 families were engaged in seaweed farming.

Every day, from dozens of islands across the Philippines, bags of seaweed arrive at Mr. Dakay's sprawling warehouses. The seaweed is dried and processed into a powder called carrageenan, an ingredient in dozens of food products from hams and hotdogs to jellies, breads, beers, noodles, chocolate milk and ice cream. Increasingly, the world's supply of carrageenan is coming from the Philippines, and a growing percentage of that from Mr. Dakay's company, the Shemberg Marketing Corporation, its name derived from the first initial of the elder Dakay's eight children.

While Shemberg is the largest of the seaweed producers and refiners, nearly a dozen other companies here in Debu are involved in the processing of seaweed. Last year, it commandeered nearly half of the $65.6 million Philippine market in seaweed products, or about 10 percent of the global demand for refined and semi-refined seaweed products. . . .

Mr. Dakay pulled his sunglasses from his shirt pocket. "Finally things are going right in the Philippines," he said, alluding to economic reforms under President Fidel V. Ramos. He turned before heading out into the blazing Cebu sun and added: "Everything has changed in the last three years. Now everyone can do business. That's what we're doing."

From "They Plow the Waves for the Squire of Seaweed," by Edward A. Gargan, June 5, 1995, *New York Times*, p. A4.

CHINESE-FILIPINOS

Chinese-Filipinos make up barely 1.5 percent of the population in the Philippines, but have become dominant in the world of business and trade. The city of Mandaue, in Cebu, has become the headquarters of a seaweed empire.

FIGURE 8.2

CULTURAL COMMODITIES

What one culture considers valuable, another may not. Seaweed, for example, had been part of the diet of the people of Cebu, in the city of Mandaue, in the Philippines for generations, but not many other societies were interested in using this commodity as food. They did, however, use carrageenan, a product of processed seaweed as an ingredient in many food products. Benson U. Dakay developed a method of farming the crop, and his company now supplies about 10 percent of the global demand for seaweed products. These workers are sorting the plants.

changed, and consumed is not limited to tangible things. Intangibles, too, may be defined as commodities. Navajos, for example, consider the sacred chants used in their curing ceremonies to be personal property, and an individual must pay an appropriate price to be taught a chant known to another. Northwest Coast Indians of North America considered titles of nobility to be a form of property, the ownership of which had to be validated by gift giving. North Americans also assert ownership over the expression of ideas and songs in their copyright laws.

The Cultural Definition of Value

Cultures also differ in how much value they place on any commodity. The same things are not of equal worth everywhere. The sacred zebu cow of Hindu India would not command a high price at a North American cattle auction, and the dogs that so many North Americans esteem as household pets are seen as too dirty to be pets by Iranians.

Supply and Demand as a Cultural Construct. The law of supply and demand is widely discussed in U.S. commerce as if it were a law of nature. Such a view of supply and demand overlooks the fact that the value of a commodity is, in many cases, culturally defined. Sahlins (1976), for instance, has pointed out that cut for cut, meat in U.S. culture is priced higher the less closely the animal from which it comes is symbolically associated with human beings. Thus, dogs are named and live within the house like one of the family, so the eating of their meat, though perfectly nutritious, is tabooed. Horses, too, are named, but they live outside the house and work for people like servants instead of living with them as kin. Americans somewhat grudgingly admit that horses are edible, but are not commonly eaten in the United States. Pigs and cattle are clearly defined as foods, but the pig, which lives closer to the human domain as a barnyard animal and scavenger of human food scraps, usually commands a lower market price than the cow. It must be remembered that Sahlins's theory cannot be applied directly to other cultures, nor to all cultures of the United States in the mid-1990s, a time when the price of pork is higher than that of beef in at least some parts of the country and at certain times of the year. But the underlying idea that the desirability of an animal as food is inversely related to its symbolic closeness to humans still applies, at least *generally*, to most food tastes in the United States.

The Profit Motive as a Cultural Construct. In the United States, people often speak of the profit motive as a basic economic incentive. Indeed, one theme of this text has been that material benefits are important predictors of customs. However, the profit motive concept is often used to imply that *material* benefit is the sole motivator in economic transactions. This extreme view, common in U.S. society, over-

KWAKIUTL BARTERING: BIDDING UP THE PRICE

A narrow, materialistic view of the profit motive can make customs in which people seek to enhance their social rank and reputation at material cost seem irrational. Consider for example the case of the Kwakiutl, whose potlatch giveaway competitions were described in chapter 2 (see p. 52). For the Kwakiutl, prestige was a major factor to be considered in important economic transactions. After all, paying too low a price could mark one as poor, and selling high could give one the reputation of stinginess. The hallmark of Kwakiutl bartering was for the buyers to insist on paying a price high enough so that their honor was enhanced. One such transaction was the exchange of blankets for a *copper*, an engraved flat piece of metal which was a major symbol of wealth among the Kwakiutl. Benedict (1934) describes a purchase in which the buyers began with an offer that represented only a fraction of the copper's worth. Then the seller, praising himself, demanded more and more, reminding the would-be buyers that the price must reflect the current owner's greatness. Each demand was accepted by the buyers, until finally the seller was satisfied with a presentation of blankets, beautiful boxes to put them in, and three canoes, the entire offer valued at four thousand blankets:

> The owner answered, "I take the price." But it was not done. The purchaser now addressed the owner of the copper, saying: "Why, have you taken the price, chief? You take the price too soon. You must think poorly of me, chief. I am a Kwakiutl, I am one of those from whom all your tribes all over the world took their names. You must always stand beneath us." He sent his messengers to call his sister, his princess, and gave to his rivals two hundred blankets more, [a final payment known as] "the clothes of his princess." (p. 197)

By paying more than the seller had been willing to accept, the buyer's honor was enhanced by his demonstration of wealth. From examples such as this we can see that the old British advice, "Buy cheap, sell dear," would not be a useful guide to the practice of trade in every culture.

(see reference map p. 52)

---

looks the important role of culture in defining value. Efforts to obtain valued commodities are not limited to the acquisition of material things. People also work to obtain intangible goods. For instance, people may willingly accept material loss for spiritual merit or for increased social honor such as prestige, respect, admiration, personal honor, mana, luck, or a reward after death. Any view of the profit motive as nothing more than the principle that people will always try to maximize their immediate material gain in any exchange of goods is much too narrow.

PRODUCTION: THE CONTROL AND USE OF RESOURCES

Just because a resource is available to people does not mean that they have the right to use it. In every culture, the right to exploit resources is divided up among the members of a society based on concepts such as use rights and ownership.

Use Rights

The right to use a resource may belong to individuals or groups. For instance, according to Allan Holmberg (1950), the Sirionó, who (before they adopted a sedentary lifestyle based on agriculture) were a nomadic hunting people of eastern Bolivia, marked wild fruit trees with a notch as a sign that their finders had claimed the right to harvest the fruit for at least the current season. The Waorani, who are horticultural villagers in Ecuador, have more complex customs concerning the ownership of wild trees. They value the fruit of the wild chonta palm, but the trunk is impossible to climb because it is ringed with spiky thorns. When a wild chonta palm is discovered, its finder claims it by planting a cecropia tree next to it. Years later, when the cecropia is large enough, the owner harvests the chonta fruit by climbing the cecropia. The fruit is shared with other members of the village, but the chonta is considered to be owned by its finder, and is even inherited by the families of its original discoverer.

The right to use a resource may also be based on such social status characteristics as rank, age, or sex. Use right may be allocated

FIGURE 8.3

SAIGON MARKET

Vietnam is finding a growing prosperity in providing animal products for its southeast Asian neighbors. In their cultures, tiger eyes are said to improve vision; tiger penis boiled in soup enhances virility; meat of a bear's paw provides strength; rhino horn dissolved in broth is a treatment for high blood pressure and strokes. On the other hand, environmentalists fear that the growing need for these products is threatening the world's rarest animals. In this market in Ho Chi Minh City, some animal parts have been preserved in wine.

by rules such as "first come, first served." This is common, for instance, among seminomadic foragers where it is more efficient for each group to simply begin its foraging in a location that is not already being used than to compete with others who began their work first. Another example of use rights is the treatment of beaches on the East Coast of the United States, where only those who own or rent a cottage on or near the shore have the right to use the adjacent beach.

Ownership

The right to use and the right to deny use rights to others temporarily is called **ownership**, a right that is held even when it is not being exercised. Thus, people are expected to obtain permission to use property owned by others. Ownership itself can be given, bought, or sold.

Division of Labor

Production is never accomplished by requiring everyone to perform the same work. In all societies that anthropologists have visited, the labor of production is divided up by age and gender. In horticultural and pastoral societies, one also finds the beginnings of occupational specialization by age, gender, and group. Specialization becomes increasingly important the larger and denser the local groups become; it is particularly important in large industrialized societies throughout the world today.

Age and Gender.   Where specialization is limited to age and gender differences, the various productive forms of work are thought of as simply roles that males and females of various ages play as members of their families and local groups. Work as an activity is not divorced from one's family or community relationships and is not thought of as a specialized activity to be done for hire. Children are socialized to help the adults in their productive activities and are gradually given greater responsibilities in these tasks until they achieve adult proficiency. In most societies, the contributions of children add to the total productive resources of the family. The most productive years tend to be from puberty until the beginning of old age, when intensive work efforts are often replaced by more organizational and managerial roles.

It is common in societies throughout the world for gender differences in the division of labor to be based on the expectation that routine and domestic labor will be done by women and the heavier and nondomestic labor will be done by men. For example, men are more often expected to hunt larger game animals, fish in offshore waters, herd large animals, clear the

(Continued on p. 200)

ownership the right to use property and the right to deny use rights to others as long as one owns the property

SHOSHONE VS. PIONEER CONCEPTS OF LAND IN THE GREAT BASIN

The aboriginal Shoshone of the United States Great Basin were a foraging people who occupied a desert environment. Their territory was a sparse land with food resources that supported only about one person per 50 square miles. So their society was fragmented into small groups. Throughout most of the year, the Shoshone wandered in search of food in family groups of only four or five people. When families happened upon one another in their nomadic quest for food, they might visit and even cooperate in communal net hunts if one of the families had a net, and if they were lucky enough to have come together when large enough numbers of jackrabbits were also in the area. Luck of that kind, however, was the exception rather than the rule. Most of the time it was more economical to remain distant enough from other families and not compete for the same limited resources. Naturally, the Shoshone conception of their relationship to the land was not one of ownership. Instead, they thought of themselves as merely users of the resources within their native lands, and the right to use a resource could not be permanently owned by a migratory people who, throughout most of the year, had to be continually on the move in order to survive. The Shoshone culture's rule governing the control of natural resources might be translated as "first come, first served."

In the 1840s, Mormon pioneers entered the Great Basin as settlers, bringing with them an agricultural technology. Their way of life was a sedentary one that exploited the ability of the soil to raise planted crops in enough abundance to support large, permanent populations. Such farmers have a different relationship to the land than migratory foragers. Farmers who live in permanent houses near the fields they plan to work for years have a special attachment to the land. They expect to own the food that they produce, and the idea of ownership of land rather than temporary use rights is likely to be a part of their culture's ideology.

In many parts of the U.S. frontier, there was a natural conflict between these two different concepts of the human relationship to nature. In the Great Basin, the conflict took a special twist. Mormon pioneers sought to avoid the direct hostility that had occurred elsewhere when arriving settlers had simply taken possession of land by force. Under a motto of "Better to feed the Indians than to fight them," many of the immigrants offered to "buy" agricultural land from the Shoshone. The Shoshone willingly took the goods offered them and went on their way. The Mormon farmers were bemused when the Shoshone returned a year or so later and tried to "sell" them the same land again.

As might be expected, the Shoshone view of the matter was quite different. To them the land was not something to be owned, bought, or sold. They had merely given up their temporary use rights to the foreigners in return for the goods given to them. Imagine their surprise when they again passed through their traditional hunting lands and found that the foreigners had not merely passed through but had settled down, fencing the land, and even hoarding the food they got from it. The Shoshone regarded this as a most improper way of acting, for they valued the act of sharing and looked upon generosity as a defining quality of human beings.

SHOSHONE

The aboriginal Shoshone were a foraging people who occupied a desert environment in the Great Basin of the United States. They valued the land and its resources as things to be used by whoever expended the effort.

FIGURE 8.4

BRAZILIAN AVON SALESWOMEN
Many Brazilian women are finding financial rewards and emotional independence as salespeople for Avon beauty products. Eliana Maria Machado da Silva, who oversees 1,000 Avon ladies, here balances a box of cosmetics as she steps to shore on the job with Iraci Macedo da Costa Queiroz.

land in preparation for planting, do the heavier work of house construction, and manufacture stone and metal implements as well as goods for trade. Women frequently cooperate in communal hunts of smaller game, gather aquatic foods near the shores, herd smaller animals, weed and harvest gardens, take primary charge of domestic chores such as cooking and childrearing, weave textiles, and make pottery. However, these common ways of dividing up the work of men and women are certainly not the only conceivable ones, and they are not necessarily rigidly enforced in societies where they are the usual ones. There are many societies that assign individual activities to women and men differently than most others do. For instance, among the Toda of southern India, men prepare the meals; among the Dani of New Guinea, men are the weavers of household textiles; and among the Great Basin Shoshone, where men were nominally called the hunters, women actually did most of the work during the communal rabbit hunts. So, although common physiological differences may often play a part in defining the roles of men and women, it is clear that biology does not control economic gender roles in any fixed or necessary way.

Occupational Specialization. In societies without domesticated food resources, work tends to be unspecialized except by age and gender. Limited specialization exists only to the degree that certain individuals devote more of their time than others to tasks such as basket making or weaving. The products of their labor are then exchanged for other things that they need. Domestication typically brings greater control of the food supply, allowing local groups to be larger and more sedentary than those of societies that survive by foraging for wild foods. Societies with domestication tend to have additional specialized roles such as food producers, potters, political specialists, warriors, religious specialists, and traders. In societies where food production has been industrialized, the percentage of persons involved in food production can be quite small and the number of other types of occupational specialization is particularly large.

Specialization by Group. In food-producing societies, entire groups may also specialize in producing crops indigenous to their environment, which they then exchange for other foods they need. Thus, in the Andean empire of the ancient Inca civilization, villagers who lived between sea level and 11,000 feet grew maize and potatoes. Between 11,000 and 14,000 feet, potatoes were the primary crop. Above 14,000 feet, villagers specialized in raising llamas, alpacas, and quinoa, a grain capable of growing at high altitudes. The specialized crops of different altitudes could be easily transported from one part of the empire to another with the aid of llamas as pack animals.

Social groups such as families or age mates may also work together in some specialized productive activity. So for example, among the pig-herding Tsembaga Maring discussed in chapter 6, children and young adults specialized in tending the pigs, while adults worked the fields to produce root crops such as sweet potatoes.

Occupational Groups in the United States. An important measure of one's position within the U.S. class system is one's occupation. The U.S. economy is based primarily on market exchange. Rather than producing goods for direct exchange, most people are employed by someone else. In return, they are compensated with an income that they then exchange for the services and goods that they require. The size of

(Continued on p. 202)

BRAZILIAN WOMEN FIND NEW OPPORTUNITIES AS AVON SALESWOMEN!

Padding down cow paths in flip-flop sandals or paddling a canoe through piranha-infested creeks, Iraci Macedo da Costa Queiroz lugs from door to door what rain forest dreams are made of: Mesmerize cologne, Forever Fragrance perfume and Cool Confidence deodorant.

With no doorbells to ring at the riverside shanties in stilts, this Avon lady of the Amazon claps her hands and calls out cheerily "Hi, honey! I'm here!"

"Women want to give me chickens, manioc flour—but what am I going to do with a chicken?" this veteran, 52-year-old saleswoman exclaimed on the job one recent morning as her son piloted a motor launch across a quiet Amazon tributary where baby pink dolphins played in the sunlight.

Far from being a lone missionary for smelling nice in the tropics, Mrs. Queiroz works at the end of a computerized, 2,500-mile long supply chain, part of a national web that last year boosted Brazil over Mexico to become Avon's largest market outside the United States. Offering food for sociological thought, Avon's sales army in Brazil—478,000 "beauty consultants"—is more than double the size of Brazil's Army: 200,000 soldiers.

The power of Latin cosmetics has not been lost on Avon, the world's largest cosmetics company. With sales increasingly stagnant in the United States and Europe, Avon now enjoys its fastest growth in the developing world. The beauty star is Brazil, where Avon's sales are expected to hit $1 billion this year, more than double the 1993 level. . . .

To blanket Brazil, Avon recognizes that there are many Brazils.

São Paulo, in the developed south, has gone through a social transformation similar to that of the United States. Doorbells ring during the day to empty apartments: women are at work. Additionally, many urban apartment buildings are encased in high security. Building guards do not allow door-to-door sales. To reach these upper-income urban markets, Avon advertises on cable television, providing a toll-free number for orders.

At the other end of the map, Avon ladies working Amazon mining camps routinely trade a jar of Renew for three grams of gold dust.

"Some of my route I do on foot, some I do on canoe," said Mrs. Queiroz who lives in this municipality, a flood plain without roads.

Although river travel is picturesque—a school boat filled with uniformed school children passed as Mrs. Queiroz talked—her route can be hazardous. Over the last year, two local children fell into rivers and were killed by swarming piranhas. The rivers also abound with poisonous water snakes and the Amazon's black caiman, a relative of the alligator. Last year, an Avon lady was badly injured after her outboard motor failed and she went over a waterfall. . . .

Avon advocates argue that, in the universe of Brazilian female poverty, Avon offers a new option beyond traditional money-making opportunities: cook, maid, babysitter, primary school teacher or prostitute.

"For housewives, there is emancipation," said Eliana Maria Machado da Silva, who oversees 1,000 Avon salewomen in this corner of the Amazon. "They start to have their own financial life. They discover themselves, they gain self-confidence."

Carefully coiffed despite her rough rural rounds, this 32-year-old sales director showed great care when stepping out of an unstable river launch to the safety of dry land.

"Last year, I won a trip to Italy, Greece, Egypt and Israel," continued Miss da Silva, an ambitious Amazonian whose formal education stopped at high school. "This year, I hope to win a trip to New York."

From "Who Braves Piranha Waters? Your Avon Lady!" by James Brooke, July 7, 1995, *New York Times*, p. A4.

SOUTH AMERICAN SALESWOMEN

Piranhas, water snakes, and the black caiman, a relative of the alligator, are just some obstacles women face who sell Avon products in the Amazon. In an economy that has given women the financial opportunity to become independent and self-confident, Brazil now outranks Mexico as Avon's largest market outside the United States.

TABLE 8.1

PERCENT REPRESENTATION OF WOMEN IN OCCUPATIONS, 1993

Occupations	Percent
All occupations	45.8
Managerial/professional	47.8
Executive, administrative, managerial	42.0
Teachers, college and university	42.5
Teachers, except college and university	75.1
Professional specialist	53.2
Technical/sales/administrative support	63.8
Sales workers, retail, and personal service	64.9
Administrative support, including clerical	78.8
Information clerks	94.3
Service workers	59.5
Personal service	80.7
Precision production, craft, repair	8.6
Operators, fabricators, laborers	24.5
Farming, forestery, fishing	15.4

Source: U.S. Bureau of the Census, *Statistical Abstract of the United States: 1995* (115th ed.), [Table No. 637, pp. 408–409], 1994, Washington, DC: U.S. Government Printing Office.

their personal income depends largely, though not entirely, on the prestige ranking of their income-producing status.

The least prestigious and least well paid of the economic statuses are **unskilled laborers**. They usually are paid by the hour or by the quantity of goods that their work produces. Unskilled laborers are often hired for part-time or seasonal work, such as food bagging at supermarkets, waiting on tables at restaurants, and harvesting crops on farms. Many of these jobs are held by young people who are not yet economically self-sufficient, by a disproportionate percentage of ethnic minorities, and by migrant workers.

Pink-collar occupations are jobs traditionally held by women: waitress, sales clerk, secretary, telephone operator, and public school teacher (see Table 8.1). There is some variation

in the prestige and incomes associated with these jobs, but in the main they fall below average in both measures. This category of low-level human service and information-processing jobs has been the fastest growing of the occupational categories since about 1950. Between 1945 and 1980, tens of millions of jobs opened up in this category. Since these were low-paid and new rather than having previously been held by men, women readily obtained these jobs without being seen as competing with men for jobs (Harris, 1981). In the past 15 years the percentage of women employed in the better-paid, higher-status occupations has been gradually increasing but still remains low.

Blue-collar workers are manual laborers other than farm workers. Although they command little prestige, some of these statuses have access to above-average incomes due to the economic importance of the commodities and services that they control. Examples of blue-collar workers are garbage collectors, dockhands, factory workers, taxicab and bus drivers, janitors, and supervisors of manual laborers.

White-collar occupations are clerical workers, sales workers, technical workers, managers, and administrators. Their work is primarily the providing of services. Although many of these occupations are fairly prestigious and relatively well paid, over the years many white-collar offices have become more and more like factories in the repetitive nature of the routine work.

Professionals are typically self-employed providers of services whose work generally requires a graduate-level university degree. Included in this category are the most prestigious nongovernmental occupations such as medical doctors, lawyers, scientists, and university faculty. These highly ranked positions, as well as highly ranked governmental positions, have generally been dominated by men (see Table 8.2).

---

unskilled laborers low-paid workers, including part-time or seasonal workers, who are usually paid by the hour or for the quantity of goods they produce

pink-collar occupations service occupations that are largely held by women

blue-collar workers nonfarm manual laborers

white-collar occupations service-providing occupations such as clerical, sales, managerial, and administrative jobs

professionals self-employed, college-educated service providers

Historically, the simplest means to climb to a higher position within the class system has been through the educational system, since higher-ranked occupations have generally required a higher level of education than lower-ranked ones. Indeed, it is common for many U.S. employers to require an educational background in prospective employees that goes far beyond what is actually needed for the work itself. This system, in which education is strongly rewarded as a means of raising one's rank within the class system, keeps potential workers in school for a longer period of time before they begin full-time work than might otherwise be the case. Along with other factors, this has kept the number of people in the U.S. labor pool, and therefore the U.S. unemployment rate, lower than it otherwise would have been.

Although opportunities for upward social mobility have been high in the United States, so have the chances of moving down in the occupational ranks. For instance, a decline in the demand for a product or service can make it impossible for a person who is qualified for a high-ranked occupation to obtain employment, and persons already employed may lose their positions. Thus, engineers who are educationally too specialized in their skills to move readily from one high-ranked position to another may find themselves bagging groceries, and recent university graduates may be forced to accept employment driving cabs. A great deal of personal anguish may accompany such downward shifts in social rank.

TABLE 8.2	
U.S. OCCUPATIONS HELD PREDOMINANTLY BY ONE GENDER, 1993	
Occupation	Percent Held
Nine Jobs Where Men Are Scarce	*by men*
Prekindergarten and kindergarten teachers	2.3
Dental assistants	2.2
Secretaries	1.1
Receptionists	2.8
Registered nurses	5.6
Child-care worker (outside private households)	1.0
Welfare service aides	17.9
Textile sewing machine operators	4.2
Librarians	11.7
Six Jobs Where Women Are Scarce:	*by women*
Surveyor and mapping scientists	5.0
Aerospace engineers	7.5
Lawyers	22.9
Police and detectives	12.0
Clergy	11.4
College and university teachers	42.5

Source: U.S. Bureau of the Census, *Statistical Abstract of the United States: 1995* (115th ed.), [Table No. 637, pp. 408–409], 1994, Washington, DC: U.S. Government Printing Office.

DISTRIBUTION

The movement of resources or goods from where they are found or produced to where they will be used is referred to as **distribution**. There are three major economic systems by which distribution is controlled: reciprocity, redistribution, and markets.

Reciprocity

The system of exchange in which goods or services are passed from one individual or group to another as gifts without the need for explicit contracting for specific payment is called **reciprocity**. Unlike buying and selling, reciprocity does not involve bargaining over what is to be given in return. There is merely

the understanding that the sharing is mutual and will eventually be evenhanded.

Reciprocity is the sole form of economic distribution in bands and tribes, where the small number of people in each local community makes gift giving a sufficient procedure to meet everyone's economic needs. The mutual sharing of surpluses in the form of reciprocal gift giving within the local community equalizes wealth and eliminates lean times for indi-

---

distribution movement of resources or goods from where they are found or produced to where they will ultimately be used

reciprocity sharing of surpluses with the understanding that the party receiving the gift will respond in kind in the future

FIGURE 8.5

RECIPROCITY

Social interdependence in most hunter-gatherer societies is the basis for reciprocity, the giving and taking of goods without the exchange of money. These San hunters are drying strips of meat before distributing them to others.

vidual members. The trait of generosity, so characteristic of band peoples, is actually a very effective economic device for ensuring the survival of the entire group. When a hunter shares excess food after a successful hunt, for example, it is a kind of insurance against future times of need. Every hunter is bound to experience some periods of poor luck in the chase. Those with whom a hunter has shared food or other useful goods in the past will make return gifts of their own later surpluses to ensure the continuation of his good will in the future. In the long run, the economic system of reciprocity maintains a balance in the distribution of goods. No one prospers at the expense of others, but neither does anyone need fear the specter of starving alone during the inevitable periods of personal failure or illness when hunting is not possible.

The enforcement of reciprocity is based primarily on the desire of the participants not to be excluded, rather than on formal sanctions. So long as everyone involved participates to everyone else's satisfaction, the rules of the exchange do not even need to be discussed. However, a group or individual that fails to engage in a fair share of gift giving may be censured or excluded by the others. In economically more complex societies, reciprocity is found within families and between acquaintances, and it typically involves symbolic goods and services such as holiday greeting cards or parties; in very simple societies, the gifts that are shared may be life-sustaining ones, such as food. In such cases, participation is likely to be self-enforcing even if it is not mandatory, since exclusion from the system may be life-threatening. As noted by Sahlins (1972), reciprocity takes three basic forms: generalized reciprocity, balanced reciprocity, and negative reciprocity.

Generalized Reciprocity. Gifts given with no expectation of immediate exchange are part of **generalized reciprocity**. The persons involved are most likely to be motivated by a sense of obligation toward the welfare of the others. For instance, in families, goods and services are provided for children by their parents even though the children may not reciprocate in kind even later in life. Generalized reciprocity may also be exemplified by the care that is given to elderly or incapacitated people who are unable to respond with a return of goods or services of equal value.

The feeling of obligation that minimizes an expectation of an immediate return of favors can be based on a sense of community as well as on the bonds of kinship. In foraging societies, generalized reciprocity is the basic economic mechanism for ensuring that everyone within the local community, nonrelatives included, is provided for. Where generalized reciprocity is practiced, generosity is likely to be an expected characteristic of normal behavior. Thus, for example, in the language of the foraging Shoshone of the intermountain region of the United States, the word *dzaande* meant both *good* and *generous*. The good human was a generous person, and since generosity in sharing was understood to be a natural attribute of the normal person rather than an unexpected or surprising behavior, no word or phrase existed that was equivalent to the English "Thank you!"

---

generalized reciprocity gift given with no expectation of immediate exchange

FIGURE 8.6

BALANCED RECIPROCITY

A more immediate exchange of goods and services is expected in a system of balanced reciprocity. These Mennonite farmers spend their time and labor *helping their neighbor in a traditional barn raising with the expectation that they each will also be helped when the need arises.*

Balanced Reciprocity. Between persons who lack a sense of kinship or obligation to help one another with no expectation of return, but who each have something that the other would like to have, **balanced reciprocity** is likely to occur, in which a return gift is expected within a relatively short time. Although the bond between the two parties is not so great as is present where generalized reciprocity is practiced, the desire to maintain good relations is great enough that haggling over the exchange is not necessary, since both parties try to respond with something of equal value. Balanced reciprocity is commonly practiced by members of neighboring communities that each specialize in the production of different goods or that control different resources. Even without direct bargaining, balanced reciprocity may be maintained to the benefit of both groups. At appropriate opportunities each group gives what it has in surplus to recipients known to desire such a commodity. Although no immediate return is demanded, the gratefulness of the recipients and their continued interest in the commodity will ensure that they

will reciprocate within a reasonable time with gifts of their own.

Balanced reciprocity may include the exchange of services as well as goods. For instance, the Quechua-speaking peoples of the South American Andes in pre-Spanish times had a concept of reciprocal work obligations between communities known as the *mink'a*. Members of a *mink'a* group cooperated in performing difficult work such as harvesting, canal repair, or housebuilding. American *barn raisings* and *harvest bees* of frontier days were a similar form of balanced reciprocity of services.

Probably the most organized example of balanced reciprocity of both goods and services in a complex society operated within the caste system in India. In each local community, individuals were organized into a system of occupations deemed appropriate to members of the various castes. This *jati system* provided for the economic needs of all members of the commu-

(Continued on p. 207)

---

balanced reciprocity gift given with expectation of a return gift shortly

THE KULA RING

Malinowski (1922) described the classic example of balanced reciprocity in his account of the Kula ring, a ceremonial exchange system between members of a ring of islands in Melanesia. In Kula trade, there were only two kinds of valuables that were exchanged: long, red shell necklaces called *soulava* and white shell bracelets called *mwali*. Both were passed from island to island around the ring as the necklaces were traded for the bracelets. The necklaces moved only clockwise around the islands and the bracelets were traded only counterclockwise.

The necklaces and bracelets exchanged in the Kula ring were objects of prestige that gave evidence of their owners' participation in the Kula system. Each necklace or bracelet carried with it a personal history of its past ownership, so, like an heirloom, its value increased with age. Each owner kept a particular necklace or bracelet only for a year or so and then gave it as a gift to a trade partner. Men who participated in Kula expeditions had specific trade partners on islands in either direction. When they traveled on a Kula

expedition, they were received as honored guests by their partners, and bracelets and necklaces were given ceremoniously with appropriate ritual speeches accompanying each bestowal. If, at that time, a partner had no object of equivalent prestige, it was understood that he was expected to work to acquire an appropriate gift to give in return on a later expedition.

Uberoi (1962) has discussed a number of social functions of the Kula ring. For instance, since the exchange of Kula valuables was a form of balanced reciprocity, trade partners should not profit at one another's expense from the exchange. What then motivated the islanders to participate in the long and sometimes dangerous sea voyages that the Kula ring required? Certainly there was an element of socializing and entertainment in the process. The Kula gift giving helped to maintain an amicable relationship between long-standing trade partners from different islands. Trading partnerships were inherited by another family member at the death of a partner and thus perpetuated friendly relationships over the generations among residents of potentially competing islands. Trading expeditions kept alive the traditions of the islands as the gift givers recited the histories and legends associated with each Kula item bestowed.

Over time new participants were introduced into the Kula exchange system. Scoditti (1983) has noted that younger men took part in Kula expeditions after they had been given necklaces or armbands by relatives or in return for building canoes. Of course, the necklaces and armbands received in this way were likely to be among the less prestigious ones. With frequent and long participation, the reputation of younger traders could rise as they acquired more valued armbands and necklaces. Campbell (1983) has suggested that possession of valuable Kula objects also symbolized high social rank, since the most valued items were usually owned by the more experienced participants who were good navigators, respected expedition organizers, and—in earlier times—successful warriors.

Finally, Kula expeditions were occasions for practical as well as ceremonial exchanges. Foodstuffs, tools, and other items of economic importance were bartered by participants in the expedition to the benefit of all. Since the islands in the ring specialized in the production of different commodities, the Kula ring played an important economic role in the lives of its participants, even though it appeared to have only ceremonial significance.

KULA RING

An example of balanced reciprocity, Kula trade took place in the islands of Melanesia. Two kinds of valuables were exchanged: red shell necklaces and white shell bracelets. The Kula exchange enhanced the prestige of the traders and guaranteed that trading partners would be available in the long run.

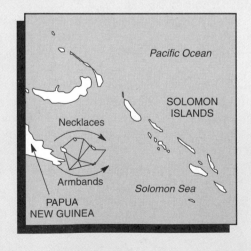

nity because each person was obligated to provide goods or services to everyone else. The miller ground grain for all of the farmers, while the farmers provided some of the food they produced to all members of the community. The barber cut hair, and the weaver gave gifts of fabric to other members of the community. Each occupation benefited others without direct and immediate payment, and so long as everyone received as well as gave, the needs of all could be met.

Negative Reciprocity. When at least one group or individual in a reciprocal exchange system attempts to get more than it gives, we speak of **negative reciprocity**. Negative reciprocity varies from simple miserliness or "Yankee shrewdness" on the part of one participant, through deceit in bargaining, to outright theft; the profit motive takes precedence over generosity. This form of reciprocity is most common among strangers within the same communities or members of different communities, especially those that differ in cultures. The traditional Apache raiding of their more sedentary neighbors exemplifies a pattern of negative reciprocity in which the neighboring groups were viewed not so much as enemies to be exterminated as a kind of resource to be exploited.

One of the most interesting examples of negative reciprocity that has been noted by ethnographers is a form called *silent trade*. In this kind of exchange, there need be no direct interaction between the trading partners once the relationship is established. Each simply leaves surplus goods known to be of use to the other at a place where they will be found. Each occasionally checks the cache site to see if anything has been left and, if so, leaves something near the offered goods. The original party may consummate the exchange by taking the goods left near the offered commodities, or may refuse to do so to indicate that the amount left by the second party was insufficient. In the latter case, the second party may add to the goods left behind or may simply retrieve them to call off the transaction. The Mbuti Pygmy foragers of the Ituri Forest carried out trade of this kind with horticultural villagers who lived outside the forest. In return for garden produce, iron knives, and pots the Mbuti partner would leave game and other forest foods. Similar silent trade has been noted in a variety of other cultures in different parts of the world, such as the Semang foragers and Malay farmers of the

Malay Peninsula. Silent trade was a particularly useful form of barter among neighboring groups that did not speak a common language.

Redistribution

The second major economic system for the distribution of goods and services is **redistribution**, where commodities are contributed by all members of the social group to a common pool from which they are then distributed to where they will be used. While reciprocity is a two-party affair involving givers and receivers, redistribution requires an intermediary, a third party who coordinates the process and exercises control over the flow of goods and services. The mediating individual or group is likely to gain both prestige and power from the position of control over whatever is exchanged in this economic system. Examples of systems of economic redistribution in complex societies include taxation, social security, retirement funds, unemployment compensation, and insurance.

Redistribution, like reciprocity, is an economic practice within families around the world, occurring when their members save for a common goal. However, as a major societal mechanism within the economic system beyond the family, redistribution is not present in all societies. Service (1962) believes that redistribution developed in sedentary agricultural societies that occupied distinctly different ecological zones in which local residents specialized in producing certain types of food.

Harris (1974) also ties the rise in importance of redistribution to the presence of food domestication, but he thinks that yearly differences in productivity rather than local specialization is the central cause. He sees redistribution as merely part of a larger set of economic practices that encourage food growers to work hard enough to produce surpluses in most years. The extra produce is normally channeled to a production manager who redistributes the goods. The underlying payoff in such a system

---

negative reciprocity one group or individual in a reciprocal exchange system attempts to get more than it gives

redistribution contribution of commodities by all members of a group to a common pool from which they will be distributed to those who will use them

FIGURE 8.7

WOMEN'S WEALTH

Trobriand Island women accumulate their own wealth and prestige in the form of skirts and banana-leaf bundles. While the woman's brother gives yams to her husband to increase the husband's stature, he is, in turn, expected to accumulate bundles and *skirts for his wife so that she can repay this debt when a member of her family dies. The quantity and quality of bundles and skirts distributed are thus a measure of the wealth and political power of the dead person's lineage.*

comes in lean years when climatic conditions or other crises lead to poorer-than-expected harvests. Furthermore, neighboring communities are not always affected by the same difficulties and may lend a helping hand at such times, if they have been beneficiaries of the suffering community's previous redistributive investments.

Those who manage the redistribution of goods and services are typically rewarded with prestige and sometimes with power and wealth. Anthropologists have been particularly interested in two kinds of redistribution managers found in societies of middle-range complexity: charismatic entrepreneurs and chiefs.

Bigmanship. The economic entrepreneurs of horticultural societies are men and women who engage in **bigmanship**, economic production and gift giving to achieve public recognition and respect. These "big men" and "big women" are not true officials who have power to demand the cooperation of others; rather they are prominent individuals within their community, charismatic leaders who encourage relatives and other members of their commu-

nity to follow their lead in the production of surplus goods. Then a festive gathering of conspicuous generosity and hospitality that promotes the prestige of the host group and its entrepreneur is held for followers of other economic leaders.

Chiefs. In somewhat larger horticultural or agricultural societies in which social ranking becomes important, the role of bigmanship merges with that of the local political official, the chief. The **chief** is a person of authority and prestige who is the major political official and the economic manager of the local community.

(Continued on p. 210)

---

bigmanship economic entrepreneurship by persons in horticulture societies who encourage economic production and gift giving in their communities to achieve public recognition and respect

chief presiding redistributive and political official of a chiefdom society or of a subdivision of a chiefdom, whose legal authority extends in at least some areas over members of families other than his or her own

BIG WOMEN IN THE TROBRIAND ISLANDS

When Annette Weiner (1988) studied the Trobrianders, she found that women as well as men obtain prestige and social power through the production and distribution of wealth. Men carve, garden, and fish; women manufacture and control red skirts and banana-leaf bundles that are important forms of wealth.

According to Weiner, "Skirts and bundles have economic value, and their major use as payment to mourners after a death directly incorporates the wealth of men" (p. 28). Men provide their sisters with yams from their gardens that economically benefit the sisters' husbands, since yams are a form of wealth used by Trobriand men to achieve status. A man's entire kin group is obligated to repay this debt to his wife's family when he dies in the form of gift giving which consists of the skirts and banana-leaf bundles that women own because they symbolize the wealth and status of the widows' relatives. Thus, the giveaways that are sponsored by women are even more important than those of men.

Weiner describes vividly the first women's bigmanship competition she observed:

As we entered the village, no one paid attention to yams or even to the men who were cooking. All the excitement was being generated by the activities coming from the central plaza, where hundreds of women sat or stood surrounded by as many baskets; I saw that the baskets were filled with something I had never read or heard about—banana-leaf bundles.

Women were completely involved in sorting out their bundles and arranging piles of red fiber skirts. One woman seemed to be in charge, and she continually took bundles into the center, threw them on the ground, and called out someone's name. Other women rushed to the center, adding their bundles to the pile. Finally, another woman gathered them all up and carried them to her own basket. The same throwing and retrieving went on for hours. Sometimes the pile was small, with only about thirty bundles; at other times several hundred were given, with ten or so skirts thrown on top. Women laughed and shouted among themselves; occasionally they argued over a particular distribution. A few women insisted that I throw down some bundles myself, and I was told, 'Our bundles are just like your money.'

. . . Although men did not participate in any of the action in the center of the village, they remained in the village throughout the day, sitting on the house verandas and casually watching the proceedings. When the distribution finally was over, however, they then entered the plaza to give yams to those women who now stood with empty baskets. (pp. 29–30)

The importance of women's bigmanship activities is indicated by the fact that the wealth acquired by Trobriand men is subordinated to their obligation to help their wives amass women's wealth which has no utilitarian value. Its only function is to enhance the reputation of women's relatives. Yet, if their husbands do not satisfy their wives' kin by spending much of their wealth on the accumulation of women's goods for their wives, the brothers-in-law reduce the economic support to their sisters. When an important member of a woman's kin group dies, she may need to use all of her husband's yams to pay for the production of skirts and banana-leaf bundles that she will give away at her relative's funeral. If her husband refused to support her bigmanship participation at such an occasion, he would be insulting her relatives, and they would decrease contributions of yams to his wife. In the long run, his ability to participate in male competitions would be undermined. So women's production of the wealth by which they achieve rank takes priority over the accumulation of men's wealth by their husbands.

TROBRIAND WOMEN

In the region of Papua New Guinea, women of the Trobriand Islands gain social power and prestige through the manufacture and control of red skirts and banana-leaf bundles, which are important forms of wealth.

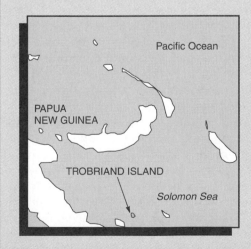

FIGURE 8.8

YAM PRODUCTION

The men of the Trobriand Islands raise yams not for themselves but to give to their sister's husband and to use as a medium of exchange. As they, in turn, receive yams from their brothers-in-law, they are expected to use them to acquire skirts and banana-leaf bundles for their wives. These yams are being stored in the yam house of the chief to whom these men are related by marriage.

Unlike the leaders in bigmanship activities, the chief does not generally participate in the productive work of the redistributive economy. Instead, the chief is a full-time political official whose duties include coordination of the redistributive practices.

In redistribution involving chiefs, festive occasions may still be celebrated using goods collected in the chief's warehouse. A more important role of redistribution, however, emerges in this system: the use of the centrally controlled goods to finance public works and services. A significant portion of the redistributive economy is channeled into such activities as building and maintaining irrigation projects, supporting a local police force or militia, and similar undertakings that enhance the general welfare of the community.

A redistributive economy that is controlled by full-time officials clearly lends itself to potential abuse. It is true that the ability of chiefs to siphon off redistributive goods for their own use allows the chiefs and their relatives in many such societies to form a social elite with special prerogatives and a higher standard of living than that of other members of society. But there is a surprisingly large number of cases in which prestige comes to the chiefs and their families only in proportion to how well they use the goods they control for the benefit of others. In these groups, chiefs may expend more than they take in and live in poverty but receive great respect in return.

Markets

The market economy is the third major approach to exchange, one that has become the major economic force in the industrialized societies of the world. The concept of the **market** is based on the idea of direct exchange, that is, buying and selling as opposed to mutual gift giving of valued items or services.

Marketing may occur spontaneously in any society, but it is most developed in sedentary societies in which the large number of people involved makes it convenient to establish traditional marketplaces to carry out the exchange. Especially in larger societies where marketplaces may bring together strangers and persons who see each other infrequently, market exchange, like negative reciprocity, may place little emphasis on mutual obligation, since each party becomes responsible for his or her own welfare in the transaction. Thus, self-interest rather than generosity often becomes the guiding principle. This, of course, is moderated, particularly in small-scale societies and even smaller communities within larger societies, by the fact that market exchange may be part of a long-term relationship between the parties.

Barter. In smaller societies that have market systems, exchanges may be primarily the trading of one object or service for another, a form of exchange called **barter**. In barter a potter and a farmer might exchange a water vessel for

---

market a system of distribution for goods and services based primarily on the use of established locations

barter form of exchange of goods by trading

YAPESE STONE MONEY

The symbolic nature of money is well illustrated by an old anthropological story about the Yapese people of the Caroline Islands in the Pacific. On the island of Yap, large, doughnut-shaped stones were used as special-purpose money for major ritual exchanges between villages. Since the stones were large, they were not easily transported; therefore they were not used in everyday transactions. However, on important occasions that warranted the use of a large number of human laborers, a stone might be moved from one village to another.

On one occasion when one of the stone cartwheels was being rafted across a lagoon between two villages, the vessel sank with its precious cargo. Try as they might, there was just no way to recover the stone from the sea bottom where it still lies. The crisis was overcome when the Yapese recognized some often overlooked facts: the real value of money is not due to its intrinsic worth but is assigned to it for the convenience of its users; and since the value of money is symbolic rather than intrinsic, physical possession of the symbol of value is not necessary to its use. Both villages agreed that although the stone could not be recovered, everyone knew where it was, so its ownership could still be transferred from one group to the other!

YAPESE MONEY

On the island of Yap in the Pacific, the medium of exchange was, at one time, large doughnut-shaped stones. They were not easily transported and thus were not used for everyday transactions. Eventually they became symbols of a medium of exchange.

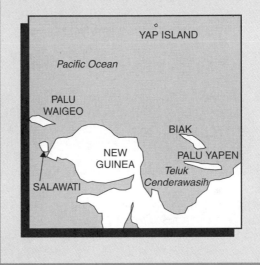

a bag of grain, or an itinerant worker might chop firewood in return for a meal and night's lodging.

Money. When the goods that people need are produced close at hand, barter can be the basic form of exchange, but when this is not the case or when goods and services must be obtained from many different specialists, the concept of money may be employed to obtain goods. Since **money** is fundamentally a *symbol* of value, in order to transform anything into money the parties involved only need a mutual agreement that a particular item will be a designated standard of value. It is usually best for the common medium of exchange to be both rare and portable; it should not require less effort to obtain money than to produce the goods and services for which it is exchanged. Gold and jewelry have these characteristics, but even printed paper or electronic bits of data will work. The key is simply that people agree to

accept the paper or electronic signals in lieu of the commodities they wish to exchange. Additionally, something of value in its own right may be used as money. For instance, in many parts of the world, salt or spices have been used as money. But their utilitarian value in such cases, their ability to make transactions possible when one person has nothing to barter that the other needs at the moment, is merely an enhancement of their real value.

Money may be either specialized or generalized. **Special-purpose money** (Bohannan, 1963) is a medium of exchange that is restricted to the buying and selling of a single commodity or at most a restricted number of designated

---

money standard medium of exchange that has a mutually agreed-upon value

special-purpose money medium of exchange restricted to the buying and selling of a single commodity

FIGURE 8.9

SPECIAL-PURPOSE MONEY

When an item is designated as a specific means of exchange for a particular category of goods, it is considered special-purpose money. These may consist of things such as shells, brass rods, pigs, or *anything a society designates. The Yapese people of Micronesia at one time used huge stone disks, like that at the left, as special-purpose money. Today, its presence in the village is a mark of prestige.*

commodities. Coins or tokens that can only be used for gambling, operating video games, or paying for bus rides, and stamps or coupons that are saved to exchange for premiums are examples of specialized money. Bohannan (1955) reports that among the Tiv, metal rods were used as a special-purpose money for buying cattle, slaves, or white cloth, all items of prestige within the Tiv economy. Subsistence goods, on the other hand, were exchanged by barter. Among native North Americans of the Northwest Coast, blankets were a special-purpose money for food, but were not a medium of exchange for other items. In various parts of Melanesia, shells are a medium of exchange for stone tools, pottery, and pigs, but not for other everyday commodities.

A universal medium of exchange, one that is not restricted in its use for only certain commodities but that can be used to buy and sell any item, is **general-purpose money**. General-purpose money is particularly useful when local populations are so large that people obtain most of the things they need to meet their daily needs by buying and selling.

When many different kinds of items are regularly bought and sold, both barter and the need for several special-purpose monies can be inconvenient ways of doing business. In such situations, a single general-purpose money may replace the other forms of exchange for most transactions.

The Productive Base of the U.S. Economy

The people of the United States are supported by an industrialized technology based primarily on fossil fuel burning and water-powered generators. About 46 percent of the population make up the employed civilian labor force of about 120 million. Another 20 million are government workers. The U.S. economy is productive enough that only about 20 percent of the labor force is involved in the production of goods, while the rest are service providers.

---

general-purpose money universal medium of exchange used to buy and sell any item

Food is produced for the entire society by only 3.3 percent of the labor force, a decline from 38 percent in 1900. High productivity has led to a relatively low demand for labor throughout most of U.S. history. As a result, the United States has rarely had an unemployment rate less than about 6 percent of the labor force except in time of war, and the unemployment rate often has risen well above 10 percent.

CONSUMPTION

In foraging bands there is little difference in the wealth and lifestyle of individuals from one local group to another because they all engage in the same basic productive activities. There are few specialized economic activities that supply goods to only some individuals, and reciprocity tends to level out even temporary wealth differences that may arise from time to time due to fluctuations in productivity of a local environment. But, with the development of food domestication and the occupational specializations that generally arise with it, opportunities increase for some individuals, families, and local groups to consistently control more wealth than do others in the same society. It is axiomatic that the more complex and productive a society's economy is, the more opportunities arise for differences to develop in **consumption**, the final use of goods and services.

Subsistence Economies

People regularly consume most of what they produce in a **subsistence economy**. This is the usual economic form in foraging societies and in simple food-domesticating tribes, because not enough surpluses are produced for a permanent exchange of goods to obtain what is needed. Rather, each family produces goods for its own consumption, its own **subsistence income**, and there is little need for trade. Thus, in subsistence economies, permanent differences of wealth are unlikely to arise.

Status Income

When surplus goods are consistently available, the big men or chiefs who control the distribution process thus acquire a high social rank. The control of goods over and above subsistence needs is called **status income**. In the case of big men, most of such wealth is given as gifts to other groups in return for the prestige such gift giving brings. Both the redistribution of wealth to the needy within a local community and the channeling of some surpluses to host neighboring groups as a source of prestige is also a practice in many chiefdoms. However, chiefs sometimes use part of this surplus wealth to raise their own standard of living and that of their relatives above that of their subordinates. In such cases, the actual consumption of surplus goods by the elite becomes a symbol of their high standing. The use of status income as a display of social rank, a practice called **conspicuous consumption**, is found in many chiefdoms and is a characteristic of the elite in all societies in which market economies predominate. The high standard of living enjoyed by the British monarchy, the European "Upper Ten Thousand," or the U.S. "jet set" typifies the use of income as conspicuous consumption.

SOCIAL AGENTS OF ECONOMIC CONTROL

Economic processes such as decision making about what to produce, what resources to use, and who will do the work is controlled by various people in various ways. In small-scale societies such as bands and tribes, control over productive work may be vested in the community as a whole, in the kin groups of society, or in special associations. In tribes and chiefdoms, the redistributive decision makers include individuals whose influence is based on prestige and power. In complex societies, decision-making power over production and distribution is often in the hands of members of the upper social classes, but exercised indirectly through

---

consumption final use by a society of goods and services

subsistence economy economy in which people consume most of what they produce

subsistence income goods produced by each family for its own consumption

status income goods produced over and above subsistence needs

conspicuous consumption the acquisition and use of a surplus of goods as a way of competitively demonstrating one's success and prestige

THE IMPACT OF AIDS ON AFRICA'S ECONOMY

AIDS has struck indiscriminately in the African continent, affecting not only prostitutes, factory workers, navvies [unskilled laborers], lorry drivers, dockers, migrant plantation workers and miners but engineers, technicians, company executives, chartered accountants and teachers.

An oil company in Ivory Coast recently hired 39 new staff. Why 39? Because that was the number of people already on its payroll of about 200 who were expected to die of AIDS within a year.

A cotton-producing company in Bangui, capital of the Central African Republic, will soon find itself with no one at the helm: its director committed suicide when he entered the final stages of the disease, and his two deputies are both HIV-positive. It is hard to see how they can be replaced in a country that trains fewer than 100 managers a year.

Africa is quietly slithering into an AIDS-stricken economy. The disease is draining the continent's lifeblood—those who produce and procreate. When they die, they leave orphans and elderly parents, shrivelled crops, vacant posts and often irreplaceable funds of experience. It has placed a gigantic question mark over Africa's ability to develop. It is a disaster on a traumatic scale, one to match that of the slave trade. . . .

A survival economy is gradually taking shape, which challenges traditional patterns of solidarity, disrupts social groups and has to come to terms with the pressing needs of those companies that have not yet gone under. . . .

Companies respond in different ways to the problem of HIV-positive staff. Some set up "commando teams" of workers who, on a one-off basis, stand in for absent or unwell staff; others appoint people to act as "understudies" to sick employees.

This duplication of jobs can pose problems. Fit employees complain about having to work for the same salary as sick ones. And while it is relatively easy to replace a manual worker, the employer's task becomes much more complicated when it is a question of training a new accountant or boiler mechanic. This can result in tensions and malfunctions. So companies create "dead-end" jobs, such as coffee-bag sorter or garment checker, which will be abolished when their incumbents die.

In Zimbabwe firms recruit apprentices and train them with a view to replacing staff later. This is cynically known as "predictive" staff management. . . .

These days, potential investors scrutinise a firm's percentage of HIV-positive staff just as they do profit ratios and risks of political instability. AIDS can weigh in the balance when a foreign company decides not to start up operations in a country, or to pull out.

"Unless you are prepared to hire infected personnel, you might as well leave straight away," says one such operator, adding that in many manager-hungry African countries the only people who are capable of filling a skilled job are already HIV-positive.

But the AIDS epidemic has not just hit factories and workshops. It is cutting swathes through Africa's main activity, farming. While west Africa has so far escaped the worst, the situation is drastic in the wooded and lake-covered central and eastern regions, wherever a road or a railway precludes isolation.

The World Bank believes that the economic impact of AIDS will prove a major obstacle to development well into the next century.

AIDS in Africa is not just a medical issue. The nine million people who are HIV-positive are fewer in number than the 110 million who have malaria, and the population explosion is unlikely to be affected in the short term by the deaths of AIDS sufferers. But the epidemic is not just killing people: it is gnawing away at whole economies. And they are economies which already have only a tiny share of the wealth of nations.

From "AIDS Deals a Harsh Blow to Africa's Economy" by Eric Fottorino, December 4, 1994, *Guardian Weekly;* reprinted from *Le Monde,* November 10, 1994.

---

their control of corporations or governmental bureaucracies.

Community Control of Production

In foraging bands in which the local groups are quite small and consist of members of only a few different families, decisions about the production and allocation of needed goods are sometimes a matter of discussion by the entire local group. This is especially true among foragers such as the Arctic Inuit, the Great Basin Shoshone, and the Yahgan and Ona of Tierra del Fuego, who spend much of the year in very small local groups. It is also common among groups such as the Andamanese Islanders or

Mbuti pygmy in which the local community of 20 or 30 persons functions like an extended family.

Kin Control of Production

The local kinship group is the most common institution for controlling production and allocation of goods among most foragers, horticulturalists, and pastoralists. Among foragers, this is merely a matter of the members of the nuclear family deciding about their daily needs and how best to fill them. Among pastoralists, who typically have larger local populations than do foragers, it is often the extended family that exerts ownership over the basic means of livelihood such as the fields and herds. Thus, for instance, among the horticultural Hopi of the southwestern United States, gardens were owned by kinship groups rather than by the individual woman who managed them day to day. Although she controlled the produce of her allotted plot, she could not dispose of the land without permission of her kinship group.

Association Control of Production

In other tribal societies, associations that cut through family lines and residential areas within a community may control important parts of production. For instance, the Cheyenne bison hunters of the North American Plains relied heavily on sudden kills of large numbers of migrating bison in cooperative hunts. A single hunter who began to shoot too soon could frighten the herd and spoil the success of the hunt for the rest of the community. So control of the hunt was vested in the Cheyenne military association, who could police the responsibility of hunters by punishing those who did not abide by the rules that governed the bison hunt. The Tahitian islanders in Polynesia used several specialized associations or guilds for the production of expensive commodities such as chiefs' houses and boats. Chiefs' houses were built on a grand scale and could attain a length of nearly 400 feet. While a house was being erected, the carpenters of the guild were fed by the chief who was having the house built. Each guild was governed by its own chief, and the builders were respected specialists who were divided into ranks based on their training and experience. The guilds had special emblems, deities, and ceremonies that set them apart from others, and different guilds competed with one another to achieve prestige and social recognition for the quality of their work.

Corporation and Governmental Decision Making. Associations of employers and employees that produce goods or provide services and that are legally entitled to act as a single person with rights of ownership are **corporations**. Corporations can outlast the lifetimes of their individual members, so they can produce more than any individual and can develop tremendous economic power as their productive properties increase. Corporations may be privately or governmentally owned, but in either case those who make decisions about what corporations produce and at what prices they sell their goods and services are members of the higher social classes.

The balance of power between governmental officials and private individuals in the control of the means of production varies among complex societies. In some cases, the economic decision making of private owners of corporations is only loosely regulated. This allows the owners to play a major role in the economic life of such societies. One common outcome of this way of organizing economic decision making is a competition between corporations for sales. If the basic needs of consumers are being met by the system of production, competition in the marketplace may increase for nonessential items. In such a **consumer market**, the economic focus is on convincing consumers to purchase nonessential goods and services that enhance their standard of living rather than simply meet their basic needs. They make life easier and more comfortable. Nonessentials, especially those that do not improve consumers' standard of living, may still be marketed successfully because the buyers gain higher status by demonstrating their ability to purchase them. In its extreme, buyers may engage in conspicuous consumption, the use of goods merely as a display of their wealth.

---

corporation association of employers and employees that is legally entitled to act as a single person to produce goods or provide services

consumer market market in which basic needs of consumers are met by the system of production, and competition for sales may focus on nonessentials

Social Class

Social class also plays a role in controlling the production and distribution of goods in complex societies. Commonly, members of the higher social classes have the greatest control over the means of production and receive the greatest share of goods. Members of the social elite may sit on corporate decision-making boards. They also have greater influence than do other persons on government policy makers, to the benefit of their corporations.

Social Class and Production in the United States

Ideologically, people in the United States have not traditionally viewed their society as one made up of separate classes. Yet, as in other industrialized societies, the people of the United States do not all have equal access to the goods or services produced by its labor force. For instance, in 1992 the median income of U.S. households was $30,786. At the same time, 25 percent of the people had incomes of less than $10,000, while 4.6 percent received $75,000 or more. U.S. society, in other words, is socially stratified into classes that differ in their share of the country's wealth and in influence on decisions about the production of commodities. The U.S. class system is somewhat ill-defined, in that the U.S. ideology itself has traditionally denied the very existence of a class system as a formal structure. Polls have indicated that some 80 percent of people in the United States claim membership in the middle class. Interestingly, this figure includes both some persons who by technical standards would be considered members of the lower class and others who are technically of upper-class background. The traditionally high level of mobility within the class system has made it easier for people in the United States not to recognize that distinct classes exist.

The Changing Context of Economics

As the effects of industrialization continue to spread around the world at the expense of technologically less complex ways of life, the cultures of the world are becoming more and more economically and politically interdependent. In many places, established economic patterns have been forced to change by external political forces or internal environmental factors. In this broader context, our future depends on what happens abroad as well as at home. Our relations with developing nations are likely to remain in a continuing state of flux as industrialization spreads and new power blocs and coalitions develop with the goal of ensuring the political and economic self-interest of developing nations. How we shall fare in this process will depend largely on a recognition that our own national self-interest is not likely to be furthered in the long run by a narrowly ethnocentric view of the other cultures with which we share the world.

CHAPTER SUMMARY

1. Cultures differ in what they define as useful or valuable and in how much worth a given commodity may be thought to have.

2. Commodities may include intangible things such as sacred stories or titles of nobility.

3. Economic systems in all cultures are constructed out of the same rules that govern the production, distribution, and consumption of valued goods and services.

4. Production or obtaining commodities involves concepts of use rights, ownership, and a division of labor.

5. Societies such as the United States where production is industrialized are characterized by an unequal distribution of wealth and status.

6. Distribution involves some combination of reciprocal exchange, centralized redistribution of goods, and markets.

7. Patterns of consumption depend on how much the producers use themselves, how commodities are used in increasing the prestige of some members of society through different levels of status income, and conspicuous consumption.

8. All societies have ways of controlling the economic system. Control may be divided between members of the community, may re-side in the kinship group, or may be effected by associations such as guilds, corporations, or groups of governmental officials.

9. As the limits to growth are approached, the U.S. mainstream seems to be turning toward an emphasis on security, social stability, and more conservative use of resources.

ANNOTATED READINGS

Blumberg, R. L. (Ed.). (1991). *Gender, family, and the economy: The triple overlap.* Newburg Park: Sage Publications. Examines the interrelationship of gender, domestic life, and the economy.

Brumfiel, E. M. (Ed.). (1994). *The economic anthropology of the state.* Lanham, MD: University Press of America. A collection that examines the relations between the state and household economy, state-controlled production, and the limits of state intervention.

Ensminger, J. (1992). *Making a market: The institutional transformation of an African society.* Describes the process by which a market economy was introduced into the economy of the Oromo, a group of Kenya pastoralists.

Halperin, R. H. (1994). *Cultural economies: Past and present.* Austin: University of Texas Press. Presents a cross-cultural approach to the analysis of economic processes in cultural systems.

Harris, M. (1981). *America now: The anthropology of a changing culture.* New York: Simon & Schuster. A provocative look at the effects of technological and economic change in U.S. culture since World War II.

Haskel, T. L., and Teichgraeber, R. F. (1993). *The culture of the market: Historical essays.* New York: Cambridge University Press. Essays that discuss the role of culture in the social aspects of commerce.

Moore, J. H. (Ed.) (1993). *The political economy of North American Indians.* Norman, Oklahoma: University of Oklahoma Press. A collection of essays that examine the politics of American Indian history as economic conflict between native modes of production and the capitalist market system.

Plattner, S. (Ed.). (1989). *Economic anthropology.* Stanford, CA: Stanford University Press. A collection of articles about economic behavior and institutions in foraging, horticultural, and market-based societies.

Taylor, C. C. (1992). *Milk, honey, and money: Changing concepts in Rwandan healing.* Washington, DC: Smithsonian Institution Press. Analyzes the economics of folk medicine among the Hutu of Rwanda.

Weiner, A. B. (1992). *Inalienable possessions: The paradox of keeping-while-giving.* Berkeley: University of California Press. Analyzes women's roles in ceremonial exchange in Oceania.

CHAPTER NINE

Marriage and the Family

CHAPTER OBJECTIVES

After reading this chapter, you should be able to:

Analyze the defining characteristics of marriage.

Explain the basic functions of marriage.

Define the four basic types of marriage.

Explain the adaptive characteristics of each marriage type.

Define the five types of atypical marriage.

Discuss the various forms of same-sex marriage.

Explain the types of rules that influence choice of marriage partner.

Discuss the economic factors in marriage negotiations.

Define the forms of the family and the household.

Define the five basic postmarital residence rules.

Explain the adaptive significance of each of the postmarital residence rules.

Discuss the characteristics of the U.S. family.

◄ *Figure 9.1 Royal Wedding Marriage as a social, economic, and sexual union between two or more people is common in most cultures of the world. However, the rules and customs that govern marriage differ from culture to culture. In traditional Japanese attire, Crown Prince Naruhito recently married Masakó Owada, a Harvard graduate and former diplomat. They promised to loosen up the ancient dynasty.*

Marriage is a social, economic, and sexual union that takes many forms. In this chapter you will be introduced to the most common marriage forms such as monogamy, polygyny, polyandry, and group marriage, as well as to less common forms such as symbolic, non-sexual, fictive, and same-sex marriage. You will learn about the common rules that govern and restrict the choices of potential marriage partners, and the ways in which marriages are negotiated in traditional societies. Finally, the contrast between nuclear and extended families will be introduced, and you will learn how three or more generations of kin can be united into a single family by different patterns of postmarital residence customs.

Something borrowed, something blue. Till death do us part. For time and all eternity. *Tali*-tying. Ghost marriage. Co-marriage. In all societies people form marriages, but in each there are different styles, rules, and customs.

MARRIAGE

Sex and reproduction are cultural as well as biological phenomena. In all societies, there are customs governing how and under what circumstances they should occur. Marriage plays a central role in these customs. Typically, people marry to legitimize sexual unions and to facilitate childrearing. Nevertheless, the reasons for marrying are diverse, and the families created by marriage differ in many ways from society to society. Ethnographers have reported marriages that are contracted by parents before the birth of a child, marriages that have no public ceremony, marriages that establish no common residence, and marriages between more than two persons, to name but four examples. What, then, are the minimum defining characteristics of marriage? While the rituals and customs surrounding marriage may differ around the world, the concept of **marriage** may be universally defined as a socially accepted sexual and economic union involving a lasting commitment between two or more people who have parental rights and obligations to any children of the union.

Functions of Marriage

The apparent universality of marriage as an institution suggests that it fulfills a variety of functions in the maintenance and perpetuation of human social life. These functions include channeling sexual behavior into stable relationships, fulfilling the economic needs of marriage partners, perpetuating a society's kinship groups, and providing an institution for the care of children until they become self-sufficient.

Committed Sexual Unions. Marriage is more than just a sexual union, since sexual relationships can exist without either a commitment to fidelity or a long-term involvement. Legitimate sexual relationships are recognized in many societies outside the bonds of marriage. For instance, data from the Cultural Diversity Data Base (White, 1987) indicate that only 27 percent of 146 societies surveyed have customs that imply the importance of female virginity at the time of marriage (p. 30). Societies may also approve of sexual relationships outside of marriage between persons who are already married to others. The Cultural Diversity Data Base indicates that only 44 percent of a sample of 109 societies forbid extramarital sex for both husbands and wives (p. 31).

The Toda of southern India recognized the legitimacy of formalized sexual liaisons between a married woman and certain other men, such as priests, to whom she was not married, so long as the woman's husband gave his approval. For the husband to refuse such requests was considered bad form. The Kalinga of the Philippines institutionalized the taking of mistresses by married men. Children born to the mistresses normally inherited smaller portions of the family property than did the children of the wife. This practice was not followed by all families, but if a wife were barren, taking a mistress was the only legitimate means of perpetuating the man's family without divorce and remarriage—so the wife would often help her husband in the selection of a sexual partner. Gregerson (1983) reminds us that sacred prostitution—often performed as part of the rites of

(Continued on p. 222)

_____

marriage a rite of passage that unites two or more individuals as spouses

SEX AND REPRODUCTION AMONG THE NAYAR OF INDIA

Although marriage is commonly said to be a cultural universal, there is at least one major group within a larger society, the Nayar of Kerala State in southern India, that has no marriages as they have been defined in this chapter.

According to Gough (1959, 1961), the nineteenth-century Nayar were a landowning caste whose men by tradition pursued the occupation of soldiers who hired themselves to the rulers of several neighboring kingdoms. This meant that men were often away from home for extended periods of time. Among the Nayar, children were members of their mother's family and household. Land was owned by a group of relatives who were related through the female line and who lived together as a household. This group, called the *taravad*, was headed by the eldest male of the household.

Each Nayar taravad had a special partnership with several others in the community. At intervals of every 10 or 12 years, the girls of each taravad would go through what was called the *tali*-tying ceremony with a man selected from the linked taravads, who tied a *tali*, a gold ornament, around the neck of the girl. Although it was considered a marriage ceremony, it also marked the transition of the girl into adulthood. Sexual relations were permitted if the girl was old enough; however, the "husband" had no further obligations to his "bride," and her only responsibility to him thereafter was to perform a ceremony at his funeral. Thus, this marriage was essentially a symbolic one.

Having gone through the tali-tying ceremony, the woman was now entitled to enter into *sambandham* relationships with other men of the same or of a higher caste than her own. These, too, might be called "marriages," but they also lacked most of the defining features of marriages elsewhere. Preferred partners were men of the higher-ranking Namboodri Brahmin caste who could not, by rules of their own caste, accept the children of the Nayar "wives" as their own heirs.

The first of these sambandham relationships began with a simple ceremony, as did any others that were intended to involve a lasting sexual relationship. Temporary relationships with other sambandham partners involved no ceremony. Sambandham "husbands" were allowed to spend the evening with their "wives" and were expected to bring small gifts with them at each visit, but a common residence was not established. The Nayar woman continued to live with her own taravad, where her brothers took responsibility for the costs of rearing her children. The woman's taravad benefited from her sambandham rela-tionships in several ways: the woman's children became members of her own taravad and constituted the next generation of her family, and she might receive various services from each of her husbands, who were likely to have a variety of occupations.

Children born to a Nayar woman were legitimate only if paternity was acknowledged by one or more of her sambandham husbands. The designated father was usually one of the men who had been sexually involved with her during the appropriate time for the child's conception, but might also be the man who was currently in the role of a "visiting husband." The fatherhood ceremony consisted of the payment of the midwife's fee, but the "father" had no further economic or social responsibilities for rearing the child. The failure of any of the husbands to acknowledge paternity was considered evidence that the woman had fathered the child with a man of a lower caste or a Muslim or Christian, an offense that was punishable by death or banishment of both the mother and child.

NAYAR

Marriage among the Nayar of southern India consisted first of a *tali*-tying ceremony, which then allowed the young men from the nearby *taravads* and the young girl to have sexual relations. Subsequent *sambandham* marriages also allowed for sexual relations and established paternity. Neither marriage allowed for a common residence.

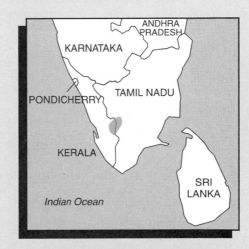

FIGURE 9.2

FAMILIES OF MARRIAGE PARTNERS

Marriage generally creates two sets of in-laws, the families of the partners who assume obligations to the couple as well as to each other. They may provide an economic and emotional support for the cou-ple. In this receiving line at a Christian wedding in Tokyo, Japan, the married couple and their families greet the guests.

a god in a sacred setting such as a temple—was accepted in much of the ancient Near East, India, and Greece. The Greek historian Herodotus reported that "every Babylonian woman must have sexual intercourse with a stranger in the temple of Mylitta [a variant of Ishtar or Astarte, a goddess Herodotus equates with Aphrodite] once in her life" (Gregerson, 1983, pp. 163–4). Though sexual unions such as these may be socially approved, they cannot be considered examples of marriage because they lack the public commitment to a lasting relationship and to sexual fidelity that is a defining feature of marriage.

What differentiates the sexual relationship of marriage from nonmarital sexual relationships is a commitment of the partners to one another and to their socially acknowledged partnership. Typically, the commitment to the marriage relationship includes the social expectation of a commitment to fidelity by at least one of the partners. White's (1987) Cultural Diversity Data Base indicates that 88 percent of societies expect sexual fidelity by wives and 56

percent have the same expectation of husbands. Although a double standard about extramarital sex exists in over half of the societies in White's sample, none accepts extramarital sex by both spouses (p. 31). Thus, marriage always includes some expectation of fidelity by at least one of the spouses.

One effect of an expectation of fidelity within marriage is to minimize the potentially disruptive effects of sexual competition. When people marry, the role change typically defines them as inappropriate sexual partners for members of the unmarried group within which courtship is a common pursuit. Being part of a stable relationship thereby permits each partner to devote time, previously taken up by the courtship process, to other pursuits.

Types of Marriage

Marriages take several forms. Four basic types seem to exist: monogamous, polygynous, polyandrous, and group marriages. These four types differ in the number of persons of one or both sexes who form the marriage relationship and in the circumstances under which each tends to be the idealized form of marriage.

Monogamy. In **monogamous marriages** two persons are joined as spouses. Monogamous marriages are the most common form of marital unit in all societies, even where other forms may be idealized as more desirable. Yet the Cultural Diversity Data Base indicates that only 14 percent of a sample of 180 societies *restricted* marriage to the monogamous form and that another 19 percent prefer monogamy without forbidding other marriage forms (p. 22). Even in those societies in which monogamy is the norm, individuals may be involved in more than one marriage during their lifetimes. For instance, despite the ideal of marriage as a long-term commitment, divorce is quite common in many societies, especially before the birth of a first child. In societies such as the United States in which monogamy is the accepted form of marriage, a high rate of divorce and remarriage creates a particular pattern called **serial monogamy**, in which individuals have more than one spouse, but at different times.

Polygyny. If men or women are permitted to marry more than one spouse at the same time instead of serially, the form of marriage is referred to as **polygamy**. Polygamous marriages may involve one husband and several wives or one wife and several husbands. These two varieties of polygamy differ markedly in a variety of ways. The form of polygamy in which one man is married to more than one woman at a time is technically referred to as **polygyny**. This was actually the *preferred* form of marriage in 83.6 percent of 185 societies surveyed by Ford and Beach (1951). The highest frequency of polygynous families is found in societies in frontier areas; in societies where warfare in common; in societies in which the ratio of adult women to men is high (a condition that is common in either of the two preceding circumstances); and in groups where rapid growth of families is beneficial to family survival. Since the ratio of male to female children is about equal in all societies, relatively few men actually are able to practice polygyny even in societies where it is the preferred marital form. It is practiced most commonly by individuals of high social standing, while most men of lower social standing remain monoga-

FIGURE 9.3

POLYGYNY
While marriage takes many forms, it is a universal phenomenon. This Togolese chief, here posing with a number of his wives, practices polygyny.

mous. Since it generally takes some time and effort to achieve the social standing that makes it possible for a man to have more than one wife, polygyny often involves an age difference between spouses, with older men taking much younger wives. White (1988) has demonstrated that polygyny is organized into two basic patterns: sororal polygyny and male-stratified polygyny. In **sororal polygyny**, or **male-ranked polygyny with related co-wives**, a man marries two or more closely related women, often sisters. In societies that practice this form of polygyny, social ranking is primarily a matter

---

monogamous marriage form of marriage where one man and one woman are joined as husband and wife

serial monogamy a marriage pattern in which individuals of either sex may have only one spouse at a given time, but through divorce and remarriage may have several spouses during their lifetime

polygamy form of marriage where a person is permitted to have more than one spouse at the same time

polygyny form of marriage in which a man has more than one wife

sororal polygyny form of polygyny in which the wives are sisters

male-ranked polygyny with related co-wives a more descriptive term for sororal polygyny

FIGURE 9.4

A POLYANDROUS WEDDING CEREMONY

One variation in the structure of marriage is the polyandrous type in which one woman marries two men.

This Nepalese woman, in the veil, is marrying the two brothers on the left.

of individual achievement. A small number of men, such as outstanding hunters, warriors, or shamans, demonstrate their success by marrying a second or third wife. Since male labor is the major contribution to the subsistence income of the family, and extra wives are a drain on the man's wealth, he exchanges his individually achieved wealth for wives, and his ability to support them demonstrates his high social rank.

Male-stratified polygyny or **wealth-increasing polygyny** is more common in societies in which there are hereditary classes. In this form of polygamy, a small number of men who hold positions of rank and authority, often older men of wealthy families, marry a larger number of wives, perhaps 20 or 30. In these societies, the labor of women is often economically valuable, and each new wife increases the wealth of the family and its social prominence. The greater wealth and improved social standing make it easier for the husband to acquire yet another wife. In contrast to sororal polygyny, where the wives and their husbands often reside together, these wives often have their own residences so that their economic ac-

tivities can be carried out with a minimum of direct competition between co-wives.

Polyandry.   It is rare for a woman to have several husbands, as in a **polyandrous marriage**. It is the idealized family type in probably less than 0.5 percent of the world's societies. The most common form of polyandrous union is one in which a woman is simultaneously married to several brothers, a form known as **fraternal polyandry**. It is advantageous where resources are extremely limited. Polyandrous unions have been reported among southern Indian and Tibetan peoples where land is at a premium and cannot easily be further subdivided from one generation to the next. It was

---

male-stratified polygyny form of polygamy in which a small number of men of high rank and authority marry a larger number of wives

wealth-increasing polygyny male-stratified polygyny

polyandrous marriage form of marriage in which one woman has more than one husband

fraternal polyandry form of polyandry in which the husbands are brothers

POLYANDROUS AND GROUP MARRIAGES AMONG THE TODA

The Toda of Southern India, described in detail by Rivers (1905), were one of the few peoples of the world among whom polyandry and group marriages were the rule. Marriages were arranged by parents when children were as young as two or three years of age. A marriage united the girl not only to the boy for whom she was originally selected but also to any brothers he might have, including those born after the ceremony. Thus, a Toda wife typically had several husbands who were usually brothers, although she might also enter marriage with other men. Since a woman was considered to be the wife of any of the brothers of a man she married, if brothers entered into marriage with more than one woman, the result was a group marriage in which several women might be wives simultaneously to several men.

Both polyandry and group marriage made it infeasible to keep track of biological paternity, so this concept was unimportant to the Toda. However, since Toda families were patrilineal, fatherhood in its social sense was important. Therefore, the Todas employed a ritual of fatherhood, a ritual that designated a particular man as the social father of any children a woman bore for a period of years, whether or not he was their natural father.

Since fatherhood was established by a ritual act, the concept of adultery was irrelevant to the Toda view of family relations. Not only was sexual infidelity by a wife not grounds for divorce—since it would not have affected the legitimacy of a child's rights to inherit from the socially defined father—but it was also so unimportant a concept that there was not even a word for adultery in the Toda language.

(see reference map p. 265)

also practiced by the Shoshone of the Great Basin, where a man might temporarily share his wife with a younger brother until he was old enough to make his own way as an independent hunter with his own family. Just as polygyny is only practiced by a minority of men where it is the preferred marital form, only a minority of women are actually able to practice polyandry in societies where it is the preferred form of marriage. In fact, since each polyandrous marriage requires more than one husband, many women are never able to marry. In polyandrous societies where the wealth of a family is based on the husbands' cooperative agricultural labor, unmarried women are economically disadvantaged and may have to enter low-ranked occupations to survive. The importance of male labor in these societies also makes it likely that female infanticide will be practiced.

Group Marriage. When several males are simultaneously married to several females, their union is called **group marriage**. Group marriage and polyandry typically occur together, but group marriage and polygyny do not. This is because polyandry and polygyny are not simple mirror images of one another. Women in polyandrous families in some ways have higher status than those in polygynous families. For instance, the sexuality of plural wives in polygynous families is often jealously guarded by their husbands, but not in a polyandrous society in which married women will have plural mates as a matter of course. On the other hand, no such contrast exists for husbands in these two family types. Polyandrous societies typically have no rules against husbands sometimes marrying plural wives, something that wives in polygynous societies are not likely to be permitted to do. When one of a woman's husbands in a polyandrous society marries another woman—often a sister of the original wife—the new bride also becomes the wife of co-husbands in the original marriage as well. Such simultaneously polyandrous and polygynous families are also considered group marriages.

Atypical Marriages

In addition to the four basic patterns of marriage, a number of other patterns also exist. These marriage forms may be rare or quite common, depending on the society in question,

---

group marriage form of marriage in which two or more men are married to two or more women at the same time

CO-MARRIAGE AMONG THE INUIT OF NORTH ALASKA

INUIT

The Inuit of North Alaska practiced co-marriage, in which, by mutual agreement, the husbands and wives had sexual intercourse with each other's residential spouse. This established a situation of mutual support and obligation among the families, crucial to survival in the harsh Arctic environment.

According to Burch (1970, 1975), the Inuit of North Alaska once engaged in monogamy, polygyny, polyandry, and a nonresidential form of group marriage that he calls *co-marriage*. Co-marriages were typically contracted to create a kind of fictive sibling relationship between the same-sex partners. This quasi-siblinghood continued into succeeding generations, since the children of both couples in a co-marriage were considered siblings, and their children in turn were accepted as cousins. Thus, co-marriages established long-lasting cooperative bonds between people and their descendants who resided in different locations, a very useful practice in a highly mobile society in which autonomous nuclear families might lack a network of relatives to call upon for help wherever they traveled.

A co-marriage was established when, by mutual agreement, the husbands and wives had sexual intercourse with each other's residential spouse. This formality established a co-husband relationship between the men and a co-wife relationship between the women, relationships that included a continuing obligation of mutual aid similar to that of siblings. Such relationships were both emotionally and practically important among the Inuit, since siblings had strong moral responsibilities toward one another, and life in the cold, arctic environment they occupied could be a difficult one for small foraging families when other relatives were not available for cooperative activities.

---

but are not the generally preferred type in any society. They lack one or more of the usual defining characteristics of marriage such as a sexual or economic relationship between the partners, a long-term commitment, reproduction, or even a living spouse. Atypical marriages include symbolic marriages, nonsexual marriages, fixed-term marriages, fictive marriages, and several forms of same-sex marriage.

Symbolic Marriages. As we have seen, marriage is normally created in all societies as a vehicle for establishing economic and social ties between kinship groups and for providing a means of perpetuating the group. However, under some circumstances societies may sanction the establishment of marriages in which these functions do not apply. Such **symbolic marriages** may serve other purposes, as when

religious specialists consider themselves married to a deity. The Roman Catholic nun who wears a ring symbolic of her status as a bride of Christ, and who is therefore taboo to others as an object of romantic love, is a Western example of a participant in a symbolic sacred marriage. Mormon religious practice provides another striking example of symbolic marriage: It includes a contrast between a "marriage for time" and a "marriage for eternity." A temporal marriage is one performed outside a Mormon temple. Such marriages end at the death of one partner, lasting only "till death do us part." Eternal marriages, on the other hand, are performed only in a Mormon Temple and are be-

---

symbolic marriages those marriages not establishing economic and social ties between kinship groups lieved to be valid "for time and all eternity" in the eyes of God. An outgrowth of this belief is the practice of performing vicarious marriages between deceased persons and their surviving spouses or even between two deceased persons who were married only temporally while alive. This system of symbolic marriage has a polygynous bias in the Mormon subculture, since a woman whose "eternal husband" has predeceased her may remarry "for time" only, while a man may enter into several "eternal marriages" serially, if one or more of his wives dies before him. When a man who has entered several "eternal marriages" dies, Mormons believe that he will be reunited with all his wives after death.

Nonsexual Marriages.

Marriages sometimes fulfill their usual economic, kinship, and even childrearing functions in the absence of a sexual union between the partners. Such **nonsexual marriages** can occur for a variety of reasons. For instance, in societies that have class differences, they may occur for the political or economic benefit of the marriage partners or their relatives, as when a royal marriage is negotiated to stabilize a political alliance between two societies. Among Mormon pioneers in the United States, an elderly woman sometimes entered into a nonsexual marriage as a plural wife for companionship or economic security in a precarious environment. In such a role, she might participate in the domestic life of the family, help with housework, and share childrearing responsibilities with her co-wives.

Fixed-Term Marriages.

Temporary marriages, such as the fixed-term marriages of Iran, legitimize a sexual relationship in which the usual marriage characteristics, such as economic obligations or the expectation of childrearing, may be minimized. In fixed-term marriages, the length of time of the marriage is agreed upon before it begins, so that it will come to an end after a specified period of time or whenever the activities that make it convenient for the couple to remain together have run their course. For instance, fixed-term marriages came into existence in Islam in order for soldiers to have legitimate sexual partners while they were fighting in foreign wars for long periods. At the end of the husband's military duty, his temporary marriage was dissolved, and he was free to return home with no further obligation to the divorced wife.

Fictive Marriages.

A marriage can exist legally without a family being established in order to allow one or both partners to obtain social benefits that would be unavailable otherwise. Such a marriage is called a **fictive marriage**. For instance, immigration and naturalization quotas in the United States have resulted in the practice of marriages between U.S. citizens and potential immigrants or resident aliens for no purpose other than to facilitate the immigration or acquisition of citizenship by the noncitizen partner. In such a case, the parties to the marriage may not establish a common domicile or sexual relationship; indeed, they need not be acquainted before the marriage nor see each other again afterwards. This particular example of fictive marriage is one that is legally rejected by U.S. immigration authorities, and those who are involved may be punished by law, but analogous fictive marriages do exist in societies where they are openly accepted as valid means to an end. For instance, among the Kwakiutl it is possible for a man to marry the male heir of a chief as a means of inheriting certain privileges from the father-in-law. When there is no heir to marry, a man may marry the chief's arm or leg as a legally valid way of becoming an inheritor.

Probably the most widespread forms of fictive marriage are the levirate and the sororate. The **levirate** is the obligation of a dead man's next of kin, usually one of his brothers, to marry the dead man's widow. Commonly, at least the first child of this union is considered to be the offspring of the first husband. This custom is especially important in societies that stress the importance of the line of descent through males, since it provides a way for men who die without heirs to have descendants. It also cements anew the marriage alliance between the two families whose children were originally united in marriage. At the same time, it provides the widow with someone who will continue to perform the

(Continued on p. 229)

_____

nonsexual marriages marriages that fulfill economic, social, and kinship functions without sexual union between the partners

fictive marriage legal marriage established to allow both partners to acquire social benefits without a family being set up

levirate a rule that requires kin of a deceased man to provide his widow with another husband, often one of the deceased man's brothers

GHOST MARRIAGE AMONG THE NUER OF THE SUDAN

Evans-Pritchard (1951) described an interesting form of fictive marriage practiced by the Nuer, a cattle-herding people who live in the savanna region of the Upper Nile in the Sudan. **Ghost marriages** (see p. 229) occur when the close, married or unmarried, male kinsman of a man or boy who died before he had any legal heirs, marries a woman in the name of the deceased relative. The living vicarious husband gives the family of the bride a number of cattle, as the deceased man would have done had he married the woman while he was still alive. Legally, the woman will be the ghost's bride, and all of the children she bears will be his. However, the vicarious husband will be treated in all other respects as if he were the woman's real husband, something that is not true in the case of the levirate. As with the levirate, the purpose of a ghost marriage is to bear children who will be heirs to the deceased husband. However, ghost marriage differs from the levirate in several important ways. A leviratic marriage unites a widow with a surrogate for her deceased husband. The wife in a ghost marriage is not the widow of the deceased, but she becomes his wife through a marriage ritual with a living surrogate after the death of the ghost husband, whom she, in most cases, might never have known while he was alive.

Ghost marriages among the Nuer are almost as common as simple marriages between a man and woman, partly because each ghost marriage tends to create anew the circumstance which requires ghost marriages in the first place: a man who enters a ghost marriage as the vicarious husband obtains no descendants through that marriage; he may well die before he is able to found a lineage of his own, and it will be up to one of his brothers or nephews to enter a ghost marriage in his behalf. Thus the Nuer "solution" to the "problem" of men who die without children perpetuates the very situation it is intended to eliminate. Such a situation suggests that some pragmatic benefits may accrue to Nuer families who practice ghost marriage.

How might Nuer ghost marriage benefit the living? An answer to this question is suggested by other customs related to ghost marriage. The Nuer not only assert that a dead man may be the legal father of children born long after his death, but also that a ghost may continue to own property. When a man dies without heirs, any cattle he may have owned do not revert to the larger family herd, but remain *ghok jookni,* "cattle of the ghost." Such cattle are sacred and may not properly be used for any purpose other than as payment to a bride's family for her bearing of children in the name of the ghost. This restriction has further implications: according to Evans-Pritchard (1966), "When Nuer raid a herd to seize cattle in compensation for some injury they will not take cattle reserved for the marriage of a ghost" (p. 111). So the idea that uninherited cattle remain the property of the dead benefits the survivors because such property is still under their control and can be used for several things. The cows may be milked while they are held in trust for the deceased owner, they may be used to obtain a wife for one of their living sons so long as he enters a fictive marriage in behalf of the dead owner of the cattle that pays for the marriage, and they cannot be taken from the family in payment of debts as their other cattle can. Thus ghost marriage is, in reality, part of a larger web of cultural concepts that includes some economic benefits similar to those of family trusts in the United States.

NUER

The Nuer of the Upper Nile of the Sudan engage in ghost marriages to provide legal heirs for the deceased relative. The woman is the legal bride of the dead man even though the ceremony and practical aspects of the marriage are conducted by the dead man's relative.

NUER WOMAN MARRIAGE

Evans-Pritchard's (1951) study of the Nuer of the Sudan reported a form of marriage that he called "woman marriage," in which one woman marries another. She does so exactly as a man does, paying a bride price of cattle, to her bride's family. The female husband in such a family acquires cattle, just as her brothers do, when her own kinswomen marry, and she may inherit cattle from her father as if she were a son. Children born to her own wife through the services of a man she chooses for that purpose "are called after her, as though she were a man" (p. 109). Her children address her as "father," and she is "treated by her wives and children with the same deference they would show to a male husband and father" (p. 109). When her daughters marry, she receives the cattle that are normally given a father in payment of the bride price.

Woman marriages may also occur when a female relative of a deceased man marries a wife in the name of the dead kinsman. According to Evans-Pritchard, "The persons involved in a marriage of this kind are the dead man, his kinswoman who marries a wife in his name, the wife, and the man who is brought in to cohabit with the wife" (p. 111). The children of this union are legally those of the dead man and will inherit from him.

(see reference map p. 228)

duties of a husband. The **sororate** is a similar custom in which a widower, or sometimes the husband of a barren woman, marries his first wife's sister. Again, at least some of the children born to this second marriage are considered children of the first wife, a particular benefit in societies where ancestry is traced primarily through women. Like the levirate, the sororate ensures that the marriage tie between the two in-law families will not be dissolved by the death of one partner and that the survivor will continue to have a mate.

Same-Sex Marriage. Just as legitimate marriages may exist without a sexual component, nonreproductive marriages may still fulfill the other functions of marriage and be socially accepted. Marriages of this type include those by persons past their reproductive years and same-sex marriages, both of which are legitimate in a large number of human societies. **Same-sex marriages** consist of both male-male and female-female relationships.

A same-sex marriage between partners of more or less equal age is called a **homophilic marriage**. Although only Denmark, Greenland, Sweden, and Norway currently extend most of the legal benefits to which married persons are entitled to same-sex couples, committed gay male and lesbian relationships fit the anthropological definition of homophilic marriage. Homophilic marriage is the most common form of committed same-sex relationship in industrialized nations. Same-sex marriages in the same generation have been socially accepted in many nonindustrialized societies, but, unlike homophilic marriages, they involve a gender-role change in one partner, who adopts a pathic gender. This entails undertaking some of the roles usually assigned to members of the other sex and practicing transvestism and cross-sex or gender-mixed dressing, as exemplified by the *berdache* among American Indians in North America (see chapter 5). Such relationships have been called **pathic marriages** (Gregerson, 1983) or **intragenerational marriages** (Adam, 1986). Homophilic and pathic marriages may be regarded as culturally patterned variants of same-sex intragenerational relationships.

Societies that historically accepted pathic marriages differed from those that did not in a number of ways. Those that accepted pathic re-

---

ghost marriages (p. 228) fictive marriages where a married or unmarried close male kinsman of a man or boy, who died before he had any legal heirs, marries a woman in the name of the deceased

sororate a rule that requires the kin of a deceased woman to provide her widower with another wife, often one of the deceased woman's sisters

same-sex marriages marriages between two males or two females

homophilic marriage same-sex marriage without transvestism or change in sex role by one of the partners

pathic marriages same-sex marriages involving gender-role change in one partner

intragenerational marriages pathic marriages

FIGURE 9.5

SAME-SEX MARRIAGE
New York City allowed unmarried couples to register as "domestic partners" in 1993. This acknowledgement of primarily same-sex relationships gives the couple many of the same rights as those who are married. Diane Flood Goldstick, left, and Patricia Flood Goldstick were the second couple to celebrate their official union.

lationships were more likely to have a variety of social traits that are associated with flexibility and adaptability to changing economic circumstances (Crapo, 1987). These included bilateral descent, ambilocal residence or the absence of patrilineal kin groups (see chapter 10) when virilocal residence (see p. 238) was followed, and social rank based on individual achievement rather than birth into a high-status descent group. Male labor was particularly important in the food-getting activities of these societies, but women had relatively high status both politically and domestically. Wealth-depleting polygyny was common and was one indicator that a male was particularly successful as a provider, since the major source of income was male labor. Pathic same-sex marriages between either males or females were common in societies with these characteristics, although male pathic relationships were somewhat more widespread in the world's nonindustrialized cultures. In societies in which pathic marriages were found, individuals entered the pathic gender that led to same-sex marriage in two different ways. Some individuals adopted the pathic gender because they were inclined to do so, but in other cases families reared a male or female child as a pathic individual. Therefore pathic persons

should not simply be understood as persons with the same-sex sexual orientation, since some individuals were socialized into the pathic gender from childhood.

In societies that accepted same-sex marriages, a pathic male commonly entered marriage as the second "wife" of an already heterosexually married man. This increased the status of the family, which, by the addition of the pathic wife, became polygynous. A pathic marriage is a relatively easy way for a man to become a polygynous husband, because, in addition to doing women's work, the gender-crossing wife can help produce income that husbands are usually responsible for alone. The pathic wife may actually increase the income of the family and improve the husband's chances of being able to afford a third wife even sooner.

Lesbian pathic marriages have been commonly under two circumstances. First, they were found in many of the same societies in which gay male pathic marriages occurred. But they were sometimes found in the absence of male pathic marriages, where polygyny was not a usual marriage form. In these societies, a daughter might be raised as a pathic child by a family that had no son, because the economic contributions usually made by a son, such as food obtained by hunting, were vital to family survival. As an adult, a pathic daughter who had learned the roles that usually were carried out by males was permitted to marry in the role of a pathic husband in a lesbian marriage.

One other form of same-sex marriage is found in a variety of the world's cultures, a form that has been labeled **mentorship** (Herdt, 1981) or **intergenerational marriage** (Adam, 1986). Mentorships are same-sex relationships between older and younger partners in which the older person has the role of husband to the younger same-sex wife. Mentorships often come into existence as a way of solidifying an important social bond such as an economic or political patron-client, master-apprentice, or teacher-student relationship by which younger members of society are socialized into specialized adult skills or knowledge. The younger apprentice may, at the same time, aid his mentor in his pursuit of higher status within the male community. Unlike pathic marriages,

mentorship form of marriage between an older, socially established partner and a younger spouse of the same sex

intergenerational marriage mentorship

which may be lifelong relationships, mentorship marriages are usually temporary unions that end when the apprentice-wife graduates into adult life and, potentially, enters into the same kind of relationship as mentor to a younger apprentice. It is usual for both male and female husbands in gay male and lesbian mentorships to be married simultaneously in heterosexual relationships.

Male mentorships are often a part of the military training system in male-dominant, warlike societies, and may be associated with specialized religious training, where younger males are secluded from contact with females. They may also be common in societies in which men play a socially dominant role and exercise sexual rights over persons of lower rank, such as women, youths, and slaves (Adam, 1981, 1986). The mentorship marriage occurs during a period of sexual segregation of young men from young women. This minimizes competition between younger and older men for wives, making it easier for high-status, older men to marry a large number of younger women.

In societies with male mentorships, the preferred form of heterosexual marriage is polygyny of the wealth-increasing variety, in which the most highly ranked, older men have a large number of wives whose work is a major source of income for the husbands (Crapo, 1987). This form of heterosexual polygyny symbolizes the husband's high social standing and perpetuates his power by ensuring that he will have many children. Since wives in societies that practice wealth-increasing polygyny typically have low status, the position of wife within a male mentorship reinforces the younger male's situation as a socially subordinate person in the male status hierarchy. However, it also provides him with an acceptable sexual outlet during his period of segregation from women and makes the temporary taboo on heterosexuality for young men easier to follow.

Unfortunately, very little is known about female mentorships. A few researchers have suggested the presence of ritualized intergenerational lesbian relationships in Melanesian cultures in which lactating women nurse prepubescent girls to transmit the life force symbolized by milk (Harrison, 1937; R. Kelly, 1976; Godelier, 1982; Keesing, 1982; Schwimmer, 1984). Anthropologists have reported female mentorships on Carriacou in the Caribbean (Blackwood, 1985) and in Lesotho in southern Africa (Blacking, 1978; Gay, 1985; Mueller,

1977). In both of these areas, husbands are away from home for prolonged periods as wage laborers, while wives remain home and have responsibility for the running of household affairs. Women in these settings sometimes enter a relationship with a younger woman for both affection and help in household work.

MARRIAGE CHOICE

Each culture includes various rules that influence the choice of marriage partners. Some of these rules restrict the choices that may be made by proscribing certain persons as possible partners. Other rules require marriage within defined social categories. Some define particular kinds of persons as preferred partners. All three kinds of rules help to narrow the range of appropriate mates from which the selection is made.

Incest Taboo

One rule that seems to be found in almost all cultures is the **incest taboo**, which forbids sexual intercourse between parents and their children, between brothers and sisters, and frequently between other kin as well. There are a few cultures in which exceptions to this rule exist. For instance, the Hawaiian royalty, the kings and queens of ancient Egypt, and the Inca emperors were expected to violate the incest taboo in order to perpetuate their lineages by brother-sister marriages. But societies such as these are rare, and all others forbid sexual contact between parents and children and between siblings. Indeed, most nonindustrialized societies have included a much broader range of kin and even fictive kin, such as nursemaids, under the prohibition.

Nevertheless, there are variations in how effectively incest taboos are enforced. Gregory Leavitt (1989) has noted that as societies become technologically and socially more complex and as trade institutions develop, the number of relatives included in the incest taboo declines and punishment becomes less severe.

---

incest taboo a rule that forbids sexual behaviors between designated kin, including but not limited to intercourse between parents and children and between siblings

A variety of theories have been proposed for the existence of an incest taboo in societies throughout the world. These have included biological instinct theories, psychological theories, more recent sociological ideas, and political and economic theories. Anthropological theories have emphasized the social functions of the incest taboo and, until recently, have given little attention to issues of the "politics" of incest as an abuse of power within the family.

Biological Theories. The earliest explanations of the incest taboo simply attributed its universality to "instinct." This idea has generally been discarded on the grounds that if there were an instinctive avoidance of incest, rules against it would not be necessary, and incest would be unlikely to occur. In fact, incest does occur. For instance, the U.S. Bureau of the Census (1994) reported that in 1993 public social service and child protective service agencies throughout the United States received 328,790 reports of child sexual abuse. In about one-fifth of the cases, the perpetrator was a family member.

Later biological theories emphasized the possible detrimental genetic effects of incest on human groups, but they have not generally remained popular for two reasons. First, most societies have limited knowledge about the nature of biological heredity, and second, it is doubtful that the harmful effects of close inbreeding on a species with fertility rates as high as are typical of human societies could cause its extinction. Therefore, most theorists have looked elsewhere to explain the universality of the incest taboo.

Psychological Theories. A psychological approach still advocated is based on Westermark's (1889) notion that "familiarity breeds contempt," that children who are reared together are simply not likely to be sexually attracted to one another due to a kind of "boredom factor." Several studies have suggested that young people are more likely to prefer strangers. For instance, unrelated children reared in the communal dormitories of certain Israeli kibbutzim have a demonstrated tendency to marry persons from other communities. Detractors of these studies argue, on the other hand, that by the time these children are old enough for mate selection, they have been dispersed due to the universal military obligation and would thus automatically choose someone outside their community. Studies of quasi-sibling marriages in Taiwan in which the bride-to-be is raised from childhood by the in-law family have shown such marriages to have higher rates of infertility, impotence, and divorce than other Taiwanese marriages (A. Wolf, 1966). Although there may be some merit to the idea that sexual attraction is greater between strangers than between persons reared together, this approach is more relevant to sibling incest taboos than to parent-child sex prohibitions and also fails to address the fact that incest does occur.

Sociological Theories. The sociological approach emphasizes the role of the taboo in preventing the role confusion that incestuous relationships could have within families if they were acceptable (Starcke, 1976; Malinowski, 1939). If, for instance, a daughter were also a co-wife of her own father, conflict could arise about when it would be appropriate to play a subordinate or equal role with respect to either the mother or the father. This approach is generally regarded as overly simplistic in failing to recognize that humans generally manage to juggle a lot of potential role conflicts without tremendous difficulty. For instance, newly married children hosting their parents in their home could experience role conflict over who should play the dominant role in the new setting, the parents in their traditional role or the children as hosts and family heads. We manage to live with such conflicts and usually work out satisfactory accommodations. Therefore, role conflict alone does not adequately explain the universality of the incest taboo.

A recent variant on Malinowski's sociological approach has arisen among feminist anthropologists, who emphasize the role of gender and relative age differences in social power as a cause of incest. In most societies, male roles have greater access to power than do female roles, and older persons have greater power than younger ones. Both parent-child and older sibling violations of the incest taboo can be examined as inappropriate uses of social power by one individual to gain sexual access to another that would otherwise be denied. From this perspective, the purpose of the incest taboo is to protect the rights of the less powerful members of the family relationship. It is during the period of childhood socialization that children acquire the foundations of trust that serve as the basis for successful interpersonal relationships with other people throughout the rest of their lives. For persons whose position in their family relationship is less powerful, incest undermines their ablity to trust others and form bonds of emotional intimacy. It is therefore a form of victimization; the more powerful individuals in incestuous relationships act on their own needs instead of meeting the needs of the victims who are dependent on them.

Economic and Political Theories. Economic and political implications of the incest taboo maintain a lot of popularity among anthropological theorists (e.g., White, 1948; Harris, 1968). The most common argument insists that prohibiting incest is an indirect means of forcing each new generation to marry outside the natal family. If sex is unavailable between parents and children or between siblings, then marriage between these persons is also impossible. Sexual partners must be found outside the family of origin, and these relationships—when legitimized as marriages—become the basis for economic and political alliances between the in-law families, who may be called upon for aid in times of economic need or political strife, such as when feuds erupt between neighboring families. Families that allow incest tend to be isolates that eventually lose out in competition with families that are more powerful through the marriage alliances. In effect, the incest taboo codifies the rule of "Marry out or die out." This approach sees the incest taboo as a cultural rule that has adaptive value, and it is supported by recent research that indicates that incest is more common among geographically or socially isolated families.

Exogamy Rules

When marriages are of practical significance to a family, the culture often has formal guidelines about whom a person ought or ought not to marry. Such rules increase the likelihood that the practical well-being of the kin group will be fostered. The most common examples of such marriage guidelines are **exogamy rules** that require marriage outside designated groups such as one's own lineage or clan.

Rules of exogamy are more than mere extensions of the incest taboo. Where incest taboos specifically govern sexual behavior, rules of exogamy do more than this: they govern marriage rights. Therefore they may exclude from consideration for marriage a broad circle of persons with whom sex is not necessarily forbidden. Thus, rules of exogamy may require marriage outside one's own residential unit as

FIGURE 9.6

EXOGAMY RULES

The rules of exogamy ensure that marriage will occur with an individual outside one's own lineage or clan. The rule is traced back to a time when it was advantageous politically and socially to extend relationships outside of one's group. In preparing for a marriage between two Bedouin groups, this sister of the groom, in a symbol of camaraderie, assumes her brother's role and embraces the bride.

well as outside one's own family. In some societies the local unit is divided into two groups, or moieties, which are each exogamous—so that members of one moiety always marry persons from the opposite moiety, each of which has reciprocal rights and obligations to the other. For instance, members of one moiety may host a funeral when a member of the opposite moiety dies.

Endogamy Rules

On the other hand, **endogamy rules** require that both marriage partners be members of a certain kinship, social, or local group. For instance, a rule of endogamy may require marriage into one's own village, church, or social class. In the traditional castes of India, marriage partners were strictly limited to members of one's own caste, and among the traditional Bedouin, there was a preference for endogamous marriage within one's own patrilineal lineage.

---

exogamy rules rules forbidding an individual from marrying a member of the kinship, residential, or other specified group to which he or she belongs

endogamy rules rules requiring marriage within specified kinship categories or other specified social or local groups to which one belongs

Marriage preference rules single out specific kin as ideal marriage partners. Although the exogamy rules of most societies promote marriage beyond the circle of one's cousins, there are many that in fact prefer marriage between cousins. Most of these cultures have a rule of preferential marriage between **cross cousins**—cousins who are linked by parents of opposite sex, who are usually brother and sister. In both patrilineal and matrilineal systems of reckoning kinship, cross cousins belong to different lineages. With such marriages, members of each family gain in-laws outside their own lineage to whom they can turn for aid in times of need. A common form of cross-cousin marriage is one in which a brother and a sister marry cross cousins who are also sister and brother to each other. In societies where the inequality of the sexes is marked, this is often described as two men exchanging sisters. In such cases, marrying one's brother-in-law's sister does create an added social bond between two men that may benefit them both politically and economically. **Sister exchange**, or, more accurately, **bilateral cross-cousin marriage**, links two lineages over many generations. This system is called "bilateral" because a man's wife is both his mother's brother's daughter and his father's sister's daughter.

A less intense pattern of intermarriage between two lineages is one in which a male of one lineage marries a woman from another lineage in one generation, and his daughter marries into that lineage a generation later. This permits his sister to marry into a third lineage, thereby extending the marriage alliances into an even greater circle of people. This system has been called **patrilateral cross-cousin marriage** because, from the male's point of view, the preferred marriage is with one's father's sister's daughter. Patrilateral cross-cousin marriage permits many lineages to be linked into a circle in which marriage partners flow between lineages in alternate directions every other generation.

An even more common pattern is one in which several lineages are linked into a circle in which the women of each lineage always marry in one direction around the circle, while their brothers marry into the lineage next to theirs in the opposite direction. This marriage system is like the patrilateral marriage system, but the direction of marriages is asymmetrical and does not alternate each generation. This system also is known as **ma-**

trilateral cross-cousin marriage, since a wife is always a mother's brother's daughter to her husband.

The rarest form of preferential cousin marriage is marriage with a **parallel cousin**, a cousin who is one's mother's sister's child or one's father's brother's child. **Patrilateral parallel-cousin marriage**, that is, marriage between a man and his father's brother's daughter, is found among many Arab societies, where it is called **bint'amm**. This rule is useful in maintaining solidarity within a lineage, since a man and his father's brother's daughter belong to the same lineage (Barth, 1954; Murphy & Kasdan, 1959). It is especially helpful, for instance, among Arab Bedouins, where members of the same lineage may be dispersed from one another for long periods of time.

NEGOTIATING MARRIAGE

In many tribal societies, chiefdoms, and nonindustrialized states, marriages have generally been arranged by parents of potential spouses. Arranged marriage characterizes societies in which the family is an important political group within its community or the basic unit of economic production, and it is also typically found where income-producing resources are inherited. Marriage establishes a connection be-

---

marriage preference rules systems that single out certain kin as ideal marriage partners

cross cousins cousins who are related through parents of the opposite sex who are usually brother and sister

sister exchange form of cross-cousin marriage in which a brother and sister marry cross cousins who are also sister and brother to each other

bilateral cross-cousin marriage more descriptive term for sister exchange

patrilateral cross-cousin marriage marriage between a male and his father's sister's daughter

matrilateral cross-cousin marriage marriage between a male and his mother's brother's daughter

parallel cousins cousins whose common parents are either two brothers or two sisters

patrilateral parallel-cousin marriage (bint'amm) marriage between a male and his father's brother's daughter

bint'amm patrilateral parallel-cousin marriage

WEDDING SHOWERS IN THE UNITED STATES

Bridal showers have long been a prenuptial tradition in most parts of the United States. They have usually been given for the bride by a close friend or member of the wedding party such as a bridesmaid or maid of honor, or by a more distant relative such as a cousin or aunt. The word "shower" most likely originated with the idea of "showering" the prospective bride with gifts that would be useful in setting up a new household. As such, functional items such as small kitchen appliances and bathroom or bedroom items have been popular gifts. The shower has been part of the process of role change for a young woman in moving from single daughter in her parents' house to married woman and mistress of her own home. It has therefore been symbolic of a new life, that of the married couple together and ultimately of the children that would be born to the couple. Games played at showers have often been symbolic of the bride's fertility and future reproductive role. For instance, the bride's comments as she opened the presents might be written down or tape-recorded and later read or listened to by the group. The words have been interpreted not as comments on the gifts that she had received but as statements with sexual meanings, and they might be introduced as what the bride would say to her new husband on their wedding night.

The wedding shower has contrasted with the future bridegroom's bachelor party, which has symbolized the end of the young man's life of sexual freedom, independence, and responsibility solely for himself. It has traditionally been held on the night before the wedding and had the reputation—commonly based more on fiction than fact—of being an orgy of drunken revelry and sexual indulgence by the prospective groom. Often, bachelor's parties have actually been organized and paid for by the prospective groom himself and might involve a relatively sedate dinner at a restaurant with his friends, brothers, and father as guests.

Traditional wedding showers have become somewhat less common in recent decades, as two-income families have become widespread and women's marital roles have shifted from homemaker and mother toward those befitting a more independent partner within marriage. There has been an increase in the prevalence of coed showers where the prospective bride and groom are both guests of honor, celebrating the beginning of their marital partnership. At the same time bachelorette parties have also become popular, at which more risqué gifts are given than were traditional at wedding showers and which, like the traditional bachelor's party, represent one last fling of freedom.

With the increased number of second marriages and of marriages by couples who have been living together and therefore already have the basic household necessities, there has also been an increase in the popularity of theme showers such as champagne and wine showers, lingerie showers, and barbeque showers. Gift selections at such showers are based less on the traditional needs of newlyweds than on the shower's individual theme.

---

tween the spouses' families with important economic and social implications for both. In the eyes of the parents, the mutual attraction of the potential spouses may be considered but is likely to be less important than the pratical implications of the match for both sets of in-laws. Negotiations before marriage between the two families tend to emphasize such issues as the size of the payment one family may make to the other and the work and domestic skills of the future spouses. Less rational matters such as the feelings of the prospective bride and groom for one another are not given as much weight as in societies where large kinship groups are not the major economic and political units of society. Neither the couple's sexual gratification nor their emotional compatibility is of great interest to their respective families.

Rather, the couple to be married form a link by which those families are joined in their society's larger political and economic arena.

Bridewealth

In perhaps three-quarters of the world's societies, marriage negotiations involve the determination of how the prospective groom's family shall recompense the family of the bride-to-be for the loss of her productive and reproductive services (Coult & Haberstein, 1965; Murdock, 1957). This compensation may consist of gifts, known alternatively as the **bridewealth**,

---

bridewealth goods transferred from the groom's kin to the bride's to recompense them for her loss

FIGURE 9.7

DOWRY

This traditional dowry presentation in what was Czechoslovakia illustrates one way a bride brings a certain amount of wealth with her into the marriage. It both ensures that some of her family property will remain in her family and that the bride will be financially cared for in the event of her husband's death or desertion.

bride price, or **progeny price**. The bride's status as a married woman and the status of her children will be greater if the bridewealth compensation is a high one; but the outcome of the bridewealth negotiation will also be influenced by the relative importance of the two negotiating families. Bridewealth is found in 60 percent of those societies that anthropologists have investigated. It is particularly common among simpler food-producing societies, such as tribal horticulturalists and noncommercial pastoralists, those that raise animals only for their own use.

Bride Service

Alternatively, compensation to the bride's family may take the form of a period of work to be performed by the groom for his wife's family, in which case it is known as the **bride service**. The bride service has been reported in about 24 percent of societies that anthropologists have studied. It is particularly common among foragers who lack the accumulation of wealth necessary for paying bridewealth.

Bridewealth is paid at one time or over a short period at the beginning of the marriage, permanently validating the marriage. By contrast, bride service continually recompenses the

bride's family, either over a fixed prolonged period or over the entire course of the marriage. In the words of Schlegel and Eloul (1988), in bride service, "marriage is in a constant state of economic negotiation." Nevertheless, even when the bride service is performed for a fixed period of time, the spouses usually have sexual access to one another from the beginning of the period of service, and the legitimacy of children is not affected by being born before the end of the service. Under the custom of bridewealth, however, children may not be considered fully legitimate, particularly in respect to inheritance rights, until the entire progeny price has been paid.

Dowry

In the **dowry**, the benefits flow in the opposite direction from those of the bridewealth or bride service. Here, goods belonging to the bride's family accompany her into the marriage. The wealth is most often controlled by the bride within her new family, but it sometimes is held in trust for her by her husband or his relatives, or it may simply become the property of the husband's family (Goody & Tambiah, 1973). In this case, it is apt to be perceived as a compensation for the economic burden of supporting the woman. Thus, the dowry is not a mirror image of the bridewealth or bride service, even though it flows in the opposite direction. Like bridewealth and bride service, dowry reflects the status of the woman in a marriage. The first two forms are more likely when a woman's status is high; the dowry is more likely when a woman's status is low (Schlegel & Barry, 1986).

The dowry is most common in agricultural or pastoral societies in which commodities are produced for market exchange and in which there are significant wealth differences between families. The dowry may be viewed as a kind of advance on a woman's inheritance from her own family; it keeps the wealth within the fam-

---

bride price bridewealth

progeny price bridewealth

bride service service performed by the groom for the family of the bride to recompense them for her loss

dowry a payment from the family of a bride to the family of her husband to compensate them for their acceptance of the responsibility of her support

FIGURE 9.8

GIFT EXCHANGE

At this wedding in Wenjang, China, guests bring gifts in baskets. Gift giving is part of a system of gift exchange that emphasizes the ties of future interaction that will exist between the families and their children. In gift exchange, the families share items of nearly equal value, whether they be yams, cattle, or silver.

ily by ultimately benefiting the grandchildren of the donors.

Indirect Dowry. Goody (1973) has noted a variant of the dowry that he has called the **indirect dowry**, a payment of goods made by the groom or his family to the bride, either directly to her or to her father, who then passes it to her. Sometimes the father may keep some of this payment before passing the rest on to his daughter, to cover the costs of the marriage preparations or to recompense him for having raised the girl. As with the dowry, the goods that go to the bride in the indirect dowry are intended to provide security for her and her children, especially if she becomes widowed. Coming from her husband's family, the payment may symbolize their commitment to the well-being of the daughter-in-law in her new home.

Gift Exchange

Sometimes the flow of goods between the families who are party to a marriage goes in both directions. Called **gift exchange**, this reciprocal sharing of objects of more or less equal value between the two families emphasizes the ties of future interaction and mutual aid that will characterize the relationship between the families.

Women Exchange. Schlegel and Eloul (1988) have pointed out that gift exchange is not perfectly balanced, since one family loses a child, while the other gains a relative by marriage. However, there is one system that overcomes this imbalance. **Women exchange** is a system in which no gifts are passed between the families. Instead, each family gives a female, usually a daughter, as a bride to the other

---

indirect dowry payment of goods made by the groom or his family to the bride either directly to her or indirectly through her father

gift exchange reciprocal exchange of gifts between families who are party to a marriage

women exchange the practice of families' exchanging women in marriage rather than exchanging gifts, so that each loses a daughter but gains a daughter-in-law

family. Since each family loses a daughter but gains a daughter-in-law, the exchange between the two families is completely balanced.

POSTMARITAL RESIDENCE

Although marriage joins two kinship groups as allies, the couple joined by the ritual of marriage may be more involved in the daily life of one of their parental kinship groups than the other, depending on where they set up their new residence.

Virilocality

According to research by Murdock (1957), in about two-thirds of the world's societies newly married couples are expected to set up residence in or near the husband's family. This form of residence, called **virilocality** or **patrilocality**, is most often found where the solidarity of the male group is very important. Naroll (1973) found that the best single predictor of virilocality was the man's predominance in food production. Its likelihood is increased by other factors that strengthen males' solidarity: for example, it is more likely where hunting is a primarily male activity; where food production requires heavy labor; where internal warfare (see chapter 11) involves fighting between neighboring groups that share a common culture and language; where men have more than one wife; where men wield authority in a political organization that is a source of prestige; or where male accumulation of property is a sign of rank.

Uxorilocality

The second most common residence pattern is **uxorilocality**, formerly known as **matrilocality**. Uxorilocality is found in about 15 percent of societies and involves the setting up of a residence in or near the residence of the bride's family (Coult & Haberstein, 1965; Murdock, 1934). This is most likely to be practiced where food is provided by simple gardening in environments that do not require heavy labor and in warlike societies where belligerence is most common between distant groups.

Bilocality

A third residential pattern is **bilocality** or **ambilocality**: residence may be in the home area of either the bride or the groom. This form of residence is practiced in 5 to 10 percent of societies, particularly where cooperation within large kinship groups is important. It also permits flexibility of choice in societies where land may be limited.

Neolocality

In **neolocality** the couple sets up a residence in some new place apart from either family. This residence pattern provides maximum flexibility in electing a place to live and is most common when the nuclear family of two parents and their children is economically independent and responsible for its own survival. Only about 1 in 20 societies emphasizes neolocal residence. It is most common in industrialized societies.

Avunculocality

In **avunculocality** the couple takes up residence in or near the house of the groom's mother's brother. This form of residence is common in less than 5 percent of societies and occurs only in matrilineal societies where the men of the matrilineage must stay together, as when warfare is common.

---

virilocality (patrilocality) custom of newly married couples setting up residence with or near the groom's family

patrilocality virilocality

uxorilocality (matrilocality) the custom of newly married couples setting up residence with or near the bride's family

matrilocality uxorilocality

bilocality (ambilocality) the custom in which a newly married couple may elect to set up residence with or near either the bride's or the groom's family

ambilocality bilocality

neolocality the custom of newly married couples setting up residence in a new location apart from either spouse's family

avunculocality the custom of newly married couples establishing residence with or near the groom's mother's brother

THE SAMOAN EXTENDED FAMILY AND HOUSEHOLD

Ella (1895) and Mead (1928) described the traditional Samoan family system, which provides a marked contrast to North American families and households. Among the Samoans, a single household was led by a *matai* or headman, a titled member of the family selected to act as their patriarchal head. The *matai* had life-and-death authority over members of the household and was responsible for carrying out religious rituals for the family. As family head, he also owned the land that was worked by the family members and assigned them their share to work.

Within the extended family group, children were tended by their older siblings. The mothers were thus freed for other activities, and all adult relatives were viewed as having rights over the children of the group. Besides baby-tending, boys under eight or nine years of age and girls who had not yet attained puberty were expected to help adults in many other ways, contributing to the work and welfare of the household. On the other hand, if the demands of the family became too great, children were free to leave home and take up residence with other relatives in another household that they found more congenial.

(see reference map p. 97)

FAMILY

Marriage legitimizes a sexual union and provides an institutionalized means for producing the next generation. Some group must be charged with the responsibility for rearing the children born from the marriage union. The group in which children are raised is known as the **family**. This group need not be structured solely around the individuals who are united to one another in marriage. When the family does consist of parents and their children, it is called a **nuclear family**. This is the family type that is most familiar to peoples of Western societies in recent times, and it is also typical of foraging societies. However, as the sole basis for households, it is a rare family form.

Almost all societies throughout most of human history have had more complex family forms than the nuclear family. These more complex family forms, known collectively as **extended families**, include more individuals than a husband and wife and their children. They are formed when the married couple sets up their residence with one of their families. Extended families usually include three generations: either a pair of grandparents, their sons, the wives of their sons, and all the children of their sons, or a pair of grandparents, all their sons and daughters, and all the children of their daughters. These two basic types of extended family may be further elaborated, depending on the marriage forms involved, since the extended family may include plural spouses in the parental and grandparental generations.

Extended families may live under a common roof or in several closely assembled dwellings. Thus, they may make up a single **household** (residential unit) or several households. In any case, the number of individuals involved in childrearing responsibilities will be much larger in extended families than in nuclear families. Therefore, extended families are likely to have more formally established rules regarding the rights and obligations of various family members to one another than do societies in which nuclear families are the norm.

Family in the United States

People in the United States often refer to the family as the basis of their society. In a culture in which individuals must compete with one another for success, the family is one of the few relatively safe havens of close emotional ties and cooperation. However, the actual role of family in U.S. society is minimal in contrast to

family the group consisting of married persons, their children, and other relatives who reside with them

nuclear family the form of family that consists only of married persons and their children

extended families families that include two or more nuclear families and often their parents, who reside together

household a group of people who share a common residence

that in most other societies, and single-parent families are very common.

The Limited Role of the Family.   The U.S. family has lost most social functions beyond the basic socialization of children and the consumption of goods. Unlike families in peasant cultures, U.S. families typically are not production units, but rather consumption units. In a sense, the U.S. family could be defined as the group that eats together, but, since the rise of television, even this definition of the family might be invalid.

Even with industrialization, earlier U.S. families often were held together by the presence of a mother whose work was home-centered. Before the development of effective contraceptive techniques, it was simply easier for the wife to rear her children at home until about the age of 40, and for the husband to seek employment outside the home. With increasingly effective birth control technology, the childbearing period between the birth of the first child and the last child has declined from about 18 years in 1900 to about 6 years in 1980, and the average number of children born to a couple is now less than 2. As the economic importance of domestic production declined, and the U.S. housewife was left in a dependent economic role, she began to seek employment outside the home. Today, over 60 percent of U.S. women are employed outside the home.

Fragmentation of Families.   The extended family household that is still common in many parts of the world and which was once common in the United States is rare today in the United States. As industrialization progressed and job mobility increased, the extended family was gradually replaced by the nuclear family as an increasing number of children established their own households near their places of employment. Since World War II, new economic conditions have created a variety of forms for the U.S. nuclear family. The household consisting of a nuclear family composed of two married parents, several children, and a single income provided by the husband—idealized as the norm in the 1950s—is no longer the predominant family form in the United States. Today, nuclear families consist not only of this traditional type but also of single-parent families, "blended" families that consist of previously married parents and children from the previous marriages as well as the current one, and families in which the heads of household are unmarried. According to the U.S. Bureau of the Census (1995), there were 68,144,000 families in the United States as of 1993. Of these, 78 percent were headed by a married couple. Over half of this group of families relied on two incomes. The remaining 14,973,000 families were headed by a single parent.

CHAPTER SUMMARY

1. Marriage is a socially accepted sexual and economic union that unites members of previously separate families in a committed relationship that typically involves child-rearing expectations.

2. The most commonly recognized marital types are monogamous, polygynous, polyandrous, and group marriages.

3. In many societies there are also symbolic, nonsexual, fictive, fixed-term, and same-sex marriages.

4. Since marriages unite separate families into an in-law relationship with each other, their creation has practical implications for more persons than just the spouses.

5. The choice of marriage partner is restricted in all societies by rules such as endogamy, exogamy, and marriage preference rules.

6. In most societies, the creation of a new marriage traditionally has also involved various practical considerations, such as the payment of goods or service to the family of the bride and the dowry.

7. The size of the family is directly related to customs that govern where a newly married couple is expected to set up their residence.

8. The family established by marriage may vary in size from the nuclear family that is common in Western societies today to the more traditional extended family that has been common in most of the world since the rise of food domestication.

9. In the United States families are often assumed to be the core of society, but they have little power and often are broken by divorce.

ANNOTATED READINGS

Blackwood, E. (Ed.). (1986). *The many faces of homosexuality: Anthropological approaches to homosexual behavior.* New York: Harrington Park Press. An exceptional collection of essays on the cultural patterns of homosexuality in a variety of different cultural contexts.

Ember, M., & Ember, C. R. (1983). *Marriage, family, and kinship: Comparative studies of social organization.* New Haven, CT: HRAF Press. A collection of cross-cultural studies that test various explanations of human social organization.

Fox, R. (1968). *Kinship and marriage: An anthropological perspective.* Baltimore, MD: Penguin. One of the easiest-to-follow texts that have been produced on kinship and marriage.

Frayser, S. G. (1985). *Varieties of sexual experience: An anthropological perspective on human sexuality.* New Haven, CT: HRAF Press. One of the most recent attempts to use cross-cultural data to examine the diversity of human sexual customs through time and across cultural boundaries, using data from Murdock and White's Standard Cross-Cultural Sample. This book includes important discussions of marriage, family, child-rearing, and divorce.

Gregerson, E. (1983). *Sexual practices.* New York: Watts. A well-illustrated and informed discussion of the major topics of the cross-cultural study of human sexuality.

Needham, R. (Ed.). (1972). *Rethinking kinship and marriage.* London: Tavistock. A collection of essays that focus on the cross-cultural study of kinship and marriage customs.

Pasternak, B. (1976). *Introduction to kinship and social organization.* Englewood Cliffs, NJ: Prentice Hall. One of the standard sources on kinship, this book contains information about theories of marriage and the family.

CHAPTER TEN

Kinship and Descent

After reading this chapter, you should be able to:

Explain the relationship of kinship to descent.

Explain the varieties of cognatic (or nonunilineal) descent.

Explain the varieties of unilineal descent.

Outline the characteristics of the various kinds of unilineal descent groups.

Describe the various kinds of ambilineal descent groups.

Explain the functions of moieties.

Describe bilateral (or noncorporate) descent groups (kindreds).

Discuss the evolution of descent groups.

List the six common types of kinship terminologies.

Explain the building blocks of kinship terminologies.

Explain the conditions that foster each of the six common kinship terminology systems.

Analyze the concept of fictive kinship.

◀ *Figure 10.1 Kinship Kinship is a cultural system by which we identify all the members of our family both present and past. Three generations of the Best family sit for a Mother's Day portrait at the Photographic Center of Harlem. At left is Maritta Best, with her mother, Edith, and Brian Dunn, Edith's grandson. The Kente cloth in the background is from Ghana. Like the Scottish tartans, its colors determine what specific region one's family is from. The fan Edith is holding is a symbol of the Ibo tribe of Nigeria. Though she doesn't own it, Edith felt it represented her family's heritage.*

Human beings all over the world distinguish their kin from other people. In this chapter, we will see how the concept of kinship is based on various ways of thinking about how children are descended from one or both of their parents and how these parent-child descent ties are used to build up networks that define people related to one another by kinship. You will learn to recognize different descent systems, some based on the concept of descent from only one parent in each generation and others based on the concept of descent from both parents. We will then consider how different kinds of kinship groups can grow out of these different ways of viewing those related to us. Finally, you will be introduced to the most common kinship terminologies, the systems for naming relatives that are related to the ways in which people think about descent.

Brother, can you spare a dime? I'm my own grandpa. Sister Sledge. Auntie Mame. Uncle Vanya. Is my mother's new husband's ex-wife's daughter my stepsister? When my mother's sister married a man who already had children, did they become my cousins? If I married a widow and my new stepdaughter married my father, would my father's new son be my half brother or my stepgrandson? How we are related to each other depends on which system of kinship our society utilizes.

KINSHIP

Kinship is a very human concept. It is the way we keep track of our relationships to our **kin**, those who are connected to us by some combination of descent and marriage. Those kin who are related to us by **descent**, that is by the connections between parents and their offspring, are our **consanguines**. You are one of my consanguinal kin if we can find a chain of connected parent-child ties that stretches from you to me. My children are linked to me, their common parent, by a chain one link long. Any two of my children are related to each other by a chain of two similar links, one link connecting one of them to me and the other link connecting me to the second child. My only niece is my mother's eldest daughter's daughter: she is

three parent-child links away from me among my consanguinal kin. Kin who are related through marriage link are known as **affines**. My affinal relatives are the consanguinal kin of my spouse or the spouse of any of my consanguinals. They are, in other words, my in-laws.

In any human community, some people are thought of as "kin" and others as "not kin," and a particular society's way of defining who are kin may not give equal weight to all connections between parents and their offspring. As we shall see, for instance, in many societies, children may be thought of as kin to only one of their parents. Thus, more formally, **kinship** is a system for classifying people who are deemed to be related through culturally defined parent-child ties or marriage ties.

DESCENT RULES

The cultural recognition of children as kin of one or both of their parents is the basis of the concept of descent. It is understood in most cultures as a biological relationship between children and parents. While in some societies, such as Canada and the United States, descent is reckoned through both parents, in others it is traced only through fathers or only through mothers.

Bilateral Descent

If parents came in only one sex, it would be a lot simpler to define our kin. Since they come in two varieties that play different roles in the production of children, the story becomes more complex. For instance, a brother-sister relationship can be traced by the links to a common mother or by links to the same father. Either way works, and contemporary U.S. culture, like that of the Siberian Chukchee or the U.S. Great

---

kin relatives based on descent and/or marriage

descent the cultural recognition of kinship connections between a child and one or both of his or her parent's kin

consanguines kin related by ties of descent

affines kin related through a marriage link

kinship a system for classifying people who are related to one another by ties of descent or by ties of marriage

FIGURE 10.2

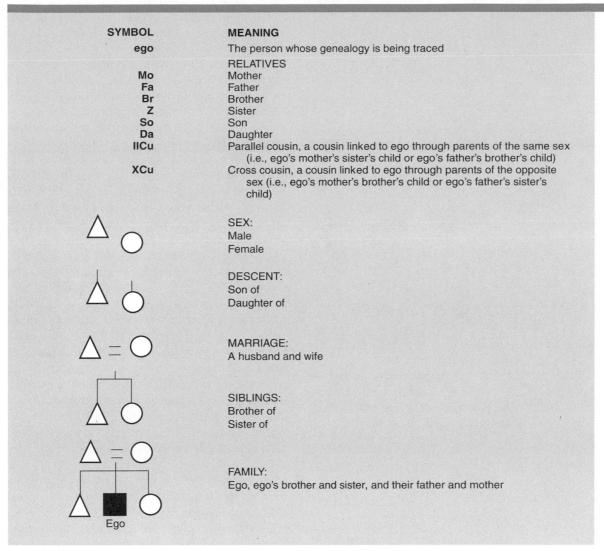

SYMBOL	MEANING
ego	The person whose genealogy is being traced
	RELATIVES
Mo	Mother
Fa	Father
Br	Brother
Z	Sister
So	Son
Da	Daughter
IICu	Parallel cousin, a cousin linked to ego through parents of the same sex (i.e., ego's mother's sister's child or ego's father's brother's child)
XCu	Cross cousin, a cousin linked to ego through parents of the opposite sex (i.e., ego's mother's brother's child or ego's father's sister's child)

SEX:
Male
Female

DESCENT:
Son of
Daughter of

MARRIAGE:
A husband and wife

SIBLINGS:
Brother of
Sister of

FAMILY:
Ego, ego's brother and sister, and their father and mother

Ego

INTERPRETING KINSHIP DIAGRAMS

Kinship diagrams are drawn using a variety of standard symbols. Those shown here are among the most common, and will be used later in this text. The simple family diagram at the bottom could be easily expanded using the same symbols to show ego's uncles, aunts, and cousins. Can you figure out how to do it?

Basin Ute, considers either chain to be equally valid. So it lets me simply say that my sister and I share the same parents and lets it go at that. This system is based on the principle of **bilateral descent**, a rule that asserts that we are equally descended from both parents and lets us count relatives on both our mother's and father's side of the family. The bilateral system is a common approach. In about 36 percent of societies, people consider links through both parents as equally valid ways of reckoning their own kin.

Ambilineal Descent

A variation on the bilateral theme is the idea that we may consider ourselves descended through parents of either sex, but we must choose only one parent for each link that connects a group of relatives. This system, followed in less than 1 percent of societies, is

---

bilateral descent a system of tracing descent lines equally through both parents

FIGURE 10.3

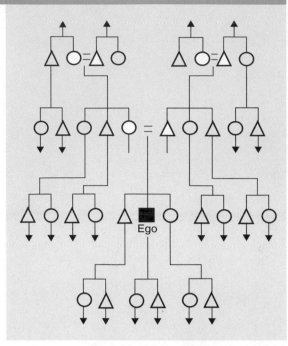

BILATERAL DESCENT

In bilateral descent, ego is considered to be descended equally from both parents and, therefore, from an increasing number of ancestors on both sides of ego's family, as shown in white.

FIGURE 10.4

AMBILINEAL DESCENT

Ego's relatives are shown in white. In ambilineal descent, ego's ancestors can be traced through either the father or mother, but not both. Membership in the traditional Scottish clans was based on genealogies that were traced in this way.

ambilineal descent. Using the concept of ambilineal descent, a child might be designated as a relative of either the mother's kin or the father's kin, but not both. A decision has to be made in each generation about which parent's group the children will be part of, but the connection may be established through the father in one generation and through the mother in another. The ancient Scottish clans were built up in such a way, so that the relatives who made up a particular clan all could trace themselves back to the founding ancestor of the clan, but not consistently through parents of the same sex.

When grouped by bilateral descent, relatives spread out on both sides of a person's family, creating two groups of equally related kin for each person. In the ambilineal approach, a less predictable group of relatives is created, one made up of individual families who belong to the entire group in some cases because the father is a member and in other cases because the mother is a member. These two descent systems are sometimes referred to by the general terms **cognatic** or **nonunilineal descent** systems.

Unilineal Descent

Most societies have a narrower way of building up a group of kin that follows a principle called **unilineal descent**, descent through a single sex line, either the father or the mother, rather than through both parents equally. About 44 percent of all societies that anthropologists have studied, including the ancient Greeks, the Lau of Fiji, the Mission Indians of southern California, and the Mossí of the Sudan, follow the system of reckoning kin by insisting that kin are only those who are joined by *father*-child ties. This rule for grouping relatives is called **patrilineal descent**, since it defines children as offspring of their fathers only.

ambilineal descent a system of tracing descent through a parent of either sex, choosing only one parent for each link that connects a group of relatives

cognatic (nonunilineal) descent a system of tracing descent bilaterally or ambilineally

nonunilineal descent cognatic descent

unilineal descent a system of tracing descent through a single sex line rather than through both parents equally

patrilineal descent a system of descent traced through fathers only

Patrilineality is commonly followed in situations that require male solidarity, for instance in work requiring heavy cooperative labor or in feuding between neighboring groups.

On the other hand, the Navajo of Arizona and New Mexico, the Tuareg of the Sahara Desert, and the Caribbean Goajiro are equally convinced that mother-child links alone should be used. Their approach to counting kin is based upon the principle of **matrilineal descent**. It is shared by about 15 percent of the world's societies. Matrilineality is an effective means of unifying groups of women as decision-making bodies. It is commonly followed as a principle of kinship in societies where men are often absent from the local community.

In about 5 percent of societies, a person may have two separate sets of kin, one designated only through mothers and the other only through fathers. Such a kinship-determining rule, called **double descent** or **double unilineal descent**, may be a useful way of keeping track of relatives if, for instance, some property—say, houses and gardens—is inherited from the parent of one sex and other property—say, religious rituals and gardening tools—is passed down through the opposite line. Just as patrilineal and matrilineal descent may coexist, ambilineal or bilateral descent may co-occur with matrilineal or patrilineal descent so long as there is some socially useful reason for keeping track of each group.

FIGURE 10.5

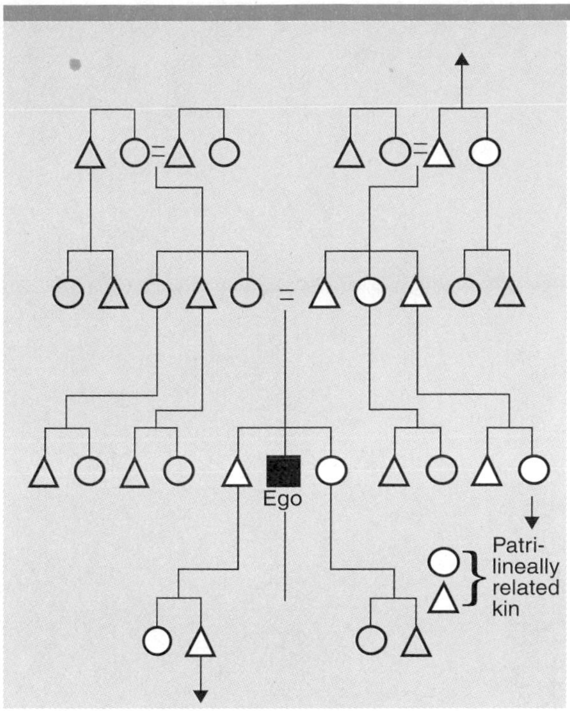

PATRILINEAL DESCENT

In patrilineal descent, a chain of father-child ties links ego to his or her ancestors. Each generation within the descent line consists of siblings who belong to the line of their father and his siblings. Only children of males will continue the line. The children of female members of a patrilineal descent line will belong to their husbands' descent lines. Ego's patrilineal relatives are shown in white.

DESCENT GROUPS

In all societies, there are social groups whose membership is based on descent. Membership in descent groups may be defined either by the sharing of a common ancestor or by the sharing of a common living relative. Groups whose members share a common ancestor are called **lineal descent groups** or **corporate descent groups**. Descent groups whose members share a living relative are associated with bilateral descent and are called **bilateral descent groups**.

Lineal Descent Groups

There are two kinds of lineal descent groups: unilineal and ambilineal. **Unilineal descent groups** are social groups that are based on either patrilineal or matrilineal descent reckoning. **Ambilineal descent groups** are groups

whose members trace their relationship to the common ancestor by using ambilineal descent rules. Both unilineal and ambilineal descent groups share one important characteristic: they

---

matrilineal descent a system of descent traced through mothers only

double descent (double unilineal descent) a system of tracing two separate sets of kin, one designated through mothers only and the other through fathers only

double unilineal descent double descent

lineal descent groups groups whose members share a common ancestor

corporate descent groups lineal descent groups

bilateral descent groups groups whose members share a living relative

unilineal descent group a system of tracing social groups based on a matrilineal or patrilineal descent system

ambilineal descent group a system of tracing social groups based on an ambilineal descent system

FIGURE 10.6

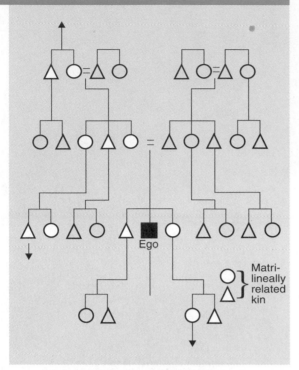

MATRILINEAL DESCENT

In matrilineal descent, a chain of mother-child ties links ego to his or her ancestors. Each generation within the descent line consists of siblings who belong to the line of their mother and her siblings. Only children of females will continue the line. The children of male members of a matrilineal descent line will belong to their wives' descent lines. Ego's matrilineal relatives are shown in white.

are corporate groups, or organizations that continue to exist even though their individual members change over the generations, and they can legally perform social functions such as owning property, conducting ceremonies, regulating marriages, disciplining their own members, or engaging in legal processes or warfare with other groups. Corporate groups are typically named to symbolize their existence as a social entity.

Lineages.   A **lineage** is a kin group that traces its descent from a known common ancestor. When members trace their genealogical ties to the common ancestor through matrilineal descent, it is known as a **matrilineage**; a lineage based on ties of patrilineal descent is a **patrilineage**. Lineages that are formed using an ambilineal descent principle are called **cognatic lineages** or sometimes **ramages** or **septs**. In all three cases, the lineage continues to exist as

generations pass. Older members may die, and new members may be born, but so long as the common ancestry is remembered, the surviving members can view themselves as part of a common body of relatives that can carry out common goals. Lineages are typically named for the common ancestor from which its members are descended.

Since each successive generation may produce more surviving offspring than made up the previous generation, a lineage may gradually increase in the size of its living membership. Thus, lineages as small as 30 or 40 people may grow to encompass thousands of members. Since growing populations tend to spread out from the location of their ancestral homelands, local segments of a lineage may become involved in activities in which it would be unwieldy and unnecessary to call together all members. So, growing lineages often fission into smaller sublineages over the generations.

Clans.   As generations pass, lineage membership may reach such numbers and such distance from the common ancestry that their exact genealogical ties are no longer remembered, even though surviving members of the total group still regard themselves as relatives. A corporate kinship group of this type is called a **clan** or sometimes a **sib**. Clans may also be differentiated by the rule of descent through which membership is defined. Thus, anthropologists speak of either **matriclans**, **patriclans**, or **cognatic** (or **ambilineal**) **clans**, depending on the descent rule.

---

lineage a kinship group whose members can trace their lines of descent to the same ancestor

matrilineage a system of tracing descent lines through mothers

patrilineage a system of tracing descent lines through fathers

cognatic lineages (ramages, septs) lineages formed using an ambilineal descent system

ramages cognatic lineages

septs cognatic lineages

clan kinship group whose members believe themselves to be descended from a common ancestor far enough in the past that they cannot trace their specific genealogical ties to one another

sib clan

matriclan clan based on matrilineal descent

patriclan clan based on patrilineal descent

cognatic clan (ambilineal clan) clan based on ambilineal descent

HOW A PERSON CAN BE HIS OWN GRANDFATHER

I married a widow who had a daughter. My father visited our home frequently, fell in love and married my stepdaughter. Thus my father became my son-in-law, and my stepdaughter my mother, because she was my father's wife. My stepdaughter had also a son; he was of course my brother and at the same time my grandchild, for he was the son of my daughter. My wife was my grandmother, because she was my mother's mother. I was my wife's husband and grandchild at the same time; and as the husband of a person's grandmother is his grandfather, I was my own grandfather.

From an advertisement by Rudolph Oak Hall, 404 Main Street (Dry Goods, Clothing, Gents' Furnishing Goods, Boats, Shoes, Trunks, Valises, Etc., and Millinery), Fayetteville, Arkansas, 1903.

The common ancestor of a clan may be so far removed in time that his or her identity may no longer be remembered accurately. As the ancestor's life story is passed down the generations, it may become altered and embroidered with tales that represent the values of clan members more than historical fact. The ancestor may take on heroic proportions and as portrayed by succeeding generations may become more mythological than real. The process by which the folk memories of an important person may become increasingly filled with symbolism that can elevate him or her to a superhuman level is one that operates even in literate societies. In the United States, for instance, children hear mythologized stories of George Washington's inability to tell a lie, and about his having thrown a silver dollar across a river that is, in some versions, Virginia's smaller Rappahannock and, in others, Washington, D.C.'s nearly mile-wide Potomac. Abraham Lincoln, the Great Emancipator, is remembered as having freed all the slaves in the United States, rather than as just having promised freedom to Southern slaves who joined the Union in fighting the Confederates. When such stories continue to be embellished over many generations, a time may come when it becomes difficult to identify the historically real from the mythological, and the stories about clan ancestors in traditionally nonliterate societies are frequently so filled with superhuman elements that it is impossible to demonstrate that the founder of the clan really existed except in folklore. Indeed, a symbolic ancestor of an existing clan may not even be a human at all. For instance, symbolic clan ancestors are often important animals, plants, or, less often, geographical features in the en-vironment, such as the Bitter-Water or Salt clans of the Navajo.

Clans may have tens or even hundreds of thousands of members. By virtue of their large membership, clans can be very powerful organizations. Like lineages, they are corporate groups that perform a variety of social functions, such as carrying out major ceremonies, owning land or other property, maintaining peaceful relationships between their individual members and the lineages that make them up, handling the legal matters, and regulating the marriage options of their members.

Phratries. In addition to lineages and clans, there can also be larger unilineal descent groups within a society. A group of clans thought to be related by kinship at a level higher than the clan ancestors is called a **phratry**. It does not necessarily grow from a common ancestral clan. The kinship connection between the clans of a phratry may be merely a social fiction that allows its members to interact as a larger corporate group. That is, a phratry is a group of two or more clans whose members believe and act as if they are somehow related, whether they are really related or not.

Moieties. Sometimes the kinship groups of a society are organized into two major categories or groups, called **moieties**, from a French word meaning "half." Each moiety in this kind of organization is a unilineal kinship group that

---

phratry group of clans thought to be related by kinship

moiety one of two basic complementary social subdivisions of a society

NAVAJO CLANS

The Navajo who reside in Arizona and New Mexico are a pastoral people who herd sheep and grow corn and other crops in a dry desert region. They number today about 200,000 people who occupy a reservation territory of more than 25,000 square miles. Though individual families may live miles apart, their unity is aided by a continued reliance on matrilineal clan membership as a source of economic and social cohesion. In the 1940s Kluckhohn and Leighton (1946) found that the Navajo had approximately 60 clans, each bearing the name of a locality; the number of clans remains the same today. Each clan is likely to have members who live in different communities, and a given local group may be composed of families who belong to 15 or 20 different clans.

A Navajo is born a primary member of the mother's clan, but members of the father's clan are also considered to be relatives, so a Navajo might describe him- or herself as "born to Bitter-Water [the mother's clan] for Salt [the father's clan]." Clans play an important role in regulating marriage; Navajos are traditionally forbidden to marry either members of their own matriclan or of their father's matriclan. This rule forces marriages to link members of different clans in each generation and is one of the means for maintaining ties of allegiance between members of the various clans in a community.

Considering that there are a large number of Navajos and the clans are spread over a large territory, each Navajo is likely to have many relatives whom he or she has never met. Two Navajo strangers who later discover that they belong to a common clan have the same familial obligations of hospitality and mutual help toward each other as they do to their previously known relatives.

Traditionally, the clan also was responsible collectively for the crimes and debts of its members. This fact, of course, meant that the clan also had authority to control irresponsible behavior in its members. Grazing land, for instance, could not be freely bought or sold by individual persons without permission of other clan members. Clans also controlled inheritance; goods passed to children from the members of their mother's clan.

Family loyalty still receives support from the traditional clan system of shared economic responsibilities in spite of the fragmenting effects of employment of many Navajos in the industrialized economy of the non-Navajo society that surrounds them. For instance, a Navajo religious ceremony—which might be necessary for the curing of an illness, the return of a family member after a period of residence at a nonreservation university, or the celebration of a girl's passage into adulthood—may cost a thousand or more dollars to carry out, an expense that can be too costly for a single household to bear. Such expenses may be supported mutually by nearby members of the person's clan for whom the ritual must be held, a practice that reinforces a tremendous sense of family loyalty, encourages reciprocal responsibilities, and gives cohesion to contemporary Navajo family life. Contemporary clans continue to regulate marriage choices and the inheritance of property.

NAVAJO

The Navajos, most of whom live in Arizona and New Mexico, still rely on traditional matrilineal clan membership as a source of economic and social cohesion as well as for marital regulations. Navajos are forbidden to marry within either their own matriclan or their father's matriclan.

may consist of a clan or phratry. Moieties usually play a role in the regulation of marriage, by the requirement that the members of each moiety take their spouses from the opposite group. According to Lévi-Strauss (1967), the relationships between moieties may "range from the most intimate cooperation to latent hostility," and in addition to providing spouses for

FIGURE 10.7

SCOTTISH CLAN

The tartan, a cross-checkered repeating pattern of stripes or lines woven into a woolen cloth, has come to have great significance in tracing the ancestry of *a Scottish clan. The earliest tartan was designed for the Highland 42nd Regiment of Foot, or Black Watch.*

one another's members, "sometimes their role is confined to activities of a religious, political, economic, ceremonial, or merely recreational character" (p. 10). Thus, the two moieties of a society may play other socially reciprocal roles such as providing funerals or hosting feasts for each other. Moieties may also facilitate social specialization by playing complementary roles. For instance, among the Toda of southern India, the clans of one moiety owned all of the sacred herds of dairy cattle and the dairies in which they were kept, but the dairymen of the sacred herds, who were the priests of Toda society, could be chosen only from the other moiety.

Combinations of Lineal Descent Groups. More than one kind of lineal descent group may operate simultaneously within the same society. For instance, lineages may be the only descent group present in a society; a clan may exist without lineages being differentiated within it; or a clan may be subdivided into identified lineages, each of which carries out activities within the entire clan. Lineages, clans, and phratries may be organized into moieties. As a matter of fact, with one exception, any combination of lineages, clans, phratries, and

moieties may occur in a particular society. The exception is merely that when phratries are present, there must also be clans, since phratries are defined as groups of two or more clans.

Bilateral Descent Groups

A **kindred** consists of all relatives on both the paternal and maternal sides of the family who are known to one living individual, referred to as ego. Because a kindred is not determined by its members' relationship to a single common ancestor, their relationships are defined bilaterally, rather than unilineally. Brothers and sisters will have the same kindred, but other relatives will have kindreds with somewhat different members. For instance, if kindreds included only first and second cousins, then my own second cousin's kindred would include *their* second cousins, who would be too distantly related to me as fourth cousins to be part of *my* kindred.

A person may call upon her or his kindred for aid and support, and kindred can act to-

---

kindred a kinship group in a bilateral descent system that consists of the known relatives of a living individual

FIGURE 10.8

LA GRANDE FAMILLE

A kindred consists of all relatives on both the paternal and maternal sides of the family who are known to a single individual. This family gathers *for a photo at the wedding of a son in Charente Maritime, France.*

gether as a group on behalf of the individual or siblings to whom they are all related. Although a person might call all of the members of his or her kindred together on an occasion like an American "family reunion," the members do not usually think of themselves as a group at other times. When the brothers and sisters who share the same kindred die, their kindred no longer has a uniting focus, so it typically ceases to exist. Thus, kindreds do not have the inherent quality of being corporate groups that exist beyond the lifespans of the individuals who are born into and die out of them. Neither are they normally responsible for such corporate responsibilities as owning property or conducting religious ceremonies. Rather, their existence is usually ephemeral.

Kindreds are most common in circumstances in which small family groups are more adaptive than larger ones and in which individual mobility is high. Thus, they are typical of industrialized societies such as those of North America, where children do not normally inherit their homes and occupations from

their parents and may even have to leave their hometowns to obtain employment. Kindreds are also typical of foraging societies, since small family groups that pursue a migratory life can more readily obtain the wild foods they need to survive in most environments than can larger, permanent family organizations such as lineages or clans.

The Evolution of Descent Groups

The oldest and simplest of human social systems, those founded on foraging economies, do not usually have corporate descent groups. Economic cooperation between intermarried families may create a local extended family of bilaterally related kin in the next generation, but when growth in the local kindred group makes food getting difficult, a breakup of the group is likely to occur. Since their lifestyle is based on a wandering quest for food, conditions do not foster the easy perpetuation of ongoing kinship ties between neighboring groups over many generations. Nor is there any specific need to do so. Within a generation or two, bilateral kindreds may still be called together for common economic or political action such as family reunions or for the distribution of property upon the death of a family member, but conditions that call for the development of permanent unilineal descent groups do not seem to be present in most such societies.

On the other hand, unilineal descent groups are common in horticultural, pastoral, and agricultural societies. In such societies, when an extended family divides, each smaller group of relatives is likely to establish its new residence within easy access of the other. This pattern of geographical and social dispersal can easily support the formation of lineages or other corporate descent groups as generations pass, if it is economically or politically advantageous to do so. For instance, lineages, clans, and phratries lend themselves readily to the maintenance of cooperating family-based military groups when warfare is an important feature of social life.

Interestingly, larger, socially more complex and specialized societies sometimes shift again toward a bilateral descent system. Where lineages and clans are the basic social building block, these kinship groups typically perform many of the governmental functions that are carried out by specialized nonkinship groups in some of the more complex societies. Thus, for instance, if a society develops a political system that takes over the military role previously played by unilineal descent groups, then bilateral descent reckoning is likely to replace the lineal system that existed before. Similarly, increasing social complexity can fragment matrilineal descent groups because geographical and occupational mobility increases the viability of smaller, economically independent nuclear family groups. Both of these conditions are common in the most industrialized societies of the world today where bilateral descent is the rule.

KINSHIP TERMINOLOGY

Kinship terminology is the system people use to identify the distinctions among relatives that are important in their lives. Kin terms may classify relatives in many different ways. For instance, kinship terminologies of various societies commonly take into account (1) the contrast between paternal and maternal relatives; (2) generation; (3) differences in relative age; (4) sex; (5) the contrast between descent ties and marriage ties; (6) the difference between a person's own descent line and a linked descent line; and (7) when descent lines are noted, the sex of the linking relative. Thus, actual kinship terminologies are highly varied. Nevertheless, individual systems can be grouped into six common types, called *Hawaiian, Eskimo, Omaha, Crow, Iroquois,* and *Sudanese.* The first two of these are types found in societies with bilateral descent systems, in which relatives on the maternal and paternal sides of the family are equally important in a person's life. The others tend to be associated with societies that use unilineal descent reckoning.

Hawaiian

This is the simplest kinship terminology in the sense that it is the system with the fewest terms. In the **Hawaiian kinship terminology** system, the key distinction is one of generation. Relatives are not distinguished by side of the family (e.g., "aunt" may be either a mother's sister or father's sister). One's affinal (related by marriage) descent line is not distinguished from linked or collateral descent lines, those that parallel one's own line back to a common ancestor. Thus, in Hawaiian kinship terminology, cousins are called by the same kin terms as are one's siblings, commonly translated as "brother" and "sister"; and one's father, father's brother, and mother's brother are all referred to as "father"; and mother, mother's sister, and father's sister are likewise designated by a single term. In its simplest form, Hawaiian kinship terminology may not make any distinction by sex, reducing the system to three basic kin terms: parents, siblings, and children.

The Hawaiian kinship system is especially common where extended families or some other form of corporate descent group, within which the nuclear family does not function autonomously, live and work together. It is more common in societies that make use of bilateral or

---

Hawaiian kinship terminology the simplest kinship designation, using the terms parents, siblings, and children

ambilineal rather than unilineal descent systems (Textor, 1967). In other words, Hawaiian terminology emphasizes the cohesion of the extended family or corporate groups, distinguishing relatives only by the generational differences that are important in the etiquette of family interaction in all societies. The Hawaiian system automatically extends the field of persons who have the same kinds of rights and obligations as members of one's own nuclear family. Thus, on the death of a child's biological father, there are likely to be several other men who will be expected to take responsibility for the childrear-

ing activities that the child's "real" father would have performed. Similarly, the incest taboo is extended to cover a much broader range of relatives, such as cross cousins, than is typical in other systems.

Eskimo

This kinship terminology is the second general type of bilateral kinship system. It is the type with which most North Americans are familiar. In **Eskimo kinship terminology**, the terms for mother, father, brother, and sister are not used for any relatives outside the nuclear family, and the terms for other relatives such as aunt, uncle, or cousin are the same for the maternal and paternal sides of the family. Cross cousins— children of siblings of the opposite sex—and parallel cousins—children of siblings of the same sex—are not distinguished by different terms, and cousin terms may not even differ by sex.

The simplicity of Eskimo terminology befits the types of societies in which it is typically found. In these societies, including most foraging or industrialized societies, an individual's most important relatives are her or his closest relatives. Thus, Eskimo terminology is commonly associated with economically independent nuclear families, bilateral descent, and kindreds rather than with unilineal or ambilineal descent and lineages, clans, or other corporate descent groups. Data compiled by Murdock (1967) for 71 societies in which Eskimo terminology was used indicated that only 4 had large extended families, and only 13 had unilineal descent groups. In fact, the other 54 had no corporate descent groups.

The remaining major kinship systems are those associated with unilineal descent systems. They distinguish between maternal and paternal kin, but differ in other ways.

Omaha

This kinship terminology is an example of a **bifurcate merging** system, one that derives

FIGURE 10.9

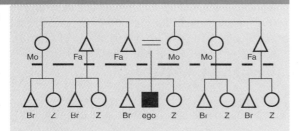

HAWAIIAN KINSHIP TERMINOLOGY

Hawaiian kinship terminology is most common in societies in which an extended group of relatives joined by bilateral descent live together and share work and child-rearing obligations. Its main emphasis is on distinguishing the members of the family's two adjacent generations—the generation of the parents and the generation of the children. Ego calls his or her parents and their siblings by the same two terms, translatable as "mother" and "father" and calls his or her cousins by terms that can be translated as "brother" and "sister."

FIGURE 10.10

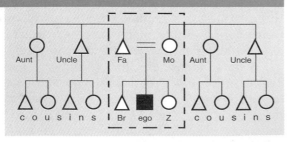

ESKIMO KINSHIP TERMINOLOGY

Eskimo kinship terminology is most common in societies that trace relationships bilaterally and in which the isolated nuclear family—a husband and wife and their own offspring—is the economically independent work-group of society. This kinship system emphasizes the separateness of ego's nuclear family (ego's parents and siblings) from other relatives by contrasting mother and father with aunts and uncles and by contrasting brother and sister with cousins.

Eskimo kinship terminology bilateral kinship system in which terms for mother, father, brother, and sister are not used for relatives outside the nuclear family

bifurcate merging kinship terminology derived from contrast between maternal and paternal relatives using a small number of kin terms to refer to many different kin

its kin terms from two major characteristics: the contrast between paternal and maternal relatives (hence, "bifurcate") and the use of a small number of kin terms to refer to many different kin within each of these two groups (hence, "merging"). The Omaha system is found in societies that have patrilineal descent systems. In the **Omaha kinship terminology** system, members of one's mother's patrilineage are distinguished only by sex regardless of generation. Thus, one term is used for all males of that group (e.g., for mother's brother and mother's brother's son) and another for all females including ego's mother, her sister, and her brother's daughter. In ego's own patrilineage, father is merged with father's brother. Parallel cousins in both lineages are merged with ego's brother and sister, and their children are called by the same term as ego's own children. The bifurcation is a useful way of contrasting the lineage of ego's mother from that of ego's father, while the merging of terms for parents and their same-sex siblings has the effect of emphasizing lineage cohesiveness. Since the mother's lineage is relatively unimportant in ego's daily life, generational differences in status can be ignored, but in ego's own patrilineage—which is the important corporate group in life—men of the father's generation are distinguished from men of ego's own generation in recognition of their likely differences in power and honor.

Crow

The Crow system is also a bifurcate merging system, but it is the mirror image of the Omaha pattern. Named for a Native North American society, **Crow kinship terminology** is found in many matrilineal societies throughout the world. In it the relatives of ego's father's matrilineage are distinguished only by sex, regardless of age or generation, while generational differences are noted within ego's own matrilineage. As with the Omaha system, Crow kinship is highly compatible with a powerful unilineal descent system, in this case emphasizing the importance of the matrilineal kin organization.

Iroquois

Like the Omaha and Crow systems, **Iroquois kinship terminology** is a bifurcate merging

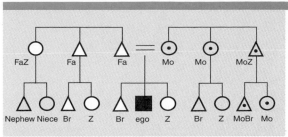

FIGURE 10.11

OMAHA KINSHIP TERMINOLOGY

Omaha kinship terminology is most often associated with patrilineal descent reckoning. Its terms for relatives contrast those related to ego through patrilineal descent ties (noted in white) to the equivalent relatives of his or her mother's patrilineal group (indicated with a dot). The terminology is more elaborate for ego's own patrilineal relatives than for ego's mother's patrilineal relatives for whom the same terms (Mo and MoBr) are used in both generations.

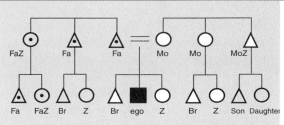

FIGURE 10.12

CROW KINSHIP TERMINOLOGY

Crow kinship terminology is most often associated with matrilineal descent reckoning. Its terms for relatives contrast those related to ego through matrilineal descent ties (noted in white) to the equivalent relatives of ego's father's matrilineal group (noted with a dot). The terminology is more elaborate for ego's own matrilineal relatives than for his or her father's matrilineal relatives for whom the same terms (Fa and FaZ) are used in both generations.

Omaha kinship terminology patrilineal descent system where mother's patrilineage is distinguished only by sex, regardless of generation

Crow kinship terminology matrilineal descent system where father's matrilineage is distinguished only by sex, regardless of generation

Iroquois kinship terminology bifurcate merging system like the Crow and Omaha systems but in which there is no merging of generations in the lineage that marries into ego's lineage

FIGURE 10.13

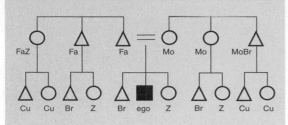

IROQUOIS KINSHIP TERMINOLOGY

Iroquois kinship terminology tends to be found in societies that use unilineal descent reckoning, especially among those that trace ancestry through matrilineal descent. Societies that follow the Iroquois system instead of the Crow or Omaha systems are believed to place less importance on the solidarity of their unilineal kinship groups and are more willing to permit marriage with cousins on either side of the family. For this reason, paternal and maternal cross cousins are not distinguished from one another, and in some variants of the Iroquois system, parallel cousins are not called "brother" and "sister" as shown in this figure but by another term—thereby indicating their acceptability as potential spouses for ego.

system. It, too, assigns different terms for maternal and paternal relatives, while merging father with father's brother and mother with mother's sister. The terms for parallel cousins are similarly merged with the terms for brothers or sisters. Unlike the Omaha and Crow systems, however, the Iroquois system does not merge generations in the lineage that marries into ego's lineage. Instead, ego's cross cousins in both lineages are merged, minimizing the

FIGURE 10.14

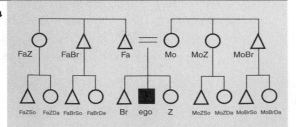

SUDANESE KINSHIP TERMINOLOGY

Sudanese, or descriptive, kinship terminology is common in societies that trace descent patrilineally when status distinctions between individual members of both ego's patrilineage and ego's mother's patrilineage are important. Accordingly, the Sudanese system uses a different term for each relative in each patrilineage.

lineage contrast for members of this one group of kin.

Like Omaha and Crow, Iroquois kinship is most often found in societies with unilineal descent, and it is particularly common in matrilineal societies. Crow, too, is associated with matrilineal social organizations, but Leslie White (1939) suggested that the Crow and Omaha patterns are most likely to develop in a society that is firmly unilineal, while the Iroquois system is most likely in either an incipient or weakening unilineal descent system. Goody (1970) has added the idea that the Iroquois pattern is likely to develop when circumstances favor marriage with either maternal or paternal cross cousins rather than with just the cross cousins of one side of the family.

Sudanese

This kinship system has the largest number of kin terms, so it is sometimes also called **descriptive kinship terminology**. Like many kinship systems, **Sudanese kinship terminology** distinguishes parallel cousins from cross cousins. In addition to the nuclear family terms for mother, father, brother, sister, son, and daughter, this system includes cousin, uncle, and aunt terms that distinguish maternal from paternal relatives.

Referring to each relative by a separate term suggests that the distinctions are culturally relevant. In other words, when descriptive terminology is present, a person's behavior is expected to be different toward each relative. For instance, a person would have a different relationship with a maternal cross cousin than with a paternal cross cousin. Relatively few societies have circumstances in which such diversity of kin relations is necessary, so the descriptive kinship system is a rare one. When it does occur, it is in association with patrilineal descent. Sudanese terminology occurs most often in North Africa.

---

descriptive kinship terminology Sudanese kinship terminology

Sudanese (descriptive) kinship terminology kinship system occurring mostly in North Africa that distinguishes maternal and paternal relatives by separate sets of terms

GODPARENTHOOD AMONG THE CHAN KOM MAYA

The village of Chan Kom in the Mexican state of Yucatan was studied in the 1930s by R. Redfield and Villa Rojas (1934). Its 250 people were Maya Indians whose customs had been influenced by 300 years of Spanish colonial domination. One European custom adopted by the people of Chan Kom was the *padrinazgo*, the choosing of godparents for their children at important ceremonial transitions during the life cycle.

The most important godparents were selected at the time of a child's baptism. The godfather, or *padrino*, and godmother, or *madrina*, took on the obligation to act as parents to the child and to aid it in growing up. In return they were treated with particular respect by the child's parents.

Godparents who had less responsibility were chosen for later changes in the life cycle of the child. The second such event was at the time of the *hetzmek*, the native Maya celebration of the change from infancy to childhood, which occurred when the child was old enough to be carried on its mother's hip instead of in her arms. Godparents were also chosen in preparation for marriage. The same-sex godparent instructed the bride or bridegroom in the marriage ritual and gave advice about the responsibilities that came with marriage. Marriage godparents might also admonish their godchildren at later times for not living up to their marriage responsibilities.

Godparents provided support for community values throughout the lives of their godchildren and so helped them to follow the customs of Chan Kom. Parents and godparents also entered into a kind of fictive kinship relationship called the *compadrazgo*, or coparenthood. This relationship involved formality

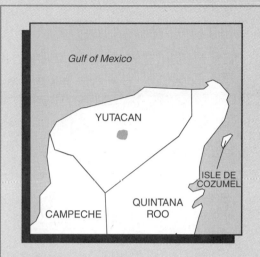

CHAN KOM MAYA

The Maya Indians who lived in the village of Chan Kom in Yucatan, Mexico, adopted the European custom of choosing godparents for their child. Godparents aided the parents in both the physical and spiritual care of the child.

and the expression of mutual respect and concern for one another's welfare. By extending the sense of intimate kinship obligations to the field of nonrelatives, coparenthood helped to further integrate the community throughout the village.

FICTIVE KINSHIP

Sometimes societies create relationships that are thought of as more or less equivalent to kinship relationships between persons who would otherwise not be considered relatives by either descent or marriage. These so-called **fictive kinship** relationships include adopted relatives who become legal equivalents of those who are relatives by birth. They also include persons thought of as ceremonial or quasi-relatives, whose relationships are secondary to those based on descent or marriage. Such ceremonial kinship relationships are established to fulfill special purposes such as establishing a stable economic bond between two persons or pro-

viding foster parents upon the death of the biological parents. Thus, in addition to fully adopted relatives, fictive kin include various kinds of "blood brotherhood" and coparenthood or "godparenthood." Among the Rwala Bedouin, for instance, men sometimes established a brotherhood of *akh* relationship with persons such as traders who were not a part of their own residential groups. This relationship created an obligation to protect the outsider's property. If a raid by one group against the other resulted in the loss of camels by someone

---

fictive kinship socially created kinship relationships involving individuals who are not otherwise considered relatives either by descent or marriage

FIGURE 10.15

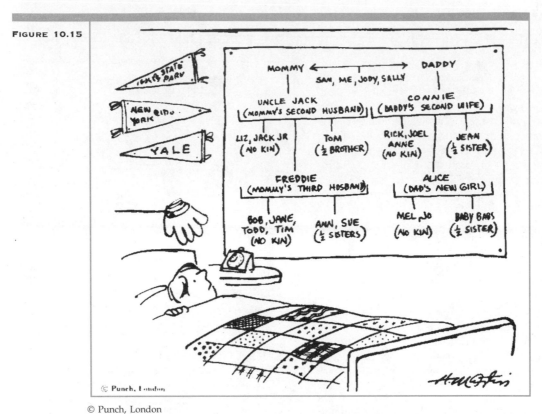

© Punch, London

FICTIVE KINSHIP

In many societies, people establish relationships with others that are not based on descent or marriage. These provide a support system in difficult times in addition to kin. Thus, godparenthood, blood brotherhood and sisterhood, and adoption all give the people involved a sense of belonging and security.

who had an *akh* in the raiding group, the *akh* was bound by honor to recover and return those animals from his own kin. This fictive kin relationship made it easier for traders to travel safely from group to group to conduct trade, an activity that was beneficial to both the traders and the Bedouin.

In societies such as Canada or the United States where kinship relationships are not central to most people's economic lives or political activities, there are fewer situations in which fictive kinship is useful. So there are few powerful contemporary North American examples of the important roles that fictive kin can play as quasi-relatives. In some ways sororities and fraternities create a sibling-like emotional bond among their members, and some groups such as the Masons and Eastern Star have explicit rules for giving aid to a fellow member who is in need.

But the sense of family-like camaraderie or obligation is likely to be more or less restricted to special occasions, such as scheduled meetings for all members. The custom in some North American religions of members' referring to one another with the friendly title of "Brother" or "Sister" is generally little more than a convention, rather than an indication of real involvement in one another's daily affairs. Probably the best example of fictive kinship in contemporary North American cultures is the relationship of godparent to child in some religious traditions. Godparents are expected to undertake a commitment to a child's spiritual upbringing. In other words, especially in regard to the child's religious life, godparents have responsibilities for the child much like those of the child's close kin, and a similar emotional involvement.

CHAPTER SUMMARY

1. The ways in which people think about kinship depend upon how they conceive of descent.

2. Children may be thought of as offspring of their mother, their father, or both. Thus, systems of kinship may be based on matrilineal, patrilineal, ambilineal, or bilateral descent.

3. Groups of people thought of as relatives may be organized into corporate groups such as lineages, clans, phratries, or moieties, or into noncorporate kindreds.

4. The various kinds of kinship groups are related to the economic and social conditions in which they are found.

5. Kinship terminology, of which there are six common types, tends to reflect the kinds of conditions with which people must cope as they work together as relatives.

6. The six patterns of kinship terminology are related, though not perfectly, to the kinds of descent systems that are found in each society.

ANNOTATED READINGS

Collier, J. F., & Yanagisako, J. (1987). *Gender and kinship: Essays toward a unified analysis.* Stanford, CA: Stanford University Press. A collection of articles illustrating recent approaches to kinship that view women and men as equal partners in kinship and marriage.

Keesing, R. M. (1975). *Kin groups and social structure.* New York: Holt, Rinehart & Winston. A study of kinship theory for advanced students.

Graburn, N. (1971). *Readings in kinship and social structure.* New York: Harper & Row. Articles on a wide range of topics and perspectives concerning kinship and society.

Pasternak, B. (1976). *Introduction to kinship and social organization.* New York: Macmillan. Includes an evaluation of theories of kinship and residence.

Schneider, D. M. (1980). *American kinship: A cultural account.* (2nd ed.). Chicago: University of Chicago Press. A symbolic interpretation of U.S. kinship.

Schneider, D. M., & Gough, K. (Eds.). (1961). *Matrilineal kinship.* Berkeley, CA: University of California Press. Discussions of kinship in a number of matrilineal societies.

Schusky, E. L. (1982). *Manual for kinship analysis.* (2nd ed.). New York: Holt, Rinehart & Winston. A short course on the basic tools of the trade for recording and analyzing kinship systems. A good starting point for the student who wants an overview of the basics.

Schusky, E. L. (1975). *Variation in kinship.* New York: Holt, Rinehart & Winston. Another good introduction to kinship, descent, and residence.

CHAPTER ELEVEN

Politics and Culture

◄ *Figure 11.1 Political Authority Through its political system a society exercises power to maintain order internally and to negotiate with other societies. Chief Counselor Bafut of Cameroon attends a gathering of chiefs of several villages. He seems well prepared to record the event.*

Nowhere is political power, the ability to make and implement decisions about public goals, shared equally by every member of society. Whether people share power broadly throughout the entire community, divide power between their family organization and specialized associations, or place power in the hands of full-time governmental officials depends largely on the size and complexity of their societies. But whatever its form, there is always some system for maintaining social order and reestablishing order when rules have been broken. Some combination of childhood socialization, values, morality, religion, rewards for conformity, and threats of punishment is used everywhere to create an ordered society, although never with perfect success. When conflicts do arise, there are a variety of ways, both peaceful and violent, by which people seek to reestablish an orderly life.

Divine kings. Senators. Chiefs. Taboos. Sanctions. Burning at the stake. Song duels. Electrocution. War. If someone steals your dog or cat, would you consider that a greater personal misfortune than if someone steals the radio out of your car? If a golf ball breaks your car window, is the player or the manufacturer of the golf club responsible for the damage? Who should decide on an appropriate punishment or recompense? How should the decision be enforced? Every society establishes a system by which it maintains some order.

TYPES OF POLITICAL ORDERS

According to Swartz, Turner, and Tuden (1966), **politics** is the way in which power is achieved and used to create and implement public goals (p. 7). As such, politics is involved in organizing and controlling human social behavior. It is through its political system that a society exercises power to maintain order internally and to regulate its relations with other societies. Those to whom the right to power is delegated are said to have **authority**, the right to legitimately use force or threaten the use of force to achieve social goals. In the study of politics, it

is important to consider how power is delegated, since not every use of power in society is legitimate.

Anthropologists have noted a variety of ways in which political power is channeled in different societies. Complex societies have full-time political systems with officials who monopolize the legal authority to govern others. Simpler societies make use of other mechanisms for creating and implementing common goals. For instance, governing authority may be vested in the local community, in the family organization, in voluntary associations, or in officials whose authority is limited to those areas not governed by the family, community, or voluntary associations.

Bands: Government by Community

Societies in which people survive by foraging for wild foods in small local groups are **band** societies. They consist typically of 50 or 60 people who cooperate in economic activities. Since most political problems affect the entire local group, it is generally the seat of legal authority. When a legal problem arises, the entire community will discuss the issue in a kind of town meeting until everyone has had ample opportunity to express an opinion. The consensus that evolves out of the give and take of group discussion is the band equivalent of law.

As one example, the handling of homicide by the nineteenth-century Inuit of the northern coasts of North America illustrates the legal role of the community in a band society. The Inuit occupied a harsh environment that placed heavy demands on them. In a territory that offered few plant foods, hunters were under great stress to provide for their families. Game included some rather formidable animals such as the polar bear and large sea mammals that were not easily taken. It is little wonder that successful Inuit hunters were strong-willed and aggressive men. In spite of rules of etiquette

(Continued on p. 264)

politics manner in which power is achieved and used to create and implement public goals

authority the right, delegated to a person or persons, to use force or threaten the use of force legitimately

band a seminomadic, kinship-based society with no full-time government, economically based on a foraging subsistence technology

THE GREAT BASIN SHOSHONE: A BAND SOCIETY

Steward (1938) described the native culture of the Great Basin Shoshone. They occupied a territory that stretched all the way from near Death Valley, California, through central Nevada, northern Utah, and southern Idaho to central Wyoming. It generally is believed that the Shoshone moved into the Great Basin from somewhere near the Death Valley area some 1,000 years ago. Throughout their territory, the Shoshone spoke dialects of the same language, closely related to those of their Great Basin neighbors, the Northern and Southern Paiute and the Ute, who practiced a similar way of life.

The Shoshone were a highly mobile people who hunted game and gathered wild plant foods in a sparse desert environment. Variations in rainfall made the location and amount of plant and animal foods highly variable from year to year. The Shoshone spent much of the year in search of food, wandering in small groups of one to three nuclear families. During the spring and summer months, their food consisted of foraged seeds, berries, roots, and small game such as insects, larvae, rodents, and other small mammals.

Occasionally, several families who usually hunted separately would come upon a large congregation of rabbits. If one of the families owned a rabbit net, a collective hunt would be held. The rabbit net was about 8 feet high and several hundred feet long. It was laid out in a great semicircle, and everyone would fan out to drive the rabbits toward the net. When the rabbits became entangled in the net, they would be clubbed or shot. These hunts provided both meat and furs which, cut into strips and woven into capes, provided warmth in the cold winter season. Similar communal hunts were held when antelope were available. After the hunt was completed and the meat eaten, families would again go their own ways in the search for food.

During the winter months, 20 to 30 families would camp in the same vicinity. Winter was a time for socializing. Dances and gambling were popular recreations. The most common dance was a communal one in which men and women arranged themselves in a great circle and side-stepped in one direction. This dance was believed to have some general health benefits for those who participated.

At the end of the winter, families began to disperse, some having added a new member or two by marriage. New wives left their families of birth and traveled with the families of their husbands. The Shoshone were flexible about their marriage forms, and although most marriages were between one man and one women, both men and women occasionally had more than one spouse. When a man married several women, it was preferred that they be sisters. Marriages created kinship ties between families that were widely dispersed.

Cooperation within and between families was the basis of Shoshone economic and political life. There was no governing authority outside the family. Property was limited to what people carried with them as they traveled, so there was little conflict over property rights. What few conflicts arose could usually be settled within the group on the basis of familial authority. Conflicts between different families were most often concerned with witchcraft accusations or wife stealing. These might be settled by a feud, but the wandering way of life lent itself to conflict avoidance or even to settling of conflicts by each family's simply going its own way rather than pursuing the matter.

Shoshone religion focused on the acquisition of spiritual power, called *puha*, which increased its possessor's skill, luck, and strength. *Puha* could be used to make love or gambling magic, to ensure the success of a hunt, and to cure or to kill. Religious specialists, who devoted more time than others to the acquisition and use of *puha*, were known as *puhakanten*, "power possessors." Some *puhakanten* had the particular ability to attract antelope. Their skill was especially useful during communal antelope drives, since they could help draw the antelope into the corral. Other *puhakanten* devoted themselves to the curing of illnesses when called upon to do so. These spiritual healers were likely to have had a visionary experience in which they acquired a spirit ally known as a *puha newepea* or "power partner." During curing ceremonies, the healer would alternately chant and smoke tobacco until his spiritual ally would come and endow him with the power to cure.

Shoshone religious beliefs included creation stories, known as Coyote stories, in which anthropomorphic animals were the central characters. Coyote, the creator of human beings, was a Trickster, a deity who enjoyed playing practical jokes. Human beings entered the world by escaping from a bundle that he had opened in spite of having been told to leave it closed. He later obtained pine nuts for the hungry Shoshone by stealing this food from wealthier tribes to the north. Coyote stories were enjoyed during the winter encampments but not at other times, since their telling could bring on a storm.

(see reference map p. 199)

FIGURE 11.2

SHOSHONE WINNOWING

The Shoshone wandered in search of their food supply from season to season. This woman on the Lemhi Reservation, Idaho, in 1904 is winnowing wheat using the traditional Shoshone method.

that demanded humility, politeness, and generosity, tempers sometimes did get out of hand, and violent deaths involving disputes about food and women were not rare.

Homicides were often dealt with by the families of the deceased. Revenge killings were legitimate, but might in turn lead to vengeance by the original killer's kin. So ultimate legal authority was vested in the community as a whole. It dealt with aggressive repeat offenders who were seen as threats to the common welfare. Boas (1888) described the role of community law enforcement among one group of Inuit:

> There was a native of Padli by the name of Padlu. He had induced the wife of a native of Cumberland Sound to desert her husband and follow him. The deserted husband, meditating revenge . . . visited his friends in Padli, but before he could accomplish his intention of killing Padlu, the latter shot him. . . . A brother of

the murdered man went to Padli to avenge the death of his brother; but he also was killed by Padlu. A third native of Cumberland Sound who wished to avenge the death of his relatives was also murdered by him.

> On account of all these outrages the natives wanted to get rid of Padlu, but yet they did not dare to attack him. When the *pimain* (headman) of the Akudmirmiut learned of these events he started southward and asked every man in Padli whether Padlu should be killed. All agreed; so he went with the latter deer hunting . . . and . . . shot Padlu in the back. (p. 582)

Because the entire community had acted as a judicial body and authorized the killing, it was a legal execution, and they had no need to fear any retribution by Padlu's relatives.

Leadership in Bands. As might be expected, band societies lack sufficient resources to support any full-time educational, economic, religious, military, judicial, legislative, or executive specialists. All leadership is charismatic. That is, a man or woman becomes a leader in some activity because of a personal talent in that area. Leadership also is unofficial; it is maintained only so long as a person demonstrates the qualities of excellence that draw a following. Charismatic leadership confers no authority, no power to coerce. A leader can only lend advice or take the initiative. Coming from a man or woman of respected abilities or wisdom, the advice or action is apt to be followed by others. The leader in the hunt, for example, is likely to be a man of proven ability in locating, tracking, and capturing game; a leader in political matters is respected because of his broad experience and proven wisdom. In both cases, however, as abilities decline, so does the leader's following.

Tribes: Government by Families and Associations

Societies with simple food domestication technologies that support local populations and that are small enough to need no full-time governmental authorities are known as **tribes**. Le-

(Continued on p. 266)

tribe a semisedentary kinship-based society without a full-time government; most often economically based on a simple food domestication subsistence technology, either horticulture or pastoralism

THE TODA: A TRIBAL SOCIETY

Rivers (1901) described the Toda, a pastoral tribe of India. The Toda lived on a high plateau in southern India. They made their living by herding buffalo. Since they practiced no agriculture, the Toda supplied neighboring tribes with dairy products from their herds in return for farm products, pottery, ironware, and other goods and services. As might be expected, buffalo were extremely important to the Toda. Cows were individually named, and their pedigrees were carefully remembered. Some herds were regarded as sacred and were tended by special dairymen at sacred dairy temples. The ancestors of these sacred herds played an important role in the creation myths of the Toda, who believed that when the first 1,600 sacred buffalo were created by one of the gods, the first human appeared holding onto the tail of the last buffalo—an apt symbol of the Toda's economic dependence on their herds.

Although families and clans were the main decision-making bodies among the Toda, their pastoral way of life had created a population density that was too great for all problems to be settled without some mechanism that superseded clan membership. This mechanism was an incipient government organization, a tribal council known as the *naim*. Its five members always came from certain families of specific clans. Lacking the authority of the true governments of more complex societies, the *naim* had no voice in criminal matters. Its primary functions were to regulate ceremonies and to settle disputes between individuals, between families, and between clans.

Population growth was limited by the Toda's location. Their land was bounded on all sides. In the southern directions, cliffs dropped from 3,000 to 5,000 feet. To the north were agriculturalists. With no room for expansion, the Toda had sought to solve the problem of population growth by limiting the number of women and therefore the number of children born in each generation. This was accomplished by the practice of infanticide, in which unwanted infants, especially girls, were suffocated shortly after birth. This led to a surplus of men in each generation. To rectify this imbalance the Toda practiced polyandry, a form of marriage in which one woman has more than one husband.

Marriages were arranged, and they occurred between children as young as two or three years of age. The girl was considered to be the wife of the boy with whom the marriage ceremony was performed and of all his brothers, including those born thereafter. Until she was 15 or 16, the bride lived with her own parents. Shortly before puberty, she had to be initiated into sex by a man selected from the group to which her family did not belong, that is, to a man whom she would not be permitted

to marry. If this ceremonial loss of virginity did not occur before puberty, the bride was stigmatized for life, and her marriage would be canceled.

Since a woman could have many husbands, fatherhood had to be designated on some basis other than that of biological paternity. Thus, among the Toda, a man became a father by performing an important ritual. A man and a pregnant woman went into the forest, where the man carved a niche in a tree, placed an oil lamp into it, promised the woman a calf, and ceremonially presented her with an imitation bow and arrow. She held the bow and arrow to her forehead and watched the lamp until it burned out. Afterwards, he prepared a meal, and the two spent the night together. From this time forward, he would be the father of all children to whom she would give birth, until some other man performed the same ceremony with her to supersede him as father of her children. Although usually one of a woman's husbands held the status of father of her children, it was possible for a man who was not one of her husbands to perform the bow-giving ceremony with her.

TODA

A tribal society in southern India, the Toda made their living herding buffalo. The main decision-making government bodies were families and clans. As population grew, a tribal council was formed that regulated ceremonies and settled disputes when asked to do so. The decision of this *naim* superseded all others.

gal authority is held by the families of the local group and by voluntary associations, or **sodalities**, whose members are drawn from at least several of the families of the community. Family law typically rules in domestic matters such as the contracting or dissolving of marriage and the punishment of family members for violation of one another's rights. Voluntary associations often play a role in the military defense of the local community and in policing the community itself, at least in matters that are not traditionally regarded as within the realm of family law.

The tribes of the North American plains illustrated well the political role of voluntary associations. Each community typically had a dozen or so military societies. In some tribes, young men graduated from one society into the next as they aged; in others, they had to choose which they would join. The military associations exercised legal authority as governing agencies by preserving order during hunts and while camp was being moved, and by punishing lawbreakers. But they also performed social, recreational, and economic roles in hosting feasts and dances, holding intersociety competitions, keeping tribal traditions, and providing information about the location of buffalo herds.

Policing Role. Among Plains Indians, each military society usually held policing authority for only a year, so that this responsibility was rotated among the associations of a community, and no one monopolized the right to police power. Enforcement of tribal laws by military societies was also limited to crimes that harmed the community welfare. Thus, on communal buffalo hunts, someone who began to shoot too soon and frightened the herd away before others were prepared was likely to be punished. The emphasis was on making the culprit an example to discourage similar behavior by others. Public punishments included the destruction of a wrongdoer's property, banishment from the camp, and death.

The Plains Indians relied heavily on the migratory buffalo that passed through their territories each year, and competition for this valuable resource brought the highly mobile, horseback-hunting tribes into recurrent conflict. The military associations protected their communities against other plundering tribes. The greatest defenders of the tribe in each military society were rewarded with honor and the plunder of war. In ceremonial meetings, these warriors recounted their exploits in battle, and it was from these men that the more formal political leaders were selected for the tribe.

Social Roles. Plains military societies also played an important role in public recreation. They performed dances as public exhibitions and generally interacted with the audience in their celebrations. For their own members, the military associations provided fraternal camaraderie and a place in which deep friendships could evolve.

As in bands, leadership in tribes is charismatic. It is achieved by an individual's personal ability to convince others that his or her unique qualities make him or her especially worthy of being followed. Thus, leadership is based on skill rather than the power of an inherited status. By and large, tribal society is egalitarian like the band society, in that every individual has more or less equal opportunity to obtain the necessities of life and the esteem of others in leadership activities. Leaders include the charismatic entrepreneurs discussed in chapter 8 who stimulate local economic productivity through the process of bigmanship.

Chiefdoms: Government by Officials

A society that unites a number of villages under the legal control of a government that recognizes the right of families to exercise some autonomous legal authority is a **chiefdom**. A chiefdom's governmental official, called a chief, can legitimately use force in matters that concern the common welfare. However, kinship groups such as the family exercise a great deal of legal autonomy. For instance, laws that govern marriage and divorce are typically matters of family law, just as they are in bands and tribes. Similarly, the enforcement of laws concerning petty theft is often a responsibility of kinship groups in chiefdoms, as in bands and tribes. However, major crimes that concern the entire community, such as grand theft, homicide, or insults to the dignity of a chief, are typically punishable by the government officials

---

sodality voluntary associations whose members are drawn from several tribal families

chiefdom a society, often of many villages, that has a government capable of coordinating social action within and between villages but in which governmental authority is balanced by the legal autonomy of families in many areas who have authority over nonrelatives in legal matters. Thus, chiefdoms have a true professional government, but one whose officials do not monopolize all legal authority to govern society. Their authority is balanced by that of each community's kinship groups, who govern themselves in those areas that most directly affect them.

Each community in a chiefdom is likely to have a chief who acts as its political head, and groups of villages usually will be unified under a district chief of higher rank than the local village ones. In some legal matters, members of the community may expect the chiefs or their delegated representatives to play the role of mediator between the conflicting parties, with the goal of reestablishing peaceful relations. In other cases, the chief may have the authority to determine guilt or innocence and exact punishment for an offense without consulting the members of the offender's family. The position of chief is therefore a true office, and its holder has authority to legitimately wield power over others with whom the chief has no known kinship ties.

The office of chief is most often hereditary, although which relative of a deceased chief will inherit the office may be decided by the surviving family members. In some cases, the community as a whole may have some say in the selection of the new chief from the group of possible heirs. Chiefdoms are typically theocratic societies in which the office of the chief is legitimized by both religious and secular authority. Indeed, some of the higher-ranking political officials may be considered sacred.

In chiefdoms, governmental authority includes the right to tax and to redistribute produce. This makes possible everyday functions of government such as military defense, local community policing, judicial activities, and drafting labor for public works projects. Probably the most important function of chiefs, however, is economic: to redistribute goods and provide services. All families in the community are expected to contribute a portion of their annual produce to the warehouse. The chief then sees to it that these goods are redistributed, generally at community feasts or festivals, to those most in need. A chief's power and prestige are often directly proportionate to his or her generosity. Indeed, the level of gift giving expected of a chief may exceed the total contributed by other families, so that the wealth of the chief's family is gradually drained to the benefit of less prestigious families.

FIGURE 11.3

ZULU CHIEFS
Most societies that are organized into chiefdoms consist of several communities, each headed by a chief. In post-apartheid South Africa, conflicts have arisen between President Nelson Mandela, who seeks to expand the authority of the government into rural areas, and the 300 or so chiefs of the Zulus, who wish to maintain their autonomous authority. Chief T. D. Ntombela, pictured above, also a member of the legislature of the province of Kwa Zulu/Natal, recently argued against the central government's attempted financial support of the chiefs. He believes that a chief enjoys both the mandate of heaven and the confidence of his tribesmen, who alone are empowered to remove him.

Simple chiefdoms lack true social classes in which people's rank depends on the importance of their occupations. Neither are they egalitarian, since their kinship groups are ranked in a social hierarchy in which some families have greater social power and prestige than others. For this reason, chiefdoms are sometimes called **rank societies** (Fried, 1967; Service, 1962, 1978). Political offices are usually inherited so that they remain within certain families, and the highest-ranking families normally have control over the most important political offices.

---

rank societies kinship groups in a chiefdom that are ranked in a social rather than occupational hierarchy

THE RWALA BEDOUINS: A PASTORAL CHIEFDOM

According to Musil (1928), the Rwala had the largest and most powerful tent-dwelling Bedouin chiefdom of the northern Arabian peninsula. Although much of their life was organized around the concept of kinship, the Rwala also had officials with authority beyond the boundaries of their own kin. These chiefs or *sheikhs* were officers whose positions were inherited within particular patrilineal lineages. In addition to local *sheikhs* whose authority was felt throughout an entire camp, there were regional chiefs as well, whose authority derived from a lineage of greater prominence than those of the local chiefs. There was also a paramount chief or *sheikh*, often called a "prince," over all the Rwala. His main duties were to conduct relations with the national government and with chiefs of other Bedouin peoples, but he had little power over the internal politics of the Rwala themselves.

Life in the camps was largely governed by kinship. Each man saw himself as the center of a group of relatives, or kindred, known as the *ahl*. A man's *ahl* consisted of all his sons and their sons, his father and grandfather, and their brothers. This group of relatives had strong obligations to him and could bear the guilt for his misdeeds. People were also organized into larger kinship groups called *feriz* that included relatives who traced their ancestry through their fathers back to a common male ancestor. Marriages were pref-erably within one's *feriz*. In particular, a man was encouraged to marry his father's brother's daughter or his father's father's brother's son's daughter. A woman could marry no other man unless her designated cousin waived his prior claim. The marriage preference system counteracted the fragmenting effects of the Bedouin pastoral adaptation to a desert environment, kept inheritable property from being dispersed, and increased their solidarity (Barth, 1954; Murphy & Kasdan, 1959).

The Rwala made their living by herding camels, which could provide transportation, milk for food, and hides and hair for manufacturing items. Camels were traded to merchants in return for cash, weapons, clothing, and other necessities. Trade was important, for the desert environment did not permit the Bedouins to be completely self-sufficient.

Warfare was a central fact of Rwala life, and it tinged many other aspects of their culture. The main reason for warfare, which consisted most often of surprise night raids on the enemy camp, was to retrieve animals that had been stolen. Weaker groups of Bedouins and villagers paid protection tribute (*khuwa*) to more powerful ones such as the Rwala. The receiver of this protection "tax" was bound to protect those who paid it and to restore any property that was stolen from them by raiders. The Rwala enjoyed war, because it

---

Beyond the superior social rank of chiefs' families, some chiefdoms may develop a true class distinction between chiefs and common-ers that cuts across communities (Earle, 1978). These complex chiefdoms also develop specialization in leadership roles and a more centralized political hierarchy. According to Henry T. Wright (1987), the political organization of chiefdoms varies in complexity along a continuum. In simple chiefdoms, political control is in the hands of a local elite, and there is only one level of political authority above that of the local community. Complex chiefdoms are those in which the competition for leadership at the higher level has created a class of chiefly competitors. As a result, these chiefdoms "characteristically cycle between one and two levels of [political] hierarchy above the level of the local community" (p. 43). In complex chiefdoms the community where the paramount chief resides is larger than those of the ordinary chiefs, partly because it is also the residence of his followers, who make up his power base, and partly because it is a center for major social rituals. Complex chiefdoms also have settlements of intermediate size that are controlled by subordinate chiefs. It is in the smallest settlements, however, that the primary work of subsistence production is done.

Those who belong to the chiefly class occupy their own segregated neighborhoods within their communities or live in separate communities reserved for the noble group. The burials of chiefs are also in segregated community locations often near where major rituals occur; as in simple chiefdoms, these burials are much more ornate than those of commoners. The economic role of chiefs as managers of redistribution shifts in complex chiefdoms from the distribution of goods to all families within the community to extracting tribute from the common class within producing communities

was an opportunity not only to win booty but also to display their skill and courage. Old age was rare for males, since over 80 percent of Rwala men died as a result of warfare.

Blood feuds were also common among the Rwala. Kin were obligated to avenge the murder of a relative, and the murderer's kin shared the guilt to the third generation. The avengers therefore could take the life of a relative of the actual culprit, should they happen on one before finding the murderer. Vengeance of this kind was legitimate, a matter of family law. Guilty parties were not permitted to defend themselves against avengers, but instead had to seek the protection of a powerful *sheikh* who aided them in reaching a traditional place of refuge, where they stayed until the avengers agreed to accept a blood price of horses, camels, and weapons to compensate them for the death.

Today, the Bedouin, who number about five million, live a more settled life. Camels for the most part have been replaced by Toyota trucks for transportation, and tents have given way to cinder-block houses. Sheep and goat herds remain an important source of livelihood for many Bedouin, but other occupations and sources of income have also been adopted. Some engage in dry farming. Others derive income from the tourist market. Members of the older generation sometimes complain that younger people know too little about herding and are only skilled at repairing trucks and televisions.

RWALA BEDOUINS

Living in the northern Arabian peninsula, the Rwala Bedouins organized their government around a hierarchy of local and regional chiefs with a paramount chief who had authority to negotiate with the national government and with chiefs of other Bedouin tribes. He had, however, little power over the internal politics of the Rwala.

and redistributing some of this tribute to the lower chiefs. As chiefdoms increase in complexity, the redistributive goods exacted as tribute shift from basic subsistence goods toward commodities produced by specialists. These economic specialists, who produce prestige goods—which are not available to commoners—may be supported either by the food producers in their communities or, alternatively, by the chiefs with payments gained from the tribute paid by the food-producing class.

States: The Official Monopoly of Law

Because chiefdoms vary in their degree of social complexity and the power of their governments, the social differences between a complex chiefdom and a small state society may be slight. The defining difference is essentially one of political ideology: a **state** is a political unit

in which a centralized government *monopolizes* the right to exercise legal force and control the affairs of local communities. It has power to levy taxes, pass laws, and draft people into work or war.

The principle that a state monopolizes the legitimate use of force is well illustrated by Ashanti law. The Ashanti, described by Rattray (1923, 1929), made up a West African state in what is now Ghana. The Ashanti state was ruled by a divine king who, like Louis XIV of France, represented the very source of the state's authority. So sacred was the king's personage that cursing him was punishable by a heavy fine. Indeed, to curse the king was such a terrible thing that it could only be spoken of by the euphemism, "to bless the king."

state a society with a centralized government that monopolizes the legal authority to use force

Only the divine king or his duly authorized representatives had the authority to use any force. Since any crime involved the use of force, it was, in a sense, theft of the king's authority and an insult to the sacred ancestors that he represented. All crimes were punishable by death.

The view that crimes were punishable primarily because they undermined the authority of the state and only secondarily because they victimized others led to another interesting aspect of Ashanti law. Suicide, like murder, involved taking the life of an Ashanti. Like murder, it was a contemptible affront to the king and the ancestors. So the body of a suicide was tried and, if found guilty, decapitated. By so doing, Ashanti law symbolically demonstrated the sanctity of the state's authority. Odd as this legal custom may seem to North Americans, it is not very different in principle from U.S. and Canadian customs in which persons who attempt suicide may be confined in mental hospitals by judicial order for violating the law by having tried to kill themselves. Although North Americans speak of such confinement as "hospitalization" for "treatment of a mental disorder," the symbolic aspects of the customs are similar. Both the Ashanti and North Americans punish suicide offenders through a judicial process.

Origins of State Societies.   According to Fried (1967), social stratification of the type characteristic of chiefdoms is inherently unstable because of the competition for political authority and its control over basic resources. In his opinion, this instability can bring about the dissolution of political authority and the return to a simpler social organization, but on a few occasions the political struggles may "evolve more power institutions of political control than ever were called upon to maintain a system of differential ranking" (p. 226). In his view, the state arises in the attempt by chiefs to maintain social order in a setting of political conflict. Thus, the state utilizes coercive mechanisms such as the army, police, and militia, which serve to maintain its monopoly on legal authority.

In those places where the first states evolved from chiefdoms, several widespread social changes marked achievement of this new social type. In the words of Jonathan Haas (1982), these included "major innovations and additions not only in art styles and settlement patterns, but also in monumental architecture and other labor projects, in recording and calendrical systems, and in religion" (p. 123).

The major change in subsistence activities between the chiefdom and the state society is the development of more intensive agriculture in the state society. This difference is due to innovations in agricultural technology. Not only are the plow and draft animals almost always present in societies that support a state-level political organization, but agricultural technology is generally much more complex in these societies as well. Irrigation systems, for example, play such a major role in the agriculture of most states that one scholar, Karl Wittfogel (1957), has suggested that it was the need to control and regulate water resources that led to the rise of the world's first states. This view has not been widely accepted, because it places too much emphasis on the single factor of irrigation at the expense of others, such as population growth, trade, diplomacy, and warfare. But it reminds us that irrigation was an important technological development in increasing the productivity of the state's subsistence activities.

Robert Carneiro (1970) suggests that states arise in circumscribed environmental zones—areas surrounded by mountains, deserts, or other natural barriers to easy emigration—when population growth causes increased social competition for natural resources. This competition leads to social stratification and the domination of some groups by others. Centralized political power creates elites who are able to exact tribute and taxes from the dominated groups. Circumscribed habitats make it difficult for those who are losing in the competition to withdraw to other areas.

According to Carneiro (1970), once states develop, they tend to expand at the expense of neighboring chiefdoms, tribes, and bands whose smaller populations make them less powerful. Members of a state society may number in the millions, owing to the food supply provided by truly intensive agriculture. They live in densely packed towns and cities in which little or no agriculture may be practiced. They also live in more rural communities of smaller size that specialize in the production of particular kinds of food, which can be exchanged for the nonagricultural products of the larger communities.

GENDER AND POLITICS

In societies throughout the world, political offices are held predominantly by men. But even in societies in which men hold most positions of political power, women have a degree of political power and influence. In patriarchal societies in which men are economically and socially dominant, women's power and influence is indirect, but in more egalitarian societies it can be formally institutionalized. For instance, in some egalitarian societies the political organization has been characterized by a joint male-female system of authority, and in some the greatest solidarity at the local village level has been among women.

Matrifocal Societies

Women have had the greatest political power in those societies in which they are the economic producers and control economic resources. Nancy Tanner (1974), a specialist in the anthropology of legal processes, investigated **matrifocal societies**, where the primary solidarity relations involve women. She found that women in these societies were decision makers at least as assertive as men, in addition to playing the preeminent economic role. Female relatives were in frequent contact with each other through mutual-aid groups that were a source of power and support that was not dependent on men. In these societies, most women generally occupied central kinship positions within their families of birth. For instance, the role of a mother in the family was typically more important than that of a wife.

In contemporary nation-states, women have also achieved high political positions, but not to the degree that is typical of matrifocal societies. For instance, Kim Campbell of Canada, Golda Meir of Israel, Corazon Aquino of the Philippines, Indira Gandhi of India, and Margaret Thatcher of Great Britain have all held positions as prime minister or president of their respective countries. Yet, worldwide statistics indicate that women continue to be numerically underrepresented in governmental offices. According to geographers Joni Seager and Ann Olson (1986), even in the Scandinavian countries, in Ghana, and in Panama, where women have the highest rates of representation in their national government, they hold only about one in four elected positions (p. 115).

The Iroquois. The Iroquois of the North American Great Lakes region have often been cited as a society whose culture defined women and men as equals. According to the nineteenth-century anthropologist Lewis Henry Morgan (1851), Iroquois children belonged to their mothers' families. Husbands were in-laws within their wives' households and had no authority over their wives or her children. Houses and gardens were owned by women and inherited by daughters, so women were not economically dependent on men. The highest governmental officials were a council of fifty chiefs, or *sachems*. These offices were hereditary within the maternal families; they most often went from a man to his younger brother or to a sister's son, but the actual choice was made by a vote within the family. Since only women were permitted to select the candidates for other family members to accept or reject, Iroquois women exercised the authority of political office in this way. Although only males were chosen to fill these offices, it was usually possible for a family to select an infant as a sachem. Functionally, such a choice amounted to electing the infant's mother to the office, since she fulfilled all the regular duties of a sachem on behalf of her son until he became mature enough to exercise the authority of his office.

The Dahomeans. According to historian Karl Polanyi (1966), women in the West African kingdom of Dahomey, which is now the republic of Benin, played even more prominent roles in political office than did Iroquois women. In the Dahomey government, every office held by a male had a corresponding position that was held by a female who was responsible for overseeing the work of the male official. Men held their offices in various places throughout the kingdom, while the women resided at the royal palace, where they could report to the king. Men who served the king could only see the king if they were accompanied by the women who maintained oversight of their work. Even the king had such a counterpart, the Queen Mother, whose status was higher than that of

---

matrifocal societies societies in which the primary solidarity relations involve women

the king. The Dahomean army had a similar organization. In the 1800s, the Dahomean army consisted of nearly equal numbers of male and female warriors and officers. The elite military corps that guarded the palace was comprised of about 2,500 celibate women warriors. The Dahomean joint male-female system for organizing the government and the military functioned very effectively to perpetuate the authority of the king by insulating him from male competitors.

The Lobedu. According to Eileen J. Krige and J. D. Krige (1943), the Lobedu of what is now Mozambique and some of their neighbors vested supreme authority in queens. The Lobedu queens had no military groups to enforce their authority. Instead, they held their office because of their religious power to bring rain to their people and to withhold it from their enemies. Thus, the Lobedu queen was the source of her subjects' welfare and general prosperity, and they regarded her as sacred. Her life was filled primarily with religious responsibilities and ritual prohibitions designed to perpetuate the well-being of her nation, and at the end of a reign of approximately 40 years she was expected to commit ritual suicide—a custom that was done away with in the 1950s. A judicial system consisted of women who were appointed by the queen to represent the various districts of the nation.

The Lobedu queen was not permitted to marry, although she might bear children whose "father" would be selected from among her relatives. She was expected to maintain a "harem" of women who were bestowed upon her as "wives" by local chiefs and nobles of her society and sometimes by foreign leaders. This custom created a network of political alliances that ensured loyalty and good relations between other important officials and the Lobedu queen, who became a "son-in-law" to the wife-givers. The queen sometimes created similar advantageous political ties with Lobedu men by arranging marriages between them and women of the harem. In implementing these customs, the Lobedu queen played roles very similar to those that were elsewhere played by kings who entered marriages primarily for political reasons.

The Ibo. Kamene Okonjo (1976) has described a similar female-male political organization among the Ibo of Nigeria, who had two monarchs, a queen and a king. Each exercized authority in their own areas of responsibility. The king's responsibilities primarily involved the lives and activities of men, while the queen was consulted on matters that affected women. Men and women had separate political organizations that paralleled each other in form and function. For instance, women settled disputes among women, but made decisions that affected both women and men. Margery Perham (1937) documented how in 1929 Ibo women exercised their political power by rioting against the British colonial government to express their dissatisfaction with policies that they deemed harmful to women's interests in Nigeria. Called the "the women's war" by the Ibo, this political action influenced about 2 million people over an area of 6,000 square miles.

INDIGENOUS PEOPLES AND POLITICS

Political power is not always equally shared by every social group. Minority statuses are typically not as influential in political life as are nonminorities. Indigenous peoples are commonly the most disenfranchised groups (see chapter 7). The extreme lack of political influence of indigenous peoples can be illustrated by the case of Native Americans in the United States. In mid-1995 there were about 1,918,000 people in the United States legally defined as American Indians. The impact of minority status on indigenous Americans is clear: Native Americans have the lowest life expectancy, at 63 years, and the highest unemployment rates, about 50 percent, of any ethnic or racial group in the United States. They also fall below the nation as a whole in average income, housing, and education.

Originally, Native Americans were the only inhabitants of the lands now under control of the U.S. government. Now, they find themselves in the unusual position of being citizens both of the United States and of tribal groups that the Supreme Court has called "domestic dependent nations" of the United States (*Cherokee Nation v. Georgia*, 5 Pet. 10 [1831]). This ambiguous legal state of affairs stems from the political history of relations between the U.S. government and the original Native American

FIGURE 11.4

PRESIDENT BILL CLINTON GREETS SOME TAOS PUEBLO NATIVE AMERICANS

Native Americans lack political power in a land which once belonged solely to them. Many are in the unusual position of being citizens both of the United States and of their own tribal group. Thus, they are governed in part by federal bureaus, in part by the states in which they reside, and in part by their own tribes. These Taos Pueblo Indians performed their version of the national anthem in Los Alamos, New Mexico, prior to an address by President Bill Clinton. He then greeted the performers as did Governor Bruce King (center) and Senator Pete Domenici, both of New Mexico.

societies that it conquered as it expanded its borders.

From the viewpoint of Native Americans, the founders of what was to become the United States entered North America as immigrants. Although the incoming population was originally small, its numbers grew rapidly from continued immigration and a high birth rate, and its economic and political power increased based on the development of industry and technology. Initially, the U.S. government formally recognized the sovereignty of Native American tribes. The Northwest Ordinance of 1787, ratified by the First Congress in 1789, declared, "The utmost good faith shall always be observed towards Indians; their lands and property shall never be taken from them without their consent."

Nevertheless, as the immigrant population expanded across much of the North American continent, its citizens entered lands occupied by Native Americans, who found themselves overwhelmed by U.S. military power. When Native American societies did attempt to regulate their relations with the U.S. government and minimize the loss of their own lands and cultural identities by the negotiation of treaties, they were at first treated as foreign nations. Thus Native American tribes typically ceded some of their lands to the United States while reserving other lands to themselves, and the United States acknowledged Native American sovereignty over their own lands, while sometimes promising economic aid and educational rights to the tribal groups in return for the ceded lands.

Native American–U.S. relations never remained as clear-cut as the contents of these treaties suggest, however. The expansion of the U.S. domain eventually engulfed the various Native American territories and left Native American societies in a more powerless position than that of other peoples who had entered into treaties with the United States. In 1823, the Supreme Court declared that the U.S. government had the right to govern Native Americans, saying that "the discovery and conquest gives the conquerors sovereignty over and ownership of the lands obtained" (*Johnson v. McIntosh*, 21 U.S. 542). Thus, lands that Native Americans thought that they had reserved to themselves through treaties became officially administered as parts of the United States itself. Tribes were no longer to be treated as sovereign nations within their own territories, but as dependent peoples of the U.S. government. This process was formalized when the U.S. Congress unilaterally passed legislation in 1924 that declared all Native Americans born within the territorial limits of the United States to be U.S. citizens.

Following the extension of U.S. citizenship to Native Americans, it was easy to forget that "reservations" were U.S. lands that had been held in trust for Native Americans who had not yet adjusted to mainstream U.S. life. U.S. treaty obligations to residents of Native American lands came to be seen by many non–Native Americans as "special treatment" by the federal government. There followed a period during which tribes were encouraged to disincorporate as tribal entities in return for settlement of claims that they had unsuccessfully pursued for lands lost to states and to the federal government. Some tribes ceased to exist under this policy. Others remained. Today, there are still 287 Native American reservations in the United States, governed in part by the tribes, in part by federal bureaus, and in part by the states in or next to which they are located.

The uneasy mix of governing powers that controls the destinies of reservation residents is a continuing source of conflict, both among Native Americans and between reservation governments and non–Native American political bodies. For instance, Crees and other tribes whose traditional lands straddled the U.S.-Canadian border were guaranteed the right to pass unimpeded from one country to the other by an early treaty between the United States and Canada. This right is still in force, although U.S. border officials occasionally express annoyance at its use by Native Americans whose vehicles are immune to the searches that may legally be made of other vehicles that cross the border.

Many times the legal conflicts over Native American rights become major court cases be-

cause of the economic interests that are at stake. For instance, treaties with the Lumhi and several other tribes in the state of Washington have guaranteed them free and unregulated fishing rights. These rights have been challenged by representatives of the commercial fishing industry and by government agencies concerned with recreational fishing, both of which have economic interests in the maintenance of fishing quotas that those treaties prevent them from imposing on members of the tribes. In Utah, important legal cases have been fought in the 1980s over whether the state government has the right to tax oil companies for oil produced by wells on the Ute Indian reservation, and over the right of the tribe to exercise police authority over predominantly non–Native American towns that lie within the Ute reservation. In 1989, the Ute government declared that the federal government and the state of Utah had abrogated their contractual obligation to build irrigation projects on the reservation in return for rights to irrigated water that flows from the reservation—opening the way for the tribe to withhold that water in the future. In Idaho, a conflict continues that threatens a major source of revenue for the Shoshone and Bannock of the Fort Hall Reservation. For years, sales of goods such as cigarettes at untaxed prices have been an important attraction for tourist dollars on the reservation. The Idaho state government is now asserting that this practice is illegal, and that the tribe must collect state taxes on all such sales. The tribal government, on the other hand, asserts that the state of Idaho has no authority over tribal business practices, since reservation lands are not legally part of the state. A similar conflict is occurring between the state of New York and two Indian tribes, the Mohawks and the Seneca.

Sometimes the conflicting views of Native American authority to govern their own lands have reached the point of forceful and even violent confrontations. For instance, in 1986 the city of Scottsdale, Arizona, refused to renegotiate the rights for non–Native Americans' use of the Pima highway, an important commuter road on reservation land. In response, the tribe eventually closed the highway to further use by non–Native Americans. Bonfires and barricades stopped the flow of traffic until the city government capitulated. More recently, in July 1989 the New York state police sealed off the St. Regis reservation because Mohawk American Indians had continued to open gambling

(Continued on p. 276)

LEGAL GAMBLING ON INDIAN RESERVATIONS

In the United States, about 150 gambling casinos and bingo parlors represent a billion-dollar-a-year source of income on Native American reservations, where about 50 percent of the population is unemployed. Although all but two states permit some form of legal gambling, the flow of revenues from states into the reservations has been politically controversial. In 1988 the U.S. Congress passed the Indian Gaming Regulatory Act, which made gambling on Native American reservations dependent on the status of gambling in the states in which the reservations are located. Under this law, if states have legal gambling, then they must negotiate "in good faith" with tribal governments about allowing gambling on the reservations as well. The issues often turn on what constitutes "good-faith" negotiating by the states and on identifying the forms of gambling that fall into the same class as those allowed under state law. Several tribes have filed lawsuits against states to attempt to force them to negotiate compacts with the tribes. In one such case, the U.S. District Court decided against the Ponca tribe, ruling that the state of Oklahoma could not be forced to conclude a gambling compact with the tribe. Under this interpretation of the law, states would be able to prevent gambling on Native American reservations simply by refusing to sign a compact with the tribes.

On April 4, 1992, U.S. Interior Secretary Manuel Lujan sent a memo to then-president George Bush's chief of staff to indicate that he had reversed his earlier position in support of legalized gambling on Native American reservations. He argued that the policy might be interpreted as being contrary to the Bush administration's position on family values, especially in states that opposed gambling.

Eight days after Secretary Lujan's memo was reported in the news media, FBI agents began a series of raids on reservations in Arizona to enforce the new rules on reservation gambling. Gaming is legal in Arizona, but the state has refused to accept gambling machines on reservations, where gambling generates $45 million a year for Native Americans. Casinos, a major source of family income for some tribes, were closed on the Fort McDowell–Yavapai reservation near Phoenix, the Tohono O'odham and Pascua Yaqui reservations near Tucson, the Tonto Apache reservation in Payson, and the Yavapai reservation near Prescott. On the Fort McDowell reservation, FBI agents entered casinos and loaded $3 million worth of video gambling machines into eight moving vans. Yavapai on that reservation responded by blocking exits from the parking lot with cars, trucks, and road-grading equipment. Af-

ter Arizona governor Fife Symington negotiated a truce, 30 federal agents were allowed to leave the casino in which they had taken refuge. Native Americans kept the parking lot under a 24-hour watch, while they continued to negotiate their right to gaming on the reservation.

On May 12, 1992, Governor Symington told representatives of seven Indian tribes that he would favor letting tribes reinstitute the same type of gambling that they had had before the raids. Negotiations regarding gambling resumed after Indians agreed to allow the FBI to warehouse the video slot machines until a formal agreement was reached with the state. After three months of negotiations, the FBI returned the 349 machines to the Fort McDowell reservation, under an agreement that they would not be used for gambling until the negotiations with the state were concluded. The tribe placed the gaming machines in a warehouse just outside a casino. Along with the machines, the FBI also presented the tribe with a bill for $104,102 for storage of the machines during the three months that the federal agency had held them. Many Indians on reservations, where unemployment rates are typically about 50 percent, regard the economic development represented by the jobs and income generated by casinos as supportive of family values. For instance, the Mashantucket Pequot Reservation in Connecticut is the home of an Indian tribe which runs the Foxwood Casino, currently the only casino in the state. This makes the casino extremely profitable, with yearly revenues of over $800 million to $900 million. The income has permitted the 320-member tribe to buy thousands of acres of land in cities near the reservation. The Department of the Interior has granted them permission to expand the reservation by more than 20 percent by annexing 247 acres of land lying within the boundaries of the town of Ledyard.

Pequot tribal wealth has also made its government politically influential. The tribe is one of the largest private employers in Connecticut. It voluntarily gives more than $130 million a year to the state in exchange for a monopoly on slot machines, it is one of the largest single contributors to the Democratic National Committee, and also donates heavily to state party committees in Connecticut. The rapid expansion of tribal holdings in neighboring towns, its assertion of tribal immunity from local taxation and control, and its political influence has been threatening to many non-Indian local residents, who have been particularly angered by the potential loss of local control over the 247 acres the tribe is planning to annex.

casinos to tourists from New York, a state that does not allow gambling. After several raids of the reservation casinos by state police, a Mohawk group called the Sovereignty Security Force blocked the main highway in protest against state and federal agencies that they believed were intervening illegitimately in the internal affairs of the tribe by attempting to prohibit gambling, a source of millions of dollars of revenue that the tribal government had authorized. New York state troopers responded with checkpoints of their own on roads into the reservation. As of May 1995, New York state troopers were still posted on the reservation, and the casinos had still not been reopened.

The unusual legal situation of indigenous peoples in the United States involves a complicated tangle of conflicting views about who has sovereignty over reservation lands. Tribal, state, city, and federal governments are all involved. Sometimes the tribes themselves are factionalized over who best represents their interests, and within the federal government conflicts sometimes arise about which government body is responsible for determining policy towards reservations. For instance, the Bureau of Indian Affairs is usually the dominant federal party, but in some cases, policies that influence American Indian lands adjacent to national forests or parks are set by the National Forest Service or National Park Service. Since vast sums of money are often at stake in these conflicts, they are likely to continue.

SOCIAL CONTROL: THE IMPOSITION OF ORDER

All societies have a variety of mechanisms by which the social behavior of people is controlled to maintain order or to reestablish order once rules have been broken. Social efforts to create orderly behavior begin at birth and continue through life. Some mechanisms for bringing about and maintaining conformity with acceptable behavior include early teaching of accepted customs and instilling values that motivate people to conform. Other mechanisms are punishments for rule violations and rewards for conformity. Malinowski (1926) pointed out that rules may be obeyed for a number of reasons: they may be followed be-

cause violating them brings public ridicule; because playing by the rules brings more rewarding interaction with others; because they are sacred, and supernatural punishment will result from breaking them; or because they are matters of law enforced by the machinery of society. They may also be self-enforcing due to their practical utility.

Socialization

The basic way we learn to fit into a social order is in our childhood **socialization** or **enculturation**. We learn about our culture, and we come to see the common expectations that others have about our behavior. Those habits that are learned early in life set the pattern for later relationships outside our home and community. Effective socialization can head off problems by establishing patterns of behavior that others find acceptable.

Values.   Part of socialization is learning to feel that some ways of behaving are better than others. **Values** may be defined as our attitudes or feelings about right and wrong behavior. This broad category may then be divided into various types such as moral, spiritual, or environmental values. **Moral values** are the attitudes or rules that govern our relationships with our fellow human beings. **Piety** or **spiritual values** define our relationship to the supernatural and may be reflected in the following of specific religious rules of behavior such as the Jewish kosher laws, rules against blasphemy, or rules about working on a sacred day. **Environmental values** deal with our relationship to our physical environment, so that concerns would in-

---

socialization or enculturation the process of learning a culture and the role-playing skills necessary for social life

enculturation socialization

value a feeling that something is either good or bad, moral or immoral; an ideal that people long for but do not necessarily pursue; often opposed to drives

moral values attitudes or rules that govern our relationships with our fellow human beings

piety attitudes that define our relationship to the supernatural

spiritual values attitudes that define our relationship to the supernatural

environmental values attitudes that define our relationship to the environment

FIGURE 11.5

WITCH TRIAL, SEVENTEENTH CENTURY

Witchcraft and sorcery, uses of supernatural power to work evil, are thought to have existed in many cultures throughout the world. Witches were accused of causing sickness, death, crop failure, and all sorts of other ills. The witch trial portrayed in this lithograph took place in Salem, Massachusetts, in 1692.

clude pollution and the protection of endangered species. Although morality and environmental values may be understood in purely practical terms, such as the need for an orderly social life or an awareness that needed resources are limited, people may accept them because they are supported by religious teaching or simply because they are traditional. Note, for instance, that the Judeo-Christian Ten Commandments begin with rules of piety such as "Thou shalt have no other gods before me" but also include moral rules such as "Thou shalt not steal."

Religion and Social Control

Another major force for the maintenance of social order is religion. The rites of passage that symbolize stages in the life of the individual as a member of society are typically religious rituals. Myths and legends also contribute an aura of sanctity to a way of life and increase people's respect for the social order. Taboos and ceremonial obligations further structure life in ways that demand predictable conformity from members of a community. Finally, in some so-

cieties, religious ideology directly mandates a moral life with the promise of supernatural rewards for proper social conduct and punishments for wrong living.

The role of religion in maintaining social order is illustrated by the Hopi Indians of the southwestern United States. As embodiments of evil among the Hopi, witches were called *Two Hearts*. They loved darkness, death, and other things that humans despise. Witches were put to death if they did not confess their evil deeds. So the accusation of witchcraft was a powerful force in bringing people into line with acceptable behavior.

The Hopi were a communally oriented society in which support of common values was prized over individual prowess. The person who excelled too much or too often might be suspected of being a witch. Thus, a child who won more races than others would be advised to run more slowly in other races so that others would not feel envy. In a society in which generosity and sharing were valued, the accumulation of too much personal wealth might also lead to suspicion of witchcraft. In this case, a suspect might sponsor a communal festival in which he or she distributed goods to others, an act that eliminated the surplus wealth and curried the favor of others simultaneously. Essentially any deviance was an invitation for suspicious gossip, and this suspicion helped pressure people into conforming behavior, much as the legal system in state societies is intended to do.

Rewards

Societies do not rely on punishments alone to maintain social order. Rewarding acceptable behavior also encourages conformity. The praise and esteem of other members of the community is one such reward. Promotions and salary increases provide incentives to support corporate goals. Similarly, various forms of public recognition reward contributions to the social group. In addition to money, honor, and respect, people may be rewarded with greater power within the military, police, or judicial system.

Gossip and Community Pressure

The esteem of others is valued by most people, so gossip and community pressure can be a powerful force in keeping people in line. The key to the effectiveness of gossip is that word eventually gets back to the person being criticized. The nonconformist then has the opportunity to try to regain the respect of others by changing the behavior that others have found unacceptable. Direct confrontation is another form of community pressure that is sometimes resorted to when gossip has failed.

Law

Order is also maintained through **law**, the cultural rules that regulate behavior through the threat of punishment (Hoebel, 1954). Legal rules may be formally defined and codified into a recognized body of laws, but they may also be said to exist informally, defined by custom rather than code. Pospisil (1972) has demonstrated that law in all societies has four characteristics: legal authority, universal application, legal rights and duties, and sanction. **Legal authority** is the right to compel others to obey the law by the use of force, by the threat of force, or by punishment. All societies vest legal authority in one or more individuals

who are charged with the responsibility to maintain order. They may be political specialists, heads of voluntary associations, designated members of a community, or heads of families. **Universal application** is the principle that the legal authority should apply the same laws uniformly in similar situations. It is this expectation of consistency that invests legal systems with tradition. Of course, legal authorities may violate this principle, but the inconsistent application of law, or favoritism, is regarded as an abuse of power in all societies. **Legal rights and duties** are the rules that define relationships between persons by specifying what recompense an injured person is entitled to receive and that legal authorities are expected to follow in enforcing contracts between persons when one or both believe their rights have been violated. Finally, **sanction** is the action taken by legal authorities when the law has been violated. A sanction may be either a punishment or the loss of a privilege or benefit to which a person was entitled before breaking a law, and may include such things as ridicule, ostracism, corporal punishment, or fines.

Case Study: U.S. Politics

The U.S. political system has historically been dominated by two major political parties, and one commonly hears political issues discussed as if U.S. voters' viewpoints can be simply summed up as either liberal and conservative. However, the actual political makeup of the U.S. population is more complex than this suggests. A 1987 Times Mirror survey of political attitudes in the United States found that there were three areas of personal orientation and six areas of value commitment on the basis of which the major U.S. voting blocks may be distinguished. The important differences in personal orientation involve (1) religious faith; (2)

---

law cultural rules that regulate human behavior and maintain order

legal authority the right to compel others to obey the law and to punish those who violate it

universal application principle that legal authority should apply the same laws uniformly in similar situations

legal rights and duties rules that define relationships between people by specifying the type of recompense an injured person should receive

sanction action taken by legal authorities responding to violations of law

degree of alienation, the sense of powerlessness and distrust of government; and (3) personally felt financial pressure. For instance, politically active voters tend to be more religious than average, and both Democrats and Republicans have important religious constituencies among their party members. The political value differences that divided groups of U.S. voters are (1) the degree of their tolerance for people with different lifestyles and the expression of non-mainstream ideas; (2) the importance they place on social justice for minorities and the needy; (3) the level of their anticommunism; (4) the stress they place on faith in their country's ability to solve its problems; (5) their attitudes about the size and effectiveness of government; and (6) their feelings about the power and influence of business corporations.

The Times Mirror survey found that a full 11 percent of the pool of potential voters in the United States are totally uninvolved in public affairs and politics. These people never vote. They tend to be young and poorly educated. Their greatest concerns are unemployment, poverty, and the threat of nuclear war.

The Republican Party. The Republican Party is most staunchly supported by two main groups: *enterprise Republicans* and *moral Republicans*. Enterprise Republicans are affluent, educated individuals who are particularly probusiness and antigovernment in their values. This group is almost exclusively white. Moral Republicans are mainly middle-aged people with middle incomes who hold strong and very conservative political views on social and foreign policy issues. They are strongly anticommunist and antiabortion and favor prayer in the public schools and the death penalty. They also favor social spending by government except when it is specifically targeted for minorities. Moral Republicans are regular churchgoers, and many are born-again Christians. Like enterprise Republicans, they are largely white.

The Democratic Party. The backbone of the Democratic Party is a coalition of five different groups: *New Deal Democrats, Sixties Democrats,* the *partisan poor,* the *passive poor,* and *seculars.* New Deal Democrats are older citizens who have moderate incomes and little financial stress. Many are of blue-collar and union background. Almost a third of this group are Catholics. They favor restrictions on abortion and

support school prayer and social spending except for minorities. The Sixties Democrats are a well-educated group that includes a large number of females and blacks. They favor government spending on social programs, specifically those for minorities, and they tend to be somewhat less anticommunist than other groups. The partisan poor are a very low-income group who are strongly concerned with issues of social justice. They favor social spending but oppose tax increases. They also favor the death penalty and school prayer, but are divided on the abortion issue. The passive poor feel less economic pressure than the partisan poor and are less critical of their society. They favor social spending, oppose cuts in defense spending, and are moderately antiabortion. The seculars are well-educated, mostly white, and generally middle-aged. They are the only nonreligious group in the political spectrum. They strongly support personal freedom, favor cuts in military spending, and oppose school prayer, antiabortion legislation, and increased aid to minorities.

There are three remaining voting groups. These are the *upbeats,* the *disaffecteds,* and the *followers.* Upbeats are young, optimistic persons who have great faith in their country. They too are largely white. Their main political concerns are the budget deficit and other economic issues, and they lean toward Republican candidates in their voting. Disaffecteds also lean toward the Republican Party. They are alienated, pessimistic, and skeptical of both big business and big government, but they are promilitary, support capital punishment, and oppose gun control. Followers usually lean toward Democratic candidates but sometimes support Republicans. They have little faith in their society, but tend also to be uncritical of either government or business.

The political rhetoric of the two-party system emphasizes the differences between the ideologies of the parties, as if there were no middle ground. Yet the U.S. electorate is extremely diverse, and both parties include people with important value differences. The election of a candidate from either party requires the support of a coalition of these different groups, and the wooing of the upbeats, disaffecteds, and followers is particularly important to both parties.

The 1992 presidential election illustrates the diversity of the electorate. Dissatisfaction with the country's economic performance and

FIGURE 11.6

LAW ENFORCEMENT

Many societies maintain order by investing the authority to make rules and regulate behavior in the family, an individual, or a community council. This

Cherokee Indians' tribal council meets to discuss issues that affect their nation.

job cutbacks led to strong voter turnout, especially among the traditional Democratic party supporters. Governor Bill Clinton received about 82 percent of the African American vote in this election and got some support from enterprise Republicans. Among the crucial swing voters, the upbeats and followers, also influenced by economic issues, voted for Clinton, after having supported Reagan and Bush in the previous elections. Many of the disaffecteds, on the other hand, moved toward third-party candidates, the most well-known being H. Ross Perot, a prominent businessman. Another important variable in this election was gender. Women, especially those who were single parents and influenced by concerns about economic needs, education, and reproductive choice, voted in record numbers for the Democratic candidate.

Thus, the political rhetoric of liberal versus conservative tends to oversimplify a complex state of affairs. The centrist tendencies of both political parties may be seen best in the actual day-to-day practice of U.S. legislators after their election, when mutual respect, compromise, bipartisan cooperation, and statesmanship are commonly emphasized.

THE RESOLUTION OF EXTERNAL CONFLICT

In all societies conflicts occur, and in all societies there are customary ways of trying to resolve them. Peaceful conflict resolution may rely heavily on the good will of those involved, whereas violent resolution may be based on the socially accepted use of force by legal authorities.

Peaceful Conflict Resolution

Antagonistic parties may sometimes resolve their conflict if both decide that it is no longer in their best interest to continue or that their losses have been restored. Even when an injury cannot itself be made right, compensation may be accepted because the payment symbolizes an admission of responsibility by the wrongdoer and allows the injured party to withdraw from the conflict honorably. For instance, the concept of compensation has been applied in many societies, even for major acts such as murder. It was called wer-gild, or "man-payment," in Anglo-Saxon England before the Norman invasion of 1066. According to Evans-Pritchard (1940), the same idea was practiced by the Nuer of the Sudan in recent times. Among the Nuer the payment took the form of cattle given by the family of the murderer to the surviving relatives. Civil actions in court in which parties sue for compensation for injuries play a similar role in contemporary state societies.

Negotiation. Peaceful resolution of conflict requires communication between the parties involved. Negotiation can be carried out by the disputing parties themselves, but it is often accomplished through **mediation**, which is negotiation carried out by a go-between. It is generally easier than direct negotiation between parties, providing the mediator is neutral. A mediator has no authority to enforce a decision on those involved in a conflict. Instead, as he draws on the desire of the parties involved to avoid a continuation or escalation of their dispute, he also relies on his own prestige and his ability to mobilize community pressure to influence the parties to settle.

Among the Nuer, the person holding the prestigious status known as leopard skin chief had no official authority over others but had ritual responsibilities and served as a mediator between families that were in dispute. The position of leopard skin chief was held only by a much-respected male whose home could be a sanctuary to which a murderer might flee for safety while a conflict was being resolved. He performed a ritual purification of the murderer and then approached the family of the murderer to determine the number of cattle that they were willing to pay to the family of the deceased. Then he visited the aggrieved family to see if they would accept the offer. If the immediate relatives pressed for retaliation, the leopard skin chief might seek the support of more distant relatives to encourage them to accept a settlement. Usually a settlement of about 40 cattle was accepted. Since an unrecompensed death could lead to a feud between the families, the role of mediator was an important one in maintaining social order.

Community Action. Community action is another approach to conflict resolution. The entire community would be mobilized to respond to and resolve the conflict in societies that lacked complex kinship organizations and that were small enough to have a vested inter-

FIGURE 11.7

LEOPARD SKIN CHIEF

The Nuer, tribal cattle herders, turned to a mediator to settle disputes between segments of the tribe in a blood feud. The leopard skin chief used threats of supernatural retribution to persuade both sides to come to a peaceful solution while providing refuge in his village for the accused until the matter was solved.

est in resolving the conflict among all members of the local group.

Courts. A **court** is a formalized institution that asserts authority over parties in a dispute and over persons accused of violating the law. A court has power to decide cases and impose sanctions. Courts are part of political systems in which governing authorities have the right to exercise control over persons outside their own kinship group, so true courts are found only in chiefdoms and states, societies with centralized political officials.

Religious Institutions. According to Black (1976), when governmental agencies of law enforcement are weak, then other means of social

(Continued on p. 283)

mediation negotiation between conflicting parties carried out by a neutral third party
court formalized institution that asserts authority over parties in a dispute and over persons accused of violating the law

INUIT SONG DUELS

INUIT

The Inuit who inhabited Greenland had several interesting methods of resolving conflicts. The most unusual, perhaps, was the song duel. The combatants composed songs deriding their opponent, and performed them in front of an audience who ultimately decided the winner by applause and laughter.

Native Greenlanders had various ways of resolving personal conflicts, including head butting, wrestling, and boxing contests. Perhaps the most interesting method was the song duel described by Rasmussen (1922), quoted in Hoebel (1954). When an individual lacked the physical strength to challenge an opponent to a test of strength, the song duel was an alternate way of seeking justice. It was carried out in front of other members of the community. Following traditional rules for composing the songs, the parties to the conflict would alternately sing insults against each other. The songs would outline the grievance or defense and deride the other person. The audience participated by their laughter and applause. As the duel wore on, the audience's laughter sided more and more against one party until the public ridicule was too great for the loser to endure and he would withdraw.

Hoebel recounted a case of a divorced man whose wife married another. The first decided he wanted his wife back and sought to get her by publicly shaming his rival in a song duel that he began with words that accused his rival of wife stealing:

Now shall I split off words—little, sharp words

Like the wooden splinters which I hack off with my ax.

A song from ancient times—a breath of the ancestors

A song of longing—for my wife.

An impudent, black-skinned oaf has stolen her,

Has tried to belittle her.

A miserable wretch who loves human flesh—

A cannibal from famine days.

The rival then responded:

Insolence that takes the breath away

Such laughable arrogance and effrontery.

What a satirical song! Supposed to place blame on me.

You would drive fear into my heart!

I who care not about death.

Hi! You sing about my woman who was your wench.

You weren't so loving then—she was much alone.

You forgot to prize her in song, in stout contest songs.

Now she is mine.

And never shall she visit singing, false lovers.

Betrayer of women in strange households.

Such singing continued back and forth, each contestant hoping to win over the audience and thereby defeat his rival. Songs might be prepared and rehearsed in advance, and in some areas the relatives of each contestant provided a backup chorus in support of their own family member.

INUIT BAND AUTHORITY

Inuit bands had no centralized authority figure who made decisions for the group. Instead, the community as a whole, or the best qualified member in a given situation, took the lead in such matters as organizing a whale hunt, distributing the meat, and arranging an equitable solution to a dispute.

control are likely to be more important. As he puts it, "Law varies inversely with other social control" (p. 6). Religion is one of the more prominent social institutions that plays a role in social control. The most well-known examples of religious mechanisms for conflict resolution in a legal setting are oaths and ordeals. **Oaths** are ritual acts of swearing innocence on pain of punishment by deities. Where religious belief is strongly held by people, oaths can be a powerful force in determining guilt, since the guilty may fear supernatural retaliation too strongly to take a false oath. **Ordeals** are tests of guilt or innocence in which parties in a conflict are challenged to undertake a dangerous or painful act with the understanding that supernatural influences will grant them success only if they are innocent. Again, the guilty are likely to refuse such tests or fail them, because their religious convictions undermine their confidence. For instance, the Philippine Ifugao people tested the innocence of persons accused of criminal acts by requiring them to reach quickly into a pot of boiling water and remove pebbles from the bottom. The arm of the person who underwent the ordeal was smeared with

grease so that if he acted quickly enough, his arm would not be burned. Those who acted out of a confidence born of innocence probably were more likely to pass this test than were those whose guilt made them hesitate. Similar tests were reported in medieval Europe and for the Tanala of Madagascar, and in these cases the arms of the accused were unprotected from the boiling water by grease. However, a period of several days was allowed to pass before the arms were examined; this lapse of time presumably favored the innocent who acted with less hesitation than the guilty, since those with less severe scalds were more likely to have healed by then.

Violent Conflict Resolution

Conflicts cannot always be ended peacefully. There are a variety of forceful ways in which people attempt to regulate their relationships

---

oaths ritual acts of swearing innocence on pain of punishment by deities
ordeals tests of guilt or innocence by enduring dangerous or painful acts

FIGURE 11.9

RETRIBUTION

Sanctions are formal and informal controls designed to regulate social behavior. When a crime of great magnitude is committed, some societies demand retribution, as do these armed dancers in Papua New Guinea, who participate in regulated combat in order to avenge a murder.

with one another, including retribution, feuds, raids, and warfare.

Retribution. In many simple societies that have no centralized governmental authority for the enforcement of law, the responsibility for the punishment of wrongs is the legitimate authority of the person whose rights have been violated. In such cases, law enforcement is synonymous with **retribution**, the personal use of force to redress wrongs. Retribution as a legal principle is not the same as anarchy, since it is legitimate in societies that condone it only when other members of the community recognize that the aggrieved party has a valid complaint that deserves redressing. Crime, anarchy, and other uses of power that are not condoned by the larger community will be seen as illegitimate and punishable.

Feuds. Armed conflicts between two kinship groups that are initiated by one of the groups to avenge a wrong are called **feuds**. The most common cause of feuds is the murder of a member of one of the groups. Feuds may occur between kinship groups that reside in the

same community as well as between neighboring groups from different communities. They are most common in societies in which bodies of related males, called **fraternal groups**, work together and feel obliged to protect one another's common interests.

Raids. Organized violence by one group against another to achieve an economic benefit is called a **raid**. Raiding is generally a more recurrent and ongoing process than feuding, since the latter is stimulated by a specific grievance and may eventually be settled. The economic advantage gained in raiding is likely to be a continuing motivation for this organized violence. Its goal is not to eliminate or even subjugate the enemy permanently, but rather to accomplish a limited objective such as the acquisition of food, cattle, or other valued goods. Where raiding is common, the enemy is likely to be treated as a resource that must be left available for future exploitation.

War. The most extensive form of organized violence is **war**, armed combat between political communities. The nature of war differs according to the complexity of the societies involved. For instance, warfare is least common in those band societies in which individual, communal, or plant-focused foraging is the basis of subsistence, more common in bands with animal-focused foraging, and most common in food-producing societies. Otterbein (1970) examined cross-cultural data of 50 societies and found that those with more centrally organized political institutions had more complex military organizations, more effective weapons and tactics, and greater mortality in their engagements than societies with little or no political centralization. In general, warfare was less complex among bands and tribes than among chiefdoms and states. For instance, the former societies

---

retribution personal use of force to redress wrongs, usually in simple societies with no centralized governmental authority

feuds armed conflicts between kinship groups initiated to avenge a wrong

fraternal groups groups of related males who work together and feel obliged to protect one another's common interests

raids organized violence by one group against another to achieve an economic benefit

war organized armed conflict between political communities

lacked professional soldiers, which were typical in the latter. The tactic of surprise was more characteristic of simpler societies, while warfare was generally more formally arranged and conducted in complex societies.

Otterbein found that the purposes of warfare also differed for the two groups. In bands and tribes, those fighting in wars were individually motivated to participate because of personal grudges. So battles tended to consist of many simultaneous fights between individuals with little group strategy. Defense of one's own village and the benefits of plunder were the motives for war in bands and tribal societies. Of course, more complex societies fought wars for these reasons as well, but they were also influenced by motives less characteristic of warfare in bands and tribes. Enhancing one's prestige and that of one's family was an especially common motivation in chiefdoms, in which competition for prestige was a prominent characteristic. On the other hand, prestige was a less common motive in states where social ranking was more stable and was based on a person's membership in a particular social class. While warfare carried out to achieve economic and political control over other communities was a motive found in some of the more complex chiefdoms, it was especially characteristic of states.

War and Gender.   Otterbein (1970) also distinguishes between **internal warfare**, in which the combat is between neighboring political communities that share the same culture, and **external warfare,** in which the conflict is between political communities with different cultures. Internal warfare is especially common among foraging bands and horticultural tribes, while external warfare is more commonly practiced by more complex chiefdoms and state societies. According to Divale and Harris (1976), internal warfare is particularly associated with the systematic subordination of women. Harris (1974) has summarized the impact of this form of warfare on male and female roles:

> Male supremacy is a case of "positive feedback," or what has been called "deviation amplification"—the kind of process that leads to the head-splitting squeaks of public-address systems that pick up and then reamplify their own signals. The fiercer the males, the greater the amount of warfare, the more such males are needed. Also, the fiercer the males, the more sexually aggressive they become, the more exploited are the females, and the higher the incidence of polygyny—control over several wives by one man. Polygyny in turn intensifies the shortage of women, raises the level of frustration among the junior males, and increases the motivation for going to war. The amplification builds to an excruciating climax; females are held in contempt and killed in infancy, making it necessary for men to go to war to capture wives in order to rear additional numbers of aggressive males. (p. 87)

Since female children are often unwanted in these societies because they lack social power but still need to be fed, **female infanticide** has been the major means of population control in most societies throughout human history. Divale (1972) studied foraging and horticultural societies that practiced warfare and found that the ratio of boys to girls aged 14 and under was 128 to 100. Since throughout the world about 105 boys are born for every 100 girls, the extra 23 boys per 100 girls in Divale's sample indicates a higher death rate among girls in these societies.

The female subordination that occurs with internal warfare does not accompany external warfare, in which men are absent from home for prolonged periods while fighting with distant enemies. Women in these societies are likely to be ranked high, since it is they who make the day-to-day economic and internal political decisions of the village while the men are away. In such societies, the gardens and houses are often the property of women, female infanticide and polygyny are likely to be uncommon, and inheritance is usually through the line of female ancestry. The power of men over their wives is minimized by their lack of ownership over their wives' home and gardens as well as their lack of authority over their wives' children, who are members of their mothers' families, not their fathers'. The male head of the household is not a woman's husband but

---

internal warfare fighting between peoples who share the same language and culture

external warfare warfare which is fought for prolonged periods in locations distant from the warriors' home with enemies who speak a foreign language and follow an alien way of life

female infanticide the killing of female infants; a major means of population control in societies that primarily engage in internal warfare

her brother, who belongs to her own family. In these societies women often have great influence on the political decisions that lead to war and that influence its conduct. Their economic roles are also an important source of power. For instance, Iroquois women in the late eighteenth century were able to control men's wartime activities by withholding the food used to provision long wartime expeditions.

Causes of War. There are diverse theories about the cause of warfare. Ember (1982) examined cross-cultural data and found that scarcity of resources such as food and fuel was one predictor of the frequency of warfare. Vayda (1976) pointed out that slash-and-burn horticulture stimulates internal warfare in many societies, because taking land that has already been worked by neighboring groups may be easier than clearing new land and preparing it for cultivation. Warfare allows horticulturalists to expand geographically when population growth overtaxes local abilities to produce enough food. Divale and Harris (1976) suggested that internal warfare is part of a system that helps to limit population growth, because warfare fosters male dominance, subjugation of women, a preference for male offspring, and therefore high rates of female infanticide, which has a major impact on population growth.

Naroll (1966) examined possible causes of the frequency of warfare. He determined that a high degree of military sophistication was not associated with lower frequencies of war. In fact, societies with a sophisticated military force were not only more aggressive than militarily less organized societies, but they were more likely to be attacked as well.

THE RESOLUTION OF INTERNAL CONFLICT

Mediation, feuds, and warfare are typical means of resolving the conflicts that may occur between societies such as tribes, chiefdoms, or states. Within the boundaries of societies with similar political or cultural views, however, conflicts may arise that necessitate a different pattern or means of resolution. Internal conflicts include crimes such as theft and murder, acts that all societies regard as disruptive. But internal conflicts may also overturn a govern-

ment. Revolution and rebellion are dramatic forms of conflict that seek to redress the wrongs that members of a society perceive are being perpetrated by its government.

Crime

No society is free of **crime**, the harming of a person or of personal property by another. But societies do differ in the frequency and likelihood of various kinds of crime and in how they deal with it. People who live in small groups have little opportunity to harm another member of the group while remaining anonymous and profiting by the act. In large societies crime is more feasible because the perpetrator can remain anonymous. The motivation, however, to violate others' rights for personal gain is certainly not accepted by everyone in such societies, so population growth alone cannot be thought of as the cause of the greater rates of crime in such societies. Rather, it appears that the individuals most likely to resort to crime in large societies are those unable to fulfill the values that a society's culture encourages. Two related factors that differentiate people in this respect are social class and income.

A study carried out by the United States National Commission on the Causes and Prevention of Violence (USNCCPV, 1969) found that violent crimes were 11 times more common in cities of over 50,000 people than in rural areas, and most crimes were committed by young, low-income males who lived in urban slums. Poverty, unemployment, poor education, and inadequate housing seemed to be major factors that created motives for criminal behavior. People in such conditions were unlikely to achieve success by legitimate means, and were therefore more likely than other members of society to undertake illegitimate actions to improve their condition.

Crime varies in frequency from extremely low levels in societies such as the !Kung San foragers of southern Africa (Lee, 1979, 1984) and the Semai horticulturalists of the Malay Peninsula (Dentan, 1968), where crime has been described as almost nonexistent, to societies such as the Yanomamö (Chagnon, 1983), in which about 23 percent of the men of each generation die violently. Nevertheless, people in all societies have some concept of crime and con-

crime the harming of a person or personal property by another

sider some harmful acts to be legitimately punishable. Theft, assault against members of one's own community, and murder are probably regarded as crimes everywhere.

Although theft is probably regarded as wrong in every society, the definition of theft differs from culture to culture. In many societies, personal property may be freely borrowed without asking unless the owner expressly indicates that an item is not to be taken. This is particularly likely in societies in which generous sharing of resources is common. For instance, Goldman (1972) described property rights among the Cubeo, a horticultural tribe of the Colombian Amazon Basin:

> The attitude of the Cubeo toward personal possessions is best described as casual. They are not indifferent to objects but they regard strong proprietary feelings as improper. Among kin objects circulate freely; the closer the tie between people the more active the exchanges. Sisters exchange ornaments and trinkets and men borrow freely from one another with or without permission. They seem to be most free with objects of economic utility, such as a canoe, weapons, implements, and somewhat more possessive with objects of personal adornment. (pp. 75–76)

In this context of rather nonchalant attitudes about property rights and borrowing, Goldman recounted an interesting story about borrowing among the Cubeo:

> On one occasion a visitor from an upriver sib [kinship group] rose to leave, after having spent most of the day in amiable talk, and in a most casual voice said, 'I will take my spear with me.' A young man then went to his quarters and fetched the spear, which the visitor took as he departed. The young man explained that he had been at this man's house during a drinking party. He saw the spear and admired it and took it home without saying anything about it. Theft to the Cubeo is not a matter of purloining an object. It is entirely a matter of attitude. They ask, in a manner of speaking: Is the taking of an object an act of friendship or of hostility? (p. 76)

Societies also differ in the likelihood of theft. For instance, in foraging bands of 50 or 60 people, it would be difficult if not impossible to steal the personal property of another and remain undetected. Furthermore, it is generally advantageous to let others borrow one's tools rather freely, since the fruits of everyone's labor will benefit the entire group. Thus, the very motive for theft can be undermined by cultural practices such as the custom in many hunting and gathering societies of leaving implements outside the hut when it is permissible for others to use them.

Homicide is universally regarded as a criminal act, but cultures vary in what they define as homicide. There is probably no society in which the taking of some human life by someone is considered under all circumstances to be murder. Killing is an accepted part of warfare wherever war is found, and avenging a murder by killing the murderer is typically accepted in most societies. Nevertheless, the intentional taking of another life without justification, however justification happens to be defined, is considered murder practically everywhere. An interesting exception to this general rule was reported by Jenness (1922), who asserted that among Copper Eskimo men, the likelihood of their killing at least one person was so high that only repeated offenses were considered to be murder. This was an important distinction, since murder was a capital offense and taking the life of everyone who had killed just once would have been impossible.

Legal Response to Crime.   In simply organized societies, the enforcement of legal rights is largely left in the hands of individuals and their families. Where the magnitude of the crime threatens to disrupt the community permanently, corporal punishment, confiscation of property, ostracism, or even death are possible sanctions. Bands and tribes are likely to act in ways that are designed to return the group to the balance it had before a law was broken, a concept known as **restitution**.

The exacting of legal punishment has followed the principle of retribution in many societies. For instance, Beattie (1964) reported that the Berbers of North Africa expected exact equivalence in revenge for a death: "So if a man in one group kills a woman in another, the object of the injured group will be not to kill the murderer, but to kill a woman on their opponent's side" (p. 175). This is the same principle of an eye for an eye that was set forth in Hammurabi's famous code:

---

restitution behavior intended to restore the group to the balance it had before a law was broken

When a patrician has destroyed the eye of a member of the aristocracy, they shall destroy his eye. If he has broken another patrician's bone, they shall break his bone. . . . If a patrician has knocked out a tooth of a seignior of his own rank, they shall knock out his tooth. . . . If a patrician struck another patrician's daughter and has caused her to have a miscarriage, he shall pay ten shekels of silver for her fetus. If that woman has died, they shall put his daughter to death.

Law enforcement in complex societies tends toward an emphasis on punishment of the criminal. This is probably because crime in societies with full-time law enforcement officials tends to be viewed as a threat to the legitimacy of the government's authority. The reaction of the enforcement system in such societies is to eliminate, imprison, or otherwise punish the wrongdoer; punishment typically becomes more important than seeing that restitution is made to the victim. In recent times in the United States and other industrialized countries, efforts have been made to pass various victim compensation laws, but the predominant emphasis in industrialized societies remains punishment; it is still regarded as the victim's obligation to seek recompense through civil suits.

Rebellion and Revolution

The most dramatic forms of internal conflict are rebellion and revolution. **Rebellion** is an organized and violent opposition to the legitimacy of a society's current governing body. It is most likely to occur when a significant number of those who are subject to the government's authority feel themselves to be disenfranchised or inadequately represented by their leaders. Rebellion seeks to influence the policies of government and how they are carried out, but it does not attempt to change the nature of the governmental system itself. **Revolution** is the organized use of force to alter the very form of government. It is fostered by the same conditions that lead to rebellion, but it is likely to occur when those involved view the very system of government as the source of its illegitimate policy and practices. Both rebellion and revolution have much in common with warfare, since all three represent conflicts, often violent ones, between at least two groups, each of which asserts the legitimacy of its own right to use force for its own political ends.

---

rebellion organized and violent opposition to the legitimacy of a society's current governing body
revolution organized use of force to alter the very form of government

---

CHAPTER SUMMARY

1. Politics, the use of social power to implement public goals, takes different forms in human societies.

2. Governing authority may reside in the local community, a typical trait of band societies.

3. Authority may be vested in the kinship group and in specialized associations that draw their members from the entire community, as in the world's tribal societies.

4. Authority may reside with full-time officials who make up a specialized govern-

ment, which shares legal authority with its society's kinship groups, as in chiefdoms, or which claims a monopoly over all legitimate uses of political power, as in states.

5. However they are organized, political systems have a variety of mechanisms for maintaining social order and for reestablishing order when rules are broken.

6. These mechanisms include socialization, values and morality, religion, rewards and punishments, informal community pressure, and law.

7. Law, the most formal means for enforcing obedience to the rules of social life, includes both peaceful and potentially violent means for resolving conflict.

8. Extreme levels of violence such as warfare and rebellion occur when conflicts exist either between governments or within a single society.

ANNOTATED READINGS

Brumfiel, E. M. (1994). *The economic anthropology of the state*. Lanham, MD: University Press of America. An examination of economics, politics, and the state.

Gailey, C. W. (1992). *Dialectical anthropology: Essays in honor of Stanley Diamond*. Gainesville, FL: University Press of Florida. A collection of essays in Marxist anthropology.

Gledhill, J. (1994). *Power and its disguises: Anthropological perspectives on politics*. Boulder, CO: Pluto Press. A text on the political anthropology of power.

Helms, M. W. (1993). *Craft and the kingly ideal: Art, trade, and power*. Austin, TX: University of Texas Press. An analysis of the interconnections among craftmanship, commerce, and kinship.

Llewellen, T. C. (1992). *Political anthropology: An introduction*. Westport, CT: Bergin & Garvey. A basic overview of political anthropology.

McGlynn, F., & Truden, A. (Eds.). (1991). *Anthropological approaches to political behavior: Contributions from ethnology*. Pittsburgh, PA: University of Pittsburgh Press. Essays on politics and power.

Nader, L. (Ed.). (1965). The ethnography of law. *American Anthropologist, 67* (Supplement), pp. 3–32. An important synthesis of anthropological viewpoints on the study of law.

Nader, L., & Todd, H. F., Jr. (1978). *The disputing process: Law in ten societies*. New York: Columbia University Press. An important collection of ethnographic descriptions of how disputes are settled in a cross section of the world's societies.

Ross, M. H. (1993). *The culture of conflict: Interpretations and interests in comparative perspective*. New Haven, CT: Yale University Press. An examination of intergroup relations and psychological aspects of conflict.

Sanders, W., Wright, H., & Adams, R. McC. (1987). *On the evolution of complex societies: Essays in honor of Harry Hoijer*. Malibu, CA: Undena Publications. A collection of essays that explore the uses of archaeological data regarding the emergence of early states.

Smith, S. (1995). *World in disorder, 1994–1995: An anthropological and interdisciplinary approach to global issues*. Lanham, MD: University Press of America. Examines the economics and human ecology of contemporary political conflict.

van Bakel, M. A., Hagesteijn, R. R., & van de Velde, P. (Eds.). (1986). *Private politics: A multi-disciplinary approach to "big-men" systems*. Leiden, Netherlands: E. J. Brill. Essays that examine political leadership and economic aspects of power.

PART FOUR

Ideology and Symbolism

CHAPTER TWELVE
LANGUAGE AND CULTURE

Language is a complex symbolic verbal system for communicating ideas. Nonverbal communication—gestures, facial expressions, and posture—are highly expressive of emotion and can also transmit ideas to others. We learn what part the human brain plays in language, how other animals communicate, and the structure of language.

CHAPTER THIRTEEN
RELIGION AND CULTURE

Religion may be defined as a system of beliefs about the supernatural and a pattern of rituals that helps maintain social order and reduces individual anxiety about those parts of the natural world over which we have too little control. Religion helps us make sense of a puzzling universe. Religious organizations give people a sense of togetherness and unity.

CHAPTER FOURTEEN
CULTURE, PERSONALITY, AND PSYCHOLOGICAL PROCESS

As studied from an anthropological perspective, personality is an expression of various roles that society considers appropriate for the statuses that individuals hold. How well we play our assigned roles is critical to our subjective well-being and to how others judge our mental health. Different kinds of emotional distress are the basis for the specific kinds of deviant behavior found in any society and defined by its culture.

CHAPTER FIFTEEN
AESTHETICS AND CULTURE

The human condition includes the ability to experience pleasure in a variety of ways. The expression of those experiences is the basis for play, recreation, and various forms of art. Painting, music, dance, and storytelling all provide status, economic gain, ritual comfort, or political power.

Humans have built a superstructure of culture, using their ability to communicate, to explain their place in the universe, to understand the concept of their own mind and its relationship to others in a society, and to create and enjoy beauty. Chapter 12 looks at patterns of language and learning, the system of symbolizing and communicating meaningful ideas to others. Chapter 13 discusses the most abstract of symbolic systems, the varieties of religious ideologies and rituals that societies develop to give meaning to their place in the universe. Chapter 14 focuses on the individual's relationship to culture, illustrating how it shapes personality, influences states of consciousness, and identifies psychological disorders. Chapter 15 describes the ways that various cultures define beauty and discusses how art forms function in society.

CHAPTER TWELVE

Language and Culture

◀ *Figure 12.1 Communication Cultural patterns of life are communicated by a complex system of signs and symbols. When this system is disrupted by voluntary or forced migration, families must adapt to a new language and a new culture. The children may find it particularly difficult when they attend a new school. While bilingual education takes place in many schools in the United States, as an effort to help these children adapt, it remains a controversial issue. These two girls, native Arabic speakers, attend a bilingual second-grade class in Dearborn, Michigan.*

Human ways of life are far more varied and complex than those of other animals. This complexity is facilitated by our distinctive ability to communicate the intricacies of these lifeways to each new generation of our group. Unlike other animals, we tend to portray our concepts by highly arbitrary but mutually accepted symbols, such as those embodied in languages. In this chapter, we will examine this capacity of symbolizing, which is fundamental to the origin and perpetuation of human cultures.

Dude. Boombox. Cyberspace. Jive. Lift. Bonnet. All words of the English language. Would you understand what they meant if you were 18 years old? Or 80? Lived in California? London? In all parts of the world, and at all ages, humans learn to communicate with each other using a complicated system of vocal sounds that symbolize complex concepts. Symbolic language is the primary ability that distinguishes us from other primates.

HUMAN COMMUNICATION

Analyzing one's experiences, whether internally in thought or externally in communication, involves the manipulation of concepts. **Communication** is the transfer of information embodied in concepts or ideas from one person to another using observable objects or events such as gestures or spoken words to represent those concepts.

Signs and Symbols

Human communication is a process by which we express meaning simultaneously with signs and with symbols. **Signs** are events such as tears, smiles, clenched fists, or agitated gestures that are spontaneous expressions of our feelings, needs, or concepts requiring little conscious effort or learning to master. Thus, when human beings smile spontaneously as a sign of happiness, they use the same facial muscles in all societies around the world. The use of natural signs that express our inner feelings or needs is a form of communication that we

share with other animals. Since signs are spontaneous outward expressions of our inner states, we often learn rather easily to recognize the meanings of signs used by other species. For instance, when a dog crouches and tenses its muscles, growls, and bares its teeth, these signs of potential aggression are readily understood not only by dogs and other animals but also by humans.

Symbolic communication is the most distinctive of all human behavioral attributes. It is the use of symbols in communicating that sets us apart from other animals and that serves as the foundation for the extremely complex ways of life found in all human groups. **Symbols** are objects or events such as national flags or spoken words that have no inherent significance and whose meanings exist only because their users have agreed that they will represent certain other objects or events (White, 1971). Thus, symbols have no innate meaning, and their use and interpretation must always be learned.

The relationship between a symbol and what it represents is not determined by the inherited biological tendencies of the communicator to relate one to the other. Furthermore, a symbol need not share any physical similarities or physical proximity with its referent. There is, for instance, no reason dictated by human biology or the physical properties of the wavelengths of light that red had to be used to mean "stop" or green to mean "go" in traffic signals, nor is there any compelling reason in human biology or in geometric properties for a stop sign to be octagonal rather than triangular in shape. There may be causal factors in one's history or environment that influence the form of a symbol, but its meaning is essentially arbitrary. Any symbol therefore may be used to designate any referent. Since the meanings of symbols are a matter of social convention or consensus rather than nature, they can change quite readily even within the lifetimes of their

(Continued on p. 296)

communication the transfer of information from one person to another using objects and events as signs or symbols

sign an object or event whose meaning is biologically disposed or based on a similarity or a tendency for two things to occur together in nature

symbol an object or event that represents another object or event because of the agreement among people that it will do so

HUMAN COMMUNICATION WITH AND WITHOUT SYMBOLS: HELEN KELLER

The dramatic impact that symbols have on human behavior is well illustrated by the case of Helen Keller, a person in whom the acquisition of symbols and, hence, the ability to communicate symbolically was delayed until she was almost 7 years old. Stricken by illness at the age of 19 months, Helen was left both blind and deaf. Helen lacked the senses through which we normally learn the arbitrarily agreed-on meanings of our communicative acts and through which we usually perceive those symbolic acts themselves. Nevertheless, she needed to communicate and did so by her own signs, acts whose meanings were implicit in the quality of the acts themselves. In her own words:

> My hands felt every object and observed every motion, and in this way I learned to know many things. Soon I felt the need of some communication with others and began to make crude signs. A shake of the head meant "No" and a nod, "Yes," a pull meant "Come" and a push, "Go." Was it bread that I wanted? Then I would imitate the acts of cutting the slices and buttering them. If I wanted my mother to make ice cream for dinner, I made the sign for working the freezer and shivered, indicating cold. (Keller, 1954)

About 3 months before Helen's 7th birthday a teacher, Miss Anne Sullivan, arrived to attempt to train her to communicate by finger spelling. Gradually, Helen learned to spell several words, but she simply used these as she had previously used her own self-invented signs. That is, she had not yet recognized the essence of symbols: since their meaning is arbitrarily assigned by their users, a symbol may be created to refer to anything. In the words of Anne Sullivan:

> Helen has learned several nouns this week. "M-u-g" and "m-i-l-k" have given her more trouble than other words. When she spells "m-i-l-k" she points to the mug, and when she spells "m-u-g," she makes the sign for pouring or drinking, which shows that she has confused the words. She has no idea yet that everything has a name. (Keller, 1954, p. 253)

In a month of intense teaching, Helen learned only 25 nouns and 4 verbs. Here is her own description of this period of her slow learning of the finger-spelling signs:

> The morning after my teacher came she led me into her room and gave me a doll. The little blind children

at the Perkins Institution had sent it and Laura Bridgman had dressed it; but I did not know this until afterward. When I had played with it a little while, Miss Sullivan slowly spelled into my hand the word "d-o-l-l." I was at once interested in this finger play and tried to imitate it. When I finally succeeded in making letters correctly I was flushed with childish pleasure and pride. Running downstairs to my mother I held up my hand and made the letters for doll. I did not know that I was spelling a word or even that words existed; I was simply making my fingers go in monkey-like imitation. In the days that followed I learned to spell in this uncomprehending way a great many words, among them *pin, hat, cup* and a few verbs like *sit, stand,* and *walk.* But my teacher had been with me several weeks before I understood that everything has a name. (p. 35)

Helen's slow rate of sign learning was superseded by a remarkably accelerated rate of learning that began when her inborn symbolic abilities became activated in a single dramatic incident. This change was recorded by her teacher in the following excerpt of a letter:

April 5, 1887

> We went out to the pump-house, and I made Helen hold her mug under the spout while I pumped. As the cold water gushed forth, filling the mug, I spelled "w-a-t-e-r" in Helen's free hand. The word coming so close on the sensation of cold water rushing over her hand seemed to startle her. She dropped the mug and stood as one transfixed. A new light came into her face. She spelled "water" several times. Then she dropped on the ground and asked for its name and pointed to the pump and the trellis, and suddenly turning around she asked for my name. I spelled "Teacher." Just then the nurse brought Helen's little sister into the pump-house, and Helen spelled "baby" and pointed to the nurse. All the way back to the house she was highly excited, and learned the name of every object she touched, so that in a few hours she had added thirty new words to her vocabulary. Here are some of them: *Door, open, shut, give, go, come,* and a great many more.

> *P.S.—I didn't finish my letter in time to get it posted last night; so I shall add a line. Helen got up this morning like a radiant fairy. She has flitted from object to object, asking the name of everything and kissing me for very gladness. . . . I thought my heart would burst, so full was it of joy.* (Keller, 1954, pp. 256–57)

FIGURE 12.2

HELEN KELLER

Unable to communicate by speaking and unable to hear, Helen Keller (1880–1968) learned the meaning of words through the complicated method of her teacher forming letters in her hand. This photograph, taken in the early 1950s, shows the hand of her companion signing letters in Helen's hand. Helen became a tireless lecturer for the rights of the deaf.

users. Because people can freely assign new meanings to objects or actions, they can communicate extremely complex and subtle messages to one another.

Human vs. Nonhuman Communication

Homo sapiens is not the only animal species that communicates. Many nonhuman animals make use of both biologically innate and learned signs in communicative acts. However, the creation and use of symbols is characteristic of humans alone, and the human use of symbols is central to our most conscious efforts to communicate. Acts such as smiling or crying have rather natural meanings as signs, but they can be consciously manipulated and used in ways that alter their natural meanings and transform them into sym-

bols, as when we smile sarcastically or feign tears or a sad expression to communicate a feeling that we are not really experiencing.

In human beings, only the simplest of meaningful signs—those that communicate simple feelings in unconscious or unintentional ways—are biologically preprogrammed. For instance, we express heightened interest in whatever we are observing by an increase in the dilation of the pupil of the eye, a change controlled on an unconscious level by the autonomic nervous system (the part of the nervous system that controls the functioning of involuntary actions such as the beating of the heart). This sign, though unintentional, is communicative, and other persons perceive the change and respond to it. Similarly, the increased muscle tension that signals rising anger is often communicative enough to cause an observer to act more carefully.

In some other animals, even complex communications may be governed by biologically controlled behavioral tendencies. For instance, a fighting timber wolf may indicate its submission by freezing its stance and exposing the vulnerable area of its throat to the attacking fangs of its opponent. This act might seem highly inappropriate and dangerous in the heat of battle, yet the timber wolf has a biological predisposition to signify its acceptance of defeat in this way. And the sign receives the appropriate response: although the victor grasps the throat of its victim with its mouth as if to bite, its muscles tremble as if strained by the effort to control its enraged attack, and it does not bite to kill. If the submitting wolf remains rigid and unmoving, it will not be bitten, and the victor will continue to strain as if it desires but is unable to bite until, finally exhausted, it releases its hold and begins to walk away. Even now, if the submitting wolf starts to move, a renewed attack will begin until the sign of submission is given again. The process may be repeated several times until the loser manages to escape from the repeated attacks of the gradually tiring dominant animal.

NONVERBAL COMMUNICATION

The two most active forms of interpersonal communication are nonverbal communication and language. **Nonverbal communication** consists of the messages that we convey to each other without words or beyond words alone. Often it is an unconscious expression of our emotions and may not even be intended as communication. It ranges from grins and hugs to the space that we place between ourselves and others in conversation and our handling of time (as in arriving early or late for an appointment). Although nonverbal communication does not include the words that we speak, it does include various qualities of speaking such as our speed of talking, intonation, pitch, and volume, all of which express how we feel about what we are saying.

Nonverbal Signs

The simplest forms of nonverbal communication are physiological signs, not symbols. For instance, blushing, which communicates embarrassment, is a direct reflection of one's emotional state and is controlled by the autonomic nervous system. Smiling, although it can be consciously controlled and assigned other symbolic meanings in special contexts, is also more generally a direct reflection of happy feelings. As such, it can be observed in deaf-blind individuals as well as in others. Slumping posture will signal submission or defeat without conscious effort; prolonged eye contact can indicate aggression or interest in maintaining contact; staring blankly while avoiding eye contact may signal fear or a desire not to interact. Nonverbal signs communicate the same meanings in every culture. Samoan, Navajo, or Chinese, we all express happiness with the same spontaneous smile, confusion with a distinctively human knit brow, and boredom with a yawn.

Culturally Patterned Nonverbal Symbols

In contrast with nonverbal signs, our nonverbal symbols, such as parting gestures, flirtatious uses of the eyes, and hand gestures of contempt, vary from culture to culture. For instance, throughout Europe when people want to point out the location of something they gesture in the appropriate direction with their hand. The finger closest to the thumb, appropriately called the "pointing finger" in colloquial English, may also be extended. Shoshone Indians of the North American Great Basin still use their traditional gesture, pointing with their lips. Many North Americans use a "thumbs up" gesture to express their feeling that things are going well. In Japan this gesture would likely be interpreted to mean "boss" or "father." The German who points to the side of his forehead communicates the same idea—"crazy!"—that the North American may convey by tracing a circle next to the head with the index finger. North Americans point at their chests to indicate "self"; Japanese point to their noses with the same significance.

Our most common nonverbal symbolic communications tend to be performed with the highly visible upper extremities of the body—the hands, arms, shoulders, head, and parts of the face. They are often used in situations of purposeful communication: (1) where verbal communication is impossible, as when persons are too distant from one another to hear one another well; (2) where verbal communication is inappropriate, as when the actor wishes to send the message to only one member of a group (but knows others would overhear a verbal message), or when the sender feels that a verbal communication would be too direct or strong in impact; and (3) where their use will provide added emphasis while speaking verbal symbols.

Cultural variations in such symbols may inhibit full communication between people of different cultures, even on a nonverbal level. Greeting is not signified everywhere by a handshake: a kiss, an embrace, or a nose rub will do as well. Among the Toda of India, a woman indicates respect in greeting an elder kinsman by kneeling and lifting his foot to her forehead (Murdock, 1969). A wave of the hand that the European would interpret as a farewell might elsewhere be used as a request to approach. Such differences can lead to misunderstandings between well-intentioned persons from different societies who do not realize that their behaviors are only arbitrarily endowed with meaning and that the same behaviors might denote something different to people from another society.

---

nonverbal communication all transfer of information beyond words alone, involving such things as volume, pitch, tone of voice, and speed when speaking, as well as non-oral things such as gestures, posture, and use of space and time

FIGURE 12.3

ANDAMANESE GREETING AND PARTING CUSTOMS

Andaman Islanders of either sex greet each other after absences of a few weeks by one sitting in the lap of the other and weeping. Since their etiquette demands crying as a means of expressing sentiment, the Andamanese learn to shed tears on demand.

Proxemics

Even the distance we place between ourselves and others conveys subtle nonverbal meanings. Edward Hall (1959) has studied the ways in which people symbolically structure the spatial relationships between themselves and others. He refers to the study of people's use of the space around them as **proxemics**. One finding of proxemic research is that the distance people choose to place themselves from others while communicating with them illustrates how they feel about the interaction. According to Hall, there are four main distances to which North Americans adjust themselves in their business and social relations: intimate, personal, social, and public.

Intimate distance, which is reserved for occasions when caressing and touch are appropriate, varies in the United States from direct contact to 1½ feet, where persons are still close enough to touch one another easily. We experience others in this zone intensely by many of our senses. They fill our field of vision, their breathing is audible, and we are aware of their presence by the senses of touch and smell as well. This intimate awareness often leads us to experience the other as an extension of our own self rather than as a separate entity. Intimate distance is normally regarded as too close to be used by adults in public. In crowded situations such as elevators or subways, when one is forced to remain within the intimate distance of strangers, individuals communicate that they are not intentionally intruding on the intimate zone of others by staring impersonally at a distant spot.

The second meaningful zone to which North Americans adjust themselves, called **personal distance**, indicates a close friendship. It extends from 1½ to 4 feet. A husband and wife

---

proxemics the study of how people structure the space around them when interacting with others

intimate distance the distance from their bodies that people reserve for those with whom they are intimate enough to permit casual touching

personal distance the distance to which people adjust themselves when interacting with close friends

generally place themselves within the first half of each other's personal zone in public or conversational situations, while other friends will normally occupy the farther half of this zone. In many other cultures, the distances for this personal zone are somewhat closer than they are in the United States or northern Europe. This can make it difficult for persons of differing cultural backgrounds to communicate their interest in one another. An Anglo-American may feel ill at ease if a stranger from another society adopts a distance that in the stranger's homeland indicates friendship but which to the Anglo-American seems overly intimate or pushy. When the Anglo-American backs away to a distance at which he or she feels comfortable among friends, the other may mistakenly interpret the nonverbal communication as disinterest. Such misunderstandings can be avoided only if one becomes aware that even the most habitual of human behaviors, because they are very specific and symbolic, have no universal meanings but vary from society to society.

Beyond personal distance is **social distance** of 4 to 12 feet, which is used in more impersonal interactions of a cordial type such as in business transactions. **Public distance**, which is greater than 12 feet, is the final zone. The usual distance placed between a teacher or public speaker and most audiences is 12 to about 25 feet. Distances greater than this are used to distinguish important public figures.

Hall (1959) has studied several societies and has found that the distances to which people adjust themselves for intimate, personal, social, or public activities are not the same in every society. For instance, among Germans personal space is expanded to include visible areas far beyond the North American's 4-foot space. People are expected to greet formally anyone of their acquaintance who comes into sight and is within hailing distance. This is reflected in the German preference for solid doors that clearly separate each room in homes and work places, a preference that contrasts with the common North American preference for rooms connected by doorways that have no closeable doors. Typically, the traditional German home or apartment has a lockable door on every room, including the kitchen, allowing Germans to indicate their personal space with a definite boundary. The North American walk-through floor plan with kitchen and dining areas open to and clearly visible from the living room would strike the traditional German family as strange, indeed. Arab homes, on the other hand, are much more open than those in North America. Privacy there is obtained not by physical boundaries but by withdrawal from communication, which may simply mean moving outside personal distance. To North Americans who identify their "selves" with their bodies, this constant physical intimacy in the openness of the living space might seem an invasion of their persons. Yet Arabs, many of whom have had to adjust to higher population densities in which contact with strangers is difficult to avoid, have learned to isolate their sense of personal identity deeper within their bodies than North Americans do.

Kinesics

Nonverbal communication often accompanies speech, providing the context within which speech is interpreted. Signs such as posturing of the body, gestures, and the use of the eyes communicate the level of interest and involvement in others present or in the subject being discussed. Nonverbal communication with its subtlety and complexity provides information about emotions such as love, hate, fear, dependency, submission, dominance, interest, disinterest, or boredom. It therefore defines and expresses the nature of the relationship. Without a successful nonverbal relationship between people, verbal communication may become impossible. For instance, if body movements are too unsynchronized with one another, or if they indicate hostility, successful verbal communication may be impossible.

The study of the body movements that complement speech as a means of communication is called **kinesics**. Ray Birdwhistell (1970) has developed a system for recording those movements with precise detail. He has discovered, for instance, that the human face can make a quarter of a million different expressions. For study purposes, however, 26 symbols are enough to record the basic facial positions.

---

social distance the distance to which people adjust themselves when interacting in impersonal situations such as business transactions

public distance the distance reserved for separating people whose interaction is not intended to perpetuate a social relationship

kinesics the study of the body movements that accompany speech as a component of communication

FIGURE 12.4

NONVERBAL COMMUNICATION

Nonverbal communication can be as subtle as the lifting of an eyebrow, or the turning of a shoulder, providing a context within which speech can be interpreted. Nonverbal signs, however, such as a fist raised high in the air, or a high five, can also be conscious, obvious efforts to communicate an emo- *tional state. Here, a Bosnian Serb soldier flashes his culture's three-finger victory sign from a window in downtown Pale in September 1995. The building is reinforced with wooden logs to withstand NATO bombs. The slogan on the wall reads "Comrade Tito," the name of the former Communist leader of Yugoslavia.*

Birdwhistell's system for recording the movements of the entire body uses less than 100 symbols. He has demonstrated that the ability of the human brain to process visual data about other people's body movements is astounding. He estimates that people are capable of processing as many as 10,000 bits of information or percepts per second.

Some nonverbal signs can be brought under more or less conscious control and can become overlaid with symbolic significance that will alter their basic significance as signs. Yet such nonverbal signs still tend to reflect the emotional state of the speaker and thus are limited in their use as a productive communication system. The more usual role of nonverbal communication is to define a relationship between two or more persons and a topic of communication by sending simple, often unconscious messages about how those involved feel about themselves, about each other, and about the ideas being expressed in language (Watzlawick, Beavin, & Jackson, 1967).

LANGUAGE

Language is a symbolizing system that does not rely on body signs in order to communicate. Language is therefore said to be an "open" system of communication because its subject matter is unlimited. New messages can be invented to express anything that can be thought. Language can be used to communicate about not only those feelings, things, and persons that are visible at the moment, but also those that are invisible because they are displaced in space or time, as well as things that are nonexistent. Language is a **metacommunication system**—one that can be used to communicate about the process of communication itself. In the following sections, we will examine the distinction between speech and language, the bio-

---

metacommunication system a system of communication that includes the capacity to communicate about itself logical basis of humans' capacity for language, the origin of language, the structure of language, the interactions between language and culture, the processes by which languages change and diverge from each other, and the politics of language.

Language vs. Speech

Within the human supply of symbolic skills, language, the most systematically organized component, stands out. **Language** is the shared system of rules that guides the production of **speech**, the audible symbols that people use to communicate. Every language system is made up of three sets of shared rules: (1) rules for forming the particular speech sounds used in the language, (2) rules for putting the sounds of speech together into words that symbolize concepts, and (3) rules for putting the words together into sentences that portray the relationships between concepts. The existence of a system for organizing speech symbols increases the amount of information that can be communicated with those symbols. For instance, each of the words "boy," "dog," "bit," and "the" communicates an image or a concept. But it is the word order of the sentence "The dog bit the boy" that lets the same words communicate more than just a list of ideas. The way those words are organized within the sentence enables the hearer to decipher the relationships between the images and concepts that they represent. The existence of a rule-governed structure for organizing sounds makes speech symbols possible, and the rules of sentence formation allow us to communicate effectively with those symbols.

When children begin learning language, they not only learn the vocal symbols of the speech that they hear uttered by others around them, but they also discover the meaningful pattern to the arrangement of these speech sounds. The number of sentences that can be spoken in any language is effectively unlimited. But the existence of a system that governs the organization of words into sentences makes it unnecessary for children to actually hear and memorize each separate sentence before they can communicate any idea they wish to express to someone else (Chomsky, 1971). Having a socially shared pattern for representing concepts by a series of vocal symbols makes it possible (1) to produce new sentences that one has never heard before, (2) to communicate about new concepts, and (3) to correctly interpret new utterances that one hears for the first time.

The Biological Basis of Language

The exceptional linguistic ability of humans—an ability that has allowed the creation and perpetuation of complex cultures—is made possible by a biologically inherited, specialized set of structures in the brain. The human brain is a complex affair, as yet imperfectly understood. It consists of three major subdivisions: (1) the **brain stem**, which regulates involuntary processes such as breathing and heartbeat and controls basic drives such as hunger; (2) the **cerebellum**, which coordinates muscular activity; and (3) the **cerebral cortex**, the largest and most recently evolved part of the brain, which monitors the senses, controls mental activities, and initiates voluntary activities (see Figure 12.6 on p. 304).

The cerebral cortex is the area of the brain that analyzes sensory experiences and initiates conscious action. Seen from above, it is divided in half into two major components or hemispheres. Each hemisphere is creased by numerous folds. The specialized language mechanisms of the cerebral cortex are located on only one side of the cerebral cortex—on the left hemisphere for almost all individuals.

Below one of the major creases is **Wernicke's area**, the section of the cortex that receives incoming information about speech sounds. It seems to be the seat of comprehension of speech, of interpreting the meanings of words as well as of formulating verbal messages. Here, concepts are translated into their corresponding word representations.

(Continued on p. 304)

language a system of rules that govern the production and interpretation of speech

speech the audible symbols that people use to communicate

brain stem the parts of the brain that regulate involuntary processes such as breathing and heartbeat

cerebellum the part of the brain below and behind the cerebral hemispheres of the brain that functions in the coordination of muscular activity

cerebral cortex the surface layer of the two large hemispheres of the brain that functions in the analysis of sensory experiences and initiates conscious action

Wernicke's area the part of the cerebral cortex involved in processing speech sounds

COMMUNICATION IN NONHUMAN PRIMATES

Is language unique to the human species? We are now attempting to understand the communication patterns and language potential of other animals, including our own closest relatives. Biologically speaking, human beings are members of a group of animals known as *primates* that consists of the apes, the monkeys, and the small tree-dwelling prosimians. As a group, the primates tend to be social and communicative animals. Nevertheless, the uniqueness of human language is apparent when one compares it with the communication systems of the other primates.

According to Altmann (1973), "For the most part . . . the social signals of monkeys and apes are not semantic: the messages do not stand for something else. They are simply social signals to which a response is given. In this they are much more like the cry of a newborn infant than they are like the speech of human adults" (p. 87). Similarly, Marler (1965) observes, "It begins to appear that a repertoire of from about 10 to about 15 basic sound-signals is characteristic of nonhuman primates as a whole. In some it may prove to be smaller or larger, but it is doubtful if the limits will be exceeded by very much. . . . Comparison with other highly vocal groups of vertebrates that have been closely examined reveals an approximately similar repertoire size" (p. 558). Thus, the nonhuman primates do not seem much different from other comparable animals in their vocal communicative abilities. Symbolic language seems to be a distinctively human trait.

In recent years, the limits of nonhuman primate communicative abilities have begun to be explored through attempts to teach various forms of language to chimpanzees (Mounin, 1976), possibly the most similar to human beings in their biological characteristics. These efforts have revealed a striking capacity in chimpanzees to expand their communication skills. One such study was started in 1966 by Allen and Beatrix Gardner with the chimpanzee Washoe (1969, 1985). A major problem in earlier attempts to teach a human language to chimpanzees had been the chimpanzee's difficulty in forming the sounds used in human speech (Kellog, 1968; Hayes & Nissen, 1971). The Gardners overcame this problem by teaching Washoe a modified version of **American Sign Language (ASL)**, the gestural language of the deaf in North America. Chimpanzees naturally make use of a variety of gestures when communicating in the wild, and the Gardners' use of ASL proved to be a breakthrough. Within four years, Washoe had mastered more than 130 signs of ASL. In addition to using signs appropriately to name objects (e.g., dog, flower, or shoe), attributes (e.g., red, dirty, or funny), and actions (e.g.,

give, want, or drink), Washoe learned to combine signs into sequences such as "give" + "tickle." The Gardners and Washoe's later trainer, Roger Fouts, claim that Washoe has mastered something equivalent to grammar in human language. In six successful studies they believe that they have proven that chimpanzees have at least a basic ability to use language in the human sense. Others disagree. Herbert Terrace (1979) has worked with chimpanzees and has also analyzed videotapes of human/chimpanzee sign language interaction. He and his colleagues claim that many of the apparent examples of chimpanzees' combining signs into grammatical sequences are not spontaneous but have resulted from the chimpanzees' responding to subtle cues that the trainers gave (Terrace et al. 1979). Duane Rumbaugh, H. Warner, and Ernst Von Glasersfeld (1977) began training chimpanzees to communicate by pressing keys embossed with geometric signs. They agree with Terrace that chimpanzees can learn to associate signs with objects and actions and to use signs to make simple requests, but that the chimpanzees taught ASL do not demonstrate a grasp of grammar (Savage-Rumbaugh, Rumbaugh, & Boysen, 1980; Savage-Rumbaugh et al. 1983). Rather, they merely string together any signs they know that are relevant to the situation in which they are making a request. Savage-Rumbaugh and her colleagues (1980) assert that the most important difference between chimpanzee communication and that of human children is that chimpanzees make requests but do not spontaneously begin to describe their environment. They make sequences like "give orange me give eat orange me eat orange give me eat orange give me you," but they do not make comments such as "The orange is cold" or "The orange juice is sticky" while they are eating the orange (p. 60).

Another primate language training study has been carried out by Francine Patterson with a gorilla named Koko (1978; see also Hill, 1978). Like Washoe, Koko has been taught American Sign Language. Her vocabulary is over 400 words. It includes words for emotions, such as sadness and shame, that Koko uses to communicate about her own feelings. She has spontaneously used descriptive phrases, such as "finger bracelet" for ring, to refer to things for which she had learned no word from her trainer, an ability that also had been demonstrated by the chimpanzee Washoe; she has been caught lying, when she tried to blame a human for something she had broken, and she has mastered sign language well enough to take an intelligence test designed for human beings, scoring in the low-average range!

FIGURE 12.5

CHIMPANZEE SIGNING

In several different experiments chimpanzees have been taught to converse with their trainers, using American Sign Language. Here this chimpanzee asks to hug the cat and gets his wish.

We have much to learn about nonhuman primate communication skills—what they have in common with and how they differ from human language. Considering the abilities that nonhuman primates have demonstrated, an intriguing question that remains to be answered is why they have not put these skills to use in the wild, where their communication with one another seems limited to a small number of signs that have very natural expressive meanings. One project now under way that may eventually help us answer questions like this one began at the Institute for Primate Studies in Oklahoma. There, a group of chimpanzees—including Washoe—who had learned American Sign Language were placed together on an island to see if they would use ASL with, and learn signs from, one another, and whether or not their skills would be passed on to the next generation (Linden, 1974). In 1980 the project was moved to Central Washington University, where the study of communication between chimpanzees has continued. Roger Fouts and his colleagues have reported that by 1984 Washoe's adopted offspring, Loulis, had learned 28 signs from her mother (Fouts, Fouts, & Schoenfeld, 1984); by October 1995 the number had reached 80 (R. Fouts, personal communication, October 1995).

In evolutionary terms, chimpanzees and gorillas are our closest living relatives. Perhaps they do have the same basic symbolic capacities as human beings, but the controversy about how closely their communication skills parallel our own continues. The communication skills of these nonhuman primates are tremendously impressive, but whether they can use the "languages" that they have been taught symbolically and not just as systems of meaningful signs remains to be seen. So far none of the primates in these studies has demonstrated that they have Helen Keller's distinctively human insight that *everything* can be given a name.

American Sign Language (ASL) a system of hand gesture symbols used by hearing-impaired persons for communicating; a true, though nonvocal, language that has its own grammar and vocabulary

FIGURE 12.6

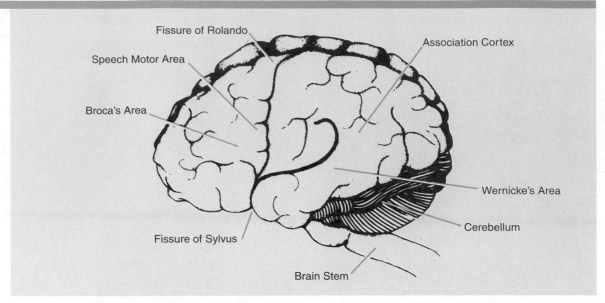

THE SPEECH CENTERS OF THE HUMAN BRAIN

Without the complex structures in the brain, humans wouldn't have the ability to transform sensory experiences into speech. The speech centers are located in the left hemisphere of the cerebral cortex. Wernicke's area receives speech sounds and interprets them as meaningful. The association cortex co-ordinates information from other sensory stimuli to allow the brain to select a proper verbal response. Broca's area and the speech motor area control the grammatical sequence of words and the physical movements necessary to produce speech.

From Wernicke's area, the information is passed on to a larger region of the cerebral cortex called the **association cortex**. It coordinates information from various other parts of the cerebral cortex—such as the hearing centers, the visual centers, and the centers of physical sensation—with the vocal message, and it provides Wernicke's area with the conceptual information that guides its selection of the appropriate word symbols.

From the association cortex, the linguistic message is sent forward to an area in the front half of the cerebral cortex known as **Broca's area**. There, the brain organizes the message grammatically and controls information about the sequences of movements necessary for the production of speech. Broca's area is directly in front of an important fold in the cerebral cortex known as the **Fissure of Rolando**, which controls the voluntary movements of various parts of the body. The part of the Fissure of Rolando directly next to Broca's area is the **speech motor area**. This area controls the movement of the vocal cords, tongue, jaws, and lips. Thus, Broca's area seems to be directly in charge of causing this area of the brain to move the vocal apparatus in the proper sequences to produce the speech sounds of the message.

There are no *direct* connections between the parts of the association areas that deal with vision, those that pertain to hearing, and those that are related to the motor activities of speech. Lancaster (1968) has pointed out that in monkeys and apes the only way of making these connections involves another region of the brain known as the **limbic system**, which consists of some of the deeper and evolutionarily older areas of the cortex that deal with emotional experience. This may be why vocal communication in the nonhuman primates such as the apes and monkeys is limited to the

association cortex the area of the cerebral cortex that coordinates information from various other parts of the brain

Broca's area the part of the cerebral cortex involved in organizing words into grammatical sequences

Fissure of Rolando a vertical fold in the surface of the brain that separates the motor areas, which control conscious muscle movement, from corresponding areas, which receive sensory information from various parts of the body

speech motor area the part of the cerebral cortex that controls the production of speech sounds

limbic system areas within the brain that deal with emotional experience

expression of internal motivational states. In human beings, on the other hand, indirect connections that do not involve the limbic system (and emotion) can be made between the areas of the association cortex, which are connected with the other sensory centers, and the association areas connected to the speech centers (DeVore, 1965). This gives humans the unique ability to withhold vocalizations in moments of emotional excitation and to communicate vocally about facts of no immediate emotional significance to the speaker, abilities of fundamental importance for symbolic communication.

The Origin of Language

Very little is known about how human language abilities evolved. Unfortunately, spoken language leaves no imprint that can be searched for directly, and humans only began to record language in written form a few thousand years ago. So our investigation of the very beginnings of language must look at indirect evidence. Investigating the fossil record of early human forms for evidence of biological characteristics necessary for speaking is one method. Another is determining how people who do not speak the same language have sometimes developed new languages, called creoles.

Biological Evolution and Language.
Clearly, our nearest living relatives, chimpanzees and gorillas, do not use spoken symbols as humans do when speaking. Since it is unlikely that completely sophisticated language skills emerged suddenly, it is commonly assumed that the foundations from which modern languages evolved developed sometime after the separation of the human line from that of the apes about 4 to 6 million years ago. Communication among early human ancestors such as the australopithecines of 2 to 4 million years ago probably had much in common with nonsymbolic communication in the apes, consisting of vocal calls and gestures. The important question is when and under what circumstances the communication of our ancestors might have taken on the symbolic and, therefore, "open-system" qualities that are characteristic of all modern languages. Some researchers believe that studies of the evolution of the brain and vocal tract may help us pinpoint the transition.

The human brain achieved its modern size among Neanderthals at least 100,000 years ago, and Dean Falk (1975) and Philip Tobias (1983) pointed out that Broca's area was well developed in Neanderthals. Several kinds of archaeological evidence strongly suggest that Neanderthals practiced religious rituals. For instance, at several sites they stored cave bear skulls and leg bones with ceremonial care, and their gravesites indicate carefully prepared burials. Such behavior implies abstract thought and a level of communication that other animals do not demonstrate.

What is not clear, however, is whether Neanderthals' communicative abilities were as sophisticated as human languages are today. Philip Lieberman and E. S. Crelin (1971) studied reconstructions of the Neanderthal vocal tract and found that their throats and mouths were not organized in a way that would have permitted them to produce the sounds found in all modern languages. Jeffrey Laitman (1984) and Lieberman (1984) argue that the modern physical form was not achieved until about 40,000 years ago.

Pidgin and Creole Languages.
There are several situations that bring people together who speak no common language. For instance, in colonial days, masters of plantations might need to communicate with laborers who spoke another language, or in the early days of trading, shipboard life often brought together a crew of many different nationalities who needed to work and communicate together. These and similar situations have given rise to the development of **pidgin languages**, which are simplified versions of one language or a combination of several. Pidgins are simpler in grammar and smaller in vocabulary than the natural languages that children learn in childhood. However, they have sometimes become the second-generation native languages of entire populations, in which case they invariably develop the greater grammatical sophistication and larger vocabularies that are necessary for use in everyday life. Such true languages that have developed out of pidgins or through the efforts of speakers of several different languages are called **creoles**. There are over a hundred creole languages spoken in the world

---

pidgin languages simplified versions of one language or a combination of several

creoles true languages that have developed out of pidgins

today. They include Haitian Creole, Hawaiian Creole, São Tomense of Equitorial Guinea, and Srinam of Suriname.

Derek Bickerton (1983) has investigated creoles and has found that they all have a number of characteristics in common. Their grammatical qualities may reflect that of early human language. For instance, in almost all creoles adjectives function as verbs, so there is no need for a "to be" verb to join a subject with an adjective. Thus, in Guyanese Creole "He is tired" is simply "i wiiri." Creoles express future and past tenses by the addition of a particle, such as "shall" or "was" between the subject and the verb, and all have adopted the use of double negatives such as in Papia Kristang "non dag na bait non kyat" (literally, "no dog no bite no cat"), which translates into English as "No dog bit any cat." All creoles also make use of intonation to indicate the difference between questions and statements.

The traits that all creoles have developed may tell us something about the origins of language itself. It was suggested some time ago by the linguist Noam Chomsky (1965) that all natural languages share an underlying grammatical system. Chomsky's views were based on his studies of noncreole languages. He found that certain fundamental grammatical patterns of all languages are variations on a relatively simple, universal system of grammar. This led him to suggest that human children are born with an innate capacity to learn language. According to Bickerton, the notable uniformities among creoles support this idea, and the situations in which creoles emerge make it likely that the basic, innate language patterns are likely to be followed more closely than in languages with longer histories. Thus, in his opinion, the shared grammatical qualities of creoles are likely to be the very ones that were present in the earliest forms of human language.

THE STRUCTURE OF LANGUAGE

Anthropological linguists who are interested in the structure of languages have shown that all languages have definite patterns in the sounds that their speakers use, in how those sounds are combined to form symbols, and in how those symbols are organized into meaningful utterances. These three structured parts of language are called phonology, morphology, and syntax.

Phonology

The study of sounds used in speech and the rules for producing the sequences of sounds that occur in a particular language is called **phonology**. The human vocal apparatus is capable of forming a large number of different sounds, but the range of sounds actually produced in human languages is relatively small. Although there are at least 3,000 languages in the world, it is possible to record any human language using the **International Phonetic Alphabet**, which consists of fewer than 100 sound symbols.

The description of a specific language begins by using some of the symbols of this alphabet to record the **phones**, sounds made by speakers of the language. This record is called a **phonetic description** of the language. A phonetic transcription of a language records more sound detail than would seem necessary to native speakers. A simple phonetic transcription of verse from the well-known English poem, "The Walrus and the Carpenter" by Lewis Carroll, looks like this:

> ðə tʰãym hæz kʰʌm
> ðə wɔlrʌs sɛd
> tʰu tʰɔk əv mɛ̃ni θĩŋz
> əv šuz æ̃nd sĭps
> æ̃nd silĩ̃ wæks
> əv kʰæbəǰəz æ̃nd kʰĩŋz
> æ̃nd way ðə si ɪz bɔylĩŋ hat
> æ̃nd wɛðər pʰɪgz hæv wĩŋz.

It is difficult to read a phonetic transcription of one's native language without practice, because it records more information than is needed by fluent speakers who are uncon-

---

phonology the study of the rules that govern the production and the organization of the sounds of a particular language

International Phonetic Alphabet (IPA) a standard alphabet of nearly 100 sound symbols used by linguists throughout the world for writing phonetic transcriptions of languages

phones smallest sound units of a language

phonetic description a description pertaining to the smallest units of sound actually produced by speakers of a language

scious of many of the predictable sound patterns in their speech. In every language, some of the phonetically recorded sounds are not meaningfully distinct from one another. Instead, they are simply variants, or **allophones**, of a more general sound called a phoneme of that language. For instance, a native English speaker is likely to say that the letter *t* in the words "top" and "stop" are the same sound. In fact, this is not the case. In the first word the pronunciation of the *t* ends with a definite explosion of air that is not present following the *t* in the second word. This difference can be demonstrated by pronouncing each word while holding the end of a strip of paper against the upper lip. The paper will flutter only when the word "top" is pronounced.

Once it is determined how the phones of a language are grouped into phonemes, it is possible to record the language phonemically, using a smaller alphabet designed especially for that language. A **phonemic alphabet** is made by using only one symbol for each phoneme of the language. The **phonemes** of such alphabets are the smallest meaningful units of sound in a language; substituting one phoneme for another can change the meaning of a word. Thus, if the word *stop* is pronounced so that the *t* is followed by the explosion of air found in its allophone in the word *top*, the word will still be heard by listeners as *stop*. However, substituting the phoneme *l* for *t* will create a different word, "slop."

A phonemic alphabet records the distinctions in sounds that are psychologically relevant to the native speakers of a language, so it spells words the way they seem to sound to native speakers. In a phonemic transcription of spoken English, the word *hiss* would be written as *his*, and the word *his* would be written as *hiz.* Typically, only between 20 and 45 phonemes are necessary for writing a language. English, for instance, has 45 phonemically distinct sounds. Since the 26-letter alphabet used by English speakers for writing their language is not phonemically accurate, English speakers must learn a complex system of spelling to decipher the conventions they use in writing their language.

Grammar

The analysis of the regular and predictable ways that the sounds of a language are combined to form meaningful utterances is called **grammar**. It has two subdivisions, morphology and syntax.

Morphology. The first of these, **morphology**, is the study of how phonemes are combined into the smallest meaningful units, called **morphemes**. *Alligator, love*, and *Arkansas* are **free morphemes** because they can stand alone as words in sentences. English morphemes such as *-s*, meaning "plural," and *pre-*, meaning "before," are called **bound morphemes** because they cannot serve as words in sentences. Bound morphemes only occur as suffixes or prefixes of other morphemes. Sometimes several morphemes carry the same meaning; for instance *-s, -z* (written as an *s* in English), *-en*, and *-ren* all mean "plural." Such morphemes are considered variants of one another, since it is predictable which will be chosen by English speakers to pluralize another morpheme. Thus, *child* combines acceptably only with the plural morpheme *-ren*. Morphemes that carry the same meaning in this way are called **allomorphs** of one another.

Syntax. The second subdivision of grammar is **syntax**. It is the study of the rules for combining morphemes into complete and

---

allophones phonetically variant forms of a single phoneme

phonemic alphabet a written record of speech that uses an alphabet composed of only one symbol for each phoneme of the language

phoneme the smallest psychologically real unit of sound in a language

grammar the analysis of the regular ways that the sounds of a language are combined to form meaningful utterances; includes morphology and syntax

morphology the study of how phonemes are combined into the smallest meaningful units of a language

morpheme the smallest meaningful sequence of sounds in a language

free morphemes morphemes that can stand alone as words in sentences

bound morphemes morphemes that cannot stand on their own as complete words

allomorphs variants of a single morpheme that have the same meaning but different phonological structure

syntax the study of the rules for combining morphemes into complete and meaningful sentences

meaningful sentences. All languages do an adequate job of expressing meanings, but each language has its own distinctive rules that control how one goes about expressing those meanings. Although we each find the conventions of our own language quite natural, seeing how differently other languages operate can give us some idea of the fact that what seems natural to us as native speakers is merely one of many possible conventions.

Languages such as English use word order to indicate differences between the actor and the acted-upon. For instance, there is an important difference of meaning between the two English sentences, *The dog bit the child* and *The child bit the dog*. In many languages, the distinction between subject and object is instead indicated by subject and/or object suffixes. For instance, in the Latin sentence *Canis infant-em momordit* (literally, "Dog child-object bit"), the suffix *-em* indicates the object. Languages that distinguish subjects and objects in this way can become quite free in their word order. Thus, in Latin *Infant-em momordit canis* could also be used to mean "The dog bit the child." Often, in languages that do not rely on order to indicate subject-object relations, differences in order may convey differences in emphasis. In the two Latin sentences just used, the first might be translated as "The *dog* bit the child," while the second would be "The dog bit the *child*." Some languages have special ways of marking an emphasized word. For instance, in the Andean language Quechua the bound morpheme *-qa* indicates the emphasized topic of a sentence: *Alqu wawa-ta-qa k'ani-rqa* (literally, "dog child-object-topic bite-past"), which might be translated as "The dog bit the *child*," but *Alqu-qa wawa-ta k'ani-rqa* would be "The *dog* bit the child."

Quechua greatly elaborates the process of modifying single words with suffixes to express complex meanings. Thus, the two-word Quechua sentence *Mana kasu-wa-na-yki-chiq-ri-chu* (literally, "Not obey-me-for-you-plural-nicely-question") means "Is it not for you to obey me nicely?" Other languages such as Chinese use but one morpheme per word, so that the Chinese equivalent of "The dog bit the boy" would be *Gǒyǎo le shǎohái* (literally, "Dog child bite completed"), the time of the action being specified by a particular word *le* that indicates that the action of the verb *yǎo* is completed.

The many languages of the world differ tremendously in their phonologies and grammars. Despite the great diversity in how languages organize a small number of sounds into meaningful sentences, all languages seem equally able to express ideas. As natural as your own language may seem to you after years of use, it is no more fundamentally human than others. Like all symbolic systems, languages convey meanings effectively simply because their users have learned the same conventions for interpreting those meanings.

LINGUISTIC RELATIVITY

Any idea can be symbolically expressed in any language. Nevertheless, the vocabulary and grammatical variations of different languages do have an impact on (1) which things speakers habitually notice, label, and think about, and (2) how speakers will ordinarily organize their expression of the relationships between these things (Sapir, 1949). The idea that language influences thought processes is expressed in the theory of **linguistic relativity**, sometimes called the "Sapir-Whorf hypothesis" after two of its originators. According to linguistic relativity, what a people habitually think about is a reflection of what the current vocabulary of their language encourages them to notice, and at least some aspects of how people think will be affected by the grammatical relationships demanded by their language. Most anthropological linguists today agree that linguistic relativity should not be understood to mean that language structure *determines* how we think, but that language does have some effect on what we think about most readily and on how we think much of the time.

Effects of Morphology

Benjamin Lee Whorf was an originator of the idea that the superficial and arbitrary grammatical patterns that distinguish one language from another influence the ways in which its speakers habitually think about the world. His strongest argument is that the morphology of a language can have an effect on its speakers' tendency to notice some things readily while

linguistic relativity the idea that the characteristics of a language influence the way that its speakers think

failing to pay attention to others. For example, Whorf (1971a) pointed out that one place in which industrial fires frequently begin is the room in which so-called "empty" containers are stored. The word *empty* is a symbol that refers to two somewhat different concepts: it is used to mean (1) "containing only residues, gases, vapor, or stray rubbish," and also, in a more basic sense, to mean (2) "vacuous, inert, or containing nothing." Managers who label the room as a storage area for "empty containers" understand the word in its more specialized association with the first concept; workers are likely to behave around these containers of sometimes volatile residues and gases as if they were inert and vacuous. A worker, for example, who would never consider lighting a cigarette near a "full" gasoline drum might casually do so near an "empty" one, never stopping to think that the volatile gasoline fumes that remain in the empty containers are much more likely to ignite explosively than is the liquid gasoline of the full containers. According to Whorf, the use of a single symbol that represents two different concepts is not uncommon in hazardous situations.

Whorf (1971b) argued that people's names for things often influence how they behave around those things even more than the physical traits of the things themselves. He cited the blower as an example. Physically, a fan is a machine that simply causes air to move. Yet when it is used to make air pass through a room—such as a room for drying materials—because it is called a *blower*, workers are likely to install it so that it *blows* air into the room instead of *pulling* air out of it. The former method of installation is no more efficient and is much more hazardous than the latter, since an electrical fire in the machine itself will be blown into the room. Once begun, the fire will be fanned by a blower installed in this way as long as it continues to function.

Sometimes labels are changed either to avoid undesirable conditioned responses or to produce a specific result. Thus, unpopular wars are called "pacification programs," and the U.S. War Department was renamed the "Defense Department." Similarly, tuna did not become a popular food in the United States until one company began to label it "Chicken of the Sea." And those who wished to support what they called "decriminalization" of drug use or prostitution soon recognized that it was better to use that label rather than "legalization" for

their legislative proposals. Western science provides a further example of the conditioning effects of verbal symbolic labels: European scientists noted that when they "added heat" to an object, its weight did not change. So for years they searched for evidence of other "weightless substances" before they realized that heat, even though it is labeled by a noun, is actually a process rather than a substance.

This relationship between our words and our ways of conceptualizing things exists for languages besides English. For instance, in the Navajo language, the word for Mexican is *Naakaii*, which combines the root verb *naakai*, which means "(they) go about in a group" and the suffix *-ii*, which means "the ones." The fact that the word Naakaii is etymologically plural is the source of a conceptual quandary—to speak of a Mexican as a single person would be a contradiction in terms. This is illustrated by the Navajo sentence that means "That Mexican is walking about." In Navajo, this sentence is *Éi Naakaii naagha*, which literally means "That those-who-they-walk-about-in-a-group he-walks-about." An acquaintance of mine once described listening to a group of Navajos discussing whether it is possible for there to be a single Mexican, that is, a Mexican who stays alone and does not go about in a group.

Effects of Syntax

Syntactical processes also may affect how speakers of a language think about the world and how they behave, although the influence of syntax is probably not as great as the effects of morphology. Nevertheless, one finds numerous examples of correlations between a society's way of thinking about what reality is like and the grammatical characteristics of its language. For instance, if the English sentence "The dog was kicked by the man" is translated literally into Navajo, it becomes *Łííchą́ą́* (dog) *hastiin* (man) *biz-tał* (the former by the latter was-kick). However, this Navajo sentence has two problems: it is ungrammatical (Creamer, 1974), and to native Navajo speakers it is also absurd (Witherspoon, 1977). The absurdity occurs because the Navajo passive implies that the object allows itself to be acted upon (a meaning not implied by the English passive), and in the Navajo worldview the human, being more intelligent than a dog, would be responsible for the dog being kicked. The passive construction, by implying that the dog "allowed" itself to be kicked by the man, portrays the dog as the more intelligent and responsible party!

Rom Harré (1984) cites examples of Inuit grammar that parallel Inuit ideology. If the Inuit respond to the question "Who is preparing dinner?" their answer, *uva-nga*, does not translate as "I am" but as "The being here-mine." The English "I hear him" becomes in Inuit *tusarp-a-ra*, literally, "his making of a sound with reference to me." In general, where English grammar portrays a person as an "entity" who has attributes and intentions and who initiates actions, Inuit designates a person as the "location" at which qualities and relations occur. This characteristic of Inuit grammar mirrors and supports Inuit social life, in which one's position within the group is much more important than one's characteristics as an individual. Responsiveness to others is the hallmark of Inuit social interaction: when one person laughs, all laugh; when one cries, everyone cries. According to Harré, "At least with respect to a large and varied catalogue of public performances, individual feelings, intentions, and reasonings play a very minor role" (p. 88).

Such parallels between syntax and culture are best viewed as systems like that of the chicken and its egg: it is not clear which came first. Syntax may change to reflect the culture in which the language is spoken, but the habits of thought embodied in that syntax may help to maintain conformity to the rules of the culture by making those rules feel very natural to those who speak the language.

Language, then, seems to have an effect on the way people relate to the world. It is a conscious vehicle of habitual thought. The vocabulary of any language selects segments of reality that its speakers must become aware of when they learn to use their language. And the grammar is a built-in logic system that leads its users to relate the parts of the world to one another in the same way that the grammar organizes the relationships between the words that stand for those parts of the world.

LANGUAGE CHANGE

Since languages are symbol systems, they are highly susceptible to change. Language change may occur as the language is passed, by learning, from one generation to the next. A language may also change as its speakers are influenced by their interaction with speakers of other languages. In the following sections, these processes of linguistic change will be described in detail.

Changes over Time

Since the sounds used to form the verbal symbols of a language have no necessary connection with the meanings of those symbols, it is possible for both the sounds and the meanings attached to them to change as time passes. Likewise, the customary ways of organizing the verbal symbols into meaningful word order to communicate relationships between the concepts may also change as time passes. Thus, with the passage of time, languages may change in their sound system, their semantic or meaning system, and in their grammatical system. Consider, for instance, the differences between contemporary versions of the Lord's Prayer and this Old English version written in the ninth century:

> Faeder ūre, thū the eart on heofonum, sī th īn nama gehālgod. Tobecum thīn rīce, Gewurthe thīn willa on eorthan swā on heofonum. Urne gedaegh-wāmlican hlāf syle ūs to daeg. And forgyf ūs ūre gyltas, swā swā we forgyfath urum gyltendum. And ne gelaed thū ūs on costnunge, ac ālys ūs of yfele. Sothlīce. (quoted in Kispert, 1971, p. 19)

Since language change involves the systems that language comprises, changes occur in systematic or patterned ways. For instance, the change of one sound to a new one expresses itself in every word of the language in which that sound occurs. Compare a list of Old English words of about 1,000 years ago with their modern English equivalents:

Old English	Modern English
hus	house
mus	mouse
ut	out
hu	how

In this list, the Old English *u* represents a sound that would be pronounced approximately as *uw* (or *oow*). Today English speakers consistently pronounce these words with the vowel sequence *ao*, variously written as *ou* or *ow* in contemporary spelling. That is, the Old

English sound *uw* has become *ao* in Modern English, consistently changing the pronunciation of all English words in which it occurs.

Processes of Change

Change in language also occurs when words are borrowed by the speakers of one language from other languages with which they come in contact, especially those spoken by their politically and economically more powerful neighbors. For instance, following the Norman invasion of England in 1066, English speakers began to be influenced by the Old French language of the more powerful Normans. Today, about half of the vocabulary of the English language traces its origins to borrowed Old French words. Approximately 2½ centuries after the invasion, an early historian, Robert of Gloucester (1300), described in his *Chronicle* the effects of the language of the Norman rulers on English:

> Thus cōm, lǫ, Engelǫnd intō Normandïes hǫnd; And thē Normans ne cōuthe spęke thǫ bot hor owe spęche, And spęke French as hii düde at hǫm, and hor children düde alsǫ tęche,

> Sǫ that heie men of this lǫnd that of hor blōd cōme Hǫldeth alle thülke spęche that hii of hom nǫme; Vor bote a man conne Frenss me teleth of him lüte. Ac lowe men hǫldeth tō Engliss, and tō hor owe spęche zhüte. (quoted in Emerson, 1923, p. 210)

> (Lo, thus England came into Normandy's hand; and the Normans speak nothing but their own speech, and spoke French as they did at home, and did so teach their children,

> So that high men of this land came of their blood Hold the same speech that they received of them; For except a man knows French men speak little of him. But low men hold to English, and to their own speech yet.)

Those English speakers who had the most contact with the Norman rulers began to adopt Old French terms for elements of Norman life. The speech of the English commoners was less influenced. For instance, contemporary English has inherited a distinction between the cooked and live forms of several meat animals. *Mutton*, *pork*, and *beef* were adopted into English from Old French (*moton, porc,* and *boef*) for use when serv-

ing foods to the Norman rulers. When the animals were still alive and in the keeping of the English peasants, they were called by their original English names, *sheep, swine,* and *cow.* These latter three terms have their counterparts, not in French, but in the German words *Schaf, Swein,* and *Kuh,* a derivation that reflects the recent separation of English and German from a common ancestral language. Similarly, the word *roast* represents a borrowing from Old French— *rostir* was a verb used by cooks when speaking about preparing meat for their Norman rulers. This aristocratic term did not, however, replace the original English word *bake,* which continued to be used in the peasant households for the same method of preparing meat; they became alternative terms for essentially the same procedure. *Bake* itself stems from the same original word as the German word *backen,* which means "to bake or roast." Notice that in modern English, one still "roasts pork" (both words being of Old French origin) or "bakes ham" (both Germanic words). Although the foods themselves and the cooking procedures may be identical, the two idioms reflect two socially different speech contexts (Leaf, 1971).

Dialects

Changes in language occur gradually with the passage of time. Yet, at any given time, the need to communicate effectively within a social group necessitates a certain degree of mutual sharing in the sounds used to form words, in the meanings of words, and in the grammatical patterns for combining them. So a language changes in the same way for all members of the group. However, when a group is subdivided, either geographically or socially, the members of each subgroup tend to communicate more frequently with each other than with others. One result of such isolation is that new ways of speaking that arise in one of the new groups may not necessarily pass over into the others. Thus, a language originally spoken in the same way by several groups can gradually change until it is made up of separate **dialects**, mutually intelligible variants of a language shared by different social groups. For instance, the English now spoken in Great Britain differs

dialects geographical or social subdivisions of a language that differ systematically from other subdivisions of the same language in their vocabulary, grammar, and phonology

BLACK ENGLISH VERNACULAR

William Labov (1972) studied the everyday speech of African Americans in Philadelphia, New York, and other urban centers in the United States and recorded the patterns of an English dialect technically called **Black English Vernacular** or BEV. It differs in several ways from **Standard English**, the dialect taught in U.S. schools and used by most people in the United States at least on formal occasions.

One notable difference is the common omission in Black English of forms of "to be." This rule allows a statement such as "You are fast" to be expressed more succinctly as "You fast." Although this deletion of "to be" is not used in Standard American English, it is not at all unusual. For instance, subject and predicate complements are not joined by a "to be" verb in Russian, Hungarian, or Arabic. Black English Vernacular also makes use of various forms of the double negative. For instance, Standard English "There wasn't much I could do" becomes "Wasn't much I couldn't do" in BEV, and "When it rained, nobody knew it did" becomes "When it rained, nobody don't know it didn't."

According to Labov, Black English Vernacular is a dialect "that is more different from most other English dialects than they are from each other" (p. 36). However, like any other dialect, most of its grammatical rules are those shared by all dialects of English. Its difference from Standard English is one of degree, not kind.

---

from the varieties of English spoken in the United States and Australia, although all three forms developed from a single language spoken but a few hundred years ago by residents of and emigrants from Great Britain.

Dialects of the same original language can gradually become so different that their speakers are no longer able to understand one another. English and German, for example, were at one time in history a single language. Called **Proto-Germanic** by modern students of language, it was spoken on the mainland of Europe in what is now northern Germany by peoples known as the Angles and the Saxons. Those who left the mainland about 1,500 to 2,000 years ago became a separate social group in the British Isles, where their isolation allowed the language to change in different ways than it did on the mainland. Since the process of change was systematic in both groups, one finds a system of consistent parallels between the two "daughter" languages, German and English. Compare, for instance, the initial sound of the following word lists from German and English, and notice that the German z (written as uppercase Z in the case of nouns), which is pronounced ts, is consistently a t sound in English:

German	English
zu	to
zwanzig	twenty
zwölf	twelve
zwitschern	twitter
Zinn	tin

Basic Vocabulary

The tenacity of Germanic words for household objects suggests that domestic terminology may be somewhat more stable and resistant to externally induced language change than other parts of a vocabulary. The part of a language that best reflects its internal history consists of words learned by individuals early in their lives in their home setting. Such words are frequently used in normal speech situations. The habit of their use is not easily overcome, and foreign terms are not likely to supplant them (Gudschinsky, 1956). The part of a vocabulary that has these qualities is known as the **basic vocabulary** of a language. It includes the words most commonly used to express such concepts as *father, mother, brother, sister, head, hand, foot, eat, water, drink, fire, house, earth, sky, sun, moon,* and *star,* as well as others that designate basic elements of people's social, biological, and physical environments.

By comparing the basic vocabularies of two languages, it is possible to determine whether

---

Black English Vernacular the everyday speech patterns of African Americans studied in urban centers

Standard English the dialect taught in U.S. schools and used by most people in the United States at least on formal occasions

Proto-Germanic the language from which both English and German are descended

basic vocabulary the part of a vocabulary that one learns early in life in the home setting

FIGURE 12.7

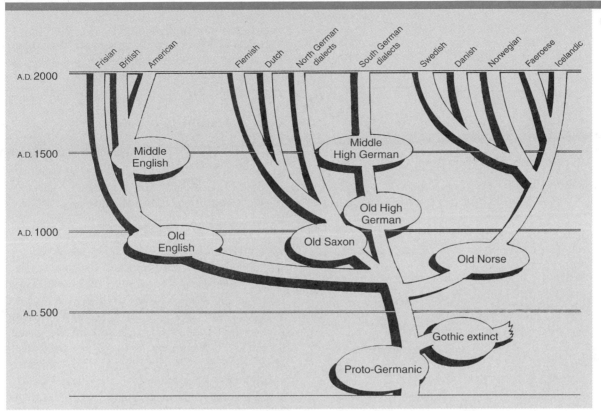

THE FAMILY TREE OF NORTHERN EUROPEAN LANGUAGES

The root or parent language of Northern European languages is called Proto-Germanic. It in turn is derived *from an earlier Proto-Indo-European base, the ancestor of many languages in India as well as Europe.*

they developed from the same common ancestral language, proof that may not be evident in comparing the entire contemporary vocabularies of the languages. For instance, the fact that over 50 percent of the English vocabulary is derived from French does not indicate that both languages arose recently from a common ancestral language. This distinction becomes clear only when one examines the *basic* English vocabulary. In this more stable part of the vocabulary, English words generally have their closest counterparts not in French but in the Germanic languages spoken in the region from which the Anglo-Saxon immigrants to England originally came. This common origin of English and German is illustrated by the following basic vocabulary lists:

English	*German*
father	Vater
mother	Mutter
brother	Bruder
sister	Schwester
hand	Hand
house	Haus
mouse	Maus
water	Wasser
sun	Sonne
moon	Mond
fire	Feuer

LANGUAGE FAMILIES

Such lists of basic vocabulary terms make it possible to compare how many of these items the languages share. It is assumed that the more of these stable items two languages have in common, the more recently they began diverging from a single parent language to become separate languages in their own right. Using this assumption, it is possible to reconstruct a family tree of related languages such as the one that compares the languages of northern Europe in Figure 12.7. The branches on this language family tree correspond to major historical occurrences in the societies that

FIGURE 12.8

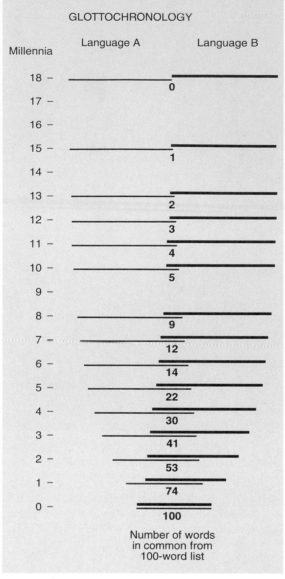

GLOTTOCHRONOLOGY

Millennia	Language A	Language B
18 –		0
17 –		
16 –		
15 –		1
14 –		
13 –		2
12 –		3
11 –		4
10 –		5
9 –		
8 –		9
7 –		12
6 –		14
5 –		22
4 –		30
3 –		41
2 –		53
1 –		74
0 –		100

Number of words
in common from
100-word list

GLOTTOCHRONOLOGICAL CHANGE

Human vocabulary shares a common ancestral language or protolanguage. After a period of one thousand years any given language will replace 14 percent of its original vocabulary with new terms. This chart graphically portrays the divergence of languages over a period of time.

led to the separation of the speakers of the original language into separate subdivisions. Thus, the point where Old English separates from the other branches that arose from Proto-Germanic corresponds to the migration of the Anglo-Saxons from the northern German coast to the British Isles about 500 C.E. After this time the islanders were no longer in sufficiently intense communication with their mainland counterparts to maintain language unity. This

family of languages diverged from a single common ancestral language that contemporary linguists call **Proto-Indo-European**. It was spoken about 5,000 years ago. The languages of other parts of the world have also been grouped into similar language families.

Glottochronology

Morris Swadesh and Dorothy Lee developed a method in the 1950s to estimate the minimum number of years since the divergence of any two related languages. **Glottochronology** made it possible to assign dates to the various branches in a language family tree. By comparing the basic vocabularies of languages that belong to different language families and have had long written histories, researchers discovered that about 14 percent of a 100-word basic vocabulary was replaced by new words every 1,000 years in all the languages that had been examined in nonisolated societies (Gudschinsky, 1956). Thus, the rate of change in the basic vocabulary, being a constant, could be used to compute the length of time that two languages have been diverging from one another. Since about 14 percent of the basic vocabulary of a parent language will be lost in any daughter language after 1,000 years of change from that original state, each daughter language will maintain a different 86 percent of the original vocabulary. Consequently, if one compares lists of 100 basic vocabulary items for two contemporary languages and discovers that they share about 74 basic vocabulary items (86 percent of 86 items), then one may calculate that they were in fact a single language 1,000 years ago. Two languages will share about 55 (74 percent of 74) of the original 100 basic vocabulary items after 2,000 years of separation and about 41 items (74 percent of 55) after 3,000 years of separation (see Figure 12.8).

Since the number of similarities between the vocabularies of any two related languages decreases with the passage of time, glottochronological evidence with which such relationships can be proven becomes sparse beyond the first 5,000 years. For instance, two languages

---

Proto-Indo-European the ancestral language from which most of the contemporary languages of Europe, Iran, and India have developed

glottochronology a technique for calculating the minimal length of time that two related languages have been diverging from a common ancestral language will share only about 14 of a 100-word basic vocabulary after 6,000 years of divergence. After 12,000 years the number of shared words is likely to be only 3. In addition, two unrelated languages can occasionally independently develop similar-sounding words with the same meaning or similar meanings by chance. Such accidental similarities also occur in about 3 cases in every hundred. For instance, the Shoshone word for "die" is *tiai-* and its word for "deer" is *təhəya*, but these similarities between English and Shoshone can simply be attributed to chance. Thus, beyond about 10,000 years of divergence, glottochronological comparisons of related languages are very difficult to establish with certainty.

Language Macrofamilies

Despite the limitations of current statistical techniques for establishing relationships between languages, some linguists have tried to establish even more ancient relationships between the world's various language families. The most ambitious effort so far began in the 1960s, when Soviet scholars suggested the existence of a macrofamily of languages that they called Nostratic. The Nostratic macrofamily united the Indo-European language family with the largely northern European language family called Uralic, the Altaic family of western and northern Asia, the Dravidian languages of India, and the northern African and Middle Eastern Afro-Asiatic family. Originally greeted with skepticism among most other linguists, the hypothesis of a Nostratic macrofamily remains controversial but continues to inspire research. In 1994 Allan Bombard and John Kerns published a compilation of about 600 reconstructed Nostratic word roots derived from comparisons of words belonging to contemporary languages that they believe are descended from Nostratic. Other linguists, such as Donald Ringe (1995), assert that the cross-language comparisons of the Nostratic macrofamily proponents are not yet strong enough to say that they are not merely chance similarities.

Contemporary World Languages

Most estimates indicate that there are at least 3,000 languages spoken in the world today; some estimates indicate there are closer to 5,000. The exact number is difficult to determine because the dialects that make up a language can be very similar to one another or so distinct that two linguists might not agree on whether they should be called dialects or separate languages. Consider German and Dutch. Although speakers of Bavarian German dialects would be unable to comprehend the dialect spoken in a German village in Schleswig-Holstein near the border of Denmark, the change from one local dialect to the next is too gradual to claim that there is more than one German language in the country. Similarly, the dialects spoken in small towns on either side of the German and Dutch borders may be so similar that the inhabitants of both towns can understand one another; yet people speak of German and Dutch as if they were separate languages. In fact, some southern German dialects differ more from the nationally preferred way of speaking the modern standard German "language" (which is mostly based on northern German dialects) than some northern dialects in Germany differ from Dutch.

Some languages are spoken by relatively few native speakers. For instance, only a few thousand people speak Shoshone today. On the other hand, some languages are spoken by many societies with very different cultures. Such languages may cross the borders of modern nation-states and be spoken by millions of people. For instance, English is one of the official languages of India as well as the native tongue of peoples inhabiting lands as scattered as England, Canada, South Africa, the Falkland Islands, and Jamaica.

The languages spoken by the largest numbers of people today are those that have become the national languages of major nations. The Beijing dialect (formerly called Mandarin) of China is spoken by more than 950 million people. English is the next most commonly spoken language of the world, with about 470 million speakers.

In some parts of the world, many different languages are spoken by people who differ relatively little in their culture. Canada maintains two nationally recognized languages, French and English; political speeches and advertising must be carried out in both. In Nigeria about 400 languages are spoken, of which only one, English, has been designated as an official language. Such a diversity of spoken languages can create enormous political problems in administering governmental affairs throughout the country. The elevation of one or more languages to official status is intended

FIGURE 12.9

MARIE SMITH

Marie Smith, 72, who lives in Anchorage, Alaska, is the last native speaker of the Eyak language. Of Alaska's 20 native Inuit and Indian languages, 17 are essentially moribund since not a single child is learning them, and almost all of them have fewer than 1,000 speakers each. Only two native Alaskan languages are still being learned by children: Siberian Yupik, with 1,000 speakers, and Central Yupik, with 10,000 speakers (Diamond, 1993). This situation mirrors the kind of language extinction occurring around the world.

to alleviate some of these problems. Since government business is largely conducted in an official language, speakers of other languages are expected to learn one of the official languages or find an interpreter when they wish to deal with government administrators. Where national languages exist, they are likely to be the ones used in the school system, with the idea that all citizens should learn to use the national language or languages. Although the selection of one of a society's languages as an official one may simplify some of the problems of governing a linguistically diverse country, the designation of a single official language is not without its

problems. For instance, speakers of a nonofficial language may find themselves at a political or economic disadvantage compared with others who speak the national language. Such circumstances can lead to political rivalries and conflicts that are difficult to resolve.

Language Extinction

Although there are at least 3,000 languages in the world today, not all of them have a large body of speakers. Only about 200 are spoken by more than a million people. Many languages are spoken by fewer than a thousand people, and the number of the world's languages declines each year. For instance, when Columbus crossed the Atlantic there were about 300 languages spoken in North America. Today only 207 survive. Of the approximately 300,000 people who speak a native North American language, about a third are speakers of Navajo. The remaining languages average fewer than 1,000 speakers each, but for many the numbers are much smaller. Alaska offers a typical example of the decline of indigenous North American languages. Of its 20 native languages, there are only 2 that are still being learned by children. Of the 187 native languages outside Alaska, 149 are no longer being learned.

The decline of languages in North America is not unique. The same thing is happening throughout the world, and the total number of human languages is actually declining at an accelerating rate. Jared Diamond (1993) estimates that at the current rate of language extinction the total number of human languages will drop to just a few hundred within the next 2 centuries.

LANGUAGE POLITICS

Language can reflect political differences or acquire political significance as people from different geographical or cultural areas interact. Two examples of the politics of language are judgments about the acceptability of a dialect or language and the use of language as a symbol of nationalism.

Prestige Dialects

Since different social groups often speak different dialects, inability to speak the dialect of a society's elite may become a means of identifying those who do not belong to the elite and thus of discrimination. According to Pierre Bourdieu (1982, 1984), speaking the dialect of the politically powerful or of the wealthy class can become a necessary skill for those who wish to participate within these areas of social life. So the dialects of such groups sometimes take on the reputation of being superior to others. Dialects with a reputation of being inherently better than others are called **prestige dialects**.

Prestige dialects are a phenomenon of socially stratified societies such as chiefdoms and states in which social ranking is used to distinguish the power and influence of different groups. Thus, foraging societies such as the Great Basin Shoshone lacked prestige dialects, but they are common in the world's contemporary nation-states. In countries that have one traditionally accepted prestige dialect, it is often a dialect spoken in the capital city. In France, it was a dialect of Paris that became the national standard of "good French." In England, it is the dialect spoken by the monarch. In the United States, where the capital was created as an unconnected district not based on a previously existing population center, the nationally preferred dialect taught in the school system does not belong to any particular part of the country. It is somewhat of an amalgam and is most often spoken by television and radio newscasters.

Language and Nationalism

In contemporary countries that are made up of peoples who speak more than one language, intergroup politics similar to those that give rise to prestige dialects influence language preferences in the political arena. In Canada, for instance, English is the dominant language used for most economic and political transactions in most of the country, while French plays a dominant role in the province of Quebec. The country as a whole recognizes both languages as "official" national tongues for the conduct of government business, and products sold in stores throughout the country carry labels that repeat the same information in French and English. In Quebec, the one Canadian province in which French-speaking citizens have greater political and economic influence than English speakers, French has the legal

FIGURE 12.10

POLITICS AND LANGUAGE
Gordon McIntyre, an English-speaking minority in the town of Huntingdon, in the province of Quebec, Canada, has been fighting a ruling that required all outdoor commercial signs to be French only. He argued that many people in his town wouldn't understand that "salon funéraire" meant funeral home, the business that he operates. The United Nations Commission on Human Rights in Geneva ruled in his favor on the grounds that the law violated his freedom of expression rights. Until the province complies with the ruling, McIntyre simply adds the English words to the French.

status of being the official language of the provincial government.

The political loyalties that are symbolized by preference for one language or another can be powerful enough to express themselves in public hostility between members of different language communities within a country. For instance, competition between native French and English speakers in Canada has erupted into open conflict on more than one occasion and has been the basis for a secessionist movement within Quebec aimed at founding a separate, French-speaking country. Language as a politi-

---

prestige dialects dialects with the reputation of being inherently better than others cal rallying point of this kind is not unique to Canada. For instance, the Basque separatist movement in Spain and France has involved a long history of armed conflict based on the demands of specific language-speaking groups. The United States has seen two recurring political issues during periods of large-scale immigration by non-English-speaking people: whether or not English should be officially declared the country's national language, and which language should be used in school to teach children who do not speak English or are less proficient in English than in another language.

BILINGUAL EDUCATION IN THE UNITED STATES

The 1990 U.S. Census indicated that 31.8 million U.S. residents speak some language other than English at home. The most widely spoken language other than English is Spanish, which is the first language of 17.3 million Americans. The large immigration of Cambodians during the 1980s has made Mon-Khmer the fastest-growing language. The second fastest is French Creole, spoken by Haitian immigrants.

The diversity of first languages spoken by children in the United States has tremendous practical implications for public education. In the nineteenth and early twentieth centuries, English was the sole language of instruction in the public education system, and it was simply assumed that non-English-speaking children would have to learn English to participate in school. For instance, American Indian children were routinely taken from their homes and sent to distant boarding schools to be socialized into the dominant English-speaking way of life. These schools actually forbade the children to speak their native language, and the children were severely punished for doing so even outside the classroom.

Recent decades have seen a growing recognition that bilingualism can be an asset to the child rather than a liability that should be eliminated. In 1968 the U.S. Congress passed the first Bilingual Education Act. As amended in 1978, it requires equitable treatment of students who have limited English proficiency; there are currently between 3.5 and 5.5 million such students in the public school system. In 1991, 2.3 million children were enrolled in limited-English-proficiency (LEP) classes in grades K–12, and almost 43 percent of U.S. school districts offered some form of bilingual education. Bilingual education includes both classes in which instruction is in a language other than English and classes in English as a second language (ESL).

CHAPTER SUMMARY

1. The basis for the complexity of human cultures is our ability to form and communicate concepts.

2. Signs are communications that express our feelings directly.

3. Symbols are forms of communication in which one thing is arbitrarily used to represent another, according to socially agreed-on and learned conventions.

4. Human communication is highly symbolic and therefore extremely flexible.

5. While some nonverbal messages, such as our gestures, facial expressions, body language, and distances from each other, are spontaneous signs of our emotions, even nonverbal communications may be symbolic.

6. Verbal communication—language—is totally symbolic, for speech sounds, written words, and ways of arranging them are uniquely and arbitrarily assigned symbolic meanings within each culture.

7. The capacity for creating and using complex language systems seems to reside within certain areas of the human cerebral cortex.

8. Some nonhuman primates may have similar language capacities as humans, though more limited ones, but these primates do not use their capacities unless they are carefully taught to do so.

9. Languages and cultures are so closely linked that the forms and patterns of our speech both affect and reflect how we perceive the world.

10. Languages, like their cultures, change over time with influences from other cultures and their languages.

11. The part of a language that is most resistant to change is its basic vocabulary, which consists of household words taught and used from childhood.

12. Differences and similarities in basic vocabularies allow linguists to trace the historical growth of language families into the many languages and dialects spoken in the world today.

ANNOTATED READINGS

Abu-Lughod, L. (1986). *Veiled sentiments: Honor and poetry in a Bedouin society.* Berkeley, CA: University of California Press. Discusses the uses of Arabic poetry among Egyptian Bedouins.

Appel, R., & Muysken, P. (1987). *Language contact and bilingualism.* London: Edward Arnold. Examines what happens when different languages interact.

Bourdieu, P. (1984). *Distinction: A social critique of the judgment of taste* (R. Nice, Trans.). Cambridge, MA: Harvard University Press. Discusses the politics of language and the role of language as a source of access to economic and social benefits.

Birdwhistell, R. L. (1970). *Kinesics and context: Essays on body motion communication.* Philadelphia: University of Pennsylvania Press. An exposition of the techniques used for analyzing body movement in nonverbal communication.

Carroll, J. B. (Ed.). (1956). *Language, thought and reality: Selected writings of Benjamin Lee Whorf.* Cambridge, MA: M.I.T. Press. The primary writings of Whorf on the effects of language on thought and action.

Greenberg, J. H. (1968). *Anthropological linguistics: An introduction.* New York: Random House. A good nontechnical introduction to anthropological linguistics.

Hall, E. T. (1959). *The silent language.* Greenwich, CT: Fawcett Publications. An interesting look at the rules for nonverbal communications in a variety of cultures.

Labov, W. (1972). *Language in the inner city: Studies in the Black English Vernacular.* Philadelphia: University of Pennsylvania Press. The classic investigation of Black English Vernacular that destroyed the myth of the natural superiority of Standard English.

Lakeoff, R. (1975). *Language and women's place.* New York: Harper & Row. An examination of gender differences in language and related social implications.

Lenneberg, E. H. (1967). *The biological foundations of language.* New York: John Wiley. The basic text on the biological basis of language.

Lieberman, P. (1984). *The biology and evolution of language.* Cambridge, MA: Harvard University Press. Examines the fossil evidence for the origin of language.

Mandelbaum, D. G. (Ed.). (1968). *Selected writings of Edward Sapir in language, culture and personality.* Berkeley, CA: University of California Press. A well-chosen collection of the classic writings of the father of American anthropological linguistics.

Trudgill, P. (1983). *Sociolinguistics: An introduction to language and society* (Rev. ed.). New York: Penguin Books. A short introduction to the various roles that language plays in social relationships, including gender, class, and ethnicity.

CHAPTER THIRTEEN

Religion and Culture

After reading this chapter, you should be able to:

Critique the various definitions of religion

Analyze the ways in which people conceive of the supernatural and their relationship to it.

Discuss the relationship between religion and practical aspects of human survival and cultural adaptation.

Define the structure and diversity of religious ideology.

Define the relationship between religious ideologies and social organization.

Analyze the nature and functions of ritual.

Explain the different forms of religious social organization.

Illustrate the role of borrowing in religious change.

Explain the role of religion in the U.S.

Describe the revitalization movement.

Discuss the social and psychological functions of religion.

Analyze the cognitive characteristics of religious thought.

◀ *Figure 13.1 Shiva Vishapaharana Religious beliefs and rituals take many forms around the world but include a basic belief in supernatural beings and power, a symbolic expression of feelings, and ritualistic behavior in order to influence the supernatural. In the Hindu system, Brahma is the Lord of Creation, Vishnu is the Preserver, and Shiva is the Destroyer. This bronze sculpture of the Eastern Chalukya dynasty (642–ca. 1075) depicts Shiva Vishapaharana, the Lord who Swallowed the World Poison.*

Religion is an organized system of shared supernatural beliefs that gives meaning to perplexing parts of human society and its environment and a system of rituals by which human beings strive for greater control over themselves and their social and natural environments. Psychologically, the beliefs and rituals of a particular religion symbolically express the kinds of stresses and anxieties that are common among the members of that society. In this chapter we will examine both the psychological and the social aspects of religion.

Ghosts. Demons. Angels. Witches. Buddha. Shaman. Christ. Do you whistle in the dark as one way of dealing with the unknown silence? Do you sleep with a night-light? Do you avoid stepping on cracks in the sidewalk or walking under ladders? Do you light candles to ward off the demons of darkness in your soul or your world? Every culture has evolved a system of symbolic beliefs and rituals that it uses to define its place in the universe.

THE DEFINITION OF RELIGION

Religious beliefs and rituals take so many forms across the world that anthropologists have found it difficult to define religion in a way that encompasses them all. They have agreed, however, that the major characteristics of a global definition of **religion** include belief in supernatural beings and supernatural power, symbolic expression of feelings, and rituals performed both individually and in groups for the purpose of positively influencing the supernatural powers.

Belief in the Supernatural

Religious beliefs differ from the ordinary day-to-day beliefs that grow out of a mechanistic view of things. Religious beliefs portray the world supernaturally rather than scientifically. They postulate a world of humanlike beings and powers: gods, angels, demons, ghosts, or forces that respond to rituals and other symbolic acts and that inspire special feelings, such as awe and dread. Anthropologists have attempted to explain the emotionally powerful supernatural beliefs and symbolic rituals of religion in various ways. Their different approaches to analyzing religion have led to a variety of different but complementary definitions.

Belief in Supernatural Beings. Sir Edward Burnett Tylor (1871), a nineteenth-century Victorian scholar, provided one of the first anthropological definitions of religion: a belief in supernatural beings such as the soul, ghosts, spirits, and gods. According to Tylor, religion functions to provide human beings with explanations of perplexing phenomena such as unconsciousness, sleep, dreams, and hallucinations. Early humans, Tylor contended, created the idea of the soul to account for such phenomena. Unconsciousness, fainting, sleep, and even death could be explained as the soul's departure from the body; dreams could be memories of the soul's experiences as it travels outside the body during sleep; and visions or hallucinations could simply be apparitions of souls and other spirit beings. The idea of the soul also implied the possibility of other spiritual entities such as ghosts, genies, angels, and gods.

Although Tylor's views were useful in pointing out the role that religion plays in providing people with ways of understanding the experiences for which they have no pragmatic explanations, his perspective was narrow. For Tylor, religion was a product of the human intellect; its relationship to emotional life was unimportant.

Belief in Supernatural Power. An even greater limitation of Tylor's definition was its ethnocentric narrowness in excluding from the realm of religion the belief in formless supernatural powers. Robert Marett (1909) raised this criticism of Tylor and introduced the Melanesian word **mana** to refer to the concept of spiritual power. Mana, which might be thought of as a kind of supernatural electricity, may reside in objects such as a rabbit's foot, a four-leaf clover, in powerful natural phenomena such as

---

religion belief in supernatural power, symbolic expression of feelings, and rituals performed in order to influence the nonhuman realm

mana supernatural power or force

thunderstorms, or in anything strange, rare, or dangerous. In doses too large, it can cause harm, illness, or even death, but properly channeled it can be used by human beings to accomplish ends that are unattainable by other means. Mana can increase one's luck, skill, and ability to gain knowledge of hidden things. It is the force behind magic; it is the holiness in the ground around the burning bush; it is the sacredness of the Host in the Eucharist; it is Luke Skywalker's Force. As the embodiment of spiritual power in its rawest form, mana inspires the sense of awe and reverence that people of every religion experience when they perceive themselves to be in the presence of the Holy. Though mana makes things more powerful than they normally would be, it does not come and go of its own accord. Like its secular equivalent, electricity, it must be manipulated by human beings to benefit from its power. However, unlike electricity, the manipulation of mana is accomplished through rituals.

Marett believed that the concept of mana was one of the simplest and most widespread of religious ideas. He asserted that it was a more ancient religious concept than the belief in spiritual beings, and that it arose not from intellect but from the emotions.

Where mana plays a prominent role in religion, the concept of taboo is also likely to be important. A **taboo** is a rule that forbids contact with sacred or dangerous things, those filled with so much mana that careless contact with them may harm the unwary. The term was derived from a Polynesian word, *tapu* or *tabu*, which means both forbidden and sacred. Polynesian chiefs were sacred, and their bodies contained so much mana that it was taboo for commoners to touch them, since to do so might kill an ordinary person. Since Tylor's definition failed to encompass mana, an important aspect of religious practice and ideology, Marett broadened it by defining religion as the belief in supernatural things in general.

Recently, a number of anthropologists have attempted to clarify some ambiguities of the word **supernatural**, which has almost always been a central element in Western anthropologists' definitions of religion. Traditionally, the supernatural has been understood to be a realm that transcends the natural senses. It consists of things that are believed to be very powerful but that do not seem to conform to the normal laws that govern the behavior of things in the world. Since the dichotomy between a natural

and a supernatural realm has long played a central role in the distinction between science and religion in Western culture, few have felt that the term "supernatural" needed further clarification. However, Cohn (1967) has pointed out that the distinction between a natural and a supernatural realm is not made in most of the world's religions. Neither is there a word in most of the world's languages that translates as "religion." How, then, have anthropologists decided to call behavior religious when they were studying cultures in which there is no word for religion and no explicit concept of a supernatural realm?

Anthropomorphism.   Anthropologists have adopted several different ways of defining the concept of the supernatural. One approach has been to find an alternative concept; another has been to broaden the idea of religion by dropping the concept of the supernatural from its definition. An example of the former approach is found in the work of Stewart Guthrie (1980), who undertook a major survey of the studies of religion and showed that the common denominator in all religious thinking is **anthropomorphism**—assigning human qualities to things that are not human in order to create beliefs in those beings and powers that traditionally have been called supernatural. Thus the concept of anthropomorphism can take the place of the supernatural in the definition of religion, which may be described as a system of (1) beliefs in which the nonhuman realm is portrayed as having humanlike qualities, including the ability to respond to symbolic communication; (2) feelings related to those beliefs; and (3) ritual practices that elicit and control those feelings and are carried out either to portray the beliefs or to influence the universe by symbolic communication.

Symbolic Expression of Feelings

The second approach to bypassing the problem of the supernatural, that of dropping the con-

---

taboo a rule forbidding contact with sacred things, those containing mana

supernatural that which transcends the natural, observable world

anthropomorphism using human qualities to explain the nonhuman realm; interpreting or acting toward the nonhuman realm as if it were human, especially as if it were able to respond to symbolic communication

cept altogether, has usually involved emphasizing the emotional side of religion over its cognitive aspect, an expression of feelings, not beliefs. An early example of such an approach to religion is embodied in the work of the French anthropologist Émile Durkheim (1912/1915), who focused on the feelings that religion creates in a community of people. To him religion was a system of beliefs and practices pertaining to **sacred** things, by which he meant things that inspire feelings of awe, respect, or reverence because they are set apart and forbidden.

Durkheim was concerned with the question of what lies at the root of religious ideas and what maintains them through the generations. He suggested that sacred things and religious ideas about them are symbolic representations, or metaphors, for those aspects of society and culture that inspire feelings of respect, fear, and awe among its members. Durkheim believed that by maintaining and manipulating these feelings in symbolic form, religion perpetuated the sentiments that people must have toward their society if it is to survive. He illustrated his belief in the intimate connection between a religion's sacred symbols and society's fundamental institutions by examining the native people of central Australia. These foraging people lived in local groups, each of which belonged to one of a number of different clans. Each clan, which united local groups that were dispersed over large areas, was named for a species of animal or plant that was sacred to its members and symbolized the unity of the dispersed clan members. As the clan **totem**, this species was believed to be spiritually related to clan members; their souls were believed to be the same kind of spirit as that of their totem species. On certain occasions clan members came together from diverse areas to perform rituals that were intended to increase the numbers of the clan's totem species. By participating with one another in this religious ritual, the members of the clan reinforced their common social bond. Thus, religious rituals intended to influence the clan's sacred totem simultaneously perpetuated the solidarity of the clan itself. Durkheim believed that the synonymity between sacred symbols and the basic institutions of social life is not unique to the religion of central Australians but is typical of every religion. Thus, in Durkheim's view each religion is best understood as a society's symbolic worship of itself.

A more recent definition of religion that emphasizes its role in expressing feelings to lend stability to society was formulated by Clifford Geertz (1966): "A religion is (1) a system of symbols which acts to (2) establish powerful, pervasive, and long-lasting moods and motivations in [people] by (3) formulating conceptions of a general order of existence and (4) clothing these conceptions with such an aura of factuality that (5) the moods and motivations seem uniquely realistic" (p. 4). By eliminating the supernatural from his definition, Geertz has broadened the traditional concept of religion to include any ideological system that people turn to as the ultimate source of their most deeply held feelings. Geertz's definition emphasizes similarities in the deep commitment and behavior of followers of theologies such as Islam or Christianity and of adherents of political ideologies such as Marxism.

Geertz's approach, like that of Durkheim, focuses on the role of religion in validating people's allegiance to their society and culture. Religion, in this view, consists of important symbols that affirm a culturally valued worldview by providing people with ritual settings in which they will feel that those valued beliefs are true even though they may be challenged by experiences outside the religious setting. Thus, for instance, religion can rescue people's faith in spite of disasters, tragedies, and personal difficulties that might otherwise challenge it. Religious concepts that explain life's evils as "God's will," punishment for sin, the results of witchcraft, or in terms of similar religious ideas help people cope with the difficulties of life that might otherwise undermine their social commitments. According to Geertz, it is especially by participating in religious rituals that people repress any contradictions between the world as it ought to be and the world as it is.

Ritual Behaviors

Other anthropologists have shifted their interest away from both beliefs and feelings toward the ritual behaviors that are always a part of the prac-

(Continued on p. 326)

_____

sacred the quality of inspiring feelings of respect, awe, and reverence that is possessed by things set apart and forbidden

totem a plant, animal or, less commonly, nonliving thing that is a sacred symbol of the unity of a social group

INDIA'S SACRED COW

Religious beliefs often serve practical purposes, though these purposes may not be obvious. Such is the case with the sacred cows of India.

Since the British colonial occupation of India, the English phrase "sacred cow" has stood for any custom that is maintained in spite of all rational reasons for its change. The zebu cow, held sacred by Hindus of India, symbolizes gentleness, life, and India itself. The cow is so greatly revered that its protection was written into the constitution. The cow may be neither killed nor molested as it wanders the streets. To the British, for whom cattle were an important food resource, it seemed the height of folly for a society in which hunger and even starvation were significant social problems to support cow reverence instead of cow eating. In spite of the thinly veiled ethnocentrism in this opinion, there is some intuitive merit to the idea that protection of the cow is irrational when its use as food might alleviate a major social problem.

Marvin Harris (1974), who believes that the material conditions of life have a greater impact on an ideology than an ideology does on those conditions, has argued that the custom of cow reverence is integrated with other facts of Indian life in such a way that using cows for food would create more problems than it would solve. Those whose only contact with cattle is the meat section of their local supermarket may be unaware of the great expenditure of resources that goes into the raising of cattle as food. In the United States, for instance, beef cattle are fed from farm-grown foods. Three-fourths of the agricultural land in the United States is devoted to growing food for cattle. Since U.S. farmers are still able to produce sufficient food for domestic consumption and export, this cost is well within their means. In India, though, the establishment of this kind of beef industry would remove acreage from the production of food for human beings. The result would be the displacing of millions of farmers and an increase in food costs and hunger.

Indian farmers pen their cows at night but allow them to wander during the day, scavenging their own food. Eating the weeds and plants that they find away from the farm, the cows consume things that are not edible to humans for about four-fifths of their diet. The custom of permitting cows to range freely greatly reduces the amount of labor and feed that farmers must devote to the upkeep of their animals. Allowing cows to wander and fostering cow love benefits the poorest farmers who otherwise could not afford to own a cow or keep it during times of hardship.

Although the cow is not food for its owner, it is an important part of that farmer's means of food production. Teams of oxen are harnessed to pull plows. Cows provide a small amount of milk for their owners and a few milk peddlers. Cattle also produce dung, which is valuable as fertilizer and fuel in India, a country with little oil, coal, or wood. Cattle dung takes the place of expensive petrochemical fertilizers. It is also burned within the home. Finally, when cattle die from natural causes, the meat is not wasted, for most of it is eaten by members of the lowest castes. The custom of cow worship ensures that the meat reaches the tables of those who could least afford to buy it if it were a market item sought by all.

Perhaps someday beef will be routinely eaten in India, but under current circumstances beef eating would not be cost effective, whereas cow reverence is. Far from being a case of the irrationality of religious symbols, the sacredness of the zebu cow in India reflects the real importance of the cow as a resource and means of livelihood in India under the current economic conditions.

FIGURE 13.2

SACRED COW OF INDIA

The zebu cow is sacred to Hindus of India not only because of what it symbolizes but also because it is economically and ecologically more sound to preserve it than to slaughter it. These cows share the road with automobiles and the sidewalk with people.

tice of religion. **Ritual** differs from other sorts of behavior in three important ways: it is symbolically meaningful; it is often performed in a repetitive, stereotyped, and predictable way; and it has the intent of manipulating nature through the power of symbols rather than by mechanical means. Typical of those who view ritual as the central element of religion is Anthony F. C. Wallace (1966), who contends that ritual is performed to bring about or to prevent changes in human beings or in nature. Religious beliefs give meaning to rituals by explaining and interpreting them and by directing the energy of the ritual performance.

IDEOLOGY IN RELIGION

Religious ideology, which comprises the supernatural beliefs and sentiments of society, is more diverse than most kinds of nonreligious ideology, because religious beliefs and feelings are typically less restricted than beliefs and feelings about nonreligious matters by practical consequences of immediate concern in daily life. For instance, our ideas about how to make and use the tools upon which our society depends for survival must conform to the facts of physics relevant to their effective functioning. Thus, it will not be difficult to recognize a bow and arrow no matter what part of the world it comes from, and ideas about how to make and use this weapon will have much in common in all societies.

The realities of social life, however, typically leave more room for diversity of thought and values than do the ideologies of technologies. So, for instance, gender roles or economic institutions may vary greatly from one culture to another and even across time within the same society. Nevertheless, social customs are rarely without some practical consequences that set limits on their potential diversity. Thus, despite the cultural diversity of gender roles, all societies must incorporate sexual reproduction into their customs or become extinct, and all economic systems must produce the necessities of life and adequately distribute them to the members of society.

In contrast with matters of ideology that pertain to technology of social organization, religious ideology belongs to the arena of expres-

sive culture (see p. 389), the realm of such activities as play and art, in which the beliefs and feelings that guide our actions are least directly constrained by immediate practical considerations. This permits tremendous diversity in those areas of ideology that make up any society's expressive culture. Thus, that which is sacred in one society may be profane in the ideology of another, and the things that inspire reverence in the people of one society may have no religious significance in another.

Diversity of Beliefs

Consider first some examples of religious diversity. Chastity, sexual fidelity, and even celibacy are venerated in some religious traditions. But in southern India from the ninth or tenth centuries until the twentieth century, sexual intercourse was a religiously acceptable means of attaining the highest state of spiritual ecstasy, and temple dancers called *devadaasii* shared themselves sexually with priests and other devotees as a sacred act.

Not all witches fly on broomsticks. The Nyakyusa, a farming and herding people of Tanganyika, believe that there are witches living as pythons in the bellies of their human victims, whose insides they gnaw away to satisfy their cravings for flesh (Wilson, 1951). Cannibalism was a sacred act among several peoples in the not too distant past, notably among the Kwakiutl of the British Columbia coast, where the Cannibal Society was the highest-ranked religious association. Among the Aztec of Middle America, cannibalism may have played a role in the system of human sacrifice by which the Aztec gods were placated. Estimates of how many people—mostly enemy soldiers—the Aztec sacrificed to the gods and then devoured every year range from about 15,000 to 250,000 people.

Souls come in many sizes and shapes depending on their cultural definition. Among the Shoshone of the U.S. Great Basin, the soul was thought to be shaped like a small ball of feathers that resided in the forehead. The Jívaro, who were native to the forests of Ecuador, be-

---

ritual behaviors, often performed in repetitive and stereotyped ways, that express people's anxieties by acting them out and that may be performed with the desire to influence supernatural beings or powers to achieve greater control over the natural world

lieved that a person could have three kinds of souls: the *nëkas*, the *arutam*, and the *muisak*. The nëkas was an ordinary soul that resided in the bloodstream and perpetuated the individual's personality after death. The arutam was a power-conveying soul that had to be acquired by prayer and fasting. It protected the possessor from death as long as it was not lured away by magic. The muisak was an avenging soul that came into being only at the death of a powerful warrior with a special kind of power-conveying soul. Once it was formed, it sought to kill the murderer.

Many people have worshipped both female and male deities. Others have venerated various types of animals or worshipped deformed children or other humans as deities. The adherents of some North American religions believe themselves immune to poisons, the bites of venomous snakes, or the weapons of enemies as long as they exercise sufficient faith, practice the rituals of their religion assiduously, or wear the proper charms. The possibilities of religious belief have been limited only by human imagination. From the unicorns of medieval European folklore to the cannibalistic stone giants of contemporary Shoshone stories, if something can be imagined, it has probably been a part of the religious ideology of some people somewhere.

The Adaptive Basis of Religious Beliefs

Despite the intriguing diversity among religions, each exists within a larger social environment to which it must adapt. Religious beliefs and feelings must at least be compatible with the ways of thinking and the values that are held by its adherents as they participate in their daily lives. No religion is likely to flourish if it demands beliefs or attitudes that are incompatible with those that are necessary for survival, whether in the economic, political, or reproductive lives of its members. Thus, many differences in religious ideologies may be accounted for as adaptations of culture to differing environmental, technological, and social circumstances.

Environment. Religious symbolism draws heavily on features of the natural environment that are important to the survival of groups. Thus, in aboriginal Australian religions, one important concept was that every human was

FIGURE 13.3

FEMALE DEITY

The artifacts and murals at Knossos on the island of Crete indicate that in the seventeenth century B.C.E. one sacred being was a female deity with women acting as her clergy. She is depicted with snakes encircling her body or holding snakes, as shown in this ivory and gold carving. The serpent was a symbol of wisdom and prophetic counsel.

born with a special spiritual relationship with a particular food animal. For Ituri Forest Pygmies, the forest, as the source of all necessary resources, was religiously personified as the spiritual parent of humans, and religious rituals such as the christening ceremony emphasized the tie between humans and the forest. And throughout India, where cattle pull the plow and provide dung to fertilize the fields and fuel the cooking fires, the cow is religiously venerated.

The connection between environment and religion runs deeper than the mere borrowing of symbolism from the environment. Cultural ecologists and cultural materialists have determined that religious beliefs and practices help societies adapt to different environmental circumstances. For instance, Omar Khayyam Moore (1965) has argued that when hunting peoples such as the Montagnais-Naskapi of the barren plateau of the Labradorian Peninsula use divination to decide where to hunt, their technique randomizes their choices. Thus, although the religious practice may not improve their chances of hunting success in the short term, it reduces the likelihood of overhunting their already scarce food resources for a long-term benefit.

Technology.   One famous proponent of a deterministic view, Leslie White (1971), contended that the degree to which people view the world around them in religious terms is inversely related to the complexity of their technology. The more complex it is, the more they relate to the world in mechanistic rather than spiritual ways. In other words, as people develop direct, pragmatic control over their environment, they become less likely to seek help from supernatural powers.

Growth in technological complexity also tends to accompany growth in population and increasing social complexity and specialization. These factors make it increasingly likely that people will feel lost in a sea of strangers, and that they lack the power they would like to have in day-to-day social life. When such people are alienated from the mainstream secular values of their society, they are also less likely to believe in the supernatural. Since religious rituals reaffirm people's commitment to the fundamental goals and values of their society, stresses experienced by the socially alienated tend to be channeled into coping mechanisms other than traditional religion, an adaptation referred to as secularization.

Secularization is the process by which nonreligious beliefs expand within an ideology at the expense of religious ways of thinking. It is a natural result of the more complex technologies and the greater level of social specialization that results from increased population densities. The users of these technologies learn to think of the parts of their environment that their tools allow them to manipulate in a pragmatic and matter-of-fact way. Compared to peoples who rely on rainfall for their food supply, those utilizing crop rotation, the plow, fertilization of the soil, and efficient irrigation systems are unlikely to think of the growth of crops as dependent upon mysterious spiritual forces. As the number of specialists grows, people are apt to become increasingly aware that many of their survival needs are fulfilled through the services of other human specialists, a perception that can also breed a secular view of life.

Secularization can also occur within the religious organization itself. Where technologies produce an economic base that supports a variety of religious specialists such as full-time theologians, religious belief tends to place more stress on organized rational doctrine; characteristics such as religious ecstasy and altered states of consciousness are likely to be less valued. Thus, when there are full-time religious practitioners who specialize in the performance of rituals, the congregation moves toward less active participation. The congregation also may be motivated largely by a secular desire to be accepted as a conforming member of society rather than by an immediate spiritual need for the rituals.

Social Organization.   Social organization also affects religious ideology. Guy Swanson (1960) tested the notion that religious beliefs are symbolic representations of what he calls the "sovereign groups" of society, the groups that have "original and independent jurisdiction over some sphere of life" (p. 20) and, thereby, the power to inspire respect and compliance in their members. Using a sample of 50 societies from around the world, he found that strong statistical relationships existed between several common religious doctrines and social traits that could logically be expected to be symbolized by those doctrines.

Swanson found that **monotheism**, the belief in a high god, a supreme being who either created and ordered the universe or at least maintains order within it now, is most likely to be found in societies in which the sovereign, decision-making groups are organized hierarchically so that one of them is superior in rank to at least two levels of groups below it. In such societies, the supreme sovereign group, like a

---

secularization the process by which nonreligious beliefs expand within an ideology at the expense of religious thought

monotheism the belief in a high god, a supreme being who either created the physical universe and other spiritual beings and rules over them or who at least maintains the order of the universe today

FIGURE 13.4

INDONESIAN BURIAL VAULTS

These Indonesian burial vaults in Lemo village, Tana Toraja, are carved into rock, with wooden effigies, or Tau-Taus, of the deceased displayed in their own clothes. Indonesians believe the earth-bound spirit of the deceased inhabits the Tau-Tau.

supreme god, can create and maintain order among subordinates.

The belief in superior (but not supreme) gods who control environmental areas of the universe, such as the weather, the oceans, or agriculture, is called **polytheism**. According to Swanson, polytheism reflects specialized purposes in human affairs. A society with many unranked occupational specialties is more likely to have a polytheistic religion than is a society with few such specialties. Similarly, societies with distinct social classes are more likely than egalitarian societies to have polytheistic religions. For example, traditional Indian society with its hereditary social castes and numerous jati occupations (see p. 66) had equally diverse, specialized polytheistic deities.

According to Swanson's research, **ancestral spirits** are believed to remain active in human affairs when the kinship organizations that perpetuate the purposes and goals of their deceased members are more complex than the transitory nuclear family. Belief in **reincarnation** is most common in societies in which continuity from one generation to the next is maintained by small, isolated groups whose members are economically interdependent and occupy a common settlement smaller than a village.

Belief in some form of **human soul**, the embodiment of an individual's personality and personal memories, is almost universal. But

(Continued on p. 331)

---

polytheism the belief in superior (but not supreme) gods, each of whom controls or rules over some major aspect of the universe

ancestral spirits souls of ancestors who remain interested and involved in affairs of their descendants

reincarnation the belief that the soul of a human being may be repeatedly reborn into the human group to which it previously belonged or as an animal that may be symbolically associated with that group

human soul the supernatural part of the human being that is believed to animate the human body during life or perpetuate the individual's memories or life goals after death

THE HOLINESS CHURCH

"And these signs shall follow them that believe: In my name shall they cast out devils; they shall speak with new tongues; they shall take up serpents; and if they drink any deadly thing, it shall not hurt them; they shall lay hands on the sick, and they shall recover" (Mark 16: 17–18). Some fundamentalist Christian churches in Appalachia, a coal-mining region in the eastern United States, take these verses to heart and contrast themselves with others who "do not accept the *whole* Word of God." The religious services of the Holiness churches involve much more active and emotionally charged participation of the congregation than is common in the more staid middle-class churches.

In the Holiness way, the emotional experience of the presence of God as the Holy Ghost is a crucial test of the validity of religion. It can be experienced in a variety of ways: loud music and hymn singing are accompanied by dancing, speaking in tongues, spontaneous preaching by any individual who feels inspired to do so, drinking strychnine, and handling poisonous snakes such as timber rattlers and copperheads.

For members of the Holiness churches, the snake is not a symbol of evil, but of God's power over life and death. Handling snakes is a test of faith and a proof of God's love for the faithful. Mary Lee Daugherty (1976), who studied the Holiness churches of West Virginia, interpreted snake handling as their central sacrament. In her view the ecstatic experience of handling serpents counterbalanced the dreariness of a life of poverty and provided a means for experiencing the power of God's protection in a dangerous environment:

> The land is rugged and uncompromisingly grim. It produces little except for coal dug from the earth. Unemployment and welfare have been constant companions. The dark holes of the deep mines into which men went to work every day have maimed and killed them for years. The copperhead and rattlesnake are the most commonly found serpents in the rocky terrain. . . . Mountain people have suffered terrible pain and many have died from snakebite. Small wonder that it is considered the ultimate act of faith to reach out and take up the serpent when one is filled with the Holy Ghost. (p. 232)

Generally, members of the snake-handling churches are drawn from the poorer, working-class members of Appalachia. They experience a high unemployment rate. According to Daugherty, "The handling of serpents is their way of confronting and coping with their very real fears about life and the harshness of reality . . . in years gone by and, for many, even today" (p. 235). Handling serpents and drinking poison safely also demonstrates that they are valued by God, even if they are not held in high esteem by society.

Serpent handlers know that God sometimes lets even the faithful die from snakebites as a demonstration of the very real danger that they face when they demonstrate their faith in His power over death. Contrary to what outsiders might expect, however, relatively few serpent handlers have died from snakebite. Many have survived numerous bites, and those who have been bitten frequently are praised for their faith and courage.

HOLINESS CHURCH

Trusting that Jesus will protect them, some members of the Holiness Church handle poisonous rattlesnakes during the singing and dancing that characterize their service. Fundamentalists in the strictest sense, members are centered in the poor Appalachian towns of the southeastern United States.

FIGURE 13.5

SERPENT HANDLERS

Members of the Church of Lord Jesus in Jolo, West Virginia, handle dangerous rattlesnakes and drink strychnine as a part of their worship service. The act for them is not *only a test of faith but also a way of affirming the words of the Bible: "They shall take up serpents; and if they drink any deadly thing, it shall not hurt them."*

Swanson distinguishes between societies in which the soul is believed to be lodged in the individual's body and those in which the soul transcends the body. The belief in souls intimately tied to the individual's body is more common in societies with (1) many different sovereign groups to which everyone must belong, (2) situations in which individuals with conflicting objectives that cannot be reconciled by such means as courts must work together as a group, (3) situations in which groups of individuals whose relationship is not based on their common consent must cooperate to achieve the members' common goals, (4) large-sized settlements, (5) debts, or (6) no sovereign kinship group. All these social traits increase the degree to which individuals are set apart and are socially distinct from each other. Where these traits are absent, the soul is more likely to be conceived as an impersonal vitalizing essence, part of a transcendent spirit that animates everyone.

Although all societies have moral and ethical rules that govern the conduct of individuals toward each other, not all societies use the threat of supernatural punishments for the violation of their moral rules. **Supernatural sanctions for violations of moral rules** are most frequently seen where interpersonal dif-

ferences in wealth are prominent, that is, where different groups within society benefit unequally from those rules.

According to Swanson, **sorcery**—the use of rituals to harm another person supernaturally—is most common in societies in which individuals must interact with each other but in which socially approved means for one individual to control another do not exist. In an earlier study of sorcery, Beatrice Whiting (1950) showed that it was most likely to be practiced in societies that lack "individuals or groups of individuals with delegated authority to settle disputes" (p. 90), leaving retaliation by peers as the main tool of social control. In addition, beliefs in sorcery and **witchcraft**—a related

supernatural sanctions for violations of moral rules punishments for immoral acts by spiritual agencies as opposed to human agencies. In most societies, the enforcement of morality is a strictly human responsibility, rather than a religious preoccupation

sorcery the learned use of rituals to magically control the supernatural realm to achieve human goals

witchcraft the innate ability to influence supernatural forces, usually to operate in ways that are harmful to others, without the necessity of using rituals

phenomenon in which the evildoer has an innate ability to harm others without using rituals—are most common in societies that engender severe anxiety about the expression of aggression or sexuality in children during their socialization (Whiting & Child, 1953).

Religious Feelings

Supernatural things are believed to be a source of great power that can be influenced for human ends. Whether perceived as gods, spirits, or mana, they have the quality of being both nonhuman and humanlike in their response to symbols. Because they are both powerful and mysterious, they are capable of inspiring strong feelings in humans who approach them. Rudolf Otto (1923) described these intense feelings as the uncanny or eerie sense of awe and dread that people sometimes experience when they are confronted by mysterious things. Such feelings are easily interpreted as a perception of a transcendent, supernatural presence that can fascinate even while it may be feared.

The "religious thrill" of the ecstatic experience, often associated with a state of trance, is typically thought to be caused by the overpowering presence of supernatural beings or power. Religious ecstasy is accompanied by unusual behaviors such as convulsions and **glossolalia**, a behavior that can vary from groaning to uttering unintelligible sequences of sounds that are commonly called "speaking in tongues" by followers of some North American religions, such as the Holiness churches. Similar ecstatic states have been described in non-Western cultures. For instance, Ruth Benedict (1934) described the dance of an initiate into the Cannibal Society, the most sacred society of the Kwakiutl Indians of British Columbia: "He danced wildly, not able to control himself, but quivering in all his muscles in the peculiar tremor which the Kwakiutl associate with frenzy" (p. 180). Similar behavior is found in the spirit possession trances of many cultures around the world, such as the Shoshone and Koreans (see discussion later in this chapter).

RITUAL IN RELIGION

Of the many cultural arenas in which ritual behavior is common, such as play and art, religion is the most publicly encouraged system for the ritual expression of people's concerns and anxieties.

This section will examine the three main roles of ritual in religion: (1) to unite a community emotionally; (2) to portray or act out important aspects of a religion's myths and cosmology; and (3) to influence the spiritual world and thereby the natural world for human beings or, conversely, to help human beings adjust to the conditions of the natural and spiritual realms. These roles of ritual as symbolic communication may be present simultaneously in a single ritual and are not always clearly distinguished in the minds of the participants themselves.

Ritual as Communitas

Victor Turner (1969) has emphasized the role of ritual in helping people achieve a sense of unity with each other, a kind of social relationship that he calls **communitas**. During the state of communitas, the normal structure and hierarchy of society is forgotten, and members of the group experience themselves as a community of equals whose individuality may even be submerged into a general sense of fellowship. According to Turner, the experience of communitas is a source of deeply felt bonding and allegiance between a group's members—a kind of "mystery of intimacy"—that every society needs (p. 139). However, communitas is also potentially dangerous and disruptive to society, since it challenges the basic system of social hierarchy, rank, and power differences as they are usually experienced in day-to-day interaction. The dangers that communitas might otherwise pose to society's power structure are restrained by the fact that this state is typically achieved only during the ritual process.

Rituals, Turner noted, are often described as having three phases. In the first phase, sometimes described as a period of "separation," the participants in the ritual may be literally removed from their normal place of work to a place set apart for the purpose of disentangling themselves from the web of symbols that define the ordinary reality of their culture. The middle phase of a ritual is often described as a period

---

glossolalia behavior in religious ecstasy that may include groaning and uttering unintelligible sounds
communitas Turner's term for a social relationship achieved through ritual in which people feel a sense of unity with each other

of pilgrimage within a spiritual landscape. Turner calls this transition stage between the beginning and end of a ritual the **liminal period**. It is during the liminal phase of a ritual that communitas is characteristic of the participants' feelings toward each other. Finally, participants in rituals are returned to an awareness of the mundane world of normal social life during the phase of reintegration. This tripartite pattern of ritual is particularly common in the rites of transition that societies commonly use to mark the status changes that occur during the life cycle. However, liminality, the state of being "betwixt and between," is also found in social settings where people experience themselves as marginal or inferior in the eyes of others. Thus, people with low-ranked or marginal social statuses—such as slaves, prostitutes, or street people—may experience a strong sense of camaraderie such as is experienced by mainstream members of society only during the communitas of the ritual process.

Ritual as Portrayal

Rituals often involve symbolic portrayals of myths. The Christian ritual that is sometimes called the Sacrament of the Lord's Supper, in which wine and broken bread are shared by members of a congregation, may remind people of the final meal that Jesus and the disciples had together before Jesus' arrest and crucifixion. At the same time, the broken bread and the wine may symbolize or become the body and the blood of Jesus, who Christians believe died as a vicarious sacrifice on behalf of humankind. In addition, the ritual may represent purification and renewal of the spiritual bonds that unite members of the congregation with their religion as they receive and eat the sacramental meal. Similarly, the baptism by immersion that is practiced in some Christian churches may represent simultaneously a washing away of sin; a portrayal of the death, burial, and resurrection from the dead that most Christians believe Jesus experienced; the spiritual death and renewal by which the individual enters the Christian religion; or the individual's own future death, burial, and hoped-for reawakening to a life beyond the grave. Part of the beauty of a ritual for its participants lies in the multiplicity of meanings it may have for them, a characteristic that may give them the feeling that the ritual embodies meanings transcending those of ordinary symbols.

Ritual as Influence

Rituals are also performed to influence the supernatural for the sake of human beings. The purposes of such rituals—for instance, regaining health or avoiding illness, protecting oneself in times of danger, discovering a lost watch, bringing rain in times of drought, winning at gambling, or winning someone's love—are as diverse as are human needs. The role of rituals may be perceived as only mildly influential or as powerfully effective. The former type, called **petitionary rituals** by anthropologists, are often most prominent in religions that emphasize the worship of powerful deities who may choose to decline the request. In such religions, petitionary rituals may combine expressions of praise and thanksgiving with requests for desired benefits, since a good relationship with the supernatural being may increase the chances of the petition being positively received.

On the other hand, rituals that are considered powerful and effective, even compulsive of the supernatural, and therefore more likely than mere petition to achieve the desired results, are called **magic.** This should not be confused with nonreligious stage "magic," which even the audience may recognize as nothing more than skilled illusion. Magic of the religious variety is ritual that its audience truly believes will work by virtue of its ability to coerce supernatural beings or powers such as mana. Unlike petitionary rituals, which include general guidelines to be followed but often involve much personal latitude in how they are performed, magical rituals are presumed effective only if they are performed correctly. Therefore, magic is typically executed with mechanical precision, and with great care and attention given to its details.

In earlier times, anthropologists treated magic as a system based on supernatural beliefs that was somehow different from religion, or they ethnocentrically contrasted the magic

---

liminal period transition stage between the beginning and end of a ritual

petitionary rituals ritual requests for supernatural aid that are believed to increase the likelihood of the requested result but not guarantee it

magic the use of rituals that, when performed correctly, are believed to compel—as opposed to simply making requests of—the supernatural to bring about desired results

that they described in non-Western societies with the religions of Europe, which emphasized petitionary rituals. Today, we consider such contrasts too sweeping and instead describe magic as one variety of religious ritual. In other words, we think of rituals as falling along a continuum whose endpoints are petition and compulsion, with magic falling nearest the compulsive end of the scale. Usually, rituals are more coercive when people feel an urgent need to have more control over events than they have by nonreligious means. Magic, in other words, is more typical of religious behavior when the successful outcome of the magical act is crucial to the performers.

Law of Similarity. Sir James Frazer (1922) noted long ago that magic the world over seems invariably to make use of the same two principles: imitation and contagion. **Imitative magic** acts out or portrays what it is intended to accomplish. It uses a principle that Frazer called the **Law of Similarity**. This principle seems to be based on the idea that performed activities similar to the desired outcome increase the probability of its occurrence. Thus, magical rituals that follow this principle imitate the thing that they are designed to bring about. Christians who immerse a convert in water to "wash away sin" and Pueblo Indians who whip yucca juice into frothy suds to "bring rain" are both making use of the Law of Similarity. So is the child in the United States who takes care to step over the cracks in the sidewalk, following the admonition in the childhood rhyme, "Step on a crack, and you break your mother's back"—in which there are similarities in the sound of the words "back" and "crack" and in the appearance of the line of sidewalk blocks and the line of vertebrae in the spinal column.

Law of Contagion. The idea that once two things have been in contact with each other they will remain in contact on a spiritual level, so that the magical manipulation of one will also affect the other, is called the **Law of Contagion. Contagious magic** follows this law. It may be performed on anything that has had contact with the person to be influenced: a lock of the person's hair or a piece of his or her clothing are ideal; fingernail or toenail clippings, dirt from under the nails, or excrement will do just fine; even dirt from the bottom of a footprint will help. In magic designed to

harm, the magical poison can simply be poured into the victim's footprint itself. The Law of Contagion is one reason why many people all over the world have two names, one for public use by others and a true, private name known only to themselves and perhaps a few close relatives. Since the name is an extension of the self, so the logic goes, to know someone's true name is to be able to use it as a form of contact in speaking a magical spell. In some parts of the world, when illness is thought to have been magically induced, the victim will customarily change his or her name as a part of the cure. This denies the sorcerer the chance for continued mischief by magical contact through the victim's name.

Often, magic employs elements of both the Law of Similarity and the Law of Contagion at the same time. My grandmother in Arkansas, for example, practiced the custom of protecting her children from tetanus by carefully washing the farmyard nail that had been stepped on, covering it with lard, and placing it on the kitchen windowsill. This magical ritual made use of the object that had inflicted the wound—the Law of Contagion—and treated it in a way that she believed would prevent germs from reaching it—the Law of Similarity.

Divination. An important use of rituals to obtain supernatural aid or knowledge is **divination**. Methods of divination can be very creative. They may include examining the entrails of animals for unusual signs, considering the flight direction of birds or the shapes formed by molten lead poured into water, or checking the lines on people's hands or the date of their birth. These methods have been used to answer such questions as, Where is my lost watch? Who committed a particular crime? What kind

---

imitative magic attempted ritual coercion of the supernatural realm by use of the Law of Similarity

Law of Similarity the principle that things that are similar to one another are spiritually identical and can be used in rituals to influence a desired outcome

Law of Contagion the principle that things that have been in contact remain supernaturally in contact or that contact between things can be used to transfer mana from one to the other

contagious magic ritual coercion of the supernatural realm by the use of the Law of Contagion

divination the use of ritual to obtain answers to questions from supernatural sources

THE AZANDE POISON ORACLE

Evans-Pritchard (1937) described an interesting system of divination that uses poison. The Azande, who live in Sudan, Zaire, and the Central African Republic, consult the poison oracle on all important matters—in order to diagnose the cause of an illness, to decide how to conduct vengeance by magic most safely, or to determine who has used magic against them. The poison oracle is also consulted to find out if a journey may be undertaken safely and to prepare for any dangerous or socially important activity.

Consulting the poison oracle usually occurs in the bush far from the homestead to maintain secrecy and to avoid people who have not observed the taboos necessary for the oracle to work. Participants must not have sexual intercourse, smoke hemp, or eat elephant's flesh or a number of other foods for several days before consulting the oracle.

The diviner, who with only rare exceptions is a male, scrapes a hole in the ground and places into it a large leaf to hold the *benge*, or oracle poison. He fashions a brush of grass to administer the poison to chickens, several of which are brought by each questioner. When everyone is seated, it is decided how each question will be framed to provide the most information. The diviner then pours water into the leaf bowl and adds the powdered poison. After mixing the paste with his brush, the diviner squeezes the liquid from the brush into the beak of one of the chickens. While several doses are given, the questioner asks the first question repeatedly, ending each time with a request for the poison to kill or to spare the fowl if the answer is affirmative. For instance, a question about whether adultery has occurred might be followed by the questioner's saying:

> Poison oracle, poison oracle, you are in the throat of the fowl. That man his navel joined her navel; they pressed together; he knew her as woman and she knew him as man. She has drawn *badiabe* [a leaf used as a towel] and water to his side [for ablutions after intercourse]; poison oracle hear it, kill the fowl. (p. 138)

The poison used is a red powder prepared from a jungle creeper. The alkaloid that it contains has effects similar to strychnine. Some chickens seem unaffected by it. Others die immediately or soon after it is administered.

In poison oracle divination, there are always two tests of each question, one framed positively and the other negatively. One chicken must die and another must survive to confirm an answer to a question. If both live or if both die, the oracle must be consulted at another time to obtain an answer to the question.

AZANDE

The Azande, who live in the Republic of the Sudan, Zaire, and the Central African Republic, consult an oracle on important matters of politics or health. The diviner forces poison into the beak of a chicken as he seeks an answer to his question. For a definitive response, one chicken must die, and another must live.

of person should I marry? Methods of divination fall into two main categories: those in which the results can be easily influenced by the diviner and those in which they cannot. The former include practices such as reading tea leaves or interpreting an astrological sign, casting the *I Ching*, spreading *tarot* cards, or randomly selecting a Bible verse; each gives the diviner a good deal of latitude for subjective interpretation. These methods permit the diviner's knowledge of the client's circumstances to play a role in providing answers that are psychologically satisfying to the customer.

Methods that give responses that the diviner is unable to control include such techniques as casting lots or checking whether an object floats on water. Like flipping a coin, these tend to randomize the answers. This approach to divination is especially useful when conflicting secular information causes confusion or when divergent opinions must be resolved.

Affecting Health.   Influential magic also may be used to cause ill health. Illness is a problem with which people must cope in all parts of the world. Although health-related magic is most common in societies that lack complex secular medical technologies, one finds religious rituals for the curing and causing of illness in all the world's societies.

According to Forest Clements (1932), there are six major theories of disease in the world's societies: natural causes, magic, the intrusion of disease objects into the victim's body, soul loss, spirit possession, and taboo violations. Each of these is associated with an appropriate approach to curing the illness.

Those diseases or infirmities that are thought to be the result of natural causes are treated by pragmatic techniques such as setting broken bones and using herbs.

When magic is used to bring about illness or death in a victim, the sorcerer's favored materials may include things that have been in intimate contact with the victim, since they invoke the Law of Contagion (see p. 334) and direct the magic more surely to its intended victim than the Law of Similarity alone might. Magic-caused illnesses must be cured by corresponding countermagic.

Sending a foreign object, called a **disease object**, into the body of a victim by magic is another favored technique of sorcerers and witches for bringing about illness or death. When a foreign object such as a barbed stick or a stone is believed to have been supernaturally projected into the victim's body, thereby causing pain and illness, the object is removed by massage and sucking.

The fourth cause of illness is **soul loss**, a malady commonly found where independence and self-reliance are important social values. When a soul has left a person's body—whether dislodged from the body by a sudden fright, simply lost during its nightly wanderings, or stolen by another's magic—the body is left without the vitality that it needs to survive. If this is believed to be the cause of the victim's ill health, a healer must coax the wayward soul back into the patient's body or recapture it and bring it back.

Spirit possession, the control of a person's behavior by a spirit that has entered his or her body, is common in societies where people are expected to be dutiful and compliant rather than independent and assertive. It requires a ritual of exorcism to remove the offending spirit (see also chapter 14).

In many cultures, especially those in which people are expected to learn many rules, it is believed that illness may come not as punishment but simply as a natural consequence of breaking a supernatural rule. Thus **taboo violation** may include not only willful rule breaking but also rule breaking that is accidental or even done without the actor's awareness. So the rule breaker is not necessarily held morally responsible for the act, as in the Western concept of **sin**, but he or she may still suffer the consequences. For instance, Apache Indians of the southwestern United States believe that illness may result from using firewood that has been urinated on by a deer, even though one is unlikely to know whether or not this is the case. Furthermore, in some societies the illness that follows a taboo violation may strike someone other than the rule breaker—a relative or a neighbor, for instance. When taboo violation is thought to be the cause of illness, confession will play a role in the cure.

What determines whether people will believe that the malicious acts of others, such as sorcerers or witches, are the cause of illness, or will attribute illnesses to other causes? As has been noted, Beatrice Whiting (1950) and Guy Swanson (1960) have cited the presence of societal conflicts and the absence of effective social means of resolving them as major causes of the belief in sorcery to work harm. Specific conflicts surrounding sexual jealousy also have been suggested as a basis for witchcraft and

---

disease object an object such as a barbed stick or stone that is magically cast into the body of a victim to cause illness

soul loss in primitive societies, the belief that the departure of the soul from the body, usually caused by a sudden fright, causes the body to weaken and die

spirit possession a trance in which individuals feel as if their behavior is under the control of one or more spirits that have entered their bodies

taboo violation the breaking of a supernatural rule, whether intentional or not; often believed to be a cause of illness

sin a form of taboo violation in which the rule breaker is morally responsible for the act

sorcery. On the other hand, the belief that illness may be caused by nonhuman spiritual beings (spirit possession) seems to symbolize anxiety about the kind of social role one is expected to play. Bourguignon and Greenberg (1973) found that spirit possession is most common in societies in which people are expected to be submissive and compliant, and that spirit loss is most common in societies in which people are socialized to be independent and self-assertive. Illness as a result of taboo violation is found in societies in which conformity to rules is important. For instance, taboo violation is an important cause of illness among the arctic Inuit, whose environment can be quite deadly if one is lax or careless in following the established rules of life.

Death by Magic. In some cases, victims of sorcery actually die. Anthropologists have tried for decades to understand the phenomenon of death by magic.

Cannon (1942) analyzed cases of so-called **voodoo death** and suggested that the actual cause of death in such cases may be prolonged shock induced by extreme fear. Cannon quotes Herbert Basedow (1925), who graphically described the terrifying effect of sorcery by **bone-pointing** (see Fig. 13.6) in Australia:

> A man who discovers that he is being boned by an enemy is, indeed, a pitiable sight. He stands aghast, with his eyes staring at the treacherous pointer, and with his hands lifted as though to ward off the lethal medium, which he imagines is pouring into his body. . . . His cheeks blanch and his eyes become glossy, and the expression of his face becomes horribly distorted, like that of one stricken with palsy. He attempts to shriek but usually the sound chokes in his throat, and all that one might see is froth at his mouth. His body begins to tremble and the muscles twist involuntarily. He sways backwards and falls to the ground, and after a short time appears to be in a swoon but soon after he begins to writhe as if in mortal agony, and, covering his face with his hands, begins to moan. After a while he becomes more composed and crawls to his wurley [hut]. From this time onwards he sickens and frets, refusing to eat, and keeping aloof from the daily affairs of the tribe. Unless help is forthcoming in the shape of a counter charm administered by the hands of the *"Nangarri"* or medicine-man, his death is only a matter of a comparatively short time. If the coming of the

FIGURE 13.6

BONE-POINTING

A man in the Northern Territory, Australia, shows how the magic bone is pointed at a victim while he is being "sung." It is said that when a victim learns of the ritual, even though it is done in secret, he or she may actually die.

medicine-man is opportune, he might be saved. (Cannon, 1942, p. 181)

Normally, both fear and anger stimulate the sympathetic nervous system, which regulates the inner organs and the circulatory system. This stimulation prepares the body for prolonged muscular exertion by discharging adrenalin and accelerating the heart rate, by constricting blood vessels during the exertion, and by dilating the bronchioles within the lungs so that more oxygen may be available to the muscles and more carbon dioxide may be expelled. All of these changes prepare the body for the muscular action that may be necessary for the escape from danger. However, when the energy thus made available cannot be used for a prolonged period, the physiological stress of remaining in this state of preparedness for intense action will eventually result in exhaustion and damage to the bodily organs, which may result in death. As Hans Selye (1976) pointed out in his description of the stress response, which he termed the **General Adaptation Syndrome,**

---

voodoo death death that occurs following a magical ritual performed to kill

bone-pointing a magical ritual for killing in which a sharp bone or stick is pointed at or ritually cast into the body of the intended victim

General Adaptation Syndrome the nonspecific changes that occur in the body as a result of stress, as it mobilizes itself to act against the cause of the stress

THE IROQUOIS FALSE FACE SOCIETY

FALSE FACE SOCIETY

To cure sick people in their community, members of the Iroquois False Face Society wear ceremonial masks while they sprinkle the patient with ashes and shake a turtle carapace rattle to dispel the illness. The masks represent spirit forces that heal.

The False Face Society is a powerful religious curing society among the Iroquois of the northeastern United States. Their cures are accomplished with the use of wooden masks representing various spirits worn by the members of the society during its ceremonies. The masks characteristically have distorted features created by carving the face into the trunk of a live tree (see Fig. 13.7). During the carving, prayers are made to the spirit force that it represents. After tobacco is burned before the mask, it is cut free, painted, and decorated with hair made from corn-silk or horsehair.

Curing ceremonies take place at the request of the patient's family in the longhouse where they live. The members of the False Face Society don their masks and travel in a group to the patient's house. As they come, they mimic the spirits represented by the masks. Upon entering the patient's house, they sprinkle the afflicted person with ashes and shake their turtle carapace rattles over him or her to drive away the illness. In return for their work, members of the False Face Society are paid with gifts and food.

these are nonspecific changes that occur in the body as a result of any stress, and even adaptation to a stress-producing event eventually ends in a state of exhaustion. Adaptation to unusual levels of stress cannot go on indefinitely.

In fear-induced shock, the prolonged constriction of the small blood vessels occurs especially in the extremities and the abdominal viscera. The lack of an adequate supply of oxygen in the visceral capillaries causes their thin walls to become more permeable, and blood plasma escapes into the spaces surrounding these small blood vessels in the abdomen. This reduces the volume of blood available in the circulatory system until adequate circulation is no longer possible. The result is a lowering of blood pressure, which in turn leads to a deterioration of the heart and other organs that normally ensure an adequate circulation of blood to the body. If the cycle is not broken, death is inevitable. Victims themselves often speed up the process by ceasing to eat and drink, thereby adding even greater stresses to the body. H. D. Eastwell (1982) has

argued that dehydration may be the actual cause of death. Since stress that is brought on by fear of sorcery cannot be eliminated by any practical action, death may indeed result unless the fear can be eliminated by a ritual cure.

Reo Fortune (1932) gave a graphic account of the use of sorcery to kill among the Dobuans, inhabitants of the Melanesian Islands near New Guinea. The sorcerer and one or more assistants approached the area of the victim's garden in the forest. They rubbed their bodies with magically powerful herbs to make themselves invisible and then crept to the edge of the clearing where the victim was working in the garden. Suddenly, with a characteristic scream, the sorcerer jumped into the clearing. The victim, taken by surprise, would recognize what was happening from the cry and actions of the sorcerer. He or she would be overcome by fear and fall immediately into a faint. The sorcerer was then free to prance about and dramatically act out, in symbolic form, the surgical opening of the victim's abdomen and the magical removal of the entrails and vital organs. After closing the magical wound, the sorcerer would ask the victim, "What is my name?" The victim could not respond, ensuring that the sorcerer would not be identified.

After the sorcerer departed, the victim gradually recovered enough to stagger home and crawl up the ladder to his or her house. Relatives, recognizing the expression of shock and fear on the victim's face, knew what had transpired and began to make arrangements for the funeral. The victim lost all appetite and could die from shock within the next few days.

Spiritual Healing. Just as ritual is believed to play a prominent role in the causing of illness or even death, religious power is called on in many societies to cure illness. Curing illness is the primary concern of shamans, or inspired religious healers (see p. 342). In societies in which shamans are able to congregate in sufficient numbers, they may form organizations in which they discuss their practices, cooperate with one another in curing patients, and initiate apprentices into the shared secrets of the trade. For instance, among the Iroquois, a Native American people who lived in northern New York and were described extensively by Morgan (1851), various illnesses were treated by the members of specialized medicine societies. Among these were the False Face Society, the Bear Society, the Pygmy Society, the Otter Society, the Chanters for the Dead, and the Eagle Society. Each specialized in the treatment or prevention of particular ills and had its own songs and rituals. Those who asked a particular society for a cure became members of that society if the cure was successful, as did persons who dreamed that they must join a society, since such a dream was believed to have been a message from the supernatural. Thus, following a cure, individuals acquired a new social status and were expected to play a role in the curing of others who became afflicted by the same disease.

THE SOCIAL ORGANIZATION OF RELIGION

A hallmark of religion is ritual involvement with others. By participating in the religious rituals of their society, people express a sense

FIGURE 13.7

FALSE FACE SOCIETY
The members of the Iroquois False Face Society perform rituals to cure the sick. They wear masks that have been carved from the trunk of a tree and shake their turtle carapace rattles over the patient as they dance in order to drive out the evil spirits causing illness.

of togetherness, unity, and belonging. This group aspect of religious practice fosters deeper loyalty to one's society. To be sure, all religions include rituals that individuals may perform for their own benefit: private prayer to petition the spirits and gods for aid; magic to achieve the same ends more coercively; taboos that are followed to avoid misfortune; and positive acts that foster luck, skill, and safety. However, no religious system is built solely from these individualistic ritual activities. All religions have at least part-time religious specialists who perform rituals for others, and some are organized into more complex communal or ecclesiastical religious groups (Wallace, 1966).

Ritual Specialists

Ritual may be performed by any adherent of a religion, but all religions also have some individuals who specialize in the use of spiritual power to influence others. These include shamans, sorcerers, priests, and witches.

Shamans. The most common kind of ritual specialist in human societies is the inspired,

BECOMING A SHAMAN AMONG THE AVAM SAMOYED

Where shamans are formally initiated by others of their kind, the initiation ceremony often enacts a kind of symbolic death, followed by a journey through the spirit world where the novice is trained and given the powers of a shaman and rebirth into the human world. This formula is well

AVAM SAMOYED

Becoming a shaman involves a formal initiation in most societies. Among the Avam Samoyed of Siberia, the ritual includes a symbolic death, a journey through the spirit world where the initiate is trained, and a rebirth into the human world.

illustrated in a story told by Popov (1936) about the vision of a Siberian Avam Samoyed man who received the power to cure. While he lay near death from smallpox, his sickness spoke to him on behalf of the Lords of Water and gave him a new name, Diver. After climbing a mountain, Diver met a naked woman, the Lady of Water, who took him as her child and suckled him at her breast. Her husband, Lord of the Underworld, gave him two guides who led him to the Underworld. There he learned of the diseases, both physical and mental, from which people suffer. Then he visited the Land of Shamanesses where voice is strengthened, since song is used in cures. On an island in one of the Nine Seas, he found the tree of the Lord of the Earth. There he was given the wood for making three of the drums that shamans use in their ceremonies. After he received instruction in the medicinal use of seven herbs and in other techniques for curing, he was told that he must marry three women.

Then the initiate was led to another high mountain where he met two women clothed in the hair of reindeer. Each gave him a hair to be used when he used his power to influence reindeer. He crossed a great desert to another mountain. There he was dismembered, and his body parts were boiled in a great cauldron by a naked man who forged his head on an anvil that was used to forge the heads of great shamans. This man taught him to divine whether a cure would be successful, reassembled his body, gave him new eyes capable of seeing into the spirit world, and pierced his ears so they could hear the speech of plants. After all these things, he awoke and found that during the 3 days of his coma, he had been so close to death that he had almost been buried.

charismatic medical-religious curer called a **shaman**. The term shaman was originally taken from a seminomadic Siberian people called the Chuckchee, among whom shamanism was a male occupation. According to Waldemar Bogoras (1907), Chuckchee shamans were generally men who were socially withdrawn, listless, and prone to falling into trances before entering the shamanic career. Chuckchee shamans were expected to adopt the dress of women as a symbol of their sacred status. Some took on the behavior of women and entered into sexual relationships or marriages with men as well, and

these shamans were thought to be the most powerful.

Mircea Eliade (1964) has shown that the central feature of shamanistic practice is the ecstatic experience achieved in trance. In the trance state, shamans may send their spirits on errands in service to their clients, or they may invite powerful spirits to enter their bodies and

---

shaman part-time religious practitioner who is believed to have access to supernatural power that may be used for the benefit of specific clients, as in healing or divining

give them power. In spirit travel and possession trances, shamans experience the ecstasy of visions of a world not seen by ordinary eyes. Noll (1985) has argued that what sets the shaman apart from other people is his skill in entering trances and experiencing visions. By practicing visual imaging, the shaman becomes able to have more vivid and lively visions, and he learns to control when the visions begin and end and what their content will be. L. P. Peters and D. R. Price-Williams (1980) describe the trance as similar to a waking dream and guided imagery. Further, Price-Williams (1985) believes that the true shamanistic trance involves passing over from simple visual imaging into an altered state of consciousness in which the shaman experiences personal "participation and immersion in the imagery content" (p. 656).

Sorcerers. The antisocial equivalent of a shaman is the **sorcerer**, a person who uses supernatural power to harm human beings, causing misfortune, illness, and even death. As dangerous as a sorcerer may be, acknowledged practitioners of the art may be tolerated by their neighbors, since their noxious powers may occasionally be sought by others. A sorcerer might, for instance, be hired by persons who believe themselves to have been wronged by others and who seek vengeance by sorcery. Since individuals who discover that they have been cursed by a sorcerer may seek the removal of that curse by making amends for the wrong of which they have been accused, the sorcerer's role in society is sometimes similar to that of the law enforcers in societies that have centralized governments.

Among the Navajo of the southwestern United States, it is said that a curer may be seduced by the dark side of power. No human being is wholly good or wholly evil. In the Navajo view, we each have both qualities or, more accurately, the capacity to do both good and evil. According to Witherspoon (1977), the goal of Navajo life is to bring one's impulses under control so that one grows and develops through a complete life in a condition of *hózhó*—the state of beauty, harmony, good, and happiness—and then dies naturally of old age and becomes one with the universal beauty, harmony, and happiness that make up the ideal positive environment.

A person's *ch'indi*, or potential for evil, can be controlled by rituals that restore one to a state of *hózhó*. Although the state of inward beauty achieved through living in outward harmony with the ideal environment can be disrupted by contact with dangerous (*báhádzid*) things or by the sorcery of others, perhaps leading to illness or to death, such states can be countered by a traditional ritual chant, or "Sing," of which there are over 60. These channel positive supernatural power by reenacting the Navajo creation myths.

Navajo singers, the curing shamans of the Navajo, can also learn to use the power of ritual to harm other people. Initiation into the world of sorcery carries a high price: the initiate must consent to the death of a close relative. In using rituals to upset the ideal balance of life in others, the sorcerer's *ch'indi* grows stronger and may overwhelm him. Sorcerers live a life that inverts the ideals of the Navajo: they gather at night in places avoided by others to do their rituals; they dig up corpses to grind their bones into poisons; and they don the skins of wolves and transform themselves into animals. Skinwalkers, as they are called, can travel great distances faster than ordinary humans can imagine. They cast their poisons into the smoke holes of their victims' hogans or magically shoot harmful substances into their bodies.

Witches. Shamans and sorcerers share the world of supernatural power with **witches**, men or women who are believed to have spiritual powers for good or ill. Unlike shamans or sorcerers, who must learn the rituals with which they work, witches are thought to be born with their power. Thus, the evil of a witch may do its damage to others even without the witch's conscious intent. Since witches are different from ordinary humans they are often viewed as the epitome of evil and described in terms that invert the normal qualities of human beings: they are said to love the night, to commit incest and kill their own relatives, and to travel on their heads instead of their feet or fly as fireballs through the sky. The presence of persons believed to be witches may not be tolerated, and those convicted of being witches are likely to be killed. Because of this, societies with actual practicing witches are uncommon.

---

sorcerer practitioner of magical rituals done to harm others

witches persons believed to have the innate supernatural ability to harm others without the use of ritual

FIGURE 13.8

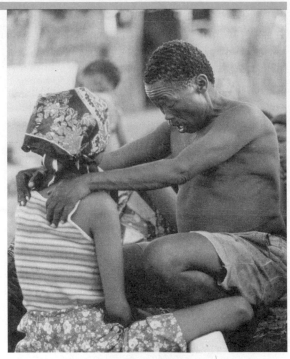

KALAHARI SAN SHAMAN

Shamans are specialists primarily in healing. Extensive training gives them both physical and spiritual knowledge in eliminating the causes of illness. The rituals shamans use may vary from culture to culture but involve chanting, smoking, massaging the body of the patient, and entering a trance state. This Kalahari San shaman, while in a trance, lays his hands on the patient in order to cure her.

Priests. Religious practitioners who have been trained to perform rituals for entire congregations are called **priests** to distinguish them from their more charismatic counterparts, the shamans. Whereas shamans serve individual clients when called upon to do so, priests perform rituals for a congregation on a full-time or at least regular basis. Priests may be organized into a professional priesthood, a bureaucracy that both organizes the activities of its members and regulates the ritual calendar of the congregations. Unlike shamans, who often are highly charismatic individuals who follow the inspiration of the moment in modifying their ritual performance to fit the needs of their clients, priests maintain the traditional ritual forms that they have learned.

Shamanic Religions

Of all forms of religious organization, **shamanic religions** are the socially simplest and perhaps the oldest. They are based on rituals performed both by nonspecialists and the shamans. Shamans may perform rituals to divine the future or to gain answers to their clients' questions. As spirit mediums, they may be called on to increase the success of a hunt, the fertility of the game, or the growth of crops. The charms that they make protect their clients from harm or increase their luck and skill. However, shamans are best known for their skill at manipulating the supernatural to cure illness. Their spiritual powers do not differ in nature from those that nonspecialists may use on their own behalf, but their special status grows out of their reputation for greater skill at manipulating these powers. In addition to their spiritual powers, shamans often possess an impressive body of knowledge about the natural medical effects of a broad range of native plants and other curative materials and techniques. Shamans also draw upon their patients' awe and reverence for religious power, thereby increasing the patients' confidence in the likelihood of recovery.

On the reservation in Nevada where I did my fieldwork, a Shoshone *puhakanten*, literally a "possessor of power," still cured the sick. The shaman's spiritual power was brought to him by a spirit partner, a *newe puha-pea*, the Eagle, who first appeared to him in a vision and gave him the power to cure.

When a prospective patient approached this shaman, the first task was to determine whether he would be able to perform the cure. At the direction of his spirit partner, certain cases—such as those that he diagnosed as cancer—had to be referred to a medical doctor. To facilitate the diagnosis, the individual who consulted him would be given an "eagle wing," a fan made of eagle feathers to place above his or her bed that night. That evening, the shaman would consult his spirit partner for a diagnosis. On the next day, he would either accept or reject the petitioner as a patient, depending on the diagnosis.

---

priests religious practitioners who perform rituals for the benefit of a group; are often are full-time specialists whose emphasis is on preserving the established ritual forms, rather than on inspiration and innovation in the application of their rituals

shamanic religions religions in which the only ritual specialist is the shaman, and which contain only shamanic and individual ritual practices

A cure usually begins at sunset in the shaman's home. It is sometimes attended by other interested members of the community. Attendance at a curing ceremony is believed to foster good health in general among those who participate. The patient, who has bathed that morning at sunrise in a local hot spring, provides tobacco that is smoked by the shaman as part of the ceremony. After smoking, the shaman begins a chant that he was taught by his spirit partner in his first vision. This chant is a call to the Eagle to come down from his mountain abode and enter the shaman to give him power to cure his patient's illness. He alternately smokes, chants, and massages the patient's body to remove the illness. Following the ceremony, the patient may be given some tasks to perform to complete the cure. For instance, a patient who is suffering from nosebleeds may be required to collect the blood and dispose of it on a red anthill. Patients are required to abstain from alcohol to ensure the efficacy of the cure.

Korean religious tradition also includes an important role for shamanic rituals, which are performed by a class of female shamans called *mansin*. They obtain their power by becoming possessed by powerful spirits and deities, during which time they carry out rituals that benefit both individuals and groups. They divine the causes of both psychological and physical illnesses, undertake the cures, communicate with the spirits of the dead, placate angry gods, and purify villages plagued by evil spirits.

Brian Wilson (1980) has described a *kut*, or spirit possession ritual, conducted by a *mansin* to cleanse a village of angry spirits that had caused a series of tragic deaths, a murder and several suicides. The shaman, whom Wilson calls Mansinim, had diagnosed the cause of the problems as the village's tutelary spirit, who was angry because some members of the community had cut down some trees. According to Wilson:

> Mansinim began the *kut* with the *pujong*, or ritual cleansing of the [village] shrine and surrounding area of all polluting elements. While the *paksu* (male shaman) who was working with her this day beat a rapid beat on the drum and gong and chanted the invocational *tokkyung*, Mansinim walked around the concrete *sonang* shrine with salt water and ashes and sprinkled the surrounding area using her *Changgun* sword to sprinkle the water. Then

> she took a bowl of salt and walked around the shrine and sprinkled the salt to drive away any harmful spirits that might have been lurking about. She took two cymbals (*para*) attached to each other by a strip of white cloth and began beating them in a slow, almost funereal rhythm. She walked out in the field, clanging the cymbals, and when I later asked why she said it was to notify the gods and spirits that she was here and that the *kut* was about the begin. The field was marked off with straw rope from which were fluttering red, blue, and green bits of cloth. She marched toward an old tree beside which were the two guardian posts inscribed with the customary *ch'onha tae changgun* [male general of heaven] and *chisang yo changgun* [female general of the earth]. She circled the tree three times and bowed, then walked to the base of the mountain overlooking the village and bowed to *San Sin* [the Mountain God]. Walking back to the *sonang*, still clanging the cymbals, she bowed before every tree along the side of the path.

> She entered the *sonang* shrine and bowed. Then she put on the red vest and blue sash of [the god] *Sinjang*, the Arrester, and her hands, pressed together in a prayer-like position, began shaking. This is the outward sign that the god has possessed her. She took the sword and trident and began jumping in front of the *Sonang* shrine. Inside the little house-like shrine was the offering of a pig tied to an upright stone. The stone is the *sonang* spirit which guards the village. The villagers say it was miraculously washed up during a flood and deposited in the village.

> The *paksu* changed the beat to a dance rhythm and Mansinim took the divinatory flags and danced with them, circling the shrine. Then she danced with a fan and bells. She danced over to the chairman of the Elders' Association and pulled him into the shrine, where he bowed and placed a money offering at the foot of the stone. Mansinim fanned him with both fans. The gods were pleased.

> She took the *sin tae* (spirit stick used in divination) and danced with it. A bow signaled the end of that *kori* [one segment of the ceremony].

> After lunch the *kut* resumed. Mansinim put on the blue vest and black hat and the *Taegam* [Greedy Provincial Official] danced. Then she put on the *Changgun* ["General's"] costume, took two swords and danced with them inside

the shrine compound. Her motions became very mannish and brusque. She stopped dancing and her body shook. *Changgun* had descended. She took her sword and tried to balance it on the flat end of the handle but the wind kept blowing it over. She went out and got the trident while the *paksu* picked up the beat with drum and gong. This time the trident stood, a sign of the favorable presence of *Changgun*. Her body shook again and she began dancing, becoming more animated as she danced and then she began jumping. Finally she faced the assembled villagers and the General spoke to them through her:

You are ungrateful! (*kwaessim hada*) Do you know which General has come down? *Tosol Changgun* ["Heavenly General"] has come down in order to help the people who live in this mountain valley. I come to this village letting three *mansins* go ahead, In order to make a success of human wishes. Because three mansins fervently pray, Because all the spirits cooperate to make a success of human wishes, Because villagers ask the *Son Hwang* [the tutelary spirit of the *sonang* shrine] spirit for their wishes, Because villagers offer a whole *ssiru* [steamed rice], Because villagers offer a whole pig and pray fervently, Don't worry, I will solve your problem, I will also open the door to a bright future.

Later in the afternoon, at the end of the *kut*, Mansinim drove the offending *subi* [goblins], *magwi* [demons], *kwisin* [ghosts] and other evil spirits into a dead branch to which had been tied pieces of red and green cloth. With the chairman of the Elders' Association trailing behind she ran across the field and then across another field to the foot of a hill where she untied and burned the colored cloth and 'planted' the tree in the hillside. (pp. 8–10)

Lewis (1971) pointed out that spirit possession is a religious practice in which socially powerless members of society are able to assert themselves in ways that society ordinarily forbids and "press their claim for attention and respect" (p. 32). This view of the psychological role of spirit possession seems valid when applied to the *kut* because in Korea, the social roles of women provide few opportunities for achieving high public status. In a discussion of the role of the *mansin* in Korea, Wilson (1980) has painted a poignant portrait of how Mansinim sought the fulfillment that was denied her because of her gender.

Mansinim had had a difficult life: her father had died when she was 3 years old, and she worked as a housemaid as a teenager. She entered into an arranged marriage with a man she had never met, and had to live alone in a bomb shelter when her husband went into the army during the Korean War. After the death of two of her children, she suffered from dizzy spells and fits of crying, and was frequently ill. After a violent quarrel with her husband about an affair he had been having, she found her calling as a shaman when she became possessed by the spirit of her mother-in-law during a *kut* ceremony. Wilson has noted that similar hardships seem characteristic of many of the female shamans whose lives he studied.

Yet according to Wilson, Mansinim's role as a shaman was not simply the manifestation of psychological stresses. As a shaman, Mansinim came to be possessed by a variety of powerful spirits and deities such as Tosol Changgun. During her states of possession on ceremonial occasions, Mansinim was able to abandon her prescribed role of submissive woman and speak with a religiously legitimated power and authority usually reserved for men in Korean society. In Wilson's opinion, her dominant behavior when possessed fit her natural predispositions in a healthier way than any other role available to her.

Possessed of a god, Mansinim was able to express a part of her personality that was otherwise forbidden by her culture. Thus, Mansinim's shamanistic religion offered her a healthy outlet for parts of herself that, if denied, might have been a source of psychic distress.

Communal Religions

A more complex form of religious organization tends to be found in societies that have slightly larger local groups than those in which shamanic religions predominate. In societies with larger social groups, **communal religions** serve to celebrate the cohesiveness of the group or ease the transition of individuals from one status to another by publicly proclaiming that change in a rite of passage. Like shamanic religions, they are found in societies where people survive by foraging wild foods. For instance,

---

communal religions religions that include the performance of rituals by groups of lay practitioners, shamans, or individuals

THE RAIN-BRINGING RITUAL OF THE JIGALONG PEOPLE

According to Tonkinson (1974), the most important yearly ritual of the Jigalong people of the western Australian desert is the rain-bringing ritual, called *Ngaawajil*. This ritual reenacts the story of Winba, an old snake-man ancestral being, and other rainmaking beings, controllers of rain, clouds, thunder, lightning, hail, and other elements of the weather. If the people perform, the annual return of the rains is ensured, as is the increase in the kangaroo and other game animals that depend on the rains for water in the desert environment where the Jigalong people live and hunt.

Since the ritual lasts for many days and consists of a number of ceremonies performed simultaneously in different locations, it requires the cooperation of five male and four female groups, each with its own name, insignia, and ritual responsibilities. Throughout the ritual there is a division of the participants into the two-generation-level moieties of Jigalong life, groupings that both unite members of alternate generations (grandparents and grandchildren) and separate members of contiguous generations (parents and children). Thus, the ritual reinforces a major aspect of Jigalong social life by incorporating the moiety division into the structure of the ritual.

The ritual activities occur at two locations: the camp, where men, women, and children participate together in the ritual, and the "men's country" away from the camp, where only initiated males are involved in the ceremonies. At the camp, men and women of appropriate status prepare food for the participants, and members of each moiety engage in chanting and throwing water at members of the other moiety. Away from the camp, the ritual requires two groups or stacks of sacred objects such as rainbow stones to encourage the rain-

making ancestors to bring the rains. These objects are sprinkled with blood symbolic of rain, covered with down feathers symbolic of clouds, and "fed" with ceremonial food and water. The desire for rain is communicated to the rainmaking ancestors by rainmaking snakes believed to live in the piles of sacred objects.

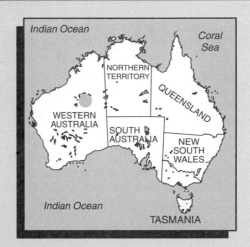

JIGALONG PEOPLE

The Jigalong people of the western Australian desert depend heavily on rain for their subsistence. Thus, they perform a yearly ritual reenacting the story of Winba, a snake man, and other rainmaking spirits in order to ensure that the rains will come.

communal religions were common among aboriginal Australians. They are also found in societies where horticulture and pastoralism are practiced and within nation-states that have incorporated older foraging, horticultural, and pastoral societies within their boundaries.

The group rituals permit broader social participation in the shared concerns of the community or of groups of specialists than do individual or shamanic rituals. The rituals that

are most often celebrated in communal religions include rituals to increase the fertility of game or ensure success in hunting; annual rituals to influence the weather, the fertility of crops, and the harvest; social rituals to celebrate changes in status or reinforce the importance of social divisions by sex or age; and ceremonies to reenact the mythology of the group or commemorate cultural heroes, ancestral spirits, or particular deities.

FIGURE 13.9

ECCLESIASTICAL PRIESTS

Priests function as ritual specialists for their congregations in ecclesiastical religions. In 1977 some Western ecclesiastical religions began to admit women to the priesthood, but not without controversy. In 1994 the Anglican Church of the United Kingdom ordained the first women to the priesthood. These women deacons are arriving at Bristol Cathedral in London, England, for their ordination.

Ecclesiastical Religions

The **ecclesiastical religions** make use of individual, shamanic, and communal rituals, but they add to them a series of rituals performed by priests. In ecclesiastical religions priests may perform some shamanistic roles, such as confessor, counselor, and faith healer. However, the priestly hierarchy may not be tolerant of some shamanistic activities, such as seances, faith healing, prophecy, and psychic readings by separate specialists. The hierarchy of priests often frowns on similar behavior in the lay congregation as well and may forbid such practices as spirit possession trances and ecstatic speaking in tongues by members of the congregation. Ecclesiastical religions tend to be found in agriculturally based societies, particularly in those with large enough populations to support a variety of full-time specialists.

Polytheism and Monotheism. Ideologically, the earliest recorded ecclesiastical religions had polytheistic beliefs in which a variety of high gods each required the service of special religious practitioners. Wallace (1966) has called these early ec-

clesiastical religions the **Olympian religions** to distinguish them from the later monotheistic religions. In monotheism the supernatural pantheon of ranked gods is superseded by a conception of the highest deity as a truly supreme being, if not the only god in the pantheon. The ancient Greeks, Egyptians, Babylonians, and Romans followed the Olympian pattern, while monotheism is represented today by Judaism, Christianity, Islam, and modern philosophical Hinduism, in which all of the gods of earlier Hindu tradition are said to be merely various manifestations of a single, all-encompassing deity.

Religion in the United States. People in the United States tend to view the universe in mechanistic terms, and, historically, a scientific worldview has been central to their approach to everyday problems. The government recognizes no official religion; the Bill of Rights of the U.S. Constitution guarantees separation of church and state. Nevertheless, the U.S. government has traditionally fostered religion in general, granting tax-exempt status to churches and their properties, while citizens have tended to view membership in a church, synagogue, or equivalent religious organization as evidence of full allegiance to the community. The church was once the center of local community life, and people in the United States still tend to participate in religious activities more frequently than do most Europeans.

As of 1991, 68 percent of people in the United States hold formal membership in a religion, and about 42 percent attend religious services in a typical week (U.S. Bureau of the Census, 1994, Table 75). Most belong to Christian churches, Protestant denominations being the most common. Judaism is the most visible non-Christian religion in the United States, but one also finds Buddhists and Muslims in most communities, as well as adherents of several other religions. Indigenous varieties of Christianity are also popular. Native American religion

---

ecclesiastical religions religions that include not only individual, shamanic, and communal ritual practices but also a coordinating body of priests who perform rituals on behalf of congregations

Olympian religions polytheistic ecclesiastical religions in which the gods or supernatural beings may be loosely ranked but in which no one of the supernatural beings is truly supreme over the others

MORMON PRIESTHOOD AND PANTHEON

Mormonism was founded in 1824 in the eastern United States by a charismatic leader, Joseph Smith, following a series of visionary experiences, including a visitation by God the Father and Jesus. As of the beginning of 1995, the religion claims about 9 million members worldwide and is growing at a rate of about a third of a million each year.

Mormonism is an ecclesiastical religion. Its priesthood, which is held only by male members of the church, is organized into a complex hierarchy, presided over by a president who is also referred to as the *Prophet, Seer,* and *Revelator* of the church. As the presiding official of the church, the Prophet is believed to receive direct guidance from God whenever this is necessary for the work of directing the church. Below the Prophet is the Quorum of Twelve Apostles, which is presided over by its own president and two counselors. Below this level are intermediary officers down to the local congregations, called *wards*. The presiding official of the ward is the *bishop*. The bishop is a nonpaid minister, as are all local members of the priesthood. His responsibilities are not to deliver weekly sermons, but to organize and preside over each Sunday's worship services and all other business of the ward. In this work he is aided by his own counselors and a series of priesthood quorums within the ward.

The local priesthood quorums are themselves organized into an age-graded system divided into two major components, the lower or Aaronic Priesthood and the higher or Melchizedek Priesthood. Boys are typically inducted into the Aaronic Priesthood at the age of 12 as deacons. Their assignments include passing the Sacrament to members of the ward during the Sacrament meeting each Sunday. At 14 boys are ordained teachers and are permitted to prepare the sacramental bread and water used in the service. Sixteen-year-olds become priests, at which time they receive the authority to bless the Sacrament and to baptize. Eighteen-year-olds receive the full authority of the Melchizedek Priesthood as elders, including the authority to confirm a baptized person as a member of the church and, by the laying on of hands, to give that person the right to receive direct and personal guidance through the Holy Ghost. At this time, it is expected that worthy males will spend a 2-year period as unpaid, full-time missionaries for the church. For most, the next major change occurs at age 45, when men are inducted into a high priest's quorum.

The women's organization is an auxiliary program, since all policy-making and governing authority is vested in the priesthood. The men's and women's organizations are structurally equivalent, but they differ in authority and responsibility, with the women specializing in supportive service roles. Mormon ecclesiastical values reflect the secular differentiation of male and female roles. According to Shepherd and Shepherd (1984), Mormons are taught to idealize a family pattern in which the husband, as the family's sole source of income, plays a presiding role and in which the wife, as counselor to her husband, specializes in domestic responsibilities.

In addition to a Father in Heaven, Mormon theology includes a divine Mother in Heaven (Heeren, Lindsey, & Mason, 1984). However, her role in Mormon theology is an auxiliary one, like that of the women's organization within the church or of the wife within the idealized Mormon family. She is never explicitly mentioned in Mormon scriptures, she has no governing authority within the Godhead, and she is not approached in worship in any rituals of the church.

The recurring pattern of presidents and two counselors within the church structure mirrors Mormon theology, which includes a divine pantheon of many gods presided over by God the Father, Jesus Christ, and the Holy Ghost. Jesus, the firstborn spirit child of God, and the Holy Ghost, another spirit son of God, are believed to be fully separate individuals from the Father. Their role in the Godhead is much like that of the counselors to the earthly Prophet of the church. Thus, church organizational structure reproduces forms that Mormons think of as divine in origin and that reinforce the value of a presiding role for males.

---

and organized witchcraft are found throughout the country, but these have not entered the mainstream consciousness to the same degree as the other organized religions. About 5 percent of people in the United States espouse no religious belief, and another 5 percent who do assert a belief in God or a universal spirit express no preference for a particular religion (*Gallup Report*, 1985, pp. 13, 50). Interestingly, the tendency in the United States to emphasize membership and participation in religious organizations rather than insist on a specific religious belief is also found among nonbelievers: for instance, the American

Atheists have formed their own quasi-religious organization.

Bellah (1967), a Harvard sociologist who has specialized in the study of religion, has proposed that the basic religious dimension of U.S. life is a **civil religion** that coexists with the formally organized religions. While it draws predominantly from Christianity and Judaism for its symbolism, it is integrated into social and political life. Its God is the author of order, law, and morality and is actively involved in history, especially in U.S. history, much like the God of ancient Israel. According to Bellah, the symbolism of civil religion portrays the United States as the modern equivalent of the biblical Israel and the Founding Fathers as the inspired prophets of U.S. history. The Declaration of Independence, the Constitution, and Abraham Lincoln's Gettysburg Address are the three sacred documents of U.S. civil religion. The first two grew out of the Exodus from Europe, the symbolic Egypt from which God led people to the American Promised Land, which God set up as a light to all the world. Whereas Washington was the American Moses, Lincoln was the counterpart of Jesus, the wise and compassionate hero who counseled love of neighbor and whose life was taken by his enemies. Lincoln's Gettysburg Address, the New Testament of sacred political literature, is built around themes of death and rebirth such as "these honored dead," "conceived in liberty," and "a new birth of freedom." Bellah describes the sacred calendar of the U.S. civil religion as consisting of Memorial Day, on which U.S. communities honor their martyred dead, Thanksgiving Day, which integrates the family into the civil religion in a ceremonial feast of thanks to God for the bounties of U.S. life, and the less overtly religious holidays of the Fourth of July, Veterans Day, and the birthdays of Washington and Lincoln. The recent addition of Martin Luther King Jr.'s birthday to U.S. holidays, to symbolize and encourage interracial respect, may be viewed as an extension of the sacred calendar.

RELIGIOUS CHANGE

Religion tends to be a conservative institution that normally functions as a stabilizing influence within society by emphasizing the impor-

tance of tradition and perpetuating beliefs and rituals that have been handed down from the past. Yet religion does change. Usually, religious beliefs and practices lag behind social change, and then make small adjustments when the discrepancies grow too large.

Syncretism

Religion is not immune to the influences of diffusion. One way religions change is by borrowing beliefs, practices, and organizational characteristics from other religions, a process called **syncretism**. The idea of one religion's being receptive to ideas and rituals that have their origins in a different religious tradition is likely to surprise people raised in Western cultures, where most religions portray themselves as deriving solely from a specific body of exclusive ancient scriptures. However, most of the world's many religions have been open to the idea of borrowing practices and beliefs from other religions on the assumption that "If it works for them, maybe we should try it too." And despite the common formal attitudes, religious borrowing does occur within western religions as well.

The Haitian religion of *voudou* (voodoo) is an excellent example of one that has combined many elements of religious traditions from Africa and Europe into a synthesis of beliefs and practices that meet the needs of its contemporary adherents. For instance, the Christian deity, called by its African name, Bondye, is accepted as the only god, while many traditional African deities are viewed as his intermediaries with humans. Many of these, while identified with traditional Catholic saints, are, nevertheless, referred to by their African names. Saint Patrick, associated with the expulsion of snakes from Ireland in European tradition, is called Dambella, the Dahomean rainbow serpent

---

civil religion a system of religious beliefs and values that is integrated into the broader, nonreligious aspects of society and is shared by its members regardless of their affiliation with formally organized religious organizations; in the United States, a system of largely Judeo-Christian religious symbolism within which the U.S. political system is portrayed as divinely sanctioned and members of U.S. society are viewed as God's modern chosen people

syncretism the borrowing of beliefs, practices, or organizational traits by one religion from another

ZUÑI ART AND ROMAN CATHOLICISM IN NEW MEXICO

The Roman Catholic religion has been adopted by many of the people of Zuñi, New Mexico. Just as European Christianity has incorporated many of its pre-Christian symbols such as Easter eggs and Christmas trees into its practice, so too have Zuñi Catholics maintained ties with their cultural heritage within their new religious context. Our Lady of Guadalupe Church on the Zuñi Indian Reservation combines European and Mexican symbolism, imported by missionaries from Mexico in the 1500s, with murals that celebrate traditional Zuñi religious symbolism.

Above the altar, the Zuñi artist, Alex Seowtowa, has painted a Christ figure dressed in Zuñi blankets and wearing turquoise jewelry. Beneath his feet is a rain cloud, an important symbol to the Zuñi, whose ancestors were desert-dwelling horticulturalists. The rain cloud is not painted in the soft, cottony billows preferred by traditional European religious artists, but has the abstract shape that marks it clearly as a Zuñi rain cloud. Along the walls, above the Stations of the Cross, which depict different parts of the story of the Crucifixion, are murals of Zuñi kachinas who are mediators between human beings and the divine.

When paintings of kachinas were first introduced into the art of Our Lady of Guadalupe Church, they were portrayed as disciplinary figures to encourage parishioners to be attentive during the Mass. Seowtowa's artistic renovation of the church's walls, which he began in 1970, has introduced a more contemporary message. Since the north is associated with cold in Zuñi myths, the north wall of the church is adorned with kachinas from the Shalako ceremony held in November that portrays the return of the kachinas to the Zuñi after a period of absence. People put away anger for this happy occasion of renewed contact with the divine and receive the kachinas with respect and dignity. On the south wall are kachinas from Zuñi ceremonies at other seasons with equally positive connotations for the worshipers.

Tourists who visit the Zuñi church are sometimes surprised at the "non-Christian" images that adorn it. However, they fail to understand that they are similar to the syncretism in their own version of Christian symbolism. Their inclusion of the story of the Little Drummer Boy into the celebration of Christmas, their children's hunt for eggs at Easter time, and their images of angels as cute little cherubs or as beings with wings do not strike them as an incongruous mixing of one tradition with another. In this they are no different from the Zuñi, for whom ancient cultural imagery blends with their contemporary worship in a harmonious and beautiful whole (Niebuhr, 1995) *(see reference map, p. 49).*

---

deity. The Yoruba spirit Ogun, who was associated with metal and metalworking, has become the Voodoo patron of soldiers. His day of special ceremonies is the Catholic feast day of Saint James the Elder, the first martyred apostle, who was known as one of the "Sons of Thunder" because of his unruly temper. It is through "serving the spirits" by spirit possession rituals that followers of voodoo seek to influence the supernatural realm for human benefit, since Bondye is too important to be directly involved in helping people. Because voodoo draws heavily on Catholic symbolism and practice, its members also feel comfortable participating in Catholic Church ceremonies, which often include voodoo activities.

Revitalization Movements

Revolutionary change can also occur in religions through a process that Anthony Wallace (1966) called a **revitalization movement**, which he described as a "conscious, organized effort by members of society to construct a more satisfying culture" in response to unusual social and cultural stresses (p. 30). According to Wallace, revitalization movements are frequently the bases of new religions, often millenarian in outlook, that promise a return to a more stable and harmonious society.

Revitalization movements typically involve four stages, which Wallace termed the steady state, the period of increased individual stress, the period of cultural distortion, and the period of revitalization. The steady state is the normal moving equilibrium of any culture during which change is relatively slow and incremental. A culture can be pushed out of its usual

---

revitalization movement a change in religion that represents a conscious effort to construct a more satisfying culture

FIGURE 13.10

SYNCRETISM

In Our Lady of Guadalupe Church on the Zuñi Reservation in New Mexico hang portraits of the Virgin Mary. Above the pictures of the Stations of the Cross, depicting scenes of the Crucifixion, are murals of more than two dozen life-sized kachinas, *the spirit beings of Pueblo culture. The artist, Alex Seowtowa, a Roman Catholic Indian, finds no contradiction in combining the traditions of his Pueblo culture with those of Christianity.*

steady state by forces such as "climatic and biotic change, epidemic disease, war and conquest, social subordination, or acculturation" (p. 159). Such forces cause a growing number of individuals to experience individual stress because they interfere with society's ability to meet people's needs. During the period of increased individual stress, crime and illness increase, individual deviance increases, and society appears increasingly disorganized.

A period of cultural distortion can arise if some members of society respond to the increasing stresses by organizing special interest groups that no longer support the established social order. Instead, the special interest groups struggle to obtain the old benefits of life for their members through previously unacceptable behavior. The period of cultural distortion is a time of widespread "alcoholism, venality

in public officials, the 'black market,' breaches of sexual and kinship mores, hoarding, gambling for gain, 'scapegoating' by attacking other groups or a central bureaucracy, and similar alienated behaviors which, in the preceding period, were still defined as individual deviances" (p. 159). At such times, the old religious rituals, beliefs, and values may be less than satisfying to many, since they are too rooted in earlier, less stressful times to help people cope with new, current problems.

The period of revitalization begins when an "individual or group of individuals constructs a new, utopian image of sociocultural organization" (p. 160). This often occurs when a man or woman who was personally distressed by the lack of order in society undergoes a hallucinatory experience perceived by the distressed person as a religious revelation from a super-

FIGURE 13.11

SIOUX GHOST DANCE

The Ghost Dance ritual originated among the Plains Indians in the nineteenth century as a response to the encroachment of the non-Indian on Indian lands. In each version of the dance, the idea was to destroy the non-Indians and bring back to life the spirit of the dead Indians. The Sioux warriors wore Ghost Dance shirts in the belief that they would be protection against bullets. This 1890 drawing by Frederic Remington portrays a Ghost Dance performed by the Ogallala Sioux at the Pine Ridge Agency, South Dakota.

natural source. It seems to account for society's turmoil and provides a series of new religious rituals that are intended to help people cope with the new problems that the old religions appear to have failed to address.

When the prophet of the new religion preaches the message to others, those who have been trying unsuccessfully to cope with the same widespread social ills may accept it as a divinely revealed answer to their problems. In fact, converts may be attracted so quickly that the revitalization prophet cannot personally coordinate the activities of the growing organization. At this point, a group of full-time disciples may be appointed to do that. The rapid growth of the new religion is often perceived as a threat by those members of society who still have a vested interest in the old, established institutions, such as the government and the previous religious organization. Sometimes the conflict that develops out of this perceived threat ends in the destruction of the new movement by its opponents, but sometimes the re-

vitalization movement achieves dominance and establishes a new steady state.

Revitalization movements were common in many parts of the world among indigenous peoples after they were contacted by the technologically and militarily more powerful European societies. They have included the so-called Cargo Cults of Melanesia and Australia and several nativistic religious movements among American Indians, such as the Handsome Lake religion of the Iroquois, the Ghost Dance religion of the U.S. Great Basin region, and the Native American Church, which has spread to many parts of the United States. Similar millenarian Christian movements also have histories that follow the pattern of revitalization movements. They include Mormonism, Seventh-Day Adventism, the Reverend Sun Myung Moon's Unification Church, Bhagwan Shree Rajneesh's utopian movement in Rajneeshpuram, Oregon, the Reverend Jim Jones's People's Temple settlement in Guyana, and David Koresh's Branch Davidian group in Waco, Texas.

WHY ARE PEOPLE RELIGIOUS?

Although cultures differ considerably in their religious beliefs, practices, and organizations, there is no known human culture from which religion is absent. There is archaeological evidence that religion has been practiced by our ancestors since at least the time of the Neanderthals, 100,000 years ago. These people prepared graves and buried their dead carefully. Like many of the world's peoples today, they covered the corpse with red ochre, a practice that gives it a lifelike color. Often they also included in the grave a supply of tools, food, and flowers. Such practices imply belief in an afterlife where the tools and food could be used by the deceased.

Besides burial practices, Neanderthalers engaged in another practice that seems to have had a religious significance: the ceremonial arrangement of cave bear skulls within specially prepared storage areas. In caves in both Switzerland and France, archaeologists have found cube-shaped chests that were made by lining a pit with stone and covering it with massive stone lids. The skulls and other bones of cave bears had been placed within these chests in a carefully arranged way that indicates that this creature must have had great significance to these earlier hunters. In Drachenloch Cave in Switzerland, other cave bear skulls were left in niches along the cave wall.

Since the cave bear was a powerful and dangerous predator and less formidable game was available to Neanderthal hunters, it is unlikely that the cave bear was hunted simply for its food value. A stronger religious motivation is suspected to have guided the hunt and ritual disposition of these trophies, perhaps as a symbol of spiritual control over animals as a source of food. Such ceremonial treatment of the cave bear by the Neanderthalers has parallels in ritual practices among several hunting peoples such as some Siberian tribes and the Ainus of Japan as late as the turn of the century.

In trying to explain the universal existence of religion, anthropologists have usually considered the role that religion plays in making our social life more successful and the psychological benefits that religion gives us as individuals. The question of whether people are also responding to a true supernatural realm is not itself accessible to anthropological study.

The Maintenance of Social Order

Religion teaches people that they have a place in the universe and a relationship to it. Through the ideology of a religion and through its rituals, people gain a sense of identity and a feeling that life is meaningful. The practice of a religion creates greater solidarity among its participants, enabling them to work more effectively together and accomplish more.

Religion provides guidelines about how human life should be properly conducted and what values should be held. In so doing, it motivates people to follow the customs of their society even in the absence of practical insights about how their actions may benefit it. For instance, farmers suffering the effects of a prolonged drought may, after several failures, be too discouraged to dig yet another well until a "water witch" assures them of the presence of water at some location. Without such religious sources of motivation, the short-term costs of trying one more time in the face of the previous failures might seem to outweigh the potential long-term benefits.

Social rules necessary to the maintenance of order may be supported by the threat of supernatural punishments for their violation or supernatural rewards for their acceptance. This can be especially beneficial in a society that lacks secular means of ensuring obedience to the rules. Viking men were promised the reward of Valhalla for valor in warfare, and Aztec warriors were assured that death in battle led to an eternity in the most glorious of the Aztec heavens, that of their war god, Huitzilopochtli. Among the Rwala Bedouin of northern Saudi Arabia, the pains of Hell awaited those who lied, and for the ancient Egyptians a similar fate was reserved for the stingy.

In situations in which disagreement might be divisive, religion may provide the means to achieve consensus without hard feelings. For instance, divination can be used to find the answer to a question about which the group is hopelessly divided. That solution then can be accepted by all without loss of face.

Finally, the rituals of religion provide emotional release from stresses that might otherwise lead to socially disruptive behavior. When Zuñi farmers blame their crop failures or illness on the malevolent activities of sorcerers in another town and take action to protect themselves through rituals, they may be sparing themselves the strife that might otherwise disrupt their own village if they took out their frustrations on neighbors or relatives.

The Reduction of Anxiety

In addition to benefits to society at large, there are psychological benefits for the individual in the practice of religion. People do not always have as much control over their lives or circumstances as they need to feel secure. When this is the case, the performance of rituals for control through supernatural means can alleviate debilitating anxiety. This is especially true when the anxiety stems from problems for which no secular remedies are known. More than one anthropologist has noted parallels between shamanistic curing rituals and Western psychotherapeutic practices.

In frightening situations, religion can be a source of strength in enabling one to stand up to one's fears and overcome them. The prayer uttered privately or the blessing given by another before a dangerous act is undertaken may provide just enough confidence to ensure success. Guilt can be overcome by acts of penance and sacrifice, and shame may be counteracted by demonstrations of piety that restore one's reputation. People who are unable to remove unjust obstacles in their lives can release their anger by acting it out with rituals that direct the power of magic against the source of their frustrations. At times of loss, religion may console the grieving. In these and other ways, religion helps people cope with troubling emotions.

The Cognitive Role of Religion

Religion's role in shaping beliefs is to give people answers to important questions for which they have no scientific or definitive answers: Why do I exist? What will become of me after I die? What are the sun, moon, and stars, and how did the earth itself come into existence? Who were the first humans, and how did they originate? To such questions, religious ideology usually provides satisfying answers based on supernatural authority.

Although science is not equipped to answer existential questions about the meaning and purpose that life should have, it can often provide utilitarian answers to practical questions. The rise of scientific specialists in Western societies led to new answers to many questions that had previously been handled by religious leaders. This sometimes resulted in social conflict between advocates of science and advocates of religion, which, as society became more secular and dependent on rational explanations for natural phenomena, gradually resulted in a major loss of social and political influence by religious professionals. Education, for instance, increasingly came under the control of secular educators. A natural byproduct of the conflict between science and religion in Western culture was the development of the idea that scientific and religious ideologies are fundamentally different, perhaps even irreconcilable. This idea is dramatically illustrated in the ongoing attacks on scientific knowledge about the age of the earth or about human evolution by Christian fundamentalist religious leaders in the United States who reject the notion that scientific insights should be allowed to influence their interpretation of Scripture.

It is true that science and religion differ in the methods and assumptions that they employ to create new ideas. However, it is an error to assume that the cognitive processes involved in religious thinking differ radically from those applied in science. Guthrie (1980) has shown that "people hold religious beliefs because they are *plausible* [emphasis added] models of the world, apparently grounded in daily experience" (p. 181). Guthrie believes that anthropomorphism (using human qualities to explain the nonhuman realm) is fundamental to religion and that it is anthropomorphism that all religions have in common. According to Guthrie, such anthropomorphic explanations are plausible for three reasons: (1) humans are complex and multifaceted, so similarities can be found between many phenomena and some parts of the human condition; (2) human beings are likely to be found wherever the human observer may be; (3) humans are the most important factor in the human environment. Therefore, anthropomorphic models are readily used by human beings to interpret their experiences, and it is these models and interpretations of the universe as created and governed by unseen humanlike beings that we call religion.

In Guthrie's view, our understanding of our experiences is initially ambiguous, but by interpreting experiences in human terms, we reduce this ambiguity. Whether we do so religiously or scientifically does not matter. We understand new things by finding similarities between them and things we already understand. Thus, by thinking of nonhuman phenomena in human terms, the hallmark of religious thinking, we create plausible explanations for the unknown.

CHAPTER SUMMARY

1. Religion is found in all cultures but is subject to greater diversity than any other aspect of culture.

2. Universal aspects that define religion in all societies are the belief in supernatural beings, the belief in supernatural power, the symbolic expression of feelings, and ritual behavior.

3. The great diversity in belief systems may be related to variation in people's social, environmental, and technological contexts and may be seen as helping them adapt to those particular circumstances.

4. Ritual behaviors may serve any of three general functions: uniting a community emotionally, portraying human needs or sacred beliefs, or influencing the supernatural. Rituals may be the province of solo practitioners—shamans, sorcerers, or witches—in small-scale societies.

5. In somewhat larger societies, religion is often a communal matter, with group ceremonies.

6. In large, socially stratified societies, religious specialists are commonly full-time practitioners, organized into the hierarchical systems that characterize ecclesiastical religions.

7. The majority of people in the United States belong to some religious group, and it has been argued that most also subscribe to a patriotic "civil religion."

8. New religions often arise during times of social stress as revitalization movements that offer solutions to society's problems.

9. Religion seems to help maintain social order, reduce individual anxiety, and help people make sense of the often puzzling world around them.

ANNOTATED READINGS

Carmody, D. L., & Carmody, J. T. (1993). *Original visions: The religions of oral peoples.* New York: Macmillan. A brief, introductory overview of the religions of traditional societies.

Evans-Pritchard, E. E. (1956). *Nuer religion.* Oxford: Clarendon Press. Based on years of intensive study by one of the greats in British anthropology, this is a classic study of religion in an African society.

Furst, P. T. (Ed.). (1972). *Flesh of the gods: The ritual use of hallucinations.* New York: Praeger Press. A collection of articles on the use of hallucinogens to achieve altered states of consciousness in religious settings.

Guthrie, S. (1993). *Faces in the clouds: A new theory of religion.* New York: Oxford University Press. A detailed analysis of the role of anthropomorphism in religion.

Lehmann, A. C., & Myers, J. E. (1993). *Magic, witchcraft, and religion: An anthropological study of the supernatural* (3rd ed.). Palo Alto, CA: Mayfield. A thorough and up-to-date collection of articles on religion.

Morris, B. (1987). *Anthropological studies of religion: An introductory text.* Cambridge, England: Cambridge University Press. A readable overview of the explanations of religion by the founders of the various schools of thought within the social and behavioral sciences.

Pandian, J. (1991). *Culture, religion, and the sacred self: A critical introduction to the anthropological study of religion.* Englewood Cliffs, NJ: Prentice Hall. An attempt to formulate an anthropological approach to the study of the relationship between religious symbolism and the symbols with which individuals construct their own identity.

Saler, B. (1993). *Conceptualizing religion: Immanent anthropologists, transcendent natives, and unbounded categories.* New York: E. J. Brill. An in-depth look at the many ways religion has been defined by anthropologists.

Sharon, D. (1978). *Wizard of the four winds: A shaman's story.* New York: Macmillan. An insightful biography of a Peruvian shaman.

Swanson, G. E. (1960). *The birth of the gods: The origin of primitive beliefs.* Ann Arbor, MI: University of Michigan Press. An often overlooked but important exploration of the Durkheimian view of religious belief as a reflection of the organization of society.

Worsley, P. (1957). *The trumpet shall sound: A study of "cargo" cults in Melanesia.* London: MacGibbon & Kee. The classic comparative study of religious revitalization movements in Melanesia.

CHAPTER FOURTEEN

Culture, Personality, and Psychological Process

After reading this chapter, you should be able to:

Explain the relationships among personality, socialization, and social roles.

Discuss the relationships among childrearing practices, personality, and a society's secondary institutions.

Explain the role of socialization in culturally patterned gender differences.

Analyze the concept of face-work.

Analyze the relationship between role playing and emotional distress.

Explain the nature and causes of trance.

Discuss cultural functions of trance states.

Explain the roles of ritual in expressing and alleviating stress.

Explain the nature and causes of deviance.

Discuss culture-specific mental disorders.

◀ *Figure 14.1 Culture and Personality In Kyrgyzstan, the Central Asian land that was once a Soviet republic, the people are reestablishing their cultural identity by celebrating Manas, a legendary folk hero. He lives through an oral epic 20 times longer than the Iliad and the Odyssey combined, which is recited by storytellers called Manaschis. While not everyone is convinced that this great warrior actually existed, he is the symbolic essence of an indigenous hero, a necessary icon with which to replace the old Soviet pantheon. The wing of his hunting eagle shades the head of this elderly Kyrgyz during the ceremonies.*

We like to think of ourselves as unique individuals, yet we tend to be somewhat similar to other people in our society. Our personalities are not merely our own. They are shaped to a great extent by our culture. In this chapter, we will look at how culture provides the limits within which we can express our unique qualities. Culture also provides various ways for interpreting deviant behavior. Such behavior may be valued as creative or it may be stigmatized. Deviant behavior grows out of attempts to relieve the stresses peculiar to life in each society. If these attempts do not fit within the bounds of what others consider normal behavior appropriate for our roles, we may be labeled mentally ill.

Stressed out. Cool. Yuppie. Druggie. All-American. Are you self-confident? Shy? Bright? Frightened? Do you listen to Metallica? Or Mozart? Do you play the violin? Or enjoy basketball? Do you drink Coke? Or Pepsi? Who we are and who we become depend on numerous influences both in our family and our culture.

CULTURE AND PERSONALITY

In the 1920s, a number of anthropologists began to study the relationship between culture and human psychology. Their school of thought came to be known as **culture and personality** for its emphasis on the close parallels between each society's culture and the common personality characteristics of its people. This early period in the study of culture and its impact on individuals had two thrusts: configurationalism and national character studies.

Configurationalism

The leader in culture and personality studies was Ruth Benedict (1932), a student of Franz Boas. She suggested that each culture molded personalities in distinctive ways. Because of the harmony between a culture and the basic personality type it engendered, culture could be seen as a "personality writ large." Culture, then, is to a society what the personality is to an individual. According to Benedict, each culture is a unique, integrated whole with a distinctive configuration of values and customs that are analogous to "individual psychology thrown large upon a screen, given gigantic proportions and a long time span" (p. 24), a view of culture that is known as **configurationalism**. As an example, Benedict characterized the Pueblo societies of the southwestern United States as having a culture that stressed the values of emotional balance, moderation, and cooperation, a configuration she named *Apollonian*, after the Greek god of sunlight, music, and poetry (1928, 1934). The socialization of Pueblo individuals based on these values almost guaranteed that their personalities would all be similar. Benedict contrasted the Pueblos with the culture of the Plains Indians, in which emotional extremes were valued. Their customs included the pursuit of valor in warfare as a way of achieving high status and religious practices such as self-torture, vision quests, and the use of drugs to achieve ecstatic experiences, a configuration that she called *Dionysian*, after the Greek god of wine. These cultural traits resulted in the socialization of individuals into much more aggressive and emotive personalities than were found among the Pueblos.

As another example, Margaret Mead (1928), a student of Ruth Benedict, looked specifically at the adolescent development of young women in Samoa. She found that Samoan adolescence was not characterized by the same turmoil and rebellion that was common among adolescents in the United States. She concluded that the emotionally smoother transition between childhood and adulthood in Samoa was a result of values that stressed harmony and cooperation and customs that permitted their children to learn about and explore their sexuality in a more casual way than was possible in the United States.

Socialization and Personality. Our culture is incorporated into our personality through the

---

culture and personality anthropological study of relationship between culture and human psychology

configurationalism Benedict's view of culture as a configuration of values and customs that influence individual psychology

FIGURE 14.2

SOCIALIZATION

Socialization is a process by which the customs of a society are passed down from one generation to the next, particularly during childhood. These Ya̧no- *mamö boys have learned how to cook lizards, a common food in their culture.*

process of **socialization**, which also guarantees that a culture will be passed from one generation to the next. Much of this socialization occurs during our childhood. Every society has its own customs by which children are raised toward adulthood. For instance, Mead (1950) pointed out that the warlike, aggressive Iatmul of New Guinea encouraged aggression in their children by allowing them to cry for long periods before feeding them and then frustrating their attempts to take food. The nearby Arapesh, on the other hand, having a peaceful way of life, indulged their children.

The importance of childrearing customs in influencing the development of personality traits has been illustrated by Cora DuBois (1944). She reported that Alorese children in Indonesia received very inconsistent care from infancy. Mothers had to return to work in the fields within two weeks after the birth of a child, and infants received little attention until they were nursed when their mothers returned late in the afternoon. Once an Alorese child learned to walk, it received even less attention during the day. Weaning occurred before the birth of another child and was promoted by teasing, punishment, or even by sending the

child to stay with relatives. As one might expect, Alorese children grew up to be suspicious and pessimistic, with shallow friendships. Alorese religion and art reflected their upbringing. Like parents, Alorese gods were not to be relied on. They had to be placated to avoid their anger. But this was done grudgingly, and religious art was only carelessly crafted, without devotion. Frustration and resentment were central themes of Alorese folk tales and stories.

Abram Kardiner (1939), an influential psychoanalyst, popularized the concept of the **basic personality structure**, which he defined as the "adaptive tools of the individual which are common to every individual in society" (p. 237). While difficult to define, personality involves the distinctive ways in which a person behaves, thinks, and feels, based on his or her cognition of self. A personality structure is derived from primary family care and values and from institutions in the culture that satisfy basic needs

socialization the process of learning a culture and the role-playing skills necessary for social life

basic personality structure the distinctive ways in which a person behaves, thinks, and feels based on his or her cognition of self

and tensions not met by the primary care institutions. Thus, some anthropologists believed that all people in a certain culture would behave, think, and feel in a similar fashion. Other anthropologists, especially those in the 1950s and later, who compiled statistical data about the prevalence of personality traits in various societies, took a position that allowed for variation in the personalities of members of any society by substituting the concept of **modal personality type** for basic personality structure. It refers to the most frequent personality traits that are found in a society as statistically measured by several different types of personality tests.

Primary Institutions.   Kardiner's model of the interaction of culture and personality held that children's personalities are most directly influenced by a society's **primary institutions**, those involved in childrearing. During childhood, our personality is shaped by factors such as how we are fed and cared for, the degree to which we are touched and comforted, how long we are nursed, how we are weaned and toilet trained, and how and what we are taught about human sexuality. Thus, according to John Whiting and Irvin Child (1953), "The economic, political and social organs of a society—the basic customs surrounding the nourishment, sheltering and protection of its members—seem a likely source of influence on child training practices" (p. 310).

Secondary Institutions.   Kardiner further argued that people's personalities shape the **secondary institutions** of society, those most central to the ideology of a culture, such as religious beliefs and rituals, myths, folktales, humor, recreation, and art styles.

Robert LeVine (1973) has suggested that the relationship between primary and secondary institutions is influenced by an intermediate level that he calls a society's **maintenance system**, the economic and social structure that results from a society's adaptation to a particular environment. It is this system, according to LeVine, that determines the society's childrearing practices, which—mediated by the biological needs, drives, and capacities of these children—result in the development of their personalities. As children grow into adulthood, the basic patterns of their personalities influence how they work and play and are the source of cultural products such as fantasies, forms of recreation,

and perceptions of the world as benevolent or dangerous.

Subsistence Patterns.   The impact of subsistence patterns on personality development has been investigated by Herbert Barry, Irvin Child, and Margaret Bacon (1959), who compared agricultural societies with those in which people survive by hunting and gathering. They found that the cultures of agricultural societies are more likely to stress compliance in children, while hunting and gathering people are more likely to teach their children to assert themselves as individuals. Whereas self-reliance is an important survival trait among hunters, following an established routine seems more important in the daily lives of agriculturalists. Children who play with and scatter the stored food reserves of agricultural peoples or who get underfoot in their more crowded settlements are not likely to be well tolerated.

National Character

While the culture and personality school of anthropology was developing its model of how socialization influenced personality and how personality, in turn, influenced other aspects of a culture, some members of this field produced a series of studies that came to be known as national character studies. Like the configurationalist descriptions of nonindustrialized societies, **national character studies** were an attempt to identify the psychological characteristics of entire societies, but the focus was on entire nations. A common theme in national character studies was the view that childrearing customs had a major impact on adult per-

---

modal personality type the most common or typical pattern of personality traits in a society

primary institutions the primary care groups related to childrearing, including feeding, weaning, sexual training, and subsistence patterns

secondary institutions the institutions in social life that satisfy the needs and tensions not met by the primary institutions, including taboo systems, religion, rituals, folk tales, and techniques of thinking

maintenance system the parts of the economic and social structure of a society that determine its childrearing practices

national character studies an attempt to identify the psychological characteristics of entire societies

sonality traits. For instance, the supposedly strict and early toilet training experienced by Japanese children was claimed to be the foundation for the extreme wartime aggressiveness of Japanese soldiers. The Russian swaddling, the tight wrapping of infants that constrained their arm and leg movements, was said to be the reason why adult Russians had little self-control and were given to long periods of brooding followed by outbursts of rage.

National character studies were a product of World War II and of efforts of some U.S. anthropologists to help their government better understand the Japanese (Gorer, 1943; LaBarre, 1945; Benedict, 1946). Since direct fieldwork was impossible, these anthropologists carried out their study of Japanese culture indirectly, by examining Japanese Americans, Japanese films, and previously published documents about Japan. These studies portrayed the Japanese culture as one that instilled obsessive-compulsive traits in its people, characteristics that were manifest in great concern for ritual, order, and cleanliness. Other national character studies were carried out on countries such as the United States (Mead, 1942; Gorer, 1948/1964), Russia (Gorer & Rickman, 1949), and England (Gorer, 1955).

Criticisms of the Culture and Personality School

The early culture and personality studies have been subject to criticism because both the configurationalist studies and the national character studies tended to gloss over individual differences within any society and to overgeneralize consistencies of personality. Thus, Benedict's portrayal of the Zuñi was flawed by its failure to acknowledge the existence of conflict, alcoholism, or suicide, all of which did occur among the Zuñi despite cultural ideals to the contrary. Mead did discuss several examples of young women whose adolescence was not as conflict free as she had portrayed it as being in many Samoan women's lives, but Harris (1968) has pointed out that Mead portrayed these women as deviants, not as examples of personality differences (p. 410).

Culture and personality studies have also been criticized for their lack of methodological rigor. The absence of fieldwork in the wartime national character studies introduced errors. For instance, later studies demonstrated that Japanese families were typically less concerned

with toilet training than were Americans. The portrayals of cultural characteristics in this early period were also highly impressionistic, a problem that resulted from cultures being described as if every member of society shared exactly the same understandings of their way of life. Thus, culture and personality studies such as Benedict's portrayals of the Zuñi and Kwakiutl have been criticized for failing to recognize the widespread cultural diversity and personality differences that exist in all societies. Furthermore, culture and personality studies were not based on random samples of members of the societies that were being studied, but relied heavily on the intuitions of the investigators when they described the "typical" personality characteristics of a society. For instance, Mead's study of Samoan women was based on interviews of only 50 individuals from neighboring villages, and half of the young women were not yet past puberty. In addition, the validity of supposed causal links between childrearing customs and adult personalities was not tested by examining cross-cultural data on other societies with the same childrearing practices. Methodological weaknesses were especially problematic in national character studies, where the peoples being studied were political enemies, and ethnocentric judgments were a particularly common source of error. Thus, discussions of rituals in Japanese life were defined with terminology, such as compulsiveness, that was developed within Freudian psychology to characterize a psychological disorder.

PSYCHOLOGICAL ANTHROPOLOGY

Efforts to overcome the methodological and conceptual weaknesses of earlier culture and personality research led to new approaches to the study of the relationships between culture and the individual, beginning in the 1950s. These more modern approaches make up today's diverse field of **psychological anthropology**, which has abandoned global characterizations of

---

psychological anthropology an empirical approach to data collection that emphasizes statistical correlations between culture and psychological processes

cultures and intuitive generalizations about personality and has adopted a more empirical approach to data collection that emphasizes statistically testable links between specific aspects of culture and particular psychological processes. Psychological anthropology has taken two major forms. In the first, studies use cross-cultural fieldwork to make comparisons of specific psychological characteristics among different groups within the same culture or among members of different cultures. In the second, cross-cultural survey research emphasizes tests of particular hypotheses about customs and psychology that rely on statistical comparisons of similar data from a large number of societies. Whereas the first approach relies on fieldwork studies, often by teams of researchers, the second approach makes heavy use of the Human Relations Area Files (HRAF) data derived from traditional ethnographies of the world's cultures.

Cross-Cultural Fieldwork

An excellent example of cross-cultural fieldwork by a team of researchers is a project that was headed by Walter Goldschmidt (1965). It investigated the influence of subsistence activities on personality in four East African societies, the Hehe, Kamba, Pokot, and Sebei. The Hehe and Kamba had some historic connection and shared a common language, Bantu. Similarly, the Pokot and Sebei, though distinct, also spoke a common language, Kalenjin, and had some historic continuities. Each of these societies had communities based on pastoralism and communities based on horticulture. Based on data collected by asking questions and by recording responses to inkblots and color slides, the team demonstrated that each of these societies had distinct cultural characteristics. For instance, the Hehe data showed them to be aggressive, formal, mistrusting, and secretive. The Kamba showed psychological traits of extreme male dominance, fear of poverty, and restrained emotions. The Pokot were particularly concerned with cattle, beauty, and sex. And the Sebe were concerned with health and showed more jealousy and hostility than the other groups.

By comparing the pastoral and horticultural communities in each of the four East African societies, one of Goldschmidt's team members, Robert Edgerton, was able to demonstrate certain similarities that distinguished pastoralists from cultivators regardless of which society or cultural tradition they belonged to or which language they spoke. He found that the pastoralists were direct and open in their communication, realistic in their outlook, and constricted and controlled in their emotions, while the horticulturalists in all groups tended to be indirect, abstract in their views, more anxious and less able to deal with their emotions as well as less able to control their impulses (1965). Fieldwork studies such as this one have been valuable sources of data about the cultural variables that influence personality differences among groups, since they examine the mechanisms of personality formation in specific, real-life contexts.

Cross-Cultural Surveys

Whiting and a number of his colleagues have made extensive use of the Human Relations Area Files developed by George Murdock to test a variety of hypotheses regarding relationships between specific customs and personality traits. These studies have generally followed a model derived from Kardiner (see p. 359).

Whiting and Child (1953) were the first to use the HRAF in an important study of personality. They described a relationship connecting childhood experiences to beliefs and religious practices regarding illness in societies that lacked complex medical technologies. For instance, they found early punishment of aggression to be cross-culturally correlated with a strong belief in sorcery and witchcraft as causes of illness. Similarly, George Wright (1954) has found that in societies where children are severely punished for aggression, the theme of aggression is particularly common in their folk tales. In a similar way, proverbs, riddles, and jokes seem to reflect the psychological preoccupations of a people.

Today, psychological anthropology is a highly varied field within anthropology. Psychological anthropologists specialize in the study of such diverse topics as the relationships between culture and emotions, the development of cognitive skills, the influence of language on perception and on cultural differences in how people classify and understand themselves and their environment, psychological universals in symbolic aspects of culture, and cultural similarities and differences in psychiatric disorders.

PERSONALITY

In psychological terms, **personality** may be defined as our consistent pattern of behaviors, resulting from internal mechanisms. Although we generally think of our personality as something located within ourselves, anthropologists are more interested in examining it in relation to a complex external cultural system and social pressures. From an anthropological perspective, personality represents an individual's pattern of behavior that results from the various social roles that he or she has learned to play. Whereas psychologists tend to be interested in the consistent ways of behaving regardless of the role being played, anthropologists are more likely to be interested in how differences in the individual's style of behaving vary from role to role, depending on the time, place, or social context of the role playing. In this chapter, we will examine the various approaches anthropologists have taken to analyzing the relationships between personality, social roles, and culture.

Personality and Social Roles

Culture defines the nature of a society, the kinds of roles the participants may adopt, and, hence, the ways that people can interact. For instance, among the Cheyenne of the North American plains, the **Contrary Warrior** was expected to interact with others in a different way from other Cheyenne (Grinnell, 1961; Llewellyn & Hoebel, 1941). When Contraries wished to affirm something, they were required to say "No"; to deny, they said "Yes"; when they were asked to go away, it was anticipated that they would approach. Contraries were chosen from the bravest of warriors. They were thought to be possessed of visionary power and inspired other warriors to fight their hardest. To set the status of the Contrary apart from others, Contraries were expected to do all things backwards, displaying buffoonery even during otherwise solemn occasions.

Status-Appropriate Roles. Patterns for behavior are laid down in the culture's ideology as rules outlining the **status-appropriate roles** that people may play when interacting with one another. Personality therefore can be seen as a cultural phenomenon as well as an internal, psychological one—that is, as a cultur-

ally controlled pattern in an individual's role playing. Whenever people interact in settings where one of their statuses is appropriate, they normally manifest those parts of their personality that embody the roles of that status.

Each human group is made up of several statuses that the group defines as mutually compatible. When a person attempts to enter a new group, members interact with the newcomer to determine her or his potential to hold a status that the group recognizes as appropriate. This process determines which roles of the group's various statuses the newcomer is capable of playing. In initiating the process, newcomers "present face," that is, communicate to the others the possible social value they claim for themselves. Once admitted to the group, individuals are expected to play a role that supports that **face**, or social standing. They will be evaluated by the others based on how well they continue to live up to that initial self-portrayal.

Face-Work. Much of our day-to-day social interaction is aimed at promoting and protecting our own face and the face of other members of our group. In general, the more highly ranked our social status, the more effort others will expend to protect our face. Erving Goffman (1955) has described as **face-work** the process by which we are maintained in the roles we have been assigned to play. Often, when one first behaves in a way that contradicts the face one has initially espoused, such violations are ignored, and no damage to face occurs. It is then possible for a person to return to the usual role, and social interaction continues according to the normal game plan. If, however, a violation of the norms is brought to public attention—that is, if it becomes publicly

---

personality a consistent pattern of behavior related both to inner forces and to external, cultural, and social pressures

Contrary Warrior a Cheyenne status that required the reversal of all normal behaviors, reserved for the bravest warriors

status-appropriate roles the ways of behaving that are expected of an individual who holds a particular social status in a specific culture

face the positive social value a person can contribute to a group; social standing

face-work interaction in which effort is directed to maintaining or returning behavior to roles considered appropriate for members of a group; efforts to maintain or reestablish face

SORORITY RUSH: AN EXAMPLE OF ESTABLISHING FACE

Whether we are being interviewed for a job, discussing the news of the day with a group of potential new friends, or joining a sorority, our first interactions with others are an attempt to demonstrate that we can be of value to them. If we convince the group that we can fill a role that would benefit it, and if the group convinces us that we have something to gain from playing that role, then we will be taken into the group. Depending on how formally the group is organized, the process may be more or less highly structured, but it is essentially the same in content wherever it occurs.

Consider the case of sorority rush, a more formal example of face-work. On the Utah State University campus, Greek Rush Week begins on Monday, when the three sororities set up a registration table in the Student Center. Young women who wish to join a sorority pay a registration fee to demonstrate the seriousness of their intent. They fill out an application giving their names, hometowns, grade-point averages, and interests, as well as identifying immediate relatives who have been sorority sisters. On Tuesday, applicants attend a movie that explains the Greek system: the philanthropies engaged in by each House, the intramural sports played between the Houses, the parties and social events that each hosts, and the activities of Greek Rush Week. The applicants are then divided into groups of 30 or 40 for House Tours through the three sorority Houses near the campus.

During the next three days of Greek Rush Week, the applicants and sorority sisters become more familiar with each other. The sisters must study all applicants' information, learning their names and as much as possible about them. On Wednesday they host half-hour "Halloween Parties" for each group of applicants. The activities include singing and dancing. The applicants and House sisters meet personally at this time. On the next day each House invites a smaller group

to return to a "Beach Party." This group includes only those applicants in which each House is most interested. At this party, the sorority sisters talk with the applicants, trying to become better acquainted personally. After the party, the sisters meet to hold an open discussion and vote on each applicant.

On Friday an even smaller group of the most preferred applicants are invited to return to the "Preference Party." The selectiveness of the process works both ways, for even if the applicants are invited by all three Houses, they may attend only two events. Preference Day is the most intimate and emotional of the three days. The goal of the House at this party is to show the value of the sorority to its members, to communicate the closeness of the sisters and how they feel about each other. There is singing, and the senior sisters give talks about what the sorority means to them.

After the Preference Parties, the applicants must indicate their first and second choices of a House on a signed document. Once it is signed, their choices cannot be changed. The sisters of each house write the names of their top choices, and all applicants are ranked based on the total votes they receive. The Greek Council meets and compares the lists from each House with the preferences of the applicants, and each applicant is assigned a House.

On Saturday the applicants pick up the "bids," which inform them which house they have been assigned. They go immediately to the sorority House, where the sisters are waiting outside for them. They are greeted with songs and a welcoming party. At a formal ceremony, applicants now become Pledges, a status they will hold for about eight weeks. At the end of that period, if the Pledge wishes to finalize her entry into the House, she will be initiated into the status of a full member.

labeled as a violation of one's expected "normal behavior"—some work must be done to repair one's damaged face if one is to be accepted again as a fully participating member of the group.

This repair process generally follows a definite sequence, which Goffman has characterized as (1) the challenge, (2) the offering, (3) the acceptance, and (4) the thanks. In the challenge, the person who has injured or threatened another's face is confronted with the warning

that the threatened face will be defended. In the offering, the offender (or, occasionally, another person) is permitted to make amends, perhaps by indicating that the apparent threat was meaningless or unintentional, that it was only a joke, or that it had been unavoidable. The offering may also take the form of excusing the actor from responsibility, as when one attributes an otherwise serious violation of rules to intoxication, fatigue, or illness. At the same time, compensation may be offered to the offended party, and the offender may take on a self-imposed punishment. The recipient of the offering may now indicate acceptance of its sufficiency for reestablishing the original symbolic balance of the group. If this is done, the offender expresses thanks for the forgiveness.

As individuals manifest their personal qualities in social interaction, their behavior is constrained by culturally defined rules for maintaining social order. The personality traits that are considered normal are those that can be integrated successfully into the interactions. Behaviors that consistently disrupt social exchanges are likely to be seen as abnormal or deviant. Each society exists in a unique environment and has particular techniques for obtaining what its people need to survive there. Thus, the cultural ideals of "normal" interaction will be defined differently from society to society.

Individuality and Deviance

Although a culture's ideals and rules for behavior work to create conformity, none of us is identical to anyone else, and each of us brings to the group our own unique predispositions, including how we each respond to socialization. Thus, the actual behavior of individuals varies somewhat from the expectations embodied in their culture about how people should act in various situations. The ways in which individuals may successfully deviate from their culture's rules and the degree of deviation that is tolerated by others differs from culture to culture.

Deviance. To most people, the word *deviance* has a rather negative connotation. In a more technical context, however, it is not limited to negative behavior. **Deviance** is merely behavior that differs sufficiently from what is expected to be noticed (Becker, 1963, Erikson, 1962, Scheff, 1966). Deviance may be welcomed and praised or rejected and punished. Thus, **creativity** may be considered a kind of deviance from cultural expectations, but it generally results in a valuable new contribution to society and may be rewarded. It is also true that deviation from cultural norms may bring public censure and **stigma**, the loss of rank that accompanies the social rejection of persons who have violated accepted role behavior. For instance, writers or actors sometimes have been imprisoned or confined in mental hospitals by

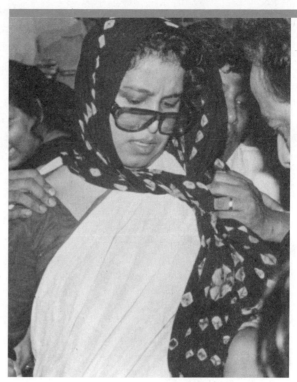

FIGURE 14.3

CULTURAL DEVIANCE

What one culture might interpret as creative license, another might interpret as insubordination. One recent example involves the Bangladeshi writer Taslima Nasrin. Angry Muslims have been demanding her death, not only because, they claim, she blasphemed the Koran by calling for a more liberal interpretation that would, in effect, give women more rights, but also because of the language she has used in her poetry and newspaper columns. Having fled to Sweden in 1994, she remains in hiding.

governments who perceived their political commentaries as "traitorous," "pornographic," or "insane."

INADEQUATE ROLE PLAYING

Failure to play our roles as we are expected to may bring us personal distress as well as

(Continued on p. 367)

deviance behavior that differs enough from what society expects that others notice and react to it

creativity deviance that results in valuable new contributions to society

stigma loss of rank that accompanies the social rejection of persons who have violated accepted role behavior

TABLE 14.1   EMOTIONAL RESPONSES TO INADEQUATE ROLE PLAYING

Problem (Context of Stress)	Individual's Interpretation of the Role Playing Difficulty	Individual's Physiological and Behavioral Responses to Tension State**	Individual's Subjective Feeling
UNKNOWN DANGER, NON-SPECIFIC AROUSAL	"I need to act but I don't know what to do. I cannot cope with this."	generalized visceral tension, hyperventilation, breathlessness, tightness of chest, stomach spasms, diarrhea or constipation, rapid heartbeat, respiratory distress, fainting, nausea, sweating, tremor and agitation	ANXIETY (includes frenzy, helplessness, inner conflict, worrying, feelings of loss of self-control)
KNOWN DANGER	"I have too little power."	*facial pallor, coldness of hands and feet, rapid and shallow breathing, rapid heartbeat, immobilization or retreat	FEAR (includes terror, apprehension)
HARM TO ANOTHER	"I have used too much power."	head lowered (lower than in shame), gaze averted with only quick glances at other people, avoidance of eye contact, wringing of hands, face takes on "heavy" look with tightness around eyes, dryness of mouth, tightness of sphincter muscles, preoccupation with concepts of fault and wrongdoing	GUILT (includes self-reproach, remorse)
REJECTION, LOSS, ISOLATION	"I have too little esteem; I am worthless."	*sadness with or without tears, headaches, nasal congestion, swelling of eyes, feelings of hopelessness	GRIEF (includes loneliness, sadness, sorrow, pensiveness)
LOSS OF FACE	"I have claimed too much esteem, and others know it."	*blushing, lowering or covering of face, gaze averted down and to one side, confusion, body curved inward on itself, curled up, makes self look smaller, eyes closed	SHAME (includes embarrassment, shyness, contriteness, sheepishness, mortification)
FRUSTRATION	"Someone/something stands in my way."	*violence of movement or speech, repetitiveness	ANGER (includes hate, rage, annoyance)

In a given situation, when we fail to respond in a manner appropriate to our status or role, we experience emotional distress.

*Source: "The Distancing of Emotion in Ritual," by T. J. Scheff, 1977, *Current Anthropology, 18* (3), 483–506.
**Alternatively, any of these may be realized as emotionless and/or distraction.

Note: Ideas about power and esteem adapted from *A Social Interactional Theory of Emotions* by T. D. Kemper, 1978, New York: John Wiley and Sons.

stigma. Every status has a culturally defined rank. To maintain face, the holder of each status is expected to use a particular amount of power and to receive a certain amount of honor. Failure to play one's roles in a way that uses the appropriate level of power or demands the appropriate amount of honor results in emotional distress for the role player.

The most basic form of this subjective distress is **anxiety**, a general sense of powerlessness and foreboding. Depending on the context in which the stress occurs and on how the individual interprets the situation, anxiety may alternate with more focused distressful feelings (see Table 14.1). Anxiety will take the form of the more concrete emotion **fear** if the sufferer feels that he or she is playing a role with insufficient power to remain safe from the negative effects of some specific problem. Anxiety alternates with **guilt** when stress arises from an awareness that one is exercising more power than is personally acceptable. **Grief** or sadness may be present when the stress-causing situation is understood by the sufferer as the inability to obtain voluntary esteem from others. Alternatively, anxiety may take the form of **shame** or **embarrassment** when there is a possibility that the present esteem of others may be withdrawn, that is, when the stress stems from discovering that one is receiving more honor than one's skills deserve. Any of these four negative, concrete emotions—fear, guilt, grief, and shame—may be avoided if the sufferer has learned to respond to others with anger instead. We feel **anger** when we hold another person responsible for causing our own distress.

Stress

Stress is the body's attempt to prepare itself to take action against any problem, whether it is organic (e.g., a change in brain chemistry), psychological (e.g., learned habits that make it difficult to interact successfully with others), or external (e.g., a major life crisis, such as a divorce). Normally, we prefer to channel the energy mobilized by stress into direct attempts to eliminate the problem. This pragmatic response may not be possible, however, if (1) we have not correctly identified the problem, (2) we have not learned a means of dealing with it adequately, (3) we lack the skill to take action successfully, or (4) we have no opportunity to take action. In such cases, we may begin to ex-

perience anxiety, conscious awareness, and preoccupation with the stress we feel. Depending on how we interpret the situation, anxiety may be a general, nagging sense of foreboding, or it may take on the more concrete form of one of the distressful emotions: fear, guilt, grief, shame, or anger. Some persons so control the expression of anxiety that they experience **affectlessness**, a kind of emotional lethargy.

The Trance State

One common result of intense or prolonged anxiety is the experience of **trances**, which are sometimes also called **altered states of consciousness**. These are subjective states of mind in which experiences are interpreted not in terms of the normal symbolic categories of one's culture, but in various ways common to all human beings. Trances may be rather mild and undramatic experiences, such as the state of daydreaming or fantasy that we all engage

---

anxiety a distressful subjective awareness of stress; a general sense of powerlessness and foreboding without awareness of a specific danger

fear a distressful emotion characterized by concerns about inadequate power to protect oneself from specific danger

guilt a distressful emotion characterized by remorse for having used too much power and having harmed another

grief a distressful emotion characterized by a sense of loss, sadness, and failure to obtain esteem from others

shame (embarrassment) a distressful emotion characterized by a sense of personal ineptness resulting in damage to one's reputation and loss of esteem

embarrassment shame

anger an emotional state during which another person is held responsible for one's own distress; may substitute for anxiety, fear, guilt, grief, or shame in situations in which those emotions might otherwise be felt

stress a physiological response to any demand, characterized by the body's preparing itself for action

affectlessness the complete control of emotion resulting in lethargy

trance (altered state of consciousness) subjective state of mind where experiences are not interpreted in terms of normal symbolic categories of one's culture

altered state of consciousness trance

ANGER AND VIOLENCE AMONG THE SEMAI OF MALAYSIA

The Semai horticulturalists of central West Malaysia were described by Dentan (1968) as a society whose people were so unaggressive in their customs that they had no need for police, judges, or jails. The very idea of physical violence was so horrifying to them that their word for "hit" would be translated as "kill" (p. 58).

In the Semai culture, people learned that anger made them prone to accidents. So instead of getting angry, victimized persons preferred to seek redress for their grievances in ways that did not show anger, such as approaching the offender and asking for compensation. The other person was under some pressure to acknowledge his fault and make amends to avoid further responsibility for accidents that might befall the already injured person. Even when social problems were not adequately resolved, violence rarely resulted. The injured party might spread gossip and otherwise insult the wrongdoer. These acts were enough pressure for some to resolve the problem finally, but even if they failed, escalation of the hostility did not occur among the Semai.

In support of his description of a society without violence, Dentan noted that the Semai could not remember an instance of homicide, and he could find no instance of murder, attempted murder, or maiming among the Semai from 1956 through 1968. In Dentan's opinion, violence actually seemed to terrify the Semai. They reacted to force with passivity or flight and learned to keep a tight rein over aggressive impulses.

The Semai had no authority figures, even in their families. Parents never coerced their children into specific kinds of behavior, but let them follow their own inclinations. The Semai believed that to pressure children would make them unhappy and, therefore, accident-prone. To teach their children to avoid unacceptable behavior, the Semai used fear in the form of threats of physical punishment. But the threatened blow was never realized; it would be frozen inches away from the child or transformed, at worst, to a slight tap.

That it was situational forces and not just personality that molded people to crime or conformity was illustrated by a further fact about Semai behavior. During the 1950s, the Malaysian government was involved in military conflict with Communist guerrilla forces. When Semai men joined the British military forces and participated in combat, some individuals became noted for the extremes of their fervor in battle. But when the circumstances of warfare led them to kill other human beings, their acts of violence caused them such psychological distress and disorientation that, in order to deal with it, they entered a trance-like state they termed *buul bhiib,* or "blood drunkenness." During the mental dissociation that accompanied this state, they sometimes participated in extremely violent fighting. In Dentan's words:

A typical veteran's story runs like this. "We killed, killed, killed. The Malays would stop and go through people's pockets and take their watches and money. We did not think of

in occasionally when we are tired or bored with our current environment. They also may be rather vivid and dramatic occurrences, such as hypnotic trances or dreams.

Psychologist Arnold Ludwig (1966/1972) describes 10 major characteristics of altered states of consciousness:

- alterations in thinking
- disturbance of the sense of time
- change in emotional expression
- change in body image
- distortions in perception
- change in the perceived meaning or significance of things
- a sense that the experiences cannot be described
- hypersuggestibility

- a sense of loss of control (in some cases)
- feelings of rejuvenation (in some cases)

Most of these changes may be results of stress, which may inhibit the usual role of the left hemisphere of the cerebral cortex in initiating action and controlling a person's behavior.

Biological Explanations of Trances.   To understand altered states of consciousness, we must first look at the effects of stress on the human brain. In the discussion of a biological basis of language (see chapter 12), we noted that the cerebral cortex is divided into two major halves or hemispheres, and that the left hemisphere has specialized centers that make possible the symbolic skills embodied in language. Stress,

watches or money. We thought only of killing. Wah, truly we were drunk with blood." One man even told how he had drunk the blood of a man he had killed. (pp. 58–59)

Robarchek and Dentan (1987) have pointed out that many of the Semai who behaved violently were men who had experienced the murder of a number of influential Semai by Communist terrorists. In Robarchek and Dentan's opinion, the Semai soldiers were simply "people with little or no prior experience in either committing or dealing with violence, transplanted from an egalitarian, peaceful society into one that taught and rewarded killing, where they were trained in military behavior, including how to kill" (p. 361). In the "heat, fear, and excitement of a sudden firefight" they did what they had been trained to do against enemies they believed had harmed and killed their own neighbors and friends. Most importantly, the state of "blood drunkenness" that these men experienced was an expression of their horror at their own behavior. Contrary to the implications of its English translation, "blood drunkenness" was a state of mind that was characterized not by a frenzy of blood lust or desire to kill, but "an acute state of nausea, fear, disorientation, and disgust which the sight of human blood evokes among the Semai" (p. 361).

Violence and its accompanying "blood drunkenness" were not typical of Semai soldiers. As a matter of fact, the original Semai unit of over 300 soldiers killed only an average of one person a year over a 20-year period. It is true that some Semai were certainly capable of extremes of violence when they were removed from their normal

SEMAI

Living in central West Malaysia, the Semai are a nonviolent people. In solving social problems, they simply ask for, and expect, compensation for whatever fault was committed against them. They react to force with passivity or flight and learn to control their own aggressive impulses.

cultural environment. But even these Semai veterans were disgusted by their own extreme behavior and were at a loss to explain it. Their traditional nonviolent self-image remained intact when they returned to civilian life, and they reverted to their former gentle and timid style of life.

however, interferes with the symbolic capacity of the human organism. The right hemisphere, which takes the lead in nonsymbolic behavior, plays the dominant role during the expressive acts that are common in rituals since it communicates by direct representation with signs.

The changes in thinking that are common in altered mental states include increased difficulties in concentration, attention, and memory, all of which are results of stress. There is also a shift away from thinking in terms of cause and effect—a left-hemispheric way of organizing thought—toward a mode of thought in which opposites may coexist, a hallmark of communication by signs: a smile may indicate friendship or sarcasm, tears may signal sorrow or joy, and laughter may express either relief from stress or mounting embarrassment.

The ordering of information in a sequence, such as a chronological listing of events, is a left-hemispheric trait. The experience of time as a passage of events one after another at a constant, measurable pace is alien to the way in which the right hemisphere orders its memory of events. Therefore, the disturbed time sense common in altered mental states may be a result of a shift away from the predominant influence of the left hemisphere's symbolic conceptualization of time.

Perceptual distortions take their most dramatic form as **hallucinations**, which are like

---

hallucination a realistic-seeming experience—much like a vivid waking dream—that may include vision, hearing, the sense of touch, smell, and/ or taste in the absence of external causes

vivid dreams in a waking state. According to Buchsbaum (1979), studies of how the left and right hemispheres communicate suggest that hallucinations may result from the failure of the left hemisphere to suppress incoming fears of the right hemisphere, normally, a result of an inhibitory chemical, **serotonin**, produced in the brain during waking hours (Goleman, 1978; Jacobs, 1978). Both dreams and daydreams are normally produced by brain stem stimulation on a 90-minute cycle (Krupke & Lavie, 1975; McCarley, 1978), and daydreams may be the waking state manifestation of dreams in a washed-out form. Under stressful circumstances, the levels of serotonin in the brain may decline, allowing daydreams to be experienced in the vivid form of hallucinations.

The change in the perceived meaning or significance of things experienced during altered states is called the **eureka experience**, a sudden sense of deep insight into things "as they really are." It occurs because the right hemisphere analyzes experiences not by breaking them up conceptually into parts that are then related to one another by abstract logic, but by weighing the experience in its totality and finding answers in sudden flashes of insight. The left hemisphere solves problems and discovers meaning by the symbolic process of analysis.

Producing Trance States. Ludwig (1966/1972) reports five main ways of producing altered states of consciousness: (1) a prolonged reduction of sensory input and/or motor activity; or (2) the opposite condition, namely, sensory and/or motor overload; (3) prolonged increased alertness or mental involvement; or (4) the opposite condition, a prolonged decrease in mental alertness or involvement; and (5) changes in body chemistry. The first of these may be exemplified by trances induced by solitary confinement, so-called "highway hypnosis," (the detached state sometimes experienced by motorists on long, boring stretches of road), or the sensory deprivation associated with *kayak angst* (see p. 378). Examples of the second process are brainwashing, the trances of whirling dervishes, and either a frightening encounter or incessant tickling that leads to *latah* (see p. 376). Increased alertness as a path to altered mental states may be caused by fervent prayer or sentry duty. Decreased alertness is used in some forms of meditation to achieve a mystical mental state. Changes

in body chemistry include all the drug-induced altered states of consciousness. All of these conditions interfere with the normal functioning of the central nervous system and produce stress, the source of signalized ritual behavior accompanied by altered states of consciousness.

Trance and Ideology. Interestingly, altered states of consciousness may play a part in the development of the ideology of a culture. Whenever people attempt to describe or account for the experiences they have had during an altered mental state, they must use the medium of language, a left-hemispheric system of communication. Whatever the particular beliefs by which people make sense of altered state experiences, these beliefs invariably involve some degree of what Leslie White (1971) has called a confusion between self and not-self. It may manifest itself in one of two ways: either (1) that which lies outside the individual is considered an extension of the individual, as when lightning is said to be nature's response to a sinful thought; or (2) that which actually occurs within an individual, such as a dream or a hallucination, is spoken of as a truly external event such as the experiences of one's soul which is believed to have left one's body. Thus efforts to explain trance experiences may give rise to religious beliefs such as spirit travel or powers and beings that respond to human thought and actions.

CULTURAL SHAPING OF ALTERED STATES OF CONSCIOUSNESS

To the extent that altered states of consciousness are responses to stress, they may be culturally shaped in two dimensions. One dimension is the cultural nature of the stress itself; the other is the way in which altered states of consciousness are culturally defined. One example of how cultural definitions of trance influence its

---

serotonin a chemical produced in the brain during waking hours that inhibits the production of dreams or hallucinations

eureka experience a sense of intensified meaningfulness of experiences that sometimes occurs during an altered state of consciousness

THE TRANCE STATE

The trance state, or altered state of consciousness, results in changes in perception of time, space, or body image. It may be induced by drugs, stress, sen- *sory deprivation, or sensory overload. This trance dance in the village of /Aotcha, Namibia, depicts spiritual travel.*

role in society is the use of dreams to control the supernatural.

Dream-Control of the Supernatural.

D'Andrade (1961) compared societies in which people attempt to contact and control the supernatural through dreams with those societies in which dreams play no such role. He found that societies in which young men move far from their parents when they marry are more likely to make such use of dreams. He suggests that this may be a response to the loss of a parent as a source to turn to in times of need. Societies that have the capacity to store food are less likely to use dreams for supernatural purposes than those that do not preserve food. Since the latter is also likely to emphasize independence and self-reliance as a natural consequence of its small accumulation of foodstuffs, Bourguignon (1974) regards the use of dreams to control supernatural power as a response to stresses generated by the lack of human support that the expectation of self-reliance implies.

Socialization and Trance States

Bourguignon and Greenbaum (1973) have noted that different cultural patterns lie behind

two different forms of trance, **spirit travel trance** and **spirit possession trance**. The first is characterized by passivity or even unconsciousness during the altered mental state, which is interpreted as a "trip" in which the spirit leaves the body and communes with supernatural entities. Possession trances, on the other hand, involve a great deal of bodily activity, thought to be under the control of a spirit visitor. These trances are often entered with the aid of repetitive chants and dancing. Unlike participants in spirit travel trances, people who engage in possession trances often experience amnesia about what they said and did while possessed. In spirit travel trances, hallucinations may be vividly recalled and drugs are more likely to be used as an aid to entering the trance.

The spirit travel trances are most likely to be found in societies that place the heaviest stress on independence and assertion. Spirit possession trances, on the other hand, are most

---

spirit travel trance a trance in which individuals experience themselves as leaving their bodies
spirit possession trace a trance in which individuals feel as if their behavior is under the control of one or more spirits that have entered their bodies

FIGURE 14.5

DIAL "S" FOR SOOTHSAYER

In attempting to deal with stress and anxiety, some people turn to others for advice. Combining African tradition and Western marketing techniques, Liza Khumalo of Johannesburg, South Africa, is a star among the new breed of telephone diviners. She wears the traditional sangoma of the soothsayer, a woolen wig, arranges her tools, including shells and bones, and sits by the phone waiting for customers who pay about $2 a minute to get answers to their questions.

common in societies where compliance is expected. Thus, Bourguignon and Greenbaum believe that the type of trance that is more common in a culture is the kind that will most effectively reduce the kind of stress common in that culture. For example, in cultures in which people normally are expected to behave in an independent way, spirit travel trances permit them to be taken care of physically by others while they are on a spiritual trip. The spirits that they visit offer help and assistance in a way that is not generally available in normal social settings, thereby fulfilling dependency needs that go unsatisfied in the participants' day-to-day social life. By contrast, in cultures where people usually are compliant and de-

pendent, some may satisfy their normally unfulfilled desires for power and autonomy during a spirit possession trance in which they take on the personalities of the powerful, dominant spirits that animate their bodies. During these possession states they can behave in ways that their normal roles do not permit, speaking boldly and acting powerfully. Later, they are not held responsible for behaving aggressively, since they did so in the role of a passive vehicle for the spirit that controlled them and may even claim no recollection of their own trance behavior.

According to Whiting and Child (1953), spirit travel trances were especially common in North America, where they were found in 94 percent of the native societies examined. In contrast, only 25 percent had spirit possession trances. In sub-Saharan Africa, on the other hand, only 36 percent had spirit travel trances, and spirit possession trances were about as common as in North America—26 percent. This may reflect a greater emphasis on self-reliance in traditional North American cultures and a corresponding greater role for fulfilling one's responsibilities to the community in many African cultures.

Emotional Distress and Ritual

Prolonged or intense anxiety may also result in changes in behavior. The behavioral changes that often accompany spontaneous trances begin with a breakdown of old patterns of behaviors leading to the violation of the unspoken, taken-for-granted rules of a culture. Sometimes such altered behavior may result in a creative new solution to the original problem. More often it does not. In such cases, our rule breaking settles down into highly expressive actions such as a grimace or clenched fists that portray how we feel about the unresolved problem. Whenever it recurs, we are likely to respond with the same expressive acts. Thus, stress-induced rule breaking coalesces into **ritual**, stereotyped repetitive behavior that expresses problems by acting them out. Although ritual acts have no pragmatic effect on the original problem, they

---

ritual behaviors, often performed in repetitive and stereotyped ways, that express people's anxieties by acting them out; may be an attempt to influence the supernatural realm to achieve greater control over the natural world

do have the psychological effect of reducing our anxiety.

Ritual and the Control of Anxiety. We all spontaneously use rituals when we experience stress that we have not learned to handle in any practical way. Many of our rituals are organized into culturally established patterns that are shared by many people and thought of as *religious* acts. In times of crisis, these religious rituals are available as a source of comfort. Rituals give us something to do when we feel that we must act but do not know what to do. They permit us to channel some of the excess energy of stress into physical action and thereby relieve some of the physiological problems of stress. An even more important role of rituals is to distract us from the stress sensation by focusing our attention elsewhere.

Religious rituals are especially effective in this, since they are supported by an ideology that people believe is a source of supernatural power that can help solve their problems. Following major disasters, such as the 1985 earthquake in Mexico or the 1992 hurricane in Florida, individuals often seek comfort from grief and fear through prayer, both privately and in groups. More idiosyncratic rituals also appear, spontaneously created and carried out with the same emotional benefit of relief from anxiety. For example, people sweeping the steps of a now-demolished house reassure themselves that order can be maintained in the midst of chaos. Others gain solace after the death of loved ones by temporarily denying the loss in word and deed—by preparing food for them as usual at mealtime or even by talking to them as if they were still there. We reassure ourselves in much the same way when we bring flowers or gifts to the bed of someone in a coma, keeping alive the hope of recovery by ritual communication. Rituals give us real benefits in emotionally trying situations; while they may not solve the problems that cause us stress, they do help us continue to function in spite of it.

Sometimes, however, our rituals fail to allay our worries sufficiently. When this happens, we may elaborate upon them in a vain attempt to gain control over the anxieties that they have not succeeded in eliminating. Then our rituals can interfere with other parts of our lives and become part of a vicious cycle in which we function less and less effectively. It is these rituals that others are most likely to see as evidence

of insanity. John Nemiah (1975) has reported the case of a young man whose rituals began over his anxiety about not performing well on the job but eventually interfered with his performance:

> A man of 32 who worked on the assembly line of an electronic concern developed the following compelling ritual: before he could solder one piece to another, he had to tap on the workbench 3 times with his left hand and 3 times with his right, followed by stamping 3 times on the floor first with his left foot, then with his right. For a time this merely slowed down his work performance, and he was able to continue his job.
>
> Gradually, however, an element of doubt crept into his mind. After completing a sequence of tapping and stamping, doubting thoughts would flash into his consciousness: "Did I really do it right? Am I sure I tapped 3 times? Did I stamp with my left foot first?" In response to these questions, he had to repeat the ritual to make sure it was perfectly done; but, the more he performed it, the greater his doubt. Before long, almost his entire working day was taken up by his rituals, and he was forced to leave his job. (p. 1246)

Social Stress and Deviant Personality

People who suffer the stigma and emotional distress that can accompany inadequate role playing may occasionally experience spontaneous altered states of consciousness and find themselves engaging in ritual behavior that expresses their distressful feelings. Sometimes, however, individuals become habituated to ritualized behavior and trance states, and this interferes even more with their ability to play acceptable social roles. Such individuals may find themselves reassigned to deviant master statuses, such as "immoral," "possessed," or "insane."

Deviant Statuses. A **deviant** is a person who has been given this label by others for his or her role-playing errors. The specific deviant status assigned will depend on the way in which a person misuses socially assigned power and prestige. The user of an excess of power will be seen as *hostile* and will be described as being

---

deviant a person who has been labeled a rule violator by others for his or her role-playing errors

prone to anger. The person who consistently uses less power than expected will be seen as *timid* or *fearful*. One who claims the right to an unrealistically high level of esteem will be viewed as *conceited* or *megalomaniacal*. The overly self-denigrating individual will be labeled as *depressive* or *insecure*. Each culture elaborates these four basic categories with labels for subtypes that occur with high frequency. For instance, in U.S. culture the special term for the person who manifests the hostile use of power by insulting the value of another person is *catty*. One who uses an excess of power to prevent another from terminating a conversation, while remaining overtly oblivious to his or her own violation, will be called a *bore*.

Categories of Cultural Rules.   Rule violations in the use of culturally appropriate levels of power and prestige are common enough in all societies so that every culture is likely to specifically label and define realms within which violations of rules can be grouped. For instance, in the United States, rule violations will be seen as violations of *law* if they result in harm to persons or property. Violations of rules of prestige, which differentiate members of one class from another, are violations of *etiquette*. *Aesthetic* standards are current values about beauty. They include judgments about what things may be compatibly organized together. For instance, North American aesthetic standards preclude the use of Greek columns on a ranch style house, although I suspect that if one grew up with such a style it would not seem strange. As do all symbolic categories, aesthetic standards change. For instance, before the film *Flashdance*, wearing a torn sweatshirt in public was considered unaesthetic in most of North America. Law, etiquette, and aesthetics are but three of a much longer list of formally labeled North American rule categories.

The precise list of rule categories varies, of course, from culture to culture, and categories that are important in one society may be absent from another. The one universal fact, however, is that, regardless of how long the list may be, there will always be rules left over that belong to none of the categories. These may be said to make up the *miscellaneous* or **residual rules** of that culture. Although they comprise a leftover category, residual rules are important, since they play a central role in concepts about the most deviant statuses in a society.

Violations of Residual Rules.   Even if a residual rule category is not formally named, the violation of any of these rules elicits a reaction from members of society in which the violator is labeled *insane*. The violation of legal rules may be abhorred. But such violations are punished at least in part because most members of society can conceive of situations in which they themselves might be tempted to violate the rights of others. Likewise, violation of etiquette is undesirable, but this "poor taste" is understood as evidence of a failure to achieve a desirable level of social ranking, something that not everyone is expected to be able to accomplish. The residual rules, on the other hand, are the rules that are taken for granted, conformity to which is assumed to come naturally to all normal individuals.

Residual rules are the social prohibitions that need not be taught; it literally "goes without saying" that they are not to be done. The list is, for any culture, an open-ended one that could be added to *ad infinitum*. For example, it is doubtful that any North Americans have ever been taught not to remove their shoes and juggle them while carrying on a conversation with a minister. Yet most if not all would immediately recognize such behavior as a rule violation were they to witness it, especially if the actor, on being queried, failed to provide an acceptable rationale for her or his behavior; he or she would be likely to be judged insane.

Stress and Residual Rule Breaking.   In the opinion of Scheff (1966), the causes of residual rule breaking are diverse. They include (1) organic sources such as genetic, biochemical, and physiological problems; (2) psychological sources, such as problems in upbringing and training or maladaptive habit patterns that interfere with one's own success; (3) external stress such as drug ingestion, danger, lack of food and sleep, or sensory overload; and (4) volitional acts of innovation or defiance. The common denominator of all these causes is that residual rule breaking is likely to occur when the individual is experiencing stress, regardless of its sources. Stress is a physiological state that has been studied for years by Selye (1976), who defines it as the nonspecific response of the

---

residual rules miscellaneous, normally unspoken rules that people are expected to follow to avoid violating the pattern or style of behavior that is expected in the culture

body to any demand. In the beginning stages of the stress state, the human body is mobilizing itself for action. This state of readiness involves such general bodily changes as increased movement, heightened blood pressure, excess perspiration, and accelerated heartbeat.

When one's culture has provided no normal response to a stressful situation, residual rule breaking does have the potential of being adaptive. By doing things that are not in the usual behavioral repertoire of the culture, the stressed person may discover a creative practical solution to the original stress-inducing problem. In such cases, residual rule breaking may be a source of cultural innovation and change. However, such innovations will be adopted by society at large only if enough others are trying to cope with the same kind of problem and therefore recognize the benefit of the innovation (Wallace, 1961). When this is not the case, people are likely to regard the residual rule breaking as a startling and undesirable form of deviance from the usual behaviors that they expect.

MENTAL DISORDERS AND CULTURE

The concept of insanity is found in cultures throughout the world and may be viewed as a cultural process as well as a psychological one. An analysis of the cultural process involved in defining insanity casts light on the conditions in which a person is given the master status of being insane.

Insanity

As a cultural process, there are two criteria, both of which must be present, for a person to be regarded as insane. The first is the characteristic of residual rule breaking, which Edgerton (1976) has described as a state in which "a person's thought, emotions, or behavior appear to others in his society to be unreasonable or irrational, or when his ability to cope with the ordinary demands of life are impaired" (p. 63). As a case in point, Edgerton reports the example of "an elder Sebei man of Uganda who for some years spent most of his waking hours hanging upside down from the limb of a tree or a rafter in his house. His only comments

were: 'I have a chicken in my head' or 'I have countless wives.' Most Sebei easily agreed on labeling him psychotic" (p. 64). This example illustrates the condition of a residual rule breaker who cannot control his deviant behavior. The second criterion is the judgment that a person lacks control over his or her deviant behavior (Miller, 1974; Murphy, 1976). Thus, **insanity** may be defined as role playing in which a person engages in residual rule breaking that others believe he or she cannot control.

Typically, the insane status that such people acquire is one of the most highly stigmatized in all societies. People who hold this master status are considered the antithesis of whatever their societies regard as normal. Thus, for instance, languages as diverse as Shoshone and English express the idea of insanity with a word that means "not sane." The Chippewa of northern Wisconsin and northeastern Minnesota, the Cree of northern Manitoba, and the Montagnais-Naskapi of northern Quebec referred to any severe form of insanity as the generic term *windigo* or *wiitiko*, terms that were also names for a mythological giant cannibal with a heart of ice.

Dissociative Disorders and Culture

In **dissociative disorders**, an overwhelming anxiety, fear, or sense of powerlessness may be avoided by dissociating oneself from awareness of their causes. Normally, consciousness, memory, one's sense of identity, and perception function together in an integrated way. However, in dissociative disorders the usual integration of these parts of a personality is disrupted, and a person may experience a sense of detachment from his or her mental processes or body. Dissociative disorders may also involve amnesia in which distressful memories are blocked out of conscious memory without the direct awareness of the afflicted individual.

---

insanity process by which a person acquires and maintains deviant master status of residual rule breaker

dissociative disorders (hysteria) mental disorders in which anxiety is avoided through the nonvoluntary loss of integration among consciousness, memory, sense of identity, and/or perception of the environment

Seymour Parker (1962) has summarized the traits common to cultures in which **hysteria**, an older term for dissociative disorders, is prevalent: (1) early socialization is not severe and there is a high level of need gratification; (2) there is a corresponding emphasis on communalistic values and expectations of mutual aid; (3) the female role is ranked markedly below that of the male; and (4) the religious system often provides models of hysteria-like behavior in spirit-possession rituals. In other words, childrearing practices foster high expectations that others may be relied on to fulfill one's dependency needs; therefore, self-reliance does not reach a high level and a person's self-esteem is contingent on the interpretation of his or her value in the eyes of others. Women, however, are repeatedly reminded that their status is inferior to that of men in both esteem and power. By and large, women in these societies therefore transform their day-to-day stress into negative self-worth. They also, then, are more likely than men to react to sudden dangers with fright that may lead to dissociative breaks with reality. Similarly, symbolic reminders of their inferior status may lead stressed women to fall into dissociative trances.

Social outcasts of either sex are not supported in their self-esteem by these societies. Rather, the communities use subtle and not-so-subtle sanctions to withdraw their support from deviant individuals. For the individual whose self-esteem is dependent on the support of others, this can be disastrous. For example, in traditional Chinese societies, the woman who fails, either out of laxity or poverty, to make the expected offerings to the dead could find herself losing the needed support of her community, leading to great anxiety. Since a married woman leaves her own family to reside with her husband and his kin, she also lacks support from her own kin at times of emotional stress. The dissociative reaction that results is believed by those around her to be a manifestation of spirit possession. In performing a cure, the community would reintroduce her into its good graces and the hysteria would subside.

Men who are less active than others or who fail in the pursuit of traditional male goals in these societies are more likely than others to develop anxiety about their inadequate personal power. When arctic hysteria (see p. 377) struck men, it usually struck those whom Edward Foulks (1972) described as " 'nervous' young men aspiring to become shamans," that

is, young men who were somewhat marginal in secular male pursuits and wished therefore to become spiritual healers (p. 11).

Culture-Specific Forms of Dissociative Disorders

Although the basic psychological mechanisms by which dissociative states are produced may be common to all peoples throughout the world, the specific ways in which dissociative disorders are experienced and communicated are influenced by cultural interpretations of human behavior. Anthropological fieldworkers have reported a variety of culturally specific forms of hysteria in non-Westernized traditional societies.

Amok, which is a dissociative reaction, is found in New Guinea (Langness, 1965; Newman, 1964). Only young men ages 25 through 35 seem to be afflicted. After an initial depression, the victim enters a phase of anxiety and depression in which experiences take on an unreal quality, and the victim broods over offenses by others. Finally, in a burst of energy, the victim "runs amok," screaming and attacking people and their property. During this stage, the sufferer seems delirious and sometimes unable to hear what others shout at him. After exhausting himself, the victim returns to consciousness but has no memories of what he has done. Among the Gururumba of New Guinea, the individual who was affected by amok was not expected to recompense the victims for the losses he inflicted on them, for his behavior was believed to have been beyond his control, caused by the bite of an aggressive ghost or some similar factor. Additionally, his susceptibility to the disorder was seen as evidence of a weakness in his ability to deal with the normal stresses of Gururumba social and economic life. Therefore, payment of his previous economic debts was no longer vigorously sought by others. Disorders similar to amok were also reported in Malaya, Indonesia, Polynesia, and the Sahara.

Latah, a hysterical dissociation brought on by a sudden startling encounter with danger-

---

hysteria dissociative disorders

amok a culture-specific hysterical disorder in which young men attack other people and destroy property

latah a culture-specific hysterical disorder that is characterized by uncontrollable imitation of the actions and speech of others

ous things or by being tickled, was found in Southeast Asia and Mongolia (Aberle, 1961; Van Loon, 1926). After an initial fright reaction, such as tremor and collapse, the victim engaged in compulsive imitation of the actions and speech of others. In Southeast Asia and Indonesia, latah was most common among women, but in Mongolia it was more likely to afflict men.

Imu, which is perhaps simply a variety of *latah*, was found among the aboriginal inhabitants of northern Japan, the Ainu (Winiarz & Wielawski, 1936). Like latah in Southeast Asia, imu mainly afflicted women. Brought on by a sudden frightening experience, such as hearing a loud sound or being bitten by a snake, it begins with an aggressive or fearful startled reaction, followed by automatic obedience to suggestions given by others or its opposite, negativism, and the compulsive imitation of sounds and gestures until the victim is exhausted.

A similar disorder, **arctic hysteria** or **amurakh**, was found among the Yakut and Tungus of northeastern Siberia, where it also was most common among women (Czaplicka, 1914). Like its counterparts elsewhere, it involves compulsive imitation of sounds and gestures. At least in the form experienced by spiritual healers, or shamans, the original attack is brought on by a sudden fright.

Another dissociative disorder was found among the northern native Greenlanders (Foulks, 1972; Gussow, 1960; Wallace, 1972). This affliction is known as **pibloktoq**. After a period of irritability and withdrawal, the victim becomes highly agitated, violent, and talkative. Some victims may tear off their clothing and run naked into the snowfields. Finally, after collapsing from exhaustion and falling into unconsciousness, the victim may recover from the attack with no memory of it. Researchers found it to be somewhat more common in women than in men.

Since pibloktoq was most common in the winter, increased life stresses caused by coping with the rigorous arctic winter in small communities might be a triggering factor in this disorder. However, Wallace (1972) has argued that the basic cause of pibloktoq was the Greenlanders' calcium-deficient diet. Since vitamin D—produced by the body when it is exposed to sunlight—is necessary for the body to absorb calcium from food, the seasonal increase in pibloktoq could be explained by the decreased sunlight in winter. Calcium deficiency would impair the functioning of the central nervous system, producing the pibloktoq symptoms of

FIGURE 14.6

CULTURE-SPECIFIC FORMS OF DISSOCIATIVE DISORDER

Culture may play a role in the manifestation of dissociative disorder. In some Inuit areas where the environment causes stress and sunlight is decreased, the disorder may take the form of pibloktoq, where the victim becomes highly agitated, violent, and may run naked into the icy cold snow.

nervous excitability and distortions in thought processes. Other researchers (Foulks, 1972) failed to find significant differences in the serum calcium levels of pibloktoq-prone and normal Greenlanders, so Wallace's calcium deficiency hypothesis remains controversial.

Hsieh-ping is a dissociative disorder found in traditional Chinese societies (Wittkower & Fried, 1957). Sufferers, most commonly women, are believed to be possessed by spirits of dead relatives or friends to whom they have failed to offer the proper respect. It includes symptoms of tremor and disorientation, with clouding of consciousness, delirium, speaking in tongues, and hallucinations.

---

imu a hysterical disorder found among the Ainu of northern Japan, characterized by automatic obedience or negativism and uncontrollable imitation of sounds and gestures

arctic hysteria (amurakh) a culture-specific hysterical disorder that is characterized by compulsive imitation of sounds and gestures

amurakh arctic hysteria

pibloktoq a culture-specific hysterical disorder characterized by agitated attempts to flee the presence of other people

hsieh-ping a culture-specific hysterical disorder that is characterized by tremor, disorientation, clouding of consciousness, delirium, speaking in tongues, and hallucinations

Saka is a dissociative disorder found among Wataita women in Kenya (Harris, 1957). Sometimes preceded by restlessness and anxiety, an attack begins with convulsive movements in which the upper body trembles and the head shakes from side to side. Occasionally, the victim may repeat actions or sounds thought to be in a foreign tongue. A trance or loss of consciousness and rigidity of the body may follow. Attacks may be precipitated by the sight, sounds, and smells of men or foreigners or even by things associated with them, such as a train whistle or the smell of a cigarette.

Social Roots of Dissociative Disorders.

Each of the dissociative disorders is ideologically patterned in such a way that the people among whom it is found understand the symptoms according to their culture's unique system of meanings. Yet all these disorders share several important characteristics with the varieties of hysteria described in the Western psychiatric tradition. For instance, in most of these cases, the affliction is more likely to strike women than men, a finding that may reflect women's traditional lack of socially granted power. In those cases where men are victims, they have often failed in the goal-oriented masculine roles of their culture, where power is expected to be exercised successfully. Attacks are often set off by a sudden frightening shock or by other stimuli that may call the victims' attention to how little power they have compared with others. Attacks are followed by great agitation and even violent behavior that is powerful in form, if not in fact. Alternatively, instead of violent agitation, one may find its opposite: behavior that dramatizes the powerlessness of the victim, such as automatic obedience or robot-like imitation of others' sounds and gestures. In either case, the behavior is generally performed in a mentally clouded, disoriented state of mind. Finally, after termination of this intense and ritualized drama of powerlessness, the victim, who may fall exhausted into a state of unconsciousness or sleep, is likely to experience amnesia concerning the attack itself.

Other Culture-Specific Disorders

Besides the dissociative disorders, anthropologists have described other disorders that are uniquely shaped by specific cultures. Among these are kayak angst, susto, koro, and frigophobia.

Kayak Angst. Found among the indigenous people of western Greenland, **kayak angst** strikes males while they are alone and the sea is calm (Freuchen, 1935; Gussow, 1963; Honigmann & Honigmann, 1965). The stress results from physical immobility and environmental monotony in a potentially dangerous situation. The reaction begins with confusion, dizziness, and blurring of vision and depth perception. The victim becomes immobilized by fear of capsizing the kayak, a fear that is increased by a sudden chilling of his lower body, which he believes to be caused by water entering the kayak. These attacks may recur and be so incapacitating that the man may refuse to leave shore again, in spite of the economic importance of doing so.

Kayak angst has characteristics that are common in the phobic disorders of Western cultures. In *phobias*, conscious awareness of the true source of anxiety is avoided by displacing fear onto some object that is symbolic of whatever produces the anxiety. The overtly feared object is often something regarded as completely harmless by nonphobic individuals. Phobics may fear kittens, dirt, open fields, closed-in spaces, or almost anything else.

Susto. Most common in Latin America, **susto**, sometimes called **espanto** or **pasmo**, illustrates what Western psychiatry calls an *anxiety disorder* (Rubel, 1960). Such a disorder may involve a chronic state of tension and mild apprehension or, alternatively, temporary but acute and terrifying paniclike reactions that are not associated with any real danger. Susto typically begins following an experience of shame from failure to meet an important social obligation. The victim, whose soul is believed to have been lost because of a sudden fright or some other spiritual cause, becomes withdrawn, listless, and irritable. In ad-

---

saka a culture-specific hysterical disorder that is characterized by repetition of actions or sounds believed to be a foreign language, and loss of consciousness with body rigidity

kayak angst a culture-specific phobic disorder that is characterized by an inordinate fear of being at sea in a kayak

susto (espanto, pasmo) a culture-specific anxiety disorder with depressive features, interpreted by the victim as caused by soul loss

espanto susto

pasmo susto

dition, the victim loses appetite and experiences rapid heartbeat, nausea and vomiting, diarrhea, and restless sleep troubled by nightmares. Susto seems to combine some elements of depression with its primary symptoms as an anxiety reaction.

Koro.   This disorder parallels the Western disorder of *hypochondriasis*, a condition characterized by intense preoccupation with physical health, magnifying the sensations of normal bodily fatigue, aches, pains, and a recurring but unfounded fear that the sufferer's complaints are evidence of some dire disease. **Koro** has been associated most commonly with China and other parts of east and southeast Asia (Hsien, 1963, 1965; Yap, 1963, 1965). Koro attacks often follow a sudden fright. Male victims report that their penis feels cold, numb, and no longer a part of themselves. They fear that it is shrinking and being absorbed into their abdomen, leading to death. Among women, the fears center on the belief that their breasts are being similarly absorbed and that they will die. The cultural parallel of this anxiety about masculinity or femininity is clear: the traditional ideology of Chinese culture classified all things as masculine and feminine on the basis of the *yin* and *yang* or "female" and "male" essences they contain. In China, koro is believed to be caused by an imbalance of yin and yang in the victim. For instance, it is believed that koro can be brought on in men by the loss of semen through masturbation or frequent sexual intercourse, since semen is held to be a source of yang, which represents masculine vitality and strength. Like susto, koro is an anxiety reaction.

Frigophobia.   The Chinese disorder termed **frigophobia** or **pa-ling** is a culturally patterned *obsessive-compulsive disorder* in which anxiety is manifest through repetitive thoughts and acts that are symbolic of the underlying anxiety. Frigophobia involves an obsessive-compulsive need to change clothing repeatedly and to wear it in several layers to avoid heat loss from the cold and from winds (Kiev, 1972; Yap, 1951). The attendant fear of the cold and wind is rationalized by the victim of pa-ling by the belief that either of these may upset the balance of yin and yang necessary to health, and that the resulting loss of vital essence may lead to death. In contrast to the normal use of layered clothing in China, sufferers of frigophobia may spend so much time changing clothes that they

are unable to function in their normal responsibilities.

It is clear from these examples that the culture-specific disorders have much in common with one another. Indeed, the underlying psychological process seems to be the same. Individuals who are faced with stresses that they are unable to relieve by pragmatic action experience emotional distress and begin to manifest that stress by breaking the residual rules of their cultures. These various culture-specific disorders differ from one another mainly in their overt manifestations: the responses to stress are symbolic behaviors that are appropriate to the particular culture.

CAUSES OF MENTAL DISORDERS

Some people use altered states of consciousness as coping mechanisms for dealing with stress and then return to their normal behaviors; others get lost in altered states. What prevents some individuals from maintaining an acceptable social role while suffering from stress? The failure may be due in part to individual characteristics that make some people unusually susceptible to the effects of stress. It may also be due in part to the nature and level of the stresses involved. Finally, it also may be due to the social reactions of others who do not give the individual the opportunity to escape from the anxieties that stress creates.

Individual Susceptibility

Those who prefer to examine insanity from a psychological or biological perspective argue that insanity is at least partially a result of objective abnormalities within the sufferer, rendering him or her incapable of dealing with stresses that most people can handle. This viewpoint is not strictly a Western one. Jane

---

koro a culture-specific anxiety disorder characterized by fear of death through loss of sexual essence

frigophobia (pa-ling) a culture-specific obsessive-compulsive disorder characterized by fear of loss of body heat

pa-ling frigophobia

ANOREXIA NERVOSA: A WESTERN CULTURE-SPECIFIC DISORDER

The unique social stresses of the modern industrialized societies also lead to culture-specific disorders, including one syndrome in which some young women literally starve themselves to death.

FIGURE 14.7

ANOREXIA NERVOSA

In American society, models such as Kate Moss, left, shown with Karen Alexander, are generally more slender than the average U.S. woman. This emphasis on physical slenderness as the standard of beauty has contributed to the culture-specific disorder of anorexia nervosa. It primarily affects young girls who starve themselves almost to death in order to achieve a slender body.

Although the disorder, termed **anorexia nervosa**, is found in Japan, it occurs primarily in western cultures such as the United States, Canada, Europe, Australia, New Zealand, and South Africa. The cultures in which anorexia nervosa is prevalent emphasize slenderness as a mark of beauty in women. Fashion models, for example, are much more slender than the average U.S. woman. The stars of our motion pictures are rarely of average build, and the overweight actress is most often found in a comic role. In North America diet foods fill an entire section of our supermarkets.

In societies in which youth and slenderness are highly valued, anxiety about weight gain and growing older is also common. For instance, as many as 0.5 to 1.0 percent of U.S. females between the ages of 12 and 18 years may suffer from anorexia nervosa. The central characteristics of this disorder are an intense fear of becoming obese, an inaccurate body image, a loss of at least 15 percent of normal body weight, and a refusal to maintain even a minimal normal body weight. The patient refuses to eat and may lose 25 to 30 percent of her body weight. Although the most common pattern is a single episode followed by full recovery, some cases are so severe and life-threatening that they require hospitalization. Among hospitalized patients, the long-term death rate is over 10 percent.

This condition also may express a fear of the transition from childhood to womanhood. Victims of anorexia nervosa are almost always female. They are frequently described as perfectionistic "model children" who commonly feel inadequate in their social roles and incompetent in their work or school performance.

Murphy (1976) points out that one element of insanity in cultures around the world is the belief that those who are truly mentally ill are *unable* to control the spontaneous rituals that plague them and the onset of their altered states of consciousness. This approach often portrays genetically inherited differences as predisposing factors that are insufficient by themselves to cause insanity. That is to say, genetic inheritance may play a role in setting an individual's level of tolerance for stress, but social stresses—which differ in form from culture to culture—are believed to be the critical triggering forces that precipitate episodes of insanity.

---

anorexia nervosa a culture-specific obsessive-compulsive disorder characterized by an unrealistic appraisal of one's own body as overweight and by self-starvation

The Social Context

Those who prefer to apply a cultural perspective to the analysis of insanity reject the notion that it is an illness (Szasz, 1970). Rather, they believe that it is more enlightening to see insanity as a social process in which problematic situations force some members of society to play the role of sick or inadequate individuals. Those who maintain this position argue that the inability to control ritualized behavior and altered states of consciousness—used in many cultures as a criterion for judging a person to be insane—need not always be the result of a real biological incapacity of the individual who plays the sick role.

Another social aspect of insanity is that the same rule violation may be ignored when engaged in by one person, excused when done by another, and seen as evidence of "mental illness" in a third. What accounts for such differences in people's reactions to norm violations?

Research in complex societies has made it clear that the higher one's rank, the easier it is to behave in unusual ways without being labeled as insane. For instance, Hollingshead and Redlich (1953) examined data about schizophrenia from New Haven and surrounding Connecticut towns. **Schizophrenia** is a striking disorder that is characterized by unusual thought processes and bizarre forms of self-expression. It is sometimes accompanied by hallucinations. Although genetic factors may play a strong role in predisposing individuals to schizophrenic disorders, their social manifestations can be viewed as problems in the process of communication, especially in role acquisition and the presentation of face. Hollingshead and Redlich found that there was an inverse relationship between social class and schizophrenia. The higher the class, the lower was the percentage of people being treated for schizophrenia. The lowest of five classes made up 17.8 percent of the community's total population, but 36.8 percent of the psychiatric population. It appears, then, that one's social rank may be a factor in determining whether one enters the socially labeled role of a schizophrenic.

The situation in which a person deviates from the norms of the group may also influence whether or not the behavior is judged insane. For instance, the individual who engages in acts of autistic reverie will not be thought insane if this silent musing is confined to times when he or she listens to music. The person who carries on half of a dialogue with what seems to be an unseen partner will not be thought to be mentally ill if there are cues such as age or setting that suggest a plausible alternative explanation—for instance, a child may talk to an "invisible playmate," and an actor or university professor may rehearse lines for a play or public address. Even the person who claims to hear voices that others do not hear or who "speaks in tongues" and makes unintelligible sounds need not be thought of as strange, if he or she does so only during the services of an appropriate religious organization. On the other hand, these same activities performed in other contexts may lead to the practitioner's being labeled insane.

Since the status of the insane is a master status with low access to both power and prestige, once people have been labeled insane they are likely to continue to be thought of as insane, irrespective of their future behavior. One U.S. researcher, David Rosenhan (1973), had himself and several other researchers admitted to a number of U.S. mental hospitals as patients. He and his coresearchers discovered that once they had been admitted, even though they behaved normally, the hospital staff, including psychiatrists, psychologists, and psychiatric nurses, failed to recognize that they were actually sane.

The implication is that the researchers' predicament mirrored what happens in social life outside institutions. Once people are branded with a deviant status associated with an altered state of consciousness, others will assume that all their actions spring from that altered state and therefore withhold power and prestige from them, severely restricting the roles they are allowed to play.

---

schizophrenia a mental disorder characterized by residual rule breaking caused by difficulty in communicating an acceptable social identity; may include hallucinations and ideas about reality that are greatly at odds with mainstream ideas

CHAPTER SUMMARY

1. From an anthropological perspective, personality is an individual's patterns of behavior that express the various social roles he or she has learned to play.

2. As children, we are socialized to fit into the patterns of our society. As we take on roles, we learn the behaviors that are considered appropriate for them.

3. These behaviors are what others perceive as our personalities.

4. Kardiner popularized the concept of basic personality structure.

5. The socialization customs of each society engender different anxieties in children, and these are expressed in various ways.

6. The socialization that is the source of our personality differences results in the patterns of male and female personality characteristics that are found in societies throughout the world.

7. The social roles that define our personalities are also not the same in every culture.

8. National character studies were an attempt to identify the psychological characteristics of entire societies.

9. The Human Relations Area Files (HRAF) is used to test a variety of hypotheses about relationships between specific customs and personality traits.

10. Each society includes different statuses, each with its own culturally defined roles. Normal day-to-day behavior in any society is a matter of trying to play those roles appropriately.

11. In every society, people deviate from their expected roles in ways that may be approved as creative or stigmatized as unacceptably deviant.

12. The stigma of inadequate role playing is often accompanied by emotional distress and sometimes by trances, altered states of consciousness that are interpreted in most societies as evidence of the influence of supernatural forces.

13. Ritual behavior is another common result of anxiety. Rituals may be used to control anxiety. Quite often they take the form of religious acts.

14. Those who have such experiences too frequently may be reassigned to a master status such as that of insane person, a status that implies an inability to control one's own behavior.

15. The insane status is found in every culture, but cultures differ in how it is understood and how it is expressed.

ANNOTATED READINGS

Barnouw, V. (1985). *Culture and personality* (4th ed.). Homewood, IL: Dorsey Press. An introductory-level text on psychological anthropology.

Bateson, G. (1985). *Naven: A survey of the problems suggested by a composite picture of the culture of a New Guinea tribe drawn from three points of view* (2nd ed.). Stanford, CA: Stanford University Press. The analysis of a Iatmul ritual that led to Bateson's revolutionary theory of schizophrenia.

Bock, P. K. (1988). *Rethinking psychological anthropology: Continuity and change in the study of human action.* New York: W. H. Freeman. A brief introduction to psychological anthropology.

Freilich, M., D. Raybeck, and J. Savishinsky. (1991). *Deviance: Anthropological prespectives.* Westport, CT: Bergin & Gavey. Emphasizes the role of culture in defining what is normal.

LeVine, R. A. (1982). *Culture, behavior, and personality: An introduction to the comparative study of psychosocial adaptation* (2nd ed.). Chicago: Aldine Press. An important viewpoint about psychological anthropology for students seeking more than a basic introduction.

Marsella, A. J., DeVos, G., & Hsu, F. L. K. (Eds.). (1985). *Culture and self: Asian and Western perspectives.* New York: Tavistock Publications. A current examination of the experience of self from a cross-cultural perspective.

Morris, B. (1994). *Anthropology of the self: The individual in cultural perspective.* Boulder, CO: Westview Press. An ethnopsychological examination of concepts of the individual, self, and self-perception.

Price, W. F., & Crapo, R. H. (1995). *Cross-cultural perspectives in introductory psychology* (2nd ed.). Minneapolis/St. Paul, MN: West Publishing. Twenty-eight vignettes about cross-cultural research that illustrate various aspects of human psychology.

Shweder R. (1991). *Thinking through cultures: Expeditions in cultural psychology.* Cambridge, MA: Harvard Univerity Press. Provides a good overview of contemporary approaches in psychological anthropology.

Simons, R. C., & Hughes, C. C. (1985). *The culture-bound syndromes: Folk illnesses of psychiatric and anthropological interest.* Boston: D. Reidel Publishing Company. The most comprehensive survey of the culture-specific mental disorders available. Each disorder is described and then analyzed in terms of contemporary Western psychiatric classification.

CHAPTER FIFTEEN

Aesthetics and Culture

After reading this chapter, you should be able to:

Discuss the cultural relativity of aesthetics.

Define and illustrate the concepts of aesthetic experience and expressive culture.

Define the nature of play and explain its psychological functions.

Explain the relationships of art to play.

Explain the roles of form, feelings, and meaning in art.

Outline the various forms of art.

Analyze the social functions of art.

◀ *Figure 15.1 Cultural Aesthetics As many people of the same culture emigrate to different parts of the world, they take much of their culture with them. As one way of preserving that culture, they organize festivals and parades, where a functional as well as expressive aesthetic is displayed. This marcher at the West Indian American Day Parade in Brooklyn, New York, displays the striking mask and face painting indigenous to his Caribbean heritage.*

The human condition includes the ability to experience pleasure in various ways. The expression of these experiences is the basis for play, recreation, ritual, and art, the most distinctive characteristics of a culture. Art is a particularly intriguing and many-faceted aspect of expressive culture in which people find beauty in the skilled production of meaningful forms as diverse as painting, sculpture, music, dance, and aesthetic forms of speaking. This chapter defines the various categories of expressive culture and analyzes the functions of art in human life.

Beauty. Pleasure. Disgust. Appreciation. Connoisseurship. Gourmet. Gourmand. Artist. Critic. Dada. "Primitivism." Kitsch. Pornography. Sensuality. Jazz. Baroque. Rap. However beauty is defined, humans everywhere react to some things as beautiful and to others as ugly. In this chapter, we will explore the nature of the aesthetic experience and the ways it is culturally patterned.

THE RELATIVITY OF AESTHETICS

The parts of an ideology that comprise the rules by which beauty is to be evaluated are called the **aesthetics** of a culture. Not all cultures have a formally articulated aesthetic, but when members of any society express aesthetic judgments, it is possible to infer the rules to which their evaluations about beauty conform.

Cultural Differences in Aesthetics

Most of the languages of nonliterate societies lack a word for art. This is because in many societies what we call art does not belong to a circumscribed sphere of life, a domain of specialists, but is integrated into the day-to-day activities of the ordinary member of society. Thus, many cultures lack a conceptual category of art as an activity or a class of objects not because of an absence of aesthetic appreciation but because art is part of daily living in these cultures. People everywhere sing, dance, and decorate themselves and the objects that they use, placing value only on the beauty they see in such acts. What they lack is not a sense of artistry but a concept of "art for art's sake." Phrased in this way, the difference between cultures that have such a category and those that do not can be readily understood in *social* terms: a vocabulary that includes the word "art" is the product of a society that has professional artists, persons who make their living by the production of objects that are valued primarily for their aesthetic qualities rather than for their common or utilitarian ones.

Aesthetic Locus.   Maquet (1986) has noted that societies may devote aesthetic effort to different areas of life, and each culture has certain areas in which aesthetic experience is more important than others. He calls such an area an **aesthetic locus** of a culture, which he defines as "the categories of objects in which aesthetic expectations and performances are concentrated" (p. 69). As examples of aesthetic loci he cites the tea ceremony of Japan, the Christian ritual of thirteenth-century Western Europe, and ancestral effigies and masks of many societies in West and Central Africa. Charles Keil (1979) describes dance as the central aesthetic locus of Tiv culture, a horticultural society in West Africa. Men's dances are displays of strength, speed, and agility. They often convey a message that mockingly portrays the effects of disease, sequences of skilled dance being interspersed with segments in which the dancers break step, stagger, and grimace as if from the effects of various dire illnesses. Their dance styles change rapidly; new steps invented by creative individuals are adopted by others and then just as quickly replaced by other fads as new styles are invented. Tiv dance troups tour the country, earning money and fame.

Diversity in Aesthetic Standards.   From culture to culture, standards of aesthetic judgment vary. For instance, Tipilit Ole Saitoti (1986), a Masai visitor to Germany, described his reaction to German chamber music:

---

aesthetics the rules by which beauty is to be evaluated in a culture

aesthetic locus the area of a culture to which a society devotes its aesthetic effort

One Sunday I was wandering along Ludwig Strasse when I struck up a conversation with a young German woman. She took me to an old church. Two men were before an audience. They held two musical instruments between their knees and shoulders and rubbed them with sticks. They produced strange melodies that rose and fell like waves.

This was the first time I had heard such music, and I was not at all impressed. At the end of each performance the audience stood up and clapped, and the men on the stage bowed their heads in appreciation. The whole thing went on and on, and I was getting bored. My companion loved the show and was very disappointed when I told her that I did not like it. She insisted, *"Das ist gut, das ist gut."* I was used to African rhythms you could dance to, such as Congolese drumbeats. The young woman and I never saw each other again. (p. 108)

A formal set of rules for evaluating the beauty or effectiveness of a work of art is most likely to exist only if a society treats the realm of art as one for specialists. For instance, Charles Keil (1979) reports that the Tiv have no word for art and no accepted principles for distinguishing such things as good carvings from bad ones. Nevertheless, they do make individual judgments about which carvings are well done and which are not. Thus, even in societies that have no such specialists, informal aesthetic standards exist implicitly in the consensus of public opinion.

In contrast with the Tiv, the Yoruba, an agricultural people of Nigeria, have a well-developed set of standards for judging beauty in art. Robert Thompson (1968, 1973) had Yoruba critics rank works of sculpture and explain the basis of their judgments. By comparing the opinions of many individuals, he found over a dozen general principles that guided Yoruba aesthetic evaluations. Some of these rules are clearly distinctive to Yoruba aesthetics. For instance, the Yoruba felt that the major parts of a sculpture should be clearly visible, as should any designs with which they were decorated. They also valued sculptures that depicted people in their prime over carvings that portrayed older people, and open-mouthed figures were considered particularly unattractive.

Not only do societies differ in the rules that govern aesthetic standards, but works of art are also not necessarily thought of as creative productions of individual artists. For instance, Paul Bohannan (1961) reported his difficulty in adjusting to the "communal" approach of the Tiv to creating and decorating objects. At one point during his fieldwork, he bought tools and tried his hand at making stools and chairs.

But I was not allowed to do it myself. The moment I rested, some bystander would take up the adze and get the work a little farther forward. I, in Western tradition, had a feeling of complete frustration because my "creativity" and my ability were being challenged. For a few days I tried to insist that I wanted to do the work myself, but soon had to give it up because everyone thought it silly and because no one could remember my foible. Eventually, several of our chairs and stools "didn't turn out too badly." I had a hand in all of them, but they are not my handiwork—the whole compound and half the countryside had worked on them. (p. 90)

This communal approach to art was not unique to making furniture. For instance, Bohannan observed the same group involvement in the decorating of personal items such as staffs:

The most astounding feature, to me, was that comparatively few of the designs were made by a single individual. As I sat watching a young man of about thirty carve a stick one day, he was called away. He laid aside his stick and the double-edged knives with which he was cutting the design. A guest came in a few moments later, picked up the stick, and added a few designs. A little later, he handed it on to someone else. Four men put designs on that stick before the owner returned and finished it. When he had done so, he held it out for me to copy and said, "It turned out pretty well, didn't it?" (p. 90)

Any society may have formally defined standards of aesthetic judgment and attribute the beauty of individual artworks to the skill of their creators. Yet, a formal aesthetic is most common in complex societies where the economy supports aesthetic specialists such as professional artists and art critics.

Hindu aesthetics illustrates the presence of explicit aesthetic standards in a society with specialists who produce and analyze art. According to Richard Anderson (1990), the Hindu

THE FOLK ART OF SWEPT YARDS IN GEORGIA, ALABAMA, AND SOUTH CAROLINA

A folk art with roots in West Africa lives on in the yards of African Americans in the rural U.S. South. Richard Westmacott (1994), a professor

FIGURE 15.2

SWEPT YARDS

Yards with no grass, swept clean with a broom made of branches gathered in the woods, were the most important "rooms" of the West African household. Slave quarters were cramped and hot, so you washed and cooked outside, and when the meal was over, everything could be swept into the fire. The tradition is carried on in the rural U.S. South through yards like Magnolia and Andrew Moses's in southeast Athens, Georgia.

of landscape architecture at the University of Georgia, has described the custom of creating swept yards decorated with flowers and shrubs among rural African Americans. The custom of sweeping the ground around houses to keep it free of grasses and weeds was brought from West Africa by slaves. In the hot southern summers, a swept yard created an outdoor room that was a cooler place for cooking than an indoor kitchen would have been. Because of its utility, the custom was readily adopted by white slave owners as well.

What distinguishes the swept yards of rural African Americans is their distinctive gardening style. Since decorative shrubbery for hedges and foundation plantings is expensive, the tradition that has been inherited from the earlier times of slavery is to plant a smaller number of shrubs and flowers that were useful as well as decorative; each plant was set out in a location chosen for its ecological soundness or where it was likely to be needed.

Yards are decorated with other objects, not just with plants. For instance, colored bottles might be used to line a walk, and stone slabs from quarries where members of a family worked might be brought home to make an outdoor table. Decorating with objects that were commonly available or no longer useful allows a lot of improvization influenced by what happens to be available. Hubcaps can be an attractive addition when nailed to a gate, or a leaky birdbath can be reused as an interesting planter.

Improvization and building an art form out of discrete elements that are not marshalled into regimented patterns is not unique to the art of swept yards, but are themes that recur in other contributions of the African American heritage to U.S. aesthetics. Similar themes can be noted, for instance, in the improvization and playful inventiveness of jazz and decorative arts such as quiltmaking.

philosophy of art was founded on the concept of *rasa*, "the sensuous pleasure that the aesthetically attuned individual may experience as a result of art—the thrill of excitement or, at the least, the soothing of grief, that can come about when a person is immersed in an art" (p. 166). *Rasa* implies an experience of oneness between the audience and a work of art, a state in which the work of art evokes one of nine basic human emotions—happiness, pride, zest (or laughter), sorrow, anger, disgust, fear, wonder, or tranquility. According to Anderson, "the capacity to feel delight is the basis of erotic art, laughter is elevated by art to become comedy, sorrow is transmuted into pathos, and anger is the basis of furious art" (p. 168). In the state of aesthetic oneness between the beholder and the work of art, a basic human emotion is transformed into a higher feeling, one in which the audience can experience itself at one with Brahma, the highest manifestation of God as Absolute Being, who transcends the limitations of the senses.

So in Hindu philosophy, the essential quality of the aesthetic experience is its ability to help people transcend the idiosyncratic qualities of personal experience and the limitations of mundane senses in order to achieve oneness with that transcendent reality. In this tradition, art does not merely serve religion in the sense of providing moral instruction or of instilling emotions appropriate to a religious setting, as might the murals in a religious building. Art can be coequal with meditation or ritual as an independent way of experiencing the divine. Indeed, according to the oldest Indian aesthetic tradition, recorded in a third-century document called the *Nāṭyaśāstra*, Brahma himself created art for the pleasure and betterment of the lesser gods and of mortals.

THE AESTHETIC EXPERIENCE AND EXPRESSIVE CULTURE

Although beauty may be defined differently from culture to culture, the **aesthetic experience**, the pleasure we feel when we recognize something as beautiful, is universal. There are many phenomena that can involve us in an aesthetic experience. Some, like a beautiful sunset, a magnificent vista, the dancing flames in a fireplace, or an awesome thunderstorm, are natural. Others, like an attractively woven basket, an ornamental rug, or an unforgettable melody, are cultural. The ability to appreciate beauty in things—the capacity to take pleasure in the senses—is a biologically based capacity that we all share.

The aesthetic experience is similar to other positive emotional states that occur in real-life settings in which emotions influence our responses as participants. In the aesthetic experience, the same emotions may be evoked even though the situation does not involve our actual participation. As observers, rather than participants, we are able to experience those emotions in a more distanced, reflective way. Thus, for instance, we experience aesthetic feelings when a work of art reminds us of one we might love, of a cause we might take pride in,

or of successes worthy of striving for. The various ways in which aesthetic pleasure is given cultural form constitute a society's **expressive culture** which includes aspects of life as diverse as play, games, festivals, sports, and the arts.

Play

Common among mammals, including humans, play has never been defined in a way that everyone accepts. It seems to be intrinsically pleasurable behavior even though it does provide practical benefits—the practice of skills that will be used in goal-oriented ways outside the setting of play. Play also has an important symbolic component in which we act out feelings and preoccupations, often in a trance-like state of mind in which fantasy and imagination overshadow the real world. So one way of defining **play** is as a stress-relieving ritualistic practice of potentially utilitarian behaviors, in which the perception of external things is altered by the participant's own fantasy. Thus, in play, a broom may become a horse to ride, or a chair may become a castle.

Although we sometimes play as adults, spontaneous play is more typical of childhood. It seems to have a number of characteristics that are particularly beneficial to children. Since children lack the experience and skills necessary for adult functioning, they are likely to experience repeated stress because of their inability to perform many tasks that they attempt. The fantasy of play provides the opportunity to practice various tasks without experiencing anxiety about lack of skill. The pleasurable quality of play provides the motivation for repetition and practice which, in turn, helps children become proficient in motor activities, including complex sequences of acts. The mental component of play allows them to externalize their fantasies. Children can thus project into the outside world those things that are of current concern to them. How this process can help to alleviate stress is most clearly seen in the case of fears. When a child pretends that a pillow is a shark or a crumpled sheet a ghost, the signs of real fear may be evoked

---

aesthetic experience the pleasure we feel when we recognize something as beautiful

expressive culture expressions of culture such as play, ritual, or the arts

play stress-relieving ritualistic practice of potentially utilitarian behaviors

FIGURE 15.3

PLAY

Play may be defined as intrinsically pleasurable be-
havior, as a symbolic practice of utilitarian skills, or
as a stress-relieving ritual. These Chinese Buddhist
monks say their prayers as they prepare for a ride
on the sky coaster at the Pacific National Exhibition
in Vancouver, Canada.

when the object is approached or brought
closer. These fear signs usually alternate with
laughter and a cathartic release as the child
suddenly retreats from the fear-evoking object.
This cycle may be repeated many times, as the
child alternately seeks to increase the level of
fear and then to discharge it. The experience
itself may involve real physiological fear. But,
as long as the child is able to remember that
the situation is only one of "make-believe," he
or she is learning that fears are controllable. As
the experience of controlled fear is generalized
to the thing represented by the play object, the
fear of that thing is gradually diminished.

A. C. Cain (1964) observed this process in
a group of children who were mental patients:

> A considerable component of the erratic be-
> havior of these children has a conscious ele-
> ment—that is, they are "playing crazy." Much,
> though by no means all, of this activity centers
> around their past experiences of and continual
> concerns about "being crazy." While playing
> crazy may be very quiet and subtle or blatant
> and obvious, identified as "pretend" by the
> child or exhaustively "defended" as crazy, it

takes varied forms: "looking odd," staring off
into space, or acting utterly confused; wild,
primitive, disorganized, ragelike states; odd
verbalizations; incoherencies; mutterings; al-
leged hallucinations and delusions; the child's
insistence that he is an animal, goblin, or other
creature; or various grossly bizarre behaviors.
Most of the children show many of these
forms of playing crazy and make clear—
though by no means reliable—announcements
that they have played crazy or intend to do
so, or speak of "just pretending."

> At times, the child is quite consciously, de-
> liberately, almost zestfully, playing crazy—he
> is under no significant internal pressure, is
> completely in control, and at the end is most
> reassured. For if one can openly *pretend* to be
> crazy, how can one really be crazy? (pp. 281–
> 282)

Play, of course, may be stimulated by
stresses other than those derived from lack of
skill, but reduction of the effects of stress—from
whatever source—is a consistent factor in play.
Indirect release from the subjective aspects of
stress accounts for another central quality of
play: the pleasure that participants derive from
it. People sometimes report that they engage in
play for the pure fun of it. But notice that this
can be understood as being equivalent to saying that when one plays, subjective distress—
the opposite of pleasure—is decreased.

Games

Games are more formally structured than spontaneous play. According to Kendall Blanchard
and Alyce Cheska (1985), a **game** is "a competitive activity that involves physical skills, strategy, and chance, or any combination of these
elements" (p. 60). J. Roberts, M. J. Arth, and
R. R. Bush (1959) view games as models of the
conflict-producing situations in society that create anxiety. Games provide an outlet for the expression of anxieties by permitting reenactment
of conflicts in a nonthreatening setting, as well
as a safe chance to practice the skills needed in
conflict situations. Societies with a simple social
organization are unlikely to use games of strategy; societies with a complex social organization
are. In simpler societies, children are encouraged

---

game a competitive activity involving physical skills,
strategy, and chance in a model of a conflict-producing real-life situation

to be assertive, so strategy is a less important social skill than in more complex societies.

Roberts and Sutton-Smith (1962) found that games of strategy are most popular where obedience is stressed in childrearing. Such games may well reflect anxiety about powerlessness among children who lack the determination to achieve many of their goals directly. Games of chance, on the other hand, are more popular in societies in which duty and responsibility are stressed during socialization. Such games may represent a form of defiance, a psychological release from anxiety about having to be responsible. These researchers also found that games of physical skill tend to be preferred when independence is emphasized during childhood socialization. Such skills help children to succeed at tasks that they undertake at their own initiative.

Festivals

Public, secular celebrations, such as festivals carried out for pleasure, are probably the most widely practiced form of adult play. Festivals occur at predictable times of year. They sometimes have religious or political overtones, but they often function as a cathartic outlet from the routine stresses of life. In contemporary nation-states, hundreds of thousands of people may gather for parades, dancing, and other forms of enjoyment at holiday celebrations such as Mardi Gras in São Paulo, Fasching in Hamburg, or New Year's Eve in New York City's Times Square and in other major cities of America and Europe. Children sometimes have special festivals, such as Halloween, reserved for their own entertainment.

Sports

According to Blanchard and Cheska (1985), **sport** is "a physically exertive activity that is aggressively competitive within constraints imposed by definitions and rules" (p. 60). Sports are more ritually patterned than games. The cultural element of sports can be seen by examining the changes that occur when a sport is borrowed from one culture by another. For instance, when cricket was taken over from the English by the Trobrianders, they transformed it to fit their own traditions of intergroup competition between villages by embellishing it with traditional warfare symbolism.

FIGURE 15.4

SKILL IN ART

While most non-Western cultures don't have a concept of "art for art's sake," they do recognize the fact that some artists have greater skill than others. Skill in art involves arranging the materials in an aesthetically pleasing manner, arranging instrumentation in a musical score, or choreographing the steps to a dance. This Inuit is preparing his sculpture in his studio.

Art

Art is more than the experience of pleasure or the manifestation of skill. It is a human product that involves skill in its production, evokes feelings, and as Jacques Maquet (1986) succinctly puts it, "is a part of a socially constructed reality" (p. 8). **Art** is, in other words, a phenomenon of culture, a symbolic expression that is meaningful within a particular cultural tradition and that evokes an aesthetic experience. Alexander Alland (1977) has suggested that art is a kind of "play with form" whose products

---

sport aggressively competitive activity played according to strict rules

art a cultural expression of feeling and meaning in a form that evokes an aesthetic experience in the participant or observer

SHOSHONE ART

Once, while I was doing fieldwork in Nevada, a Shoshone friend of mine, Dannie Millet, and I were talking about Shoshone music. He described the music that he used to sing at Fandangos, where people gathered from miles around to enjoy themselves. Songs, he said, were often accompanied by a percussion background of drums or rasps. On impulse, he decided to make a musical rasp and demonstrate it for me. It only took a minute for him to find a cottonwood branch under one of the nearby trees. Then he set about whittling a series of notches down one of its sides. Using a pot from my kitchen as a sounding board, he played and sang some traditional songs so I could hear what Shoshone music sounded like. In his younger days, he said, he had known enough songs to sing from sunset to sunrise. He graciously let me keep the rasp.

The next morning Dannie called on me unexpectedly. Although it had worked perfectly well as a musical instrument, Dannie had been dissatisfied with the instrument he had made on such short notice. The branch that he had found the day before was curved and somewhat asymmetrical. It looked like a branch with notches cut on it, not like an instrument. So that night when he went home, he had spent some time searching out a more suitable branch from which to carve a rasp that was more pleasing to the eye. He had selected a straight branch, about a foot long, and had carefully cut away its surface bark. Then he notched it evenly from one end, but left a suitable hand-hold area at the other. The finished product gave evidence of his skill as a craftsman. It didn't play any better as a percussion instrument—not, at least, to my untrained ear. But it was a better instrument, because Dannie had endowed it with a beauty his first rushed job had lacked, a visual form that demonstrated his technical skill as its maker and that was more pleasing to the eye. Here was art in its most fundamental sense, art as an expression of the artist's desire for a beauty of form that went beyond mere functionality.

are aesthetically successful and culturally meaningful (p. 39). Unlike ordinary play, it is performed with conscious attention to the meaningfulness of the acts of play or its products.

Although all art involves our senses in ways that demonstrate technical skill in its production, arouse feelings, and convey a message, these three components of art may not be equally prominent in a particular artistic product. This is true whether the work is in the visual arts such as painting or sculpture, the auditory arts such as music, or the kinesthetic arts such as dance. So artistic products of all types can be classified by their relative emphasis on feelings they arouse, the skill with which they were produced, and the meanings that they embody.

Skilled Production of Form. Although art has much in common with play, it is more than just play. The artist gives conscious attention to how the artistic activity is carried out in a way that is not present in the spontaneity of play. Therefore skill in the production of form has been held by many to be a fundamental quality of art. As long ago as 1916, Franz Boas (1940) observed that "All art implies technical skill" (p. 535). Nevertheless, as a disciplined variety of play, artistic acts are creative and innovative within the constraints of the rules that define each form and its various culturally recognized styles. The artist explores the current conventions of an established artistic style, creates new variations on the themes those rules imply, and sometimes alters those rules in creative new ways. An appreciation for the skill of its producer is also an important aspect of the aesthetic experience of the observer of art.

Artistic skill includes the artist's mastery of execution and judgment about the qualities of form of the artistic product. Skill in organizing the composition is crucial to the aesthetic experience in all forms of art. It can be found in the arrangement and choice of instrumentation in a musical score, in the choice of colors and the balance of different forms within a painting, in the choreography of dance, or in the arrangement of acts in a play.

The Expression of Feelings in Art. Artistic acts and play are both self-rewarding activities that express feelings. Both may be pleasurable and provide cathartic release from the stresses of daily life and work. Also like play, the artistic frame of mind has been described repeatedly in terms suggesting an altered state of consciousness. Artists sometimes describe their creative ideas as if they come to them from somewhere outside themselves, like revelations. In general, all creative acts are intimately related to altered states of consciousness, which in turn are responses to and statements about the stresses of life (Koestler, 1964). Like play, the acts of art are expressive of the hopes, fears, and desires of the actor, but in art, the expressive signs of the tension that exists between reality and desire are consciously refined.

All art expresses feelings as well as craftsmanship and meaning, but there are, historically, styles of art in which emotion is particularly prominent. In European history, for example, both the music of the Romantic period, which followed the more formal Baroque era of music, and the "Sturm und Drang" literature of German writers such as Lessing and Schiller are highly emotional, as are contemporary U.S. horror movies.

Meaning in Art.   In addition to the characteristics that it shares with play, art has meaning and makes an intentional statement. Because it is intended as communication, art implies an audience, real or potential, even if the audience is the artist alone. The artist transforms raw, natural signs, such as smiles and tears that have universal meanings and that are used intuitively by others, into the symbolic conventions of his or her own culture. Yet a skilled work of art may be appreciated beyond its original cultural setting. Because symbols of art are derived from natural signs, commentators sometimes speak of art as using a universal language or as making a statement that transcends the narrow confines of its society or time. Nevertheless, since the artistic transformation involves the elaboration of natural signs into a symbolic statement that is particularly meaningful within the cultural tradition of the artist, no work of art is truly universally meaningful.

Intellectual art in which the meaningful component is highly emphasized can be exemplified by propagandistic art, the drawings of political cartoonists, and iconoclastic art such as the works of Andy Warhol and the students of Dadaism. Intellectual artistry is often an important component of the verbal arts, but all forms of art make a meaningful statement. For instance, in the Western musical tradition, Bach, one of the last Baroque composers, is known for the "intellectual" nature of his music. Though his music may be admired for its beauty and the interplay of melodies, he is nevertheless particularly remembered for the re-

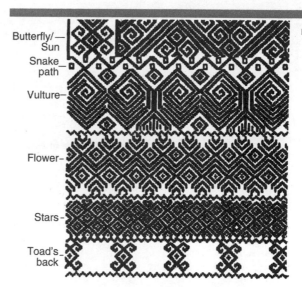

FIGURE 15.5

Butterfly/Sun
Snake path
Vulture
Flower
Stars
Toad's back

MAYAN GARMENT DESIGN

The artist communicates meaning by transforming natural phenomena into designs that are particularly symbolic of her or his culture. The traditional Mayan huipil, a rectangular hand-woven shawl, is decorated with diamond patterns that represent the cosmos, the vulture, a symbol of the weaver's community, and the toad, representing rain and fertility. The ancient weavers of these designs symbolically placed themselves at the center of the world, close to the ancestors who interceded for them with requests to the gods who control order, rain, and life on earth.

markable ways in which his music incorporated meanings for those who could discover them. For instance, in his final work, his own name is spelled out in the musical notes employed in its melody—a fact that a German listener is more likely to discover than a British or American, since the German musical scale includes an H as well as an A, B, and C.

ART FORMS

Anthropological research has looked intensely at the products of artists as accessible descriptors of a particular culture. The major categories of works of art with which anthropologists generally have dealt are visual arts, music, dance, and verbal arts.

The Visual Arts

Probably all languages have a word that stands for visual beauty. In English we say that some

CAVE PAINTINGS

In December 1994 over 300 paintings and engravings were found in a limestone cavern in a gorge near the Ardeche River in southern France. Included in the artworks were a pair of fighting rhinoceroses, a pack of lions, horses' heads, cave bears, and human handprints. Researchers were able to determine the age of the paintings by dating the charcoal pigments used in them and found that they were created 20,000 to 22,000 years ago, making them the world's oldest known artworks.

The images are sophisticated in their use of shading and the overlapping of figures to give depth to the paintings. In some cases, the natural curvature of a rock was used to give dimensionality to a painting. The unknown artists also used techniques for portraying motion, and the paintings include running and leaping animals and even animals fighting or stepping on one another. One drawing is an imaginative composite figure that combines the upright legs of a human being with the head and hump of a bison.

The sophistication of the artistic techniques indicates that art did not evolve gradually from crude beginnings, but that human artists even during the earliest period of the human species were as capable as those of later times.

FIGURE 15.6

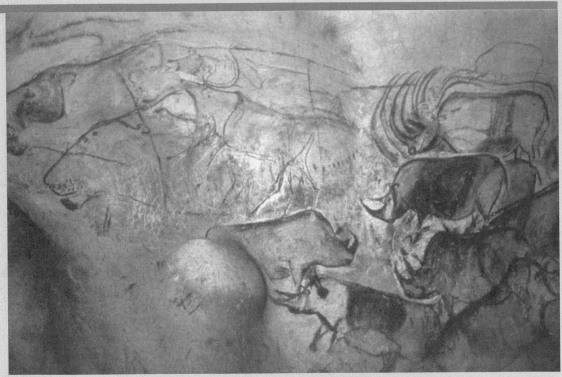

STONE AGE MURALS

In 1994 French explorers found approximately 300 paintings and engravings preserved in the darkness of an underground limestone cavern near the town of Vallon-Pont-d'Arc. Drawn in colors of red hematite, ochre yellow, and hues of charcoal, specialists believe they were made some 20,000 years ago. The technique of depicting motion is evident in the portrayal of rhinos overlapping each other, shown at the right of this detail.

things are "good looking." In Shoshone they are *caan na-pui-tyn*, literally "good itself-looking." The Navajo speak of scenery or a location as hó-zhó-ní (literally, "location-beauty-is"). So it is not surprising that there are a large variety of ways of expressing visual beauty, including decorating the human body, designing physical objects that people use, such as baskets, and expressing feelings in paintings and sculpture.

Body Decoration.   People throughout the world decorate their bodies in various ways to make themselves beautiful. Common forms of body decoration include clothing and jewelry, makeup, tattoos, and scarification. The beauty conferred by decorating the body can have a variety of purposes. For instance, personal adornment may be used to make individuals more attractive, uniforms and decorative insignia may communicate their rank or occupations, and costumes may facilitate play and recreation, sometimes by hiding people's identities and status or even by making them less attractive.

Decorative Arts. Sometimes objects are made for purely aesthetic reasons. Paintings, murals, mosaics, and sculptures may be done solely to decorate the environment of a home or workplace. In societies with professional artists, objects of this type may also be treated as "art for art's sake," and stored in museums or privately owned. Similar objects can be found in less complex societies as well. These tend to be of a more personal nature: aesthetic objects of religious significance such as medicine bundles (rabbit's feet, four-leaf clovers, or other personal religious objects); fetishes (objects containing spirits); mandalas (objects to look at while meditating); ceremonial masks; or paintings used in religious ceremonies.

John Fischer (1961) compared the pictorial art of complex, socially stratified societies with the art of egalitarian societies (those that are usually organized into small, self-sufficient communities, with little differentiation of activities, statuses, or rank). He found that, regardless of the specific symbols used, art in egalitarian societies tends to use symmetrical designs and repetition of simple features. Much of the available space is left empty, and figures are not enclosed by a formal boundary. In stratified societies, by contrast, pictures tend to be asymmetrical and composed of dissimilar elements that are integrated into the full design. The tendency is for little empty space to be left within the field of works of pictorial art, and figures are often enclosed by well-defined boundaries.

Fischer speculated that symmetry may reflect the basic similarity of the generalized statuses within the egalitarian communities; repetition of simple elements may reflect the similarity of individuals. He suggested that the asymmetrical design of the art of stratified societies may reflect the specialized differences and ranking of statuses; the integration of diverse elements into the design may mirror the high degree of specialization and integration of diverse statuses in complex societies. Fischer also suggested that the greater use of empty space in the art of simple egalitarian societies may represent their relative isolation and self-sufficiency. By contrast, the filling of empty space in the art of complex societies may stem from the lack of isolation of individuals, who learn to find security through establishing a place for themselves in the network of statuses that makes up the community. Similarly, the enclosing boundaries may represent the imposition of controls on the behavior of individuals—since many rules imposed from above is a social trait most characteristic of the socially stratified societies.

Music

The study of **music**, rhythmically organized, scaled tones that produce melodic sound, and its relationship to culture is the subject matter of a specialized subfield of anthropology called **ethnomusicology**.

Scales. A **scale** is a sequence of tones that ends with a return to a tone that has a frequency twice that of the starting tone. The European tone scale with which Americans are familiar is an octave of eight tones (CDEFGABC) in which one of two different pitch intervals may occur between each succeeding tone pair. In any sequence of eight tones of increasing pitch, the eighth will have a frequency of twice that of the first tone, which has the psychological effect of making it sound like a higher pitched version of the first. The pitch intervals between succeeding tone pairs (C-D, D-E, F-G, G-A, and A-B), called "whole steps," are twice the interval between the two remaining tone pairs (B-C and E-F), which are called "half steps," the interspersion of whole and half steps depending on the particular scale. Since the Middle Ages, European music has also employed five other tones within the octave (C#, D#, F#, G#, and A#), each of which is a half step above or below its adjacent tones.

Ethnomusicologists have discovered that very different musical scales are found in many other societies. These include scales of as few

---

music rhythmically organized scaled tones that produce melodic sound

ethnomusicology the study of music and its relationship to culture

scale a sequence of tones that ends with a return to a tone that has a frequency twice that of the starting tone

as 2 or 3 tones or more than 12. Scales of 5, 6, or 7 tones are the most common. For instance, the Japanese use a scale whose octaves are of 5 equidistant notes, the Javanese use scales of 5 and scales of 7 notes, and Arabic music uses octaves of 17 and 24 tones. Most musical scales are rooted in a single tone to which melodies frequently return and on which they end.

Barbara Ayres (1968) has found cross-cultural support for connections between childrearing practices and tonality. Noting that laboratory animals that were stressed before weaning engaged in more exploratory behavior as adults, she suggested that a similar relationship might be found in humans between early stress, such as scarification, nose piercing, or circumcision before two years of age, and extensive tonal ranges in adult music. Alan Lomax (1962) found another intriguing cultural difference in tonal ranges: the pitch interval in song was greater in foraging societies where the group had to cover larger territories in the quest for food.

Rhythm. The timing and stressing of tones within a melody is called **rhythm**. It is highly varied from society to society. For instance, rhythm may be characterized by patterns of stressed tones arranged in regular groupings, or meters. Western music traditionally relies on meters of two, three, four, or six beats, with variations in the patterns of which beats are stressed and which are unstressed. Asymmetric meters are also possible and are quite common in Asian music. Much African drum music is characterized by great rhythmic complexity in which accents, meters, or even beats change in different segments of the music.

Ayres (1973) also examined the rhythms infants are exposed to when carried, to see if these influenced the rhythm of a society's music. She found that when children are regularly carried in slings, pouches, or shawls, so that they experience the movement of walking by the person who carries them, musical rhythms tend to have regular beats. In contrast, where children are strapped to a cradle board or spend time in cradles, the rhythms of adult music tend to have irregular beats or free rhythm.

Lyrics. Musical melodies can be hummed or chanted, using nonsense syllables to sing the tones. In all parts of the world, music is sometimes conveyed with **lyrics**, words that convey a message. Music was studied in great detail by Lomax (1968), who found the songs of complex societies to be wordier than those of simple societies. He pointed out that precision in enunciation also tends to increase with social complexity. Lomax noted that choral singing and counterpoint, the addition of independent melodies above or below the main one, are most common where cooperative labor is the hallmark of work. Polyphony, the singing of two or more melodies simultaneously, is most common in societies where women contribute at least half of the food.

Dance

Rhythmically patterned human movement performed for aesthetic pleasure is called **dance**. It is typically accompanied by music or song, and often has a place in religious ritual as well as in secular life. Lomax (1968) studied dance as a cultural art form, and found that "movement style in dance is a crystallization of the most frequent and crucial patterns of everyday activity" (p. 237). For instance, the postures adopted in work frequently are found in the dance style of a society. Dance styles also vary between societies with simple subsistence technologies and those with complex food production techniques. For instance, foraging bands and gardening tribes make more use of simple up-and-down movements such as hopping and side-to-side steps such as shuffling, while the dance styles of agricultural chiefdoms and states are more likely to include movements in many parts of the body, such as the hands, arms, and torso (Lomax & Arensberg, 1977).

The Verbal Arts

The **verbal arts**, sometimes called **oral literature**, include myths, legends, rhetoric, folktales, proverbs, riddles, jokes, and other forms of art that are based on language and that enrich the human experience.

---

rhythm the timing and stressing of tones within a melody

lyrics words in a musical piece that convey a message

dance rhythmically patterned human movement performed for aesthetic pleasure

verbal arts (oral literature) various forms of speaking for aesthetic pleasure, including orating, reciting myths, and telling folktales

oral literature verbal arts

Myths. Stories that recount the origin of such things as the gods, the universe, human beings, animals, and plants are considered **myths**. They may explain how human ways of life began, the nature of death, and the afterlife. Usually myths are placed in the distant past and involve supernatural beings. For example, the Shoshone of the Great Basin desert tell of a time when the sun was so close to the earth that people were dying, and the plants of the earth were burned up so there was no food to be found. Cottontail, one of the creatures of the earth, determined to kill the sun and set things right. He took some rocks as weapons and traveled toward where the sun rises until it got too hot for him. Then he began to burrow until he got to his destination. He made a hunting blind and waited until the sun came up. When the sun arose, Cottontail threw a rock at the sun and killed him. It was so hot that Cottontail was scorched, which left him brown, as he is to this day. After a while, the sun revived, but Cottontail removed the sun's gallbladder and told the sun that he must go up higher in the sky so that all people might have light to gather food, but not be burned. Out of the sun's gallbladder, Cottontail fashioned the moon, which also went up to the sky.

According to Clyde Kluckhohn (1965), five themes seem to be found in the myths of every society: great natural catastrophes (most often by flood, but sometimes by earthquake, hurricane, or fire); monster slaying; incest (usually by brother and sister); sibling rivalry; and castration (in real or, more often, symbolic form). The list clearly deals with anxiety-related matters that must be dealt with by peoples the world around.

Legends. **Legends** are very similar to myths but usually deal with a more recent period of time. Their central characters are heroes and heroines of great stature who are usually responsible for the origin of a particular society or culture. Although they are usually regarded as real persons, they are often thought to possess superhuman qualities and to embody the central values of their society. The legendary figures of U.S. culture are noted for their individualism, self-reliance, strength, and cleverness. They stand up for their ideals against great odds, triumphing over adversity. George Washington is one legendary figure who actually existed, yet time has endowed him with stature somewhat above that of a real person.

He is remembered in U.S. folklore as being unable to tell a lie even as a child. At one time, it was said that he was strong enough to have thrown a silver dollar across the Rappahannock River. In many parts of the country, the river in this story has become the much wider Potomac. Other U.S. legends are based on purely fictional characters, like Johnny Appleseed, whose exploits included the planting of apple trees throughout the New World.

Legends are not limited to stories that claim to have been passed down from an earlier era. New legends can arise in each generation and be an active part of people's sense of their current place in the broader scheme of things. For instance, legends of a hitchhiker who admonishes people about their obligations and then vanishes mysteriously have been common for generations in the American West. In early October 1992, I heard a contemporary version of this legend by a woman who told me that an acquaintance of hers had been driving near Ogden, Utah, when she picked up an elderly hitchhiker with white hair and a white beard. He asked her if she had enough food in storage to see her through difficult times. When she responded that she did not, he told her that she should have a good food supply laid aside by January. When she next looked in the rearview mirror, he was no longer in the back seat of the car. Shocked, she pulled to the side of the freeway to ponder the remarkable incident. Shortly thereafter, a highway patrol officer stopped to see if she needed any assistance. When she recounted her experience, the officer told her that she was the sixth person who had told him the same story that day. The vanishing hitchhiker legend has a very active life. A week after I heard this particular version, the Salt Lake City newspapers reported that many people were telling variations of the same tale, and the highway patrol office had received numerous calls of inquiry. Such stories function to support an Intermountain tradition of self-sufficiency, an important social value in this U.S. subculture.

Rhetoric. Formal speech that follows the traditional rules of a particular culture is called

---

myths stories that recount the origin of such things as gods, the universe, animals, and plants

legends stories that describe heroes and heroines who are usually responsible for the origin of a culture or society

FIGURE 15.7

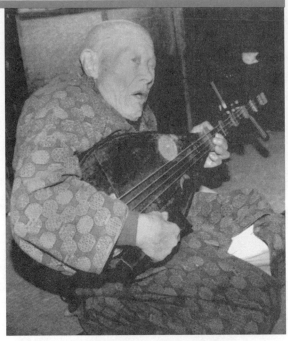

YOSHIYUKI YAMASHIKA

In 1992, at the age of 91, Yoshiyuki Yamashika was believed to be the last surviving biwa hoshi, or lute priest, of Japan. By tradition, biwa hoshi are blind men who made a living by wandering through Japanese towns chanting tales of intrigue, treachery, and loyalty, accompanied by a lute. It is believed that Yamashika knows 50 or more tales, some of which last, in the telling, for about 10 hours. In an era of satellite television, when few people are interested in hearing the stories, and no one is taking the time to learn them and become a biwa hoshi, historians and anthropologists are rushing to record as many of his tales of ancient Japan as they can.

rhetoric. Most societies acknowledge a distinction between ordinary, everyday speech and elegant speech used for special occasions. It is particularly common in societies with class differences to provide formal education, at least to the elite members of society, in styles of public speaking that are judged to be refined and aesthetically pleasing. For instance, among the Aztecs, members of the nobility received special training in public speaking, including the use of metaphors, poetry, proverbs, and other ways of embellishing their speaking. Effective speech was so highly valued by the Aztecs that they had many euphemisms for describing people's manner of talking: an argumentative person who insisted on the last word was "wooden-mouthed"; when one was too easily offended and responded by scolding others it was said that "words are

his food"; a chatterer was "swallow-mouthed," and the Aztec ruler was called the *tlatoani*, "the one who speaks," because his authority derived from his oratorical skills.

Folktales.   **Folktales** are fictional stories that are told primarily for entertainment, but also teach a moral principle or a practical lesson. Aesop's fables capture the essence of folktales told both for pleasure and to teach a lesson, as do many of Grimm's fairy tales. Folktales are commonly placed in a timeless setting and vague location. They portray the basic dilemmas with which people must grapple as they strive to attain the goals of their culture. For instance, many European folktales are built around the theme of a poor but beautiful young girl who is often mistreated by her evil stepmother or sisters but who, by some type of magic or supernatural intervention, is rescued from her life of drudgery and raised to high status as the wife of a handsome prince. Against the backdrop of European social systems in which the female role traditionally included domestic chores and economic dependence on an income controlled by fathers and husbands, such folktales can be seen as stress reduction through wish fulfillment. They also contain the moral: dutiful little girls will be rewarded. In the United States, a popular series of folktales are those about the fictional character Paul Bunyan, whose exploits included the creation of Puget Sound. The telling of Paul Bunyan stories reinforces historic U.S. values of expansiveness and pride in heroic individualism.

Folktales include many forms of storytelling and humor that communicate messages of folk wisdom, giving people a sense of their common heritage and cultural identity. This can be illustrated by the common Sufi stories about the wise fool, Mulla Nasrudin, who, through his foolish simplicity, teaches important moral principles. For instance, in one story, Nasrudin began a sermon to a crowd by announcing that he had a message of the greatest importance and asking them if they knew what he was about to tell them. When the people responded that they did not, he walked away muttering that if they were so unenlightened, it would be a waste of time trying to explain

---

rhetoric formal speech that follows the traditional
   rules of a particular culture
folktales stories told for entertainment that teach a
   moral principle or a practical lesson

it to them. When he returned the next day and posed the same question, the audience, thinking they had better answer differently than they had the day before, called out "We do! We do!" To this, Nasrudin responded, "Well, then I don't need to explain it to you!" and left. On the third day, the villagers, hoping to maneuver Nasrudin into revealing his secret, had prepared themselves by agreeing that half the crowd would say yes, but that the other half would say no. But upon receiving this mixed response to his query, Nasrudin simply said, "Then let those who know explain it to those who do not," and left. To Sufis, this tale, told with much humor at Nasrudin's failure to reveal an important message because of his own foolishly concrete interpretation of what others said to him, does contain an important message. It reiterates a Sufi belief in the foolishness of seeking truth in an intellectual treatise instead of by listening to God through one's own heart.

Proverbs.   Like myths and legends, **proverbs** embody the basic values of a culture, but in a form that can readily express issues that concern people in a particular society. Their brevity makes it possible for proverbs to be inserted into conversations, where they can be used to cast light on the topics being discussed, comment on the propriety of a state of affairs, call others to take action, or even mildly rebuke another person without direct confrontation. In accordance with the work ethic, Americans remind each other that "the early bird gets the worm." The Aztec leader who was informed about disputes among the commoners might have responded, "My task is to guard turkeys. Shall I peck at those who peck at one another?" He meant that it was no more his fault that the commoners contended among themselves than it was the fault of the turkey guardian that turkeys pecked one another. Proverbs are often highly idiomatic, using symbolism that is drawn from the life experience of a particular society. For this reason, they may be difficult for members of other societies to decipher correctly.

Riddles.   **Riddles** are mental puzzles told for entertainment. By describing common things in novel ways, they challenge hearers to exercise their ability to see similarities between common things that are not usually associated with one another. They are a source of information about the things that a people consider noteworthy in their environment, how they classify things, and what aspects of things they judge to be relevant. For instance, Aztec riddles about spindles are often related to pregnancy. Perhaps the most obvious analogy is that the spindle grows in size as it is filled, just as a woman does in pregnancy. However, a more subtle message carried by these Aztec riddles is one of classification: they reiterate the idea that the spindle is symbolically associated with the woman's role.

Jokes.   **Jokes** and other forms of humor have long been recognized for their role in helping people relieve the tensions of their way of life. Since the major anxieties differ from society to society, so does the type of humor. Consider the Inuit of northern Alaska and Canada. They live in a harsh environment that challenges the limits of their skill. The ability to endure pain and to cope skillfully with potentially disastrous situations is necessary for survival in the far north. The people's reaction to many near-disasters is one of mirth. For instance, they might laugh uproariously at the tale of a party of travelers who are spilled into the wet snow, lose their dogs when their sled tips over, or lose their sled when it slides from the trail onto rotten sea ice and breaks through. Despite the inconveniences, a true disaster has been avoided. Even those who were involved in the situation might react with immediate laughter at their relief, before settling down to the unpleasant task of retrieving their dogs and damaged goods.

The Olfactory and Gustatory Arts

Smell and taste are the chemical senses. Their evolutionary importance has often been linked to their role in the recognition of what is edible and what is not. Just as vision and hearing are important to many forms of artistic expression, the senses of smell and taste also have been sources of aesthetic experience. For instance, perfumes and scents have been used since early times to make people more attractive. The ancient Egyptians mixed perfumes into cones of butter that they placed on their heads during parties so that the melting butter would release a pleasant scent. Today, perfume production is

---

proverbs short statements that illustrate the basic values of a culture

riddles mental puzzles told for entertainment

jokes humor that serves to help relieve the stress of everyday life

TEA CEREMONY IN JAPAN

One of the most famous artistic functions of food is the role of tea in the Japanese tea ceremony called *chanoyu*, "boiling water for tea." The tea ceremony has its origins in Kyoto during the fifteenth century. The custom of drinking *matcha*, powdered green tea whipped into boiling water, had been brought to Japan from China by Japanese Zen Buddist monks trained in China during the thirteenth century. Tea was used in temples as an aid to meditation.

The aesthetic emphasis in each tea ceremony was the concept of *wabi*, or elegant simplicity, which highlighted the transience of human life and the importance of experiencing each gathering in the seclusion of the tearoom as a unique and valuable moment.

The basic pattern of a ceremony begins with the cleaning of the tearoom hut and the surrounding garden. The host lays a fire in a sunken hearth or brazier and begins to boil the water, then places a scroll and flower arrangement in the utensil alcove. To prepare the tea, the host must wipe the tea scoop and ladle with a silk cloth, remove the lid from the boiling kettle, and place it on a special stand. The host then washes the bamboo whisk and wipes the tea bowl with a cotton cloth. Two scoopfuls of tea are put into the bowl, and a ladleful of hot water is poured into it. The mixture is whisked into frothy tea that is served to the first guest as the host bows. Each guest is served in the same way, and as each finishes drinking, the host cleans each tea bowl. The host then removes the implements to their alcove and bows to the guests from the pantry.

The austerity of the tea ceremony and its symbolism of humility and simplicity are captured in a poem by Fujiwara Teika (1162–1241):

As far as the eye can see,
No cherry blossom,
No crimson leaf,
A thatched hut by an inlet,
This autumn evening.

a multibillion-dollar-a-year industry worldwide. Various kinds of incense are burned to produce an attractive scent in the rituals of diverse religions. For instance, the Aztec and Maya of Middle America used a resin called copal as well as pine pitch as an offering to the gods, and Christians, Hindus, and Buddhists throughout the world burn incense as a symbol of purification, prayer, and piety.

The enjoyment of food involves both taste and smell. In all societies, individuals express preferences for one food over another, and sometimes make judgments about how well a food has been prepared. In some cultures, the ability to make such judgments is the basis for an aesthetic of foods and eating. For instance, the French distinguish between the *gourmand* and the *gourmet*; English speakers contrast the glutton with the epicure. But even in societies that may lack terms to distinguish one who takes aesthetic pleasure in food and eating from one who merely eats without aesthetic reflection, eating is sometimes an event of special importance that is expected to bring particular pleasure.

Special attention to food preparation can have important significance in religious settings, at important family functions, and as an aspect of political ceremonies. In the United States, most families have formal practices that relate to meals on at least certain holidays, such as Passover, Christmas, or Thanksgiving Day. In tribal societies, food preparation and feasting is a common part of the celebrations hosted by big men and big women, and sharing food can be an important act in finalizing political arrangements between allies or former enemies.

In chiefdoms, the high rank of political leaders is often acknowledged by sumptuary laws that permit certain foods to be eaten only by the chiefs. For instance, Trobriand Island chiefs were ceremonially presented the finest yams as gifts from members of their wives' clans, and only chiefs were permitted to have the best gardens. In societies that have class distinctions, rules of etiquette that distinguish upper-class members of society from others always include rules about socially preferred ways of preparing, presenting, and eating foods, and sumptuary rules may also distinguish the aristocracy from commoners in the kind of foods that each may eat.

THE FUNCTIONS OF ART

Art has an effect on the individual and on a particular culture in a society. Psychologically, art enhances life by adding beauty to our surroundings. It is a source of pleasure and relaxation from the stresses of life. Socially, art plays a number of different roles by virtue of its capacity to embody symbolic significance for its audience.

Art and Social Organization

Art fulfills a number of important social functions. It is used to communicate the various statuses people hold. It can play a role in regulating economic activities. And it is almost always a means for expressing important political and religious ideas and for teaching principles that are valued in society. These and other social uses of art function to preserve the established social organization of each society.

Status Indicators

One of the social functions of art is the communication of status differences between individuals. For instance, gender differences in body decorations and dress are typical of cultures throughout the world. Age differences may be similarly indicated. Puberty rituals often include tattooing, scarification of the body in decorative designs, or even filing of the teeth to distinguish between children and adults. Social class differences in complex societies also involve aesthetic markers such as the clothing people wear and the kinds of artworks they use as decorations of their homes.

Economic Functions

Economic life, by virtue of its practical importance to our survival and to our standard of living, can sometimes be a source of conflict between groups that must carry out exchange with one another. Sometimes art, perhaps because it is valued for its nonutilitarian qualities, can play a role of maintaining harmony in such settings. This was one of the functions of the Kula Ring exchange of ceremonial necklaces and armbands among islanders such as the Trobrianders and Dobuans (see chapter 8, p. 206).

Religious Functions

Much of the dramatic and emotional impact of religion derives from its use of art. Religious rituals everywhere include song and dance performances, and the visual arts function to

FIGURE 15.8

ART AND POLITICS

Art can be utilized as propaganda when governments need to legitimize their policies or to elicit loyalty from the people. These women of the Malawi Congress Party's Women's League wear dresses decorated with the portrait of their leader, Life President Hastings Kamuzu Banda, as they greeted his return to Blantyre, Malawi's largest city, in 1993.

heighten the emotional component of religious experience in all parts of the world by portraying important scenes and symbols from religious history and mythology. In some cultures, art and religious ritual are inseparable. For instance, among the Abelam of Papua New Guinea, all art is produced for use in rituals.

Didactic Functions

Art is often employed as a means for teaching important cultural ideas and values. For instance, hymns in Western religions express theological concepts and encourage the support of specific religious values. Daniel Biebuyck (1973) has analyzed the use of art to embody moral and ethical principles by the Lega people of Central Africa. Lega ethical ideals are codified in figurines of humans and animals made of ivory, pottery, bone, wood, and wickerwork. The figurines are used in the initiation and training of men into prominent positions within Lega society. Each of these statues is associated with one or more aphorisms, a concise statement that alludes to a general ethical concept. For instance, one figure is a carved stick

> whose top is slit so as to suggest an open mouth. . . . The object illustrates the saying, "He who does not put off his quarrelsomeness will quarrel with something that has the mouth widely distended." (In other rites this idea may be rendered by a crocodile figurine with widely distended jaws.) The aphorism alludes to the disastrous effects of quarrelsomeness and meddlesomeness. (p. 217)

Thus, Lega figurines were not only works of art but also devices for teaching important moral principles to each new generation. At the same time, their ownership by older men who had achieved initiation into the highest levels of society functioned to perpetuate respect for the moral wisdom of the leaders in the established social hierarchy.

Political Functions

Art often functions to legitimize the authority of government. Mount Rushmore, in South Dakota, memorializes four U.S. presidents who were selected for their symbolic association with messages about values of individualism and democracy. The statue Mother Russia commemorates the enduring will to survive of the Russian people. The British Crown Jewels, by

virtue of their artistry and the symbolism of precious stones that originated throughout the Commonwealth, celebrate the value of the institution of the monarchy. And the ornately carved Golden Stool of the Ashante of southern Ghana, with the distinctive myth of its supernatural origins, reinforces the legitimacy of the Ashante king and the unity and stability of Ashante society. Douglas Fraser's (1972) account of the myth of the Golden Stool illustrates the interconnectedness of art and the social order. In this story, the chief priest of the first king of the new Ashanti Confederacy

> promised the king and the nation that he would call down from the skies a supernatural stool of solid gold which would enshrine and protect the soul of the nation. As a precondition to fulfilling his promise, however, he demanded that the ancestral (blackened) stools, state shields, state swords, and other regalia of all the member states be surrendered to him. This was done, and he buried them in the bed of the Bantama River in Kumasi. The purpose of this action was twofold: to ensure that no item of regalia in the new kingdom could have a longer history than the Golden Stool and hence take precedence over it, and, by depriving the formerly independent states of the relics of their respective pasts, to pave the way toward a new and broader union. (pp. 139–140)

As a statement about the legitimacy of governmental authority, art is a conservative force in society. In this role, it is intended to elicit loyalty and to stabilize society and its political system. Governments also sometimes deliberately employ this aspect of art as propaganda urging public action that supports official policy. Thus, propagandistic art embodies both didactic and political functions.

CHAPTER SUMMARY

1. Art is a culturally relative phenomenon, both in the degree to which explicit aesthetic rules exist for judging artistic beauty and in the nature of those rules.

2. In all societies, human beings take pleasure in the experience of beautiful things.

3. The aesthetic experience is culturally organized into activities such as play, recreation, ritual, and art.

4. Play is the spontaneous stress-relieving behavior in which the practice of potentially utilitarian skills is facilitated by fantasy.

5. Recreations such as games, sports, and festivals are socially organized forms of play.

6. Art is a disciplined form of play that utilizes the skilled production of forms that are both expressive of feelings and culturally meaningful.

7. The art forms of any society may be classified by the senses that they predominantly utilize.

8. Art fulfills a variety of social functions, including communicating status, facilitating economic processes, instilling rituals with meaningful feelings, supporting the political system, and teaching social values.

ANNOTATED READINGS

Alland, Alexander. (1977). *The artistic animal.* New York: Doubleday/Anchor Books. A simple introduction to the biological basis of and the cultural influences on art.

Anderson, R. L. (1990). *Calliope's sisters: A comparative study of philosophies of art.* Englewood Cliffs, NJ: Prentice Hall. A comparative study of the aesthetics of 10 societies, ranging from foragers to industrialized agriculturalists.

Anderson, R. L. (1989). *Art in small-scale societies* (2nd ed.). Englewood Cliffs, NJ: Prentice Hall. Discusses the ways art is conceptualized and how art functions in nonindustrialized societies.

Anderson, R. L., & Field, K. (1993). *Art in small-scale societies: Contemporary readings.* Englewood Cliffs, NJ: Prentice Hall. First-hand accounts by ethnographers who explore their own attempts to understand the roles and meanings of art during fieldwork in nonwestern societies.

Blanchard, K., & Cheska, A. (1985). *The anthropology of sport.* South Hadley, MA: Bergin & Gavey. An introduction to the study of sport within an anthropological framework.

Coote, J., & Shelton, A. (Eds.). (1994). *Anthropology, art and aesthetics.* Oxford, England: Clarendon Press. A sophisticated collection of articles that present a variety of anthropological approaches to art and aesthetics.

Dundes, Alan. (1980). *Interpreting folklore.* Bloomington, IN: Indiana University Press. A collection of articles on the study of folklore.

Hannah, Judith L. (1979). *To dance is human.* Austin, TX: University of Texas Press. A cross-cultural study of dance that examines the functions of dance in various kinds of social organizations.

Lomax, Alan. (1968). *Folksong style and culture* (American Association for the Advancement of Science, Publication No. 88). Washington, DC: American Association for the Advancement of Science. The groundbreaking study of folksong styles throughout the world.

Maquet, Jacques. (1986). *The aesthetic experience: An anthropologist looks at the visual arts.* New Haven, CT: Yale University Press. An anthropological approach to the visual arts that integrates the study of Western and non-Western traditions into a single model.

GLOSSARY

Page references indicate where term is defined.

acculturation the process in which one culture adapts to the influence of another culture by borrowing many of its traits 161

achieved statuses social positions that one acquires by demonstrating the necessary role-playing abilities 63

adaptation adjustment of an organism to a particular environment 137

adulthood ritual puberty ritual 94

aesthetic experience the pleasure we feel when we recognize something as beautiful 389

aesthetic locus the area of a culture to which a society devotes its aesthetic effort 386

aesthetics the rules by which beauty is to be evaluated in a culture 46, 386

affectlessness the complete control of emotion resulting in lethargy 367

affines kin related through a marriage link 244

agriculture the form of intensive cultivation that uses tools and techniques such as irrigation, animal traction, and fertilization of the soil 154

alienation dissociation of workers from ownership of things they produce, accompanied by feelings of powerlessness and boredom 166

allomorphs variants of a single morpheme that have the same meaning but different phonological structure 307

allophones phonetically variant forms of a single phoneme 307

altered state of consciousness trance 367

ambilineal descent a system of tracing descent through a parent of either sex, choosing only one parent for each link that connects a group of relatives 246

ambilineal descent group a system of tracing social groups based on an ambilineal descent system 247

ambilocality bilocality 238

American Anthropological Association major professional organization for anthropologists in the United States 10

American Sign Language (ASL) a system of hand gesture symbols used by hearing-impaired persons for communicating; a true, though nonvocal, language that has its own grammar and vocabulary 303

amok a culture-specific hysterical disorder in which young men attack other people and destroy property 376

amurakh arctic hysteria 377

ancestral spirits souls of ancestors who remain interested and involved in affairs of their descendants 329

anger an emotional state during which another person is held responsible for one's own distress; may substitute for anxiety, fear, guilt, grief, or shame in situations in which those emotions might otherwise be felt 367

animal-focused foraging fish and animal life provide basic food supply where plants are scarce 143

anorexia nervosa a culture-specific obsessive-compulsive disorder characterized by an unrealistic appraisal of one's own body as overweight and by self-starvation 380

anthropological linguists cultural anthropologists who specialize in the study of communication, human languages, and their role in human social life 19

anthropomorphism using human qualities to explain the nonhuman realm; interpreting or acting toward the nonhuman realm as if it were human, especially as if it were able to respond to symbolic communication 323

antinatalist societies societies whose customs favor low birth rates and thus permit abortion and infanticide 68

anxiety a distressful subjective awareness of stress; a general sense of powerlessness and foreboding without awareness of a specific danger 367

applied anthropology the attempt to use anthropological skills and insights to aid in the process of cultural development in nonindustrialized parts of the world or to aid in private and public policy making 20, 183

archaeologists cultural anthropologists who study the material remains of earlier societies in order to reconstruct their cultures 17

arctic hysteria (amurakh) a culture-specific hysterical disorder that is characterized by compulsive imitation of sounds and gestures 377

arid lands areas of low annual rainfall and sparse cover with low-growing desert shrubs 135

art a cultural expression of feeling and meaning in a form that evokes an aesthetic experience in the participant or observer 391

ascribed statuses social positions that one is assumed to occupy by virtue of the group into which one happens to be born—for instance, one's sex or race 63

association cortex the area of the cerebral cortex that coordinates information from various other parts of the brain 304

attitude a subjective reaction to an experience expressed in positive or negative terms 46

authority the right, delegated to a person or persons, to use force or threaten the use of force legitimately 262

avunculocality the custom of newly married couples establishing residence with or near the groom's mother's brother 238

balanced reciprocity gift given with expectation of a return gift shortly 205

band a seminomadic, kinship-based society with no full-time government, economically based on a foraging subsistence technology 140, 262

barter form of exchange of goods by trading 210

Basic Law of Cultural Evolution the concept that increases in energy harnessed or in efficiency of its use through technological change are the primary cause of cultural evolution 162

basic personality structure the distinctive ways in which a person behaves, thinks, and feels based on his or her cognition of self 359

basic vocabulary the part of a vocabulary that one learns early in life in the home setting 312

behavioral superstructure those behaviors most closely linked to a culture's ideology, including art, ritual, recreation, philosophy, and science 33

beliefs ideas people hold about what is factual or real 42

berdache a social status in which males and females adopt the role of the other sex; considered a third gender in some societies 113

bifurcate merging kinship terminology derived from contrast between maternal and paternal relatives using a small number of kin terms to refer to many different kin 254

bigmanship economic entrepreneurship by persons in horticulture societies who encourage economic production and gift giving in their communities to achieve public recognition and respect 208

bilateral cross-cousin marriage more descriptive term for sister exchange 234

bilateral descent a system of tracing descent lines equally through both parents 245

bilateral descent groups groups whose members share a living relative 247

bilocality (ambilocality) the custom in which a newly married couple may elect to set up residence with or near either the bride's or the groom's family 238

bint'amm patrilateral parallel-cousin marriage 234

biological and psychological needs the needs for nutrition, reproduction, bodily comforts, safety, relaxation, movement, and growth 28

biological anthropologists physical anthropologists 19

biological death measured by cessation of such organic functions as breathing, heartbeat, reaction to pain, or brain functioning 101

Black English Vernacular the everyday speech patterns of African Americans studied in urban centers 312

blue-collar workers nonfarm manual laborers 202

bone-pointing a magical ritual for killing in which a sharp bone or stick is pointed at or ritually cast into the body of the intended victim 337

boreal forests heavily wooded regions dominated by coniferous trees 136

bound morphemes morphemes that cannot stand on their own as complete words 307

Brahmin the highest-ranked Hindu caste, members of which are theoretically priests 66

brain stem the parts of the brain that regulate involuntary processes such as breathing and heartbeat 301

bride price bridewealth 236

bride service service performed by the groom for the family of the bride to recompense them for her loss 236

bridewealth goods transferred from the groom's kin to the bride's to recompense them for her loss 235

Broca's area the part of the cerebral cortex involved in organizing words into grammatical sequences 304

carrying capacity a particular environment's ability to support a species on the available resources 137

caste a social class determined by birth, so that an individual cannot legitimately change class membership by acquiring a new status 65

cerebellum the part of the brain below and behind the cerebral hemispheres of the brain that functions in the coordination of muscular activity 301

cerebral cortex the surface layer of the two large hemispheres

of the brain that functions in the analysis of sensory experiences and initiates conscious action 301

chief presiding redistributive and political official of a chiefdom society or of a subdivision of a chiefdom, whose legal authority extends in at least some areas over members of families other than his or her own 208

chiefdom a society, often of many villages, that has a government capable of coordinating social action within and between villages but in which governmental authority is balanced by the legal autonomy of families in many areas 266

circumcision the surgical removal of the foreskin from the penis 94

civil religion a system of religious beliefs and values that is integrated into the broader, nonreligious aspects of society and is shared by its members regardless of their affiliation with formally organized religious organizations; in the United States, a system of largely Judeo-Christian religious symbolism within which the U.S. political system is portrayed as divinely sanctioned and members of U.S. society are viewed as God's modern chosen people 348

clan kinship group whose members believe themselves to be descended from a common ancestor far enough in the past that they cannot trace their specific genealogical ties to one another 248

class a broad, ranked stratum within society made up of unrelated families that have more-or-less equal power and prestige 65

cognatic clan (ambilineal clan) clan based on ambilineal descent 248

cognatic (nonunilineal) descent a system of tracing descent bilaterally or ambilineally 246

cognative lineages (ramages, septs) lineages formed using an ambilineal descent system 248

cognitive anthropology ethnoscience 27

colonial peasants members of peasant societies that were politically and economically dependent on a foreign state that perpetuated its economic exploitation of the peasant area by military domination 178

commodities goods, services, and intangible items that are determined to be useful or valuable in a particular culture 194

communal foraging cooperative food gathering where fish and small game are meat resources and plants are easily collected 142

communal religions religions that include the performance of rituals by groups of lay practitioners, shamans, or individuals 344

communication the transfer of information from one person to another using objects and events as signs or symbols 294

communitas Turner's term for a social relationship achieved through ritual in which people feel a sense of unity with each other 332

complementary statuses a pair of statuses, each of which has roles that are different from but compatible with the roles of the other 63

configurationalism Benedict's view of culture as a configuration of values and customs that influence individual psychology 358

consanguines kin related by ties of descent 244

conspicuous consumption the acquisition and use of a surplus of goods as a way of competitively demonstrating one's success and prestige 213

consumer market market in which basic needs of consumers are met by the system of production, and competition for sales may focus on nonessentials 215

consumption final use by a society of goods and services 213

contagious magic ritual coercion of the supernatural realm by the use of the Law of Contagion 334

contextual cues culturally defined indicators such as setting, date, time of day, or the statuses of other persons present that determine which roles are appropriate and

which are inappropriate to play 65

Contrary Warrior a Cheyenne status that required the reversal of all normal behaviors, reserved for the bravest warriors 363

corporate descent groups lineal descent groups 247

corporation association of employers and employees that is legally entitled to act as a single person to produce goods or provide services 215

court formalized institution that asserts authority over parties in a dispute and over persons accused of violating the law 281

couvade a custom in which the husband acts as if he gives birth to his child 89

creativity deviance that results in valuable new contributions to society 365

creoles true languages that have developed out of pidgins 305

crime the harming of a person or personal property by another 286

cross cousins cousins who are related through parents of the opposite sex who are usually brother and sister 234

cross-cultural comparison basing general conclusions about the nature of culture and its influence on society on the comparison of a diverse sample of cultures from many parts of the world, so that those conclusions will be generally valid for the human condition as a whole 15

cross-cultural research research that bases its conclusions on data drawn from many diverse ways of life rather than just one 5

Crow kinship terminology matrilineal descent system where father's matrilineage is distinguished only by sex, regardless of generation 255

cultural anthropologists anthropologists who specialize in the study of specific cultures or of culture in general 17

cultural ecology the study of the ways in which cultures adapt to their specific habitats 30

cultural evolutionism the nineteenth-century emphasis on analyzing cultures in terms of their development through a

series of stages from savagery to civilization 6

cultural materialism approach that analyzes technological and social variables in explaining ideological facts of culture 33

cultural relativism principle that cultural traits are best understood in the context of the cultural system of which they are a part; the attempt to avoid the narrow bias of judging a custom or entire culture on the basis of one's own cultural values; the view that meanings of behaviors are best understood when interpreted in terms of the culture of the actors 7, 51

cultural universals those characteristics of human life that can be found in all human ways of life 22

culture a learned system of beliefs, feelings, and rules for living around which a group of people organize their lives; a way of life of a particular society 17, 38

culture and personality the anthropological field that studies the variety of psychological traits and personality characteristics among cultures 8, 358

culture areas geographical areas in which different societies share a complex of cultural traits due to similar adaptations to their environmental zone and to the effects of diffusion of cultural traits through those societies 7

culture of poverty an approach to life often found in situations of poverty in which actions are directed only to satisfying the needs of the present, by spending and consuming all income, because saving for the future seems futile 181

culture shock the loneliness and depression that are often experienced when one is in a foreign cultural setting 56

"culture-free" intelligence tests tests that are not biased in favor of the values and life experiences (the "culture") of any one segment of a society 80

dance rhythmically patterned human movement performed for aesthetic pleasure 396

descent the cultural recognition of kinship connections between a child and one or both of his or her parent's kin 244

descriptive kinship terminology Sudanese kinship terminology 256

developed country nation in which industrialization has become the primary basis of the economy 172

developing country underdeveloped nation undergoing industrialization 172

deviance behavior that differs enough from what society expects that others notice and react to it 365

deviant a person who has been labeled a rule violator by others for his or her role-playing errors 373

dialects geographical or social subdivisions of a language that differ systematically from other subdivisions of the same language in their vocabulary, grammar, and phonology 311

dialogic model an approach to ethnographic narrative that engages the anthropologist and natives of a culture in a give-and-take exploration of cultural meanings 27

diffusion the passage of such cultural traits as customs, artifacts, and ideas from one society to another 7, 160

diffusionism the early-twentieth-century approach to analyzing cultures that emphasized the historical reconstruction of the influences of one culture on another, in contrast to the more general evolutionary perspective of earlier anthropologists 7

direct borrowing the adopting of a cultural trait by one society from another with relatively little change in form, as exemplified by traits acquired through trade or imitation 160

discovery the development of new insights and ideas 160

disease object an object such as a barbed stick or stone that is magically cast into the body of a victim to cause illness 336

dissociative disorders (hysteria) mental disorders in which anxiety is avoided through the nonvoluntary loss of integration among consciousness, memory, sense of identity, and/or perception of the environment 375

distribution movement of resources or goods from where they are found or produced to where they will ultimately be used 203

divination the use of ritual to obtain answers to questions from supernatural sources 334

division of labor the rules that govern how the day-to-day work of life is divided among the holders of various statuses 64

domestic economy the reproductive, economic, and social behaviors that characterize life within the family or household 33

double descent (double unilineal descent) a system of tracing two separate sets of kin, one designated through mothers only and the other through fathers only 247

double unilineal descent double descent 247

dowry a payment from the family of a bride to the family of her husband to compensate them for their acceptance of the responsibility of her support 236

drives the ideals that people actively pursue, sometimes at great cost, rather than those to which they merely give lip service 47

dry-land gardening horticulture is carried out in arid environments with the aid of simple supplemental watering techniques 149

ecclesiastical religions religions that include not only individual, shamanic, and communal ritual practices but also a coordinating body of priests who perform rituals on behalf of congregations 346

economics system by which people obtain or produce, distribute, and consume material goods and services 194

embarrassment shame 367

emic analysis description of a culture as it would have meaning for an insider 22

emotion a pleasant or unpleasant subjective reaction to an experience, characterized by varying degrees of muscle tension and changes in respiration and heart rate 43

empiricism the viewpoint that conclusions should be based on careful observation and description, rather than on abstract theorizing 7

enculturation (socialization) the process by which children learn the customs, beliefs, and values of their culture 92, 276

endogamy rules rules requiring marriage within specified kinship categories or other specified social or local groups to which one belongs 233

environmental values attitudes that define our relationship to the environment 276

Eskimo kinship terminology bilateral kinship system in which terms for mother, father, brother, and sister are not used for relatives outside the nuclear family 254

espanto susto 378

ethnic group a group whose identity is based on shared customs, especially of immigrants 68

ethnocentrism the attitude that one's own culture is the only good one and that the more other cultures differ from one's own, the more inferior they are 50

ethnocide the systematic destruction of a traditional way of life 170

ethnographers cultural anthropologists who spend prolonged periods living with and describing the cultures of specific peoples 17

ethnographies descriptions of customs, beliefs, and values of individual societies 17

ethnologists cultural anthropologists who formulate general laws of culture based on the study of the ethnographies of many diverse societies 17

ethnomusicology the study of music and its relationship to culture 395

ethnoscience (cognitive anthropology) approach that aims to systematically describe a culture by analyzing the linguistic categories used by informants to discuss their society 27

etic analysis description of a culture in categories based on universal principles 22

etiquette values that govern manners and define what is considered courteous or civil ways of communicating with others 46

eureka experience a sense of intensified meaningfulness of experiences that sometimes occurs during an altered state of consciousness 370

excision surgical removal of all or part of the female clitoris 97

exogamy rules rules forbidding an individual from marrying a member of the kinship, residential, or other specified group to which he or she belongs 233

expressive culture expressions of culture such as play, ritual, or the arts 389

extended families families that include two or more nuclear families and often their parents, who reside together 239

extensive cultivation horticulture that involves the use of land for short periods followed by periods of letting the land stand idle for several years 148

external warfare warfare which is fought for prolonged periods in locations distant from the warriors' home with enemies who speak a foreign language and follow an alien way of life 285

face positive social value a person can contribute to a group; social standing 363

face-work interaction in which effort is directed to maintaining or returning behavior to roles considered appropriate for members of a group; efforts to maintain or reestablish face 363

family the group consisting of married persons, their children, and other relatives who reside with them 239

fear a distressful emotion characterized by concerns about inadequate power to protect oneself from specific danger 367

feelings subjective reactions to experiences as pleasant or unpleasant, good or bad. Feelings include emotions, attitudes, values, and drives 42

female circumcision mutilation of female genitals, including infibulation and excision, a symbol of male dominance in some societies 95

female infanticide the killing of female infants; a major means of population control in societies that primarily engage in internal warfare 285

feminist anthropology the anthropological approach that studies the relationships among social power, social honor, and gender 30, 114

feminization of poverty a growing trend in which women comprise a large proportion of the world's poor 126

feudal peasants food producers in preindustrialized societies who pay rent or perform service for the privilege of farming lands owned by local aristocratic officials, who, in turn, have obligations to provide police and military protection, judicial services, and care for the peasants in times of hardship 177

feuds armed conflicts between kinship groups initiated to avenge a wrong 284

fictive kinship socially created kinship relationships involving individuals who are not otherwise considered relatives either by descent or marriage 257

fictive marriage legal marriage established to allow both partners to acquire social benefits without a family being set up 227

fieldwork the basic tool of anthropological research in which information is gathered from the context in which it naturally occurs 10

Fissure of Rolando a vertical fold in the surface of the brain that separates the motor areas, which control conscious muscle movement, from corresponding areas, which receive sensory information from various parts of the body 304

folktales stories told for entertainment that teach a moral principle or a practical lesson 398

foraging a subsistence technology based on gathering wild plant foods, hunting, and fishing 138

formal learning learning that proceeds by admonition and correction of the learner's errors, with emotional emphasis on the importance of behaving acceptably 93

fraternal groups groups of related males who work together and feel obliged to protect one another's common interests 284

fraternal polyandry form of polyandry in which the husbands are brothers 224

free morphemes morphemes that can stand alone as words in sentences 307

frigophobia (pa-ling) a culture-specific obsessive-compulsive disorder characterized by fear of loss of body heat 379

frontier areas lands unproductive for industrialized agriculture that are opened to settlement by national governments that do not recognize the claims of the indigenous population 168

function the contribution that any one cultural trait makes to perpetuating the unity, equilibrium, and adaptation of a way of life within its environment 8

functionalism the approach to analyzing cultures by examining the mechanics of society while it is in equilibrium, as opposed to the more historical emphasis of diffusionism or the developmental emphasis of evolutionism 8

funeral ritual a rite of passage that formalizes the removal of an individual from the status of living member of the social group 104

game a competitive activity involving physical skills, strategy, and chance in a model of a conflict-producing real-life situation 390

gender social statuses assigned on the basis of cultural concepts about the sexes 108

gender stereotypes preconceived ideas about what behaviors and roles are considered "masculine" or "feminine" 109

gender stratification systematic differences in power and honor between men and women 115

General Adaptation Syndrome the nonspecific changes that occur in the body as a result of stress, as it mobilizes itself to act against the cause of the stress 337

general evolution change in the direction of increasing complexity 165

generalized reciprocity gift given with no expectation of immediate exchange 204

general-purpose money universal medium of exchange used to buy and sell any item 212

genocide the systematic extermination of a people 170

ghost marriages fictive marriages where a married or unmarried close male kinsman of a man or boy, who died before he had any legal heirs, marries a woman in the name of the deceased 229

gift exchange reciprocal exchange of gifts between families who are party to a marriage 237

glossolalia behavior in religious ecstasy that may include groaning and uttering unintelligible sounds 332

glottochronology a technique for calculating the minimal length of time that two related languages have been diverging from a common ancestral language 314

grammar the analysis of the regular ways that the sounds of a language are combined to form meaningful utterances; includes morphology and syntax 307

grasslands areas that cover 26 percent of the earth's surface, with grasses of different types 135

green revolution use of modern plant breeding to produce high-yield, fertilizer-intensive, fast-maturing crops 185

grief a distressful emotion characterized by a sense of loss, sadness, and failure to obtain esteem from others 367

group two or more individuals engaged in a common activity 62

group marriage form of marriage in which two or more men are married to two or more women at the same time 225

guilt a distressful emotion characterized by remorse for having used too much power and having harmed another 367

hallucination a realistic-seeming experience—much like a vivid waking dream—that may include vision, hearing, the sense of touch, smell, and/or taste in the absence of external cause 369

Hawaiian kinship terminology the simplest kinship designation, using the terms parents, siblings, and children 253

hermeneutic anthropology approach that examines the interaction between fieldworker and native informant 26

holistic emphasizing the full range of relations among parts of a system and the ways the operation of those parts helps to perpetuate the whole system 5

homophilic marriage same-sex marriage without transvestism or change in sex role by one of the partners 229

honor the esteem some statuses confer on those who hold them 64

horticulture cultivation of crops using simple hand tools such as the hoe and digging stick and without fertilization of the soil, crop rotation, and often without irrigation 147

household a group of people who share a common residence 239

hsieh-ping a culture-specific hysterical disorder that is characterized by tremor, disorientation, clouding of consciousness, delirium, speaking in tongues, and hallucinations 377

Human Relations Area Files (HRAF) a research data pool containing information on over 335 major societal groups, each coded for the presence or absence of about 700 cultural and environmental traits 16

human soul the supernatural part of the human being that is believed to animate the human body during life or perpetuate the individual's memories or life goals after death 329

hysteria dissociative disorders 376

ice zones regions of permanent snow and ice 136

ideal culture the ways people perceive their own customs and behaviors, often more a

reflection of their feelings and ideals about what they should be than an accurate assessment of what they are 48

ideological communication communication that reaffirms people's allegiance to their groups and creates a sense of community by asserting its ideology 41

ideology the consciously shared beliefs and feelings that members of a society consider characteristic of themselves 40

image of limited good a fatalistic outlook common in situations of peasant poverty, in which the drudgery of life is not believed to bring much reward, since the achievement of one person can only be accomplished at the expense of another 181

imitative magic attempted ritual coercion of the supernatural realm by use of the Law of Similarity 334

imu a hysterical disorder found among the Ainu of northern Japan, characterized by automatic obedience or negativism and uncontrollable imitation of sounds and gestures 377

incest taboo a rule that forbids sexual behaviors between designated kin, including but not limited to intercourse between parents and children and between siblings 231

indigenous people a group of people whose occupation of an area precedes the state political system that now controls that area, and who have little or no influence within that political system 168

indirect dowry payment of goods made by the groom or his family to the bride either directly to her or indirectly through her father 237

individual foraging men and women each gather their own plant foods, with women providing for the children 142

industrialization the process of change from an economy based on home production of goods to one based on large-scale, mechanized factory production 171

industrialized agriculture the use of an industrialized technology and other techniques such as chemical soil fertilization to obtain high levels of food production per acre 155

infibulation surgical closing of the female vulva over the vagina 96

informal learning learning by imitation 92

innovation changes in a culture as a result of discovery or invention 160

insanity process by which a person acquires and maintains deviant master status of residual rule breaker 375

intensive cultivation the use of food growing techniques that permit permanent use of the same fields 154

intergenerational marriage mentorship 230

internal warfare fighting between peoples who share the same language and culture 285

International Phonetic Alphabet (IPA) a standard alphabet of nearly 100 sound symbols used by linguists throughout the world for writing phonetic transcriptions of languages 306

interpretive anthropology approach that attempts to explain how each element of a culture relates meaningfully to its original context 25

intimate distance the distance from their bodies that people reserve for those with whom they are intimate enough to permit casual touching 298

intragenerational marriages pathic marriages 229

invention the act of combining preexisting cultural traits in new ways 160

IQ (intelligence quotient) a standardized score on an intelligence test 77

Iroquois kinship terminology bifurcate merging system like the Crow and Omaha systems but in which there is no merging of generations in the lineage that marries into ego's lineage 255

jati an occupational subcaste in Hindu society 66

jokes humor that serves to help relieve the stress of everyday life 399

kayak angst a culture-specific phobic disorder that is characterized by an inordinate fear of being at sea in a kayak 378

kin relatives based on descent and/or marriage 244

kindred a kinship group in a bilateral descent system that consists of the known relatives of a living individual 251

kinesics the study of the body movements that accompany speech as a component of communication 299

kinship a system for classifying people who are related to one another by ties of descent or by ties of marriage 244

koro a culture-specific anxiety disorder characterized by fear of death through loss of sexual essence 379

Kshatriya the second most important of the Hindu castes, members of which were the traditional warrior-rulers, nobles, and landowners 66

language a system of rules that govern the production and interpretation of speech 301

latah a culture-specific hysterical disorder that is characterized by uncontrollable imitation of the actions and speech of others 376

law cultural rules that regulate human behavior and maintain order 278

Law of Contagion the principle that things that have been in contact remain supernaturally in contact or that contact between things can be used to transfer mana from one to the other 334

Law of Cultural Dominance the principle that the cultural system that effectively exploits the energy resources of a given environment has the tendency to spread into that environment at the expense of less effective systems 162

Law of Evolutionary Potential the concept that a culture's capacity to move from one general evolutionary stage to another varies inversely with the degree of its specific evolutionary adaptation to its environment 165

Law of Local Discontinuity of Progress the idea that the successive stages of general evolutionary change are not likely to occur in the same locality 165

Law of Similarity the principle that things that are similar to

one another are spiritually identical and can be used in rituals to influence a desired outcome 334

legal authority the right to compel others to obey the law and to punish those who violate it 278

legal rights and duties rules that define relationships between people by specifying the type of recompense an injured person should receive 278

legends stories that describe heroes and heroines who are usually responsible for the origin of a culture or society 397

levirate a rule that requires kin of a deceased man to provide his widow with another husband, often one of the deceased man's brothers 227

life cycle the status changes from birth to death that are typical of a particular society 84

limbic system areas within the brain that deal with emotional experience 304

liminal period transition stage between the beginning and end of a ritual 333

lineage a kinship group whose members can trace their lines of descent to the same ancestor 248

lineal descent groups groups whose members share a common ancestor 247

linguistic relativity the idea that the characteristics of a language influence the way that its speakers think 308

lyrics words in a musical piece that convey a message 396

magic the use of rituals that, when performed correctly, are believed to compel—as opposed to simply making requests of—the supernatural to bring about desired results 333

maintenance system the parts of the economic and social structure of a society that determine its childrearing practices 360

male-ranked polygyny with related co-wives a more descriptive term for sororal polygyny 223

male-stratified polygyny form of polygamy in which a small number of men of high rank and authority marry a larger number of wives 224

mana supernatural power or force 322

market a system of distribution for goods and services based primarily on the use of established locations 210

marking the idea that the behaviors of a woman during pregnancy may influence the physical or psychological characteristics of the unborn child 86

marriage a rite of passage that unites two or more individuals as spouses 220

marriage preference rules systems that single out certain kin as ideal marriage partners 234

Marxist anthropology the study of the effects of class conflict on social and cultural change 29

master status a social status that is so important that it cannot be ignored 67

matriclan clan based on matrilineal descent 248

matrifocal societies societies in which the primary solidarity relations involve women 271

matrifocality a form of society in which high social status is assumed by females primarily because they control food production and because the male is absent much of the time 119

matrilateral cross-cousin marriage marriage between a male and his mother's brother's daughter 234

matrilineage a system of tracing descent lines through mothers 248

matrilineal descent a system of descent traced through mothers only 247

matrilocality uxorilocality 238

mediation negotiation between conflicting parties carried out by a neutral third party 281

mentorship form of marriage between an older, socially established partner and a younger spouse of the same sex 230

metacommunication system a system of communication that includes the capacity to communicate about itself 300

minorities those with a low-ranked master status, commonly but incorrectly called "minority groups" 68

mixed forests regions of conifers and broadleaf trees in temperate climates 134

modal personality type the most common or typical pattern of personality traits in a society 360

mode of production the work practices by which people apply their subsistence technology within a particular environment 33

mode of reproduction the technology and practices operating within a particular social environment that influence the size of the society's population 33

moiety one of two basic complementary social subdivisions of a society 249

money standard medium of exchange that has a mutually agreed-upon value 211

monogamous marriage form of marriage where one man and one woman are joined as husband and wife 223

monotheism the belief in a high god, a supreme being who either created the physical universe and other spiritual beings and rules over them or who at least maintains the order of the universe today 328

moral values attitudes or rules that govern our relationships with our fellow human beings 276

morality values concerning proper and improper ways of treating other human beings 46

morpheme the smallest meaningful sequence of sounds in a language 307

morphology the study of how phonemes are combined into the smallest meaningful units of a language 307

mountain lands a variety of environments, often within short distances of one another 135

multilinear evolution an approach to cultural evolution that emphasizes the divergent paths that each culture follows as it adapts to its local environment 29

music rhythmically organized scaled tones that produce melodic sound 395

myths stories that recount the origin of such things as gods,

the universe, animals, and plants 397

naming ceremony a rite of passage following birth, at which the infant is declared a member of the human group by being given a name 91

national character studies an attempt to identify the psychological characteristics of entire societies 360

natural selection the process whereby those members of a species that are better adapted to their environment contribute more offspring to succeeding generations than do other members 137

negative reciprocity one group or individual in a reciprocal exchange system attempts to get more than it gives 207

neocolonialism the contemporary world system of economic exploitation of underdeveloped nations by the developed centers of economic power, in which underdeveloped nations' participation is enforced by economic necessity rather than by political coercion. 145

neoevolutionism a view of cultural evolution that describes culture as "a mechanism for harnessing energy and of putting it to work" and that measures cultural evolution by the amount of energy that a society's technology harnesses per capita per year 28

neofunctionalism contemporary approach to studying functional processes of cultural systems, with emphasis on the ways in which conflict may be one of the mechanisms by which cultural stability is maintained 29

neolocality the custom of newly married couples setting up residence in a new location apart from either spouse's family 238

nonindustrialized (traditional) agriculture intensive cultivation using simple tools such as hoes, shovels, and animal-drawn plows 154

nonscientific beliefs beliefs that grow out of people's feelings 43

nonsexual marriages marriages that fulfill economic, social, and kinship functions without sexual union between the partners 227

nonunilineal descent cognatic descent 246

nonverbal communication all transfer of information beyond words alone, involving such things as volume, pitch, tone of voice, and speed when speaking, as well as non-oral things such as gestures, posture, and use of space and time 297

nuclear family the form of family that consists only of married persons and their children 239

oaths ritual acts of swearing innocence on pain of punishment by deities 283

Olympian religions polytheistic ecclesiastical religions in which the gods or supernatural beings may be loosely ranked but in which no one of the supernatural beings is truly supreme over the others 346

Omaha kinship terminology patrilineal descent system where mother's patrilineage is distinguished only by sex, regardless of generation 255

optimal foraging theory principle that foragers use food resources in direct proportion to the caloric effort required to obtain them 143

oral literature verbal arts 396

ordeals tests of guilt or innocence by enduring dangerous or painful acts 283

ownership the right to use property and the right to deny use rights to others as long as one owns the property 198

pa-ling frigophobia 379

parallel cousins cousins whose common parents are either two brothers or two sisters 234

participant observation the technique of cultural anthropology in which the researcher spends a prolonged period participating with and observing subjects in their natural setting, as opposed to studying them in a laboratory setting 11

pasmo susto 378

pastoralism a subsistence technology based on animal husbandry 152

pathic marriages same-sex marriages involving gender-role change in one partner 229

patriarchy a form of society in which access to social power and prestige is available primarily to men 118

patriclan clan based on patrilineal descent 248

patrilateral cross-cousin marriage marriage between a male and his father's sister's daughter 234

patrilateral parallel-cousin marriage (bint'amm) marriage between a male and his father's brother's daughter 234

patrilineage a system of tracing descent lines through fathers 248

patrilineal descent a system of descent traced through fathers only 246

patrilocality virilocality 238

peasants people who use nonindustrialized, labor-intensive techniques for producing food and who are politically and economically subordinate to a governing class of which they are not a part and with whom they have little influence 177

permissive societies those that are tolerant of childhood sexual experimentation 93

personal distance the distance to which people adjust themselves when interacting with close friends 298

personality consistent pattern of behavior related both to inner forces and to external, cultural, and social pressures 363

petitionary rituals ritual requests for supernatural aid that are believed to increase the likelihood of the requested result but not guarantee it 333

phoneme the smallest psychologically real unit of sound in a language 307

phonemic alphabet a written record of a speech that uses an alphabet composed of only one symbol for each phoneme of the language 307

phones smallest sound units of a language 306

phonetic description a description pertaining to the smallest units of sound actually produced by speakers of a language 306

phonology the study of the rules that govern the production and the organization of the sounds of a particular language 306

phratry group of clans thought to be related by kinship 249

physical (biological) anthropologists anthropologists who specialize in the study of the evolutionary origins of the human species, the relationships between the human species and other living primates, the physical variations within the human species today, and the relationships between human biology and our species' cultural capacities 19

pibloktoq a culture-specific hysterical disorder characterized by agitated attempts to flee the presence of other people 377

pidgin languages simplified versions of one language or a combination of several 305

piety values concerning the treatment of nature and attitudes that define our relationship to the supernatural 46, 276

pink-collar occupations service occupations that are largely held by women 202

plant-focused foraging gathering of plant resources that are readily available, allowing hunting expeditions far from campsite 142

play stress-relieving ritualistic practice of potentially utilitarian behaviors 389

polar lands regions of cold climates near North and South poles 136

political economy the reproductive, economic, and social behaviors that are typical of life outside the family or household 33

politics manner in which power is achieved and used to create and implement public goals 262

polyandrous marriage form of marriage in which one woman has more than one husband 224

polygamy form of marriage where a person is permitted to have more than one spouse at the same time 223

polygyny form of marriage in which a man has more than one wife 223

polyphony diversity of viewpoints within a single culture 27

polytheism the belief in superior (but not supreme) gods, each of whom controls or rules over some major aspect of the universe 329

postmodernist anthropology a humanistic approach to anthropology that rejects the notion of ethnography as a detached, scientifically objective process and proposes the view that culture is composed of a constantly changing, open-ended, and ambiguous system of meanings that are negotiated and renegotiated by members of society as they interact 26

power the ability to exercise coercion in a group in obtaining what is sought 64

practicing anthropologist anthropologist who applies anthropological approaches to analyzing and solving real-world problems 22

prairies areas with tall varieties of grass that tolerate wetter climates 135

pregnancy rituals religious rules such as taboos designed to protect the unborn child and the mother during pregnancy and childbirth or admonitions to engage in acts believed to be a positive influence on the developing child 85

prestige dialects dialects with the reputation of being inherently better than others 317

priests religious practitioners who perform rituals for the benefit of a group; are often are full-time specialists whose emphasis is on preserving the established ritual forms, rather than on inspiration and innovation in the application of their rituals 342

primary institutions the primary care groups related to childrearing, including feeding, weaning, sexual training, and subsistence patterns 360

Principle of Stabilization the concept that the more efficient a culture becomes at harnessing energy for society, the more expensive and difficult it becomes to implement new means of increasing efficiency 165

professionals self-employed, college-educated service providers 202

progeny price bridewealth 236

pronatalist societies societies whose customs favor reproduction and forbid abortion and infanticide 68

Proto-Germanic the language from which both English and German are descended 312

Proto-Indo-European the ancestral language from which most of the contemporary languages of Europe, Iran, and India have developed 314

proverbs short statements that illustrate the basic values of a culture 399

proxemics the study of how people structure the space around them when interacting with others 298

psychological anthropology an empirical approach to data collection that emphasizes statistical correlations between culture and psychological processes 361

psychological death the process by which one subjectively prepares for impending biological death 102

puberty ritual a rite of passage that formalizes the change from the status of child to the status of adult 94

public distance the distance reserved for separating people whose interaction is not intended to perpetuate a social relationship 299

races distinct biological subdivisions of a species 70

racial discrimination treating people differently based on their membership in different racial groups 71

racial prejudice an attitude made up of feelings of dislike and contempt for people who are thought of as belonging to a racial group different from one's own 71

racism culturally mandated, institutionally-supported discrimination against members of minority races that is based on and supported by cultural beliefs about innate differences between the races 71

racist beliefs beliefs that mistakenly attribute the causes of role differences to inborn racial predispositions rather than to social learning 71

raids organized violence by one group against another to achieve an economic benefit 284

ramages cognatic lineages 248

rank the relative importance of a status or group as measured by the amount of power and/or honor to which it is entitled 64

rank societies kinship groups in a chiefdom that are ranked in a social rather than occupational hierarchy 267

real culture culture portrayed in terms of the actually observable behaviors of a people 48

rebellion organized and violent opposition to the legitimacy of a society's current governing body 288

reciprocity sharing of surpluses with the understanding that the party receiving the gift will respond in kind in the future 203

redistribution contribution of commodities by all members of a group to a common pool from which they will be distributed to those who will use them 207

refugees displaced people who have been forced from their homes and means of livelihood because of the fear of political persecution 182

reincarnation the belief that the soul of a human being may be repeatedly reborn into the human group to which it previously belonged or as an animal that may be symbolically associated with that group 329

religion belief in supernatural power, symbolic expression of feelings, and rituals performed in order to influence the nonhuman realm 322

residual rules miscellaneous, normally unspoken rules that people are expected to follow to avoid violating the pattern or style of behavior that is expected in the culture 374

restitution behavior intended to restore the group to the balance it had before a law was broken 287

restrictive societies societies that do not accept childhood sexual experimentation 93

retribution personal use of force to redress wrongs, usually in simple societies with no centralized governmental authority 284

revitalization movement a change in religion that represents a conscious effort to construct a more satisfying culture 349

revolution organized use of force to alter the very form of government 288

rhetoric formal speech that follows the traditional rules of a particular culture 398

rhythm the timing and stressing of tones within a melody 396

riddles mental puzzles told for entertainment 399

rite of passage (life crisis rite) a ritual that formalizes a major change in social status 84

ritual behaviors, often performed in repetitive and stereotyped ways, that express people's anxieties by acting them out; may be an attempt to influence the supernatural realm to achieve greater control over the natural world 326, 372

role the skills, abilities, and ways of acting toward others that belong to each status of a society 63

role conflict emotional discomfort and confusion experienced in situations in which conflicting contextual cues indicate that an individual should play the roles of more than one of his or her statuses 65

sacred the quality of inspiring feelings of respect, awe, and reverence that is possessed by things set apart and forbidden 324

saka a culture-specific hysterical disorder that is characterized by repetition of actions or sounds believed to be a foreign language, and loss of consciousness with body rigidity 378

same-sex marriages marriages between two males or two females 229

sanction action taken by legal authorities responding to violations of law 278

savannas tropical areas of tall grasses and drought-resistant undergrowth 135

scale a sequence of tones that ends with a return to a tone that has a frequency twice that of the starting tone 395

scarification decorating the body by cutting designs in it and treating them with ashes or other material to ensure that they will produce raised scars 94

schizophrenia a mental disorder characterized by residual rule breaking caused by difficulty in communicating an acceptable social identity; may include hallucinations and ideas about reality that are greatly at odds with mainstream ideas 381

scientific beliefs beliefs that are based on the desire to solve the practical day-to-day problems of living 43

scrub forests regions between coasts and mountains with mild, wet winters and hot, dry summers 135

secondary institutions the institutions in social life that satisfy the needs and tensions not met by the primary institutions, including taboo systems, religion, rituals, folk tales, and techniques of thinking 360

secularization the process by which nonreligious beliefs expand within an ideology at the expense of religious thought 328

sedentarism living in permanent or semipermanent settlements 146

semirestrictive societies those that accept childhood sexual experimentation so long as those involved follow established rules of etiquette and discretion 93

septs cognatic lineages 248

serial monogamy a marriage pattern in which individuals of either sex may have only one spouse at a given time, but through divorce and remarriage may have several spouses during their lifetime 223

serotonin a chemical produced in the brain during waking hours that inhibits the production of dreams or hallucinations 370

sex biological distinctions such as the chromosomal, hormonal, or physical differences between males and females 108

sexism the belief that differences in the sex roles of males and

females are biologically determined 109

sexual dimorphism marked differentiation in size and form of the sexes 108

sexual terrorism customs that employ violence against females in order to maintain male domination 115

shaman part-time religious practitioner who is believed to have access to supernatural power that may be used for the benefit of specific clients, as in healing or divining 340

shamanic religions religions in which the only ritual specialist is the shaman, and which contain only shamanic and individual ritual practices 342

shame (embarrassment) a distressful emotion characterized by a sense of personal ineptness resulting in damage to one's reputation and loss of esteem 367

shifting cultivation extensive cultivation 148

sib clan 248

sign an object or event whose meaning is biologically disposed or based on a similarity or a tendency for two things to occur together in nature 294

sin a form of taboo violation in which the rule breaker is morally responsible for the act 336

sister exchange form of cross-cousin marriage in which a brother and sister marry cross cousins who are also sister and brother to each other 234

slash-and-burn cultivation a form of farming in which the land is prepared by cutting and burning the natural growth and in which several plots, in various stages of soil depletion, are worked in a cycle 149

sleep crawling a Samoan sexual practice in which an uninvited youth would enter a young woman's house after dark with the intent of seduction 97

social anthropology Radcliffe-Brown's approach emphasizing the importance of social interactions in determining the customs of a culture 27

social death the point at which people respond to a person with the behaviors appropriate to one who is biologically dead 103

social distance the distance to which people adjust themselves when interacting in impersonal situations such as business transactions 299

social organization the relationships between the groups, statuses, and division of labor that structure the interaction of people within society 62

social structure the part of social organization made up of groups and their relationships with each other 27, 63

socialization or enculturation the process of learning a culture and the role-playing skills necessary for social life 92, 276, 359

society a group of human beings who conceive of themselves as distinct from other such groups 38

sociobiology approach that emphasizes the role of natural selection on genetic predispositions for specific behaviors 31

sodality voluntary associations whose members are drawn from several tribal families 266

sorcerer practitioner of magical rituals done to harm others 341

sorcery the learned use of rituals to magically control the supernatural realm to achieve human goals 331

sororal polygyny form of polygyny in which the wives are sisters 223

sororate a rule that requires the kin of a deceased woman to provide her widower with another wife, often one of the deceased woman's sisters 229

soul loss in primitive societies, the belief that the departure of the soul from the body, usually caused by a sudden fright, causes the body to weaken and die 336

special-purpose money medium of exchange restricted to the buying and selling of a single commodity 211

specific evolution change in the direction of increasing adaptive specialization 164

speech the audible symbols that people use to communicate 301

speech motor area the part of the cerebral cortex that controls the production of speech sounds 304

spirit possession a trance in which individuals feel as if their behavior is under the control of one or more spirits that have entered their bodies 336, 371

spirit travel trance a trance in which individuals experience themselves as leaving their bodies 371

spiritual values attitudes that define our relationship to the supernatural 276

sport aggressively competitive activity played according to strict rules 391

Standard English the dialect taught in U.S. schools and used by most people in the United States at least on formal occasions 312

state a society with a centralized government that monopolizes the legal authority to use force 269

status a culturally defined relationship that one individual may have with one or more other individuals; the position within a group that each member holds 63

status income goods produced over and above subsistence needs 213

status pair the statuses that two people acquire when they interact, and that together form a relationship 63

status-appropriate roles the ways of behaving that are expected of an individual who holds a particular social status in a specific culture 363

steppes areas that cover stretches of southeastern Europe and Asia, with a short, hardy variety of grass 135

stigma loss of rank that accompanies the social rejection of persons who have violated accepted role behavior 365

stimulus diffusion the borrowing of the idea for a cultural trait by one society from another, with the implementation of that idea being more or less determined within the borrowing culture 161

stress a physiological response to any demand, characterized by the body's preparing itself for action 367

structural-functionalism approach based on the analytical method of social anthropology that focuses on ways in which societies' customs function to maintain their social structure 28

structuralism Lévi-Strauss's concept of the underlying unity of all cultures, represented in the tendency to think in dualities 24

subcultures the geographical or social variations that occur within the cultures of societies with large populations 39

subsistence how people obtain the necessities of life, particularly food, from the environment 138

subsistence economy economy in which people consume most of what they produce 213

subsistence income goods produced by each family for its own consumption 213

subsistence technology the tools and techniques by which people obtain food 138

Sudanese (descriptive) kinship terminology kinship system occurring mostly in North Africa that distinguishes maternal and paternal relatives by separate sets of terms 256

Sudra the lowest of the Hindu castes, made up of farm artisans, servants, farmers, and laborers 66

supernatural that which transcends the natural, observable world 323

supernatural sanctions for violations of moral rules punishments for immoral acts by spiritual agencies as opposed to human agencies. In most societies, the enforcement of morality is a strictly human responsibility, rather than a religious preoccupation 331

survivals remnants of earlier social customs and ideas that can be used to reconstruct the evolutionary past of societies 6

susto (espanto, pasmo) a culture-specific anxiety disorder with depressive features, interpreted by the victim as caused by soul loss 378

swidden horticulture slash-and-burn horticulture 149

symbol an object or event that represents another object or event only because of the agreement among people that it will 39, 294

symbolic marriages those marriages not establishing economic and social ties between kinship groups 226

symmetrical statuses a pair of statuses, each of which has the same roles to play with respect to the other 63

syncretism the borrowing of beliefs, practices, or organizational traits by one religion from another 348

syntax the study of the rules for combining morphemes into complete and meaningful sentences 307

Systema Naturae the book in which Carolus Linnaeus classified plants and animals into a hierarchical system based on their degree of similarity to one another 6

taboo a rule forbidding contact with sacred things, those containing mana 323

taboo violation the breaking of a supernatural rule, whether intentional or not; often believed to be a cause of illness 336

taigas swampy coniferous forests of the northern lands south of the tundras 136

technical learning learning that occurs when the logical rationales for specific ways of doing things—rather than emotional pressure to behave in that way—are given to the learner 93

technology tools and techniques through which human beings harness the energy available in their environment 28

teknonymy the custom of referring to a person as the parent of his or her child rather than by birth name 100

totem a plant, animal or, less commonly, nonliving thing that is a sacred symbol of the unity of a social group 324

traditional agriculture nonindustrialized agriculture 155

trance (altered state of consciousness) subjective state of mind where experiences are not interpreted in terms of normal symbolic categories of one's culture 367

transhumance a form of pastoralism in which only a part of the group moves with the herd; some stay in villages and grow crops year round 152

transvestism cross-dressing or mixed-gender dressing, a common part of the berdache gender role and of the Western transvestite status 114

tribe a semisedentary kinship-based society without a full-time government; most often economically based on a simple food domestication subsistence technology, either horticulture or pastoralism 150, 264

tropical forests regions with warm climates and abundant rainfall, plants, and animal life 135

tundras level or undulating treeless plains in the arctic and subarctic regions of North America, Asia, and Scandinavia 136

underdeveloped country nation with a largely nonindustrialized economy 172

unilineal descent a system of tracing descent through a single sex line rather than through both parents equally 246

unilineal descent group a system of tracing social groups based on a matrilineal or patrilineal descent system 247

universal application principle that legal authority should apply the same laws uniformly in similar situations 278

unskilled laborers low-paid workers, including part-time or seasonal workers, who are usually paid by the hour or for the quantity of goods they produce 202

Untouchables the lowest-status members of Hindu society who belong to none of the traditional castes and who ritually perform the polluted tasks of life 66

uxorilocality (matrilocality) the custom of newly married couples setting up residence with or near the bride's family 238

Vaisya the third-ranked Hindu caste, comprised of commoners 66

values feelings about what should be considered good, bad, moral, or immoral; the ideals that people long for but do not necessarily pursue 46, 276

verbal arts (oral literature) various forms of speaking for aesthetic pleasure, including orating, reciting myths, and telling folktales 396

virilocality (patrilocality) custom of newly married couples setting up residence with or near the groom's family 238

voodoo death death that occurs following a magical ritual performed to kill 337

war organized armed conflict between political communities 284

wealth-increasing polygyny male-stratified polygyny 224

Wernicke's area the part of the cerebral cortex involved in processing speech sounds 301

white-collar occupations service-providing occupations such as clerical, sales, managerial, and administrative jobs 202

witchcraft the innate ability to influence supernatural forces, usually to operate in ways that are harmful to others, without the necessity of using rituals 331

witches persons believed to have the innate supernatural ability to harm others without the use of ritual 341

women exchange the practice of families' exchanging women in marriage rather than exchanging gifts, so that each loses a daughter but gains a daughter-in-law 237

BIBLIOGRAPHY

Abbott, J., Johnson, R., Koziol-McLain, J., & Lowenstein, S. R. (1995, June 14). Domestic violence against women: Incidence and prevalence in an emergency department population. *JAMA: Journal of the American Medical Association, 273*(22), 1763–1767.

Aberle, D. F. (1961). "Arctic hysteria" and latah in Mongolia. In Y. A. Cohen (Ed.), *Social structure and personality: A casebook* (pp. 471–475). New York: Holt, Rinehart & Winston.

Adam, B. D. (1981). *Christianity, social tolerance and homosexuality: A symposium.* Paper presented at the Society for the Study of Social Problems, Ontario, Canada.

Adam, B. D. (1986). Age, structure, and sexuality: Reflections on the anthropological evidence on homosexual relations, *Journal of Homosexuality, 11*(3–4), 19–33.

Adams, A. (1989, Winter). Women's tales of torture. *Feminist Ethics, 3*(1), 88–89.

Alan Guttmacher Institute. (1994). *Sex and America's teenagers.* New York: Alan Guttmacher Institute.

Albert, B. (1991). A Yanomami leader speaks: A message from Davi Kopenawa Yanomami. *Anthropology Newsletter, 32*(6), 52.

Alland, A. (1977). *The artistic animal: An inquiry into the biological roots of art.* Garden City, NY: Doubleday.

Altman, S. A. (1973). Primate communication. In G. A. Miller (Ed.), *Communication, language and meaning: Psychological perspectives* (pp. 84–94). New York: Basic Books.

American Psychiatric Association. (1994). *Diagnostic and statistical manual of mental disorders* (4th ed.). Washington, DC: American Psychiatric Association.

Amnesty International. (1992). *Women in the front line: Human rights violations against women.* New York: John D. Lucas Printing.

Anderson, L. (1990). *Calliope's sisters: A comparative study of philosophies of art.* Englewood Cliffs, NJ: Prentice Hall.

Anonymous. (1987, May). Torture and mistreatment of prisoners. In *A stern, steady crackdown: Legal process and human rights in South Korea* (pp. 87–107). Washington, DC: Asia Watch.

Anonymous. (1989, Spring). Human rights violations against women in Turkey. *Interact: A Human Rights Bulletin about Women Prisoners of Conscience,* 3–10.

Ashworth, G. (1986). Of violence and violation: Women and human rights. In *Change Thinkbook II.* London: Change.

Ayres, B. C. (1968). In A. Lomax (Ed.), *Folk song style and culture* (AAAS Publication No. 88). Washington, DC: American Association for the Advancement of Science.

Ayres, B. C. (1973). Effects of infant carrying practices on rhythm in music. *Ethos, 1,* 387–404.

Bamberger, J. (1974). The myth of matriarchy. In M. Z. Rosaldo & L. Lamphere (Eds.), *Women, culture, and society* (pp. 263–388). Stanford, CA: Stanford University Press.

Barker-Banfield, G. J. (1983). The spermatic economy: A nineteenth century view of sexuality. In T. Altherr (Ed.), *Procreation or pleasure: Sexual attitudes in American history* (pp. 47–70). Malabar, FL: Robert E. Krieger Publishing.

Barnes, G. H., & Dummond, D. W. (Eds.). (1934). *Letters of Theodore Dwight Weld, Angelina Grimké Weld and Sarah Grimké, 1822–1844* (Vol. 1). New York: Appleton-Century.

Barnouw, V. (1985). *Culture and personality* (4th ed.). Homewood, IL: Dorsey.

Barry, H., Child, I. L., & Bacon, M. K. (1959). Relation of child training to subsistence economy. *American Anthropologist, 61,* 51–63.

Barth, F. (1954). Father's brother's daughter marriage in Kurdistan. *Southwestern Journal of Anthropology, 10*(1), 164–171.

Basedow, H. (1925). *The Australian aboriginal.* Adelaide, Australia: F. W. Preece & Sons.

Bates, M. (1967). *Gluttons and libertines: Human problems of being natural.* New York: Vintage Books.

Bateson, G. (1958). *Naven: A survey of the problems suggested by a composite picture of the culture of a New Guinea tribe drawn from three points of view* (2nd ed.). Stanford, CA: Stanford University Press.

Beals, A. M. (1974). *Village life in South India.* Chicago: Aldine.

Beals, A. M. (1980). *Gopalpur.* New York: Holt, Rinehart & Winston.

Bean, S. S. (1981). Soap operas: Sagas of American kinship. In S. Montague & W. Arens (Eds.), *The American dimension: Cultural myths and social realities* (pp. 61–75). Sherman Oaks, CA: Alfred Publishing Co.

Beattie, J. (1964). *Other cultures: Aims, methods, and achievements in social anthropology.* New York: Free Press.

Becker, H. S. (1963). *Outsiders: Studies in the sociology of deviance.* New York: Free Press.

Behnam, D. (1985). The Tunis conference. *Current Anthropology, 26,* 555–556.

Bellah, R. (1967, Winter). Civil religion in America. *Daedelus, 96*(1), 1–21.

Benedict, R. (1930). Psychological types in the cultures of the Southwest. In *Proceedings of the Twenty-Third International Congress of Americanists* (pp. 572–581). New York: International Congress of Americanists.

Benedict, R. (1932). Configurations of culture in North America. *American Anthropologist, 34,* 1–27.

Benedict, R. (1934). *Patterns of culture.* Boston, MA: Houghton Mifflin.

Benedict, R. (1946). *The chrysanthemum and the sword.* Boston: Houghton Mifflin.

Bernard, H. R., & Pelto, P. J. (Eds.). (1972). *Technology and social change.* New York: Macmillan.

Bickerton, D. (1983, July). Creole languages. *Scientific American,* 116–122.

Biebuyck, D. P. (1973). *Lega culture*. Berkeley, CA: University of California Press.

Binford, L. R. (1968). Post-Pleistocene adaptations. In L. R. Binford & S. R. Binford (Eds.), *New perspective in archaeology* (pp. 22–49). Chicago: Aldine.

Bird, C. (1973). *Born female: The high cost of keeping women down*. New York: David McKay.

Birdwhistell, R. L. (1970). *Kinesics and context: Essays on body motion communication*. Philadelphia: University of Pennsylvania Press.

Black, D. (1976). *The behavior of law*. New York: Academic Press.

Blacking, J. (1978). Uses of the kinship idiom in friendships at some Venda and Zulu schools. In J. Argyle & E. Preston-Whyte (Eds.), *Social system and tradition in southern Africa* (pp. 101–117). Cape Town, South Africa: Oxford University Press.

Blackwood, E. (1985). Breaking the mirror: The construction of lesbianism and the anthropological discourse on homosexuality. *Journal of Homosexuality, 11*(3–4), 1–17.

Blanchard, K., & Cheska, A. (1985). *The anthropology of sport*. South Hadley, MA: Bergin & Gavin.

Blau, Z. S. (1981). *Black children/white children: Competence, socialization, and social structure*. New York: Free Press.

Bloomfield, L. (1933). Dialect geography. In H. Hoijer (Ed.), *Language history* (pp. 321–345). New York: Holt, Rinehart & Winston.

Blount, B. G. (1974). *Language, culture and society: A book of readings*. Cambridge, MA: Winthrop.

Boas, F. (1888). *The central Eskimo* (Bureau of American Ethnology Annual Rep. No. 6). Washington, DC: U.S. Government Printing Office.

Boas, F. (1911). *Handbook of American Indian languages* (Bureau of American Ethnology Bulletin No. 40). Washington, DC: U.S. Government Printing Office.

Bodley, J. H. (1975). *Victims of progress*. Menlo Park, CA: Cummings.

Bogoras, W. (1907). The Chuckchee. In *Memoirs of the American Museum of Natural History, Vol. 11, Part 2. Religion*. Leyden, Netherlands: E. J. Brill.

Bohannan, P. (1955). Some principles of exchange and investment among the Tiv. *American Anthropologist, 57*, 60–70.

Bohannan, P. (1963). *Social anthropology*. New York: Holt, Rinehart & Winston.

Bohannan, P., & Middleton, J. (Eds.). (1968). *Marriage, family, and residence*. New York: Natural History Press.

Bombard, A., & Kerns, J. (1994). *The Nostratic macrofamily: A study in distant linguistic relationship*. The Hague, Netherlands: Mouton de Gruyter.

Boserup, E. (1965). *The condition of agricultural growth: The economics of agrarian change under population pressures*. Chicago: Aldine-Atherton.

Bourdieu, P. (1977). *Outline of theory of practice* (R. Nice, Trans.). Cambridge, England: Cambridge University Press.

Bourdieu, P. (1982). *Ce que parler veut dire*. Paris: Fayard.

Bourdieu, P. (1984). *Distinction: A social critique of the judgment of taste* (R. Nice, Trans.). Cambridge, MA: Harvard University Press.

Bourguignon, E. (1974). *Culture and the varieties of consciousness* (Addison-Wesley Module in Anthropology No. 47). Reading, MA: Addison-Wesley.

Bourguignon, E., & Greenberg, L. (1973). *Homogeneity and diversity in world societies*. New Haven, CT: Human Relations Area Files.

Breslau, K. (1990, January 22). Overplanned parenthood: Ceausescu's cruel law. *Newsweek, 115*, 35.

Briggs, J. (1970). *Never in anger: Portrait of an Eskimo family*. Cambridge, MA: Harvard University Press.

Briggs, J. (1980). Kapluna daughter: Adopted by the Eskimo. In J. Spradley & D. McCurdy (Eds.), *Conformity and conflict* (4th ed., pp. 44–62). Boston: Little, Brown.

Briggs, J. (1986). Kapluna daughter. In P. Golde (Ed.), *Women in the field: Anthropological experiences* (pp. 19–44). Berkeley, CA: University of California Press.

Brooke, J. (1995, July 7). Who braves piranha waters? Your Avon lady! *New York Times*, p. A4.

Brown, J. (1963). A cross-cultural study of female initiation rites. *American Anthropologist, 656*, 837–853.

Brown, J. K. (1970). A note on the division of labor by sex. *American Anthropologist, 72*, 1073–1078.

Brown, S. J., & Batty, J. C. (1976). Energy allocation in the food system: A microscale view. *Transactions of the American Society of Agricultural Engineers, 19*(4), 758–761.

Buchsbaum, M. S. (1979). Tuning in an hemispheric dialogue. *Psychology Today, 12*(8), 100.

Bunch, C. (1975, Fall). Not for lesbians only. *Quest: A Feminist Quarterly, 2*(2) 50–56.

Bunster, X. (1984). The torture of women political prisoners: A case study in female sexual slavery. In K. Barry, C. Bunch, & S. Castley (Eds.), *International feminism: Networking against female sexual slavery* (pp. 94–102). New York: International Women's Tribune Centre.

Bunzel, R. (1952). *Chichicastenango: A Guatemalan village* (American Ethnological Society Monograph No. 22). New York: J. J. Augustin.

Burch, E. S. (1970). Marriage and divorce among the north Alaska Eskimos. In P. Bohannan (Ed.), *Divorce and after*. Garden City, NY: Doubleday.

Burch, E. S. (1975). *Eskimo kinsmen: Changing family relationships in northwest Alaska* (American Ethnological Society Monograph No. 59). St. Paul, MN: West Publishing.

Burger, J. (1987). *Report from the frontier: The state of the world's indigenous peoples*. London: Zed Books.

Burgess, F. W., & Wallin, P. (1953). Homogamy in social characteristics. *American Journal of Sociology, 49*, 109–124.

Burling, R. (1970). *Man's many voices: Language in the cultural context*. New York: Holt, Rinehart & Winston.

Cain, A. C. (1964). On the memory of "playing crazy" in borderline children. *Psychiatry, 27*, 281–282.

Cairns, G. (1984). *Law and the status of women in Latin America: A survey* (Development Law and Policy Program Working Paper No. 13). New York: Columbia University.

Calder, J. E. (1874). Some accounts of the wars of extermination, and habits of the native tribes of Tasmania. *Journal of the Anthropological Institute of Britain and Ireland, 3.*

Callender, C., & Kochems, L. (1983). The North American berdache. *Current Anthropology, 23*(4), 443–456.

Calman, L. J. (1987, September). *Are women's rights human rights?* (Women in International Development Working Paper No. 146). East Lansing, MI: Michigan State University.

Campbell, S. (1983). Kula in Vakuta: The mechanics of *keda.* In J. Leach & E. Leach (Eds.), *The kula: New perspectives on Massim exchange.* Cambridge, England: Cambridge University Press.

Cannon, W. B. (1942). Voodoo death. *American Anthropologist, 44,* 169–181.

Carneiro, R. (1970). A theory of the origin of the state. *Science, 169,* 733–738.

Carneiro, R. (1978). Political expansion as an expression of a principle of competitive exclusion. In R. Cohen & E. Service (Eds.), *Origins of the state* (pp. 205–233). Philadelphia, PA: ISHI.

Carroll, J. B. (Ed.). (1956). *Language, thought and reality: Selected writings of Benjamin Lee Whorf.* Cambridge, MA: M.I.T. Press.

Cassirer, E. (1944). *An essay on man: An introduction to a philosophy of human culture.* New Haven, CT: Yale University Press.

Chagnon, N. A. (1983). *Yanomamö: The fierce people* (3rd ed.). New York: Holt, Rinehart & Winston.

Chambers, R. (1983). *Rural development: Putting the last first.* Essex, England: Longman Scientific & Technical.

Chandler, J. T., & Platkos, J. (1969). *Spanish speaking pupils classified as educable mentally retarded.* Sacramento, CA: California State Department of Education, Division of Instruction.

Chase, A. (1977). *The legacy of Malthus.* New York: Alfred A. Knopf.

Chomsky, N. (1965). *Aspects of the theory of syntax.* Cambridge, MA: M.I.T. Press.

Chomsky, N. (1971). Language acquisition. In J. P. B. Allen & P. Van Buren (Eds.), *Chomsky: Selected readings* (pp. 127–148). London: Oxford University Press.

Clements, F. E. (1932). Primitive concepts of disease. *Publications in American Archaeology and Ethnology* (Berkeley, CA), *32*(2).

Clifford, J. (1983, Spring). On ethnographic authority. *Representations, 1,* 118–146.

Clifford, J., & Marcus, G. E. (1986). *Writing culture: The process and politics of ethnography.* Berkeley, CA: University of California Press.

Codere, H. (1950). *Fighting with property* (American Ethnological Society Monograph No. 18). New York: J. J. Augustin.

Codere, H. (Ed.). (1967). *Kwakiutl ethnography.* Chicago: University of Chicago Press.

Coe, R. (1970). *The sociology of medicine.* New York: McGraw-Hill.

Cohen, Y. A. (1964). *The transition from childhood to adolescence: Cross cultural studies in initiation ceremonies, legal systems, and incest taboos.* Chicago: Aldine.

Cohen, Y. A. (Ed.). (1974). *Man in adaptation: The cultural present.* Chicago: Aldine.

Cohn, W. (1967). "Religion" in non-western culture? *American Anthropologist, 69,* 73–76.

Conklin, H. C. (1956). Hanunóo color categories. *Southwestern Journal of Anthropology, 11,* 339–344.

Cook, R. J. (1990, Fall). Taking women's rights seriously. *WID Bulletin, 6*(1), 22–23.

Cooper, J. M. (1946). The Yahgan. In J. H. Steward (Ed.), *Handbook of South American Indians* (Bureau of American Ethnology Bulletin No. 143, Vol. 1, pp. 97–98). Washington, DC: U.S. Government Printing Office.

Coote, J., & Shelton, A. (Eds.). (1994). *Anthropology, art, and aesthetics.* Oxford: Clarendon Press.

Corr, C. A. (1993, January/February). Coping with dying: Lessons that we should and should not learn from the work of Elizabeth Kübler-Ross. *Death Studies, 17*(1), 69–83.

Coughlin, E. K. (1995, February 17). Farming lessons from prehistory. *Chronicle of Higher Education,* pp. A10, A15.

Coult, A. D., & Habenstein, R. W. (1965). *Cross tabulations of Murdock's world ethnographic sample.* Columbia, MO: University of Missouri Press.

Cowley, G. (1989, June 26). The plunder of the past. *Newsweek, 113,* 58–60.

Crane, J., & Angrosino, M. V. (1974). *Field projects in anthropology: A student handbook.* Morristown, NJ: General Learning Press.

Crapo, R. H. (1987). *Sexuality and kinship: Factors in the cross-cultural patterning of homosexuality.* Paper presented at the annual meeting of the American Anthropological Association, Chicago.

Crapo, R. H. (1995). Factors in the cross-cultural patterning of male homosexuality: A reappraisal of the literature. *Journal of Anthropological Research, 29*(2), 178–202.

Creamer, M. H. (1974). Ranking in Navaho nouns. *Diné Bizaad Nánil'ih:* Navajo Language Review, *1*(1), 29–38.

Critchfield, R. (1981). *Villages.* Garden City, NY: Doubleday/Anchor Press.

Crosby, A. W. (1986). *Biological imperialism: The biological expansion of Europe, 900–1900.* Cambridge, England: Cambridge University Press.

Czaplicka, M. A. (1914). *Aboriginal Siberia: A study in social anthropology.* Oxford, CT: Clarendon Press.

Dahlberg, F. (Ed.). (1981). *Woman the gatherer.* New Haven, CT: Yale University Press.

Dalby, L. (1985). *Geisha.* New York: Vintage Books.

Dalton, G. (1969). Theoretical issues in economic anthropology. *Current Anthropology, 10,* 63–102.

Daly, M. (1978). *Gyn-ecology: The metaethics of radical feminism.* Boston: Beacon Press.

D'Andrade, R. (1961). The anthropological study of dreams. In F. L. K. Hsu (Ed.), *Psychological anthropology* (pp. 296–332). Homewood, IL: Dorsey.

Darwin, C. (1859). *On the origin of species.* New York: Atheneum.

Das, M. (1989). *Dowry violence against women in India.* Unpublished master's thesis, Colorado State University, Fort Collins, CO.

Daugherty, M. L. (1976). Serpent-handling as sacrament. *Theology Today, 33*(3), 232–243.

Dentan, R. K. (1968). *The Semai: A nonviolent people of Malaya*. New York: Holt, Rinehart & Winston.

Dentan, R. K. (1988). Rejoinder to Nanda. *American Anthropologist, 90*(2), 423.

Derrida, J. (1976). *On grammatology*. Baltimore: Johns Hopkins University Press.

Devale, W. T., & Harris, M. (1976). Population, warfare and the male supremacist complex. *American Anthropologist, 78*, 521–538.

Devereux, G. (1955). *The study of abortion in primitive societies: A typological, distributional and dynamic analysis of the prevention of birth in 400 preindustrial societies*. New York: Julian Press.

Devereux, G. (1967). A typological study of abortion in 350 primitive, ancient, and pre-industrial societies. In H. Rosen (Ed.), *Abortion in America*. Boston: Beacon Press.

DeVore, P. (1965). Language and communication. In P. Devore (Ed.), *The origin of man* (pp. 77–77a). New York: Wenner-Gren Foundation for Anthropological Research.

Diamond, J. (1993, February). Speaking with a single tongue. *Discover*, 78–85.

Dibble, C. E., & Anderson, A. J. O. (Trans.). (1950–1969). *Florentine codex: General history of the things of New Spain* (Vols. 1–12). Salt Lake City, UT: School for American Research and the University of Utah.

Divale, W. (1972). Systematic population control in the Middle and Upper Paleolethic: Inferences based on contemporary hunters and gatherers. *World Archaeology, 4*, 222–243.

Divale, W., Chambaris, F., & Gangloff, D. (1976). War, peace and marital residence in pre-industrial societies. *Journal of Conflict Resolution, 20*, 57–78.

Divale, W., & Harris, M. (1976). Population, warfare and the male supremacist complex. *American Anthropologist, 78*, 521–538.

Doctor, R. F. (1988). A review of the literature on transvestism and transsexualism. In R. F. Doctor, *Transvestites and transsexuals: Toward a theory of cross-gender behavior* (pp. 39–71). New York: Plenum Press.

Doerr, E., & Prescott, T. W. (1990). *Abortion rights and fetal personhood* (2nd ed.). Long Beach, CA: Centerline Press.

Douglas, M. (1966). *Purity and danger: An analysis of conflicts of pollution and taboo*. New York: Praeger Press; London: Routledge & Kegan Paul.

Douglas, M., & Isherwood, B. (1979). *The world of goods: Toward an anthropology of consumption*. New York: W. W. Norton.

Downie, D. C., & Hally, D. J. (1961). *A cross-cultural study of male transvestism and sex-role differentiation*. Unpublished manuscript, Dartmouth College.

Downs, J. F., & Bleibtreu, H. K. (1972). *Human variation: An introduction to physical anthropology*. Beverly Hills, CA: Glencoe Press.

DuBois, C. (1944). *People of Alor: A social psychological study of an East Indian island* (Vols. 1–2). Minneapolis, MN: University of Minnesota Press.

DuBois, C. (1955). The dominant value profile of American culture. *American Anthropologist, 57*, 1232–1239.

Duke, P. G., & Wilson, M. (1995). *Beyond subsistence: Plains archaeology and the postprocessual critique*. Tuscaloosa, AL: University of Alabama Press.

Dumont, J. P. (1978). *The headman and I: Ambiguity and ambivalence in the fieldwork experience*. Austin, TX: University of Texas Press.

Dumont, L. (1970). *Homo heirarchicus*. Chicago: University of Chicago Press.

Durkheim, E. (1915). *The elementary forms of the religious life* (J. W. Swain, Trans.). London: Allen & Unwin. (Original work published 1912)

Earle, T. K. (1978). Economic and social organization of a complex chiefdom: The Halelea District, Kauai, Hawaii. *Anthropological Papers of the Museum of Anthropology* (Ann Arbor, MI), 63.

Eastwell, H. D. (1982). Voodoo death and the mechanism for dispatch of the dying in East Arnhem, Australia. *American Anthropologist, 84*, 5–18.

Edgerton, R. B. (1965). Cultural vs. ecological factors in the expression of values, attitudes, and personality characteristics. *American Anthropologist, 67*, 442–447.

Edgerton, R. B. (1976). *Deviance: A cross-cultural perspective*. Menlo Park, CA: Cummings.

Eichenlaub, J. E. (1963). *The marriage art*. New York: Dial Press.

Eliade, M. (1964). *Shamanism: Archaic techniques of ecstasy*. Princeton, NJ: Princeton University Press.

Ella, S. (1895). *The ancient Samoan government*. (Australasian Association for the Advancement of Science Publication No. 5). Brisbane, Australia: Australasian Association for the Advancement of Science.

Elliot, B., & Johnson, M. (1995). Domestic violence in a primary care facility: Patterns and prevalence. *Archives of Family Medicine, 4*(2), 113–119.

Ellwood, C. (1913). *Sociology and modern social problems*. New York: American Book.

Ember, M. (1982). Statistical evidence for an ecological explanation of warfare. *American Anthropologist, 84*, 645–649.

Ember, M., & Ember, C. R. (1983). *Marriage, family, and kinship: Comparative studies of social organization*. New Haven, CT: Human Relations Area Files.

Emerson, O. (1923). *A Middle English reader*. New York: Macmillan.

Erikson, K. T. (1962). Notes on the sociology of deviance. *Social Problems, 9*, 307–314.

Evans-Pritchard, E. E. (1937). *Witchcraft, oracles and magic among the Azande*. Oxford, England: Clarendon Press.

Evans-Pritchard, E. E. (1940). *The Nuer: A description of the mode of livelihood and political institutions of a Nilotic people*. London: Oxford University Press.

Evans-Pritchard, E. E. (1951). *Kinship and marriage among the Nuer*. New York: Oxford University Press.

Evans-Pritchard, E. E. (1956). *Nuer religion*. Oxford: Clarendon Press.

Eyferth, K. (1959). Eine Untersuchung der Neger-Mischungskinder in Westdeutschland. *Vita Humana, 2*, 104–105.

Falk, D. (1975). Comparative anatomy of the larynx in man and the chimpanzee. *American Journal of Physical Anthropology, 43*, 123–132.

Faron, L. C. (1961). *Mapuche social structure: Reintegration in a patrilineal society of central Chile.* Urbana, IL: University of Illinois Press.

Faron, L. C. (1964). *Hawks of the sun: Mapuche mortality and its ritual attributes.* Pittsburgh, PA: University of Pittsburgh Press.

Faron, L. C. (1968). *The Mapuche Indians of Chile.* New York: Holt, Rinehart & Winston.

Fillmore, R. (1989). Ph.D. survey results: 1988 doctor rate update. *Anthropology Newsletter, 30*(3), 30–32.

Fischer, A. (1986). Field work in five cultures. In P. Golde (Ed.), *Women in the field: Anthropological experiences* (pp. 267–289). Berkeley, CA: University of California Press.

Fischer, J. (1961). Art styles as cultural cognitive maps. *American Anthropologist, 63,* 80–84.

Fischer, M. M. J. (1987). Beyond otherness, or the spectacularization of anthropology. *Telos, 71,* 161–170.

Fisher, J. (1972). Why do prospects fail to come up to expectations? In *The CENTO seminar on agricultural planning* (pp. 106–113). Ankara, Turkey: Public Relations Division, Central Treaty Organization.

Flannery, K. V. (1971). The origins and ecological effects of early domestication in Iran and the Near East. In S. Struever (Ed.), *Prehistoric agriculture* (pp. 50–79). Garden City, NY: Natural History Press. (Reprinted from *The domestication and exploration of plants and animals* by P. J. Ucko & G. W. Dimbleby, 1969, Chicago: Aldine)

Flynn, J. R. (1987). Massive IQ gains in 14 nations: What IQ tests really measure. *Psychological Bulletin, 101,* 171–191.

Ford, C. S., & Beach, F. A. (1952). *Patterns of sexual behavior.* New York: Harper & Row.

Fortune, R. (1932). Incest. *Encyclopedia of the Social Sciences, 7,* 620–622.

Fortune, R. F. (1963). *Sorcerers of Dobu: The social anthropology of the Dobu Islands of the Western Pacific.* New York: E. P. Dutton. (Originally published 1932)

Foster, G. (1965). Peasant society and the image of limited good. *American Anthropologist, 67,* 293–315.

Fottorino, E. (1994, December 4). AIDS deals a harsh blow to Africa's economy. *Guardian Weekly.* (Reprinted from *Le Monde,* 1994, November 10)

Foucault, M. (1977). *The archeology of knowledge.* London: Tavistock.

Foulks, E. F. (1972). *The arctic hysterias of the north Eskimo* (Anthropological Studies Issue No. 10). Washington, DC: American Anthropological Association.

Fouts, R. S., Fouts, D. H., & Schoenfeld, D. (1984, Spring). Cultural transmission of a human language in a chimpanzee mother-infant relation. *Sign Language Studies, 42,* 1–17.

Fowler, B. (1994, December 20). Recreating stone tools to learn ancient makers' ways. *New York Times,* pp. C1, C12.

Fox, R. (1967). *Kinship and marriage: An anthropological perspective.* Baltimore: Penguin Books.

Frake, C. O. (1961). The diagnosis of disease among the Subanum of Mindanao. *American Anthropologist, 63,* 113–132.

Frake, C. O. (1964). A structural description of Subanum religious behavior. In W. Goodenough (Ed.), *Explorations in cultural anthropology* (pp. 111–129). New York: McGraw-Hill.

Fraser, D. (1972). The symbols of Ashanti kingship. In D. Fraser & H. M. Cole (Eds.), *African art and leadership* (pp. 261–293). Madison: University of Wisconsin Press.

Frayser, S. G. (1985). *Varieties of sexual experience: An anthropological perspective on human sexuality.* New Haven, CT: Human Relations Area Files.

Frazer, J. (1910). *Totemism and exogamy* (Abridged ed.). London: Macmillan.

Frazer, J. (1922). *The golden bough: A study in magic and religion* (Abridged ed.). New York: Macmillan. (Originally printed in 12 vols., London: Macmillan)

Freeman, D. (1983). *Margaret Mead in Samoa: The making and unmaking of an anthropological myth.* Cambridge, MA: Harvard University Press.

Freuchen, P. (1935). *Arctic adventure.* New York: Farrar & Rinehart.

Fried, M. H. (1967). *The evolution of political society: An essay in political anthropology.* New York: Random House.

Friedl, E. (1975). *Women and men: An anthropologist's view.* New York: Holt, Rinehart & Winston.

Frisch, R. (1975). Critical weights, a critical body composition, menarche and the maintenance of menstrual cycles. In E. Watts, F. Johnston, & G. Lasker (Eds.), *Biosocial interrelations in population adaptation* (pp. 309–318). The Hague, Netherlands: Mouton.

Frisch, R., & McArthur, J. (1974). Menstrual cycles: Fatness as a determinant of minimum weight for height necessary for their maintenance or onset. *Science, 185,* 949–951.

Furst, P. T. (Ed.). (1972). *Flesh of the gods: The ritual use of hallucinations.* New York: Praeger Press.

Gallup Report. (1985, May). *Religion in America: 50 years, 1935–1985* (Reprint No. 236). Princeton, NJ: Gallup Poll.

Gardner, B. T., & Gardner, R. A. (1969). Teaching sign language to a chimpanzee. *Science, 165,* 664–672.

Gardner, B. T., & Gardner, R. A. (1985). Signs of intelligence in cross-fostered chimpanzees. *Philosophical Transactions of the Royal Society of London, B308,* 150–176.

Gargan, E. A. (1992, June 4). A single-minded man battles to free slaves. *New York Times,* p. A7.

Gargan, E. A. (1995, June 5). They plow the waves for the squire of seaweed. *New York Times,* p. A4.

Gay, J. (1985). Mummies and babies and friends and lovers in Lesotho. *Journal of Homosexuality, 11*(3–4), 97–116.

Geertz, C. (1963). *Agricultural involution: The processes of ecological change in Indonesia.* Berkeley, CA: University of California Press.

Geertz, C. (1966). Religion as a cultural system. In M. Banton (Ed.), *Anthropological approaches to the study of religion.* London: Tavistock.

Geertz, C. (Ed.). (1971). *Myth, symbol, and culture.* New York: W. W. Norton.

Geertz, C. (1972). Deep play: Notes on the Balinese cockfight. *Daedalus, 101,* 1–37.

Geertz, C. (1973). *The interpretation of cultures*. New York: Basic Books.

Ghazi, K. (1991, June 11). Inch by inch, the women let their hair down. *New York Times*, p. A4.

Gibbs, J. L. (Ed.). (1965). *Peoples of Africa*. New York: Holt, Rinehart & Winston.

Ginsburg, F., & Tsing, A. (1990). *Uncertain terms: Negotiating gender in American culture*. Boston: Beacon Press.

Goddard, H. H. (1913). The Binet tests in relation to immigration. *Journal of Psycho-Asthenics, 18*, 105–107.

Goddard, H. H. (1917). Mental tests and the immigrant. *Journal of Delinquency, 2*, 243–277.

Godelier, M. (1982). La production des grandes hommes: Pouvoir et domination masculine chez les baruya de nouvelle-guinée. In A. Verdiglione (Ed.), *Sexualité et pouvoir*. Paris: Fayard.

Goffman, E. (1955). On face-work: An analysis of ritual elements in social interaction. *Psychiatry, 18*, 213–231.

Goffman, E. (1961). *Asylums*. New York: Anchor Books.

Goffman, E. (1967). *Interaction ritual: An essay on face-to-face behavior*. Garden City, NY: Doubleday.

Goldman, I. (1972). *The Cubeo: Indians of the northwest Amazon*. Urbana, IL: Illinois University Press.

Goldschmidt, W. (1965). Variation and adaptability of culture. *American Anthropologist, 67*, 400–447.

Goleman, D. (1978). Why the brain blocks daytime dreams. *Psychology Today, 9*(10), 69–70.

Gona, D. (Ed.). (1987). *State elective officials and the legislature, 1987–1988*. Lexington, KY: Council for State Governments.

Goode, W. J. (1963). *World revolution and family patterns*. New York: Free Press.

Goodenough, W. H. (1956). Componential analysis and the study of meaning. *Language, 32*, 195–216.

Goody, J. (1970). Cousin terms. *Southwestern Journal of Anthropology, 26*, 125–142.

Goody, J. (1973). Bridewealth and dowry in Africa and Eurasia. In J. Goody & S. J. Tambiah (Eds.), *Bridewealth and dowry*. Cambridge, England: University of Cambridge Press.

Gordon, E. (1981). An analysis of the impact of labour migration on the lives of women in Lesotho. *Journal of Development Studies, 17*(3), 59–76.

Gorer, G. (1943). Themes in Japanese culture. *Transactions of the New York Academy of Sciences, 2d ser., 5*, 106–124.

Gorer, G. (1955). *Exploring English character*. London: Cresset.

Gorer, G. (1964). *The American people: A study in national character*. New York: W. W. Norton. (Originally published 1948)

Gorer, G., & Rickman, J. (1949). *The people of Great Russia*. London: Cresset.

Gough, K. (1959). The Nayars and the definition of marriage. *Journal of the Royal Anthropological Institute, 89*, 23–34.

Gough, K. (1961). Nayar: Central Kerala. In D. Schneider & K. Gough (Eds.), *Matrilineal kinship*. Berkeley, CA: University of California Press.

Gould, S. J. (1981). *The mismeasure of man*. New York: W. W. Norton.

Graburn, N. (1971). *Readings in kinship and social structure*. New York: Harper & Row.

Greenberg, J. H. (1968). *Anthropological linguistics: An introduction*. New York: Random House.

Gregerson. E. (1983). *Sexual practices: The story of human sexuality*. New York: Watts.

Gregor, T. (1982, December). No girls allowed. *Science 82 Magazine, 3*, 26–31.

Gregor, T. (1983). Dark dreams about the white man. *Natural History, 92*(1), pp. 8–14.

Grinnell, G. B. (1961). *The Cheyenne Indians: Their history and ways of life* (Vol. 2). New York: Cooper Square Publishers.

Gross, L., Aurand, S. K., & Adessa, R. (1988). *Violence and discrimination against lesbian and gay people in Philadelphia and the Commonwealth of Pennsylvania*. Philadelphia: Philadelphia Lesbian and Gay Task Force.

Gudschinsky, S. C. (1956). The ABC's of lexicostatistics (glottochronology). *Word, 12*, 175–210.

Gussow, Z. (1960). Pibloktoq (hysteria) among the polar Eskimo: An ethnopsychiatric study. In W. Muensterberger & S. Axelrad (Eds.), *The psychoanalytic studies of society* (Vol. 1). New York: International University Press.

Gussow, Z. (1963). A preliminary report of kayak-angst among the Eskimo of West Greenland: A study in sensory deprivation. *International Journal of Social Psychiatry, 9*, 18–26.

Guthrie, S. (1980). A cognitive theory of religion. *Current Anthropology, 2*, 181–203.

Haas, J. (1982). *The evolution of the prehistoric state*. New York: Columbia University Press.

Habermas, J. (1976). *Legitimation crisis* (T. McCarthy, Trans.). London: Heinemann.

Hahn, E. (1990). Raising eyebrows in Tonga. In P. R. DeVita (Ed.), *The humbled anthropologist: Tales from the Pacific*. Belmont, CA: Wadsworth Publishing Company.

Hall, E. T. (1959). *The silent language*. Greenwich, CT: Fawcett Publications.

Harding, T. G. (1960). Adaptation and stability. In M. D. Sahlins & E. R. Service (Eds.), *Evolution and culture* (pp. 45–68). Ann Arbor, MI: University of Michigan Press.

Harner, M. (1972). *The Jívaro: People of the sacred waterfall*. Garden City, NY: Doubleday/Natural History Press.

Harner, M. (1977). The ecological basis of Aztec cannibalism. *American Ethnologist, 4*(1), 117–135.

Harré, R. (1984). *Personal being*. Cambridge, MA: Harvard University Press.

Harris, G. (1957). Possession "hysteria" in a Kenya tribe. *American Anthropologist, 59*, 1046–1066.

Harris, M. (1968). *The rise of anthropological theory: A history of theories of culture*. New York: Crowell.

Harris, M. (1974). *Cows, pigs, wars and witches: The riddle of culture*. New York: Random House.

Harris, M. (1977). *Cannibals and kings: The origins of culture*. New York: Random House.

Harris, M. (1979). *Cultural materialism: The struggle for a science of culture*. New York: Random House.

Harris, M. (1981). *America now: The anthropology of a changing culture*. New York: Simon & Schuster.

Harris, M. (1986). *Good to eat*. New York: Harper & Row.

Harrison, T. (1937). *Savage civilization.* London: Victor Gollancz.

Hartmann, H. (1976). Capitalism, patriarchy, and job segregation by sex. *Signs: Journal of Women in Culture and Society, 1*(3), 137–169.

Haub, C., & Yanagishita, M. (1995). *1995 world population data sheet.* Washington, DC: Population Reference Bureau.

Hayami, Y., & Kikuchi, M. (1981). *Asian village economy at the crossroads: An economic approach to institutional change.* Tokyo: University of Tokyo Press; Baltimore: Johns Hopkins University Press.

Hayes, K. J., & Nissen, C. H. (1971). Higher mental functions of a home-raised chimpanzee. In A. M. Schrier & F. Stollnitz (Eds.), *Behavior of nonhuman primates* (Vol. 4, pp. 59–115). New York: Academic Press.

Heeren, J., Lindsay, D. B., & Mason, M. (1984). The Mormon concept of mother in heaven. *Journal for the Scientific Study of Religion, 23*(4), 396–411.

Heise, L. (1989a, March/April). Crimes of gender. *World • Watch, 2*(2), 12–21.

Heise, L. (1989b, April 8). The global war against women. *Washington Post,* pp. B1, B4.

Herdt, G. (1981). *Guardians of the flutes: Idioms of masculinity.* New York: McGraw-Hill.

Herdt, G. (1984). *Ritualized homosexuality in Melanesia.* Berkeley, CA: University of California Press. (Originally published 1982)

Herek, G. M. (1989). Hate crimes against lesbians and gay men. *American Psychologist, 44*(6), 948–955.

Herrnstein, R. J., & Murray, C. (1994). *The bell curve: Intelligence and class structure in American life.* New York: Free Press.

Herskovits, M. J. (1940). *The economic life of primitive peoples.* New York: Alfred A. Knopf.

Hill, J. (1978). Apes and language. *Annual Review of Anthropology, 7,* 89–112.

Hoebel, E. A. (1949). *Man in the primitive world.* New York: McGraw-Hill.

Hoebel, E. A. (1954). *The law of primitive man: A study in comparative legal dynamics.* Cambridge, MA: Harvard University Press.

Hofstadter, R. (1963). *Anti-intellectualism in American life.* New York: Alfred A. Knopf.

Hoijer, H. (1964). Cultural implications of some Navaho linguistic categories. In D. Hymes (Ed.), *Language in culture and society: A reader in linguistics and anthropology* (pp. 142–153). New York: Harper & Row.

Hollingshead, A. B., & Redlich, F. C. (1953). Social stratification and psychiatric disorders. *American Sociological Review, 18,* 163–169.

Holmberg, A. R. (1950). *Nomads of the long bow: The Sirionó of eastern Bolivia* (Institute of Social Anthropology Publication No. 10). Washington, DC: Smithsonian Institution.

Honigmann, J. J., & Honigmann, I. (1965). *Eskimo townsmen.* Ottawa, Ontario, Canada: University of Ottawa.

Horwood, H. A. (1969). *Newfoundland.* Toronto, Ontario, Canada: Macmillan of Canada.

Hosken, F. P. (1980). Women and health: Genital and sexual mutilation of women. *International Journal of Women's Studies, 3*(1–3), 300–316.

Hsien, R. (1963). A consideration on Chinese concepts of illness and case illustrations. *Transcultural Psychiatry Research, 15,* 23–30.

Hsien, R. (1965). A study of the aetiology of koro in respect to the Chinese concept of illness. *International Journal of Social Psychiatry, 11,* 7–13.

Hsu, F. L. K. (1961). *Chinese and Americans: A study of two cultures.* New York: Henry Schuman.

Hsu, F. L. K. (Ed.). (1972). *Psychological anthropology: Approaches to culture and personality.* Morriston, NJ: Schenkman.

Hsu, F. L. K. (1983). *Rugged individualism reconsidered: Essays in psychological anthropology.* Knoxville, TN: University of Tennessee Press.

Hymes, D. (1964). *Language in culture and society: A reader in linguistics and anthropology.* New York: Harper & Row.

Hymes, D. (1967). Models of interaction of language and social setting. *Journal of Social Issues, 23*(2), 8–28.

Ineichen, B. (1979). The social geography of marriage. In M. Cook & G. Wilson (Eds.), *Love and attraction.* New York: Pergamon Press.

Jacobs, B. L. (1978). Serotonin: The crucial substance that turns off dreams. *Psychology Today, 9*(10), 70–71.

James, P. E. (with collaboration by H. V. B. Kline). (1959). *A geography of man.* Boston: Ginn.

Jenness, D. (1922). *Report of the Canadian Arctic Expedition, 1913–1918: Vol. 12. The Life of the Copper Eskimo.* Ottawa, Ontario, Canada: National Museum of Canada.

Jensen, A. (1969). How much can we boost I.Q. and scholastic achievement? *Harvard Educational Review, 39*(1), 1–123.

Johnson, P. (1979). *The civilization of ancient Egypt.* London: Weidenfeld & Nicholson.

Jorgensen, J. G., & Truzzi, M. (1974). *Anthropology and American life.* Englewood Cliffs, NJ: Prentice Hall.

Josephides, L. (1985). *The production of inequality: Gender and exchange among the Kewa.* New York: Tavistock.

Kaplan, D. (1960). The law of cultural dominance. In M. D. Sahlins & E. R. Service (Eds.), *Evolution and culture* (pp. 69–92). Ann Arbor, MI: University of Michigan Press.

Kaplan, D., & Manners, R. A. (1972). *Culture theory.* Englewood Cliffs, NJ: Prentice Hall.

Kardiner, A. (Ed.). (1939). *The individual and his society.* New York: Columbia University Press.

Keesing, R. M. (1975). *Kin groups and social structure.* New York: Holt, Rinehart & Winston.

Keesing, R. M. (1982). Introduction. In G. Herdt (Ed.), *Rituals of manhood: Male initiation in Papua New Guinea* (pp. 1–43). Berkeley, CA: University of California Press.

Keil, C. (1979). *Tiv song.* Chicago: University of Chicago Press.

Keller, H. (1954). *The story of my life.* Garden City, NY: Doubleday.

Kellog, W. N. (1968). Communication and language in the home-raised chimpanzee. *Science, 162,* 423–427.

Kelly, R. (1976). Witchcraft and sexual relations. In P. Brown & G. Buchbinder (Eds.), *Man and woman in the New Guinea highlands.* Washington, DC: American Anthropological Association.

Kemper, T. D. (1978). *A social interactional theory of emotions.* New York: John Wiley & Sons.

Kenyatta, J. (1962). *Facing Mount Kenya: The tribal life of the Gikuyu.* New York: Random House.

Kerkhoff, A. C., & Davis, K. E. (1962). Values consensus and need complementarity in mate selection. *American Sociological Review, 27,* 295–303.

Kiev, A. (1972). *Transcultural psychology.* New York: Macmillan.

Kispert, R. J. (1971). *Old English: An introduction.* New York: Holt, Rinehart & Winston.

Kluckhohn, C. (1965). Recurrent themes in myth and myth-making. In A. Dundes (Ed.), *The study of folklore* (pp. 158–168). Englewood Cliffs, NJ: Prentice Hall.

Kluckhohn, C., & Leighton, D. (1946). *The Navaho.* Cambridge, MA: Harvard University Press.

Koestler, A. (1964). *The act of creation.* New York: Macmillan.

Kolanda, P. (1978). *Castes in contemporary India.* Menlo Park, CA: Cummings.

Kolata, G. B. (1974). !Kung hunter-gatherers: Feminism, diet and birth control. *Science, 185,* 932–934.

Kramer, S. N. (1959). *History begins at Sumer.* Garden City, NY: Doubleday.

Kressel, G. M. (1981, April). Sororicide/filiacide: Homicide for family honour. *Current Anthropology, 22*(2), 141–158.

Krige, E. J., & Krige, J. D. (1943). *The realm of the rain-queen.* London: Oxford University Press.

Kroeber, A. L. (1915). The eighteen professions. *American Anthropologist, 17,* 283–289.

Kroeber, A. L. (1917). The superorganic. *American Anthropologist, 19,* 163–213.

Kroeber, A. L. (1939). *Cultural and natural areas of native North America* (American Archaeology and Ethnology Publication No. 38). Berkeley, CA: University of California Press.

Kroeber, A. L. (1944). *Configurations of culture growth.* Berkeley, CA: University of California Press.

Kroeber, A. L. (1948). *Anthropology.* New York: Harcourt, Brace & World.

Kroeber, A. L., & Kluckhohn, C. (1952, November 1). Culture: A critical review of concepts and definitions. *Papers of the Peabody Museum of American Archaeology and Ethnology, 47.* (Reprinted by Random House, n.d.)

Krupke, D. F., & Lavie, P. (1975). Ultradian rhythms: The 90-minute clock inside us. *Psychology Today, 8*(11), 54–57.

Kübler-Ross, E. (1969). *On death and dying.* New York: Macmillan.

LaBarre, W. (1945). Some observations of character structure in the Orient: The Japanese. *Psychiatry, 8,* 326–342.

Labov, W. (1972). *Language in the inner city: Studies in the Black English vernacular.* Philadelphia: University of Pennsylvania Press.

Lacan, J. (1967). *Écrits.* Paris: Seuil.

Laitman, J. (1984, August). The anatomy of human speech. *Natural History, 63,* 20–27.

Lancaster, J. B. (1968). Primate communication systems and the emergence of human language. In P. C. Jay (Ed.), *Primates: Studies in adaptation and*

variability (pp. 447–454). New York: Holt, Rinehart & Winston.

Langness, L. L. (1965). Hysterical psychosis in the New Guinea highlands: A Bena Bena example. *Psychiatry, 28,* 258–277.

Lappé, F. M., & Collins, J. (1977). *Food first: Beyond the myth of scarcity.* New York: Random House.

Lazarus, R. S. (1991). *Emotion and adaptation.* New York: Oxford University Press.

Leach, E. (1969). *Genesis as myth and other essays.* London: Jonathan Cape.

Leaf, M. (1971). Baking and roasting: A compact demonstration of a cultural code. *American Anthropologist, 73,* 267–268.

Leavitt, G. C. (1989). The disappearance of the incest taboo: A cross-cultural test of general evolutionary hypotheses. *American Anthropologist, 91,* 116–131.

Lee, G. R., & Kezis, M. (1979). Family structure and the status of the elderly. *Journal of Comparative Family Studies, 10,* 429–443.

Lee, R. B. (1969). !Kung Bushman subsistence: An input-output analysis. In A. P. Vayda (Ed.), *Environment and cultural behavior: Ecological studies in cultural anthropology.* Garden City, NY: Natural History Press.

Lee, R. B. (1972). *The Dobe !Kung.* New York: Holt, Rinehart & Winston.

Lee, R. B. (1979). *The !Kung San: Men, women and work in a foraging society.* Cambridge, England: Cambridge University Press.

Lee, R. B. (1984). *The Dobe !Kung.* New York: Holt, Rinehart & Winston.

Lee, R. B., & DeVore, I. (Eds.). (1968a). *Man the hunter.* Chicago: Aldine.

Lee, R. B., & DeVore, I. (1968b). Population growth and the beginnings of sedentary life among the !Kung Bushmen. In B. Spooner (Ed.), *Population growth: Anthropological implications* (pp. 329–342). Cambridge, MA: M.I.T. Press.

Lehmann, A. C., & Myers, J. E. (1985). *Magic, witchcraft, and religion: An anthropological study of the supernatural.* Palo Alto, CA: Mayfield.

Lehmann, H. E. (1975). Schizophrenia: Clinical features. In A. M. Freedman, H. I. Kaplan, & B. J. Sadock (Eds.), *Comprehensive textbook of psychiatry—II* (Vol. 1, pp. 890–923). Baltimore: Williams & Wilkins.

Lehne, K. (1976). Homophobia among men. In D. David & B. Brannon (Eds.), *The forty-nine percent majority* (pp. 66–88). Reading, MA: Addison-Wesley.

Lenneberg, E. H. (1967). *The biological foundations of language.* New York: John Wiley.

LeVine, R. A. (1973). *Culture, behavior and personality.* Chicago: Aldine.

LeVine, R. A. (Ed.). (1974). *Culture and personality: Contemporary readings.* Chicago: Aldine.

Lévi-Strauss, C. (1950). *Sociologie et anthropologie.* Paris: Presses Universitaires de France.

Lévi-Strauss, C. (1967). *Structural anthropology* (C. Jacobson & B. G. Schoepf, Trans.). New York: Anchor Books. (Original work published 1958)

Lévi-Strauss, C. (1969). *The elementary structures of kinship* (Rev. ed., J. H. Bell & J. R. von Sturmer, Trans.). Boston: Beacon Press.

Lévi-Strauss, C. (1970). *The raw and the cooked*. Chicago: University of Chicago Press.

Levy, H. S. (1966). *Chinese footbinding: The history of a curious erotic custom*. New York: Walton Rawls.

Lewis, I. M. (1971). *Ecstatic religion*. Baltimore: Penguin Books.

Lewis, L. S., & Brissett, D. (1967). Sex as work: A study of avocational counseling. *Social Problems, 15*(1) 8–18.

Lewis, O. (1966, October). Culture of poverty. *Scientific American, 215*, 19–25.

Li, An-che. (1937). Zuñi: Some observations and queries. *American Anthropologist, 39*, 62–77.

Lieberman, P. (1984). *The biology and evolution of language*. Cambridge, MA: Harvard University Press.

Lieberman, P., & Crelin, E. S. (1971). On the speech of Neanderthal. *Linguistic Inquiry, 2*, 203–222.

Linden, E. (1974). *Apes, men and language*. New York: Penguin Books.

Linnaeus, C. (1956). *Systema naturae per regna tria naturae secundum classes, ordines, species cum characteribus, differentiis, synonymis, locis* (Vol. 1). London: British Museum. (Photographic facsimile of 10th ed., Stockholm: Laurentii Salvii, 1735)

Linton, R. (1936). *The study of man: An introduction*. New York: Appleton-Century-Crofts.

Livermore, M. A. (1889). *My story of the war*. Hartford, CT: A. D. Worthington.

Lizot, J. (1976). *The Yąnomami in the face of ethnocide* (International Work Group for Indigenous Affairs Document No. 22). Copenhagen, Denmark: International Work Group for Indigenous Affairs.

Llewellyn, K. N., & Hoebel, E. A. (1941). *The Cheyenne way*. Norman, OK: University of Oklahoma Press.

Lomax, A. (1962). Song structure and social structure. *Ethnology, 1*, 425–451.

Lomax, A. (1968). *Folk song style and culture* (AAAS Publication No. 88). Washington, DC: American Association for the Advancement of Science.

Lomax, A., & Arensberg, C. M. (1977). A worldwide evolutionary classification of cultures by subsistence systems. *American Anthropologist, 18*, 659–708.

Ludwig, A. M. (1972). Altered state of consciousness. In C. T. Tart (Ed.), *Altered states of consciousness* (pp. 11–24). Garden City, NY: Doubleday. (Reprinted from *Archives of General Psychiatry, 15*, pp. 215–234, 1966)

Lustig-Arecco, V. (1975). *Technology: Strategies for survival*. New York: Holt, Rinehart & Winston.

Maine, H. S. (1879). *Ancient law: Its connection with the early history of ideas, and its relation to modern ideas*. London: J. Murray.

Malinowski, B. (1922). *Argonauts of the western Pacific*. New York: Dutton.

Malinowski, B. (1926). *Crime and custom in savage society*. London: Routledge & Kegan Paul.

Malinowski, B. (1929). *The sexual life of savages in northwestern Melanesia: An ethnographic account of courtship, marriage and family life among the natives of the Trobriand Islands, British New Guinea*. New York: Harcourt, Brace & World.

Malinowski, B. (1935). On the concept of function in social science. *American Anthropologist, 37*, 394–402.

Malinowski, B. (1939a). The group and the individual in functional analysis. *American Journal of Sociology, 44*, 938–964.

Malinowski, B. (1939b). *Sex and repression in savage society*. London: Kegan Paul, Trench, Trubner.

Malinowski, B. (1945). *Dynamics of culture change: An inquiry into race relations in Africa* (P. Kaberry, Ed.). New Haven, CT: Yale University Press.

Mandelbaum, D. G. (Ed.). (1968). *Selected writings of Edward Sapir in language, culture and personality*. Berkeley, CA: University of California Press.

Mandelbaum, D. G. (1972). *Society in India*. Berkeley, CA: University of California Press.

Manson, S., Shore, J., & Bloom, J. (1985). The depressive experience in American Indian communities: A challenge for psychiatric theory and diagnosis. In A. Kleinman & B. Good (Eds.), *Culture and depression: Studies in the anthropology and cross-cultural psychiatry of affect and disorder*. Berkeley, CA: University of California Press.

Maquet, J. (1986). *The aesthetic experience: An anthropologist looks at the visual arts*. New Haven, CT: Yale University Press.

Marcus, G. E. (1986). Afterword: Ethnographic writing and anthropological careers. In J. Clifford & G. E. Marcus (Eds.), *Writing culture* (pp. 262–266). Berkeley, CA: University of California Press.

Marcus, G. E., & Cushman, D. (1982). Ethnographies as texts. *Annual Review of Anthropology, 11*, 25–69.

Marcus, G. E., & Fischer, M. M. J. (1986). *Anthropology as culture critique: An experimental moment in the human sciences*. Chicago: University of Chicago Press.

Marett, R. R. (1909). *The threshold of religion*. London: Methuen.

Marler, P. (1965). Communication in monkeys and apes. In I. DeVore (Ed.), *Primate behavior: Field studies of monkeys and apes* (pp. 544–584). New York: Holt, Rinehart & Winston.

Marsella, A. J., DeVos, G., & Hsu, F. L. K. (Eds.). (1985). *Culture and self: Asian and western perspectives*. New York: Tavistock Publications.

Martin, M. K., & Voorhies, B. (1975). *Female of the species*. New York: Columbia University Press.

Marx, K. (1961). *Economic and philosophic manuscripts of 1844*. Moscow: Foreign Language Publishing House.

McCarley, R. W. (1978). Where dreams come from: A new theory. *Psychology Today, 12*(7), 15–20.

Mead, M. (1928). *Coming of age in Samoa: A psychological study of primitive youth for western civilization*. New York: William Morrow.

Mead, M. (1942). *And keep your powder dry: An anthropologist looks at America*. New York: William Morrow.

Mead, M. (1950). *Sex and treatment in three primitive societies*. New York: Mentor.

Meggitt, M. (1964). Male-female relationships in the highlands of Australian New Guinea. In J. B. Watson (Ed.), *New Guinea: The central highlands* (American Anthropological Association Special Publication 6, No. 4, Pt. 2). Washington, DC: American Anthropological Association.

Mejer, M. (1985). Oppression of women and refugee status. In *International seminar on refugee women* (pp. 30–38). Amsterdam: Dutch Refugee Association.

Miller, S. N. (1974). The playful, the crazy and the nature of pretense. In E. Norbeck (Ed.), *The anthropological study of human play* (Vol. 6, No. 3, pp. 31–52). Houston, TX: William Rice University.

Minister of Supply and Services. (1988). *Canada yearbook, 1988*. Ottawa, Ontario, Canada: Minister of Supply and Services.

Minturn, L., & Lambert, W. W. (1964). *Mothers of six cultures: Antecedents of child rearing*. New York: John Wiley.

Montagu, A. (1974). *Man's most dangerous myth: The fallacy of race*. Fair Lawn, NJ: Oxford University Press.

Montagu, A. (Ed.). (1980). *Sociobiology examined*. New York: Oxford University Press.

Montagu, A. (1986). *Touching: The human significance of the skin* (3rd ed.). New York: Harper & Row.

Moore, H. (1988). *Feminism and anthropology*. Minneapolis, MN: University of Minnesota Press.

Moore, O. K. (1957). Divination: A new perspective. *American Anthropologist, 59*, 69–74.

Moran, M. (1990). *Civilized women: Gender and prestige in southeastern Liberia*. Ithaca, NY: Cornell University Press.

Morgan, L. H. (1851). *League of the ho-de-no-sau-nee or Iroquois*. Rochester, NY: Sage & Brothers.

Morgan, L. H. (1877). *Ancient society*. New York: World.

Moris, J. (1981). *Managing induced rural development*. Bloomington, IN: International Development Institute.

Mosher, S. (1983). *Broken earth: The rural Chinese*. New York: Free Press.

Mounin, G. (1976). Language, communication, chimpanzees. *Current Anthropology, 17*, 1–21.

Mueller, M. B. (1977). *Women and men in rural Lesotho: The periphery of the periphery*. Waltham, MA: Brandeis University Press.

Munroe, R. L., & Munroe, R. H. (1977). Male transvestism and subsistence economy. *Journal of Social Psychology, 103*, 307–308.

Munroe, R. L., Munroe, R. H., & Whiting, J. (1973). The couvade: A psychological analysis. *Ethos, 1*(1), 30–74.

Munroe, R. L., Whiting, J. W. M., & Hally, D. J. (1969). Institutionalized male transvestism and sex distinctions. *American Anthropologist, 71*(1), 87–91.

Murdock, G. P. (1934). *Our primitive contemporaries*. New York: Macmillan.

Murdock, G. P. (1950). Family stability in non-European cultures. *Annals of the American Academy, 272*, 195–201.

Murdock, G. P. (1957). World ethnographic sample. *American Anthropologist, 59*, 664–487.

Murdock, G. P. (1967). *Ethnographic atlas*. Pittsburgh, PA: University of Pittsburgh Press.

Murdock, G. P., Ford, C. S., Hudson, A. E., Kennedy, R., Simmons, L. W., & Whiting, J. W. (1961). *Outline of cultural materials* (5th ed.). New Haven, CT: Human Relations Area Files.

Murdock, G. P., & Provost, C. (1973). Factors in the division of labor by sex: A cross-cultural analysis. *Ethnology, 12*, 203–225.

Murphy, J. M. (1976). Psychiatric labeling in cross-cultural perspective. *Science, 191*(4230), 1019–1028.

Murphy, R. F., & Kasdan, L. (1959). The structure of parallel cousin marriage. *American Anthropologist, 61*, 17–29.

Musil, A. (1928). *Manners and customs of the Rwala Bedouins*. New York: American Geographical Society.

Nadel, S. F. (1952). Witchcraft in four African societies: An essay in comparison. *American Anthropologist, 54*, 18–29.

Nader, L. (Ed.) (1965). The ethnography of law. *American Anthropologist, 67*(Supplement), 3–32.

Nader, L., & Todd, H. F. (1978). *The disputing process: Law in ten societies*. New York: Columbia University Press.

Nanda, S. (1985). The Hijras of India: Cultural and individual dimensions of an institutionalized third gender role. *Journal of Homosexuality, 11*(3–4), 35–54.

Nanda, S. (1988). More dialogue on the "bloodthirsty" Semai. *American Anthropologist, 90*(2), 422–423.

Nanda, S. (1990). *Neither man nor woman: The Hijras of India*. Belmont, CA: Wadsworth Publishing Company.

Naroll, R. (1966). Does military deterrence deter? *Trans-Action, 3*(2), 14–20.

Naroll, R. (1973). Holocultural theory tests. In R. Naroll & F. Naroll (Eds.), *Main currents in cultural anthropology* (pp. 309–384). New York: Appleton-Century-Crofts.

Nash, J. (1993). *Global integration and subsistence insecurity: Comparative perspectives and strategies*. Paper presented at the Curriculum Development Institute of the Interfaith Hunger Appeal, University of Massachusetts, Amherst, MA.

Nassehi-Behnam, V. (1985). Change and the Iranian family. *Current Anthropology, 26*, 557–562.

Neale, W. C. (1976). *Monies in societies*. San Francisco: Chandler & Sharp.

Needham, R. (Ed.). (1972). *Rethinking kinship and marriage*. London: Tavistock.

Nelson, M. (1989). Why witches were women. In J. Freeman (Ed.), *Women: A feminist perspective* (4th ed.) (pp. 335–350). Mountain View, CA: Mayfield.

Nemiah, J. C. (1975). Phobic neurosis. In A. M. Freedman, H. I. Kaplan, & B. J. Sadock (Eds.), *Comprehensive textbook of psychiatry—II* (Vol. 2, pp. 1247–1255). Baltimore: Williams & Wilkins.

Neusner, J. (1979). *The Talmud as anthropology*. New York: Jewish Theological Seminary of America.

Newman, P. L. (1964). Wild man behavior in a New Guinea highlands community. *American Anthropologist, 66*, 1–19.

Niebuhr, G. (1995, January 29). Zuñis mix traditions with icons of church. *New York Times*, p. 14.

Nock, S. L., & Kingston, P. W. (1990). The political institution: The politics of abortion. In S. L. Nock & P. W. Kingston (Eds.), *The sociology of public issues* (pp. 194–213). Belmont, CA: Wadsworth Publishing Company.

Noll, R. (1985). Mental imagery cultivation as a cultural phenomenon: The role of visions in shamanism. *Current Anthropology, 26*, 443–461.

Obeyesekere, G. (1985). Depression, Buddhism, and the work of culture in Sri Lanka. In A. Kleinman & B. Good (Eds.), *Culture and depression* (pp. 134–152). Berkeley, CA: University of California Press.

O'Kelley, C. G. (1980). *Women and men in society.* New York: Van Nostrand.

Okonjo, K. (1976). The dual-sex political system in operation: Igbo women and community politics in midwestern Nigeria. In N. J. Hafkin & E. G. Bay (Eds.), *Women in Africa.* Stanford, CA: Stanford University Press.

Olmstead, F. L. (1904). *A Journey in the seaboard slave states in the years 1853–1854 with remarks on their economy* (Vol. 2). New York: Putnam.

Ortner, S. B. (1974). Is female to male as nature is to culture? In M. Z. Rosaldo & L. Lamphere (Eds.), *Women, culture, and society* (pp. 67–87). Stanford, CA: Stanford University Press.

Otterbein, K. F. (1970). *The evolution of war.* New Haven, CA: Human Relations Area Files.

Otto, R. (1923). *The idea of the holy: An inquiry into the non-rational factor in the idea of the divine and its relation to the rational* (J. W. Harvey, Trans.). London: Oxford University Press.

Palmer, I. (1985). *The impact of male out-migration on women in farming.* West Hartford, CT: Kumarian Press.

Parker, S. (1962). Eskimo psychopathology in the context of Eskimo personality and culture. *American Anthropologist, 64,* 76–96.

Pasternak, B. (1976). *Introduction to kinship and social organization.* Englewood Cliffs, NJ: Prentice Hall.

Patterson, F. (1978). Conversations with a gorilla. *National Geographic, 154*(4), 438–465.

Paul, R. A. (1978). Instinctive aggression in man: The Semai case. *Journal of Anthropology, 1*(1), 65–79.

Perham, M. F. (1937). *Native administration in Nigeria.* London: Oxford University Press.

Peters, L. G., & Price-Williams, D. R. (1980). Towards an experiential analysis of shamanism. *American Ethnologist, 7,* 397–418.

Pike, K. (1967). *Language in relation to a unified theory of the structure of human behavior* (Vol. 1). The Hague, Netherlands: Mouton.

Polyani, K. (1966). *Dahomey and the slave trade.* Seattle, CA: University of Washington Press.

Popkin, S. L. (1979). *The rational peasant: The political economy of rural society in Vietnam.* Berkeley, CA: University of California Press.

Popov, A. A. (1936). *Tavgytsy: Matgerialy po ethnografi avamskikh i vedeyevskikh tavgytzevi* (Special Publication 1, No. 5). Moscow and Leningrad: AN, Trudy Instituta Anthropologii i Ethnografii.

Pospisil, L. (1971). *Anthropology of law: A comparative theory.* New York: Harper & Row.

Pospisil, L. (1972). *The ethnology of law.* (Addison-Wesley Module in Anthropology No. 12). Reading, MA: Addison-Wesley.

Poussaint, A. F. (1967, August 20). A Negro psychiatrist explains the Negro psyche. *New York Times,* Sec. 6, pp. 52–80.

Powell, B., & Jacobs, J. A. (1983). Sex and consensus in occupational prestige ratings. *Sociology and Social Research 67*(4), 392–404.

Prescott, J. W. (1990). Personality profiles of "pro-choice" and "anti-choice" individuals and cultures. In J. W. Prescott & E. Doerr (Eds.), *Abortion rights and fetal "personhood"* (pp. 109–110). Long Beach, CA: Centerline Press.

Price-Williams, D. R. (1985). On mental imagery and shamanism. *Current Anthropology, 26*(5), 656.

Putnam, C. (1967). *Race and reality: A search for solutions.* Washington, DC: Public Affairs Press.

Rabinow, P. (1977). *Reflections on fieldwork in Morocco.* Berkeley, CA: University of California.

Radcliffe-Brown, A. R. (1952). *Structure and function in primitive society.* London: Oxford University Press.

Radcliffe-Brown, A. R. (1958). Taboo. In W. A. Lessa & E. Z. Vogt (Eds.), *Reader in comparative religion: An anthropological approach* (pp. 45–68). Evanston, IL: Row, Peterson.

Radin, P. (1937). *Primitive religion.* New York: Dover Books.

Raheja, B. (1988). *The poison in the gift: Ritual, presentation, and the dominant caste in a North Indian village.* Chicago: University of Chicago Press.

Randall, T. (1990). Domestic violence intervention calls for more than treating injuries. *JAMA: Journal of the American Medical Association, 264*(3), 939–940, 943.

Rappaport, R. A. (1967). Ritual regulation of environmental relations among a New Guinea people. *Ethnology, 6,* 17–30.

Rappaport, R. A. (1968). *Pigs for the ancestors: Ritual in the ecology of a Papua New Guinea people.* New Haven, CT: Yale University Press.

Rasmussen, K. (1922). *Grønlandsagen.* Berlin: Gyldendal'scher Verlag.

Rattray, R. S. (1923). *Ashanti.* London: Oxford University Press.

Rattray, R. S. (1929). *Ashanti law and constitution.* London: Clarendon Press.

Redfield, R., & Rojas, A. V. (1934). *Chan Kom: A Maya village* (Carnegie Institution Publication No. 448). Washington, DC: Carnegie Institution.

Reiss, I. L. (1986). *Journey into sexuality: An exploratory voyage.* Englewood Cliffs, NJ: Prentice Hall.

Ribiero, D. (1971). *The Americas and civilization.* New York: Dutton.

Rich, A. (1980). Compulsory heterosexuality and lesbian existence. *Signs: Journal of Women in Culture and Society, 5*(4), 631–660.

Ringe, D. (1995). "Nostratic" and the factor of chance. *Diachronica, 12*(1), 55–74.

Rist, R. (1970). Student social census and teacher expectations: The self-fulfilling prophecy in ghetto education. *Harvard Educational Review, 40*(3), 411–451.

Rivers, W. H. R. (1901). *The Todas.* New York: Macmillan.

Rivers, W. H. R. (1905). Observations on the senses of the Todas. *British Journal of Psychology, 1,* 321–396.

Rivers, W. H. R. (1926). *Psychology and ethnology.* New York: Harcourt, Brace & World.

Robarchek, C. A., & Dentan, R. K. (1987). Blood drunkenness and the bloodthirsty Semai: Unmaking an anthropological myth. *American Anthropologist, 89,* 356–365.

Roberts, J., Arth, M. J., & Bush, R. R. (1959). Games in culture. *American Anthropologist, 61,* 597–605.

Roberts, J., & Sutton-Smith, B. (1962). Child training and game involvement. *Ethnology, 1,* 166–185.

Roberts, S. (1979). *Order and dispute: An introduction to legal anthropology.* New York: St. Martin's Press.

Robertson, A. F. (1984) *People and the state: An anthropology of planned development.* Cambridge, England: Cambridge University Press.

Robinson, J. T. (1972). *Early hominid posture and locomotion.* Chicago: University of Chicago Press.

Rodney, W. (1972). *How Europe underdeveloped Africa.* London: Bogle-L'Ouverture Publications.

Rosaldo, M. Z., & Lamphere, L. (Eds.). (1974). *Woman, culture, and society.* Stanford, CA: Stanford University Press.

Rosenhan, D. (1973, January 19). On being sane in insane places. *Science, 179,* 250–258.

Roth, W. E. (1963). Superstition, magic and medicine. *North Queensland* (Australia) *Ethnographic Bulletin, 5.*

Rubel, A. J. (1960). Concepts of disease in Mexican-American culture. *American Anthropologist, 62,* 795–814.

Ruby, J. (Ed.). (1982). *A crack in the mirror: Reflexive perspectives in anthropology.* Philadelphia: University of Pennsylvania Press.

Rumbaugh, D. M., von Glasersfeld, E. C., Warner, H., Gill, T. V., Brown, J. V., Pisani, P., & Bell, C. L. (1977). A computer-controlled language training system for investigating the language skills of young apes. *Biological Research Methods and Instrumentation, 5*(5), 385–392.

Russell, D. E. H., & Van de Ven, N. (Eds.). (1976). *Crimes against women: Proceedings of the international tribunal.* Millbrae, CA: Les Femmes.

Sachs, J. (1992, March). Building a market economy in Poland. *Scientific American, 267,* 34–40.

Safilios-Rothschild, C. (1985). The persistence of women's invisibility in agriculture: Theoretical and policy lessons from Lesotho and Sierra Leone. *Economic Development and Cultural Change, 33*(1), 299–317.

Sahlins, M. D. (1960, September). The origins of society. *Scientific American, 203,* 76–89.

Sahlins, M. D. (1962). *Primitive social organization: An evolutionary perspective.* New York: Random House.

Sahlins, M. D. (1968). *Tribesmen.* Englewood Cliffs, NJ: Prentice Hall.

Sahlins, M. D. (1972). *Stone age economics.* New York: Aldine.

Sahlins, M. D. (1976). *Cultural and practical reason.* Chicago: University of Chicago Press.

Sahlins, M. D., & Service, E. R. (1960). *Evolution and culture.* Ann Arbor, MI: University of Michigan Press.

Saitoti, T. O. (1986). *The worlds of a Maasai warrior: An autobiography.* Berkeley, CA: University of California Press.

Sanday, P. R. (1973). Toward a theory of the status of women. *American Anthropologist, 75,* 1682–1700.

Sanday, P. R. (1974). Female status in the public domain. In M. Z. Rosaldo & L. Lamphere (Eds.), *Women, culture, and society* (pp. 189–206). Stanford, CA: Stanford University Press.

Sanday, P. R. (1981). *Female power and male dominance: On the origins of sexual inequality.* New York: Cambridge University Press.

Sapir, E. (1924). Culture, genuine and spurious. *American Journal of Sociology, 29,* 401–429.

Sapir, E. (1932). Cultural anthropology and psychiatry. *Journal of Abnormal Psychology, 27,* 229–242.

Sapir, E. (1934). The emergence of the concept of personality. *Journal of Social Psychology, 5,* 408–415.

Sapir, E. (1949). The status of linguistics as a science. In D. G. Mandelbaum (Ed.), *Selected writings of Edward Sapir on language, culture, and personality.* Los Angeles: University of California Press.

Saussure, F. de. (1959). *Course in modern linguistics* (W. Baskin, Trans.). New York: Philosophical Library.

Savage-Rumbaugh, E. S., Pate, J. L., Lawson, J., Smith, S. T., & Rosenbaum, S. (1983). Can a chimpanzee make a statement? *Journal of Experimental Psychology: General, 112*(4), 457–492.

Savage-Rumbaugh, E. S., Rumbaugh, D. M., & Boysen, S. L. (1980). *American Scientist, 68,* 49–61.

Scheff, T. (1966). *Being mentally ill: A sociological theory.* Chicago: Aldine.

Scheff, T. (1977). The distancing of emotion in ritual. *Current Anthropology, 18*(3), 483–506.

Schieffelin, L. (1983). Anger and shame in the tropical forest: On affect as a cultural system in Papua, New Guinea. *Ethos, 11*(3), 181–191.

Schlegel, A., & Barry, H. (1986). The cultural consequences of female contribution to subsistence. *American Anthropologist, 88,* 144–150.

Schlegel, A., & Eloul, R. (1988). Marriage transactions: Labor, property, status. *American Anthropologist, 90*(2), 291–309.

Schneider, D. M. (1980). *American kinship: A cultural account* (2nd ed.). Chicago: University of Chicago Press.

Schneider, D. M., & Gough, K. (Eds.). (1961). *Matrilineal kinship.* Berkeley, CA: University of California Press.

Schuler, M. (1986). Women and the law. In R. S. Gallin, M. Aronoff, & A. Ferguson (Eds.), *The women and international development annual* (Vol. 1, pp. 155–187). Boulder, CO: Westview Press.

Schusky, E. L. (1971). *Manual for kinship analysis* (2nd ed.). New York: Holt, Rinehart & Winston.

Schusky, E. L. (1975). *Variation in kinship.* New York: Holt, Rinehart & Winston.

Schwimmer, E. (1982). Male couples in New Guinea. In G. Herdt (Ed.), *Rituals of manhood: Male initiation in Papua New Guinea* (pp. 248–291). Berkeley, CA: University of California Press.

Scoditti, G. (1983). Kula on Kitava. In J. Leach & E. Leach (Eds.), *The Kula: New perspectives in Massim exchange.* New York: Cambridge University Press.

Scott, J. C. (1976). *The moral economy of the peasant: Rebellion and subsistence in Southeast Asia.* New Haven, CT: Yale University Press.

Scott, R. (1969). *The making of blind men.* New York: Russell Sage Foundation.

Scull, A. (1979). *Museums of madness: The social organization of insanity in nineteenth century England.* New York: St. Martin's Press.

Seager, J., & Olson, A. (1986). *Women in the world: An international atlas.* New York: Simon & Schuster.

Selye, H. (1976). *The stress of life*. New York: McGraw-Hill.

Service, E. R. (1962). *Primitive social organization: An evolutionary perspective*. New York: Random House.

Service, E. R. (1971). *Cultural evolutionism: Theory in practice*. New York: Holt, Rinehart & Winston.

Service, E. R. (1978). *Profiles in ethnology*. New York: Harper & Row.

Sharon, D. (1978). *Wizard of the four winds: A shaman's story*. New York: Macmillan.

Sharp, L. (1952). Steel axes for stone age Australians. In E. H. Spicer (Ed.), *Human problems in technological change* (pp. 69–90). New York: Russell Sage Foundation.

Sheffield, C. (1987). Sexual terrorism: The social control of women. In B. B. Hess & M. M. Ferree (Eds.), *Analyzing gender: A handbook of social science research*. Newbury Park, CA: Sage Publications.

Shepherd, G., & Shepherd, G. (1984). *A kingdom transformed: Rhetorical patterns with institutionalization of Mormonism*. Salt Lake City, UT: University of Utah Press.

Shipman, P. (1994). *The evolution of racism: Human differences and the use and abuse of science*. New York: Simon & Schuster.

Shostak, M. (1983). *Nisa: The life and words of a !Kung woman*. New York: Random House.

Sihler, A. L. (1973). Baking and roasting. *American Anthropologist, 75*, 1721–1725.

Simmons, L. W. (Ed.). (1942). *Sun Chief: The autobiography of a Hopi Indian*. New Haven, CT: Yale University Press.

Simons, R. C., & Hughes, C. C. (1985). *The culture-bound syndromes: Folk illnesses of psychiatric and anthropological interest*. Boston: D. Reidel

Speck, F. (1909). *Ethnology of the Yuchi Indians* (Anthropological Publications of the University [of Pennsylvania] Museum Special Issue, No. 1, Pt. 1). Philadelphia: University of Pennsylvania Press.

Starcke, C. N. (1976). *The primitive family in its origin and development*. Chicago: University of Chicago Press.

Stephens, W. N. (1963). *The family in cross-cultural perspective*. New York: Holt, Rinehart & Winston.

Steward, J. H. (1938). *Great-Basin sociopolitical groups* (Bureau of American Ethnology Bulletin No. 120). Washington, DC: U.S. Government Printing Office.

Steward, J. H. (1955). *The theory of cultural change: The methodology of multilinear evolution*. Urbana, IL: University of Illinois Press.

Stow, G. W. (1905). *The native races of South Africa: A history of the intrusion of the Hottentots and Bantu into the hunting grounds of the Bushmen, the aborigines of the country*. London: S. Sonnenschein.

Strathern, M. (1980). No nature, no culture: The Hagen case. In C. P. MacCormack & M. Strathern (Eds.), *Nature, culture and gender* (pp. 174–222). Cambridge, England: Cambridge University Press.

Stuckert, R. P. (1966). Race mixture: The African ancestry of White Americans. In P. B. Hammond (Ed.), *Physical anthropology and archaeology: Selected readings* (pp. 192–197). New York: Macmillan.

Survey of anthropology Ph.D.'s, 1990. (1991). *Anthropology Newsletter, 32*.

Sussman, R. (1972). Child transport, family size and the increase in human population size during the neolithic. *Current Anthropology, 13*, 258–267.

Svenson, F. (1980). Aboriginal peoples of Siberia. In G. Ashworth (Ed.), *World minorities in the eighties*. Sunbury, England: Guttermaine House.

Swanson, G. E. (1960). *The birth of the gods: The origin of primitive beliefs*. Ann Arbor, MI: University of Michigan Press.

Swartz, M. J., Turner, V. W., & Tuden, A. (Eds.). (1966). *Political anthropology*. Chicago: Aldine.

Szasz, T. (1970). *Ideology and insanity: Essays on the dehumanization of man*. Garden City, NY: Doubleday.

Tambiah, Y. (1986). Sri Lanka: Violence and exploitation. In M. Schuler (Ed.), *Empowerment and the law: Strategies of Third World women* (pp. 145–154). Washington, DC: Overseas Education Fund.

Tanaka, J. (1977). Subsistence ecology of the Central Kalahari !Kung. In R. B. Lee & I. Devore (Eds.), *Kalahari hunter gatherers* (pp. 99–119). Cambridge, MA: Harvard University Press.

Tanfer, K., & Horn, M. (1985). Contraceptive use, pregnancy and fertility patterns among single American women in their 20's. *Family Planning Perspectives, 17*(1), 10–19.

Tanner, N. (1974). *Marifocality in Indonesia and Africa and among Black Americans*. In M. Z. Rosaldo & L. Lamphere (Eds.), *Women, culture, and society*. Stanford, CA: Stanford University Press.

Terrace, H. S. (1979). *Nim*. New York: Alfred A. Knopf.

Terrace, H. S., Pettito, L. A., Sanders, R., & Bever, T. G. (1979). Can an ape create a sentence? *Science, 206*, 891–902.

Textor, R. B. (Ed.). (1967). *A cross-cultural summary*. New Haven, CT: HRAF Press.

Thomas, E. M. (1959). *The harmless people*. New York: Alfred A. Knopf.

Thompson, R. F. (1968). Aesthetics in traditional Africa. *Art News, 66*(9), 44–45, 63–66.

Thompson, R. F. (1973). Yoruba artistic criticism. In W. I.. d' Azevedo (Ed.), *The traditional artist in African societies* (pp. 19–61). Bloomington, IN: Indiana University Press.

Times Mirror. (1987). *The people, press and politics*. Reading, MA: Addison-Wesley.

Tobias, P. V. (1983). Recent advances in the evolution of hominids with especial reference to brain and speech. *Pontifical Academy of Sciences Scripta Varia, 50*, 85–140.

Toelkin, B. (1979). *The dynamics of folklore*. Boston: Houghton Mifflin.

Tonkinson, R. (1974). *The Jigalong mob: Aboriginal victors of the desert crusade*. Menlo Park, CA: Cummings.

Toth, E. L. (1986). *The velvet ghetto* (Research Report). San Francisco: International Association of Business Consultants Foundation.

Toth, E. L. (1989). *Beyond the velvet ghetto* (Research report). San Francisco: International Association of Business Consultants Foundation.

Turnbull, C. (1961). *The forest people*. New York: Simon & Schuster.

Turner, V. (1969). *The ritual process: Structure and anti-structure.* Chicago: Aldine.

Tylor, E. B. (1871). *Primitive culture: Researches into the development of mythology, philosophy, religion, language, art and custom.* London: J. Murray.

Uberoi, J. P. S. (1962). *The politics of the Kula ring: An analysis of the findings of Bronislaw Malinowski.* Manchester, England: University of Manchester Press.

U.S. Bureau of the Census. (1994). *Statistical abstract of the United States, 1994* (114th ed.). Washington, DC: U.S. Government Printing Office.

U.S. Bureau of Census. (1995). *Households and families, by type* (Current Population Reports, Series P-20, No. 477). Washington, DC: U.S. Government Printing Office.

USNCCPV (U.S. National Commission on the Causes and Prevention of Violence). (1969). *Justice: To establish justice, to ensure domestic tranquility. Final report.* Washington, DC: U.S. Government Printing Office.

Van den Berghe, P., & Barash, D. (1977). *Human family systems: An evolutionary view.* New York: Elsevier Science Publishing Co.

Van Gennep, A. (1960). *The rites of passage* (S. T. Kimball, Trans.). Chicago: University of Chicago Press. (Original work published 1908)

Van Loon, F. H. G. (1926). Amok and latah. *Journal of Abnormal and Social Psychology, 21,* 434–444.

van Willigen, J. (1986). *Applied anthropology: An introduction.* New York: Bergin & Garvey.

Vayda, A. P. (Ed.). (1969). *Environment and cultural behavior: Ecological studies in cultural anthropology.* New York: Natural History Press.

Vayda, A. P. (1976). *War in ecological perspective.* New York: Plenum Press.

Vayda, A. P., & Rappaport, R. A. (1968). Ecology: Cultural and noncultural. In J. H. Clifton (Ed.), *Introduction to cultural anthropology.* Boston: Houghton Mifflin.

Vetter, B. M., & Babco, E. L. (1986). *Professional women and minorities: A manpower resource data service.* Washington, DC: Commission on Professionals in Science and Technology.

Walker, E. (1972). *The emergent Native Americans.* Boston, MA: Little, Brown.

Wallace, A. F. C. (1961). *Culture and personality.* New York: Random House.

Wallace, A. F. C. (1966). *Religion: An anthropological view.* New York: Random House.

Wallace, A. F. C. (1972). Mental illness, biology, and culture. In F. L. K. Hsu (Ed.), *Psychological anthropology* (pp. 363–402). Cambridge, MA: Schenkman.

Wallerstein, I. (1974). *The modern world-system.* New York: Academic Press.

Warner, W. L. (1953). *American life: Dream and reality.* Chicago: University of Chicago Press.

Watzlawick, P., Beavin, J. H., & Jackson, D. (1967). *Pragmatics of human communication: A study of interactional patterns, pathologies, and paradoxes.* New York: W. W. Norton.

Weinberg, G. (1985). Homophobia. In O. Pocs (Ed.), *Annual editions: Human sexuality, 85/86* (10th ed., pp. 198–200). Guilford, CT: Dushkin Publishing Group. (Reprinted from *FORUM Magazine,* 1982, November)

Weiner, A. B. (1988). *The Trobrianders of Papua New Guinea.* New York: Holt, Rinehart & Winston.

Weisner, T. S., & Gallimore, R. (1977). My brother's keeper: Child and sibling caretaking. *Current anthropology, 18,* 169–180.

Werner, D. (1979). A cross-cultural perspective on theory and research on male homosexuality. *Journal of Homosexuality, 4,* 345–362.

West, J. (1945). *Plainville, U.S.A.* New York: Columbia University Press.

Westermark, E. (1889). *The history of human marriage.* New York: Macmillan.

Westmacott, R. (1994). *African-American gardens and yards in the rural South.* Knoxville, TN: University of Tennessee Press.

White, D. R. (1987). *Cultural diversity data base.* La Jolla, CA: National Collegiate Software Clearinghouse.

White, D. R. (1988a). Causes of polygyny: Ecology, economy, kinship, and warfare. *American Anthropologist, 90*(4), 871–887.

White, D. R. (1988b). Rethinking polygyny: Co-wives, codes, and cultural systems. *Current Anthropology, 29*(4), 529–572.

White, L. A. (1939). A problem in kinship terminology. *American Anthropologist, 41,* 569–570.

White, L. A. (1943). Energy and the evolution of culture. *American Anthropologist, 45,* 335–356.

White, L. A. (1948). The origin and prohibition of incest. *American Anthropologist, 50,* 416–435.

White, L. A. (1949). *The science of culture: A study of man and civilization.* New York: Grove Press.

White, L. A. (1959). *The evolution of culture.* New York: McGraw-Hill.

White, L. A. (1971). *The science of culture: A study of man and culture.* New York: Farrar, Straus & Giroux.

Whiting, B. (1950). *Paiute sorcery* (Viking Fund Publications in Anthropology No. 15). New York: Viking Fund.

Whiting, B., & Whiting, J. W. M. (Eds.). (1975). *Children of six cultures: A psycho-cultural analysis.* Cambridge, MA: Harvard University Press.

Whiting, J. W. M. (1959). Cultural and sociological influences on development. In *Growth and development of the child in his setting* (pp. 3–9). Baltimore: Maryland Child Growth and Development Institute.

Whiting, J. W. M. (1964). Effects of climate on certain cultural practices. In W. H. Goodenough (Ed.), *Explorations in cultural anthropology: Essays in honor of George Peter Murdock* (pp. 175–195). New York: McGraw-Hill.

Whiting, J. W. M., & Child, I. L. (1953). *Child training and personality: A cross-cultural study.* New Haven, CT: Yale University Press.

Whiting, J. W. M., Kluckhohn, R., & Anthony, A. S. (1958). The function of male initiation ceremonies at puberty. In E. E. Maccoby, T. M. Newcomb, & E. L. Hartley (Eds.), *Readings in social psychology* (pp. 359–370). New York: Holt, Rinehart & Winston.

Whiting, R. (1979, September 25). You've gotta have "Wa." *Sports Illustrated,* 60–71.

Whorf, B. L. (1956a). Languages and logic. In J. B. Carroll (Ed.), *Language, thought and reality: Selected writings of Benjamin Lee Whorf* (pp. 233–245). Cambridge, MA: MIT Press.

Whorf, B. L. (1956b). The relation of habitual thought and behavior to language. In J. B. Carroll (Ed.), *Language, thought, and reality: Selected writings of Benjamin Lee Whorf* (pp. 134–159). Cambridge, MA: MIT Press.

Whyte, M. K. (1978a). Cross-cultural codes dealing with the relative status of women. *Ethnology, 17,* 117.

Whyte, M. K. (1978b). *The status of women in preindustrial societies.* Princeton, NJ: Princeton University Press.

Wilson, B. (1980). *Kut: Catharsis, ritual healing or redressive strategy?* Paper presented at the Conference on Korean Religion and Society, Mackinac Island, MI.

Wilson, E. O. (1975). *Sociobiology: The new synthesis.* Cambridge, MA: Harvard University Press.

Wilson, M. H. (1951). Witch beliefs and social structure. *American Journal of Sociology, 56,* 307–313.

Winiarz, W., & Wielawski, J. (1936). Imu: A psychoneurosis occuring among Ainus. *Psychoanalytic Review, 23,* 181–186.

Witherspoon, G. (1977). *Language and art in the Navajo universe.* Ann Arbor, MI: University of Michigan Press.

Wittfogel, K. (1957). *Oriental despotism: A comparative study of total power.* New Haven, CT: Yale University Press.

Wittkower, E., & Fried, J. (1957). A cross-cultural approach to mental health problems. *American Journal of Psychiatry, 116,* 423–428.

Wolf, A. (1966). Childhood association and sexual attraction: A further test of the Westermarck hypothesis. *American Anthropologist, 72,* 503–515.

Wolf, E. R. (1964). *Anthropology.* Englewood Cliffs, NJ: Prentice Hall.

Wolf, E. R. (1966). *Peasants.* Englewood Cliffs, NJ: Prentice Hall.

Wolf, E. R. (1969). *Peasant wars of the twentieth century.* New York: Harper & Row.

Wolf, E. R. (1982). *Europe and the people without history.* Berkeley, CA: University of California Press.

Worsley, P. (1957). *The trumpet shall sound: A study of "cargo" cults in Melanesia.* London: MacGibbon & Kee.

Wright, G. D. (1954). Projection and displacement: A cross-cultural study of folk-tale aggression. *Journal of Abnormal and Social Psychology, 49,* 523–528.

Wright, H. T. (1987). Prestate political formations. In W. Sanders, H. Wright, & R. McC. Adams (Eds.), *On the evolution of complex societies: Essays in honor of Harry Hoijer, 1982* (pp. 41–77). Malibu, CA: Undena Publications.

Wright, R. (1982, Spring). The Yanomami saga. *Cultural Survival Quarterly, 6*(2).

Yap, P. M. (1951). Mental illness peculiar to certain cultures: A survey of comparative psychiatry. *Journal of Mental Science, 97,* 313–327.

Yap, P. M. (1963). Koro or suk-yeong: An atypical culture-bound psychogenic disorder found in southern Chinese. *Transcultural Psychiatric Research, 1,* 36–38.

Yap, P. M. (1965). Koro: A culture-bound depersonalization syndrome. *British Journal of Psychiatry, 111,* 43–50.

Zelnick, M., & Kantner, J. (1977). Sexual and contraceptive experiences of young unmarried women in the United States, 1976 and 1971. *Family Planning Perspectives, 9,* 55–71.

Zetterberg, P. (Ed.). *Conference on Evolution and Public Education: Resources and References.* St. Paul, MN: University of Minnesota Center for Educational Development.

INDEX

Page references in bold indicate a glossed term.

CREDITS & ACKNOWLEDGMENTS

Chapter 1 3 UN Photo; 6 The Bettmann Archive, Inc.; 7 The Bettmann Archive, Inc.; 8 The Bettmann Archive, Inc.; 9 The Bettmann Archive, Inc.; 16 Table 1.1 adapted from *Varieties of Sexual Experience: An Anthropological Perspective on Human Sexuality* by S. G. Frayzer, used by permission of Human Relations Area Files; 18 "Recreating Stone Tools to Learn the Ancient Makers' Ways" by Brenda Fowler, copyright © 1994 by the New York Times Company, reprinted by permission; 19 Mary Ann Carter for NYT Pictures; 20 Cleveland Museum of Natural History; 24 Henri Cartier-Bresson—Magnum; 30 Robert Fox—Impact Visuals; 31 © Kal Muller—Woodfin Camp.

Chapter 2 36 Michelle V. Agins—The New York Times; 39 "Where Suburban Tribes Gather for Sun and Surf" by George Judson, copyright © 1993 by the New York Times Company, reprinted by permission; 40 Frank Dougherty for NYT Pictures; 41 UN photo; 43 © David Austen—Woodfin Camp; 47 Jean-Claude Lejeune; 51 Vickie Jensen; 53 Pamela Carley; 57–58 excerpt from *Yąnomamö: The Fierce People*, 3rd ed., by Napoleon A. Chagnon, copyright © 1983 by Holt, Rinehart & Winston, Inc., reprinted by permission of the publisher.

Chapter 3 60 UN photo; 65 UPI/Bettmann; 67 Bettmann; 69 Bettmann; 72–73 "At the Racial Dividing Line" by Robin Wilson, excerpted from the *Chronicle of Higher Education*, copyright 1995, reprinted with permission; 74 UN photo.

Chapter 4 82 © Joel Gordon; 85 © 1987 Miguel Sayago—Photo Researchers, Inc.; 89 Shostak—Anthro Photo; 90 Excerpted text reprinted by permission of the publisher from *Nisa: The Life and Words of a !Kung Woman* by Marjorie Shostak, Cambridge, MA: Harvard University Press, copyright © 1981 by Marjorie Shostak; 95 Waigwa Kiboi—The New York Times; 96 "France Fights Female Genital Mutilation by African Immigrants" excerpted from "French Prosecutor Fighting Girl-Mutilation by Migrants" by Marlise Simons, copyright © 1994 by the New York Times Company, reprinted by permission; 98 Anita Bartsch—Design Conceptions; 99 © Barbara Alper—Stock•Boston; 100 UN photo by John Isaac; 102 Marilyn K. Yee for NYT Pictures.

Chapter 5 106 Reuters/Bettmann; 110 Katayon Ghazi—The New York Times; 113 reproduced by permission of the American Anthropological Association from *American Anthropologist* 75:5, October 1973, not for further reproduction; 114 The National Museum of the American Indian/Smithsonian Institution, Neg. # 34256; 118–119 "Sexual Equality in Vanatinai Society" excerpted from "Sexes Equal on South Sea Isle" by John Noble Wilford, copyright © 1994 by the New York Times Company, reprinted by permission; 120 Owen Franken—Stock•Boston; 121 Agence France-Presse; 123 American Museum of Natural History, Neg. # 125283; 124 "Sex-Based Persecution as a Basis for Asylum in the United States" excerpted from "Women Refugees Offered Asylum for Gender Violence" by Linda Wong, reprinted with permission of *Sojourner: The Women's Forum*, vol. 20(11), July 1995; 125 AP/Wide World; 127 UN photo.

Chapter 6 132 UN photo; 136 UN photo; 139 Lee—Anthro Photo; 143 Eastcott/Momatiuk—Woodfin Camp & Assoc.; 147 UN photo; 149 © Marc & Evelyne Bernheim—Woodfin Camp & Assoc.; 150 © Wendy Stone—Gamma Liaison; © 152 1992 Clark Erikson; 153 excerpted from "Farming Lessons from Prehistory," Ellen K. Coughlin, reprinted with permission from the *Chronicle of Higher Education*, February 17, 1995; 155 Keith Dannemiller for NYT Pictures.

Chapter 7 158 Sally Weiner Grotta—Stock Market; 161 James Sterngold—The New York Times; 167 Agence France-Presse; 170 AP/Wide World; 172 AP/Wide World; 174 Stephen Ferry—The New York Times; 180 Fiona McDougall—The New York Times; 183 Fiona McDougall for NYT Pictures; 186 "Home, Home on the Range, in Brazil's Heartland" by James Brooke, copyright © 1995 by the New York Times Company, reprinted by permission; 187 Patrick E. Tyler for NYT Pictures.

Chapter 8 192 UN photo; 195 "Seaweed Farming" excerpted from "They Plow the Waves for the Squire of Seaweed" by Edward A. Gargan, copyright © 1995 by the New York Times Company, reprinted by permission; 196 Edward A. Gargan for NYT Pictures; 198 David Portnoy for NYT Pictures; 200 John Maier Jr. for NYT Pictures; 201 "Brazilian Women Find New Opportunities as Avon Saleswomen!" excerpted from "Who Braves Piranha Waters? Your Avon Lady" by James Brooke, copyright © 1995 by the New York Times Company, reprinted by permission; 204 Irven DeVore—Anthro Photo; 205 Blair Seitz—Photo Researchers, Inc.; 208 Annette Weiner; 210 Annette Weiner; 212 UN Photo; 214 "The Impact of AIDS on Africa's Economy" excerpted from "AIDS Deals a Harsh Blow to Africa's Economy" by Eric Fottorino, *Guardian Weekly*, December 4, 1994, reprinted from *Le Monde*, November 10, 1994, used by permission.

Chapter 9 218 Agence France-Presse; 222 © 1983 Robert A. Isaacs—Photo Researchers, Inc.; 223 UN photo; 224 Schuler—Anthro Photo; 230 Sara Krulwich for NYT Pictures; 233 Abuhugbod—Anthro Photo; 236 Eastcott/Momatiuk—Woodfin Camp & Assoc.; 237 Cary Wolinsky—Stock • Boston.

Chapter 10 243 Jimmy Belfon Jr./Photographic Center of Harlem; 251 Eastcott/Momatiuk—Woodfin Camp & Assoc.; 252 Mark Antman—The Image Works.

Chapter 11 260 Koons—Anthro Photo; 264 Museum of the American Indian; 267 Greg Marinovich—NYT Pictures; 273 Bettmann; 277 The Granger Collection; 280 © 1984 Nancy J. Pierce—Photo Researchers; 281 J. F. E. Bloss—Anthro Photo; 283 American Museum of Natural History, Neg. # 2A3766; 284 © Fred McConnaughey—Photo Researchers, Inc.

Chapter 12 292 *Time* Magazine; 296 The Bettmann Archive, Inc.; 298 American Museum of Natural History, Neg. # 32102; 300 Sara Stankovic—Agence France-Presse; 303 H. Terrace; 316 Chick Rice—Discover Magazine; 317 Horacio Paone—NYT Pictures.

Chapter 13 320 The Nelson-Atkins Museum of Art; 325 Kit Porter; 327 Museum of Fine Arts, Boston; 329 Brian Spykerman; 331 Melissa Springer—The New York Times; 337 Australian News & Information Bureau; 339 American Museum of Natural History, Neg. # 319671; 342 Irven DeVore—Anthro Photo; 343–344 Excerpted text from "Kut Catharsis, Ritual Healing or Redressive Strategy?" by Brian Wilson, paper presented at the Conference on Korean Religion and Society, Mackinac Island, MI, 1980, used by permission; 346 Agence France-Presse; 350 Eliza Wells Smith for NYT Pictures; 351 The Granger Collection.

Chapter 14 356 Agence France-Presse; 359 Victor Englebert—Photo Researchers, Inc.; 365 Agency France-Presse; 371 Paul Weinberg; 372 Tim Zielenbach for NYT Pictures; 377 American Museum of Natural History, Negative # 232202; 380 Archive Photos.

Chapter 15 384 Chester Higgins for NYT Pictures; 388 Alan S. Weiner for NYT Pictures; 390 AP/Wide World; 391 © Eastcott/Momatiuk—Woodfin Camp & Assoc.; 393 Illustration by Elizabeth Ross from "Living Maya" by Walter F. Morris, Jr., Harry N. Abrams, Inc., 1987; 394 AP/Wide World; 398 David E. Sanger for NYT Pictures; 401 Bill Keller for NYT Pictures.

CHAPTER ONE

ANTHROPOLOGY: A DEFINITION

CHAPTER OBJECTIVES

After reading this chapter, you should be able to:

▸ *Define anthropology as a discipline.*

▸ *Describe the diversity and interrelatedness of anthropological topics.*

▸ *Outline the history of anthropology.*

▸ *Discuss the methods of anthropological research.*

▸ *Enumerate the subdivisions of anthropology.*

▸ *Analyze fieldwork in the context of the subdivisions of anthropology.*

▸ *Discuss the benefits and limitations of participant observation.*

▸ *Explain the basic ethics of anthropological research.*

▸ *Identify the uses of cross-cultural comparison.*

▸ *Explain the difference between emic and etic interpretations of culture.*

▸ *Explain the difference between humanistic and scientific approaches to culture.*

▸ *Characterize the individual approaches to explaining culture.*

REVIEW QUESTIONS

1. How does the primary goal of a humanistic understanding of the human condition differ from that of a scientific understanding? Why can humanistic approaches to anthropology be said to be similar to the work of translating a foreign language?

   _____

   _____

2. What are the primary interests of cultural ecologists, feminist anthropologists, and postmodernists?

   _____

   _____

3. What do anthropologists mean when they say that they take a *holistic* view of the human condition? How does a holistic perspective add to the breadth of anthropology?

   _____

   _____

4. Why is *cross-cultural research* important to the goals of anthropology?

   _____

   _____

5. What social forces during the fifteenth and sixteenth centuries led to the growing interest in human differences that eventually resulted in the birth of anthropology? What kinds of biases influenced the beliefs of European scholars about non-European societies before the eighteenth century?

   _____

   _____

6. What was the dominant framework for organizing ideas about human social life used by most eighteenth-century anthropologists?

   _____

   _____

7. What was Carolus Linnaeus's *Systema Naturae* and what did it contribute to the European knowledge about living species?

   _____

   _____

8. When did the idea of biological evolution of species become the dominant scientific viewpoint? What was Charles Darwin's major contribution to the study of biological evolution in his book *On the Origin of Species?*

_____

_____

9. How did the emphasis of anthropological research change under the influence of Franz Boas around the end of the nineteenth century? What is meant by Boasian *empiricism?*

_____

_____

10. Define *cultural relativism.* Why is it important to the study of other cultures?

_____

_____

11. Define *diffusion.* How did American and European *diffusionism* differ? Where were diffusionist views most dominant? In what setting did scholars first develop the concept of *culture areas?*

_____

_____

_____

_____

12. Define *functionalism.* Explain the concept of a custom's *functions.* How did Malinowski's brand of functionalism differ from that developed by Radcliffe-Brown? What criticisms have been leveled against the early functionalists?

_____

_____

_____

_____

13. What were Ruth Benedict's and Margaret Mead's best-known contributions to the history of anthropology?

_____

_____

14. What was the central interest of the *culture and personality* approach to anthropology during the 1930s?

_____

_____

15. How has anthropology changed since World War II? How has employment in anthropology changed during the past few decades?

_____

_____

16. How does the anthropological emphasis on *fieldwork* differ from the research methods of other behavioral and social sciences such as psychology or sociology? Describe the form that fieldwork takes in cultural anthropology.

_____

_____

17. Describe the characteristics of *participant observation* research. Which subdivision of anthropology uses participant observation as its basic approach to information gathering? What advantages does participant observation have over other forms of research (e.g., questionnaires or laboratory research) about human social behavior?

_____

_____

_____

18. Why is it crucial for ethnography to be carried out by both female and male anthropologists?

_____

_____

19. Explain why anthropological ethics demands that the first loyalties of fieldworkers be to the people they are studying. List three examples of kinds of research that would probably be regarded as unethical by most anthropologists.

_____

_____

20. Why do anthropologists use *cross-cultural comparison?* What is the name of the major archive of cross-cultural data?

_____

_____

21. Describe the main concerns of each of the following branches of anthropology: *cultural anthropology; archaeology; anthropological linguistics; physical (biological) anthropology.*

_____

_____

_____

_____

22. Explain the difference between *ethnography* and *ethnology*. Which of these two subdivisions of cultural anthropology would most likely involve the use of HRAF materials? In what way is the work of archaeologists similar to that of ethnographers?

_____

_____

_____

23. How does the work of anthropological linguists differ from that of linguists in other fields? How can learning a people's native language aid a cultural anthropologist studying them?

_____

_____

24. What are the three main domains of *applied anthropology?* What is the distinction between applied anthropology and *practicing anthropology?*

_____

_____

25. What is the difference between an *emic* and an *etic analysis* of a culture?

_____

_____

26. What is the basic claim of Lévi-Strauss's *structuralism?* According to Mary Douglas, how does a culture's system of symbolic classification influence people's feelings?

_____

_____

27. Define *interpretive anthropology.* What does Clifford Geertz regard as the main goal of interpretive anthropology?

_____

_____

28. Why is the role of the anthropological fieldworker such a central feature in the examinations of other cultures that are written by *hermeneutic anthropologists?* What do hermeneutic anthropologists mean by "the dialectic of fieldwork"?

_____

_____

29. How does the *postmodernist anthropologist* characterization of a culture differ from earlier ways of defining a culture, and how do postmodernists use the concept of cultural relativism? What is the *dialogic model* in postmodernist anthropology? What does the postmodernist mean by *polyphony?*

_____

_____

_____

30. What is *ethnoscience* and from what field does it draw many of its analytic methods? What is the major goal of ethnoscience and what technique plays a central role in doing ethnoscientific research? By what other name is ethnoscience sometimes known?

_____

_____

_____

31. What goals do the various scientific approaches to anthropology have in common?

_____

_____

32. What do British social anthropologists believe to be the most important factors in determining the customs of a society? What do they mean by *social structure* and *structural-functionalism?*

_____

_____

33. What are the central ideas of *Marxist anthropology?*

_____

_____

34. What similar interest is shared by *neofunctionalism* and Marxist anthropology, and how do the two differ?

_____

_____

35. What are the main explanatory variables used by *feminist anthropologists?* In what way does feminist anthropology uniquely cross-cut the boundaries between humanistic and scientific anthropology?

_____

_____

36. What is the emphasis of *sociobiology?* Which kinds of anthropologists have been most influenced by some of the viewpoints of sociobiology?

_____

_____

37. How does *cultural materialism* differ from cultural ecology? Define *mode of production, mode of reproduction, domestic economy, political economy,* and *behavioral superstructure.* What is Harris's main claim about the causes of people's customs and ideology?

_____

_____

_____

_____

_____

_____

Matching Test

Match each concept with its definition, illustration, or explication below.

a. culture
b. function
c. diffusion
d. empiricism
e. archaeology
f. ethnography
g. sociobiology
h. ethnoscience
i. etic analysis

j. functionalism
k. emic analysis
l. structuralism
m. neofunctionalism
n. *Systema Naturae*
o. cultural ecology
p. cultural universal
q. applied
   anthropology

r. physical
   anthropology
s. feminist
   anthropology
t. cultural
   evolutionism
u. cross-cultural
   research

v. participant
   observation
w. hermeneutic
   anthropology
x. interpretive
   anthropology
y. postmodernist
   anthropology

____ 1. study of humans' evolutionary origins

____ 2. study of the cultures of specific peoples

____ 3. study of material remains of earlier societies

____ 4. characteristic found in all human ways of life

____ 5. description of culture as "insiders" understand it

____ 6. passing of cultural traits from one society to another

____ 7. technique of studying subjects in their natural setting

____ 8. approach using data drawn from diverse human ways of life

____ 9. learned system of beliefs, feelings, and rules for living

____ 10. approach emphasizing the mechanics of society in equilibrium

____ 11. study of the ways in which social power interacts with gender

____ 12. study of the ways in which cultures adapt to specific habitats

____ 13. classification of plants and animals into a hierarchical system

____ 14. description of culture in terms of universally derived categories

____ 15. careful observation and description rather than abstract theorizing

____ 16. approach focusing on fieldworkers' interaction with native informant

____ 17. approach focusing on how conflict may serve to maintain cultural stability

____ 18. nineteenth-century approach emphasizing progression of culture through stages

____ 19. approach focusing on natural selection's role in creating behavioral predispositions

____ 20. contribution made by any one cultural trait to the unity and survival of the culture in which it is found

___ 21. approach emphasizing the underlying unity of all cultures, represented by the tendency to think in dualities

___ 22. approach that focuses on the meaningful relationship between each element of a culture and its original context

___ 23. approach that rejects detached, scientifically objective model of ethnography, instead emphasizing cultural flux

___ 24. approach focused on systematic description of each culture in terms of the linguistic categories used by informants to discuss their society

___ 25. anthropological subfield that aims to facilitate cultural development in nonindustrialized areas and to aid public and private policy making

---

ANSWER KEY

1. r	8. u	15. d	22. w
2. f	9. a	16. w	23. y
3. e	10. j	17. m	24. h
4. p	11. s	18. t	25. q
5. k	12. o	19. g	
6. c	13. n	20. b	
7. v	14. i	21. l	

CHAPTER TWO

CULTURE

CHAPTER OBJECTIVES

After reading this chapter, you should be able to:

▶ *Explain the nature of culture.*

▶ *Define ideology.*

▶ *Discuss ideological communication.*

▶ *Explain the relationship between beliefs and feelings.*

▶ *Enumerate the differences between real and ideal culture.*

▶ *Discuss the ways cultures may influence each other.*

▶ *Outline the various emotional reactions people have to other societies and cultures.*

▶ *Analyze the values of cultural relativism.*

▶ *Explain the causes of culture shock.*

▶ *Recognize how scientific and humanistic approaches to culture influence the ways culture is conceptualized.*

REVIEW QUESTIONS

1. Define *society* and *culture*. How are the two related? How is culture related to biology? What are *subcultures* and how does this concept relate to our contemporary view of diversity within cultures?

    _____

    _____

2. What is a *symbol*, and in what sense are the customs, objects, and events in a society symbols?

    _____

    _____

3. Define *ideology*. How does a society's ideology differ from the other beliefs and feelings of its culture?

    _____

    _____

4. What is *ideological communication* and how does it differ from other forms of communication? Give three examples of ideological communication.

    _____

    _____

5. What is the difference between a *belief* and a *feeling?* How do they influence each other? Why is it often difficult for people to distinguish between beliefs and values? What does the text mean by saying that beliefs "are imposed on us"?

    _____

    _____

    _____

6. In what sense can some of the beliefs of a society be called *scientific*, even if that society has no professional scientists? Can a society's scientific beliefs, as defined in this text, sometimes be false? What is the basic criterion, then, for distinguishing *scientific* from *nonscientific* beliefs?

    _____

    _____

7. Distinguish between the three basic kinds of feelings: *emotions, attitudes,* and *values.* Give an example of each. How did Ruth Benedict portray cultural differences in the role of emotion in human life? In her view, how was emotion handled in the Zuni versus the Dobuan cultures? What is the major criticism that has been leveled at Benedict's portrayal of cultures as expressions of particular themes?

    _____

    _____

    _____

8. Distinguish among *morality, etiquette, piety*, and *aesthetics*.

_____

_____

_____

_____

9. What is the relationship between values and *drives?*

_____

_____

10. What is the difference between *ideal culture* and *real culture?* How has this distinction played a role in some criticisms of Ruth Benedict's book *Patterns of Culture?*

_____

_____

11. Why should descriptions of culture be understood as representing only one point in time? What are some of the effects that contact between cultures can have? When two societies with different cultures interact, what factor best predicts which society and culture will change the most?

_____

_____

_____

12. How does the socialization of children into their society's culture influence their relationships to themselves and to members of other societies?

_____

_____

13. Define *ethnocentrism*. What adaptive functions might ethnocentrism have had in earlier, small-scale societies? Why do anthropology students need to learn to recognize their own ethnocentrism and try to overcome it?

_____

_____

_____

14. Define *cultural relativism*. In what sense is it an antidote for ethnocentric thinking? What feeling does it also help us cultivate? When are members of society most and least likely to adopt a relativistic way of thinking about behavior?

_____

_____

_____

15. How did Barre Toelken's experience among the Navajo help him realize that there were aspects of his own culture that he took for granted but could not really explain?

_____

16. Define *culture shock*. When is it commonly experienced by anthropologists? List some of the experiences that contributed to Napoleon Chagnon's difficulties in adjusting to fieldwork among the Yąnomamö.

_____

_____

_____

17. How is the relationship between culture and the human individual viewed differently by those who view culture as a superorganic phenomenon and those who see culture as the domain of human communication and human interaction?

_____

_____

18. What are *subcultures*? Why is it inappropriate to view even the traditional cultures of the world as independent of outside influences?

_____

_____

19. Why is it important to consider cultures both in terms of their distinctive qualities and in terms of their similarities to other cultures? What are *cultural universals*?

_____

_____

MATCHING TEST

Match each concept with its definition, illustration, or explication below.

a. piety
b. symbol
c. values
d. drives
e. society
f. beliefs

g. emotions
h. feelings
i. ideology
j. morality
k. etiquette
l. aesthetics

m. subcultures
n. real culture
o. ideal culture
p. culture shock
q. ethnocentrism
r. scientific beliefs

s. nonscientific beliefs
t. ideological communication

___ 1. actually observed behaviors of a people

___ 2. values regarding beauty and compatibility

___ 3. ideas people hold about what is factual or real

___ 4. disorientation experienced in a foreign setting

___ 5. values regarding proper treatment of other people

___ 6. represents another object or event by mutual agreement

___ 7. ideals not just formally adhered to but actively pursued

___ 8. based on desire to solve practical, day-to-day problems

___ 9. subjective positive or negative reactions to experiences

___ 10. geographical or social variations within large societies

___ 11. a people's own description of their customs and behaviors

___ 12. human group that considers itself distinct from other groups

___ 13. views people hold based on their feelings about their existence

___ 14. feelings about what should/should not be considered good and bad

___ 15. conscious, formally stated beliefs shared by members of a society

___ 16. spiritual values concerning the natural world and the supernatural

___ 17. values regarding manners and proper ways of communicating with others

___ 18. reaffirms people's allegiance to their groups and creates a sense of community

___ 19. attitude that one's own culture is the standard by which all other cultures should be judged

___ 20. pleasant or unpleasant subjective reactions to an experience, also characterized by physiological changes

---

ANSWER KEY

1. n	7. d	13. s	19. q
2. l	8. r	14. c	20. g
3. f	9. h	15. i	
4. p	10. m	16. a	
5. j	11. o	17. k	
6. b	12. e	18. t	

CHAPTER THREE

SOCIAL ORGANIZATION, BIOLOGY, AND CULTURE

CHAPTER OUTLINE

ORGANIZATIONAL PATTERNS
Groups
Statuses and Roles
Division of Labor
Rank
Contextual Cues
Master Statuses

BIOLOGICAL TRAITS AND SOCIAL STATUSES
Biology and Socially Learned Roles
Race, Cultural Ability, and Intelligence

CHAPTER OBJECTIVES

After reading this chapter, you should be able to:

▶ *Define the concept of social organization and its parts.*

▶ *Discuss the relationships between status, roles, and division of labor.*

▶ *Explain the relationship of rank to power and prestige.*

▶ *Compare and contrast the concepts of class and caste.*

▶ *Discuss the nature and functions of master statuses.*

▶ *Explain the nature of minorities.*

▶ *Explain the relationships between biology and statuses.*

▶ *Discuss the scientific fallacies of racism.*

▶ *Analyze the social functions of racism.*

REVIEW QUESTIONS

1. Define *social organization*. What are the basic component parts of a society's social organization? How does social structure differ from social organization?

_____

_____

_____

2. What are the characteristics of a *group?* How do human groups differ from the groups found in other social animals? What does the concept of *social structure* have to do with groups?

_____

_____

_____

3. What is a *status,* and what are *status pairs?* Give three examples of *complementary statuses* and three examples of *symmetrical statuses.* What pattern do you see in how statuses are named that might suggest to an anthropologist whether the people in each status pair are expected to play the same or different roles with each other?

_____

_____

_____

4. Give three examples of *ascribed statuses* and three examples of *achieved statuses.*

_____

_____

5. What are *roles* and the *division of labor?* In what kind of society is the division of labor based solely upon age and gender?

_____

_____

6. What are the two basic components of social *rank?* Define each of these elements of rank. Is it possible for a status to have a great deal of one element but little of the other? Give an example of statuses that demonstrate each possible combination.

_____

_____

_____

7. Explain the difference between social *class* and *caste.* List the most common castes in the Hindu caste system. In India how did *jatis* relate to castes?

_____

_____

_____

8. How are the roles that we are expected to play related to the circumstances in which we find ourselves? When several of a person's roles are equally appropriate to the situation, which one is commonly played? What do people experience psychologically when there are conflicting cues present about what roles to play?

_____

_____

_____

9. What is a *master status*? Give an example of a master status that has high rank and one that has low rank. What is the term for low-ranked master statuses and what is sometimes misunderstood about this term? What is an *ethnic group*?

    _____

    _____

    _____

    _____

10. Give three examples of statuses that people are given because of some biological characteristic they have. If it is true that biology is not the cause of how people behave, why do people who share a biologically defined status in life sometimes behave in the ways that people sometimes claim are biologically caused?

    _____

    _____

11. What are *races*? Why is the concept of racial purity within the human species a myth? What is *racial prejudice* and how is it related to *racial discrimination*? How is *racism* different from simple racial prejudice and discrimination by individuals? What is the fundamental error embodied in *racist beliefs*?

    _____

    _____

    _____

    _____

    _____

12. Give the three main reasons why racism, including racist beliefs, has no valid scientific basis. What social functions does racism fulfill that may help to perpetuate it in spite of its lack of scientific validity?

    _____

    _____

13. Why did racism tend to replace ethnocentrism as the main way of justifying slavery with the passage of time?

    _____

    _____

14. What was the purpose of legal restrictions on interracial marriage in the United States? When did such legal restrictions come to an end? In what other countries have governments followed policies based on racism?

    _____

    _____

15. In what sense can racism be more harmful than individual racial prejudice?

    _____

    _____

16. What is an *IQ?* What evidence is there that IQ scores are changeable, depending on social experience? How much change in average IQ scores between generations did James R. Flynn document for a number of different countries? How does this contradict the widely held belief that IQ scores are primarily a measure of a fixed, inborn biological capacity?

_____

_____

_____

17. How have IQ differences between U.S. Blacks and Whites been interpreted in a racist way? What social policy viewpoints have consistently been linked with such interpretations throughout this century?

_____

_____

18. Why does one's language background influence one's performance on an IQ test? What language effects did Chandler and Plakos demonstrate to exist among California schoolchildren?

_____

_____

19. What kinds of differences in social background are known to influence performance on IQ tests? What cultural difference did Zena Blau find to be particularly influential on IQ test performance, and why might this characteristic be expected to affect U.S. Blacks more than Whites? What happened to the average difference in IQ scores between Blacks and Whites when this trait was controlled for?

_____

_____

_____

20. How might motivation influence performance on an IQ test?

_____

_____

_____

21. How can cultural biases actually be written into an IQ test? Give an example of a test question that might favor one social group over another.

_____

_____

_____

22. How did Rist demonstrate that academic performance can be a "self-fulfilling prophecy"?

_____

_____

_____

23. What is meant by the term *"culture-free" intelligence tests?* Why can culture still influence IQ scores, even on a "culture-free" test?

_____

_____

24. What dramatic evidence was reported by Klaus Eyferth that demonstrated that the average performance difference between U.S. Blacks and Whites is better explained as a product of cultural differences than by an innate biological difference in intellectual capacity between the two groups?

_____

_____

_____

MATCHING TEST

Match each concept with its definition, illustration, or explication below.

a. role
b. race
c. group
d. power
e. class
f. honor
g. caste
h. status

i. Brahmin
j. minority
k. Kshatriya
l. status pair
m. ethnic group
n. Untouchables
o. role conflict
p. master statuses

q. contextual cue
r. racial prejudice
s. social structure
t. achieved statuses
u. ascribed statuses
v. division of labor
w. social organization

x. symmetrical statuses
y. racial discrimination
z. complementary statuses

___ 1. broad, ranked social stratum

___ 2. esteem conferred by some statuses

___ 3. the group relationships in a society

___ 4. social class determined by birth and fixed

___ 5. distinct biological subdivision of a species

___ 6. social statuses so important they cannot be ignored

___ 7. set of individuals engaged in a common activity

___ 8. group whose identity is based on shared customs

___ 9. set of individuals with a low-ranked master status

___ 10. statuses acquired by two people when they interact

___ 11. social positions based on group into which one is born

___ 12. highest-ranked Hindu caste, associated with priesthood

___ 13. lowest-status members of Hindu society not in any caste

___ 14. ability to exercise coercion in obtaining what one seeks

___ 15. culturally defined relationship that an individual has with another

___ 16. allocation of day-to-day tasks among the holders of various statuses

___ 17. skills, abilities, and ways of acting toward others attached to a status

___ 18. second-highest Hindu caste, including warrior-rulers, nobility, and landowners

___ 19. unequal treatment of people based on their membership in different racial groups

___ 20. social positions based on one's demonstration of the necessary role-playing abilities

___ 21. culturally defined indicators of which roles are appropriate to play in a given setting

___ 22. attitude of dislike and contempt for those considered to belong to a different racial group

___ 23. status pair in which each status-holder is expected to act toward the other in the same way

___ 24. status pair in which the status-holders are expected to behave in different but compatible ways

___ 25. the relationship between the groups, statuses, and division of labor that structure interaction in a society

___ 26. emotional confusion experienced when a person faces conflicting contextual cues derived from two or more of his or her statuses

---

ANSWER KEY

1. e	8. m	15. h	22. r
2. f	9. j	16. v	23. x
3. s	10. l	17. a	24. z
4. g	11. u	18. k	25. w
5. b	12. i	19. y	26. o
6. p	13. n	20. t	
7. c	14. d	21. q	

CHAPTER FOUR

THE LIFE CYCLE

CHAPTER OUTLINE

THE LIFE CYCLE
Rites of Passage
Pregnancy, Childbirth, and Naming
Enculturation, Childhood, and Adolescence
Courtship and Marriage
Parenthood
Divorce
Old Age
Death

CHAPTER OBJECTIVES

After reading this chapter, you should be able to:

▸ *Analyze the social and psychological functions of rites of passage.*

▸ *Describe the more common customs in the world concerning pregnancy and childbirth.*

▸ *Explain the three forms of learning that play a role in socialization.*

▸ *Describe the more common customs in the world concerning sexuality and puberty.*

▸ *Describe the more common customs in the world concerning marriage and divorce.*

▸ *Describe the more common customs in the world concerning old age and death.*

REVIEW QUESTIONS

1. What *rites of passage* are most often publicly celebrated as important changes during the *life cycle* in societies throughout the world? What social and psychological functions do rites of passage play?

   _____

   _____

2. What are *pregnancy rituals?* Give an example from your own culture. What societies are best known in anthropology for having cultures that have denied the role of sex in pregnancy? Why did Leach regard such culturally based beliefs as not really being based on ignorance of the biological role of sex in pregnancy?

   _____

   _____

   _____

3. According to George Devereux, how common are societies in which intentional abortions are not practiced? According to Suzanne Frayser, what was likely to make abortion more likely? What other social attitudes did Steven Nock and Paul Kingston find to be closely linked to people's attitudes about abortion? What characteristics did James Prescott find to be common among nonindustrialized abortion-intolerant societies?

_____

_____

_____

_____

4. What is the most common posture adopted by women throughout the world for giving birth? What benefits does it have over the position that U.S. women have traditionally been expected to adopt in the hospital birthing process? What were the !Kung San ideals about how childbirth should be carried out and what medical effects did these ideals contribute to?

_____

_____

_____

5. Describe the custom of the *couvade*. What kinds of societies are most likely to have such a custom, and what symbolic value might it have for them? What other custom did Munroe, Munroe, and Whiting find typically to be absent when the couvade is present? What environmental conditions are associated with the couvade?

_____

_____

_____

_____

6. How do the symbols of the *naming ceremony* reveal something about the society in which it is performed?

_____

_____

7. What are the three forms of learning that Edward Hall believes influence the *enculturation* or *socialization* of individuals? Explain how each of these learning processes affects us differently.

_____

_____

_____

8. According to Clellan Ford and Frank Beach, how do societies differ in their degree of restrictiveness about children's learning about sexual matters? Under what circumstances are societies most restrictive regarding sexual experimentation before adulthood?

_____

_____

9. What percentage of women and men in the United States have experienced sexual intercourse by age 18? How many teenage pregnancies were there in 1991? What percentage ended with abortion, and what percentage ended in out-of-wedlock births?

_____

_____

10. Which of the traditional rites of passage is *least* emphasized in North American culture? What effect may the lack of such a ritual have?

_____

_____

_____

11. What are *puberty rituals* or *adulthood rituals* and what social conditions increase the likelihood of puberty rituals for males and for females? According to Yehudi Cohn, under what circumstances are puberty rituals most likely?

_____

_____

12. When are male puberty rituals likely to be most dramatic? What painful acts are most commonly associated with male puberty initiations? According to Whiting, Kluckhohn, and Anthony, what social traits are most commonly associated with circumcision at puberty?

_____

_____

_____

13. According to J. Brown, under what circumstances are female puberty rituals (a) most common and (b) most painful? What are the two forms of "female circumcision" and under what circumstances is each most common? In what parts of the world are such customs most frequently found?

_____

_____

_____

14. What percentage of societies examined by Frayser had little or no restriction on premarital sexual relations? According to Ford and Beach, what social traits are most associated with restrictive customs regarding nonmarital sex? What social conditions increase the likelihood that a society will attempt to restrict premarital sex?

_____

_____

_____

15. What was *sleep crawling* in traditional Samoa?

_____

_____

16. Briefly describe the role of mock battle in the marriage rituals of the South African !Kung San.

_____

_____

17. When did religious marriage rituals develop in Europe? When was governmental regulation of marriage first instituted in Europe?

_____

_____

18. Define *teknonymy*.

_____

_____

_____

19. What are the most common reasons for divorce throughout the world, and what are some of the customs that make divorce less common in some societies than in others? About what percentage of U.S. marriages begun in 1989 are likely to end in divorce? What social characteristics are associated with low divorce rates cross-culturally?

_____

_____

_____

20. Under what conditions is old age likely to be associated with high social rank?

_____

_____

21. Define each of the three concepts of death discussed in the text and describe the differences between them. What common coping strategies did Kübler-Ross find to be characteristic of dying patients?

_____

_____

_____

_____

22. What are the common functions of *funeral rituals?* How do these rituals commonly influence the living in the world's societies? Briefly outline the funeral customs of the Mapuche Indians of Chile.

_____

_____

_____

MATCHING TEST

Match each concept with its definition, illustration, or explication below.

a. marking
b. couvade
c. excision
d. teknonymy
e. life cycle
f. infibulation
g. circumcision
h. social death

i. scarification
j. enculturation
k. funeral ritual
l. puberty ritual
m. sleep crawling
n. naming ceremony
o. rite of passage
p. formal learning

q. pregnancy ritual
r. biological death
s. informal learning
t. technical learning
u. permissive society
v. female circumcision

w. restrictive society
x. psychological death
y. semirestrictive society

___ 1. learning by imitation

___ 2. mutilation of female genitals (general term)

___ 3. surgical removal of the foreskin from the penis

___ 4. decorating the body with a pattern made of scars

___ 5. ritual formalizing a major change in social status

___ 6. societies tolerant of childhood sexual experimentation

___ 7. removal of all or part of the female clitoris (specific term)

___ 8. societies that do not accept childhood sexual experimentation

___ 9. process of subjective preparation for impending biological death

___ 10. custom in which the husband acts as if he gives birth to his child

___ 11. process by which children learn customs and values of their culture

___ 12. surgical closing of the female vulva over the vagina (specific term)

___ 13. typical status changes between birth and death in a particular society

___ 14. religious rules thought to ensure a successful pregnancy and childbirth

___ 15. ritual marking the change from the status of child to the status of adult

___ 16. point at which a person is treated in manner appropriate for one who is biologically dead

___ 17. custom of referring to a person as the parent of his or her child rather than by birth name

___ 18. idea that children may be influenced by things their mothers do or experience during pregnancy

___ 19. ritual that formalizes an individual's removal from the status of living member of the social group

___ 20. cessation of such organic functions as breathing, heartbeat, reaction to pain, and brain functioning

___ 21. ritual that symbolically gives an infant human status and receives him or her into the human community

___ 22. learning involving disapproval and correction of learner's errors and emphasis on rules of correct behavior

___ 23. learning that occurs when the logical rationales for specific ways of doing things are taught without emotional pressure

___ 24. societies that accept childhood sexual experimentation within the bounds of established rules of etiquette and discretion

___ 25. Samoan sexual practice in which an uninvited youth would enter a young woman's house after dark with the intent of seduction

---

ANSWER KEY

1. s	8. w	15. l	22. p
2. v	9. x	16. h	23. t
3. g	10. b	17. d	24. y
4. i	11. j	18. a	25. m
5. o	12. f	19. k	
6. u	13. e	20. r	
7. c	14. q	21. n	

CHAPTER FIVE

GENDER AND CULTURE

CHAPTER OUTLINE

SEX AND GENDER
Sexual Differences
Gender

DIVERSITY IN MALE AND FEMALE ROLES
Socialization of Gender Differences
Common Patterns in Division of Labor
Gender Roles and Subsistence

THIRD AND FOURTH GENDERS
The Berdache
The Hijra
The Transvestite

GENDER, POWER, AND HONOR
Gender Stratification
Gender in Patrilineal Societies
Male Dominance
Gender in Matrilineal Societies
Matrifocality
The Causes of Gender Inequality

GENDER AND RELIGION
Gender Symbolism
Gender in the Religious Institution

WOMEN'S RIGHTS AS HUMAN RIGHTS
Economic Exploitation
Equality in Family Law
Reproductive Rights
Violence
Political Rights

CHAPTER OBJECTIVES

After reading this chapter, you should be able to:

▶ *Distinguish between sex and gender.*

▶ *List some of the common sexual differences in humans.*

▶ *Discuss cultural differences that have existed in gender roles.*

▶ *Recognize the effects of gender stereotypes on the roles we learn to play.*

▶ *Explain the concept of third and fourth genders.*

▶ *Outline the common patterns of division of labor by gender.*

▶ *Explain the influences of kinship, economics, religion, and warfare on the relative power and honor accorded the different genders.*

▶ *Discuss the various aspects of women's rights as human rights.*

▶ *Discuss the relationships between religion and gender differences.*

REVIEW QUESTIONS

1. Explain the difference between *sex* and *gender*.

    _____

    _____

2. What are some of the important sexual differences between males and females? What cross-cultural consistencies did Beatrice and John Whiting find between the behavior of girls and boys?

    _____

    _____

3. What are *gender stereotypes?* How are they related to socialization?

    _____

    _____

4. Summarize what Margaret Mead found about differences in beliefs about men and women among the Arapesh, the Mundugumor, and the Tschambuli of New Guinea.

    _____

    _____

5. According to Behnam and Nassehi-Behnam, how have industrialization and urbanization influenced the traditional Iranian family? What influence have they had on the practice of veiling? How have religious values functioned to perpetuate gender stratification since the Iranian revolution of 1979?

    _____

    _____

    _____

6. What pattern did Murdock find cross-culturally in the kinds of work commonly assigned to men and to women? How does Brown explain the common difference in gender roles for men and women?

    _____

    _____

7. What percentage of the U.S. paid labor force is now represented by women? In the United States, what percentage of their husbands' incomes do the incomes of married women

average? What kind of subsistence base is associated with the largest contribution by women to their families' food supply? How has industrialization usually influenced the status of women?

_____

_____

_____

_____

8. Describe the northern Indian *hijra* status and the traditional North American Indian *berdache* status. What are the similarities and differences between these statuses, and what distinguishes them from the status of *transvestite* in the United States and Europe? Why is it appropriate to define statuses such as the berdache as a gender?

_____

_____

_____

9. What are the major concerns of *feminist anthropology?*

_____

_____

10. What four measures of women's social power have been suggested by Peggy Sanday? According to Sanday, under what circumstances is women's social rank usually the highest?

_____

_____

11. What is *gender stratification?* What does Carole Sheffield mean by *sexual terrorism?* What did Thomas Gregor find about the role of rape as a means of social control?

_____

_____

_____

12. What was the ideological significance of footbinding in China until the 1920s? Who originated the custom? What was its effect on the women whose feet were bound?

_____

_____

13. How common is the physical abuse of women in the United States? How widespread does the problem seem to be on a global scale?

_____

_____

14. Describe the Hindu custom of the suttee in nineteenth-century India. Who benefited from the custom?

_____

_____

15. What is purdah and for what purpose is it practiced? How does the concept of "family honor" relate to the killing of sisters or daughters described by Gideon Kressel?

_____

_____

16. Why are patrilineality and patrilocal residence often associated with gender stratification?

_____

_____

17. What is the meaning of the term *patriarchy*? According to Whyte, what cultural characteristics are typically not found in patriarchal societies?

_____

_____

18. How is women's status related to matrilineality and matrilocality? What is *matrifocality*? What kinds of inheritance and residence rules are common in matrifocal societies? How does this concept differ from that of matriarchy?

_____

_____

19. What matrifocal characteristics of the patrilineal, polygynous Ibo of eastern Nigeria gave women high status in a society that might otherwise have been expected to be patriarchal in its gender role concepts?

_____

_____

20. How common are true matriarchies? According to Sanday, in what kind of societies are beliefs about matriarchies common?

_____

_____

21. What is Marvin Harris's view about the main cause of gender inequality in nonindustrialized societies? How do Divale and Harris explain the correlation of internal warfare with an unbalanced sex ratio? What relationship exists between external warfare and women's economic and political roles?

_____

_____

_____

22. What is Lisette Josephides's view of the primary cause of gender inequality? According to Friedl, how is male dominance in his economic role in industrialized societies similar to the role of the hunter in foraging societies, and the role of the bigman in horticultural societies?

_____

_____

23. According to Heidi Hartmann, what has been the major economic mechanism that has perpetuated male control over women in capitalist societies?

_____

_____

24. What does Sanday see as the major factor in women's high rank in some societies?

_____

_____

25. According to Mary Nelson, what was the main source of antagonism toward women during the Inquisition?

_____

_____

26. How does religious symbolism frequently portray women in societies in which women are markedly subordinate to men? How does the symbolism of religious creation stories often mirror their societies' gender relations? In what kind of society are women most likely to be religious practitioners? In what kind of societies do men and women participate in separate religious organizations?

_____

_____

27. What are some examples of problems that are often perceived as "women's issues" rather than human rights issues? How has the concept of "the sanctity of the family" sometimes functioned to prevent women's rights from being protected? What are the four main ways in which women's human rights are abridged in many of the world's contemporary nations?

_____

_____

_____

28. What is meant by the *feminization of poverty?* What percentage of U.S. citizens who live in poverty today are female?

_____

_____

29. What have been some of the forms that governmental control over women's reproductive lives has taken in different countries?

_____

_____

30. What are dowry deaths and why do they occur? Why have they increased in recent times?

_____

_____

MATCHING TEST

Match each concept with its definition, illustration, or explication below.

a. sex
b. gender
c. sexism
d. berdache
e. patriarchy

f. transvestism
g. matrifocality
h. sexual terrorism
i. sexual dimorphism

j. gender stereotypes
k. gender stratification

l. feminist anthropology
m. feminization of poverty

___ 1. cross-dressing or mixed-gender dressing

___ 2. marked differentiation in size and form of the sexes

___ 3. systematic differences in power and honor between men and women

___ 4. social status assigned on the basis of cultural concepts about the sexes

___ 5. form of society in which men have primary access to social power and prestige

___ 6. belief that differences in male and female sex roles are biologically determined

___ 7. customs that employ violence against females in order to maintain male domination

___ 8. increasing tendency for women to constitute a large proportion of the world's poor

___ 9. approach emphasizing the relationships among social power, social honor, and gender

___ 10. biological distinctions—chromosomal, hormonal, or physical—between males and females

___ 11. preconceived ideas about distinctions between "masculine" and "feminine" behaviors and roles

___ 12. social status in which males and females adopt the role of the other sex; sometimes considered a third gender

___ 13. form of society in which high social status is assumed by women, who control most food production, and men are often frequently absent

ANSWER KEY

1. f	5. e	9. l	13. g
2. i	6. c	10. a	
3. k	7. h	11. j	
4. b	8. m	12. d	

CHAPTER SIX

ENVIRONMENT, ADAPTATION, AND SUBSISTENCE

CHAPTER OUTLINE

ENVIRONMENTAL DIVERSITY
Cultural and Natural Areas
Natural Environments
Carrying Capacity

BIOLOGICAL AND CULTURAL ADAPTATION

SUBSISTENCE ADAPTATIONS AND THE ENVIRONMENT
Foraging
Optimal Foraging Theory
Food Production
The Trend toward Food Domestication

CHAPTER OBJECTIVES

After reading this chapter, you should be able to:

▸ *Discuss the relationship between cultural areas and natural environments.*

▸ *Characterize the world's major natural environments.*

▸ *Explain the concept of carrying capacity.*

▸ *Discuss the concept of adaptation in the context of biology and culture.*

▸ *Define subsistence adaptation.*

▸ *Discuss foraging as a subsistence adaptation.*

▸ *Explain optimal foraging theory.*

▸ *Discuss the major theories of the origin of food production.*

▸ *Describe the kinds of food production.*

▸ *Relate the different kinds of food production to the natural environments in which they are usually found.*

REVIEW QUESTIONS

1. Why, according to Alfred Kroeber, do societies that occupy similar natural environments often share many similarities of culture?

---

2. List the eight world environments outlined by Preston James, and briefly state the main characteristics of each.

_____

_____

_____

_____

_____

_____

_____

_____

3. What are the differences between *steppes*, *prairies*, and *savannas*, and in which of the basic environments are they found?

_____

_____

_____

4. What are the differences between *ice-zones*, *tundras*, and *taigas*, and in which of the basic environments are they found?

_____

_____

_____

5. Which of the inhabited areas have the highest and lowest human population densities? Which type of environment is most and least densely inhabited by human beings today? What are the main problems for agriculture in *tropical forests?* Which food-getting strategy has been the most successful in *arid lands?* Which environments are least useful for plant domestication?

_____

_____

_____

_____

6. Define *carrying capacity*. What factor is the basic determinant of an environment's carrying capacity?

_____

_____

7. Define *adaptation*. What is the mechanism by which a species biologically adapts to its environment and how does this mechanism work? What parallel between natural processes and stockbreeding led Charles Darwin to the idea of *natural selection?* Give two examples of human biological adaptations to different environments. How does cultural adaptation differ from biological adaptation?

_____

_____

_____

8. Define *subsistence*. What are *subsistence technologies?*

_____

_____

9. Define *foraging*. How old is foraging? What are the basic tools used by foragers? What skills do Alan Lomax and Conrad Arensberg see as characteristic of foragers? Where is the greatest concentration of foragers today?

_____

_____

_____

_____

10. Describe the basic characteristics of *band* societies. What is the basic group in band societies that controls and organizes the education of children, social etiquette, and economic, political, military, and judicial practices? Why do the local groups of band societies tend to be rather small? What are the two bases for the division of labor in all band societies? Why are band societies generally not very competitive and warlike?

_____

_____

_____

_____

_____

11. List and describe the differences between the four basic types of foraging adaptation that have been outlined by Ernestine Friedl. How does the prestige of women differ in each? According to Service, Lee, DeVore, and Tanaka, how large a percentage of the calories in the diets of foraging societies can sometimes be contributed by women? What is the most common percentage contributed by women in these societies?

_____

_____

_____

_____

12. According to Colin Turnbull's description of the Ituri Forest Pygmy, how do net-hunting bands contrast with archery-hunting bands in terms of seasonal changes in their group structure?

_____

_____

13. Explain the idea of *optimal foraging theory*. According to this theory, why do foragers not usually think of insects as a food? What does the use of many different food resources by foragers generally indicate about their environment?

_____

_____

_____

14. How did the development of food production alter the lives of human beings in terms of the size of their local communities and the length of their workweeks? Why has food production often been *less* successful than foraging in meeting the nutritional needs of communities? How does childrearing generally differ between food producing and foraging societies?

_____

_____

_____

15. What is meant by the contemporary world system? How does *neocolonialism* differ from traditional colonialism?

_____

_____

16. What changes began as early as 20,000 years ago that laid the foundations for the development of food production? In what kind of environment did the move toward a more sedentary lifestyle occur?

_____

_____

17. Define *sedentarism*. Explain the views of Frisch and McArthur about the effects of sedentarism and the shift of emphasis from hunting to gathering in the ancient Near East on human population growth. What does Esther Boserup suggest as the main cause of the shift to food production? What does Robert Sussan believe to have been the cause of the shift from plant gathering to food production? Where do Lewis Binford and Kent Flannery believe the shift to food production actually occurred?

_____

_____

_____

_____

18. What is the earliest archaeological evidence we have of plant and animal domestication in the Near East?

_____

_____

19. Define *horticulture*. When did it begin? How does horticulture differ from true agriculture? How do the populations of horticultural peoples differ from those of foragers? How do they differ in their approach to government and family organization?

_____

_____

_____

_____

20. Compare and contrast *slash-and-burn cultivation (swidden horticulture)* with *dry-land gardening*. In what environments is each most common? Which involves the greater investment of human labor?

_____

_____

_____

21. What are the major subsistence activities of the Shuara (Jívaro) of Ecuador and Peru, as described by Michael Harner? Why do you think that hunting remained an important activity even though they had horticulture?

_____

_____

22. Define *pastoralism* and *transhumance*. Why do most anthropologists think that this form of food production is not as old as horticulture? List the most important domestic animals for the various pastoral areas of the world. According to Lomax and Arensberg, what effect does pastoralism often have on the environment and why does this occur? Why did pastoralists frequently have a militaristic lifestyle? What traits do the childrearing customs of pastoralists often foster in children?

_____

_____

_____

_____

23. What environments were utilized by the Northern Tungus of Siberia? What was their major food resource? What contribution did reindeer make to the Tungus diet?

_____

_____

_____

24. Define *agriculture*. How long has agriculture existed? How does *nonindustrialized (traditional) agriculture* differ from *industrialized agriculture*? Which form of agriculture requires the greater percentage of people to be involved in food production? Which form is more efficient? How does agriculture compare with horticulture in terms of the use of human labor versus tools and animal labor?

_____

_____

_____

25. What environmental zones and food-getting techniques were utilized by the Classic Maya? What agricultural tool did they lack?

_____

_____

_____

Matching Test

Match each concept with its definition, illustration, or explication below.

a. band	j. agriculture	s. carrying capacity	x. intensive cultivation
b. tribe	k. subsistence	t. communal foraging	y. subsistence technology
c. taigas	l. pastoralism	u. individual foraging	z. nonindustrialized agriculture
d. tundras	m. sedentarism	v. swidden horticulture	
e. steppes	n. horticulture	w. extensive cultivation	
f. prairies	o. mixed forests		
g. savannas	p. neocolonialism		
h. foraging	q. tropical forests		
i. adaptation	r. natural selection		

____ 1. tools and techniques by which people obtain food

____ 2. living in permanent or semipermanent settlements

____ 3. subsistence technology based on animal husbandry

____ 4. gathering by men and women of their own plant foods

____ 5. adjustment of an organism to a particular environment

____ 6. regions of conifers and broadleaf trees in temperate climates

____ 7. tropical areas of tall grasses and drought-resistant undergrowth

____ 8. areas with tall varieties of grass that tolerate wetter climates

____ 9. swampy coniferous forests of the northern lands south of arctic regions

____ 10. regions with warm climates and abundant rainfall, plants, and animal life

____ 11. the obtaining of the necessities of life, particularly food, from the environment

____ 12. intensive cultivation based on tools such as hoes, shovels, and animal-drawn plows

____ 13. subsistence technology based on gathering wild plant foods, hunting, and fishing

____ 14. employment of food-growing techniques that permit permanent use of the same fields

____ 15. a particular environment's ability to support a species on the available resources

___ 16. areas that cover stretches of southeastern Europe and Asia, with a short, hardy variety of grass

___ 17. intensive cultivation using methods such as irrigation, animal traction, and fertilization of the soil

___ 18. cooperative food gathering where fish and small game are meat resources and plants are easily collected

___ 19. economic exploitation of underdeveloped nations by the developed world that is enforced by economic necessity

___ 20. level or undulating treeless plains in the arctic and subarctic regions of North America, Asia, and Scandinavia

___ 21. cultivation of crops using simple hand tools without fertilization of the soil, crop rotation, or, often, irrigation

___ 22. seminomadic, kinship-based society with no full-time government, economically based on a foraging subsistence technology

___ 23. semisedentary society that is governed by kinship groups and economically based on extensive horticulture or pastoralism

___ 24. cultivation using land on which natural growth has been cut away and burned, usually with several plots being worked in a cycle

___ 25. horticulture that involves the use of land for short periods followed by periods of letting the land stand idle for several years

___ 26. process whereby those members of a species that are best adapted to their environment contribute the most offspring to succeeding generations

---

Answer Key

1. y	8. f	15. s	22. a
2. m	9. x	16. e	23. b
3. l	10. q	17. j	24. v
4. u	11. k	18. t	25. w
5. i	12. z	19. p	26. r
6. o	13. h	20. d	
7. g	14. x	21. n	

CHAPTER SEVEN

CULTURAL EVOLUTION AND THE CONTEMPORARY WORLD

CHAPTER OUTLINE

STUDY GUIDE

CHAPTER OBJECTIVES

After reading this chapter, you should be able to:

▶ *Discuss how cultural change occurs.*

▶ *Analyze the interrelationships among the three cultural subsystems: technology, social organization, and ideology.*

▶ *Contrast specific and general evolution.*

▸ *Explain the principles of cultural evolution.*

▸ *Discuss the nature and causes of alienation.*

▸ *Discuss the processes of acculturation, ethnocide, and genocide.*

▸ *Analyze the process of industrialization.*

▸ *Compare and contrast developed and underdeveloped societies.*

▸ *Recount the history of feudal and colonial peasantries.*

▸ *Describe contemporary peasantries.*

▸ *Explain the work of applied anthropology.*

▸ *Explain the role of population control in developing nations.*

REVIEW QUESTIONS

1. Define *discovery, invention,* and *diffusion.* What are the two kinds of diffusion, and how do they differ?

    _____

    _____

    _____

    _____

2. What is *acculturation?* When two cultures interact, what factor may cause one to be more likely than the other to undergo acculturation?

    _____

    _____

3. Explain the *Law of Cultural Dominance.*

    _____

    _____

4. What are the three major subsystems of culture? Which of the three did Leslie White regard as the most important in determining the characteristics of the rest of culture? How did White express this in his *Basic Law of Cultural Evolution?*

    _____

    _____

    _____

5. What effects did the introduction of steel axes have on Yir Yiront culture?

    _____

    _____

6. Give an example of how social change can cause alterations in the rest of a cultural system.

_____

_____

7. Give an example of how cultural change can begin within its ideological subsystem.

_____

_____

8. What effect does *general evolution* have on the balance of power between neighboring societies?

_____

_____

9. Explain Thomas Harding's *Principle of Stabilization*.

_____

_____

10. Explain Marshall Sahlins and Elman R. Service's *Law of Evolutionary Potential*. How is it related to Harding's principle?

_____

_____

11. Explain the *Law of Local Discontinuity of Progress*. Why is the first culture to make one general evolutionary leap forward likely to be at a disadvantage by the time a new general evolutionary advance becomes possible? How does this fact show up geographically over long periods of cultural evolution?

_____

_____

_____

12. Define *alienation*. Who argued that alienation develops when the work of individuals only satisfies their needs indirectly? How does the phenomenon of alienation show that we should not confuse cultural evolutionary change with *progress?*

_____

_____

_____

13. What are *indigenous peoples?* How many indigenous people are there in the world and what percent of the world's current population do they represent?

_____

_____

14. What are *frontier areas?* Why are even these territories being lost to indigenous peoples today? How does the case of the Western Shoshone illustrate that the rights of indigenous peoples are ignored even today in societies in which they hold citizenship?

_____

_____

_____

15. What is the difference between *ethnocide* and *genocide?* According to Gregor, how does the contemporary indigenous population of Brazil compare to the original Indian population of that region?

_____

_____

16. What is *industrialization,* and what effects did it have on the economic life of traditional societies?

_____

_____

17. What is the difference between *developed* and *underdeveloped countries?* How do developing countries differ from underdeveloped countries?

_____

_____

18. How do economic production and consumption differ in industrialized societies and preindustrialized ones? How does farming for one's own consumption differ from farming cash crops?

_____

_____

19. How does the world population of today differ from that of 1900 in terms of its percentage of urbanization? What percentage of the world's population is expected to be urbanized by the year 2020?

_____

_____

20. Briefly describe the major trends of world population growth since the time of *Homo erectus.* How long did it take for the human population to expand from 4 to 5 billion?

_____

_____

21. What are the major benefits of industrialization? What are some of the main costs?

_____

_____

_____

22. Define *peasants.* How did *feudal peasantries* differ from *colonial peasantries?*

_____

_____

23. How did colonial governments encourage peasants to shift from the raising of food crops for their own consumption to export crops?

_____

_____

24. In general terms, how much of the world's population today can be classified as peasants? What are the financial conditions of most peasants today? What is the irony about how most peasant cash income is spent?

_____

_____

_____

25. Identify and describe the nine types of contemporary peasants and the environments they occupy, as outlined by Jon Moris.

_____

_____

_____

_____

26. What is the _image of limited good_, and why does it make sense from the viewpoint of many people in underdeveloped communities? What is meant by the phrase _culture of poverty_? What benefits does Scott believe peasant resistance to change has for peasant communities?

_____

_____

_____

27. Why do Nelson and Water believe the circumstances of peasant life tend to be self-perpetuating?

_____

_____

28. In what sense does Popkin believe that the peasant lifestyle is a rational response to their circumstances?

_____

_____

29. What is _applied anthropology?_

_____

_____

30. Acording to Fisher, what are the common reasons for the failure of government development projects?

_____

_____

31. What does Critchfield claim about progress in world development over the past decades?

_____

_____

32. Why have many underdeveloped countries devoted so much effort to the control of population growth? How have China and Singapore exemplified countries in which population growth needs to be controlled? How has the pressure of population influenced differences in life expectancies in different parts of the world?

_____

_____

_____

MATCHING TEST

Match each concept with its definition, illustration, or explication below.

a. peasants
b. refugees
c. genocide
d. discovery
e. ethnocide
f. invention
g. innovation
h. alienation
i. acculturation
j. feudal peasants

k. green revolution
l. direct borrowing
m. industrialization
n. colonial peasants
o. general evolution
p. developed country
q. indigenous people

r. developing country
s. specific evolution
t. stimulus diffusion
u. image of limited good
v. underdeveloped country
w. Law of Cultural Dominance

x. Principle of Stabilization
y. Law of Evolutionary Potential
z. Law of Local Discontinuity of Progress

____ 1. systematic extermination of a people

____ 2. development of new insights and ideas

____ 3. nation with a largely nonindustrialized economy

____ 4. change in the direction of increasing complexity

____ 5. underdeveloped nation undergoing industrialization

____ 6. systematic destruction of a traditional way of life

____ 7. act of combining preexisting cultural traits in new ways

____ 8. changes in a culture as a result of discovery or invention

____ 9. change in the direction of increasing adaptive specialization

____ 10. nation in which industrialization has become the primary basis of the economy

____ 11. use of modern plant breeding to produce high-yield, fertilizer-intensive, fast-maturing crops

___ 12. adopting of a cultural trait by one society from another with relatively little change in form

___ 13. group of people whose occupation of an area precedes the currently dominant state political system

___ 14. process in which one culture adapts to the influence of another culture by borrowing many of its traits

___ 15. displaced people who have been forced from their homes and means of livelihood by fear of political persecution

___ 16. principle that the successive stages of general evolutionary change will usually not occur in the same place

___ 17. dissociation of workers from ownership of things they produce, accompanied by feelings of powerlessness and boredom

___ 18. process of change from an economy based on home production of goods to one based on large-scale, mechanized factory production

___ 19. fatalistic outlook common in situations of peasant poverty based on idea that one person's achievement can only come at another's expense

___ 20. one society's borrowing of the idea for a cultural trait from another, with the borrowing society determining how the idea is implemented

___ 21. principle that as a culture becomes more efficient in its resource use, further gains in efficiency become increasingly difficult and expensive

___ 22. principle that the cultural system that most effectively exploits the energy resources of a given environment will "crowd out" less effective systems

___ 23. members of food-producing societies dependent on foreign states that used military domination as a basis for economic exploitation of these societies

___ 24. people who use nonindustrialized, labor-intensive techniques for producing food and are politically and economically subordinate to a governing class

___ 25. principle that a culture's capacity to move from one general evolutionary stage to another varies inversely with its level of specific evolutionary adaptation to its environment

___ 26. food producers in preindustrialized societies who pay rent or perform service for the privilege of farming lands owned by local aristocratic officials, who have reciprocal obligations to the food producers

ANSWER KEY

1. c	8. g	15. b	22. w
2. d	9. s	16. z	23. n
3. v	10. p	17. h	24. a
4. o	11. k	18. m	25. y
5. r	12. l	19. u	26. j
6. e	13. q	20. t	
7. f	14. i	21. x	

CHAPTER EIGHT

ECONOMICS

CHAPTER OUTLINE

DEFINITION OF ECONOMIC SYSTEMS
The Cultural Definition of Commodity
The Cultural Definition of Value

PRODUCTION: THE CONTROL AND USE OF RESOURCES
Use Rights
Ownership
Division of Labor
Socioeconomic Statuses in the United States

DISTRIBUTION
Reciprocity
Redistribution
Markets
The Productive Base of the U.S. Economy

CONSUMPTION
Subsistence Economies
Status Income

SOCIAL AGENTS OF ECONOMIC CONTROL
Community Control of Production
Kin Control of Production
Association Control of Production
Social Class
Social Class and Production in the United States
The Changing Context of Economics

CHAPTER OBJECTIVES

After reading this chapter, you should be able to:

▶ *Explain the role of culture in the definition of commodities and economic value.*

▶ *Explain the roles of use rights and the ownership of resources in the process of economic production.*

▶ *Discuss the concept of division of labor.*

▶ *Discuss the economic differences among the U.S. social classes.*

▶ *Define the three forms of economic distribution.*

▶ *Relate the forms of economic distribution to the four societal types.*

▶ *Compare and contrast subsistence economies and consumer economies.*

▸ *Define status income and explain its economic functions.*

▸ *Discuss the four systems of economic control.*

▸ *Relate the four systems of economic control to the four societal types.*

▸ *Explain how population growth affects U.S. life.*

REVIEW QUESTIONS

1. Define *economics*.

   _____

   _____

2. What are *commodities?* Illustrate the role of culture in determining what is considered to be a commodity and in determining the value that a commodity has. What type of foods valued as commodities in Western societies have generally not been considered commodities in East Asian cultures?

   _____

   _____

   _____

3. What is the difference between *tangible* and *intangible property?* Give an example of intangible property from your own culture.

   _____

   _____

4. How did Sahlins illustrate the role of cultural symbolism in determining the price of cuts of meat in the United States?

   _____

   _____

5. Why must the principle of the *profit motive,* to be valid, involve more than the simple desire to maximize *monetary* gain in transactions? What motives do people have besides economic profit when they make exchanges with each other?

   _____

   _____

6. Briefly describe Kwakiutl exchanges. What brought honor to a Kwakiutl buyer?

   _____

   _____

7. What is the difference between use rights and *ownership?* How did the Sirionó of Bolivia establish their claim to the fruit of a wild Chonta palm? What was the traditional Shoshone concept of use rights over natural resources? Why was the European concept of land ownership alien to their way of thinking?

_____

_____

_____

_____

8. What two bases for *division of labor* have been used in all societies that anthropologists have studied? When do other forms of specialization become important? In which kind of society are these the only two bases for the division of labor? In what kind of society is specialization of labor most important?

_____

_____

_____

_____

9. What forms of work have most often been assigned to men and what forms have most often been assigned to women in diverse cultures around the world? In what kinds of societies are children most likely to add to the productive abilities of their families?

_____

_____

10. What are the five categories of economic statuses based on occupation that make up the U.S. system of economic classes?

_____

_____

11. What is economic *distribution?* What are the three types of distribution that anthropologists have noted?

_____

_____

12. Define *reciprocity*. When is reciprocity likely to be practiced? Why is gift giving and generosity so readily practiced in simple societies such as those based on foraging? List three examples of the role of reciprocity in your own society.

_____

_____

_____

13. List and define each of the three basic forms of *reciprocity*. Under what circumstances is each likely to be practiced?

_____

_____

_____

14. What benefits could Melanesians obtain from participating in the Kula Ring? What type of reciprocity does it represent?

_____

_____

15. Describe the *mink'a* of the Andean Quechua and the so-called "silent trade" of the Ituri Forest Mbuti Pygmies. What type of reciprocity does each represent?

_____

_____

16. Define *redistribution*. List three examples of redistribution that are practiced in your own society. What is Service's view about the origins of redistribution? What does Harris claim about the causes of redistribution and its effects on the communities that practice it?

_____

_____

_____

_____

17. How do the economic roles of "big men" or "big women" differ from those of *chiefs?*

_____

_____

18. Define *market*. How do societies that use markets for the distribution of goods and services differ from those that use only redistribution or reciprocity?

_____

_____

19. Define *barter* and *money*. What are the two kinds of money? Give an example of each from your own society. For what special purposes did the Yapese use stone money?

_____

_____

_____

_____

20. Why is the U.S. unemployment rate rarely below 5 or 6 percent?

_____

_____

_____

21. Define *consumption*. How do simple and complex societies differ in their consumption practices?

_____

_____

22. Explain the differences between a *subsistence economy* and an economy that produces *status income*. Which type is most common in band societies?

_____

_____

23. Which kind of society has the *greatest* differences in wealth and in level of consumption?

_____

_____

24. What are the four basic means that human societies have used for controlling their economic systems? Which type of society (i.e., bands, tribes, chiefdoms, and states) is associated with each mechanism? Among the Cheyenne, what group was responsible for controlling hunting by community members?

_____

_____

_____

_____

25. Define *corporation*. Describe the different ways in which government and private corporations may interact in a market economy. What pros and cons can you think of for each approach? In what sense are these two approaches to governing a market economy simply variations on a common theme?

_____

_____

_____

_____

26. Define *consumer market*.

_____

_____

MATCHING TEST

Match each concept with its definition, illustration, or explication below.

a. money
b. market
c. barter
d. economics
e. ownership
f. bigmanship
g. corporation
h. reciprocity
i. consumption
j. commodities

k. distribution
l. professionals
m. status income
n. redistribution
o. consumer market
p. subsistence
   income
q. unskilled laborers
r. pink-collar
   workers

s. subsistence
   economy
t. blue-collar
   workers
u. balanced
   reciprocity
v. white-collar
   workers
w. negative
   reciprocity

x. general-purpose
   money
y. special-purpose
   money
z. conspicuous
   consumption

___ 1. nonfarm manual laborers

___ 2. final use of goods and services

___ 3. exchange of goods and services by trading

___ 4. use of status income as display of social rank

___ 5. goods produced over and above subsistence needs

___ 6. goods produced by a family for its own consumption

___ 7. the right to use property and deny use rights to others

___ 8. workers holding service jobs traditionally held by women

___ 9. system in which people consume most of what they produce

___ 10. system of distribution focused on sales of nonessentials

___ 11. standard medium of exchange of mutually agreed-upon value

___ 12. giving of gifts with expectation of a return gift shortly

___ 13. medium of exchange that may be used to buy and sell any item

___ 14. managers, administrators, and clerical, sales, and technical workers

___ 15. goods and services defined as useful or valuable in a particular culture

___ 16. association legally entitled to act as single person with rights of ownership

___ 17. medium of exchange restricted to the buying and selling of a single commodity

___ 18. system of distribution based on direct exchange, usually at established locations

___ 19. system by which people acquire, produce, distribute, and consume material goods and services

___ 20. attempt by one group or individual in a reciprocal exchange system to get more than it gives

___ 21. movement of goods or resources from where they are produced or found to where they will be used

___ 22. low-paid workers, often part-time or seasonal, whose wages are usually hourly or on a piecework basis

___ 23. service providers, often self-employed, doing work that generally requires a graduate-level university degree

___ 24. sharing of surplus commodities based on tacit understanding that the party that received the gift will respond in kind in the future

___ 25. economic entrepreneurship by individuals who encourage economic production and gift giving to achieve public recognition and respect

___ 26. system of contribution of commodities by all members of a group to a common pool and movement of these commodities to where they will be used

---

ANSWER KEY

1. q	8. r	15. j	22. q
2. i	9. s	16. g	23. l
3. c	10. o	17. y	24. h
4. z	11. a	18. b	25. f
5. m	12. u	19. d	26. n
6. p	13. x	20. w	
7. e	14. v	21. k	

CHAPTER NINE

MARRIAGE AND THE FAMILY

CHAPTER OBJECTIVES

After reading this chapter, you should be able to:

▶ *Analyze the defining characteristics of marriage.*

▶ *Explain the basic functions of marriage.*

▶ *Define the four basic types of marriage.*

▶ *Explain the adaptive characteristics of each marriage type.*

▶ *Define the five types of atypical marriage.*

▶ *Discuss the various forms of same-sex marriage.*

▶ *Explain the types of rules that influence choice of marriage partner.*

▶ *Discuss the economic factors in marriage negotiations.*

▸ *Define the forms of the family and the household.*

▸ *Define the five basic postmarital residence rules.*

▸ *Explain the adaptive significance of each of the postmarital residence rules.*

▸ *Discuss the characteristics of the U.S. family.*

Review Questions

1. What are the defining features of *marriage* and what are their corresponding social functions? Why is no one of these characteristics sufficient by itself to constitute marriage?

   _____

   _____

   _____

2. According to the Cultural Diversity Data Base, what percentage of societies do not require sexual fidelity of both husbands and wives? What percentage accept extramarital sexual behavior by husbands, by wives, and by both?

   _____

   _____

3. Why is it difficult to define marriage in any simple way that would include the Nayar of India as a group that has marriages? What was the Nayar *taravad?* What was the role of the *tali-tying* husband, and what role was played by a *sambandham* relationship?

   _____

   _____

   _____

4. Which societies have had a role for prostitution as a sacred activity?

   _____

   _____

5. List and define the four basic types of marriage that are considered idealized forms in different societies of the world. Explain the social conditions that seem to lead to each one being preferred. What percentage of world societies restricted marriage to *monogamy?* What percentage preferred *polygyny?*

   _____

   _____

   _____

   _____

   _____

6. What is *sororal polygyny* and under what conditions is it the common form of polygyny? What is the difference between *male-ranked polygyny* and *male-stratified polygyny,* and under what different economic and political conditions does each tend to be found?

_____

_____

7. In what areas of the world has *polyandry* been most common? What is its most common form? Briefly describe the marriage customs of the Toda of southern India.

_____

_____

_____

8. What is *group marriage,* and what are the conditions under which it is usually found? What was the social benefit of co-marriage among the northern Alaskan Inuit?

_____

_____

9. What distinguishes atypical marriages from the main types of marriage?

_____

_____

10. Define *symbolic marriage* and give an example of what is meant by this term.

_____

_____

11. Define *nonsexual marriage* and give an example.

_____

_____

12. What is meant by a fixed-term marriage?

_____

_____

13. Define *fictive marriage.* In what sense are *levirate* or *sororate* marriages fictive? What was the economic function of the Sudanese Nuer *ghost marriage,* who was expected to practice it, and in what sense was it a self-perpetuating custom?

_____

_____

14. *Same-sex marriages* are currently not legally recognized in North America and Europe (except in several Scandinavian countries and Greenland). Explain why it is nevertheless anthropologically appropriate to analyze the relationship between same-sex couples as marriages.

_____

_____

15. What are the three common forms of same-sex marriage, and what social conditions seem to be associated with the presence of each? To what or whom does the term *berdache* refer?

_____

_____

_____

_____

16. In general, what are the conditions under which it is common for a male to take over the usual social roles of a female? In what cases is this role adoption generally associated with same-sex sexual orientation, and in what cases is it not generally associated with same-sex orientation?

_____

_____

17. Describe the economic benefits that woman marriage has for the Nuer.

_____

_____

18. What is the *incest taboo?* What are the four main types of theories that have attempted to explain the universality or near universality of the incest taboo?

_____

_____

19. How does the incest taboo differ from an *exogamy rule?* What is an *endogamy rule* and why can it coexist with a rule of exogamy?

_____

_____

20. What is a cross-cousin *marriage preference rule?* Describe its three most common examples. What kind of marriage preference rule was the *bint'amm* and what was its social and economic function? How common was this marriage preference?

_____

_____

_____

_____

21. Under what conditions will the families of a potential bride and groom play the major role in deciding whether the marriage will take place? When is the individual choice of the potential bride and groom most influential?

_____

_____

22. In approximately what percentage of societies are there typical exchanges of goods and services between the families that will be joined as in-laws through a marriage?

_____

23. What is the purpose of *bride price* and *bride service?* When is each likely to be practiced?

_____

_____

24. How does the *dowry* differ from the *indirect dowry?*

_____

_____

25. Define *gift exchange* and *woman exchange.* In what kinds of societies is each likely to be practiced?

_____

_____

26. Define each of the five common postmarital residence rules, and tell what the conditions are under which each is likely to be present. What percentage of societies uses each? Which is least associated with corporate kinship groups?

_____

_____

_____

_____

_____

27. Define a *family.* How does a family differ from a *household?* What are the two common forms of the family, and when is each likely to be practiced?

_____

_____

_____

28. What kind of flexibility did Samoan children have with their household?

_____

_____

29. What is the major economic function of the contemporary U.S. nuclear family? What is the current average number of children born to a U.S. couple? What percentage of U.S. women are currently employed outside the family?

_____

_____

Matching Test

Match each concept with its definition, illustration, or explication below.

a. dowry
b. family
c. marriage
d. levirate
e. polygyny
f. monogamy
g. polygamy

h. household
i. polyandry
j. bridewealth
k. neolocality
l. incest taboo
m. virilocality
n. exogamy rule

o. bride service
p. cross cousins
q. endogamy rule
r. uxorilocality
s. nuclear family
t. pathic marriage
u. sister exchange

v. extended family
w. fictive marriage
x. parallel cousins
y. symbolic
   marriage
z. homophilic
   marriage

___ 1. group of people who share a common residence

___ 2. form of marriage in which one man has more than one wife

___ 3. rule that forbids sexual behaviors between designated kin

___ 4. same-sex marriage involving gender-role change in one partner

___ 5. form of marriage in which one woman has more than one husband

___ 6. rite of passage that unites two or more individuals as spouses

___ 7. payment from the family of a bride to the family of her husband

___ 8. family that consists only of married persons and their children

___ 9. cousins whose common parents are either two brothers or two sisters

___ 10. form of marriage that joins one man and one woman as husband and wife

___ 11. form of marriage that allows a person to have more than one spouse at the same time

___ 12. same-sex marriage without transvestism or change in sex role by either partner

___ 13. marriage that does not establish economic and social ties between kinship groups

___ 14. custom of newly married couples' setting up residence with or near the bride's family

___ 15. custom of newly married couples' setting up residence with or near the groom's family

___ 16. goods transferred from the groom's kin to the bride's to recompense them for her loss

___ 17. family that includes two or more nuclear families and often more than two generations

___ 18. work performed by the groom for the family of the bride to recompense them for her loss

___ 19. group consisting of married persons, their children, and other relatives who reside with them

___ 20. cousins who are related through parents of the opposite sex, as children of a brother and sister

___ 21. custom of newly married couples' setting up residence in a new location apart from either spouse's family

___ 22. legal marriage established to allow both partners to acquire social benefits without a family's being set up

___ 23. cross-cousin marriage in which a brother and sister marry cross cousins who are also brother and sister of each other

___ 24. rule requiring marriage within specified kinship categories or other specified social or local groups to which one belongs

___ 25. rule that requires kin of a deceased man to provide his widow with another husband, often one of the deceased man's brothers

___ 26. rule forbidding an individual from marrying a member of the kinship, residential, or other specified group to which he or she belongs

---

ANSWER KEY

1. h	8. s	15. m	22. w
2. e	9. x	16. j	23. u
3. l	10. f	17. v	24. q
4. t	11. g	18. o	25. d
5. i	12. z	19. b	26. n
6. c	13. y	20. p	
7. a	14. r	21. k	

CHAPTER TEN

KINSHIP AND DESCENT

CHAPTER OUTLINE

KINSHIP

DESCENT RULES
Bilateral Descent
Ambilineal Descent
Unilineal Descent

DESCENT GROUPS
Lineal Descent Groups
Bilateral Descent Groups
The Evolution of Descent Groups

KINSHIP TERMINOLOGY
Hawaiian
Eskimo
Omaha
Crow
Iroquois
Sudanese

FICTIVE KINSHIP

CHAPTER OBJECTIVES

After reading this chapter, you should be able to:

▸ *Explain the relationship of kinship to descent.*

▸ *Explain the varieties of cognatic (or nonunilineal) descent.*

▸ *Explain the varieties of unilineal descent.*

▸ *Outline the characteristics of the various kinds of unilineal descent groups.*

▸ *Describe the various kinds of ambilineal descent groups.*

▸ *Explain the functions of moieties.*

▸ *Describe bilateral (or noncorporate) descent groups (kindreds).*

▸ *Discuss the evolution of descent groups.*

▸ *List the six common types of kinship terminologies.*

▸ *Explain the building blocks of kinship terminologies.*

▶ *Explain the conditions that foster each of the six common kinship terminology systems.*

▶ *Analyze the concept of fictive kinship.*

REVIEW QUESTIONS

1. What is *kinship?*

   _____

   _____

2. Define *descent.*

   _____

   _____

3. To what or whom does the term ego refer in a kinship diagram? What does the symbol Z stand for? What is the meaning of a triangle, a circle, and a square?

   _____

   _____

4. What is the difference between the principles of *bilateral descent* and *ambilineal descent?* Why are both classified as types of *nonunilineal (cognatic) descent* reckoning?

   _____

   _____

5. What was the system for tracing descent in Scottish clans? List the various synonyms for this descent system.

   _____

   _____

6. What are the three forms of *unilineal descent* reckoning? How does each define the parent-child relationship, and what percentage of world societies have relied on each?

   _____

   _____

7. What are the characteristics of a *corporate descent group?* What social functions do they typically fulfill in societies in which kinship is an important organizing principle for society?

   _____

   _____

8. How does a *lineage* differ from a *clan?*

   _____

   _____

9. Define *phratry.*

_____

_____

10. What is a *moiety* and how does a moiety system help to create tighter bonds of mutual interdependence within societies that use them?

_____

_____

11. How were members of Navajo clans dispersed geographically? How could this benefit individual members of a clan?

_____

_____

12. What is a *kindred?* With what kind of descent system is it associated? How does a kindred differ from a corporate descent group such as a lineage or clan? What kinds of society are most likely to have kindreds rather than unilineal descent groups?

_____

_____

13. Briefly outline the likely historical sequence in which the various descent groups came into existence. Under what circumstances is warfare likely to be associated with the presence of unilineal descent, and when is bilateral descent reckoning likely to replace lineal descent reckoning?

_____

_____

_____

14. What are the defining characteristics of the *Hawaiian kinship terminology* system? Why is this system sometimes called a generational system of kinship terminology? Under what social conditions are people likely to label their relatives in this way?

_____

_____

15. What are the defining characteristics of the *Eskimo kinship terminology* system? Why is it more familiar to you than the other systems described in the chapter? What group of relatives are particularly contrasted with other relatives by this system of kin terms? Under what social conditions do you suppose it would make most sense to people to label their relatives with this system?

_____

_____

_____

16. What is the difference between a parallel cousin and a cross cousin?

_____

_____

17. What are the defining characteristics of the *Omaha kinship terminology* system? With which form of descent reckoning is this naming system most closely linked? Examine the terms for ego's parallel and cross cousins in Figure 10.11. What do the terms suggest about which cousins ego clearly may not marry?

_____

_____

18. What are the defining characteristics of the *Crow kinship terminology* system? With which form of descent reckoning is this naming system most closely linked?

_____

_____

19. What are the defining characteristics of the *Iroquois kinship terminology* system? With what form of descent reckoning is this naming system most closely linked? According to White and Goody, how are societies that use this system different from those that use Omaha or Crow?

_____

_____

20. What are the defining characteristics of the *Sudanese kinship terminology* system? What does its extreme elaboration of different terms for different kin imply about the social relationships that its users have with different relatives?

_____

_____

21. Define *fictive kinship*. Give an example of a fictive kinship relationship from your own society. What is the Chan Kom Maya concept of the *padrinazgo*?

_____

_____

Matching Test

Match each concept with its definition, illustration, or explication below.

a. clan
b. moiety
c. kindred
d. kinship
e. lineage
f. descent
g. affines
h. phratry
i. consanguines
j. fictive kinship
k. cognatic descent

l. bilateral descent
m. unilineal descent
n. cognative lineages
o. ambilineal descent
p. matrilineal descent
q. patrilineal descent

r. lineal descent group
s. unilineal descent group
t. Crow kinship terminology
u. bilateral descent groups
v. Omaha kinship terminology

w. Eskimo kinship terminology
x. Hawaiian kinship terminology
y. Iroquois kinship terminology
z. descriptive kinship terminology

____ 1. kin related by ties of descent

____ 2. kin related through a marriage link

____ 3. group whose members share a common ancestor

____ 4. group whose members share a living relative

____ 5. system of descent traced through fathers only

____ 6. system of descent traced through mothers only

____ 7. group of clans thought to be related by kinship

____ 8. system of tracing descent bilaterally or ambilineally

____ 9. system of tracing descent lines equally through both parents

____ 10. one of two basic complementary social subdivisions of a society

____ 11. simplest kinship designation, using the terms parents, siblings, and children

____ 12. kinship group whose members trace by ambilineal descent from a common ancestor

____ 13. kinship group whose members can trace their lines of descent to the same ancestor

____ 14. system of tracing social groups based on a matrilineal or patrilineal descent system

____ 15. system of tracing descent through a single sex line rather than through both parents equally

____ 16. system for classifying people related to one another by ties of descent or by ties of marriage

____ 17. cultural recognition of kinship connections between a child and one or both of his or her parent's kin

____ 18. kinship group in a bilateral descent system that consists of the known relatives of a living individual

____ 19. matrilineal descent system where father's matrilineage is distinguished only by sex, regardless of generation

____ 20. patrilineal descent system where mother's patrilineage is distinguished only by sex, regardless of generation

____ 21. bifurcate merging system in which there is no merging of generations in the lineage that marries into ego's lineage

____ 22. kinship system occurring mostly in North Africa that distinguishes maternal and paternal relatives by separate sets of terms

____ 23. kinship group whose members believe themselves to be descended from a common ancestor without remembering exact genealogical ties

___ 24. system of tracing descent through a parent of either sex, choosing only one parent for each link that connects a group of relatives

___ 25. socially created kinship relationships involving individuals who are not otherwise considered relatives either by descent or marriage

___ 26. bilateral kinship system in which terms for mother, father, brother, and sister are not used for relatives outside the nuclear family

ANSWER KEY

1. i	8. k	15. m	22. z
2. g	9. l	16. d	23. a
3. r	10. b	17. f	24. o
4. u	11. x	18. c	25. j
5. q	12. e	19. t	26. w
6. p	13. n	20. v	
7. h	14. s	21. y	

CHAPTER ELEVEN

POLITICS AND CULTURE

CHAPTER OUTLINE

TYPES OF POLITICAL ORDERS
Bands: Government by Community
Tribes: Government by Families and Associations
Chiefdoms: Government by Officials
States: The Official Monopoly of Law

GENDER AND POLITICS
Matrifocal Societies

INDIGENOUS PEOPLE AND POLITICS

SOCIAL CONTROL: THE IMPOSITION OF ORDER
Socialization
Religion and Social Control
Rewards
Gossip and Community Pressure
Law
Case Study: U.S. Politics

THE RESOLUTION OF EXTERNAL CONFLICT
Peaceful Conflict Resolution
Violent Conflict Resolution

THE RESOLUTION OF INTERNAL CONFLICT
Crime
Rebellion and Revolution

CHAPTER OBJECTIVES

After reading this chapter, you should be able to:

▸ *Define politics.*

▸ *Analyze the political structure of bands.*

▸ *Analyze the political structure of tribes.*

▸ *Analyze the political structure of chiefdoms.*

▸ *Analyze the political structure of states.*

▸ *Analyze politics, law, and crime in the United States.*

▸ *Explain the role of gender in politics.*

▸ *Discuss the influence of minority status on political power.*

▶ *Define the basic mechanisms of social control: socialization, religion, rewards, gossip and community pressure, and law.*

▶ *Discuss the common peaceful means for conflict resolution.*

▶ *Discuss the use of power as a means of conflict resolution.*

▶ *Define and explain crime.*

▶ *Discuss the various means by which internal conflict is commonly addressed.*

▶ *Define and explain rebellion and revolution.*

REVIEW QUESTIONS

1. Define *politics*. What is the difference between *authority* and the use of power?

    _____

    _____

2. What is the typical upper limit to the size of local communities in *band* societies? Describe the political system by which people govern themselves in band societies. How do band society peoples reach decisions for the community? Why is there no need for full-time governments in bands?

    _____

    _____

    _____

3. Among the Inuit people described by Boas, what group made judicial decisions, such as trying accusations of homicide?

    _____

    _____

4. Describe the governing mechanisms of *tribes*. Why do tribal peoples require a more complex political system than band peoples? What are *sodalities* and what political roles do they play? What kinds of authority do families have in tribes?

    _____

    _____

5. How do *chiefdoms* differ from bands and tribes in their system of government? What are the two common bases for a chief's authority? What areas of society do not typically come under the authority of the government in a chiefdom?

    _____

    _____

6. Define *state*. How does the government of a state differ from that of a chiefdom? Briefly outline Robert Carniero's interpretation of the origin of states.

_____

_____

7. How did the West African Ashanti view crimes, and what was the punishment for all crimes?

_____

_____

8. According to Fried, how is the social instability of chiefdoms related to the rise of states? What changes marked the rise of the first states from chiefdoms, according to Haas? What particular need did Wittfogel believe to be the basis for the evolution of state authority?

_____

_____

9. According to Carneiro, how did environmental circumstances influence the development of the first states?

_____

_____

10. What factors tend to be associated with high levels of political power for women? What are the defining characteristics of a *matrifocal society*?

_____

_____

11. Why was the status of women particularly high among the Iroquois? What characteristic of Dahomian government gave women high social status? How was the authority of the Lobedu queen limited?

_____

_____

12. How did the Ibo government ensure that women were politically influential?

_____

_____

13. What characteristics of Native Americans demonstrate the impact of their minority status as indigenous peoples in the United States? When was citizenship extended to U.S. Native Americans?

_____

_____

14. Why has gambling on Indian reservations become a major political issue in the United States since 1988?

_____

_____

15. Give an example of how each of the following five factors operates to promote social order: *socialization*, religion, social rewards, community pressure, and *law*.

_____

_____

16. Why are *moral values* particularly central to the concepts of criminal law? Why do other types of values sometimes become subject to enforcement by law?

_____

_____

17. How do rewards as well as punishments help promote rule following? How does gossip help promote conformity to community values?

_____

_____

18. How does law differ from other means for promoting and maintaining order? According to Pospisil, what are the four universal characteristics of law?

_____

_____

19. What are the three personal orientations and six values that influence voting choices by the American electorate, according to research by Times Mirror?

_____

_____

20. What percentage of Americans are totally uninvolved in public affairs and politics?

_____

_____

21. What are the two main groups that are staunchly Republican in their voting, and what are the main political concerns of each?

_____

_____

22. What are the five main groups that are staunchly Democratic in their voting, and what are the main political concerns of each?

_____

_____

23. Define *mediation* and explain how a mediator can function successfully even though he or she has no legal authority to enforce a decision.

_____

_____

24. What were traditional Nuer penalties for murder? Describe the role of the Nuer "Leopard Skin Chief." What was the traditional penalty against the losing party of a song duel among the Native Greenlanders and Inuit?

_____

_____

25. In what kinds of societies is action by an entire community likely to be an important means of resolving conflict? How is an Inuit "song duel" similar to the action of a court in a socially more complex society?

_____

_____

26. Define *court*. What kinds of societies are most likely to have courts?

_____

_____

27. What did Black mean when he said, "Law varies inversely with other social control"? What other means for maintaining social order are people likely to use if their system of law does not function well enough to satisfy their needs? Give examples of how some of these other ways of maintaining order work.

_____

_____

_____

28. Define *oath* and *ordeal*. Describe the Ifugao use of the ordeal as a test of guilt or innocence.

_____

_____

29. What are the differences between *retribution, feuds, raids,* and *war?*

_____

_____

30. Define *fraternal group*. What relationship do they have to the legal mechanism of feuds?

_____

_____

31. According to Otterbein, what kinds of societies practice warfare that involves the greatest mortality? In what kind of societies is the tactic of surprise most common? In what kind of societies is prestige a common motive for participation in warfare? What are the three common purposes and motives for warfare in bands and tribes?

_____

_____

32. How does *internal warfare* differ from *external warfare?* What social differences exist in the kinds of societies that practice each? Which is most associated with the subordination of women and *female infanticide?*

_____

_____

33. What did Naroll find about the relationship between the degree of military sophistication and the likelihood of warfare and the likelihood of being attacked by others? What three things have Ember and Vayda found to be associated with a high likelihood for warfare?

_____

_____

34. Why is *crime* less common in socially simple societies than in complex ones? What factors may have contributed to a low rate of crime among the Semai of the Malay Peninsula?

_____

_____

35. For the Colombian Cubeo, what determines whether taking a possession without asking its owner's permission is regarded as theft? How did the Copper Eskimo define murder?

_____

_____

36. What is the basic rule for determining punishment among the Berbers of North Africa?

_____

_____

37. How does law enforcement in complex societies differ from law enforcement in simple societies? What is the most common violent but legitimate punishment for crime in societies that have no centralized government?

_____

_____

38. Define *rebellion* and *revolution*. What conditions increase the likelihood of rebellion and revolution?

_____

_____

MATCHING TEST

Match each concept with its definition, illustration, or explication below.

a. law	h. state	o. mediation	v. external warfare
b. war	i. tribe	p. rebellion	w. internal warfare
c. oath	j. ordeal	q. revolution	x. matrifocal society
d. raid	k. sodality	r. restitution	y. universal
e. feud	l. politics	s. retribution	application
f. court	m. sanction	t. moral values	z. legal rights and
g. crime	n. chiefdom	u. legal authority	duties

_____ 1. personal use of force to redress wrongs

_____ 2. harming of a person or personal property by another

_____ 3. organized armed conflict between political communities

_____ 4. organized use of force to alter the very form of government

_____ 5. cultural rules that regulate human behavior and maintain order

_____ 6. conflict between political communities with different cultures

_____ 7. society in which the primary solidarity relations involve women

_____ 8. fighting between peoples who share the same language and culture

_____ 9. ritual act of swearing innocence on pain of punishment by deities

_____ 10. action taken by legal authorities responding to violations of law

_____ 11. semisedentary kinship-based society without a full-time government

_____ 12. armed conflicts between kinship groups initiated to avenge a wrong

_____ 13. test of guilt or innocence involving enduring dangerous or painful acts

_____ 14. right to compel others to obey the law and to punish those who violate it

_____ 15. voluntary association whose members are drawn from several tribal families

_____ 16. negotiation between conflicting parties carried out by a neutral third party

_____ 17. attitudes or rules that govern our relationships with our fellow human beings

_____ 18. organized violence by one group against another to achieve an economic benefit

_____ 19. manner in which power is achieved and used to create and implement public goals

_____ 20. behavior intended to restore the group to the balance it had before a law was broken

_____ 21. society with a centralized government that monopolizes the legal authority to use force

___ 22. organized and violent opposition to the legitimacy of a society's current governing body

___ 23. principle that legal authority should apply the same laws uniformly in similar situations

___ 24. formalized institution that asserts authority over parties in a dispute and over persons accused of violating the law

___ 25. rules that define relationships between people by specifying the type of recompense an injured person should receive

___ 26. society that unites a number of villages under the legal control of a government that allows families some autonomous legal authority

---

ANSWER KEY

1. s	8. w	15. k	22. p
2. g	9. c	16. o	23. y
3. b	10. m	17. t	24. f
4. q	11. i	18. d	25. z
5. a	12. e	19. l	26. n
6. v	13. j	20. r	
7. x	14. u	21. h	

CHAPTER TWELVE

LANGUAGE AND CULTURE

CHAPTER OUTLINE

HUMAN COMMUNICATION
Signs and Symbols
Human vs. Nonhuman Communication

NONVERBAL COMMUNICATION
Nonverbal Signs
Culturally Patterned Nonverbal Symbols
Proxemics
Kinesics

LANGUAGE
Language vs. Speech
The Biological Basis of Language
The Origin of Language

THE STRUCTURE OF LANGUAGE
Phonology
Grammar

LINGUISTIC RELATIVITY
Effects of Morphology
Effects of Syntax

LANGUAGE CHANGE
Changes in Phonology and Grammar
Word Borrowing
Dialects
Basic Vocabulary

LANGUAGE FAMILIES
Glottochronology
Language Macrofamilies
Contemporary World Languages
Language Extinction

LANGUAGE POLITICS
Prestige Dialects
Language and Nationalism

CHAPTER OBJECTIVES

After reading this chapter, you should be able to:

▶ *Discuss the contrasts between symbolic communication and sign communication.*

▶ *Contrast human with nonhuman communication.*

▶ *Explain the characteristics of nonverbal communication.*

▶ *Define language.*

▶ *Explain the biological basis of language.*

▶ *Outline the structural components of language.*

▶ *Explain the concept of linguistic relativity.*

▶ *Discuss the process of language change.*

▶ *Explain the concept of language families.*

▶ *Discuss contemporary language diversity.*

REVIEW QUESTIONS

1. Define *communication*. How is communicating with *signs* different from communicating with *symbols*? Which animals are able to use signs? Which are able to use symbols?

   _____

   _____

2. In what sense is the very existence of culture based on the human ability to create and use symbols? What do you suppose human social life would be like without this ability?

   _____

   _____

3. When Helen Keller began to use symbolic communication, how was her rate of learning influenced?

   _____

   _____

4. What does *nonverbal communication* unconsciously communicate? In what three circumstances do humans most often use nonverbal communication in a purposive way? Give three examples of nonverbal symbols and their meanings.

   _____

   _____

5. Define *proxemics*. List the four categories of meaningful distances that Hall has used to describe cultural differences in nonverbal communication, and explain when each is likely to be used. What are the actual distances for each category in the United States?

   _____

   _____

6. Define *kinesics*. How is research in kinesics carried out? What did Ray Birdwhistell discover about the many facial expressions people can make and about the rate at which they can process information to interpret facial expressions?

_____

_____

7. Define *language*. What is meant when language is called an *open system* of communication?

_____

_____

8. What is meant when language is said to be a *metacommunication system?*

_____

_____

9. How is *speech* different from language?

_____

_____

10. What evidence is there from research in the abilities of chimpanzees and gorillas to learn and use *American Sign Language* to communicate that suggests that, as impressive as their communication skills may be, they do not really have the full range of symbolic abilities that human beings have who use sign language or spoken language? What use of communication did Savage-Rumbaugh particularly note as lacking in ASL-using chimpanzees?

_____

_____

11. What roles are played by the three major subdivisions of the human brain?

_____

_____

12. List and describe the functions of each of the four specialized language centers of the brain. What is the *Fissure of Rolando?* On what side of the brain are these language centers usually found?

_____

_____

13. What is the *limbic system?* What role does it play in the vocal communication of nonhuman primates versus humans?

_____

_____

14. What evidences suggest that Neanderthals might have had language abilities? What limitation seems to have existed in their vocal abilities?

_____

_____

15. What is a *pidgin language* and how does it differ from a *creole?* What do characteristics of pidgins and creoles suggest about the characteristics of early human language?

_____

_____

16. Define *phonology, morphology,* and *syntax.*

_____

_____

17. What is the *International Phonetic Alphabet?*

_____

_____

18. What is the difference between a *phone* and a *phoneme?* How many phonemes do most human languages typically have? How many are there in English?

_____

_____

19. What is the difference between a *phonetic* and a *phonemic* description of speech?

_____

_____

20. What are the two parts of *grammar?* What is the difference between a *free morpheme* and a *bound morpheme?* What is an *allomorph?*

_____

_____

21. Why is the notion that the languages of people in small-scale nonindustrialized societies were "primitive" best understood as a form of ethnocentrism?

_____

_____

22. Define *linguistic relativity.* What else is it sometimes called? How does this theory view the effect of a language's morphology and of its syntax in how its speakers tend to think?

_____

_____

23. What fraction of today's English vocabulary was borrowed from French? Why did more borrowing occur from French to English than in the other direction between 1066 and 1300?

_____

_____

24. How do *dialects* develop in a language? Describe how a single language can develop into several distinct languages.

_____

25. What is *Black English Vernacular?* How does it differ from *Standard English?*

_____

_____

26. Define *Proto-Germanic* and *basic vocabulary.* What evidence is there that English developed from a Germanic ancestor? Why then are there so many English words today that are related to French? What is the difference between the part of the English vocabulary that has many French-related words and the part that has mostly Germanic words?

_____

_____

27. What is a *language family?* Define *Proto-Indo-European.*

_____

_____

28. Define *glottochronology* and explain its underlying principles. At what rate do languages seem to lose their original words from their basic vocabularies? According to Figure 12.8 on page 314, what percentage of the original basic vocabulary would two "daughter" languages still *both* have after about 3,000 years of separation?

_____

_____

29. Why are glottochronological relationships among languages with a common ancestor more than 10,000 years ago so difficult to prove? What controversial language macrofamily has been proposed that includes the Indo-European language family and others from Asia through northern Africa?

_____

_____

30. How many languages are estimated to be spoken in the world today? Why is it difficult to be more precise? Which language has the most speakers in the world today? How many languages are spoken in Nigeria?

_____

_____

31. What is happening to the number of world languages as time passes? About what fraction of North American Indian languages still survive? How many are still being learned by children?

_____

_____

32. What is a *prestige dialect?* In what kind of societies are prestige dialects most likely to exist? How do politics influence the choice of a prestige dialect?

_____

33. How many people in the United States speak a language other than English at home? For how many is Spanish their first language? What are the two fastest growing languages in the United States? How many children in the U.S. public school system currently have limited proficiency in English? What percentage of U.S. schools offer some form of bilingual education?

_____

_____

Matching Test

Match each concept with its definition, illustration, or explication below.

a. sign
b. phone
c. symbol
d. syntax
e. pidgin
f. speech
g. creole
h. grammar

i. dialect
j. phoneme
k. language
l. morpheme
m. kinesics
n. phonology
o. proxemics
p. morphology

q. Broca's area
r. limbic system
s. communication
t. Wernicke's area
u. prestige dialect
v. glottochronology
w. phonemic
  alphabet

x. speech motor
  area
y. phonetic
  description
z. linguistic
  relativity

___ 1. smallest sound unit of a language

___ 2. audible symbols that people use to communicate

___ 3. smallest meaningful sequence of sounds in a language

___ 4. smallest psychologically real unit of sound in a language

___ 5. simplified version of one language or a combination of several

___ 6. set of areas within the brain that deal with emotional experience

___ 7. the part of the cerebral cortex involved in processing speech sounds

___ 8. system of rules that govern the production and interpretation of speech

___ 9. the part of the cerebral cortex that controls the production of speech sounds

___ 10. study of how people structure the space around them when interacting with others

___ 11. variant of a language with the reputation of being inherently better than others

___ 12. study of the rules for combining morphemes into complete and meaningful sentences

___ 13. study of the body movements that accompany speech as a component of communication

___ 14. study of how phonemes are combined into the smallest meaningful units of a language

___ 15. record of language based on the smallest units of sound actually produced by speakers

___ 16. idea that the characteristics of a language influence the way that its speakers think

___ 17. the part of the cerebral cortex involved in organizing words into grammatical sequences

___ 18. transfer of information from one person to another using objects and events as signs or symbols

___ 19. true language that has developed out of a simplified version of a language or combination of languages

___ 20. analysis of the regular ways that the sounds of a language are combined to form meaningful utterances

___ 21. study of the rules that govern the production and the organization of the sounds of a particular language

___ 22. object or event that represents another object or event because of the agreement among people that it will

___ 23. written record of speech that uses a set of elements comprising only one symbol for each phoneme of the language

___ 24. technique for calculating the minimal length of time that two related languages have been diverging from a common ancestral language

___ 25. object or event whose meaning is biologically disposed or based on a similarity or a tendency for two things to occur together in nature

___ 26. geographical or social subdivision of a language that differs systematically from other subdivisions of the same language in its vocabulary, grammar, and phonology

---

Answer Key

1. b	8. k	15. y	22. c
2. f	9. x	16. z	23. w
3. l	10. o	17. q	24. v
4. j	11. u	18. s	25. a
5. e	12. d	19. g	26. i
6. r	13. m	20. h	
7. t	14. p	21. n	

CHAPTER THIRTEEN

RELIGION AND CULTURE

CHAPTER OBJECTIVES

After reading this chapter, you should be able to:

▶ *Critique the various definitions of religion that have been proposed in the history of anthropology.*

▶ *Analyze the ways in which people conceive of the supernatural and their relationship to it.*

▶ *Discuss the relationship between religion and practical aspects of human survival and cultural adaptation.*

▶ *Define the structure and diversity of religious ideology.*

▶ *Exemplify relationships between religious ideologies and social organization.*

▶ *Analyze the nature and functions of ritual in religion.*

▶ *Explain the different forms of religious social organization.*

▶ *Illustrate the role of borrowing in religious change.*

▶ *Explain the role of religion in the United States.*

▶ *Describe the revitalization movement in religion.*

▶ *Discuss the social and psychological functions of religion.*

▶ *Analyze the cognitive characteristics of religious thought.*

REVIEW QUESTIONS

1. What three things must always be included in any comprehensive definition of *religion?*

   _____

   _____

2. How did Sir Edward Burnett Tylor define religion? What did he believe to be the main function of religion in human life? What were some of the shortcomings of his definition?

   _____

   _____

3. In Robert Marett's opinion, what was the most basic religious concept? What aspect of human experience did he believe to have been the source of religion?

   _____

   _____

4. Define *mana.* Give three examples of where this concept is used in your own culture. (Your examples may come from formal religious settings, but you may also choose examples from other parts of culture that seem to fit this concept.) Why did Marett believe that a belief in mana was more ancient than a belief in gods or spirits?

   _____

   _____

5. Define *taboo.* How is it related to the concept of *mana?*

   _____

   _____

6. How has the word *supernatural* been defined traditionally? How cross-culturally widespread is the dichotomy implied by this term? How commonly do the world's languages have a term for religion or the supernatural?

   _____

   _____

7. What is *anthropomorphism?* What difficulties are avoided by using the concept of anthropomorphic beliefs instead of the concept of supernatural beliefs in a definition of religion?

_____

_____

8. What did Émile Durkheim mean by the term *sacred?* What did he believe to be the basis of religious ideas?

_____

_____

9. According to Clifford Geertz, what is the central core of religion and how does religion influence a people's worldview and their allegiance to their society?

_____

_____

10. Briefly summarize Harris's ideas about how the Hindu veneration of the potentially edible cow may be beneficial for Hindu society in spite of a historic problem of hunger in India.

_____

_____

11. What are the defining characteristics of *ritual?* According to Anthony F. C. Wallace, why are rituals so important in religion?

_____

_____

12. Give three examples that illustrate that the religious beliefs of different societies can be very different from one another. Why are many nonreligious beliefs about things quite similar throughout the world, while religious beliefs are so diverse? How free is religious ideology from practical constraints on what people can and do believe?

_____

_____

13. According to Omar Khayyam Moore, what is the environmentally adaptive benefit of a divination ritual such as that used by the Motagnais-Naskapi of the Labradorian Peninsula to make decisions about where to hunt?

_____

_____

14. According to Leslie White, how does the growth of science and technology influence the role of religious ideology in social life? What is *secularization* and what are its two main causes?

_____

_____

15. Describe what Guy Swanson found about the social characteristics of societies in which each of the following beliefs was likely to be found: *monotheism, polytheism,* active *ancestral*

spirits, *reincarnation*, a *human soul* in each individual's body, and *supernatural sanctions for violations of moral rules*. What basic idea of Durkheim's do these findings seem to support?

_____

_____

16. What is the difference between *sorcery* and *witchcraft?* What do they have in common? According to research by Swanson and by Whiting, what social condition seems to bring about such beliefs?

_____

_____

17. What did Rudolf Otto believe to be the most central feature of religion?

_____

_____

18. Define *glossolalia*.

_____

_____

19. What are the three main roles of ritual in religion?

_____

_____

20. What does Victor Turner mean by *communitas?* What role does ritual play in creating this feeling?

_____

_____

21. What are the three common phases of a ritual? What is the *liminal period* of a ritual and how does it relate to the feeling of communitas?

_____

_____

22. How does the fact that religious rituals are symbolic acts give them the possibility of embodying what people perceive as "transcendent meaningfulness"? Give an example of a ritual with which you are familiar and show that it portrays more than one idea.

_____

_____

23. What is *magic?* How does it differ from other kinds of rituals?

_____

_____

24. Describe the two principles that are basic to magic in any society, according to Sir James Frazer.

_____

_____

25. Define *divination*. Describe the Azande use of the poison oracle for divination.

_____

_____

26. According to Forest Clements, what are the four common religious explanations for illness? What social conditions seem to make each more likely?

_____

_____

27. What is *bone-pointing*? How have scientists explained apparent cases of *voodoo death*? What is the Hans Selye's concept of the *General Adaptation Syndrome,* and how might it be related to "magical death"? What does Eastwell believe to be the actual cause of death in many cases of so-called "magical death"?

_____

_____

28. Define *shaman*. How does the role of the shaman differ from that of the *priest*? Define *sorcerer*. What is the relationship between a sorcerer and a shaman? What are Iroquois False Face Society masks? How are they made and how are they used? What experience did an Avam Samoyed have to have to become a shaman?

_____

_____

_____

29. In societies that believe in *witches*, what characteristics are these individuals usually thought to have? What characteristics of Navajo skinwalkers make them not fit completely into either the anthropological category of *witch* or *sorcerer?* Which term seems to you to fit the Navajo case best?

_____

_____

30. Define the three basic kinds of religious organizations: *shamanic religions, communal religions,* and *ecclesiastical religions*. What natural hierarchy do they form? What does this suggest about which of the three is the most ancient form of religion, and how is your answer supported by the kind of societies in which it is most often found? What kind of gods did the earliest ecclesiastical religions emphasize?

_____

_____

_____

31. What social functions do anthropologists believe religion usually fulfills? What religious story does the Jigalong rain-bringing ritual reenact? How does the performance of this ritual help define important social categories in Jigalong life?

_____

_____

32. How does religion seem to benefit people psychologically?

_____

_____

33. In spite of the differences between science and religion, Guthrie argues that religious thought processes are not radically different from human ways of thinking in other settings. What does he mean when he says that people hold religious beliefs because they are "plausible," even though they may not be scientifically correct?

_____

_____

34. In Guthrie's view, what do concepts of gods, spirits, and mana all have in common?

_____

_____

MATCHING TEST

Match each concept with its definition, illustration, or explication below.

a. sin	h. ritual	o. polytheism	v. Law of Similarity
b. mana	i. priest	p. syncretism	w. spirit possession
c. magic	j. sorcery	q. supernatural	x. communal
d. totem	k. religion	r. reincarnation	religion
e. taboo	l. witchcraft	s. secularization	y. petitionary ritual
f. shaman	m. monotheism	t. Law of Contagion	z. ecclesiastical
g. sacred	n. divination	u. anthropomorphism	religion

____ 1. supernatural power or force

____ 2. that which transcends the natural, observable world

____ 3. rule forbidding contact with sacred things, those containing mana

____ 4. use of ritual to obtain answers to questions from supernatural sources

____ 5. form of taboo violation in which the rule breaker is morally responsible for the act

____ 6. borrowing of beliefs, practices, or organizational traits by one religion from another

____ 7. learned use of rituals to magically control the supernatural realm to achieve human goals

____ 8. process by which nonreligious beliefs expand within an ideology at the expense of religious thought

___ 9. plant, animal or, less commonly, nonliving thing that is a sacred symbol of the unity of a social group

___ 10. religion that includes the performance of rituals by groups of lay practitioners, shamans, or individuals

___ 11. quality of inspiring feelings of respect, awe, and reverence that is possessed by things set apart and forbidden

___ 12. belief in superior (but not supreme) gods, each of whom controls or rules over some major aspect of the universe

___ 13. using human qualities to explain the nonhuman realm, or interpreting or acting toward the nonhuman realm as if it were human

___ 14. ritual request for supernatural aid that is believed to increase the likelihood of the requested result but not guarantee it

___ 15. belief in supernatural power, symbolic expression of feelings, and rituals performed in order to influence the nonhuman realm

___ 16. trance in which individuals feel as if their behavior is under the control of one or more spirits that have entered their bodies

___ 17. principle that things that resemble one another are spiritually identical and can be used in rituals to influence a desired outcome

___ 18. innate ability to influence supernatural forces, usually to operate in ways that are harmful to others, without the necessity of using rituals

___ 19. use of rituals that, when performed correctly, are believed to compel—as opposed to simply making requests of—the supernatural to bring about desired results

___ 20. religious practitioner who performs rituals for the benefit of a group, often as a full-time specialist whose emphasis is on preserving established ritual forms

___ 21. principle that things that have been in contact remain supernaturally in contact or that contact between things can be used to transfer mana from one to the other

___ 22. belief in a high god, a supreme being who either created the physical universe and other spiritual beings and rules over them or maintains the order of the universe

___ 23. behaviors, often performed in repetitive and stereotyped ways, that express people's anxieties by acting them out and that may aim to influence supernatural beings

___ 24. part-time religious practitioner who is believed to have access to supernatural power that may be used for the benefit of specific clients, as in healing or divining

___ 25. process in which the soul of a human being may be repeatedly reborn into the human group to which it previously belonged or as an animal that may be symbolically associated with the group

___ 26. religion that includes not only performance of rituals by groups of lay practitioners, individuals, and shamans but also a coordinating body of priests who perform rituals on behalf of congregations

Answer Key

1. b	8. s	15. k	22. m
2. q	9. d	16. w	23. h
3. e	10. x	17. i	24. f
4. n	11. g	18. v	25. r
5. a	12. o	19. l	26. z
6. p	13. u	20. c	
7. j	14. y	21. t	

CHAPTER FOURTEEN

CULTURE, PERSONALITY, AND PSYCHOLOGICAL PROCESS

CHAPTER OBJECTIVES

After reading this chapter, you should be able to:

▶ *Explain the relationships among personality, socialization, and social roles.*

▶ *Discuss the relationships among childrearing practices, personality, and a society's secondary institutions.*

▶ *Explain the role of socialization in culturally patterned gender differences.*

▶ *Analyze the concept of face-work.*

▶ *Analyze the relationship between role playing and emotional distress.*

▶ *Explain the nature and causes of trance.*

▶ *Discuss the cultural functions of trance states.*

▶ *Explain the roles of ritual in expressing and alleviating stress.*

▶ *Explain the nature and causes of deviance.*

▶ *Discuss how culture influences people's conception of mental disorders.*

▶ *Discuss the various culture-specific mental disorders.*

REVIEW QUESTIONS

1. What was the main emphasis in the field of *culture and personality* in the 1920s? What was the basic idea of the culture and personality approach called *configurationalism?*

   _____

   _____

2. Define *socialization.* To what aspects of socialization did Cora DuBois attribute the shallow friendships and suspicious, pessimistic outlook of the Alorese? What aspect of Iatmul socialization did Margaret Mead think encouraged aggression in the personalities of the Iatmul?

   _____

   _____

   _____

3. What did Kardiner mean by *basic personality structure* and *modal personality type?* Why did Abram Kardiner and those influenced by him distinguish between *primary* and *secondary institutions?* How did Robert LeVine clarify the relationship between a society's primary and secondary institutions by adding the concept of a *maintenance system?*

   _____

   _____

   _____

4. According to Herbert Barry, Irvin Child, and Margaret Bacon, how do agricultural and foraging societies commonly differ in their socialization practices?

   _____

   _____

5. What were *national character studies* and what motivated their development?

   _____

   _____

6. What have been the main criticisms of the early culture and personality studies?

    _____

    _____

7. How did *psychological anthropology* of the 1950s and thereafter differ from the earlier culture and personality approaches? What are the two major forms of research by psychological anthropologists?

    _____

    _____

8. What fieldwork evidence did Robert Edgerton obtain about personality differences between pastoralists and horticulturalists?

    _____

    _____

9. What did Whiting and Child discover by examining HRAF data about relationships between a society's socialization customs and its ideology concerning the causes and treatment of illness? What beliefs did they find to be associated with an emphasis on the punishment of childhood aggression during socialization? What parallel did George Wright find between socialization practices and a society's folklore?

    _____

    _____

    _____

    _____

10. How does an anthropological definition of *personality* differ from a psychological definition?

    _____

    _____

11. What was a *Contrary Warrior* among the Cheyenne of North America? How does this social status illustrate to you that much of what you commonly call personality traits are really learned social roles?

    _____

    _____

12. What is meant by a *status-appropriate role?*

    _____

    _____

13. How is the idea of *face* related to the concept of status-appropriate roles? What is *face-work?* Give an illustration of face-work. In what sense does sorority rush illustrate the principle that becoming a member of an existing group requires us to establish a "face" that is acceptable to the group?

    _____

    _____

14. Outline the three stages in the typical ritual by which damaged face can be repaired.

_____

_____

15. Define *deviance*. Is it necessarily negative? Define *creativity* and *stigma*.

_____

_____

16. What is *anxiety* and how does it differ from the other distressful feelings that people sometimes experience?

_____

_____

17. Define *fear, guilt, grief, shame,* and *anger,* and state the basic role-playing difficulty that leads to each feeling. In what sense are fear and guilt opposites of one another? In what sense are grief and shame opposites? How does anger differ from the other four? How does *affectlessness* parallel anger as a possible response to social stress?

_____

_____

18. Define *stress*. When does stress result in anxiety (or one of the other emotions)? What are the two main results of unrelieved anxiety?

_____

_____

19. Define *trance (altered state of consciousness)*. What is the relationship of anxiety to trance? According to Arnold Ludwig, what are the common characteristics of trances?

_____

_____

20. What connection is there between the specialized "language centers" located in the left hemisphere of the brain and trances?

_____

_____

21. Define *hallucination*. What is the possible connection between the brain chemical *serotonin* and *hallucinations?* What is the *eureka experience?*

_____

_____

22. According to Ludwig, what are the five common causes of trances? What do they all have to do with stress?

_____

_____

23. In the terminology of Leslie White, what scientifically useful distinction do people have difficulty making when they are experiencing a trance? Can you relate this idea to Guthrie's emphasis on anthropomorphic thinking as the defining feature of religion, an institution in which trance states are often important (see chapter 13)?

_____

_____

24. What relationship did D'Andrade discover between social differences and the belief that dreams could be used to influence the supernatural? How did Bourguignon interpret this relationship?

_____

_____

25. Define *spirit travel trance* and *spirit possession trance*, and explain why they tend to be common in different kinds of societies. In what sense can each be seen as a "safety valve" for the kind of stresses people must endure in different societies? Where did Whiting and Child find each of these two kinds of trance states to be most common?

_____

_____

26. Define *ritual*. What is the effect of ritual behavior on anxiety? What psychological benefit of religion does this help explain?

_____

_____

27. What is a *deviant?* Why is a deviant not simply defined as someone who breaks social rules? What does this have to do with the concept of status (see chapter 3)?

_____

_____

28. What are *residual rules* and how are they different from the other rules of a culture? What do they have to do with the concept of *insanity?* Why is the status of "insane person" a good example of a master status (see chapter 3)?

_____

_____

29. According to Scheff, what are the three main causes of residual rule breaking? What do these have to do with Selye's concept of stress?

_____

_____

30. What are the defining characteristics of *dissociative disorders (hysteria)?* According to Seymour Parker, what characteristics are typical of societies in which hysteria is prevalent?

_____

_____

31. Briefly summarize the defining characteristics of each of the culturally specific forms of mental disorders that anthropologists have described. Do the current Western psychiatric categories seem useful in classifying them?

_____

_____

32. Define the following: phobia, anxiety disorder, hypochondriasis, and obsessive-compulsive disorder. What emotions or social role difficulties seem to be most central to these disorders?

_____

_____

33. What facts about Western cultures seem relevant to understanding *anorexia nervosa* as a culture-specific mental disorder?

_____

_____

34. Define the contemporary psychiatric concept of *schizophrenia*. In terms of the social role played in schizophrenia, what does the underlying problem seem to be?

_____

_____

35. What evidence do we have of social influences on who is most likely to be psychiatrically diagnosed as suffering from a mental disorder? Does this contradict the idea that mental disorders may have some biological basis?

_____

_____

36. How did David Rosenhan's participant-observation research demonstrate the idea that cultural expectations can influence our judgments that someone has a mental disorder?

_____

_____

MATCHING TEST

Match each concept with its definition, illustration, or explication below.

a. amok	i. deviance	q. hallucination	w. modal
b. susto	j. insanity	r. residual rules	personality type
c. shame	k. face-work	s. anorexia nervosa	x. secondary
d. guilt	l. hsieh-ping	t. eureka experience	institutions
e. stress	m. creativity	u. maintenance	y. dissociative
f. trance	n. frigophobia	system	disorder
g. stigma	o. personality	v. primary	z. basic personality
h. anxiety	p. schizophrenia	institutions	structure

___ 1. deviance that results in valuable new contributions to society

___ 2. most common or typical pattern of personality traits in a particular society

___ 3. culture-specific obsessive-compulsive disorder characterized by fear of loss of body heat

___ 4. behavior that differs enough from what society expects that others notice and react to it

___ 5. physiological response to any demand, characterized by the body's preparing itself for action

___ 6. process by which a person acquires and maintains deviant master status of residual rule breaker

___ 7. culture-specific hysterical disorder in which young men attack other people and destroy property

___ 8. distinctive ways in which a person behaves, thinks, and feels based on his or her cognition of self

___ 9. parts of the economic and social structure of a society that determine its childrearing practices

___ 10. distressful emotion characterized by remorse for having used too much power and having harmed another

___ 11. loss of rank that accompanies the social rejection of persons who have violated accepted role behavior

___ 12. consistent pattern of behavior related both to inner forces and external, cultural, and social pressures

___ 13. care groups related to childrearing, including feeding, weaning, sexual training, and subsistence patterns

___ 14. culture-specific anxiety disorder with depressive features, interpreted by the victim as caused by soul loss

___ 15. sense of intensified meaningfulness of experience that sometimes occurs during an altered state of consciousness

___ 16. subjective state of mind in which experiences are not interpreted in terms of normal symbolic categories of one's culture

___ 17. distressful emotion characterized by a sense of personal ineptness resulting in damage to one's reputation and loss of esteem

___ 18. distressful subjective awareness of stress; a general sense of powerlessness and foreboding without awareness of a specific danger

___ 19. interaction in which effort is directed to maintaining or returning behavior to roles considered appropriate for members of a group

___ 20. culture-specific obsessive-compulsive disorder characterized by an unrealistic appraisal of one's own body as overweight and by self-starvation

___ 21. miscellaneous, normally unspoken guidelines that people are expected to follow to avoid violating the pattern or style of behavior expected in the culture

___ 22. culture-specific hysterical disorder characterized by tremor, disorientation, clouding of consciousness, delirium, speaking in tongues, and hallucinations

___ 23. realistic-seeming experience—much like a vivid waking dream—that may include vision, hearing, the sense of touch, smell, and/or taste in the absence of external causes

___ 24. mental condition in which anxiety is avoided through the nonvoluntary loss of integration among consciousness, memory, sense of identity, and/or perception of the environment

___ 25. institutions in social life that satisfy the needs and tensions not met by the childrearing-related care groups; include taboo systems, religion, rituals, folk tales, and techniques of thinking

___ 26. mental disorder characterized by residual rule breaking caused by difficulty in communicating an acceptable social identity; may include hallucinations and ideas about reality that are greatly at odds with mainstream ideas

---

ANSWER KEY

1. m	8. z	15. t	22. l
2. w	9. u	16. f	23. q
3. n	10. d	17. c	24. y
4. i	11. g	18. h	25. x
5. e	12. o	19. k	26. p
6. j	13. v	20. s	
7. a	14. b	21. r	

CHAPTER FIFTEEN

AESTHETICS AND CULTURE

CHAPTER OUTLINE

THE RELATIVITY OF AESTHETICS
Cultural Differences in Aesthetics

THE AESTHETIC EXPERIENCE AND EXPRESSIVE CULTURE
Play
Games
Festivals
Sports
Art

ART FORMS
The Visual Arts
Music
Dance
The Verbal Arts
The Olfactory and Gustatory Arts

THE FUNCTIONS OF ART
Art and Social Organization
Status Indicators
Economic Functions
Religious Functions
Didactic Functions
Political Functions

CHAPTER OBJECTIVES

After reading this chapter, you should be able to:

▸ *Discuss the cultural relativity of aesthetics.*

▸ *Define and illustrate the concepts of aesthetic experience and expressive culture.*

▸ *Define the nature of play and explain its psychological functions.*

▸ *Explain the relationships of art to play.*

▸ *Explain the roles of form, feelings, and meaning in art.*

▸ *Outline the various forms of art.*

▸ *Analyze the social functions of art.*

REVIEW QUESTIONS

1. Define *aesthetics*. Are there societies without aesthetics? Under what circumstances is a society not likely to have a word for art in its language? What are the four ways in which cultures differ in their aesthetics?

_____

_____

2. What is meant by *aesthetic locus*? What is the aesthetic locus of Tiv culture? If the Tiv have no formal aesthetic standards, how could Keil discover their aesthetic standards? List some of the prominent aesthetic rules of Yoruba sculpture.

_____

_____

3. According to Paul Bohannan, how do Tiv attitudes about the production of art differ from those of Americans? What is the central feature of good art according to Hindu aesthetics?

_____

_____

4. What is meant by the *aesthetic experience?* How is it related to human biology? What is *expressive culture?*

_____

_____

5. Define *play*. How is play related to socialization? How is the "make-believe" state of mind related to catharsis?

_____

_____

6. How do *games* differ from play? What kind of society and what kind of socialization practices are most associated with games of strategy? What kind of socialization practices are associated with the popularity of games of chance versus games of physical skill?

_____

_____

7. What are the characteristics of festivals?

_____

_____

8. What distinguishes games from *sports?*

_____

_____

9. What are the three defining characteristics of *art* in all cultures? What have anthropologists usually emphasized in their study of art? What characteristics of art make it possible for

works of art to be appreciated across cultural boundaries? What kind of societies are most likely to have "art for art's sake"?

_____

_____

10. According to John Fischer, what distinguishes the visual art of complex, socially stratified societies from that of simple, nonstratified societies?

_____

_____

11. Define *ethnomusicology*. What is a musical *scale?* How many tones may an octave have? According to Barbara Ayres, when are adult tonal ranges likely to be particularly large? What aspect of childrearing is associated with rhythm?

_____

_____

12. What are the three necessary elements of song? What did Alan Lomax discover about the kinds of societies that emphasize polyphony and counterpoint? What did he find about the relationship between dance movements and other aspects of social life?

_____

_____

13. Define *verbal arts*.

_____

_____

14. What is the term for stories about the origins of things? How do these differ from *legends?* What did Kluckhohn find to be the most widespread themes in these stories throughout the world?

_____

_____

15. Define *rhetoric*. Is rhetoric found only in literate societies? What are *folktales?*

_____

_____

16. What are *proverbs?* Should people of all cultures easily understand them? Why or why not?

_____

_____

17. Define *riddle* and *joke*. How do they differ in what they reveal about the culture in which they are found? Why is humor likely to be different in different societies?

_____

_____

18. What is the central aesthetic focus of the Japanese tea ceremony?

_____

_____

19. In addition to the psychological pleasure of the aesthetic experience, what social functions are commonly fulfilled by art? What do Lega figurines represent? What socially important symbolism does the Ashante Golden Stool embody?

_____

_____

20. Why should the Kula Ring not be understood as motivated purely by aesthetic concerns?

_____

_____

21. Given what you have learned about art, briefly discuss your reaction to a definition of art as "sense pleasure given culturally meaningful form."

_____

_____

MATCHING TEST

Match each concept with its definition, illustration, or explication below.

a. art	g. jokes	m. legends	s. ethnomusicology
b. game	h. dance	n. proverbs	t. aesthetic locus
c. play	i. scale	o. rhetoric	u. expressive culture
d. music	j. rhythm	p. folktales	v. aesthetic
e. myths	k. lyrics	q. aesthetics	experience
f. sport	l. riddles	r. verbal arts	

____ 1. mental puzzles told for entertainment

____ 2. timing and stressing of tones within a melody

____ 3. words in a musical piece that convey a message

____ 4. study of music and its relationship to culture

____ 5. rules by which beauty is to be evaluated in a culture

____ 6. expressions of culture such as play, ritual, or the arts

____ 7. pleasure we feel when we recognize something as beautiful

____ 8. humor that serves to help relieve the stress of everyday life

____ 9. rhythmically organized scaled tones that produce melodic sound

____ 10. short statements that illustrate the basic values of a culture

___ 11. area of a culture to which a society devotes its aesthetic effort

___ 12. aggressively competitive activity played according to strict rules

___ 13. rhythmically patterned human movement performed for aesthetic pleasure

___ 14. formal speech that follows the traditional rules of a particular culture

___ 15. stress-relieving ritualistic practice of potentially utilitarian behaviors

___ 16. stories told for entertainment that teach a moral principle or a practical lesson

___ 17. stories that recount the origin of such things as gods, the universe, animals, and plants

___ 18. sequence of tones that ends with a return to a tone that has a frequency twice that of the starting tone

___ 19. various forms of speaking for aesthetic pleasure, including orating, reciting myths, and telling folktales

___ 20. stories that describe heroes and heroines who are usually responsible for the origin of a culture or society

___ 21. cultural expression of feeling and meaning in a form that evokes an aesthetic experience in the participant or observer

___ 22. competitive activity involving physical skills, strategy, and chance in a model of a conflict-producing real-life situation

---

ANSWER KEY

1. l	7. v	13. h	19. r
2. j	8. g	14. o	20. m
3. k	9. d	15. c	21. a
4. s	10. n	16. p	22. b
5. q	11. t	17. e	
6. u	12. f	18. i	